S0-BYE-363

www.wadsworth.com

wadsworth.com is the World Wide Web site for Wadsworth and is your direct source to dozens of online resources.

At *wadsworth.com* you can find out about supplements, demonstration software, and student resources. You can also send email to many of our authors and preview new publications and exciting new technologies.

wadsworth.com
Changing the way the world learns®

Introduction to Law Enforcement and Criminal Justice

Seventh Edition

Henry M. Wrobleski, LL.B.
Formerly Law Enforcement Coordinator
Normandale Community College

Kären M. Hess, Ph.D.
Normandale Community College

Australia • Canada • Mexico • Singapore
Spain • United Kingdom • United States

THOMSON

WADSWORTH

Senior Executive Editor, Criminal Justice: Sabra Horne
Acquisitions Editor: Shelley Murphy
Assistant Editor: Dawn Mesa
Editorial Assistant: Lee McCracken
Technology Project Manager: Susan DeVanna
Marketing Manager: Dory Schaeffer
Marketing Assistant: Neena Chandra
Advertising Project Manager: Bryan Vann
Project Manager, Editorial Production: Jennie Redwitz
Print/Media Buyer: Tandra Jorgensen
Permissions Editor: Bob Kauser
Production Service: Peggy Francomb, Shepherd, Inc.
Text Designer: Harry Voigt
Photo Researcher: Mary Reeg
Copy Editor: Michelle Campbell
Illustrator: Sara Weber
Indexing: Christine M.H. Orthmann
Cover Designer: Diane Beasley
Cover Image: Officers and helicopter: Roger Tully/Getty Images; officer with laptop: Robert E. Daemmrich/Getty Images; prison door: Marks Productions/Getty Images; officer with students: Michael Grecco/Getty Images; judge with lawyers: Jeff Cadge/Getty Images.
Compositor: Shepherd, Inc.
Cover and Text Printer: Phoenix Color Corp./BTP

Printed in the United States of America
2 3 4 5 6 7 06 05 04 03

For more information about our products, contact us at:
Thomson Learning Academic Resource Center
1-800-423-0563
For permission to use material from this text, contact us by:
Phone: 1-800-730-2214
Fax: 1-800-730-2215
Web: http://www.thomsonrights.com

Library of Congress Control Number: 2002107296

Student Edition ISBN 0-534-55280-3
Instructor Edition ISBN 0-534-55284-6

Wadsworth/Thomson Learning
10 Davis Drive
Belmont, CA 94002-3098
USA

Asia
Thomson Learning
5 Shenton Way #01-01
UIC Building
Singapore 068808

Australia
Nelson Thomson Learning
102 Dodds Street
South Melbourne, Victoria 3205
Australia

Canada
Nelson Thomson Learning
1120 Birchmount Road
Toronto, Ontario M1K 5G4
Canada

Europe/Middle East/Africa
Thomson Learning
High Holborn House
50/51 Bedford Row
London WC1R 4LR
United Kingdom

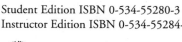

Brief Contents

Contents

Preface

Introduction to Law Enforcement and Criminal Justice was written to present an overview of the field and the numerous complexities within it. It also seeks to instill an appreciation for those who "serve and protect" our society and an understanding of this exciting, challenging profession.

The future of our lawful, democratic society depends in large part on those currently in the field of criminal justice and those preparing to enter it. Law enforcement officers have awesome power and tremendous responsibilities that must be met under constantly changing circumstances and in a way that protects individual rights and society's rights simultaneously—a tremendous challenge.

When we wrote the first edition of this text almost 25 years ago, law enforcement seemed more predictable and faced different challenges than now. In the 1970s law enforcement was focused on restoring its image after the disturbances and civil unrest of the 1960s. It saw organized crime as a major national threat. Crime fighting was its most obvious mission. Victims were seen primarily as sources of information. AIDS, crack cocaine, drive by shootings and children shooting children, domestic violence and terrorism were not perceived as problems. The first edition contained no chapters on community policing, problem-solving policing, juveniles or victims because these were not priorities. The beginnings of community policing could be seen, however, in the discussions of team policing and community service—helping citizens help themselves. The first edition also had no chapters on courts or corrections, focusing solely on the law enforcement component of the criminal justice system. The current edition recognizes the interrelationships of the components of the criminal justice system and the need for coordination among them.

Themes

As you learn about law enforcement, you will find three recurring themes in this text. The first theme is that of community or service orientation to law enforcement and the critical importance of partnerships, viewing citizens as coproducers of justice. A second theme is that of police officers as peace officers as well as crime fighters and a concern for not only criminal justice but social justice as well. The third theme is that of police officers' discretion in their role as gatekeepers to the criminal justice system.

Major Features—Context

Each chapter in the text serves as an overview of an area that could be expanded into an entire course. Not unexpectedly, the text begins with chapters that provide needed background (Section I). Our present system of law enforcement did not just magically appear. It has evolved slowly, shaped by numerous factors, including social and political influences. Chapter 1 describes the evolution of law enforcement and the criminal justice system from its ancient roots to the present system. Chapter 2 describes the laws all U.S. citizens are expected to obey and how they came to be. Chapter 3 explores crime in the United States: what types of crimes are occurring and theories about why, who commits crime and the effect it has on victims. This section provides the context within which to understand contemporary U.S. policing: its history and traditions, the laws under which it operates and which it enforces as well as the individuals who choose to disobey the laws and their victims. Policing is, at its heart, about people.

Section II helps you understand the traditional organization and functions of law enforcement, most of which can still be found within our law enforcement agencies. First, an overview of the organization, goals, characteristics and culture is presented (Chapter 4). Next, two approaches to policing gaining popularity throughout the county are introduced—community policing and problem-oriented policing (Chapter 5). This is followed by a discussion of the general functions of most agencies, patrol and traffic (Chapter 6), and the specialized assignments frequently found in larger agencies, such as investigators, SWAT teams, school resource officers and reserve officers (Chapter 7).

Section III explores important challenges to the profession in the twenty-first century. It begins with a discussion of the challenge of policing within the law, apprehending criminals without violating their constitutional rights (Chapter 8). Next, the challenges posed by gangs, drugs and terrorism, problems which have overshadowed the previous concern with organized crime, are discussed (Chapter 9). Then significant issues involved in policing are described, including discretion, discrimination, racial profiling, use of force, pursuit, liability, corruption and ethics (Chapter 10) This is followed by a discussion of departmental issues, including recruiting and retaining officers, civilian review boards, sexual harassment, unions, moonlighting, privatization of law enforcement, accreditation and professionalism (Chapter 11). The section concludes with an examination of the other two components of the criminal justice system, the courts and corrections, and how they interrelate with law enforcement. The need for collaboration and cooperation among the three components has become an important focus during the past decade (Chapter 12).

New to this Edition

This Seventh Edition has been completely updated, with the majority of sources cited being published between 1999 and 2002. The text has also been reorganized. The portion of the text dealing with criminals and victims has been moved forward to Chapter 3 so they can be kept in mind throughout the text. The community policing chapter has also been moved forward so the impact of community policing on all aspects of law enforcement can be explored throughout the remainder of the text. The chapters on courts and corrections have been combined and moved to the end of the text so they would not interrupt the discussion of law enforcement. Finally, the chapter on the juvenile justice system has been eliminated, with discussions of specific aspects of that system being incorporated within existing chapters; for example, the history of the juvenile justice system is now included in the history chapter (Chapter 1).

Relevant new information has also been included in this Seventh Edition. Most notable are the additions of considerable material on problem-oriented policing and community policing. In addition, the discussion of terrorism has been expanded to include the September 11, 2001, attack on America and its impact on the entire criminal justice system. Specific changes within each chapter include the following:

- Chapter 1—History: how southern law enforcement originated and the role of slave patrols.
- Chapter 2—Our laws: new Supreme Court precedents.
- Chapter 3—Crime: the FBI computer crime squad, hate crimes, the family as a training ground for violent behavior, cell phones and E911 technology.
- Chapter 4—Contemporary policing: the Blue Brotherhood, police subculture and code of silence.
- Chapter 5—Community policing: community partnerships created in response to terrorists' activities, private security's role in partnership with law enforcement, weapons in school and the effects of the proliferation of diversity on law enforcement.
- Chapter 6—Patrol: results of aggressive patrols, crime mapping, COMPSTAT, racial profiling, road rage, *City of Indianapolis v. Edmond* (2000) on drug check points.
- Chapter 7—Specialized roles: new guidelines for first responders to a crime scene, profilers and the future of DNA evidence.
- Chapter 8—Policing within the law: recent Supreme Court cases related to criminal procedure: *Bond v. United States* (2000) regarding luggage searches, *Dickerson v. United States* (2000) upholding Miranda, *Florida v. J.L.* (2000) regarding anonymous tips, *Illinois v. Wardlow* (2000) regarding sudden flight from police, *Illinois v. McArthur* (2001) regarding detention while executing a search warrant, *Kyllo v. United States* (2001) regarding thermal imaging and *United States v. Spinoza* (2001) regarding "knock and announce."
- Chapter 9—Gangs, drugs and terrorism: re-categorizing of gangs and gang activity, key findings of the National Youth Gang Survey, the dangers of Ecstasy, domestic and international terrorism and the role of local law enforcement.
- Chapter 10—Police conduct: expanded discussion of discretion, the federal model on use of force, new less-lethal weapons, and the police and the Americans with Disabilities Act (ADA).
- Chapter 11—Departmental issues: *Brown v. Bryan* (2000) failure to train.
- Chapter 12—Courts and corrections: community justice, restorative justice, specialized courts, community courts, community prosecution and community corrections.

How to Use This Text (Pedagogical Aids)

Introduction to Law Enforcement and Criminal Justice is more than a text. It is a learning experience requiring *your* active participation to obtain the best results. You will get the most out of the book if you first familiarize yourself with the total scope of law enforcement: read and think about the subjects listed in the Contents. Then follow five steps for each chapter to achieve triple-strength learning.

Triple-Strength Learning

1. Read the objectives at the beginning of each chapter, stated in the form of "Do You Know?" questions. This is your *first* exposure to the key concepts of the text. The following is an example of this format:

Do You Know?

- What the basic instrument of government is?

   Review the key terms and think about their meaning in the context of law enforcement.

2. Read the chapter, underlining or taking notes if that is your preferred study style. Pay special attention to all information within the highlighted area and the magnifying glass icon. This is your *second* exposure to the chapter's key concepts. The following is an example of this format:

The U.S. Constitution is the basic instrument of government and the supreme law of the United States.

   The key concepts of each chapter are emphasized in this manner. Also pay attention to all words in **bold print.** All key terms will be in bold print when they are first used.

3. Read the summary carefully. This will be your *third* exposure to the key concepts. By now you should have internalized the information.
4. To make sure you have learned the information, when you have finished reading a chapter reread the list of objectives given at the beginning of that chapter to make certain you can answer each question. If you find yourself stumped, find the appropriate material in the chapter and review it. Often these questions will be used as essay questions during testing.
5. Review the key terms to be certain you can define each. These also are frequently used as test items.

A Note: The material we've selected to highlight using the triple-strength learning instructional design includes only the chapter's key concepts. While this information is certainly important in that it provides a structural foundation for understanding the topic(s) discussed, you may not simply glance over the "Do You Know?" highlighted boxes and summaries and expect to have mastered the chapter. You are also responsible for reading and understanding the material that surrounds these basics—the "meat" around the bones, so to speak.

Exploring Further

The text also provides an opportunity for you to apply what you have learned or to go into specific areas in greater depth through discussion questions, InfoTrac College Edition assignments and Internet assignments. Complete each of these areas as directed by the text or by your instructor. Be prepared to share your findings with the class.

Good reading and learning!

Ancillaries

To further enhance your study of law enforcement and criminal justice, several supplements are available:

- **Study Guide**—A workbook that includes key concepts and terms, chapter summaries with fill-in-the-blank questions, and practice test questions in multiple choice format.
- **The Criminal Justice Resource Center http://cj.wadsworth.com**—An exceptional resource Web site containing links to over 3,000 popular criminal justice sites, jobs, news and other interesting and relevant links.
- **Careers in Criminal Justice 2.0 Interactive CD-ROM**—With this CD-ROM, students can view video profiles of actual testimonials from people in the field and link to the various career options in the criminal justice system while also learning about job requirements and salaries. Also included is FREE access to the Holland personalized self-assessment test, designed to help students determine which careers best suit their interests, as well as tips on cover letters, resumes and interviews.
- **CNN Today Video Series**—Exclusively from Thomson/Wadsworth, the *CNN Today* Video Series offers compelling videos that feature current news footage from the Cable News Network's comprehensive archives. With offerings for Introduction to Criminal Justice, Criminology, Juvenile Delinquency, and Corrections, each of these video tapes provides a varied collection of two- to ten-minute clips on such hot topics as police brutality, terrorism, high-tech crime fighting tools, registering sex offenders, juveniles behind bars, elderly inmates and much more. Available to qualified adopters, these videotapes are great lecture launchers as well as classroom discussion pieces.
- **Crime Scenes CD-ROM**—An interactive CD-ROM featuring six vignettes allowing you to play various roles as you explore all aspects of the criminal justice system.
- **Internet Investigator, Third Edition**—A colorful trifold brochure listing the most popular Internet addresses for criminal justice-related Web sites.
- **Seeking Employment in Criminal Justice and Related Fields, Fourth Edition**—This book provides specific information on many criminal justice professions, helpful tips on resumes and cover letters, practical advice on interview techniques and includes a free copy of the *Careers in Criminal Justice CD-ROM,* Release 2.0.

Acknowledgments

We would like to thank the reviewers of the Seventh Edition:

William Castleberry
University of Tennessee–Martin

Lisa Kay Decker
Indiana State University

Darek Niklas
Rhode Island College

Charles Ousley
Seminole State College

James W. Robinson
Louisiana State University–Eunice

For their valuable suggestions for the previous editions of *Introduction to Law Enforcement and Criminal Justice,* thank you to: Constance M. Bennett, Seminole Community College; Kenneth Bowser, Westfield State College; Roger Brown, Golden Valley Lutheran College; Steven Brown, East Tennessee State University; William Castleberry, University of Tennessee—Martin; Lisa Kay Decker, Indiana State University; Vincent Del Castillo, John Jay College of Criminal Justice; Rita Dorsey, Shelby Community College; David G. Epstein, Brunswick Junior College; Chris W. Eskridge, University of Nebraska; Larry Gaines, Eastern Kentucky University; James N. Gilbert, University of Nebraska; Larry A. Gould, Northern Arizona University; George Green, Mankato State University; Martin A. Greenberg, Ulster County Community College; Edmund Grosskopf, Indiana State University; Daniel Gunderson, Chippewa Valley Technical College; Burt C. Hagerman, Oakland Community College; Hill Harper, Valdosta State University; Larry W. Hensel, Tallahassee Community College; Thomas Hinze, Riverland Community College; Robert G. Huckabee, Indiana State University; Robert Ingram, Florida International University; Robert R. Ives, Rock Valley College; Paul H. Johnson, Murray State University; William Kelly, Auburn University; Leonard Luzky, Ocean City College; Sidney A. Lyle, Odessa College; Michael Moberly, Southern Illinois University at Carbondale; Glen Morgan, Lincolnland Community College; M.G. Neithercutt, California State University—Hayward; James E. Newman, Police Academy, Rio Hondo Community College; Darek Niklas, Rhode Island College; E. W. Oglesby, Fullerton College; Charles Ousley, Seminole State College; Joseph Polanski, Sinclair Community College; Frank Post, Fullerton College; James W. Robinson, Louisiana State University–Eunice; Jack Spurlin, Missouri Southern College; James Stinchcomb, Miami Dade Community College; Jack Taylor, Oscar Rose Junior College; Gary W. Tucker, Sinclair Community College; Larry Tuttle, Palm Beach Junior College; Myron Utech, University of Wisconsin at Eau Claire; Tim Vieders, Niagra County Community College; James Walsh, Mount San Jacinto College; Douglas Watson, Northern Essex Community College; David A. Wilson, Turnbull Police Department; Dawn B. Young, Bossier Parish Community College; and Gay A. Young, Johnson County Community College. Any errors in the text are, however, the sole responsibility of the co-authors.

A special thank you to Christine M.H. Orthmann for her careful proofreading of galleys and page proofs, her thorough indexing and for preparing the *Instructor's Manual* and the *Student Study Guide.* Thank you also to Joseph Wrobleski, Evelie Bakken, Diane Wrobleski, and Dawn and Jim Donald for their research assistance. Finally, we thank Sabra Horne, Shelley Murphy and Jennie Redwitz, our editors at Wadsworth; Peggy Francomb, our production editor at Shepherd, Inc.; and our families and colleagues for their support and assistance throughout the evolution of this text.

About the Authors

Henry M. Wrobleski, LLB, is the former coordinator of the Law Enforcement Program at Normandale Community College. He is a respected author, lecturer, consultant and expert witness with 30 years' experience in law enforcement. He is also the dean of instruction for the Institute for Professional Development and is a graduate of the FBI Academy.

Other Wadsworth texts Mr. Wrobleski has co-authored are *Introduction to Private Security,* 4th ed. and *Police Operations,* 3rd ed.

Kären M. Hess, PhD, has written extensively in the field of law enforcement and criminal justice. She is a member of the English department at Normandale Community College as well as the president of the Institute for Professional Development. She is also a member of the Academy of Criminal Justice Sciences (ACJS), the American Correctional Association (ACA), the American Society for Law Enforcement Trainers (ASLET), the International Association of Chiefs of Police (IACP), the National Institute of Justice (NIJ), and the Police Executive Research Forum. In addition she is a fellow in the Textbook and Academic Authors' Association (TAA).

Other Wadsworth texts Dr. Hess has co-authored are *Constitutional Law,* 2nd ed., *Corrections in the 21st Century: A Practical Approach, Criminal Investigation,* 6th ed., *Criminal Procedure, Introduction to Private Security,* 4th ed., *Juvenile Justice,* 3rd ed., *Management and Supervision in Law Enforcement,* 3rd ed., *Police in the Community: Strategies for the 21st Century,* 3rd ed., *Police Operations,* 3rd ed. and *Seeking Employment in Criminal Justice and Related Fields,* 4th ed.

Chapter 1

A Brief History: The Evolution of Law and Our Criminal Justice System

The farther backward you can look, the farther forward you are likely to see.
—Winston Churchill

Do You Know?

- What a law is?
- When and why law enforcement began?
- The significance of the tithing system, the Frankpledge system, Leges Henrici, the Magna Carta, the parish constable system and the Watch and Ward system?
- The origins of features of our criminal justice system, such as general alarms and citizen's arrests? The offices of constable, sheriff and justice of the peace? Local responsibility for law enforcement? Division of offenses into felonies and misdemeanors? Jury by peers and due process? Paid law enforcement officers? Women in law enforcement?
- What significant contributions Sir Robert Peel made to law enforcement?
- Where and when the first police department was established in England and what it was called?
- What systems of law enforcement were brought from England to colonial New England and the South?
- When and where the first modern American police force began and what it was modeled after?
- What the vigilante movement was and why it occurred?
- When and how federal and state law enforcement agencies originated in the United States?
- Who the chief law enforcement officer at the federal level is?
- What the first modern state police agency was and when it was established?
- What the five levels of law enforcement are?
- What three eras of policing have been identified? The main characteristics of each?
- What effect the spoils system had in the 1900s?
- What the Pendleton Act accomplished?
- What effect the Equal Employment Opportunity Act had?
- What four phases of development the juvenile justice system has gone through?
- What was established by the Juvenile Court Act of 1899?

Can You Define?

Bow Street Runners
community era
constable
dual system
Frankpledge system
Hue and Cry
hundreds
law
Leges Henrici
lex talionis
Magna Carta
parens patriae
parish
parish constable system
political era
proactive
professional model
rattle watch
reactive
reeve
reform era
regulators
riot act
sheriff
shire-reeve
shires
spoils system
tithing
tithing system
vigilante
Watch and Ward

INTRODUCTION

The heritage of law enforcement is a source of pride, as well as a guide to avoiding mistakes in the future. Specific dates and events are not as important as acquiring a sense of the sequence or chronology of how present-day laws and our system of law enforcement came into existence. **Law** is a body of rules for human conduct enforced by imposing penalties for their violation. Technically, laws are made and passed by the legislative branches of our federal, state, county and city governments. They are based on customs, traditions, mores and current need.

Law refers to all the rules of conduct established and enforced by the custom, authority or legislation of a group, community or country.

Law implies both prescription (rule) and enforcement by authority. In the United States, those who enforce the laws are *not* the same as those who make them. Historically, in other countries, this was not the case. Often rulers both made and enforced the laws.

This chapter discusses primitive and ancient law and its influence on the development of English law and law enforcement. This is followed by an overview of the evolution of law enforcement in England from the Anglo-Saxon tithing system, through the Norman Frankpledge system and on through the centuries up to the establishment of the London Metropolitan Police in 1829, the development of city and borough police forces and the entrance of women into law enforcement in England.

Next the continued evolution of the criminal justice system in the United States is described, beginning with a discussion of early law enforcement, including the first police forces, the city police and the vigilante movement. This is followed by a description of the various federal, state, county and local agencies established over the years. Next the overlap in these agencies is discussed, followed by a description of the three eras of policing: the political era, the reform era and the community era. The chapter concludes with a brief historical overview of the evolution of our juvenile justice system and a recap of important dates in police history.

Primitive and Ancient Law

Law enforcement can be traced back to the cave dwellers, who were expected to follow certain rules or face banishment or death. The customs depicted in early cave-dwelling drawings may represent the beginning of law and law enforcement.

The prehistoric social order consisted of small family groups living together as tribes or clans. Group living gave rise to customs everyone was expected to observe. The tribe's chief had executive, legislative and judicial powers and often appointed tribe members to perform special tasks, such as serving as a bodyguard or enforcing edicts. Crimes committed against individuals were handled by the victim or the victim's family. The philosophy of justice was retaliatory, that is, punish the offender. A person who stole the game from a neighbor's traps could expect to pay for the crime by being thrown into a pot of boiling oil or a cage of wild beasts. Other common punishments for serious offenses were flaying, impalement, burning at the stake, stoning, branding, mutilation and crucifixion.

A system of law and law enforcement began earlier than 2000 B.C. as a means to control human conduct and enforce society's rules. Keeping the peace was the responsibility of the group.

The earliest record of ancient people's need to standardize rules and methods of enforcement to control human behavior dates back to approximately 2300 B.C., when the Sumerian rulers Lipitshtar and Eshumma set standards on what constituted an offense against society. A hundred years later, the Babylonian King Hammurabi established rules for his kingdom designating not only offenses but punishments as well. Although the penalties prescribed were often barbaric by today's standards, the relationship between the crime and the punishment is of interest (see Figure 1.1). The main principle of the code was that "the strong shall not injure the weak." Hammurabi originated the legal principle of ***lex talionis***—an eye for an eye.

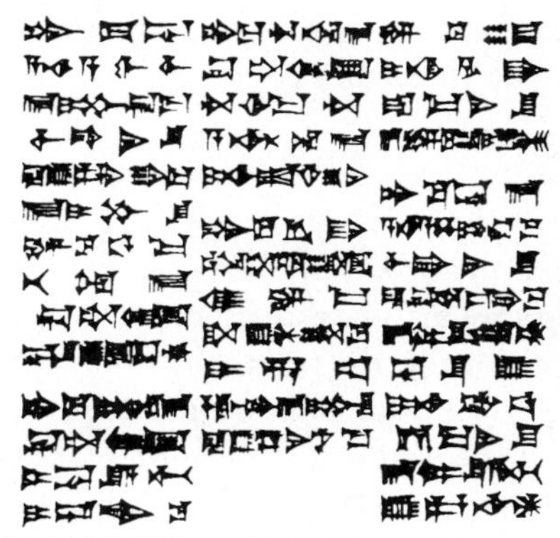

If a builder builds a house for a man and does not make its construction firm and the house collapses and causes the death of the owner of the house—that builder shall be put to death. If it causes the death of a son of the owner—they shall put to death a son of that builder. If it causes the death of a slave of the owner—he shall give the owner a slave of equal value. If it destroys property he shall restore whatever it destroyed and because he did not make the house firm he shall rebuild the house which collapsed at his own expense. If a builder builds a house and does not make its construction meet the requirements and a wall falls in—that builder shall strengthen the wall at his own expense.

Figure 1.1
From the Code of Hammurabi (2200 B.C.)

Source: Masonry Institute, 55 New Montgomery Street, San Francisco, CA 94105.

Egypt

The first accounts of a developing court system came from Egypt in approximately 1500 B.C. The court system was presided over by judges appointed by the Pharaoh. About 1000 B.C. in Egypt, public officers performed police functions. Their weapon and symbol of authority was a staff topped by a metal knob engraved with the king's name. The baton carried by the modern police officer may have its origin in that staff.

Greece

The Greeks had an impressive form of law enforcement called the *ephori.* Each year at Sparta a body of five *ephors* was elected and given almost unlimited powers as investigator, judge, jury and executioner. These five men also presided over the Senate and Assembly, assuring that their rules and decrees were followed. From the Greek philosopher Plato, who lived from 427 to 347 B.C., came the idea that punishment should serve a purpose other than simple retaliation.

Rome

Like the Greeks, the Romans had a highly developed system to administer justice. The Twelve Tables, the first written laws of the Roman Empire, were drawn up by 10 of the wisest men in Rome in 451 and 450 B.C. and were fastened to the speakers' stand in the Roman Forum. The tables dealt with legal procedures, property ownership, building codes, marriage customs and punishment for crimes.

At about the time of Christ, the Roman emperor Augustus chose members from his military to form the Praetorian Guard to protect the palace and the Urban Cohort to patrol the city. Augustus also established the Vigiles of Rome. Initially assigned as firefighters, they were eventually given law enforcement responsibilities. As the first civilian police force, the Vigiles sometimes kept the peace very ruthlessly. The word *vigilante* derives from these Vigiles.

Another important contribution from the Roman Empire was the Justinian Code. Justinian I, ruler of the eastern Roman Empire from A.D. 527 to 565, collected all existing Roman laws. They became known as the *Corpus Juris Civilis,* meaning body of law.

English Law and Law Enforcement

The beginnings of just laws and social control were destroyed during the Dark Ages as the Roman Empire disintegrated. Germanic invaders swept into the old Roman territory of Britain, bringing their own laws and customs. These invaders intermarried with those they conquered, the result being the hardy Anglo-Saxon.

Anglo-Saxons—The Tithing System

The Anglo-Saxons grouped their farms around small, self-governing, self-policed villages. When criminals were caught, the punishment was often severe. Sometimes, however, the tribe would let offenders prove innocence through battle or through testimony by other tribespeople willing to swear that the accused was innocent. Additionally, the tribe sometimes allowed criminals to pay a fine for committing a crime or to work off the debt.

Over time, the informal family groupings became more structured. Alfred the Great (A.D. 849 to 899) established that all freemen belonged to an association binding them with a certain group of people. If one person in the group committed a crime and was convicted, all group members were responsible for the person's fine. Consequently all group members were careful to see that no one in the group broke the law. Every male, unless excused by the king, was enrolled in a group of 10 families known as a **tithing.** To maintain order they had a chief tithingman who was the mayor, council and judge in one. Society was so basic that they enforced only two laws: laws against murder and theft.

> The **tithing system** established the principle of collective responsibility for maintaining local law and order.

Any victim or person who discovered a crime would put out the **Hue and Cry,** for example, "Stop, thief!" Those hearing the cry would stop what they were doing and help capture the suspect.

> The Hue and Cry may be the origin of the general alarm and the citizen's arrest.

When capture was made, the suspect was brought before the chief tithingman, who determined innocence or guilt plus punishment. Theft was often punished by working off the loss through bondage or servitude—the basis for civil law, restitution for financial loss (Lunt, 1938).

If a criminal sought refuge in a neighboring village, that village was expected to return the criminal for punishment. This cooperation among villagers eventually resulted in the formation of **hundreds,** groups of 10 tithings. The top official of the hundred was called a **reeve.**

> The hundreds also elected a **constable** to lead them in pursuit of any lawbreakers. The constable was the first English police officer and had charge of the community's weapons and horses. Finally, the hundreds were consolidated into **shires** or counties. The head of the shire was called the **shire-reeve,** the forerunner of our county sheriff.

The shire-reeve acted as both police officer and judge, traveling from hundred to hundred. The shire-reeve had the power of *posse comitatus,* meaning he could gather all the men of a shire together to pursue a lawbreaker, a practice that was the forerunner of our posse.

The Norman Frankpledge System

In 1066 William the Conqueror, a Norman, invaded and conquered England. As king of the conquered nation, William was too concerned about national security to allow the tithings to keep their system of home rule. He established 55 military districts each headed by a Norman shire-reeve who answered directly to the crown. The Normans modified the tithing system into the **Frankpledge system.**

> The Frankpledge system required loyalty to the king's law and mutual local responsibility of all free Englishmen to maintain the peace.

William also decided that shire-reeves should serve only as police officers. He selected his own judges, who traveled around and tried cases, forerunners of our circuit judges, in effect separating the law enforcement and judicial roles.

The Twelfth Century

William's son, Henry I, ruled England from 1100 to 1135 and issued the **Leges Henrici,** establishing arson, robbery, murder and crimes of violence as being against the king's peace. This set the precedent that for certain crimes a person is punished by the state rather than by the victim.

> The Leges Henrici made law enforcement a public matter and separated offenses into felonies and misdemeanors.

Henry I's reign was followed by many years of turmoil, which lasted until Henry II became king in 1154.

> Henry II established the jury system.

Henry II's jury system, called an inquisition, required people to give information to a panel of judges who determined guilt or innocence.

For the next 100 years, kings appointed enforcement officers to meet their needs. When John became king in 1199, he abused his power by demanding more military service from the feudal class, selling royal positions to the highest bidder and increasing taxes without obtaining consent from the barons—actions all contrary to feudal custom. In addition, John's courts decided cases according to his wishes, not according to law.

In 1213 a group of barons and church leaders met to call for a halt to the king's injustices. They drew up a list of rights they wanted King John to grant them. After the king refused on two separate occasions, the barons raised an army and forced him to meet their demands. On June 15, 1215, King John signed the Magna Carta.

The Magna Carta

Our modern system of justice owes much to the Magna Carta, a decisive document in the development of England's constitutional government.

> The **Magna Carta,** a precedent for democratic government and individual rights, laid the foundation for requiring rulers to uphold the law; forbade taxation without representation; required due process of law, including trial by jury; and provided safeguards against unfair imprisonment.

The Magna Carta contained 63 articles, most requiring the king to uphold feudal law. Article 13 restored local control to cities and villages, a fundamental principle of American law enforcement. Another article declared that no freeman should be imprisoned, deprived of property, sent out of the country or destroyed except by the lawful judgment of peers or the law of the land. The concept of due process of law, including trial by jury, developed from this article.

The Next 500 Years

Several interesting developments in law enforcement occurred in the following centuries. In 1285 King Edward I established a curfew and night watch program that allowed for the gates of Westminster, then capital of England, to be locked, keeping the city's occupants in and unwanted persons out. Bailiffs were hired as night watchmen to enforce the curfew and guard the gates. Edward I also mandated that groups of 100 merchants be responsible for keeping peace in their districts, again making law enforcement a local responsibility. This system of law enforcement, called the **Watch and Ward,** provided citizens protection 24 hours a day. The term *Watch and Ward* originated from the name of the shifts, with the day shift called *ward* and the night shift *watch.*

With an ever-increasing population and a trend toward urbanization, law enforcement became truly a collective responsibility. If a man's next-door neighbor broke the law, the man was responsible for bringing the lawbreaker before the shire-reeve. The hundred decided yearly who would be responsible for maintaining law and order, with responsibility rotated among community members. Inevitably some people paid other members to serve in their place, beginning a system of deputies paid to be responsible for law and order. The paid deputy system was then formalized so that those whose turn it was to pay met and appointed the law enforcers. The abuse of citizen duty to serve as watchmen was pervasive, however, and led to petty thieves and town drunks serving as watchmen.

During the fourteenth century, the shire-reeve was replaced by the justice of the peace.

The justice of the peace was assisted by the constables and three or four men knowledgeable of the country's laws. At first the justice of the peace was involved in both judicial matters and law enforcement, but later his powers became strictly judicial. The justice of the peace eventually became the real power of local government (Lunt).

With the passing of feudal times and the rise in the power of the church, the unit of local government in rural areas progressed from the hundred to the **parish,** the area in which people lived who worshipped in a particular church. Each year the parish appointed a parish constable to act as their law officer. This system of maintaining law and order in rural Britain lasted from the Middle Ages until the eighteenth century.

During the Middle Ages, the **parish constable system** was used for rural law enforcement; the Watch and Ward system was used for urban law enforcement.

Developments in urban England required a different system of law enforcement. With urbanization came commerce, industry and a variety of buildings usually made of wood, since England was primarily forest land. For purposes of fire prevention, the town guild appointed men who patrolled at night on fire watch. They assumed the coincidental responsibility of preventing people from breaking into houses and shops.

Although the Watch and Ward system was primitive and not very effective, it was adequate until the Industrial Revolution (1750) began. About the same time, famine struck the rural areas, and large numbers of people moved from the country into the towns seeking work in weaving and knitting mills and in factories. Many, however, failed to find work, and England experienced much unemployment, poverty and crime.

In addition, political extremists often incited mobs to march on Parliament. The government had no civil police force to deal with mob violence, so they ordered a magistrate to read the **riot act,** permitting the magistrate to call the military to quell the riot. This is the forerunner of our practice of governors having authority to call out their state's National Guard in times of rioting or violent strikes.

The use of a military force to repress civil disobedience did not work very well. Soldiers hesitated to fire on their own townspeople, and the townspeople, who actually paid the soldiers' wages, resented being fired on by soldiers they had hired to protect them.

In addition to unemployment, poverty and resentment against the use of military force, the invention of gin and whiskey in the seventeenth century and the subsequent increase in the liquor trade also caused a rise in violent crimes and theft. Because many constables were employed in the liquor trade, they often did not enforce regulations governing taverns and inns. In addition the London watchmen were highly susceptible to bribes and payoffs.

Henry Fielding and the Bow Street Runners

In 1748 Henry Fielding, lawyer, playwright and novelist, was appointed chief magistrate of Bow Street in policeless London. Fielding fought for social and criminal reform. He defied the law by discharging prisoners convicted of petty theft, giving reprimands in place of the death penalty and exercising general leniency.

Fielding wrote and published pamphlets and books about London's poverty-stricken inhabitants and the causes of crime, calling for an understanding and lessening of their suffering. He also urged that magistrates be paid a salary rather than depending on fees and fines for their income.

During this time thieves and robbers moved freely in London's streets, looting and rioting. Although such riots inevitably brought soldiers, they sometimes did not arrive for two or three days. Fielding suggested that citizens join together, go into the streets and trace the perpetrators of crime and instigators of mob violence *before* they committed crimes or caused destruction. Such views made Fielding one of the earliest advocates of crime prevention.

Fielding was also instrumental in establishing the **Bow Street Runners,** the first detective unit in London. This amateur volunteer force, under Fielding's direction, swept clean the Bow Street neighborhood. When these runners proved successful, other units were organized. Foot patrols of armed men guarded the city's streets, and a horse patrol combated highway robbery on the main roads up to 25 miles from Bow Street.

Although the Bow Street Runners and patrols greatly improved control in the Bow Street area of London, other parts of London were overwhelmed by the impact of the Industrial Revolution. Machines were taking the place of many jobs, causing unemployment and poverty. The cities were developing into huge slums, and the crime rate soared. Children were often trained to be thieves, and for the first time in England's history, juvenile delinquency became a problem. Developments in England had a great influence on the juvenile justice system that would later develop in the United States. Citizens began carrying weapons, and the courts used long-term prison sentences, resulting in overcrowded jails and prisons. Punishments were also severe, with more than 160 crimes punishable by death.

Despite the rampant crime, however, most Londoners resisted an organized police force, seeing it as restricting their liberty. They had fought hard to overcome the historical abuse of military power by the English kings and resisted any return to centralized military power. Then, in 1819 and 1820, two contrasting incidents helped people change their minds. The first was the Peterloo Massacre, an attack by armed soldiers on a meeting of unemployed workers that left 11 people dead and hundreds injured. This incident vividly illustrated the danger of using soldiers to maintain peace. In contrast, in the second incident, the Bow Street Runners broke up a conspiracy to murder a number of government officials. When the conspirators were executed, people saw that actions by professional peacekeepers could prevent a major insurrection.

In addition to rampant crime, Parliament was also concerned about poverty, unemployment and general conditions. Five parliamentary commissions of inquiry met in London between 1780 and 1820 to determine what should be done about the public order. It was not until Sir Robert (Bobbie) Peel was appointed Home Secretary that the first constructive proposal was brought before Parliament.

Peelian Reform

Sir Robert Peel, often referred to as the "father of modern policing," proposed a return to the Anglo-Saxon principle of individual community responsibility for preserving law and order.

> Peel's principles for reform called for local responsibility for law and order; appointed, paid civilians to assume this responsibility; and standards for these individuals' conduct and organization. His proposals led to the organization of the Metropolitan Police of London in 1829.

The name *police,* introduced into England from France, is derived from the Greek word *polis* meaning "city." The principles of Peelian Reform stated:

- Police must be stable, efficient and organized militarily.
- Police must be under governmental control.
- The deployment of police strength by both time and area is essential.
- The securing and training of proper persons is at the root of efficiency.
- Public security demands that every police officer be given a number.
- Police headquarters should be centrally located and easily accessible.
- Policemen should be hired on a probationary basis.
- The duty of police is to prevent crime and disorder.
- The test of police efficiency is the absence of crime and disorder, not the visible evidence of police action in dealing with these problems.
- The power of the police to fulfill their duties is dependent on public approval and on their ability to secure and maintain public respect.
- The police should strive to maintain a relationship with the public that gives reality to the tradition that *the police are the public and the public are the police.*

AP/Wide World Photos

During the first few years of reform, Peel encountered strong opposition was encountered. In addition to this opposition, Peel was faced with the problem of finding a building for the newly created London Police. He chose an abandoned building built many years before for visiting Scottish nobility. This building became known the world over as Scotland Yard, as immortalized by A. Conan Doyle in his Sherlock Holmes mysteries.

Peel's principles became the basis of police reform in many large cities in America. In addition, one of Peel's first steps was to introduce reform that abolished the death penalty for more than 100 offenses.

London Metropolitan Police (1829)

British police historian Critchley (1967, p.52) states: "From the start, the police was to be a homogeneous and democratic body in tune with the people, and drawing itself from the people." The London Metropolitan Police, called "Bobbies" after Sir "Bobbie" Peel, were uniformed for easy identification—top hats, three-quarter-length royal blue coats and white trousers—and were armed only with truncheons. Their primary function was crime prevention through patrol.

Unfortunately the London Metropolitan Police were not popular. Soon after the force went on street duty in 1829, a London mob assembled to march on Parliament. A police sergeant and two constables asked the mob leaders to send their people home. Rather than dispersing, the mob attacked the sergeant and constables, killing the sergeant and critically injuring the constables. A jury of London citizens, after hearing evidence clearly indicative of murder, returned a verdict of justifiable homicide. In time, however, police officers discharging their duties with professional integrity created a respect for the law.

City and Borough Police Forces (1835)

Broad public use of the steam engine and railways and better roads helped move many criminals from London to provincial cities, such as Birmingham, Liverpool and Manchester. Soon the citizens of these cities demanded some police organization similar to London's. In 1835 Parliament enacted legislation allowing (but not requiring) every city or borough (unincorporated township) of more than 20,000 people to form a police force.

Women Enter Law Enforcement

In 1883 the London Metropolitan Police appointed two women to supervise women convicts. Their numbers and functions later expanded.

In 1905 a woman was attached to the London Metropolitan Police force to conduct inquiries in cases involving women and children. Each year several more police matrons were hired.

Early in World War I, two separate movements for women police began. The Women Police Volunteers was formed and later came to be called the Women Police Service. In 1920 the group split into the Women's Auxiliary Service and the Women Patrols of the National Union of Women Workers of Great Britain and Ireland. The present official women police are largely a direct continuation of the Women Patrols (Chapman and Johnston, 1962).

Early Law Enforcement in the United States

When the English colonists came to America, they brought with them many traditions, including traditions in law enforcement. From the beginning they were concerned with avoiding anarchy:

> As the *Mayflower* rode at anchor off Cape Cod, some of the passengers threatened to go out on their own, without any framework of government. To avoid this threat of anarchy, the *Mayflower Compact* [1620] agreed that: "We . . . doe . . . solemnly and mutually . . . covenant and combine our selves together into a civil body politike for our better ordering and preservation . . . and by vertue hereof to enact . . . such just and equall lawes . . . unto which we promise all due submission and obedience" (Gardner, 1985, p.26).

The early colonial American settlements relied heavily on self-policing to assure the peace. Communal pressure was the backbone of law enforcement. The colonists were of similar background, most held similar religious beliefs, and there was actually little worth stealing. The seeds of vice and crime were present, however, as noted by Perry (1973, p.24):

> These colonists were far from the cream of European society; in many cases they represented the legal and religious castoffs. (Persons found guilty of criminal or religious offenses who were banished from Europe and exported to the New World.) Their migration served the dual purpose of removing socially undesirable persons from the Mother country and providing manpower for the outposts of imperial expansion.

Many features of British law enforcement were present in early American colonial settlements. In New England, where people depended on commerce and industry, the night watchman or constable served as protector of public order. In the South, where agriculture played a dominant role, the office of **sheriff** was established as the means of area law enforcement. Most watchmen and sheriffs were volunteers, but many were paid to serve in the place of others who were to patrol as a civic duty.

New England adopted the night watchman or constable as the chief means of law enforcement; the South adopted the office of sheriff.

Many different types of law enforcement were tried in many different parts of the country. Almost all used some kind of night watch system, with little or no protection during the day. The fastest-growing municipalities were the first to organize legal forces.

The First U.S. Police Forces

The first police forces in the United States were developed in Boston, New York and Los Angeles.

Boston

In 1631 the Boston court established a six-man force to guard the city from sunset to sunup, the first night watch in America. In 1636 a town watch was created and stayed in effect for more than 200 years. At first the primary function was to ring a bell in case of fire. In 1702 the police were to patrol the streets in silence. In 1735 they were required to call out the time of day and the weather.

New York

The first colonists in New York, then called New Amsterdam, were the Dutch who settled on Manhattan Island's south end. In 1643 a "burgher guard" was formed to protect the colony. Then, in 1653, New Amsterdam became a city (population 800), and the burgher guard was changed to a **rattle watch,** a group of night patrolling citizens armed with rattles to call for help (Bailey, 1989, p.346).

In 1664 the British took over New Amsterdam and renamed it New York. Thirty years later the first uniformed police officers replaced the nighttime rattle watch, and four years after that New York's streets were lighted.

The system of watchmen was very ineffective. Often the watchman was sentenced to patrol as a form of punishment for a misdemeanor. In addition citizens could avoid watch duty by hiring someone to take their places. Wealthy citizens came to rely on hiring others, and the men they hired then hesitated to invoke their authority against the well-to-do. By the mid-1700s New York City's night watch was "a parcel of idle, drinking, vigilant snorers, who never quell'd any nocturnal tumult in their lives; . . . but would, perhaps, be as ready to join in a burglary as any thief in Christendom" (Richardson, 1970, p.10).

Due to a continuing increase in crime during the day, New York City hired an assortment of watchmen, fire marshals and bell ringers to patrol both day and night. In 1844 a paid day watch was established, consisting of 16 officers appointed by the mayor. At this time the night watch consisted of 1,100 watchmen and was completely separate from the day force. Friction existed between the day and night forces, and they were incapable of combating the growing lawlessness in the city. Seeking a remedy, legislators from New York City visited the London Metropolitan Police Department and were duly impressed.

In 1844 New York City established the first modern round-the-clock, paid American city police force, modeled after London's Metropolitan Police.

Soon other cities followed suit, including Chicago, Cincinnati, New Orleans, Philadelphia, Boston, Baltimore and San Francisco.

Although patterned after the London Metropolitan Police, New York police officers protested wearing uniforms. Not until 12 years later did the New York police adopt a full police uniform and become the first uniformed law enforcement agency in the country. Likewise, although Fielding established the Bow Street Runners (the first detective unit) in 1750, more than 100 years passed before American police agencies recognized a need for detective units. In 1866 Detroit established the first detective bureau, followed by New York in 1882 and Cincinnati in 1886. Other important differences from the London police were that police in the United States were armed and they were under local, not national, control.

Los Angeles

In 1850 California became a state, and Los Angeles incorporated as a city with a population of 1,610. During its first year, the city elected a mayor, a city marshal and a sheriff:

> The duties assumed by the sheriff and marshal included the collection of local taxes. The sheriff's obligations required him to traverse a vast area on horseback, fighting bands of Indians and marauding desperadoes. Lacking paid assistants, the marshal was permitted to deputize citizens whenever necessary to maintain order (Bailey, pp.310–316).

In 1853 the city council established a police force of 100 volunteers, called the Los Angeles Rangers. Four years later they were replaced by the Los Angeles City Guards, who were charged with maintaining the peace. Finally, in 1869, the police force changed from a voluntary organization to a paid department.

Slave Patrols

Law enforcement in the South evolved from a different origin. By 1700 most Southern colonies, concerned by the dangers posed by oppressed slaves, established a code of laws to regulate slaves, for example prohibiting slaves from possessing weapons, congregating in groups, resisting punishment or leaving the plantation without permission.

Not surprisingly, many slaves resisted their bondage, attempting to escape or lashing out through criminal acts or revolts. The threat of harm by slaves was compounded by their growing number; in some Southern states, blacks outnumbered whites by more than 2 to 1. The white colonists' fear of this large and potentially dangerous slave population led to the creation of special enforcement officers—slave patrols (Reichel, 1999, p.82). By the mid-1700s, every Southern colony had a slave patrol, most of whom were allowed to enter any plantation and break into slaves' dwellings, search slaves' persons and possessions at will, beat and even kill any slaves found violating the slave code. Asirvatham (2000, p.2) states:

> Twentieth-century Southern law enforcement was essentially a direct outgrowth of the 19th-century slave patrols employed to enforce curfews, catch runaways, and suppress rebellion. Even later on, in Northern and Southern cities alike, "free men of color" were hired as cops only to keep other African-Americans in line [enforcing Jim Crow laws supporting segregation]. Until the 1960s black cops, by law or by custom, weren't given powers of arrest over white citizens, no matter how criminal.

Evolution of the City Police

When city police were first established, their only contact with their departments was face-to-face meetings or messengers. One early means of communication was a telephone pole light system to notify police of a call awaiting response. During the 1850s, however, telegraph networks linked police headquarters directly with their districts. Several decades later a modified telegraph system linked the patrol officers directly to the station. A fire alarm system, first introduced in Boston, was adopted for police use. Call boxes placed on city street corners were equipped with a simple lever that signaled the station that the officers were at their posts. A bell system was added that allowed the patrol officers to use a few simple signals to call an ambulance, a "slow wagon" for routine duties or a "fast wagon" for emergencies. The introduction of a special "Gamewell" telephone into the call box in 1880 made this a two-way communication system, greatly improving contact between patrol officers and their station houses.

The Civil War brought new social control problems. As centers of population became increasingly urbanized, fringe areas became incorporated suburbs of the hub city. These newly developed fringe cities had their own police forces, which fostered complex, uncoordinated relationships, compartmentalization and inefficiency.

Although cities developed police departments and maintained a certain level of law and order, this was not the case in many areas, especially the frontiers. In such areas Americans came to rely upon vigilante groups for law and order.

The Vigilante Movement

In response to the absence of effective law and order in frontier regions, as many as 500 vigilante movements were organized between 1767 and 1900 (Klockars, 1985, p.30).

The **vigilante** movement refers to settlers taking the law into their own hands in the absence of effective policing.

The first American vigilante movement occurred from 1767 to 1769 in South Carolina:

> The disorder in the South Carolina back country of the 1760's was typical of later American frontier areas. . . . Outlaws, runaway slaves, and mulattoes formed their own communities where they enjoyed their booty. . . . By 1766 and 1767 the back country was in the grip of a "crime wave," and the outlaws were almost supreme (Brown, 1991, p.61).

Because there was no sheriff or court, "respectable settlers of average or affluent means" organized as **regulators** in 1767 to attack and break up the outlaw gangs and restore order. As noted by Brown (p.60): "An American tradition had begun, for, as the pioneers moved across the Appalachian Mountains, the regulator-vigilanted impulse followed the sweep of settlement toward the Pacific."

A characteristic of the vigilante movement was that the leader was usually one of the most powerful men in the community, thus making the movement highly respectable: "Two presidents (Andrew Jackson and Theodore Roosevelt), eight state governors (including Leland Stanford, Sr., founder of Stanford Uni-

Brown Brothers

Judge Roy Bean dispensed frontier justice and cold beer in the Texas territory west of the Pecos River.

versity), and four U.S. Senators had either been vigilantes or expressed strong support for vigilante movements" (Klockars, 1985, p.31).

An uneven judicial system and a lack of jails added to the strength of the vigilante tradition. The movement was evidence of the value Americans placed on law and order and the desire to be rid of those who would break the law. It was also evidence of a basic paradox in the illegal means used to the desired end: "Perhaps the most important result of vigilantism has not been its social-stabilizing effect but the subtle way in which it persistently undermined our respect for law by its repeated insistence that there are times when we may choose to obey the law or not" (Brown, p.72).

As the country grew and its society became more complex, federal and state agencies were established to meet needs that could not be met at the local level.

Establishment of Federal Agencies

Congress created several federal law enforcement agencies to meet demands created by the nation's changing conditions. The oldest federal agency is the U.S. Marshals Office, created in 1789. Figure 1.2 illustrates the most common federal agencies.

Among the earliest federal law enforcement agencies were the U.S. Marshals Office, the Immigration and Naturalization Service, the Secret Service and the Internal Revenue Service.

The Department of Justice

The Department of Justice is the largest law firm in the country, representing U.S. citizens in enforcing the law.

The attorney general is head of the Department of Justice and the chief law officer of the federal government.

The Department of Justice's law enforcement agencies include the Federal Bureau of Investigation, the Federal Drug Enforcement Administration, the U.S. Marshals, the Immigration and Naturalization Service and the Bureau of Prisons.

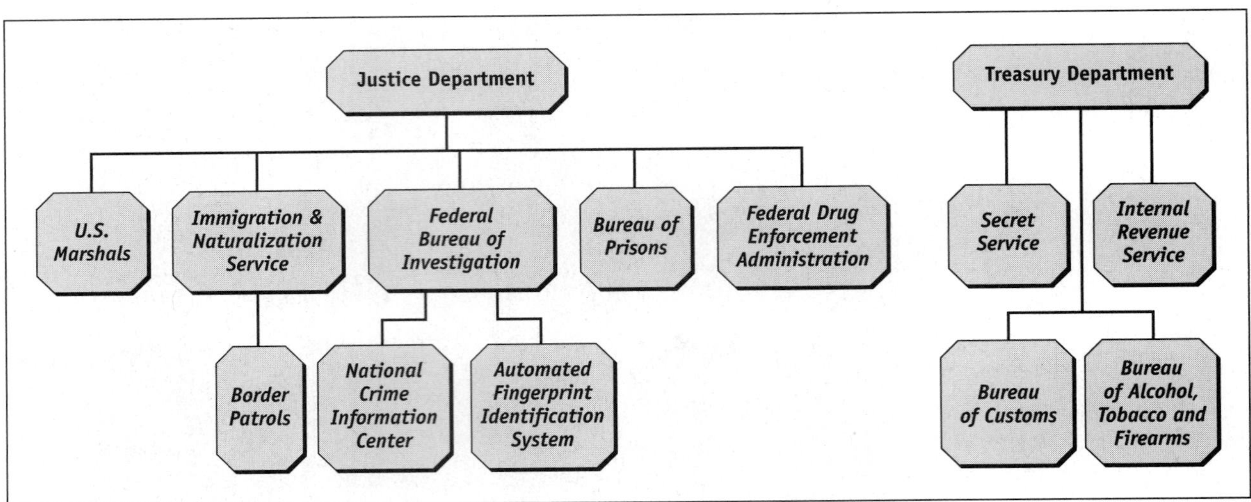

Figure 1.2
Federal Agencies

The Federal Bureau of Investigation (FBI)

Created as the Bureau of Investigation and renamed the Federal Bureau of Investigation in 1935, this is the primary investigative agency of the federal government. Its special agents have jurisdiction over more than 200 federal crimes. Their responsibilities include investigating espionage, interstate transportation of stolen property and kidnapping; unlawful flight to avoid prosecution, confinement or giving testimony; sabotage, piracy of aircraft and other crimes aboard aircraft; bank robbery and embezzlement; and enforcement of the Civil Rights Acts. The FBI also provides valuable services to law enforcement agencies throughout the country:

- The *Identification Division* is a central repository for fingerprint information, including its automated fingerprint identification system (AFIS), which greatly streamlines the matching of fingerprints with suspects.
- The *National Crime Information Center (NCIC)* is a computerized database network containing records of wanted persons, stolen vehicles, vehicles used in the commission of felonies, stolen or missing license plates, stolen guns and other stolen items serially identifiable, such as television sets and boat motors.
- The *FBI Laboratory,* the largest criminal laboratory in the world, is available without cost to any city, county, state or federal law enforcement agency in the country.
- *Uniform Crime Reports (UCR)* are periodical publications provided by the FBI which, since 1930, has served as a national clearinghouse for U.S. crime statistics. States report their monthly crime statistics to the FBI, which in turn releases information semiannually and annually regarding all crimes reported to it.

The Federal Drug Enforcement Administration (FDEA)

FDEA agents seek to stop the flow of drugs at their source, both domestic and foreign, and to assist state and local police in preventing illegal drugs from reaching local communities. They become involved in surveillance, raids, interviewing witnesses and suspects, searching for evidence and seizure of contraband.

The FDEA is charged with the full responsibility for prosecuting suspected violators of federal drug laws. It has liaison with law enforcement officials of foreign governments and highly trained agents stationed in all major cities and in 30 countries.

The U.S. Marshals

Marshals are appointed by the president and are responsible for (1) seizing property in both criminal and civil matters to satisfy judgments issued by a federal court, (2) providing physical security for U.S. courtrooms, (3) transporting federal prisoners and (4) protecting government witnesses whose testimony might jeopardize their safety.

The Immigration and Naturalization Service (INS)

The Immigration and Naturalization Service has border patrol agents who serve throughout the United States, Canada, Mexico, Bermuda, Nassau, Puerto Rico, the Philippines and Europe. They investigate violations of immigrant and nationality laws and determine whether aliens may enter or remain in the United States.

The Bureau of Prisons (BOP)

The Bureau of Prisons is responsible for the care and custody of persons convicted of federal crimes and sentenced to federal penal institutions. The bureau operates a nationwide system of maximum-, medium- and minimum-security prisons, halfway houses and community program offices.

The Department of the Treasury

The Department of the Treasury also has several agencies directly involved in law enforcement activities, including the Bureau of Customs, the Internal Revenue Service, the Secret Service and the Bureau of Alcohol, Tobacco and Firearms.

The Bureau of Customs

The Bureau of Customs has agents stationed primarily at ports of entry to the United States, where people and/or goods enter and leave. Customs agents investigate frauds on customs revenue and the smuggling of merchandise and contraband into or out of the United States.

The Internal Revenue Service (IRS)

The Internal Revenue Service, established in 1862, is the largest bureau of the Department of the Treasury. Its mission is to encourage the highest degree of voluntary compliance with the tax laws and regulations. IRS agents investigate willful tax evasion, tax fraud and the activities of gamblers and drug peddlers.

The Secret Service

The Secret Service was established in 1865 to fight currency counterfeiters. In 1901 it was given the responsibility of protecting the president of the United States, the president's family, the president-elect and the vice president.

The Bureau of Alcohol, Tobacco and Firearms (BATF)

The Bureau of Alcohol, Tobacco and Firearms is primarily a licensing and investigative agency involved in federal tax violations. The Firearms Division enforces the Gun Control Act of 1968.

Other Federal Law Enforcement Agencies

Although most federal law enforcement agencies are within either the Department of Justice or the Department of the Treasury, other federal agencies are also directly involved in law enforcement activities, such as U.S. Postal Inspectors, the Coast Guard and the armed forces military police, as well as investigators, intelligence agents and security officers for other federal agencies.

Establishment of State Agencies

Many federal agencies have state counterparts, including state bureaus of investigation and apprehension and state fire marshal divisions, as well as departments of natural resources, driver and vehicle services divisions and departments of human rights.

In 1835 the republic of Texas's provisional government established the Texas Rangers, a military unit responsible for border patrol. The apprehension of Mexican cattle rustlers was a primary task (Folley, 1980, p.88). In 1874 the Texas Rangers were commissioned as Texas police officers, with duties that included tracking down murderers, robbers, smugglers and mine bandits.

The Texas Rangers were the first agency similar to our present state police.

Massachusetts was next to establish a state law enforcement agency by appointing a small force of state officers in 1865 to control vice. The state also granted them general police powers; therefore, Massachusetts is usually credited with establishing the first law enforcement agency with general police authority throughout the state.

Most state police agencies established before the twentieth century were created in response to a limited need. This was not the case in Pennsylvania, which established the Pennsylvania Constabulary in 1905 to meet several needs: to (1) provide the governor an executive arm for help in fulfilling his responsibilities, (2) provide a means to quell riots occurring during labor disputes in the coal regions and (3) improve law enforcement services in the rural portions of the state (Folley, p.66). The Pennsylvania state police served as a model for other states and heralded the advent of modern state policing.

Today the most visible forms of state law enforcement are the *state police,* who often have general police powers and enforce all state laws, but do not usually work within municipalities that have their own forces unless requested; and *state highway patrols,* who focus their attention on the operation of motor vehicles on public highways and freeways, enforcing state traffic laws and all laws governing the operation of vehicles on public highways in the state. The highway patrols usually operate in uniform and drive distinctively marked patrol cars and motorcycles.

Development of County Agencies

The two main county law enforcement agencies are the county sheriff and the county police.

The County Sheriff

Many state constitutions have designated the sheriff as the chief county law enforcement officer. The sheriff is usually elected locally for a two- or four-year term, an obvious mixing of police and politics.

State law establishes the sheriff's powers and duties. Each sheriff is authorized to appoint deputies to assume responsibility for providing police protection, as well as a variety of other functions, including (1) keeping the public peace, (2) executing civil and criminal process (such as serving civil legal papers and criminal warrants), (3) keeping the county jail, (4) preserving the court's dignity and (5) enforcing court orders.

The hundreds of sheriff's departments vary greatly in organization and function. In some states the sheriff is primarily a court officer; criminal investigation and traffic enforcement are delegated to state or local agencies. In other states, notably in the South and West, the sheriff and deputies perform both traffic and criminal duties.

The sheriff's staff ranges from one (the sheriff only) to several hundred, including sworn deputies as well as civilian personnel. One major difference between sheriffs' offices and municipal police departments is that sheriffs often place greater emphasis on civil functions and operating corrections facilities.

The County Police

County police departments are often found in areas where city and county governments have merged and are led by a chief of police, usually appointed from within the department.

The Coroner or Medical Examiner

The office of coroner has a history similar to that of the sheriff and comes to modern law enforcement from ancient times (Adams, 1980, p.150). The coroner's principal task is to determine the cause of death and to take care of the remains and personal effects of deceased persons. The coroner need not be a medical doctor or have any legal background to be elected. In some jurisdictions, however, the coroner has been replaced by the medical examiner, a physician, usually a pathologist, who has studied forensic science.

Development of Local Agencies

Township and Special District Police

The United States has approximately 19,000 townships, which vary widely in scope of governmental powers and operations. Most townships provide a limited range of services for predominantly rural areas. Some townships, often those in well-developed fringe areas surrounding a metropolitan complex, perform functions similar to municipal police.

The Constable

Several states have established the office of constable, usually an elected official who serves a township, preserving the peace and serving processes for the local justice court. The constable may also be the tax collector, in charge of the pound, or authorized to execute arrest warrants or transport prisoners.

The Marshal

In some parts of the United States, a marshal serves as a court officer, serving writs, subpoenas and other papers issued by the court and escorting prisoners from jail or holding cells in the courthouse to and from trials and hearings. The marshal also serves as the bailiff and protects the municipal judge and people in the court. In some jurisdictions the marshal is elected; in others, appointed.

Municipal Police

The United States has more than 40,000 police jurisdictions and approximately 450,000 police officers, all with similar responsibilities but with limited geographical jurisdictions. The least uniformity and greatest organizational complexity are found at the municipal level due to local autonomy. The majority of these police forces consist of fewer than 10 officers. This level of law enforcement is the primary focus of this text.

Overlap

American police forces may be classified according to the level of government each serves. However no uniform pattern of police administration exists at any level of government, and no mechanism exists to coordinate the agencies' activities and goals.

The five levels of government authorized to have law enforcement agencies are (1) township and special district police, (2) municipal police, (3) county police, (4) state police and (5) federal police.

The preceding discussion makes evident how law enforcement in the United States did not evolve in a consistent, regulated or sequential manner, resulting in considerable duplication and overlap in providing services. Overlapping jurisdictions and potential competition when two (and often many more) forces find themselves investigating the same offense pose serious problems for law enforcement and highlight the need for education and professionalism.

The evolution of policing is much more than a history of agencies that have emerged to meet society's needs. Policing itself has evolved in how it views itself, its responsibilities and the most effective means to meet those responsibilities.

The Three Eras of Policing

Kelling and Moore (1991, pp.3–25) describe three eras of policing: the political era, the reform era and the community era.

The Political Era (1840–1930)

One basic difference between England's first police and those in the United States was that in England, bobbies could be fired. In the United States, this was not the case:

> In New York, for example, the first chief of police could not dismiss officers under his command. The tenure of the chief was limited to one year. Consequently, any early New York cop who was solidly supported by his alderman and assistant alderman could disobey a police superior with virtual impunity. So while the British were firing bobbies left and right for things like showing up late to work, wearing disorderly uniforms, and behaving discourteously to citizens, American police were assaulting superior officers, refusing to go on patrol, extorting money from prisoners, and releasing prisoners from the custody of other officers. . . .
>
> Perhaps the only good thing about the corrupt, inefficient, ineffective, and disobedient early American police is that as an institution it could not be well controlled by anyone—not even the local politicians (Klockars, 1985, p.42).

In the **political era,** police forces were characterized by a broad social service function, a decentralized organization, an intimate relationship with the community and extensive use of foot patrol.

During the political era, police got their authority from politicians and the law. This close tie to politics often caused problems.

Police Corruption

As in other countries, corruption became a problem in U.S. law enforcement. One primary factor underlying this corruption was the prevalent **spoils system,** whose motto, "To the victor go the spoils," resulted in gross political interference with policing. The winning party felt its members should be immune from arrest, given special privileges in naming favorites for promotion and assisted in carrying out vendettas against their political opponents. This system led politicians to staff many of the nation's police forces with incompetent people as rewards for support, "fixing" arrests or assuring that arrests were not made, and securing immunity from supervision for certain establishments or people.

The spoils system encouraged politicians to reward their friends by giving them key positions in police departments.

Walker (1983, p.7) notes:

> The quality of American police service in the 19th century could hardly have been worse. The police were completely unprofessional and police work was dominated by corruption and inefficiency. The source of these problems was politics. Local government was viewed primarily as a source of opportunity—for jobs, for profit, for social mobility, for corruption. . . . Selection standards for police personnel were nonexistent. Officers obtained their jobs through political contacts. . . . In 1880 most big cities paid their police $900 a year; a factory worker could expect to earn only about $450 a year.

Organizational Modifications

Reform movements began early but moved slowly against the solidly entrenched political "untouchables." Cities sought to break political control through a variety of organizational modifications, including electing police officers and chiefs, administering forces through bipartisan lay boards, asking states to assume local policing and instituting mayor-council or council–city manager municipal government.

Electing the municipal chief of police was common with the establishment of local departments. Remembering the corrupt officials who served as long as they pleased the king, the people elected police officials to serve short terms so they would not have time to become too powerful or corrupt. However this system had several drawbacks. Not only were the officials not in office long enough to become corrupt, they weren't in office long enough to become proficient in their jobs. In fact officials would just get to know their own officers and have enough experience to run the police department when their terms would expire. The position of police chief had also become a popularity contest. Furthermore, since terms were so short, officials often kept their civilian jobs and generally devoted most of their time to them, giving only spare time to running the police force. Therefore most municipalities decided that having a permanent police chief, with experience and ability, was the best way to achieve effective law enforcement. Today the elected police chief system remains in only a few cities.

In the mid-1800s administrative police boards or commissions were established. Comprised of judges, mayors and private citizens, the board served as the head of the police department, with the police chief following its orders. The rationale was that, while the chief of police should be a professional and hold the job continuously, civilian control was necessary to maintain responsibility to community needs. This system lasted many years but had serious weaknesses; board members often proved more of a hindrance than a help, and the system fostered political corruption.

In an attempt to control corrupt police agencies and the incompetent local boards behind them, some areas adopted state control of local agencies, believing such a system would assure citizens adequate and uniform law enforcement. However, most cities and states found this was not the answer because laws were not equally enforced and the system lacked responsiveness to local needs. Therefore control was returned to local government in most instances.

The next system to be tried was the commission government charter. Commissioners were elected and charged with various branches of city government. This system, also on the decline, was as inadequate as the administrative police board.

The most prevalent current local system is the mayor-council or council–city manager government. The former is very efficient when the mayor is a full-time, capable administrator. The latter assures more continuity in the business administration and executive control of the overall operations because a professional, nonpolitical administrator manages the community's affairs. In either system the police chief is selected on merit.

The Pendleton Act

In 1883 a major step toward reducing police corruption occurred when Congress passed the Pendleton Act. Prior to this act, most government positions were filled by political appointment, with those appointed commonly incapable of performing their tasks well. One government worker who was going to be replaced by President Garfield shot and killed the president. This incident caused a public outcry and resulted in passage of the Pendleton Act.

The Pendleton Act created the civil service system for government employees and made it illegal to fire or demote a worker for political reasons.

The act established a Civil Service Commission to enforce its provisions. The new laws called for a test open to all citizens and for new workers to be hired on the basis of who had the highest grades. The act also relieved government workers from any obligation to give political service or payments.

The Social Service Function

During the political era, police served a broad social service function:

> Police ran soup lines; district or precinct stations were designed to provide brief lodging for immigrant workers when they arrived in cities; police assisted ward leaders in finding work for immigrants, both in police and other forms of work; and police provided a wide variety of other services (Kelling and Moore, p.7).

The department organization during the political era was decentralized, primarily because of lack of effective communication. Toward the end of this era, the call box made communication easier and helped to centralize the police organization.

During this era, police were usually close to their community. Foot patrol was the most common strategy used, bringing the beat officer into contact with the people. Most police officers lived in the area they policed and were of the same ethnic background.

Minorities

Little has been published about minority police officers in the early history of the United States. According to Sullivan (1989, p.331), African-Americans first served as police officers as early as 1861 in Washington, DC. Most were hired in large cities, and by around 1900 they made up 2.7 percent of all watchmen, police officers and firefighters. That number declined until about 1910 when less than 1 percent of police officers were African-American.

During this era many African-American police officers rode in cars marked "Colored Police," were often hired exclusively to patrol black areas and were allowed only to arrest other black citizens (Sullivan, p.331). In addition, few were promoted or given special assignments.

During the political era, African-American officers were often segregated and discriminated against.

Women

Initially women were restricted to processing female prisoners and to positions as police matrons. Many misconceptions about a woman's ability to perform certain "masculine" tasks were dispelled as a result of changing social attitudes; yet room for improvement remained.

At the end of the 1800s, a movement to employ women as regular police officers gained support. In 1883 Marie Owen became the first woman police officer in the United States, appointed by the Detroit Bureau of Police. In 1910 the first regular policewoman under civil service was appointed in Los Angeles. Shortly thereafter, in 1912, the first woman chief of police was appointed by the mayor of Milford, Ohio. By the end of World War I, more than 220 cities employed policewomen.

A major reason for this relatively rapid acceptance of female peace officers was a change in the public's view of the police function and the newly accepted emphasis on citizen protection and crime prevention rather than exclusive concentration on enforcing laws and detecting crimes. Women were welcomed into police departments, where they were assigned to handle cases involving children and women:

> There is little doubt that early policewomen were assigned to handle children and their problems because of the female nurturing role. This role coincided with societal values that made mothers responsible for insuring that children grew up to be good citizens. Furthermore, the early policewomen's movement (1910–1930) received support from both national women's groups and prestigious civic and social hygiene associations (Hale, 1992, pp.126–127).

In 1925 August Vollmer opened the Crime Prevention Division in the Berkeley, California, Police Department. This unit was headed by policewoman

Elizabeth Lossing, a psychiatric social worker. According to Hale (p.127): "The separate roles of policemen and policewomen were emphasized by the International Association of Chiefs of Police (IACP) at its meeting in 1922 where it was recommended that policewomen meet higher education and training standards than policemen. . . . The IACP stated that policewomen were essential to police work and recommended that police departments establish separate units."

During the political era, the roles of policewomen were clearly separated from those of policemen, with women serving a protective and nurturing role.

Prohibition

The Prohibition movement (1920–1933) resulted from passage of the Eighteenth Amendment in 1919, which outlawed the manufacture, sale or transportation, including importing and exporting, of intoxicating liquor beverages within the United States and its territories. Manning (1997, p.91) suggests that Prohibition resulted in one of the most important transformations in policing in the United States:

> It placed what had been a relatively corrupt and symbiotic form of police organization in large cities in opposition to large segments of the respectable classes in the communities in which they functioned. The enforcement of Prohibition laws not only created hostility and hatred of the police and made contacts between police and public increasingly adversarial, it increased the opportunities for legally created and defined corruption.

Prohibition ended in 1933 with passage of the Twenty-First Amendment repealing the Eighteenth Amendment. The inability of the police to control consumption of alcoholic beverages might be likened to the contemporary challenge of controlling use of illegal drugs.

The Wickersham Commission and Police Professionalism

In 1929 President Herbert Hoover appointed the national Commission on Law Observance and Enforcement to study the American criminal justice system. Named after its chairman, George Wickersham, the commission devoted two of its fourteen reports to the police. Report 11, *Lawlessness in Law Enforcement,* delineated the problem of police brutality, concluding that "the third degree—the inflicting of pain, physical or mental, to extract confessions or statements—is extensively practiced." Report 14, *The Police,* concentrated on police administration and called for expert leadership, centralized administrative control and higher personnel standards—in short, police professionalism.

The Reform Era (1930–1980)

In reaction to the shortcomings of the political era, the reform strategy developed, taking hold in the 1930s and thriving during the 1950s and 1960s, before beginning to erode during the late 1970s (Kelling and Moore, p.6).

In the **reform era,** police forces were characterized by authority coming from the law and professionalism; crime control as their primary function; a centralized, efficient organization; a professional remoteness from the community; and emphasis on preventive motorized patrol and rapid response to crime.

As early as the 1920s, August Vollmer was calling for reforms in policing. Vollmer was first town marshal and then police chief in Berkeley, California, from 1905 until 1932:

> Vollmer is often called the "Father or Dean of Modern Police Administration." Some of his important contributions include the early use of motorized patrol and the latest advancements in criminalists. He suggested the development of a centralized fingerprint system that was established by the FBI; he established the first juvenile unit, was the first to use psychological screening for police applicants, and was the first to emphasize the importance of college-educated police officers (Roberg and Kuykendall, 1993, p.71).

Vollmer developed the first degree-granting program in law enforcement at San Jose State College. He also advocated that police officers serve as social service workers and that police act to prevent crime by intervening in the lives of potential criminals, especially juveniles. In addition:

> Vollmer's emphasis on the quality of police personnel was tied closely to the idea of the professional officer. . . . Another concern of Vollmer's dealt with the efficient delivery of police services. His department became the first in the nation to use automobiles and the first to hire a full-time forensic scientist to help solve crimes (Dunham and Alpert, 1989, p.27).

One of Vollmer's protégés, O. W. Wilson, became the primary architect of the reform era and the style of policing known as the **professional model.** Like his mentor, Wilson advocated efficiency within the police bureaucracy through scientific techniques. He became police chief in Wichita, Kansas, and conducted the first systematic study of the effectiveness of using one-officer squad cars. Wilson's classic text, *Police Administration,* set forth specific ways to use one-officer patrol cars, to deploy personnel and to discipline officers. Wilson also accepted a professorship at the University of California, Berkeley, and in 1947 he founded the first professional school of criminology.

The reformers sought to disassociate policing from politics. They were to become professionals whose charge was to enforce the law, fairly and impartially. The social service function became of lesser importance or even nonexistent in some departments as police mounted an all-out war on crime. Two keys to this war were preventive patrol in automobiles and rapid response to calls. This is the style of policing with which most Americans are familiar and have come to expect.

Manning (p.92) describes three changes made in the 1930s that were fundamental to altering the police role:

1. Crime statistics were linked to police professionalism through the establishment of the Uniform Crime Reports.
2. Police began to tie their fate to changes in crime rates as measured by these published figures.
3. Police began to symbolize their mission in terms of the technological means by which they were said to accomplish it.

Manning suggests: "By the mid-1930s the use of the radio, of the automobile for mobile patrol, and the collection and systematization of crime statistics began to characterize large urban departments. . . . The police eagerly espoused, displayed, and continued to seek a technologically based, rationalized crime control mandate."

Unfortunately, the war on crime was being lost. Crime escalated, and other problems arose as well. In the 1960s violent ghetto riots caused millions of dollars in damages, thousands of injuries and many deaths:

> Most of these riots were triggered by incidents in which white officers were policing in black ghetto areas. The National Advisory Commission on Civil Disorder was formed to study the situation. The resulting Kerner Report (1968) was comprehensive and scathing, and placed a large part of the blame for the riots on racism in society and the severe under-representation of blacks in police departments (Sullivan, p.333).

As a result of this report and other studies, many cities began to actively recruit minorities for their police departments. The civil rights and anti–Vietnam War demonstrations and riots had other ramifications:

> They expanded civil protest beyond the inner city to middle-class colleges, main-street America, and television. They brought large numbers of middle-class and minority protestors into open conflict with the police. When the police employed tactics that included the use of force and mass arrests against protestors, they were portrayed as agents of repression who maintained order at the expense of justice. As a result, the rational-legal bureaucratic model of policing began to be questioned by a broader spectrum of the American people (Fyfe et al., 1997, p.17).

The Law Enforcement Education Program (LEEP)

Following publication of the Presidential Crime Commission's recommendation that by 1984 all police officers be required to have at least a bachelor's degree, Congress created and funded the Law Enforcement Education Program (LEEP). This program poured thousands of dollars into police education, and by the mid-1970s, more than 1,000 academic institutions had police-related courses being offered to thousands of students nationwide. Eventually, however, LEEP was phased out of the federal budget.

Another relatively short-lived federal boost to the professionalization of law enforcement was the Law Enforcement Assistance Administration.

The Law Enforcement Assistance Administration (LEAA)

In 1968 Congress enacted the Omnibus Crime Control and Safe Streets Act; Title 1 of this act established the Law Enforcement Assistance Administration, which existed through September 1979.

LEAA worked in partnership with state and local governments, historically responsible for crime reduction and law enforcement. Congress affirmed this historical responsibility in the Act: "Crime is essentially a local problem that must be dealt with by state and local governments if it is to be controlled effectively." Of even greater significance is the statement of Richard W. Velde, LEAA administrator, foreshadowing the community policing movement: "Crime control is everyone's business. It is not just the business of the criminal justice system—of police, courts and corrections—but of all citizens who want to live in harmony and peace."

LEAA awarded more than $9 billion to state and local governments to support tens of thousands of programs and projects.

The National Institute of Justice (NIJ)

The Omnibus Crime Control and Safe Streets Act also established the National Institute of Justice as a research and development agency to prevent and reduce crime and to improve the criminal justice system. Among the institute's mandates were that it sponsor special projects and research and development programs to improve and strengthen the criminal justice system, conduct national demonstration projects that employed innovative or promising approaches for improving criminal justice, develop new technologies to fight crime and improve criminal justice, evaluate the effectiveness of criminal justice programs and identify those that promised to be successful if continued or repeated, and carry out research on criminal behavior.

Advances for Women and Minorities

A boost was given to women and minorities when the Supreme Court ruled in *Griggs v. Duke Power Company* (1971) that any tests used for employment must be job-related. Another boost was the passage of the Equal Employment Opportunity Act (EEOA) in 1972.

The Equal Employment Opportunity Act prohibits discrimination on the basis of sex, race, color, religion or national origin in employment of any kind, public or private, local, state or federal.

That same year, women began to seek positions as patrol officers. Tension and conflict resulted. Accepted as assistants to policemen, they were seldom accepted as partners on patrol:

> Clearly, policewomen on patrol have faced many obstacles from both their peers and management, who believed that they cannot perform patrol duties because they have neither the physical strength to do the job; the authoritarian presence to handle violent confrontations; nor the ability to serve as backup to their partners in high-pressure situations. Attempts by supervisors to either overprotect policewomen, or keep them from areas with high violence further reinforce the view that women are not capable of performing patrol (Hale, p.128).

During the reform era, minorities and women obtained legal equality with white male officers but still often encountered discrimination.

The Kansas City Preventive Patrol Experiment

Another event during 1972 had a great impact on eroding the reform strategy; the classic Kansas City Preventive Patrol Experiment called into serious question the effectiveness of preventive patrol or rapidity of response, the basic strategies of the reform era. The Kansas City Experiment showed that "it makes about as much sense to have police patrol routinely in cars to fight crime as it does to have firemen patrol routinely in fire trucks to fight fire" (Klockars, 1983, p.130).

Increasing Challenges to the Professional Model

The professional model faced many challenges including the inability of "traditional" police approaches to decrease crime; the rapidly escalating drug problem; the pressing problems associated with the deinstitutionalization of thousands of mentally ill people, many of whom became homeless; dealing with thousands of immigrants, some legal, some illegal, many speaking no English; and the breakdown of the family unit.

Many began asserting that the police and the criminal justice system could not control crime and violence alone:

> All of the major factors influencing how much crime there is or is not are factors over which police have no control whatsoever. Police can do nothing about the age, sex, racial, or ethnic distribution of the population. They cannot control economic conditions; poverty; inequality; occupational opportunity; moral, religious, family, or secular education; or dramatic social, cultural, or political change. These are the "big ticket" items in determining the amount and distribution of crime. Compared to them what police do or do not do matters very little (Klockars, 1991, p.250).

To attack these causes of crime, many departments turned to community-oriented policing.

The Community Era (1980–Present)

Paralleling changes being made in the business world, many police departments became "customer-oriented," viewing people within the community as consumers of police services. Just as in business it is important to know what the customer really wants and needs, so in policing it became important to know what the citizens of a community want and need.

Police forces in the **community era** are characterized by authority coming from community support, law and professionalism; provision of a broad range of services, including crime control; decentralized organization with more authority given to patrol officers; an intimate relationship with the community; and use of foot patrol and a problem-solving approach.

In contrast to policing during the reform era which was **reactive,** responding to crime after it was committed, policing during the community era is more **proactive,** seeking the causes of crime and trying to rectify those problems, thereby deterring or even preventing crime. The community-oriented approach to policing is the focus of Chapter 5. Largely because of civil service and a grassroots-inspired groundswell of general reform, most police forces have shaken the influence of corrupt politics. In contrast to conditions at the turn of the century, appointment to the forces and police administration generally are vastly improved. Police recruitment, discipline and promotion have been removed from politics in most cities.

Communications involving police service have also greatly improved. The radio and patrol car transformed the relationship between the police and the public and offered increased protection for everyone. The continuous expansion of the telephone in the 1960s and 1970s made it easier for people to call the police. Police dispatchers were added to tie radio systems directly into telephone networks. The use of fingerprint systems and the increased employment of women as police officers as well as many other advances occurred at an accelerated pace.

Despite advanced technology, which greatly improved police officers' abilities to respond to requests for aid and increased their mobility, the basic strategy of police has not altered. Crime waves in metropolitan areas prompt cities to improve their street lighting, to increase the number of police officers on the streets and to demand more severe punishment for the convicted criminals.

The human factor has assumed greater importance as police agencies cope with the tensions and dislocations of population growth, increasing urbanization, developing technology, the civil rights movement, changing social norms and a breakdown of traditional values. These factors have enormously complicated law enforcement, making more critical the need for truly professional police officers.

Today's local police officers must be law enforcement generalists with a working knowledge of federal, state, county and municipal law, traffic law, criminal law, juvenile law, narcotics, liquor control and countless other areas. However, this accounts for only approximately 10 percent of what a modern police officer does. Today's officers spend 90 percent of their time providing a variety of services while protecting life, property and personal liberty. They must be aware of human factors and understand the psychological and sociological implications of their work. They must deal with all citizens, rich and poor, young and old, in ways that maintain the community's support and confidence. This is no small responsibility.

The distinguishing characteristics of the three eras of policing are summarized in Table 1.1.

Table 1.1
The Three Eras of Policing

	Political Era 1840 to 1930	Reform Era 1930 to 1980	Community Era 1980 to present
Authorization	Politicians and law	Law and professionalism	Community support (political), law and professionalism
Function	Broad social services	Crime control	Broad provision of services
Organizational Design	Decentralized	Centralized, classical	Decentralized, task forces, matrices
Relationship to Community	Intimate	Professional, remote	Intimate
Tactics and Technology	Foot patrol	Preventive patrol and rapid response to calls	Foot patrol, problem solving, public relations
Outcome	Citizen, political satisfaction	Crime control	Quality of life and citizen satisfaction

Source: Linda S. Miller and Kären M. Hess. *The Police in the Community: Strategies for the 21st Century,* 3rd ed. West/Wadsworth Publishing, 2002, p. 14. Reprinted by permission. (Summarized from George L. Kelling and Mark H. Moore, "From Political to Reform to Community: The Evolving Strategy of Police." In *Community Policing: Rhetoric or Reality.* Edited by Jack R. Greene and Stephen D. Mastrofski. New York: Praeger Publishers, 1991, pp. 6, 14–15, 22–23.)

The Evolution of Our Juvenile Justice System

Our juvenile justice system has its roots in England's feudal period when the crown assumed the protection of the property of minors. When the feudal period ended, duties previously assumed by the overlord were transferred to the king's chancery court, which followed the doctrine of ***parens patriae.*** Under this doctrine the king, through the chancellor, was responsible for the general protection of all people in the realm who could not protect themselves, including children.

Another English common law principle that influenced our juvenile justice system was that children younger than age 7 were incapable of criminal intent. Children between the ages of 7 and 14 were presumed to still be incapable of criminal intent unless it could be shown differently. After age 14 children, like adults, were held responsible for their acts and treated according to a strict interpretation of the law. In effect age had a direct bearing on how someone who broke the law was treated.

These English common law principles were brought to the United States by the colonists and formed the foundation of the juvenile justice system they established. The system evolved through four major phases.

The four major phases in the development of the juvenile justice system were:

1. A Puritan emphasis
2. An emphasis on providing a refuge for youths
3. Development of a separate juvenile court
4. Emphasis on juvenile rights

The Puritan Emphasis

The concept of *parens patriae* and the notion that there was an age below which there can be no criminal intent were brought by the colonists to America. From the time the colonists first arrived until the nineteenth century, however, the emphasis was on Puritan values, which held that children were basically evil. Parents were responsible for controlling their children who were, in effect, their property. Children who broke the law were dealt with severely. Parents literally tried to "beat the devil" out of misbehaving children. This Puritan emphasis lasted until the 1820s.

Providing a Refuge

By the 1820s several states had passed laws to protect children from the punishments associated with criminal laws. Many states recognized the brutality of confining children in the same institutions with adult criminals. The first American institution to isolate children convicted of crimes from adult criminals was New York City's House of Refuge, established in 1825. This was the first juvenile reformatory in the United States.

In 1884 New York passed legislation allowing a trial judge to place children under age 16 who were convicted of a crime under the supervision of any suitable persons or institutions willing to accept them. During this period the state took over the parents' responsibility for their children, but not to the degree that occurred in the next phase of the system's development.

The Juvenile Court

In 1899 Illinois passed the Juvenile Court Act, creating the first juvenile court in Cook County and beginning an era of social jurisprudence. The court's primary purpose was to help wayward children become productive community members.

The Juvenile Court Act not only created the first juvenile court, it also regulated the treatment and control of dependent, neglected and delinquent children.

The Juvenile Court Act equated poor and abused children with criminal children and provided that they be treated in essentially the same way, establishing a **dual system.**

Most juvenile courts today have this same dual charge.

During this period, the philosophy of *parens patriae* was in full effect. The Chicago legislation grew out of the efforts of civic-minded citizens who saw the inhumane treatment of children confined in police stations and jails. The legislation, whose full title was "An Act to Regulate the Treatment and Control of Dependent, Neglected and Delinquent Children," included many characteristics of our current juvenile courts, including a separate court for juveniles, separate and confidential records, informal proceedings and the possibility of probation.

The Chicago legislation also required that children be given the same care, custody and discipline that parents should give them. The major goal was to save the child. This was also the first basic principle of the juvenile court—that of *parens patriae.* The state not only acts as a substitute parent to abandoned, neglected and dependent children, but also as a "superparent" for delinquent children.

In this role of superparent, the state could commit a youth found to be delinquent to a training school or some other correctional facility. The purpose was not to punish but to help reform the youth. Because this purpose was so dissimilar to the adult criminal court, a new vocabulary emerged for the juvenile justice system. Youths were not *arrested,* they were *taken into custody.* Their innocence or guilt was decided not at a *trial* but at a *hearing.*

It should be noted that many historians view the child saving movement as a means to control the lower classes, not as a means to "save the children." As Drowns and Hess (2000, p.12) state: "The child savers were not entirely

Judge Benjamin Lindsey presided in juvenile court in Denver, Colorado, from 1900 to 1927. His court stressed a caring approach "in the best interests of the child."

humanitarian, however; they viewed poor children as a threat to society. These children needed to be reformed to conform, to value hard work and to become contributing members of society."

Although establishment of juvenile courts was a tremendous advancement in the juvenile justice system, it presented some major problems. Because children were no longer considered "criminals," they lost many constitutional protections of due process in criminal proceedings. For example, often delinquents were not given notice of the charge, were not provided with a lawyer and were not given the chance to cross-examine witnesses.

Justification for the informal procedures used in the juvenile justice system before 1960 was set forth almost a century ago in *Commonwealth v. Fisher* (1905): "To save a child from becoming a criminal or from continuing in a career in crimes . . . the Legislature may surely provide for the salvation of such a child . . . by bringing it into one of the courts of the state without any process at all, for the purpose of subjecting it to the state's guardianship and protection."

By the 1960s, however, the U.S. Supreme Court began to seriously question the use of *parens patriae* as the sole reason for denying children many constitutional rights extended to adults charged with a crime, leading into the fourth phase of the juvenile justice system's development. These rights are described in the next chapter.

A Brief Recap of U.S. Policing

A fitting conclusion for this chapter is a brief recap of the sequence of events from the beginning of law enforcement in the United States to the end of the twentieth century, presented in Figure 1.3.

Summary

Our current laws and the means by which they are enforced have their origins in the distant past, perhaps as far back as the cave dwellers. Law refers to all the rules of conduct established and enforced by the custom, authority or legislation of a group, community or country. A system of law and law enforcement began earlier than 2000 B.C. as a means of controlling human conduct and enforcing society's rules. Keeping the peace was the responsibility of the group. Many features of our present system of law enforcement are borrowed from the Greeks, Romans and particularly the English.

The English tithing system (groups of 10 families) established the principle of collective responsibility for maintaining local law and order. If a law was broken, the Hue and Cry sounded, the origin of the general alarm and the citizen's arrest.

The constable was the first English police officer, and he had charge of the weapons and horses of the community. In response to a need for more regional law enforcement, the office of shire-reeve was established. The shire-reeve was the law enforcement agent for an entire county.

In 1066 William the Conqueror invaded England and changed the tithing system to the Frankpledge system, requiring loyalty to the king's law and mutual local responsibility for maintaining the peace. Under his rule the shire-reeves were limited to law enforcement, and separate judges were appointed to try cases, in effect separating the law enforcement and judicial roles. William's son, Henry I, became known as Henry the Lawmaker. His Leges Henrici made law enforcement a public matter and separated offenses into felonies and misdemeanors. Henry II established the jury system.

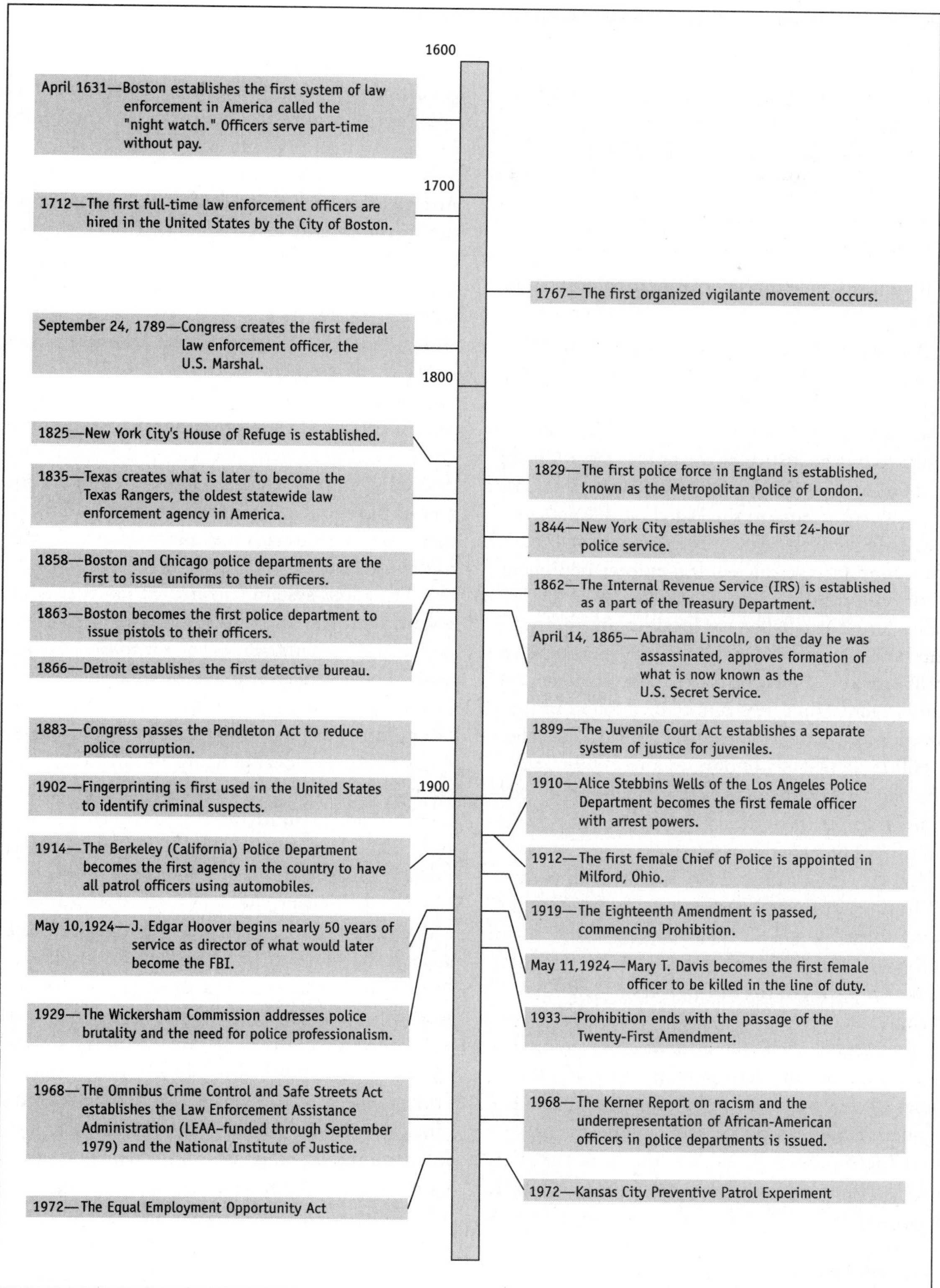

1600
April 1631—Boston establishes the first system of law enforcement in America called the "night watch." Officers serve part-time without pay.
1700
1712—The first full-time law enforcement officers are hired in the United States by the City of Boston.
1767—The first organized vigilante movement occurs.
September 24, 1789—Congress creates the first federal law enforcement officer, the U.S. Marshal.
1800
1825—New York City's House of Refuge is established.
1829—The first police force in England is established, known as the Metropolitan Police of London.
1835—Texas creates what is later to become the Texas Rangers, the oldest statewide law enforcement agency in America.
1844—New York City establishes the first 24-hour police service.
1858—Boston and Chicago police departments are the first to issue uniforms to their officers.
1862—The Internal Revenue Service (IRS) is established as a part of the Treasury Department.
1863—Boston becomes the first police department to issue pistols to their officers.
April 14, 1865—Abraham Lincoln, on the day he was assassinated, approves formation of what is now known as the U.S. Secret Service.
1866—Detroit establishes the first detective bureau.
1883—Congress passes the Pendleton Act to reduce police corruption.
1899—The Juvenile Court Act establishes a separate system of justice for juveniles.
1900
1902—Fingerprinting is first used in the United States to identify criminal suspects.
1910—Alice Stebbins Wells of the Los Angeles Police Department becomes the first female officer with arrest powers.
1912—The first female Chief of Police is appointed in Milford, Ohio.
1914—The Berkeley (California) Police Department becomes the first agency in the country to have all patrol officers using automobiles.
1919—The Eighteenth Amendment is passed, commencing Prohibition.
May 10,1924—J. Edgar Hoover begins nearly 50 years of service as director of what would later become the FBI.
May 11,1924—Mary T. Davis becomes the first female officer to be killed in the line of duty.
1929—The Wickersham Commission addresses police brutality and the need for police professionalism.
1933—Prohibition ends with the passage of the Twenty-First Amendment.
1968—The Omnibus Crime Control and Safe Streets Act establishes the Law Enforcement Assistance Administration (LEAA–funded through September 1979) and the National Institute of Justice.
1968—The Kerner Report on racism and the underrepresentation of African-American officers in police departments is issued.
1972—The Equal Employment Opportunity Act
1972—Kansas City Preventive Patrol Experiment

Figure 1.3
Important Dates in Police History

The next significant development was the Magna Carta, a precedent for democratic government and individual rights. The Magna Carta laid the foundation for:

- Requiring rulers to uphold the law.
- Forbidding taxation without representation.
- Requiring due process of law, including trial by jury.
- Providing safeguards against unfair imprisonment.

During the fourteenth century, the shire-reeve was replaced by the justice of the peace. Later, during the Middle Ages, the parish constable system was used for rural law enforcement; the Watch and Ward system was used for urban law enforcement.

Of importance to English law enforcement were the contributions of Sir Robert (Bobbie) Peel. Peel's principles for reform called for local responsibility for law and order, appointed, paid civilians to assume this responsibility and standards for these individuals' conduct and organization. His proposals resulted in the organization of the first police force in England, the Metropolitan Police of London, established in 1829. In 1883 the London Metropolitan Police appointed two women to supervise women convicts. Their numbers and functions later expanded.

The early American settlers brought with them several features of English law and law enforcement, including those found in Leges Henrici, which made law enforcement a public matter, and in the Magna Carta, which provided for due process of law. Law enforcement in colonial America was frequently patterned after England's Watch and Ward system and later after the London Metropolitan Police and the principles for reform set forth by Sir Robert Peel. The first modern American police force, modeled after London's Metropolitan Police, was the New York City Police Department, established in 1844. The vigilante movement refers to taking the law into one's own hands in the absence of effective policing.

Although law enforcement was generally considered a local responsibility, Congress created several federal law enforcement agencies, under the jurisdiction of the Departments of Justice and the Treasury, to meet demands created by the nation's changing conditions. Among the earliest federal law enforcement agencies were the U.S. Marshals Office, the Immigration and Naturalization Service, the Secret Service and the Internal Revenue Service. The U.S. Attorney General, as head of the Department of Justice, is the chief federal law enforcement officer. The beginning of state law enforcement agencies occurred with the establishment of the Texas Rangers. Law enforcement in the United States is a cooperative effort among local, county, state, federal and specialized law enforcement officers.

The three eras of policing are the political era, the reform era and the community era. In the political era, police forces were characterized by authority derived from politicians and the law, a broad social service function, a decentralized organization, an intimate relationship with the community and extensive use of foot patrol.

The spoils system encouraged politicians to reward their friends by giving them key positions in police departments. Cities sought to break political control by a variety of organizational modifications, including electing police officers and chiefs, administering forces through bipartisan lay boards, asking states to assume local policing and instituting mayor-council or council–city manager municipal government. In addition, in 1883 the Pendleton Act created the civil service system for government employees and made it unlawful to fire or demote a worker for political reasons. During the political era, African-American officers were often segregated and discriminated against. The roles of policewomen during this era were clearly separated from those of policemen, with women serving a protective, nurturing role.

Police forces in the reform era were characterized by authority derived from law and professionalism; crime control as their primary function; a centralized, efficient organization; a professional remoteness from the community; emphasis on preventive motorized patrol and rapid response to crime. During this era, in 1972, the Equal Employment Opportunity Act was passed. This act prohibits discrimination on the basis of sex, race, color, religion or national origin in employment of any kind, public or private, local, state or federal. This gave minorities and women legal equality with white male officers and prompted many women to seek patrol assignments. Despite the passage of the Equal Employment Opportunity Act, many minorities and women still often encountered discrimination.

Community era police forces are characterized by authority derived from community support, law and professionalism; the provision of a broad range of services; a decentralized organization with more authority given to patrol officers; an intimate relationship with the community; and the increased use of foot patrol and a problem-solving approach.

The juvenile justice system has developed through four phases in the United States: (1) a Puritan emphasis with severe penalties for juvenile crime (1776–1824), (2) an emphasis on providing a refuge for youths (1824–1899), (3) development of a separate juvenile court (1899–1960) and (4) emphasis on juvenile rights (1960 to present). The Juvenile Court Act equated poor and abused children with criminal children and provided that they be treated in essentially the same way, establishing a dual system.

Discussion Questions

1. What common problems have existed throughout the centuries for people in law enforcement?
2. Why was there no law enforcement during the daytime for many centuries?
3. Why did it take so long to develop a police force in England? In the United States?
4. In today's society, how has the power of the *posse comitatus* assisted and how has it worked against law enforcement?
5. At present, how does the government respond to increased crime in the United States in comparison with the responses in the seventeenth century?
6. Should police chiefs be appointed or elected?
7. What demands are made on the modern police officer that were not present 20 or 30 years ago?
8. How well are women and minorities represented on your police force?
9. Where is your regional FBI office? What facilities and services does it offer?
10. Do you feel the process of justice should be the same for juveniles as it is for adults?

InfoTrac *College Edition Assignment*

Use InfoTrac College Edition to help answer the Discussion Questions as appropriate.

- Using InfoTrac College Edition, find the article "The Rise of Juvenile Delinquency in England 1780–1840: Changing Patterns of Perception and Prosecution." This article focuses on a neglected but historically important transition, the rise to prominence of the problem of juvenile delinquency between the 1780's and the 1830's. Find 10 significant problems during this era that were studied by reformers and briefly state their effects on juveniles. Be prepared to share your analysis with the class.

Internet Assignment

Go to the Web site of the Pendleton Act and focus on *Background on the Pendleton Act.* Note the new special skills required with the introduction of typewriters. As you read the document, write down what strikes you as being the most important areas covered by the act. Be prepared to share your findings with the class.

Book-Specific Web Site

The book-specific Web site at http://info.wadsworth.com/0534552803 hosts a variety of resources for students and instructors. Included are extended activities from each chapter in which students write a policy, use critical thinking skills to make choices in response to a given scenario, use InfoTrac College Edition with direct links to articles for participation in topical discussion forums, and analyze court cases using Web links for research. Many activities can be printed or emailed to instructors. Plus, cited cases with Web links, interactive key term FlashCards, PowerPoint presentations, chapter objectives, and an extensive collection of chapter-based Web links provide additional information and activities to include in the curriculum.

References

Adams, T. F. *Introduction to the Administration of Criminal Justice,* 2nd ed. Englewood Cliffs, NJ: Prentice-Hall, 1980.

Asirvatham, Sandy. "Good Cop, Bad Cop." *Baltimore City Paper,* May 2000, p.2.

Bailey, W. G. (ed.). *The Encyclopedia of Police Science.* New York: Garland Publishing, 1989.

Brown, R. "The American Vigilante Tradition." In *Thinking About Police: Contemporary Readings,* 2nd ed., edited by C. B. Klockars and S. D. Mastrofski. New York: McGraw-Hill, 1991.

Chapman, S. G. and Johnston, Colonel T. E., Sr. *The Police Heritage in England and America.* East Lansing, MI: Michigan State University, 1962.

Critchley, T. A. *A History of Police in England and Wales.* Montclair, NJ: Patterson Smith, 1967.

Drowns, Robert W. and Hess, Kären M. *Juvenile Justice,* 3rd ed. Belmont, CA: West/Wadsworth Publishing Company, 2000.

Dunham, R. G. and Alpert, G. P. *Critical Issues in Policing: Contemporary Issues.* Prospect Heights, IL: Waveland Press, Inc., 1989.

Folley, V. L. *American Law Enforcement.* Boston: Allyn and Bacon, 1980.

Fyfe, James J.; Green, Jack R.; Walsh, William F.; Wilson, O. W.; and McLaren, Roy Clinton. *Police Administration,* 5th ed. New York: McGraw-Hill, 1997.

Gardner, T. J. *Basic Concepts of Criminal Law, Principles and Cases,* 3rd ed. St. Paul, MN: West Publishing Company, 1985.

Hale, Donna C. "Women in Policing." In *What Works in Policing,* edited by G. W. Gardner and D. C. Hale. Cincinnati, OH: Anderson Publishing Company, 1992.

Kelling, George L. and Moore, Mark H. "From Political to Reform to Community: The Evolving Strategy of Police." In *Community Policing: Rhetoric or Reality,* edited by J. R. Greene and S. D. Mastrofski. New York: Praeger Publishers, 1991.

Klockars, Carl B. *Thinking About Police: Contemporary Readings.* New York: McGraw-Hill, 1983.

Klockars, Carl B. *The Idea of Police.* Newbury Park, CA: Sage Publications, 1985.

Klockars, Carl B. "The Rhetoric of Community Policing." In *Community Policing: Rhetoric or Reality,* edited by J. R. Greene and S. D. Mastrofski. New York: Praeger Publishers, 1991.

Lunt, W. E. *History of England.* New York: Harper & Brothers, 1938.

Manning, Peter K. *Police Work: The Social Organization of Policing,* 2nd ed. Prospect Heights, IL: Waveland Press, Inc., 1997.

Perry, D. C. *Police in the Metropolis.* Columbus, OH: Charles E. Merrill, 1973.

Reichel, Philip L. "Southern Slave Patrols as a Transitional Police Type." In *Policing Perspectives: An Anthology,* edited by Larry K. Gaines and Gary W. Cordner. Los Angeles: Roxbury Publishing Company, 1999, pp.79–92.

Richardson, J. F. *The New York Police.* New York: Oxford University Press, 1970.

Roberg, R. R. and Kuykendall, J. *Police & Society.* Belmont, CA: Wadsworth Publishing Company, 1993.

Sullivan, P. S. "Minority Officers, Current Issues." In *Critical Issues in Policing: Contemporary Readings,* edited by R. D. Dunham and G. P. Alpert. Prospect Heights, IL: Waveland Press, 1989.

Walker, Samuel. *The Police in America: An Introduction.* New York: McGraw-Hill, 1983.

Cases Cited

Commonwealth v. Fisher, 213 Pa. 48 (1905)

Griggs v. Duke Power Company (1971)

Chapter **2**

The American Quest for Freedom and Justice: Our Laws

We hold these truths to be self-evident: that all men are endowed by their creator with certain unalienable rights; that among these are life, liberty, and the pursuit of happiness.

—Thomas Jefferson

Do You Know?

- What civil rights and civil liberties are?
- What the Declaration of Independence says about civil rights and civil liberties?
- What document is the basic instrument of government and the supreme law of the land?
- What law takes precedence if two laws conflict?
- What the Bill of Rights is?
- What specific rights are guaranteed by the First, Second, Fourth, Fifth, Sixth, Eighth and Fourteenth Amendments?
- What is established by the Exclusionary Rule?
- What criminal law does?
- What the difference between a felony and a misdemeanor is?
- What is usually necessary to prove that a crime has been committed?
- What civil law refers to?
- What the basic differences between a crime and a tort are?
- What Section 1983 of the U.S. Code, Title 42, stipulates?
- Where police get their power and authority and what restrictions are placed on this power and authority?

Can You Define?

actus reus
American creed
asset forfeiture
authority
bail
Bill of Rights
case law
civil law
civil liberties
civil rights
code of silence
common law
constitution
constitutional law
corpus delicti
crime
criminal intent
criminal law
custodial interrogation
double jeopardy
due process of law
ecclesiastical law
elements of the crime
equal protection
equity
Exclusionary Rule
federalism
felony
fighting words
grand jury
hearsay
hearsay evidence
incorporation doctrine
indicted
indigent
infamous crime
intent
litigaphobia
mala in se
mala prohibita
mens rea
misdemeanor

moral law
motive
negligence
ordinances
ordinary law
petition
police power
power
precedent
procedural criminal law
procedural due process
pure speech
scienter
selective incorporation
self-incrimination
social law
speech plus
statutory law
strict liability
subpoena
substantive criminal law
substantive due process
symbolic speech
tort
warrant
zones of privacy

INTRODUCTION

To assure each U.S. citizen the right to "life, liberty, and the pursuit of happiness," those who settled here established laws that all are expected to obey. The supreme law of the land is embodied in the U.S. Constitution and its Bill of Rights. Beyond that, however, each city, state and the federal government has continued to pass laws governing citizen behavior. Our system of laws is extremely complex and may be classified as follows:

- *Form*—written or unwritten common law
- *Source*—constitutional, statutory, case
- *Parties involved*—public, private
- *Offense*—criminal, civil

Each of these overlapping classifications are explored in this chapter.

The criminal/civil distinction is of interest to law enforcement officers because they must deal with those who break criminal laws and at the same time not violate the "criminal's" civil rights. Officers who do not deal legally with criminal matters may find themselves the target of a civil lawsuit. In addition law enforcement officers must be able to tell the difference between a criminal and a civil offense because they are responsible for investigating only criminal matters. Civil offenses are not within their jurisdiction.

This chapter begins with a discussion of the Declaration of Independence and the law that operated in the newly created nation. This is followed by a description of the constitutional law found in the U.S. Constitution and the Bill of Rights—the first 10 amendments, which guarantee all American citizens civil rights and civil liberties—as well as the Fourteenth Amendment, which made the Constitution and portions of the Bill of Rights applicable to the states. Following the discussion of constitutional law is an explanation of criminal and civil law. The chapter concludes with a description of police power in the United States—where it comes from and how it is restricted.

The Declaration of Independence

The Europeans' original immigration to the New World was heavily motivated by a desire to escape the religious, economic, political and social repressions of traditional European society. North America was seen as a land where people could get a new start, free to make of themselves what they chose.

Sometimes, however, reality did not fully coincide with the **American creed** of individual freedom, as seen in the treatment of Native Americans, the importation of slaves, the establishment of state churches and the repressiveness involved in such episodes as the Salem witchcraft trials. Nevertheless the spirit of liberty and justice remained strong. As noted by Myrdal (1944): "The American creed is the national conscience; a body of beliefs about equality, liberty, and justice which most Americans believe in, in spite of the fact that America has, and always has had, multiple wrongs."

In the 1760s the British began taking away rights Americans felt were naturally theirs, and the American Revolution resulted. In effect, the United States was born out of a desire—indeed, a demand—for civil rights and civil liberties.

Civil rights are those claims that the citizen has to the affirmative assistance of government. **Civil liberties** are an individual's immunity from governmental oppression.

Civil rights and civil liberties are recurring themes in America's development and reflect values that were forcefully stated in our most basic document: the Declaration of Independence. The Declaration of Independence is not only a statement of grievances against England but also a statement of alternative basic premises underlying human freedom. As Thomas Jefferson phrased it in the Declaration, the United States was demanding "the separate and equal station to which the laws of nature and of nature's God entitle them."

The Declaration of Independence asserts that all individuals are created equal and are entitled to the unalienable rights of life, liberty and the pursuit of happiness. It further asserts that governments are instituted by and derive their power from the governed, that is, the people.

The Declaration of Independence was an idealistic statement of philosophy. It broke our ties with England but did not establish how the United States should be structured or governed. Each colony developed its own means of policing and protecting itself. The colonists relied heavily on laws they had brought with them from their homelands, England in particular.

Types of Law

In addition to the classification of law introduced earlier, several types of law must be understood to appreciate their complexities and effect on criminal justice. Recall that law is a body of rules for human conduct enforced by imposing penalties for their violation. Laws define social obligations and determine the relations of individuals to society and to each other. The purpose of law is to regulate individuals' actions to conform to the way of life the community or the people's elected representatives consider essential.

Social or Moral Law

Often, obedience to law is obtained through social pressure—ridicule, contempt, scorn or ostracism. **Moral** or **social law** refers to laws made by society and enforced solely by social pressure. Moral or social laws include laws of etiquette, "honor" and morality. When moral laws break down and social sanctions fail to obtain conformity, other laws may be enacted and enforced.

Precedents: Common Law and Case Law

The beginnings of law are found in social custom. Custom is simply **precedent**—doing what has been done before. In early times custom, religion, morals and the law were intermingled. Some early customs have, over the centuries, become law. Precedent explains why many good ideas in criminal justice are so slow to materialize.

Some customs were enforced physically rather than morally, and the violator was expelled from the community, sacrificed to the gods or hanged. Other violations of custom not felt to be harmful to the whole community were punished by the injured group or the injured individual with the aid of the family (self-help, vengeance, feud). As long as such vengeance might lead to retaliation, the sanctions behind the rules of custom were still purely moral. When the community began to protect those who had taken *rightful* vengeance, however, these persons became agents of the community. This kind of self-help met early society's needs when the right to take vengeance or redress was clear. It did not provide a way to settle controversies. Therefore courts were established to interpret customs and settle controversies. Custom was replaced by judicial precedent.

In England **common law** referred to the precedents set by the judges in the royal courts as disputes rose. This was in contrast to local custom or **ecclesiastical** (church) **law.** When Parliament supplemented and modified the existing legal principles, the term *common law* described the law in force before, and independent of, any acts of the legislature.

The common law brought to the United States by the early settlers forms the basis of modern American law in all states except Louisiana, which established and kept the system of French civil law. In essence common law describes the precedent generally followed in the absence of a specific law, known in the United States as **case law.** Case law refers to judicial precedents; no specific law exists, but a similar case serves as a model. When cases not covered by the law come before the courts, the judges' rulings on previous similar cases will, for all practical purposes, be treated as law.

Statutory Law

The United States has largely replaced common law (unwritten law) with **statutory law,** that is, legislated and written law. Statutory law may be passed at the federal or state level, and at either level it includes **constitutional** and **ordinary law.**

Federal constitutional law is based on the U.S. Constitution, its amendments and interpretations by the federal courts. Ordinary federal law consists of acts of Congress, treaties with foreign states, executive orders and regulations and interpretation of the preceding by federal courts. State constitutional law is based on the state's constitution, its amendments and interpretations of them by the state's courts. State ordinary law consists of acts of the state legislatures, decisions of the federal courts in interpreting or developing the common law, executive orders and regulations and municipal ordinances.

In addition, in most states, each county and city is given the right to pass laws for its local jurisdiction, providing the law does not conflict with the state's laws. Local **ordinances** (laws) are primarily enacted to protect the community.

Equity

The need for laws to change as society changes has long been recognized, as illustrated in a letter written by Thomas Jefferson in the nineteenth century:

> . . . laws and institutions must go hand in hand with the progress of the human mind, as that becomes more developed, as more discoveries are made, new truths disclosed, and manners and opinions change with the changing circumstances, institutions must advance also, and keep pace with the times. We might as well require a man to wear still the coat which fitted him as a boy as civilized society to remain ever under the regiment of their barbarous ancestors.

Indeed, laws that once made good sense now appear ridiculous. For example, an old law in Truro, Massachusetts, states that a young man may not marry until he has killed either six blackbirds or three crows; and in Gary, Indiana, it is illegal to go into a theater within four hours of eating garlic.

Equity demands that laws change as society changes, resorting to general principles of fairness and justice whenever existing law is inadequate. It requires that the "spirit of the law" take precedence over the "letter of the law."

Equity describes a system of rules and doctrines supplementing common and statutory law and superseding laws that are inadequate to fairly settle a case. However if every locality and state were left alone, our legal system would be chaos. Fortunately our Founding Fathers foresaw this danger and wrote the Constitution of the United States, a carefully drafted document that established the workings of our democracy.

Constitutional Law

A **constitution** is a system of fundamental laws and principles that prescribe the nature, functions and limits of a government or other body. The U.S. Constitution was drafted by the Constitutional Convention of 1787 and became effective in 1789.

The U.S. Constitution, ratified in 1789, is the basic instrument of government and the supreme law of the land.

The Constitution states that the legislative, executive and judicial departments of government should be separated as far as is practical and that their respective powers should be exercised by different individuals or groups of individuals. The legislature makes the laws, the executive branch, of which law enforcement is a part, enforces the laws, and the judicial branch determines when laws have been violated.

Order of Authority of Law

If two laws conflict, a set order of authority has been established.

The order of authority of law is the federal Constitution, treaties with foreign powers, acts of Congress, the state constitutions, state statutes and, finally, common law or case law.

The Bill of Rights

The Constitution organized the government of the new nation but contained few personal guarantees. Consequently some states refused to ratify it without a specific bill of rights. In 1791 10 amendments, with personal guarantees, came into effect. They became known as the **Bill of Rights,** a fundamental document protecting a person's right to "life, liberty, and the pursuit of happiness."

The Bill of Rights refers to the first 10 amendments to the Constitution, which protect the peoples' liberties and forbid the government to violate these rights.

Individual constitutional rights are clearly specified in each amendment. Of special importance to criminal justice professionals are the First, Second, Fourth, Fifth, Sixth, Eighth and Fourteenth Amendments.

The First Amendment

The First Amendment guarantees freedom of religion, freedom of speech, freedom of the press, freedom of peaceable assembly and freedom of petition.

Freedom of Religion

Citizens are free to worship as they see fit through two guarantees: (1) no law can establish an official church that all Americans must accept and support or that favors one church over another, and (2) no law is constitutional that prohibits the free exercise of religion. The First Amendment clearly separates church and state and requires that the government be neutral on religious matters, favoring no religion above another.

Freedom of Speech

The Supreme Court has ruled that the First Amendment does not protect all forms of expression. Highly inflammatory remarks that advocate violence and clearly threaten the peace and safety of the community spoken to a crowd are not protected.

Schenck v. United States (1919) established the "clear and present danger" doctrine and serves as a guide to the constitutionality of government restrictions on free speech (and free press). The Court held: "The most stringent protection of free speech would not protect a man in falsely shouting fire in a theatre causing a panic. . . . The question in every case is whether the words are used in such circumstances and are of such a nature as to create a clear and present danger that they will bring about the substantive evils that Congress has a right to prevent." *Chaplinsky v. New Hampshire* (1942) also established that use of **fighting words** likely to cause violence will not be tolerated.

The ban on words presenting a "clear and present danger" and "fighting words" is counterbalanced by the concept of **pure speech,** speech without any accompanying action. An example is the Americanism "Kill the umpire," commonly heard during baseball season.

Unlike pure speech, **speech plus** is not protected by the First Amendment. An example of speech plus is the action taken by striking employees in a picket line. If they physically prevent others from entering or leaving a commercial building, the police may be called to assure that those who wish to enter or exit the building are allowed to do so.

Courts have recognized that **symbolic speech,** involving tangible forms of expression, such as wearing buttons or clothing with political slogans or displaying a sign or a flag, is protected by the First Amendment. The Supreme Court has also held that burning the American flag is protected by the First Amendment, as is cross burning: "Cross burning can be a symbolic act that seeks to communicate a message and therefore can also have First Amendment Protection" (Gardner and Anderson, 2000, p.235).

Freedom of the Press

The First Amendment guarantees the right to express oneself by writing or publishing one's views. The Founding Fathers recognized the importance of a free interplay of ideas in a democratic society and sought to guarantee the right of all citizens to speak or publish their views, even if contrary to those of the government or society as a whole. Accordingly the First Amendment generally forbids censorship or other restraint upon speech or the printed word. As with speech, freedom to write or publish is not an absolute right of expression. The sale of obscene or libelous printed materials is not protected.

The police and the press often come into conflict because of the Sixth Amendment guarantee of the right to a fair trial and protection of the defendant's rights. The guarantees of the First and the Sixth Amendments must be carefully balanced. The public's right to know cannot impinge upon others' rights to privacy or to a fair trial.

Freedom of Peaceable Assembly

Americans have the right to assemble peaceably for any political, religious or social activity. Public authorities cannot impose unreasonable restrictions on such assemblies, but they can impose limitations reasonably designed to prevent fire, health hazards or traffic obstructions.

Freedom of Petition

The right of **petition** is designed to allow citizens to communicate with their government without obstruction. When citizens exercise their First Amendment freedom to write or speak to their senators or representatives, they participate in the democratic process.

The Second Amendment

The Second Amendment guarantees the right to keep and bear arms as necessary for a well-regulated militia.

The Supreme Court has ruled that state and federal governments may pass laws that prohibit carrying concealed weapons, require the registration of firearms and limit the sale of firearms for other than military use. Thus it is illegal to possess certain types of "people-killing" weapons, such as operable machine guns and sawed-off shotguns of a certain length.

The right of the states to pass laws regulating firearms rests in the Supreme Court's interpretation of the Second Amendment. In *United States v. Cruickshank* (1876), the Court stated that the amendment protected only the right of the states to maintain and equip a militia and that unless a defendant could show that the possession of a firearm in violation of federal statutes had "some reasonable relationship to the preservation or efficiency of a well-regulated militia," the individual could not challenge a gun control statute on Second Amendment grounds. All federal court decisions involving the amendment have used a collective, militia interpretation and/or held that firearms control laws are constitutional.

Dozens of federal and state court decisions have held that the Second Amendment limits only the federal government, not the states, and that the right to keep and bear arms is a collective rather than an individual right.

In November 1993, the Brady Bill was passed, mandating a national five-business-day waiting period for handgun purchases and that local law enforcement officials conduct background checks of prospective handgun buyers. The law took effect in February 1994. However in June 1997, the U.S. Supreme Court ruled 5–4 in *Printz v. United States* and *Mack v. United States* that the federal government is not empowered to require state or local law enforcement agencies to run background checks on prospective gun buyers. According to the Court, the background check provision violates the principle of separate state sovereignty. Justice Scalia, writing for the narrow majority, stated: "The Federal Government may neither issue directives requiring the states to address particular problems, nor command the states' officers, or those of their political subdivisions, to administer or enforce a Federal regulatory program. Such commands are fundamentally incompatible with our constitutional system of dual sovereignty."

As of November 1, 1998, the Brady Law was modified so an applicant can receive immediate clearance to purchase a gun. The issuing police agency can contact the FBI by computer and either receive clearance or be denied a permit for the applicant. However, because many police agencies do not have the computer capability to communicate with the FBI, the new system is somewhat imperfect.

The Fourth Amendment

The Fourth Amendment requires probable cause and forbids unreasonable searches and seizures.

The Fourth Amendment has the most impact on law enforcement of any of the amendments, dictating how officers carry out their responsibilities without violating anyone's civil rights or civil liberties. The restrictions placed on law enforcement by this amendment are discussed in detail in Chapter 8. Only highlights are included here.

Searches

In most instances a police officer is not allowed to search the homes of private citizens, seize any of their property or arrest them without first obtaining a court order—a **warrant.**

The courts have ruled that in some instances it is permissible to arrest a person or conduct a search without a warrant. For example if a felony is committed in the presence of a police officer, the officer has the right to arrest the criminal immediately, without an arrest warrant. If police officers make such an arrest, they may search the suspect and a limited area surrounding the suspect to prevent the suspect from seizing a weapon or destroying evidence (*Chimel v. California,* 1969). Any evidence in plain view may also be seized.

The Supreme Court has ruled that the Fourth Amendment does not prohibit police officers from stopping and frisking a "suspicious person" if it was reasonable on the basis of the police officer's experience and the demeanor of the individual frisked (*Terry v. Ohio,* 1968).

Listening in on a telephone conversation by mechanical or electronic means is considered a search and seizure under the Fourth Amendment; therefore, such actions require probable cause, reasonableness and a warrant for their use. Congress has passed legislation that limits the use of wiretapping and bugging to the investigation of specific crimes and restricts those officials permitted to authorize them. *Katz v. United States* (1967) established that evidence of conversations overheard through electronic surveillance of a telephone booth was inadmissible because the proper authorization had not been obtained. *Berger v. New York* (1967) established that although electronic eavesdropping was prohibited by the Fourth Amendment, under specific conditions and circumstances it could be permitted.

Numerous Supreme Court cases have interpreted restrictions imposed by the Fourth Amendment. For example, in *Boyd v. United States* (1886), the Court held that the Fourth Amendment applied "to all invasions on the part of the government and its employees of the sanctity of a man's home and the privacies of life. It is not the breaking of his doors, and the rummaging of his drawers, that constitutes the essence of the offense; but it is the invasion of his indefensible right of personal security, personal liberty and private property." The findings in *Boyd* clearly suggest that evidence gathered in violation of the Fourth Amendment should be excluded from federal criminal trials and, consequently, contributed to the development of the Exclusionary Rule some 30 years later.

Exclusionary Rule

Without procedures for enforcing the provisions of the Fourth Amendment, the impressive constitutional language would be meaningless. Consequently the procedures and the power for their enforcement were vested in the courts. They must refuse to consider evidence obtained by unreasonable search and seizure methods, regardless of how relevant the evidence is to the case. Thus the phrase "innocent until proven guilty" in practice means "innocent until proven guilty by evidence obtained in accordance with constitutional guarantees."

The **Exclusionary Rule** is the direct result of the Supreme Court decision in the case of *Weeks v. United States* (1914), when the Court considered evidence seized unconstitutionally:

> If letters and private documents can thus be seized and held and used in evidence against a citizen accused of an offense, the protection of the Fourth Amendment declaring his right to be secure against such searches and seizures is of no value, and, so far as those thus placed are concerned, might as well be stricken from the Constitution. The efforts of the courts and their officials to bring the guilty to punishment, praiseworthy as they are, are not to be aided by the sacrifice of those great principles established by years of endeavor and suffering which have resulted in their embodiment in the fundamental law of the land.

In 1961 the Exclusionary Rule reached maturity when the Supreme Court, in the case of *Mapp v. Ohio,* extended the rule to every court and law enforcement officer in the nation.

Courts uphold the Fourth Amendment by use of the Exclusionary Rule, which demands that no evidence may be admitted in a trial unless it is obtained within the constitutional standards set forth in the Fourth Amendment. *Weeks v. United States* made the Exclusionary Rule applicable in federal courts. *Mapp v. Ohio* made it applicable to every court in the country.

Since 1961 the Exclusionary Rule has applied to both the federal and state courts, and evidence secured illegally by federal, state or local officers has been inadmissible in any court. The Exclusionary Rule has important implications for the procedures followed by police officers, because neither the most skillful prosecutor nor the most experienced police officer can convince a jury of a defendant's guilt without adequate and lawfully obtained evidence.

The Fifth Amendment

The Fifth Amendment *guarantees* due process—notice of a hearing, full information regarding the charges, the opportunity to present evidence in one's own behalf before an impartial judge or jury and to be presumed innocent until proven guilty by legally obtained evidence.

The Fifth Amendment *prohibits* double jeopardy and self-incrimination.

Grand Jury

The Fifth Amendment requires that before individuals are tried in federal court for an "infamous" crime, they must first be **indicted** by a **grand jury,** that is, formally accused of a crime by a grand jury. The grand jury's duty is to prevent people from being subjected to a trial when insufficient proof exists that they have committed a crime. An **infamous crime** is a felony (a crime for which a sentence of more than one year's imprisonment can be given) or a lesser offense that can be punished by confinement in a penitentiary or at hard labor.

Due Process

The words **due process of law** express the fundamental ideas of American justice. A due process clause occurs in the Fifth and Fourteenth Amendments as a restraint on the federal and state governments, respectively, and protects against arbitrary, unfair procedures in judicial or administrative proceedings that could affect a citizen's personal and property rights. Thus constitutional limitations are imposed on governmental interference with important individual liberties, such as the freedom to enter into contracts, to engage in a lawful occupation, to marry and to move without unnecessary restraints.

Due process requires timely notice of a hearing or trial that adequately informs those accused of the charges against them. It also requires the opportunity to present evidence in one's own behalf before an impartial judge or jury, to be presumed innocent until proven guilty by legally obtained evidence and to have the verdict supported by the evidence presented.

Due process requires that during judicial proceedings, fundamental principles of fairness and justice must prevail, including both substantive and procedural due process. **Substantive due process** protects individuals against unreasonable, arbitrary or capricious laws and limits arbitrary government actions. No court or governmental agency may exercise powers beyond what the Constitution authorizes. In contrast, **procedural due process** deals with notices, hearings and gathering of evidence. The vast majority of due process cases are in the area of procedural due process.

Because the Fifth Amendment is so vague, hundreds of cases have been heard. Important Supreme Court cases involving due process include *Brady v. Maryland* (1963), which held that the suppression of evidence favorable to an accused by the prosecution violates due process. *United States v. Russell* (1973) found that it was not entrapment for an undercover agent to have supplied the defendant with a scarce ingredient required to manufacture an illicit drug. In *Hampton v. United States* (1976), the Court held that it was not entrapment for undercover agents to be both providers and purchasers of drugs involved in the case.

Double Jeopardy

The Fifth Amendment also guarantees that citizens will not be placed in **double jeopardy;** that is, they will not be tried before a federal or state court more than once for the same crime. A second trial can occur, however, when the first trial results in a mistrial, when the jury cannot agree on a verdict or when a second trial is ordered by an appellate court.

Double jeopardy does not arise when a single act violates both federal and state laws and the defendant is prosecuted in both federal and state courts. Nor does a criminal prosecution in either a state or federal court exempt the defendant from being sued for damages in civil court by anyone harmed by the criminal act. This occurred in the O. J. Simpson case where Simpson was found not guilty in criminal court, but later was found responsible for wrongful death in civil court and ordered to pay restitution.

Further a defendant may be prosecuted more than once for the same conduct if it involves the commission of more than one crime. For instance if a person kills three victims at the same time and place, he or she can be tried separately for each slaying.

Double jeopardy is also an issue in asset forfeiture. **Asset forfeiture** allows the seizure of assets and property used in connection with a crime. Many police departments hesitate to use asset forfeiture for fear it would constitute double jeopardy if they also want to try the suspects in criminal court. However, as the result of two cases, *United States v. Ursery* (1996) and *Bennis v. Michigan* (1996), law enforcement can constitutionally use asset forfeiture without double jeopardy concerns. As Hartman (2001, p.6) asserts:

> Asset forfeiture remains a powerful tool for law enforcement agencies. It remedies many of the problems that often slip through the criminal justice system, such as addressing the issue of allowing a criminal to profit from crime, and it provides a remedy for the victim. In short, asset forfeiture deprives the subject of ill-gotten gains, compensates the victim, and serves the community.

Hartman (pp.3–4) cautions officers to carefully consider asset forfeiture early in an investigation to guarantee a successful outcome: "Law enforcement agencies must ensure that they use asset forfeiture only when they can demonstrate the benefits to the community." To guide law enforcement in the appropriate use of asset forfeiture, Congress has approved legislation adding due process protections to assure that property is not unjustly seized from innocent owners. Provisions of the legislation include a "*burden of proof*" clause stating that the government must establish that the property was subject to forfeiture by a "preponderance of the evidence" (Voegtlin, 2000, p.8).

Self-Incrimination

In any criminal case, every person has the right not to be a witness against him- or herself; that is, individuals are not required to provide answers to questions that might convict them of a crime. This is called **self-incrimination.** Such questions may be asked at the very earliest stages of an investigation; therefore, the Supreme Court has ruled that when an individual is interrogated in the custody of the police, the guarantees of the Fifth Amendment apply. **Custodial interrogation** can extend to questioning outside the police station.

To ensure against self-incrimination, the Court ruled, in the landmark *Miranda v. Arizona* (1966), that citizens must be warned prior to custodial interrogation of their right to remain silent, that what they say may be used against them in court and that they have a right to counsel, which will be furnished them. If these warnings are not given, any statements obtained by the questioning are inadmissible in later criminal proceedings.

Although accused persons may waive their rights under the Fifth Amendment, they must know what they are doing and must not be forced to confess. Any confession obtained by force or threat is excluded from the evidence presented at the trial. Courts have ruled that the guarantee against self-incrimination applies only to testimonial actions. Thus handwriting samples, blood tests and physical appearance and voice tests, including repeating words in a police lineup, do *not* violate the Fifth Amendment. In addition *New York v. Quarles* (1984) established an exception to the Exclusionary Rule in that if the public safety would be threatened by delaying questioning, police may question a subject in custody without first advising of the right not to self-incriminate.

The Sixth Amendment

The Sixth Amendment establishes requirements for criminal trials. It guarantees the individual's right to have a speedy public trial by an impartial jury, be informed of the nature and cause of the accusation, be confronted with witnesses against him or her, subpoena witnesses for defense and have counsel for defense.

The Supreme Court has ruled that state juries need not have 12 members and has approved state statutes that require only 6 members. Moreover the Court has ruled that jury verdicts in state courts need not be unanimous. In all jury trials the jury members must be impartially selected. The right to jury trial does not apply to trials for petty offenses, that is, those punishable by six months' confinement or fewer, such as shoplifting or minor traffic violations. Nor is a jury trial a right of juveniles.

The Sixth Amendment requires that accused persons be told how it is claimed they have broken the law so they can prepare their defense. The crime must be clearly established by statute beforehand. In general accused persons are entitled to have all witnesses against them present their evidence orally in court. Accused persons are entitled to the court's aid in obtaining their witnesses, usually by **subpoena,** which orders into court as witnesses persons whose testimony is desired at the trial. Facts not in the personal knowledge of a witness are called **hearsay. Hearsay evidence,** that is, secondhand evidence, cannot be used in criminal trials except in certain instances.

Finally, the Sixth Amendment provides a right to be represented by counsel. For many years this was interpreted to mean that defendants had a right to be represented by a lawyer only if they could afford one. The Supreme Court's first modern ruling on the right to counsel was *Powell v. Alabama* (1932), a case involving nine young black males, ages 13 to 21, charged with raping two white girls. The trial was held in Scottsboro, Alabama, where community sentiment was extremely hostile toward the defendants. Although the trial judge appointed a member of the local bar to serve as defense counsel, no attorney appeared on the day of the trial, so the judge appointed a local lawyer who reluctantly took the case. The defendants challenged their conviction on the grounds that they did not have a chance to consult with their lawyer or prepare a defense, and the Supreme Court concurred. However, in *Betts v. Brady* (1942) the Court ruled that a defendant's federal right to an attorney did *not* apply in a state Court.

Twenty years later *Gideon v. Wainwright* (1963) reexamined the holding in *Betts v. Brady.* Gideon was an indigent charged with a felony in Florida where counsel for indigent defendants was permitted only in capital cases. The trial judge denied Gideon's request for counsel, so Gideon defended himself and was convicted and sent to prison. He appealed and, in a rare occurrence, the Court agreed to hear the case and overturned *Betts v. Brady.*

Writing for the majority, Justice Hugo Lafayette Black stated:

> The fact is that in deciding as it did that 'appointment of counsel is not a fundamental right, essential to a fair trial'—the court in *Betts v. Brady* made an abrupt break with its own well-considered precedents. . . . Not only these precedents but also reason and reflection require us to recognize that in our adversary system of criminal justice, any person hauled into court, who is too poor to hire a lawyer cannot be assured a fair trial unless counsel is provided for him. This seems to us to be an obvious truth. Governments, both state and federal, quite properly spend vast sums of money to establish machinery to try defendants accused of crime. Lawyers to prosecute are everywhere deemed essential to protect the public's interest in an orderly society. Similarly there are few defendants charged with crime, few indeed, who fail to hire the best lawyers they can get to prepare and present their defenses. That government hires lawyers to prosecute and defendants who have money to hire lawyers to defend are the strongest indications of the widespread belief that lawyers in criminal courts are necessities, not luxuries. The right of one charged with a crime to counsel may not be deemed fundamental and essential to fair trials in some countries, but it is in ours. From the very beginning, our state and national constitutions and laws have laid great emphasis on procedural and substantive safeguards designed to assure fair trials before impartial tribunals in which every defendant stands equal before the law.

> This noble ideal cannot be realized if the poor man charged with a crime has to face his accusers without a lawyer to assist him. . . . Betts was an "anachronism when handed down," and it should be overruled.

The court ruled 9–0 that the due process clause of the Fourteenth Amendment requires states to provide free counsel to indigent defendants in all felony cases.

The **indigent,** that is, people who are destitute, poverty-stricken, with no visible means of support, have such a right at any "critical stage of the adjudicatory process," including the initial periods of questioning, police lineups and all stages of the trial process. In 1956 in *Shioutakon v. District of Columbia,* the courts established the role of legal counsel in juvenile court. If juveniles were to have their liberty taken away, such juveniles had the right to a lawyer in court. If their parents could not afford a lawyer, the court was to appoint one.

The Eighth Amendment

> The Eighth Amendment forbids excessive bail, excessive fines and cruel and unusual punishments.

Bail

Bail has traditionally meant payment by the accused of a sum of money, specified by the court based on the nature of the offense, to ensure the accused's presence at trial. A defendant released from custody who subsequently fails to appear for trial forfeits bail to the court. Because bail typically costs one-tenth of its amount, it is often informally considered a punishment in itself.

The Eighth Amendment does not specifically provide the right to bail, only that bail will not be excessive. In 1966 Congress enacted the Bail Reform Act to provide for pretrial release from imprisonment of indigent defendants who were confined, in effect, only because of their poverty. The act also discouraged the traditional use of money bail by requiring judges to seek other means to ensure that defendants would appear for their trial.

The leading Supreme Court decision on excessive bail is *Stack v. Boyle* (1951) in which 12 community leaders were indicted for conspiracy, and bail was set at $50,000 per defendant. The defendants moved to reduce this amount on the grounds that it was excessive, and the Supreme Court agreed:

> This traditional right to freedom before conviction permits the unhampered preparation of a defense, and serves to prevent the infliction of punishment prior to conviction. . . . Unless this right to bail before trial is preserved, the presumption of innocence, secured only after centuries of struggle, would lose its meaning.
>
> The right of release before trial is conditioned upon the accused's giving adequate assurance that he will stand trial and submit to sentence if found guilty. . . . Bail set at a figure higher than an amount reasonably calculated to fulfill this purpose is "excessive" under the Eighth Amendment.

Cruel and Unusual Punishment

Whether fines or confinement are cruel and unusual must be determined by the facts of each particular case. Clearly such excessive practices as torture would be invalid. The Supreme Court has heard numerous cases concerning cruel and unusual punishment and has held the death penalty itself to be cruel and unusual in certain circumstances if it is not universally applied:

- *Furman v. Georgia* (1972) stated that the death penalty violates the Eighth Amendment if the sentencing authority has the freedom to decide between the death penalty and a lesser penalty.
- *Gregg v. Georgia* (1976) held that the death penalty for murderers is not per se cruel and unusual punishment.
- *Rummel v. Estelle* (1980) ruled that a mandatory life sentence required by a state habitual offender statute is not cruel and unusual punishment.

The Ninth Amendment

The Ninth Amendment emphasizes the Founding Fathers' view that government powers are limited by the rights of the people and that it was *not* intended, by expressly guaranteeing in the Constitution certain rights of the people, to recognize that government has unlimited power to invade other rights of the people.

Griswold v. Connecticut (1965), a case involving the Ninth Amendment, addressed the issue of whether the right to privacy is a constitutional right and, if so, whether the right is reserved to the people under the Ninth Amendment or is only derived from other rights specifically mentioned in the Constitution. The Court in *Griswold* ruled that the Third and Fifth Amendments, in addition to the First and Fourth, created **zones of privacy** safe from governmental intrusion and, without resting its decision upon any one amendment or on the Ninth Amendment itself, simply held that the right of privacy is guaranteed by the Constitution.

The Tenth Amendment

The Tenth Amendment embodies the principle of **federalism,** which reserves for the states the residue of powers not granted to the federal government or withheld from the states. However, through the Fourteenth Amendment, many civil rights and civil liberties assured by the Bill of Rights were made applicable to the states.

The Fourteenth Amendment

The Fourteenth Amendment requires each state to abide by the Constitution and the incorporation doctrine of the Bill of Rights. It guarantees due process and equal protection under the law.

The Incorporation Doctrine

Harr and Hess (2002, p.107) explain: "Considering the Constitution was aimed primarily at limiting the power of *federal* government, it seemed inconceivable that the federal government would be kept in line only to have state authority left unbridled. The **incorporation doctrine** (also known as **selective incorporation**) prevents the inconceivable."

In *Palko v. Connecticut* (1937), the Supreme Court held that there were rights "so rooted in the traditions and conscience of our people as to be ranked as fundamental," meaning "essential to justice and the American system of political liberty." The selective incorporation doctrine holds that only those provisions of the Bill of Rights that are fundamental to the American legal process are made applicable to the states through the due process clause: "For example, if a state law were to abridge freedom of religion, it would be violating the First Amendment as applied to it through the Fourteenth Amendment" (Harr and Hess, p.107).

Due Process

The Fourteenth Amendment limits the *states'* infringement upon individual rights. The Bill of Rights does not specifically refer to actions by states but applies only to actions by the federal government. Thus state and local officers could proceed with an arrest without any concern for the rights of the accused. The Fourteenth Amendment duplicates the Fifth Amendment, except it specifically orders state and local officers to provide the legal protections of due process. An important Supreme Court case related to the Fourteenth Amendment is *Brown v. Mississippi* (1936), which stated that a criminal conviction based on a confession obtained by brutality is not admissible under the Fourteenth Amendment due process clause.

Equal Protection

The Fourteenth Amendment also prohibits denial of the **equal protection** of the laws. A state cannot make unreasonable, arbitrary distinctions between different people's rights and privileges. Because "all people are created equal," no law can deny red-haired men the right to drive an automobile, although it can deny minors the right to drive. The state can make reasonable classifications, but classifications based on race, religion and national origin have been held unreasonable.

In addition to the great body of constitutional law, criminal and civil law also are important to the criminal justice professional.

Criminal Law

Criminal law includes rules and procedures for investigating crimes and prosecuting criminals, regulations governing the constitution of courts and the conduct of trials and the administration of penal institutions. American criminal law has a number of unique features. In establishing criminal law, the federal government and each state government are sovereign within the limits of their authority as defined by the Constitution. Therefore criminal law varies from state to state. Despite the many differences, most states have a tradition derived from English common law.

Criminal law defines crimes and fixes punishments for them.

The Bureau of Justice Statistics defines **crime** as "all behaviors and acts for which a society provides formally sanctioned punishment." Crimes are made so by law. State and federal statutes define each crime, the elements involved and the penalty attached to each. The statutes that define what acts constitute social harm are called **substantive criminal law,** for example a statute defining homicide. A substantive criminal law not only defines the offense but also states the punishment. The omission of the punishment invalidates the criminal law.

In most countries crimes and punishments are expressed in statutes, with punishments including removal from public office, fines, exile, imprisonment and death. Unless the act for which a defendant is accused is expressly defined by statute as a crime, no indictment or conviction for committing the act is legal. This establishes the difference between government by law and arbitrary dictatorial government.

Criminal law in the United States generally defines seven classes of crime: offenses against (1) international law, (2) the dispensation of justice and the legitimate exercise of governmental authority, (3) the public peace, (4) property, (5) trade, (6) public decency and (7) persons. Like English law, American criminal law also classifies crimes with respect to their gravity as felonies and misdemeanors.

A **felony** is a serious crime, generally punishable by death or by imprisonment for more than one year in a state prison or penitentiary. A **misdemeanor** is any minor offense, generally punishable by a fine or a short term, usually not to exceed one year, in a jail or workhouse.

State criminal codes vary in their classification of offenses considered misdemeanors. Crimes usually defined as misdemeanors include libel, assault and battery, malicious mischief and petty theft. In some states the distinction between felonies and misdemeanors is practically discarded, the punishment for each particular crime being prescribed by statute.

Crimes have also been classified as ***mala in se*** (bad in itself) and ***mala prohibita*** (bad because it is forbidden). A *mala in se* crime is one so offensive that it is obviously criminal, for example murder or rape. A *mala prohibita* crime is one that violates a specific regulatory statute, for example certain traffic violations. These would not usually be considered crimes if no law prohibited them.

Proving That a Crime Has Been Committed

In addition to establishing what specifically constitutes a crime and the punishment for it, **procedural criminal law** specifies what must be proven and how, that is, legally within the constraints of the Constitution and the Bill of Rights.

To prove that a crime has been committed, it is usually necessary to prove:

- The act itself ***(actus reus)***—the material elements of the crime.
- The criminal mental state ***(mens rea)***—intent to do wrong.

Material Elements—The Criminal Act

Basic to the commission of a crime is the concept of *actus reus*—literally the "guilty act." The *actus reus* must be a measurable act, including planning and conspiring. What constitutes this forbidden act is usually spelled out very specifically in state statutes and is called the *corpus delicti.*

Contrary to popular belief, the ***corpus delicti*** of a crime is not the body in a murder case. It is, quite literally, the body of the crime itself—the distinctive elements that must exist for a particular crime to be proven. These **elements of the crime** make up the *corpus delicti.* Law enforcement officers are most responsible for proving that the actual act occurred—establishing the elements of a specific crime. Much more difficult to establish is the defendant's mental state.

Jeff Cadge/Image Bank

Whether a crime has been committed is decided by a judge or by a jury of the defendant's peers, as guaranteed by the Fifth Amendment. Here a jury listens to a prosecutor arguing that the defendant is surely guilty. A defense attorney will argue for the defendant's innocence.

Criminal Intent

The second key requirement of a crime is **criminal intent** or *mens rea,* literally, the "guilty mind." To convict someone of a crime, it must be proven that the defendant intentionally, knowingly or willingly committed the criminal act:

> The term *mens rea* means evil intent, criminal purpose, and knowledge of the wrongfulness of conduct. It is also used to indicate the mental state required by the crime charged, whether that be specific intent to commit the crime, recklessness, guilty knowledge, malice, or criminal negligence (Gardner and Anderson, p.36).

In some crimes intent is not an element. These are known as **strict liability** crimes. These offenses generally involve traffic violations, liquor violations and hunting violations. In strict liability crimes, defendants are liable regardless of their state of mind when the act was committed. Individuals who break traffic, liquor and hunting laws are generally not considered "criminals" and receive lesser penalties.

A liquor store owner cannot use the excuse that a minor who bought beer from the store looked at least 30 years old. A man who has consensual sex with a minor female cannot use the excuse that she said she was 21. Nor can the speeder claim ignorance of the posted speed limit or claim a faulty speedometer. Intent is not at issue—only the speed.

Intent is *not* to be confused with **motive,** which is a *reason* for doing something. Motive is not an element of any crime, but it can help to establish intent. If police officers can show why a suspect would benefit from committing a certain act, this greatly strengthens the case. A classic example is Robin Hood, who allegedly stole from the rich to give to the poor. He intended to steal, and although his motives were "righteous," he was still committing a crime. A modern example would be the actions of Dr. Jack Kevorkian, who helped people to commit suicide. Although motive is not relevant to the issue of guilt or innocence, it can affect sentencing.

Another element of a crime that must sometimes be proven is ***scienter,*** guilty knowledge making individuals legally responsible for their acts. In other words the person committing the act knew that it was a crime. For example, to be guilty of harboring a felon, the person harboring the felon has to know the person is a felon, or the person who buys stolen property has to know the property is indeed stolen.

Crimes can be categorized in many ways. You have already seen one such classification: a criminal act can be either a misdemeanor or a felony. Another common classification differentiates between violent crimes, or crimes against persons, and property crimes. Crimes against persons include homicide, rape, assault and robbery—actions that involve the use of force or the threat of force against a person. In contrast property crimes do not involve such force and include larceny, burglary, motor vehicle theft and arson. These crimes are discussed in Chapter 3. Consider next the third major type of law—civil law.

Civil Law and Torts

Although laws vary from state to state, generally such actions as trespassing, desertion of family, slander, failure to make good on a contract or similar actions against an individual would be covered under civil law.

Civil law refers to all noncriminal restrictions placed on individuals. It seeks not punishment, but restitution. The offense is called a **tort.**

> A tort is not the same thing as a crime, although the two sometimes have many features in common. The distinction between them lies in the interests affected and the remedy afforded by the law. A crime is an offense against the public at large, for which the state, as the representative of the public, will bring proceedings in the form of criminal prosecution. . . . A criminal prosecution is not concerned in any way with compensation of the injured individual against whom the crime is committed. . . . The civil action for a tort, on the other hand, is commenced and maintained by the injured person himself, and its purpose is to compensate him for the damage he has suffered, at the expense of the wrongdoer (Prosser, 1955, p.7).

Law enforcement officers recognize when a matter is covered by criminal law and when it is covered by civil law (noncriminal matters). An act can be both a crime and a tort, as was evidenced in the O. J. Simpson trial. Simpson was tried in criminal court for two counts of murder in the first degree (a crime) and found not guilty. He also faced civil suits from the families of the two murder victims for wrongful death (a tort) and was found responsible.

The distinctions between crimes and torts are as follows:

Crime	Tort
Public wrong	Private wrong
State prosecutes	Individual prosecutes
Seeks to punish	Seeks redress for injury
Criminal intent is required	Intent not necessary

The Law Enforcement Officer and Civil Liability

Citizens can bring action against the police and have been doing so with increasing frequency, as Stevens (2001, p.105) notes: "Police officers are more likely to be defendants in a civil liability suit today than at any other time in American history." This threat of civil liability greatly affects officer responses, including arrest decisions, by creating a "lawsuit paranoia" [or **litigaphobia**] that can permeate and undermine the effective operation of law enforcement agencies and can affect every law enforcement officer, both professionally and personally:

> The sad fact of the matter is that the average law enforcement officer can expect to be named party in a civil lawsuit at least once in his or her career. Some experts indicate that it is 10 times more likely that a police officer will be sued than it is that he or she will be involved in a line-of-duty shooting incident (Hill, 2000, p.47).

One reason for the numerous lawsuits is the current interpretation of Section 1983 of the Civil Rights Act.

The Civil Rights Act (Section 1983)

The U.S. Code, Title 42, Section 1983, passed after the Civil War in 1871, states:

> Every person who, under color of any statute, ordinance, regulation, custom, or usage, of any State or Territory, subjects, or causes to be subjected any citizen of the United States or other person within the jurisdiction thereof to the deprivation of any rights, privileges, or immunities secured by the Constitution and laws, shall be liable to the party injured in an action at law, suit in equity, or other proper proceeding for redress.

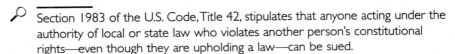

Section 1983 of the U.S. Code, Title 42, stipulates that anyone acting under the authority of local or state law who violates another person's constitutional rights—even though they are upholding a law—can be sued.

The two basic requirements for a Section 1983 action are that (1) the plaintiff must be deprived of a constitutional right and (2) the defendant must deprive the plaintiff of this right while acting under the "color of the law" (*Adickes v. Kress and Co.,* 1970). Like criminal law, civil law has levels of "intent":

- Strict liability—the wrongdoer is liable even if no harm was intended (for example, keeping wild animals).
- Intentional wrong—the person knows the act was unlawful but did it anyway.
- Negligence—the person did not set out to do harm but acted carelessly.

Intentional wrong and negligence are the two categories law enforcement officers are most frequently involved with.

Intentional wrongs that may affect law enforcement include assault, battery, excessive force, false imprisonment, false arrest, malicious prosecution, intentional infliction of emotional distress, trespass, illegal electronic surveillance, invasion of privacy, defamation and wrongful death. Later chapters introduce procedures to minimize the likelihood of a civil lawsuit for an intentional wrong.

The second category of civil charges frequently filed against law enforcement officers and their agencies is **negligence,** the failure to use due care to prevent foreseeable injury. Routine police duties that most often lead to negligence lawsuits are care of incapacitated persons, duty to render emergency aid, caring for arrestees, aiding private citizens, investigating unusual circumstances and operating emergency vehicles carelessly, for example during high-speed chases. Given the inherently dangerous nature of police work, such as the carrying of lethal weapons and the authority to drive at high speeds, officers are unquestionably vulnerable to lawsuits when mistakes or errors in judgment occur that lead to unnecessary injury of a private party. The results of such lawsuits, even when judgments are in favor of the police, can have far-reaching, long-lasting adverse effects on the officers involved and their agencies, as well as on the police profession and the community as a whole.

The leading case for police negligence is *Byrd v. Brishke* (1972), in which the plaintiff claimed to have been surrounded by about a dozen Chicago police officers who repeatedly struck him. The plaintiff could not identify the specific officers who had beaten him, but his claim was that all those present were liable since they did nothing to stop the beating. The court concurred: "We believe it is clear that one who is given the badge of authority of a police officer may not ignore the duty imposed by his office and fail to stop other officers who summarily punish a third person in his presence or otherwise within his knowledge."

Officers must also come forward with information regarding other officers' misconduct, for any evidence of a **code of silence** is enough to justify a civil rights claim against a municipality. In any departments where such a code of silence exists, civil liability is greatly increased.

Much of the civil action taken against police officers and their agencies results from the tremendous power officers have and, indeed, require.

Police Power

Without means of enforcement, the great body of federal, state, municipal and common law would be empty and meaningless. Recall that *law* implies not only the rule but also enforcement of that rule. All forms of society rely on authority and power. **Authority** is the right to direct and command. **Power** is the force by which others can be made to obey.

Police power describes the ability of federal, state or municipal governments to enforce the laws they pass by granting government agents at each level the authority to use force against those who fail to comply with the laws.

Police power is derived from the U.S. Constitution, U.S. Supreme Court decisions, federal statutes, state constitutions, state statutes, state court decisions and various municipal charters and ordinances.

Police power was defined by the Supreme Court in 1887 as "embracing no more than the power to promote public health, morals, and safety" *(Mugler v. Kansas).* For example traffic laws are passed to preserve the general safety and to make the highways safe for the motoring public. Likewise juvenile laws are passed to protect juveniles from parents, guardians, relatives or others who would endanger the youths' physical and mental welfare.

States' police powers are delegated to them by the Bill of Rights in the Tenth Amendment, giving the states those powers not delegated to the federal government.

Police power ultimately rests with the people because their elected representatives create the laws that the police enforce.

Because each state is responsible for its citizens' health, safety and general well-being, they usually assign these functions to municipal police departments in the cities and to sheriffs and constables in rural areas. State legislatures may define the powers and duties of police officers; however police officers' authority and powers cannot conflict with the Constitution.

Although the state legislature passes laws, the courts, the judicial branch of government, decide the purpose and character of the statutes, as well as whether these statutes conflict with the Constitution or are contrary to proper public policy. Acceptable police power requires that the regulations are (1) reasonable, (2) within the power given to the states by the Constitution and (3) in accord with due process of law.

Police power is restricted by the Constitution, the Fourteenth Amendment and the courts.

Many have noted the irony and inherent conflict present in our system of law enforcement—the designation of a police entity authorized to use coercive force to eradicate violence and effect a peaceful society. This paradoxical scheme often places officers, whose defining characteristic is the right to use force, in an awkward relationship with the citizens they are sworn to serve and protect.

Summary

If the fundamental values of our society are to be preserved and extended, citizens must understand and support those institutions and statutes that, in practice, reflect the principles set forth in the Declaration of Independence, the Constitution and the Bill of Rights. These documents established both civil rights—those claims that the citizen has to the affirmative assistance of government—and civil liberties—an individual's immunity from governmental oppression.

The Declaration of Independence asserts that all individuals are created equal and are entitled to the unalienable rights of life, liberty and the pursuit of happiness. It further asserts that governments are instituted by and derive their power from the governed, that is, the people.

To achieve the goals set forth in the Declaration of Independence, the U.S. Constitution was drafted as the basic instrument of government and the supreme law of the United States. The order of authority of law is the federal Constitution, treaties with foreign powers, acts of Congress, the state constitutions, state statutes and, finally, common law or case law.

Some states, however, refused to ratify the Constitution if it did not contain personal guarantees. As a result the Bill of Rights was drafted, containing the first 10 amendments to the Constitution, which protect the peoples' liberties and forbid the government to violate these rights:

- The First Amendment guarantees freedom of religion, freedom of speech, freedom of the press, freedom of peaceable assembly and freedom of petition.
- The Second Amendment guarantees the right to keep and bear arms.
- The Fourth Amendment requires probable cause and forbids unreasonable searches and seizures. Courts uphold the Fourth Amendment by use of the Exclusionary Rule, which demands that

no evidence may be admitted in a trial unless it is obtained within the constitutional standards set forth in the Fourth Amendment. *Weeks v. United States* made the Exclusionary Rule applicable in federal courts. *Mapp v. Ohio* made it applicable to every court in the country.

- The Fifth Amendment guarantees due process; it prohibits double jeopardy and self-incrimination.
- The Sixth Amendment establishes requirements for criminal trials. It guarantees the individual's right to have a speedy public trial by an impartial jury, be informed of the nature and cause of the accusation, be confronted with witnesses against him or her, subpoena witnesses for defense and have counsel for defense.
- The Eighth Amendment forbids excessive bail, excessive fines and cruel and unusual punishments.
- The Fourteenth Amendment requires each state to abide by the Constitution and the Bill of Rights. It guarantees due process and equal protection under the law.

In addition to constitutional law, the criminal justice professional must also be familiar with criminal and civil law. Criminal law defines crimes and fixes punishments for them. Crimes may be classified as felonies or misdemeanors. A felony refers to a serious crime, generally one punishable by death or by imprisonment for more than one year in a state prison or penitentiary. A misdemeanor refers to any minor offense, generally punishable by a fine or a short term, usually not to exceed one year, in a jail or workhouse. To prove a crime has been committed, it is usually necessary to prove the act itself *(actus reus)*—the elements of the crime—and prove the criminal mental state *(mens rea)*—intent to do wrong. In strict liability crimes, however, such as traffic violations, the defendant is liable regardless of intent.

Civil law refers to all noncriminal restrictions placed on individuals. It seeks not punishment, but restitution. The offense is called a tort. The distinctions between crimes and torts are as follows:

Crime	Tort
Public wrong	Private wrong
State prosecutes	Individual prosecutes
Seeks to punish	Seeks redress for injury
Criminal intent is required	Intent not necessary

Section 1983 of the U.S. Code, Title 42, stipulates that anyone acting under the authority of local or state law who violates another person's constitutional rights—even though they are upholding a law—can be sued.

Without means of enforcement, the great body of federal, state and municipal law would be meaningless. To ensure enforcement police have been given power and authority from local, state and federal sources. Police power is derived from the U.S. Constitution, U.S. Supreme Court decisions, federal statutes, state constitutions, state statutes, state court decisions and various municipal charters and ordinances. Police power ultimately rests with the people because their elected representatives create the laws that the police enforce. Police power is also restricted by the Constitution, the Fourteenth Amendment and the courts. Police have the power to enforce the laws so long as they do not violate the civil rights and liberties of any individual.

Discussion Questions

1. What specific restrictions are placed on police officers by the Bill of Rights?
2. Why has the Supreme Court said that state and federal governments can pass laws against carrying weapons when the Second Amendment specifically guarantees the right to bear arms?
3. Why were African-Americans considered "unequal" until Lincoln was president? The Constitution existed; why did it not apply to African-Americans?
4. What is the basic difference between civil rights and civil liberties?
5. In what well-known cases has the Fifth Amendment been repeatedly used?
6. What do police power and authority consist of?
7. The Declaration of Independence states that all people are created equal. Does this mean all people have the same opportunities?
8. If a person's reckless driving of a car injures another person who dies two weeks later as a result of the injuries, could the reckless driver be charged with a crime, sued for a tort, or both? How would the type of charge affect the possible consequences faced by the reckless driver?
9. Should law enforcement officers be immune from tort action?
10. Should Fourth Amendment rights be extended to include general searches?

InfoTrac *College Edition Assignments*

Use InfoTrac College Edition to help answer the Discussion Questions as appropriate.

- Using InfoTrac College Edition, locate the review by Douglas Husak of "Philosophical Analysis and the Limits of the Substantive Criminal Law." This is particularly straightforward writing to students with no previous legal background. Pick one chapter and outline its contents. Be prepared to share your outline with the class.
- Use InfoTrac College Edition to find *equality before the law* and to then locate *discrimination.* Outline how the various courts have viewed discrimination over the years.

Internet Assignment

Use the key words *actus reus* to review what is called the "guilty mind" in criminal law. Write your own definition for *actus reus,* and be prepared to compare your definition with others in your class.

Book-Specific Web Site

The book-specific Web site at http://info.wadsworth.com/0534552803 hosts a variety of resources for students and instructors. Included are extended activities from each chapter in which students write a policy, use critical thinking skills to make choices in response to a given scenario, use InfoTrac College Edition with direct links to articles for participation in topical discussion forums, and analyze court cases using Web links for research. Many activities can be printed or emailed to instructors. Plus, cited cases with Web links, interactive key term FlashCards, PowerPoint presentations, chapter objectives, and an extensive collection of chapter-based Web links provide additional information and activities to include in the curriculum.

References

Gardner, T. J. and Anderson, T. M. *Criminal Law, Principles and Cases,* 7th ed. Belmont, CA: Wadsworth Publishing Company, 2000.

Harr, J. Scott and Hess, Kären M. *Constitutional Law and the Criminal Justice System,* 2nd ed. Belmont, CA: Wadsworth Thomson Learning, 2002.

Hartman, Victor E. "Implementing an Asset Forfeiture Program." *FBI Law Enforcement Bulletin,* January 2001, pp.1–7.

Hill, Steven J. "Civil Liability in Policing: A Proactive View." *Police,* May 2000, pp.46–47.

Myrdal, G. *The American Dilemma.* New York: Harper & Brothers, 1944.

Prosser, W. L. *Handbook of the Law of Torts,* 2nd ed. St. Paul, MN: West Publishing Company, 1955.

Stevens, Dennis J. "Civil Liability and Selective Enforcement." *Law and Order,* May 2001, pp.105–107.

Voegtlin, Gene R. "Congress Approves Asset Forfeiture Legislation." *The Police Chief,* May 2000, p.8.

Cases Cited

Adickes v. Kress and Co., 398 U.S. 144, 151 (1970)
Bennis v. Michigan, 116 S.Ct. 994 (1996)
Berger v. New York, 388 U.S. 42 (1967)
Betts v. Brady, 316 U.S. 455 (1942)
Boyd v. United States, 116 U.S. 616 (1886)
Brady v. Maryland, 373 U.S. 83 (1963)
Brown v. Mississippi, 279 U.S. 278 (1936)
Byrd v. Brishke, 466 F.2d 6 (1972)
Chaplinsky v. New Hampshire, 315 U.S. 568 (1942)
Chimel v. California, 395 U.S. 752 (1969)
Furman v. Georgia, 408 U.S. 238 (1972)
Gideon v. Wainwright, 372 U.S. 355 (1963)
Gregg v. Georgia, 428 U.S. 153 (1976)
Griswold v. Connecticut, 381 U.S. 479 (1965)
Hampton v. United States, 425 U.S. 484 (1976)
Katz v. United States, 389 U.S. 347 (1967)
Mack v. United States (1997)-See *Printz v. United States*
Mapp v. Ohio, 367 U.S. 643 (1961)
Miranda v. Arizona, 384 U.S. 436 (1966)
Mugler v. Kansas, 123 U.S. 623 (1887)
New York v. Quarles, 104 S.Ct. 2626 (1984)
Palko v. Connecticut, 163 U.S. 537 (1937)
Powell v. Alabama, 287 U.S. 45 (1932)
Printz v. United States, 521 U.S. 898 (1997)
Rummel v. Estelle, 445 U.S. 263 (1980)
Schenck v. United States, 249 U.S. 47 (1919)
Shioutakon v. District of Columbia 98 U.S.App.D.C. 371(1956)
Stack v. Boyle, 342 U.S. 1 (1951)
Terry v. Ohio, 392 U.S. 1 (1968)
United States v. Cruickshank, 92 U.S. 542 (1876)
United States v. Russell, 411 U.S. 423 (1973)
United States v. Ursery, 59 Cr.L. 2191 (1996)
Weeks v. United States, 232 U.S. 383 (1914)

Chapter 3

Crime in the United States—Offenders and Victims

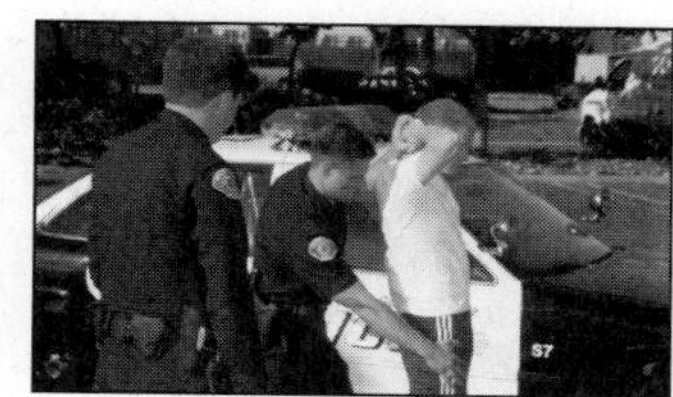

Something insidious has happened in America: crime has made victims of us all. Awareness of its danger affects the way we think, where we live, where we go, what we buy, how we raise our children, and the quality of our lives as we age. The specter of violent crime and the knowledge that, without warning, any person can be attacked or crippled, robbed, or killed, lurks at the fringes of consciousness.

—Statement of the Chairman, President's Task Force on Victims of Crime

Do You Know?

- What the three major sources of information about who commits crime are?
- What the eight Part I Index Crimes are?
- What other serious crimes present a challenge to law enforcement?
- What the most common types of white-collar crime are?
- What three key characteristics of computer-related crime are?
- What two characteristics of organized crime set it apart from other crimes committed by a group of individuals?
- What types of bias may be involved in hate crimes?
- What a ritualistic crime is and what must be investigated in it?
- What the classical and the positivist theories of crime causation state?
- What some causes of criminal behavior are?
- What groups of people are most likely and least likely to become victims of crime?
- How crime affects its victims?
- What second victimization may occur?
- How victims may become involved in the criminal justice system?

Can You Define?

aggravated assault
aggravated rape
arson
assault
battery
bias crime
burglary
career criminal
carjacking
chronic criminal
classical theory
cybercops
cybercrime
dark figure of criminality
delinquency
delinquent
determinism
direct victims
embezzle
fence
first-degree murder
grand larceny
hate crime
homicide
Index Crimes
indirect victims

justifiable homicide
larceny/theft
malice
manslaughter
motor vehicle theft
murder
negligent homicide
organized crime
petty larceny
pilfer
positivist theory
premeditated
primary victims
rape
recidivist
risk factors
ritual
ritualistic crime
robbery
secondary victims
second-degree murder
simple assault
simple rape
status offenses
statutory rape
theft
victim impact statement (VIS)
victim statement of opinion (VSO)
white-collar crime
xenophobia

INTRODUCTION

Crime is more than laws and cases. Crime involves hurtful acts committed by individuals against other individuals or their property. Until recently, however, crimes have been examined as acts against the state and prosecuted as such. This is changing. Whether it is called restorative justice or balanced justice, the system is beginning to view criminals, victims and society as all equally affected by criminal acts.

Although reported crime for 2000 showed a decrease for the eighth consecutive year, FBI statistics indicate the drop is smaller than in previous years:

> Both violent crime and property crime decreased three-tenths of 1 percent during the first six months of 2000, compared to the first six months of 1999. . . . By comparison, the overall crime index total dropped 9.5 percent between 1998 and 1999, 5.1 percent the year before, and 4.5 percent the year before that. . . .
>
> Improvements were seen in arsons, which dropped 2.7 percent; robberies, which declined 2.6 percent; burglaries, which dropped 2.4 percent; and murders, which dropped 1.8 percent. But the other major crime categories—rape, aggravated assault, larceny/theft, and motor vehicle theft—all increased slightly ("FBI's Crime Figures . . .," 2001, p.5).

While the FBI's crime index figures may seem disheartening, data from the Bureau of Justice Statistics (BJS) are more optimistic: "The violent crime rate fell almost 15 percent last year, the largest one-year decline ever recorded by the Department of Justice's (DOJ's) National Crime Victimization Survey. The survey . . . also indicated that property crime, which accounts for three-fourths of all criminal offenses, fell by 10 percent during 2000" ("Crime Rate Declines . . .," 2001, p.1). The reason for the contradictory reports lies in how the two agencies measure crime:

> The annual BJS crime victimization survey relies on interviews with a nationally representative sample of approximately 160,000 people 12 years old and older in 86,000 households about their personal experiences with crime. The FBI gathers data from more than 17,000 city, county and state law enforcement agencies on reported crime. . . .
>
> According to [the BJS's] report, only about 48 percent of violent victimizations and 26 percent of property crimes were reported to the police ("Crime Rate Declines . . .," p.5).

This chapter begins with a description of the major sources of information on crime and offers cautions on interpreting crime statistics. This is followed by an explanation of violent crimes including homicide, assault, rape and robbery; crimes against property, including burglary, larceny/theft, motor vehicle theft and arson; and crimes that are less serious in either their use of violence or the value of the property involved.

The chapter then discusses special challenges, including white-collar crime, computer-related crime, organized crime, bias crime and ritualistic crime. Next those who commit crimes are briefly described, including a discussion of why people commit crime, an examination of the biological and environmental causes of criminality, the problems of recidivism and the career criminal, as well as the juvenile offender.

The final major discussion is about those affected by crime—the victims—including an overview of victimization statistics and risk factors, followed by a discussion of a crime's effects on its victims and on indirect or secondary victims. Next the fear of victimization and how the criminal justice system may further victimize are examined. Then efforts to improve the treatment of victims, specific victims' rights during the criminal justice system proceedings, the impact of victims' rights on offenders and the rest of the system and specific programs for victims are described. The chapter concludes with discussions of the role of the police in dealing with victims and police officers as victims themselves.

Sources of Information on Crime

Several sources of information about crime are available.

The most frequently used sources of information about crime are the media, official government statistics and self-reporting surveys.

The Media

Much of what we know about crime comes from the media, which may overdramatize and distort the true extent and seriousness of the problem: "The relative infrequency of violent crime in society increases its newsworthiness and leads to its frequent appearance in crime news. Crime news thus takes the rare crime event and turns it into the common crime image" (Lawrence, 2000, p.1).

Gest (2001) examined how crime policy has evolved since the 1960s and contends the media have contributed to the failure of federal and state crime programs by headlining lurid crimes that simultaneously panic the public and encourage politicians to offer another round of quick-fix solutions. Nonetheless, the public remains fascinated by crime reports, no matter how appalling. One national survey found that the most important source of information is the local television news. Another source asserts: "When it comes to the news appetite of local media outlets, police records are a basic food group" ("Information, Please . . .," 2001, p.1).

Official Sources

The FBI's Uniform Crime Reports and NIBRS

Information about crime also comes from statistics gathered from around the country. In 1930 Congress assigned the FBI to serve as a national clearinghouse for crime statistics. The FBI's National Crime Information Center (NCIC) instituted a program called the Uniform Crime Reports (UCR). The annual publication of this program, *Crime in the United States* (2000) reports that today, more than 16,000 law enforcement agencies, serving approximately 253 million U.S. citizens, contribute data to the FBI either directly or through state UCR programs. The UCR divides offenses into two major categories: Part I and Part II **Index Crimes,** with Part I crimes being those that are most serious in either their use of violence or the value of the property involved.

The eight Part I Index Crimes are murder, aggravated assault causing serious bodily harm, forcible rape, robbery, burglary, larceny/theft, motor vehicle theft and arson.

A summary of the figures for the Part I crimes committed in 1999 is depicted in the Crime Clock (Figure 3.1). The Crime Clock should be viewed with care. Being the most aggregate representation of UCR data, it is designed to convey the annual reported crime experience by showing the relative frequency of occurrence of the Index Crimes. This graphic does not imply a regularity in the commission of the Part I offenses; rather it represents the annual ratio of crime to fixed time intervals. Figure 3.2 shows the distribution of the Part I offenses.

The Uniform Crime Reports program is undergoing major revision, moving from its current system of summary counts to a more comprehensive, detailed reporting system, the National Incident-Based Reporting System (NIBRS). This system is intended to replace the traditional eight offenses of the FBI Crime Index with detailed incident information on 46 offenses representing 22 categories of crimes (see Table 3.1). As Hoffmann (2000, p.31) explains:

> The advantage of an NIBRS program is that it reports every crime that occurs instead of just the most serious crime of an event. For instance, under the UCR/Summary requirements if two holdup men rob 18 customers in a restaurant and then shoot and kill the manager on the way out, you report just one murder. Under NIBRS you report one murder and 18 armed-robberies.

NIBRS, unlike the traditional UCR, also makes a distinction between attempted and completed crime. According to the NIBRS edition of the UCR handbook: "The ability to precisely identify when and where crime takes place, its form, and the characteristics of its victims and perpetrators is an indispensable tool in the war against crime" ("The New and Improved UCR. . .," 2000, p.1). However to date, the NIBRS has been adopted by fewer than 3,000 of the more than 16,000 state and local law enforcement agencies submitting data to the FBI ("The New and Improved. . .," p.1).

The Bureau of Justice Statistics National Crime Victimization Survey

The Bureau of Justice Statistics (BJS) National Crime Victimization Survey (NCVS) began in 1973 and, as previously described, gathers information on personal crime experience through interviews with approximately 160,000 people age 12 years and older in 86,000 households nationwide. The survey collects

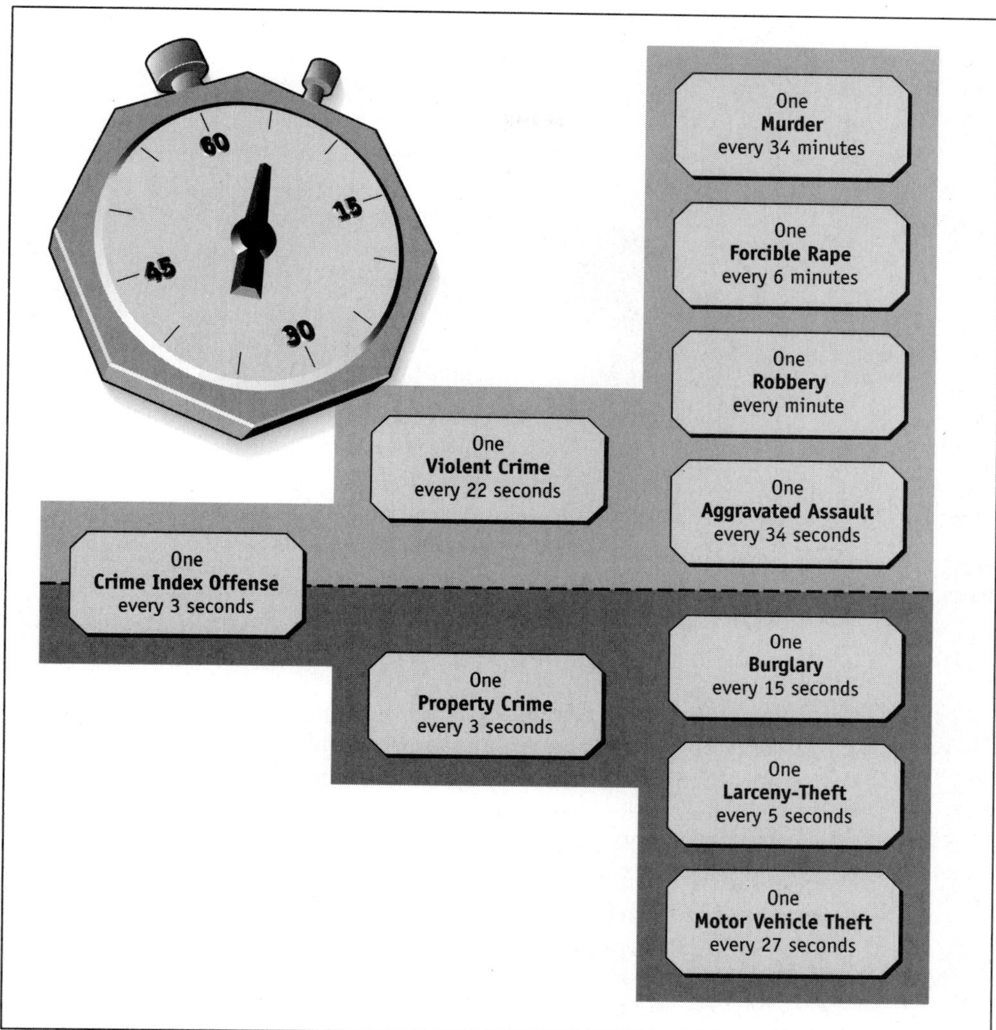

Source: *Crime in the United States, 1999.* Washington, DC: FBI, 2000, p.4.

Figure 3.1
The Crime Clock

data on crimes against individuals and households, regardless of whether they were reported to law enforcement. The data from this representative sample is then extrapolated to estimate the proportion of each crime type reported to law enforcement and details reasons given for reporting or not reporting.

The NCVS collects detailed information on the frequency and nature of the crimes of rape, personal robbery, aggravated and simple assault, household burglary, personal and household theft, and motor vehicle theft. The survey provides information about victims' age, sex, race, ethnicity, marital status, income and educational level; their offenders' sex, race, approximate age and

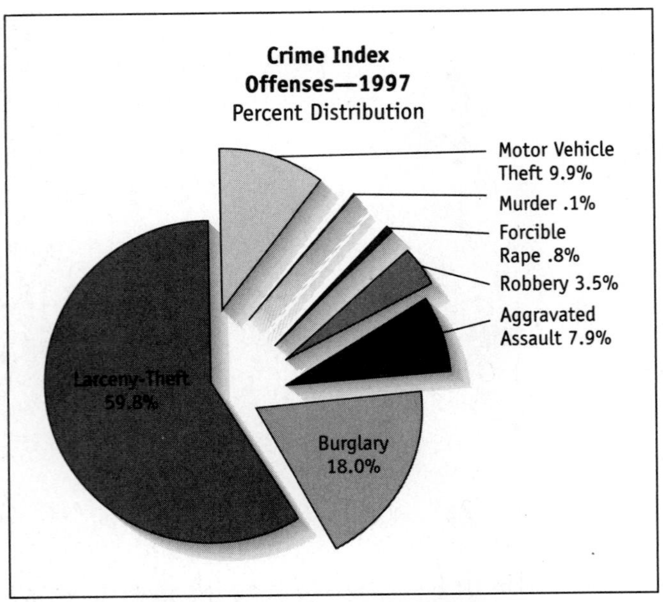

Figure 3.2
Distribution of the Part I Offenses

Source: *Crime in the United States, 1999.* Washington, DC: FBI, 2000, p.4.

victim-offender relationship; and the crimes: time and place of occurrence, use of weapons, nature of injury and economic consequences. Questions also cover the victims' experiences with the criminal justice system, self-protective measures used and possible substance abuse by offenders.

The UCR and NCVS differ significantly. As noted, the NCVS projects crime levels from a selected source of information and reports a substantially higher number of crimes than those reported in the UCR. Some analysts believe neither report is accurate and that crime is two to five times higher than either source reports.

The UCR captures crimes reported to law enforcement but excludes simple assaults. The NCVS includes crimes both reported and not reported to law enforcement but excludes homicide, arson, commercial crimes and crimes against children under age 12 (all included in the UCR Program). Even when the same crimes are included in the UCR and NCVS, the definitions vary.

Another difference is how rate measures are presented. The UCR crime rates are largely per capita (number of crimes per 100,000 persons), whereas the NCVS rates are per household (number of crimes per 1,000 households). Because the number of households may not grow at the same rate as the total population, trend data for rates measured by the two programs may not be compatible.

A Caution

Be mindful when interpreting official statistics that they reflect only reported crimes, and that these reports are voluntary and vary in accuracy and completeness. In addition not all police departments submit crime reports, and federal crimes are not included. Furthermore it is estimated that less than half the crimes committed are reported to the police. The true number of crimes, called

Table 3.1
The National Incident-Based Reporting System Group Offenses

Arson	Negligent manslaughter
Assault offenses	Justifiable homicide
Aggravated assault	Kidnapping/abduction
Simple assault	Larceny/theft offenses
Intimidation	Pocket picking
Bribery	Purse snatching
Burglary/breaking and entering	Shoplifting
Counterfeiting/forgery	Theft from building
Destruction/damage/vandalism of property	Theft from coin-operated machines
Drug/narcotic offenses	Theft from motor vehicle
Drug/narcotic violations	Theft of motor vehicle
Drug equipment violations	All other larceny
Embezzlement	Motor vehicle theft
Extortion/blackmail	Parts/accessories
Fraud offenses	Pornography/obscene material
False pretenses/swindle/confidence game	Prostitution offenses
Credit card/ATM fraud	Prostitution
Impersonation	Assisting or promoting prostitution
Welfare fraud	Robbery
Wire fraud	Sex offenses, forcible
Gambling offenses	Forcible rape
Betting/wagering	Forcible sodomy
Operating/promoting/assisting gambling	Sexual assault with an object
Gambling equipment violations	Forcible fondling
Sports tampering	Sex offenses, nonforcible
Homicide offenses	Stolen property offenses
Murder/non-negligent manslaughter	Weapon law violations

Source: Brian A. Reaves. *Using NIBRS Data to Analyze Violent Crime*. Washington, DC: Bureau of Justice Statistics Technical Report, October 1993, p.1.

the **dark figure of criminality,** is unknown. Despite these difficulties, police departments make frequent use of the information from the UCR Program.

Another caution: Any large-scale data collection program has many possible sources of error. For example in the UCR Program, a police officer may classify a crime incorrectly; and in the NCVS, a Census Bureau interviewer may incorrectly record a victim's response. Crime data is also affected by how victims perceive and recall events. In addition clerical errors may occur at any stage. Both programs have extensive accuracy checks to minimize errors.

Self-Report Surveys

Another source of data compiled every two years is the BJS document, *Report to the Nation on Crime and Justice.* This document brings together a wide range of data from the BJS's own statistical series, FBI Uniform Crime Reports, the Bureau of the Census, the National Institute of Justice, the Office of Juvenile Delinquency Prevention and many other research and reference sources. The report presents national data on crime and the criminal justice system and answers questions such as How much crime is there? Who does it strike? When? Where? Who is the typical offender? What is the government's response to crime? How are juveniles handled differently from adults? What are the costs of justice and who pays?

Regardless of the format used to compile information on crime, the need exists for crime to first be defined and classified. Major crimes are often classified as violent crimes and property crimes.

Classification and Definitions of Major Crimes

Violent Crimes

The four Part I violent crimes are murder (homicide), assault, rape and robbery. Such acts are also called crimes against persons.

Murder (Homicide)

Murder or **homicide** is defined in the UCR Program as the willful (non-negligent) killing of one human by another. The generally recognized levels of homicide are (1) first-degree, (2) second-degree, (3) manslaughter (or non-negligent manslaughter) and (4) negligent homicide. The first three categories are classified as felonies. Negligent homicide, however, is usually a misdemeanor.

First-degree murder is the willful, deliberate and **premeditated** (planned) taking of another person's life. A homicide that occurs during the commission or attempted commission of arson, robbery, rape or burglary is also usually classified as first-degree murder. **Second-degree murder** is murder that is *not* premeditated but the intent to kill is present. This charge often results from killings that do not involve weapons.

Manslaughter is differentiated from murder in that the element of **malice** is absent; the death was accidental with no original intent, hatred, ill will or disregard for the lives of others. In many states manslaughter is classified as either involuntary or voluntary. *Involuntary* manslaughter involves negligence, such as deaths resulting from automobile accidents. In contrast *voluntary* manslaughter, sometimes called second-degree manslaughter, is intentionally killing someone without previous malice but in the sudden heat of passion due to adequate provocation. For example a husband who kills another man he found in bed with his wife might be found guilty of voluntary manslaughter. Many instances of self-defense are also defined as voluntary manslaughter.

Negligent homicide refers to an accidental death that results from the reckless operation of a motor vehicle, boat, plane or firearm. **Justifiable homicide** includes killing in self-defense or in the defense of another person if the victim's actions and capability present imminent danger of serious injury or death. This classification includes killing an enemy during war, capital punishment, death caused by a public officer while carrying out a court order and deaths caused by police officers.

Assault

Assault is the unlawful attack, by one person on another to inflict severe bodily injury. Assaults are frequently committed in conjunction with rape, burglary and robbery. Several states have two distinct crimes, assault and battery. Where two crimes exist, assault refers to the threats made, whereas **bat-**

tery refers to any physical contact that occurs. If only one crime exists, it is usually assault, and battery is included within that crime. Assault may be aggravated or simple.

Aggravated assault is an unlawful attack on a person to inflict severe bodily injury or death. Assault can safely be classified as *aggravated* if a gun, knife or other weapon is used and serious personal injury is inflicted. **Simple assault,** the most frequent type, has no intent of serious injury. It may or may not be accompanied by a threat. Hands, fists or feet are the most commonly used weapons. Most simple assaults result from emotional conflicts and are classified as misdemeanors.

Rape

Rape is having sexual intercourse with a female or male through the use or threat of force. Rape may be aggravated, simple or statutory. **Aggravated rape** involves using force, threats of immediate use of force or taking advantage of an unconscious or helpless victim or a victim incapable of consent because of mental illness or a defect reasonably known to the attacker. **Simple rape** involves misleading a victim about the nature of the act being performed; for example having intercourse under the guise of a medical examination or treatment or knowingly destroying the victim's will to resist by use of a drug or intoxicant. **Statutory rape** involves sexual intercourse with a minor, with or without consent.

Robbery

Robbery is stealing or taking anything of value from the care, custody or control of a person by force or threat of force. Assault to commit robbery and attempts to commit robbery are included in the definition. Many states divide robbery into degrees.

This violent crime often results in injury to the victim. In half of the cases, robbery is accompanied by an assault upon the victim. Sometimes labeled as the most brutal and vicious of all crimes, robbery occurs in all parts of the country; its victims are people of all ages, incomes and backgrounds. Robbers may shoot, assault or torture their victims to find where valuables are located. Many victims who have refused to cooperate, and even some who have, have been ruthlessly killed.

The preferred weapon of most robbers is the handgun. Other weapons used include knives, acids, baseball bats and explosives. Armed robbers frequently attack drugstores (often for narcotics), supermarkets, liquor stores, jewelry stores, gas stations, banks, residential homes, cab drivers and pedestrians.

A new form of robbery appeared late in 1990—**carjacking,** which is taking a motor vehicle by force or threat of force. Congress enacted the Carjacking Corrections Act of 1996 to establish strict penalties for persons convicted of carjacking, with sentences up to 25 years in prison for cases involving "serious bodily injury" to a victim.

Crimes against Property

The four Part I Index Crimes against property are burglary, larceny/theft, motor vehicle theft and arson. Although these crimes do not usually involve violence, they can leave their victims feeling violated.

Burglary

Burglary is unlawful entrance into a building to commit theft or another felony. Burglary has three subclassifications: forcible entry, unlawful entry where no force is used and attempted forcible entry.

Larceny/Theft

Larceny/theft is unlawfully taking and removing another's personal property with the intent of permanently depriving the owner of the property. It includes shoplifting, pocket picking, purse snatching, thefts from motor vehicles, thefts of motor vehicle parts and accessories, and bicycle thefts. The category does not include embezzlement, "con" games, forgery, passing worthless checks or motor vehicle theft.

Larceny/theft may be classified as either a misdemeanor or a felony. It differs from robbery in that it does not involve force, threats of force or violence. The severity of punishment usually depends on the value and type of property taken, whether it was taken from a building or a person and the specific circumstances of the case.

Some states categorize larceny into degrees. **Grand** and **petty larceny** are common identifications for the value of property taken and punishment. First-, second- and third-degree larceny also indicate a certain minimum value of the property taken and various degrees of punishment. The most common type of theft is the theft of items from motor vehicles and motor vehicle parts and accessories, such as cell phones, stereos and CD/tape players, pagers, CB radios, clothing and photographic equipment.

Other common forms of larceny are thefts from underground garages where maintenance equipment, such as lawnmowers, snowblowers, lawn hoses and fertilizers, is the target. Bicycles are also common targets for thieves. Thefts from coin-operated vending machines, pocket picking, purse snatching and shoplifting are other common forms of larceny/theft.

Theft

Theft can refer to several different crimes, depending upon state statutes. It can describe a type of larceny, a theft from the person, a theft by force or a burglary. The most commonly referred to forms of theft are summarized in Table 3.2.

Motor Vehicle Theft

Motor vehicle theft is the unlawful taking or stealing of a motor vehicle without the owner's authority or permission. This definition excludes those who have lawful access to the vehicle and take it for temporary use. Motor vehicle theft includes automobiles, trucks, buses, motorcycles, motorized boats and aircraft.

The economic impact of motor vehicle theft can be great, with drivers absorbing such losses through higher insurance premiums. It is difficult to obtain a conviction for auto theft unless witnesses see the person drive the vehicle away and make positive identification. It is also difficult to prove the suspect intended to permanently deprive the rightful owner of its use. Therefore the category of "Unlawful Use of a Motor Vehicle" was created to apply to suspects who merely have possession of a vehicle reported stolen.

Table 3.2
Forms of Taking and Types of Theft

Shoplifting (retail theft) or price altering

Shoplifting—the most common form of theft in retail stores—is the taking by concealment to avoid payment for goods.

Price altering avoids payment of the full price of an object by lowering the amount on the price tag.

Taking by employee, bailee, or trustee

Employee theft of money and other objects causes large losses in business places.

Embezzlement of funds or negotiable securities that are in the custody of employees, bailees, or trustees

Snatch and run

The taking is observed and the offender flees to avoid apprehension.

Till tap

Thief opens cash register unobserved and takes cash and coins.

While store employee has cash drawer open, money is grabbed and the thief flees (snatch and run).

Taking by trick, deception or fraud (stings and scams or swindles)

Con games and operations

Deceptions and tricks to obtain property illegally

Obtaining property by false pretense

Taking by force, or the threat of the use of force (robbery)

Taking during a burglary (trespass with intent to steal or commit a felony)

Taking by extortion (threats of future violence or threats to reveal embarrassing information—blackmail)

Taking from a person

Purse snatching (a form of snatch and run)

Pickpocketing

Rolling a drunk (taking from person incapacitated by alcohol, drugs or other means)

Taking from a corpse

Taking of lost or mislaid goods or money

Taking of objects or money delivered by mistake

Example: a check for too much money is mailed to a person by mistake.

Looting

Taking property from or near a building damaged, destroyed or left unoccupied by tornado, fire, physical disaster, riot, bombing, earthquake and so on.

Taking by failure to return a leased or rented object

Example: failure to return a rented car or videotape within the time specified by state statutes or city ordinance

Taking by illegal entry into locked coin box

Vending machine, pay telephone, parking meter and so on

Smash and run

A store or other window is broken, and after snatching objects, the thief runs to avoid apprehension.

Women drivers waiting at stoplights are sometimes subjected to this tactic. The thief breaks the car window, takes the woman's purse from the front seat, and runs.

Taking by illegally obtaining or using information

Such as in the "inside trading" scandals of 1987 and 1988 involving Ivan Boesky and others. See the 1987 U.S. Supreme Court case of *Carpenter v. United States,* 108 S.Ct. 316. One of the defendants in the case was the coauthor of a *Wall Street Journal* column.

Taking by illegal use of a credit card or credit card number

Taking from a person with a superior right of possession

Persons may acquire a superior right of possession over the owner of property because of a bailment, pledge or contract. State criminal codes may make taking from a person with a superior right of possession a crime.

Theft by possession of stolen property

Ordinary theft

Taking occurs observed or unobserved by owner or other persons.

Source: Thomas J. Gardner and Terry Anderson. *Criminal Law: Principles and Cases,* 7th ed. Belmont, CA: Wadsworth Publishing Company, 2000, p.359.

One motive for auto theft is joyriding—the car is stolen, taken for a ride and then abandoned. Joyriding is often a separate charge where intent to permanently deprive is not in evidence. Autos are also stolen for revenge, for transportation, for commercial use and for use in committing other crimes, such as kidnapping, burglary and bank robbery. Autos are stolen and stripped for parts such as transmissions, engines and seats. Automobiles are also stolen, modified, given altered serial numbers and fraudulent titles and sold to an unsuspecting public.

Arson

Arson is intentionally damaging or destroying or attempting to damage or destroy by means of fire or explosion the property of another without the consent of the owner or one's own property, with or without the intent to defraud. It is a felony in all 50 states. Arson has increased more than 400 percent in the past 10 years. An estimated 1,000 people, including 45 firefighters, die each year in arson fires, and 10,000 people are injured annually. Annual damage estimates are as high as $15 billion. One of the most serious problems often encountered in arson investigations is the joint jurisdiction of firefighters and law enforcement officers. All too frequently this results in duplication of effort and inefficiency.

Part II Index Crimes

The Part II offenses consist of several other crimes that can be either misdemeanors or felonies. They include counterfeiting, curfew violations (juveniles), disorderly conduct, driving under the influence (DUI), drug abuse violations, drunkenness, embezzlement, forgery, fraud (confidence games, etc.), gambling, liquor law violations (bootlegging, etc.), loitering (juveniles), offenses against the family and children (child abuse, neglect, nonsupport), other assaults (intimidation, coercion, hazing, etc.), prostitution and commercialized vice, runaways (juveniles), sex offenses (except forcible rape, prostitution and commercialized vice), stolen property (buying, receiving, possessing), vagrancy, vandalism, weapons violations (carrying, possessing, etc.) and all other offenses (bigamy, contempt of court, the list goes on and on).

Other Crimes

Many crimes do not fall neatly into the classifications just discussed.

Other serious crimes include white-collar crime, computer-related crime, organized crime, bias or hate crime and ritualistic crime.

White-Collar Crime

White-collar crime is occupational or business-related crime. The Part I offense of larceny/theft and several Part II offenses can also be classified as white-collar crimes. These crimes often involve billions of dollars and pose an extremely difficult challenge to law enforcement officers. In recent years, several agencies, including the FBI, U.S. Secret Service and American Society for Industrial Security (ASIS), have renamed this category of crime to reflect a change in scope, now referring to it as *economic crime* (Neeley, 2000, p.2). To help fight white-collar crime the National White Collar Crime Center (NWCCC) bridges the gap between local and state criminal justice agencies and also links criminal justice agencies across international borders.

White-collar crime includes (1) credit card and check fraud including identity theft, (2) securities theft and fraud, (3) insurance fraud, (4) consumer fraud, illegal competition and deceptive practices, (5) bankruptcy fraud, (6) embezzlement and pilferage, (7) bribes, kickbacks and payoffs and (8) receiving stolen property.

Unauthorized use of credit cards (found, stolen or counterfeited) and checks results in losses of millions annually. A problem of growing concern is identity theft. In simple terms this is "the unlawful use of another's personal identifying information" (Bellah, 2001, p.222). According to Barry (2001, p.25) identity theft is America's fastest-growing financial crime. In fact, identity theft led the top 10 consumer fraud complaints of 2001, according to the Federal Trade Commission, accounting for 42 percent of the 204,000 complaints received that year ("Identity Theft . . .," 2002, p.15). Securities theft and fraud may be perpetrated by clerks acting independently, by individuals who rob messengers and steal from the mails or by well-organized rings. Most security thefts involve the cooperation of dishonest employees ("inside" people) and may involve counterfeit and bogus securities as well.

Insurance fraud losses lead to higher premiums for consumers. Because insurance is important to businesses and individuals, false claims for life, health and accident benefits affect almost everyone. Especially prevalent are fraudulent auto accident claims seeking compensation for treatments for personal injury, time lost from work and automobile repairs.

Consumer fraud, illegal competition and deceptive practices include thousands of different schemes to defraud the public, including offers for "free" articles, advice, vacations, mailing or unordered merchandise, phony contests, recommendations for unneeded repairs, "going-out-of-business" sales, unqualified correspondence schools and price fixing. Bankruptcy fraud, also called planned bankruptcy, scam or bust-out, involves purchasing merchandise on credit from many different suppliers, selling the merchandise for cash that is "hidden" and then filing for bankruptcy and not paying the creditors.

Embezzlement and pilferage, both forms of theft, are considered by many businesses to be their most serious problem. People **embezzle** when they steal or use for themselves money or property entrusted to them. To **pilfer** is basically the same, but on a much smaller scale. Cumulatively the losses from pilferage may be much greater than what some other dishonest employee might embezzle. Equally dishonest is unauthorized use of company equipment, personnel and time.

Bribes, kickbacks and payoffs are pervasive in the business world and are often used to obtain new clients, to keep old clients, to influence decisions or to obtain favors. They can involve anyone from the custodian to the company president, and they can occur in any aspect of a company's operation.

Receiving stolen property, although classified as a white-collar crime, often occurs in conjunction with such crimes as robbery and burglary. The person who buys and sells stolen property is of vital importance to most burglars, robbers and hijackers. Criminals depend on a **fence** (a professional receiver and seller of stolen property) to convert stolen goods into cash.

Computer-Related Crime

Computer crime, also referred to as **cybercrime,** is a rapidly increasing threat to American businesses and consumers:

> Stolen identities, computer viruses, child online safety, cyberstalking and harassment, network intrusion and denial of service attacks. There's a new breed of criminal emerging and threatening to overwhelm law enforcement officials. These are some of the most evasive criminals ever known, operating in an area—the Web—that is moving so far forward so fast that law enforcement agencies and judicial systems are having difficulties keeping pace (Cornell, 2001, p.55).

According to Goodman (2001, p.10): "Unfortunately, the absence of a standard definition for computer crime, a lack of reliable criminal statistics on the problem, and significant underreporting of the threat pose vexing challenges for police agencies."

As Johnston notes (2002, p.52), only 36 percent of the companies victimized reported the intrusions to law enforcement agencies. (In the survey, 85 percent detected computer security breaches within the last 12 months—from March 2001.) The FBI estimates that electronic crimes are running at least $10 billion a year.

Correia and Bowling (1999) examined how a lack of police preparedness in keeping up with technology may actually contribute to the proliferation of cybercrime and have applied Wilson and Kelling's classic "Broken Windows" theory to a new concept they call *digital disorder:*

> Attempted break-ins, trespassing, sex-related commerce, harassment, stalking, vandalism, money laundering, theft, and child pornography—surely one would agree that if these crimes were occurring in any given neighborhood, a police presence would be necessary, and without police, escalation of criminal activity would most likely continue. Yet in the neighborhood known as cyberspace, these "broken windows" abound and the police are seldom to be found. . . .
>
> Just as disorder in the physical world entices criminals, the digital variant is interpreted by the more serious cyber criminal that "no one cares" (p.229).

Cornell (p.55) reports: "The statistics indicate that cybercrime is expanding almost proportionately with the enrichments and advancements being made by the Net's existence; the FBI has seen its cybercrime caseload increase 1200% over the past five years and estimates that computer losses equate to ten billion dollars annually." Most big corporations have been victims of cybercrime, from employees' snooping through confidential files to criminal stealing of trade secrets. The most common crimes are credit card fraud, telecommunications fraud, employee use of computers for personal reasons, unauthorized access to confidential files and unlawful copying of copyrighted or licensed software. While a large portion of cybercrime is committed internally by employees, companies and private users are finding themselves increasingly vulnerable to outside hackers. According to Rataj (2001, p.43):

> Starting with the unprecedented "Distributed Denial of Service" (DDoS) attacks in February 2000, and continuing with the "Lovebug" virus in May 2000, the much-touted Internet age suffered some serious growing pains. . . . Although these attacks were carefully targeted at particular companies, without any apparent

> attempt to steal, damage or corrupt data, the apparent ease with which they were carried out had many Internet and computer-security experts worried.
>
> By late April 2000, a 15 year old boy had been arrested by the RCMP in Montreal, Canada, and charged with 66 hacking and mischief charges in relation to February's DDoS attacks on Yahoo, e-bay and Amazon.

Hall (2000, p.6) reports the estimated worldwide damage caused by the "I LoveYou" virus was $10 billion. The crime also challenged law enforcement with jurisdiction and prosecution issues, as the perpetrators were operating in one country while most of the actual victims resided in another country (Rataj, p.43).

Computer fraud may involve the input data, the output data, computer time or the program itself. *Input data* may be altered; for example fictitious suppliers may be entered, figures may be changed or data may be removed. Some schools have experienced difficulties with student grades being illegally changed. *Output data* may be obtained by unauthorized persons through such means as wiretapping, electromagnetic pickup or theft of data sheets. *Computer time* may be taken for personal use, an example of pilferage. Some employees have even used their employer's hardware and company time to set up their own computer services for personal profit. The *computer program* itself might be tampered with to add costs to purchased items or to establish a double set of records.

One area of computer crime that is becoming more publicized is sex-related computer crimes, including child pornography. Correia and Bowling point to the growing presence of sex sites on the Internet as one example of a digital broken window:

> What many perceived as simply an overabundance of "nudie" pictures on the Internet, in actuality may have served as a social cue (e.g., broken window) to others that no one cares. Such a cue may have facilitated the presence of child pornography to its current standing on the Internet and promoted the accelerated pace of organized crime participation in sex-related Internet commerce (p.230).

Computer industry experts estimate that more than 45 million children do homework assignments using the Internet ("House Passes Measure. . .," 1998, p.5). Yet many parents remain oblivious to the dangers the Internet can pose to their children. Rep. Bill McCollum, chief sponsor of the Child Protection and Sexual Predator Punishment Act (H.R. 3494), notes:

> Children are rarely supervised while they are on the Internet. Unfortunately, that is exactly what cyber-predators look for. We are seeing numerous accounts in which pedophiles have used the Internet to seduce or persuade children to meet them to engage in sexual activities. Children who have been persuaded to meet their new online friend face to face have been kidnapped, raped, photographed for child pornography, and worse. Some children have never been heard from again ("House Passes Measure. . .," p.5).

Characteristics of computer-related crime include:

- Computer crimes are relatively easy to commit and difficult to detect.
- Most computer crimes are committed by "insiders."
- Most computer crimes are not prosecuted.

AP/Wide World Photos

Thomas Foley, Sr., right, of Grand Island, NY, is escorted from Oneida County Court in Utica, NY, after being sentenced to a state prison term of two to six years under the state's computer sex law. Foley was caught on two occasions transmitting sexually explicit photos of children over the Internet to someone he believed was a 15-year-old girl, but who was actually a New York state trooper.

Unfortunately, few computer crime specialists patrol cyberspace. Those who do have been dubbed cybercops. According to Rusnell (2001, p.52), **cybercops** are highly trained police officers who investigate technological crime, and the demand for such training is growing exponentially:

> The non-profit National Economic Crime Center in Fairmont, WV, is one organization that offers this training. The center, through its National Cybercrime Training Partnership, trains 1,750 law enforcement officers a year [and is] funded by Congress through the Justice Department.

For those departments lacking funds to train and staff designated cybercops, a variety of resources and services are available:

> The Web site, www.cybercrime.gov is the closest thing you are likely to find for a one-stop resource for all things related to computer crime. The site, maintained by the Computer Crime and Intellectual Property Section (CCIPS) of the U.S. Department of Justice, is a collection of documents and links to other sites and agencies that may be of assistance in preventing, detecting, investigating and prosecuting computer-related crime (Dees, 2001, p.27).
>
> The FBI operates a computer crime squad (www.emergency.com/fbi-nccs.htm) that provides information and conducts investigations and prosecutions of computer crimes. Its National Infrastructure Protection Center (www.nipc.gov) also acts as a clearinghouse for information on cyber crime (Rataj, p.45).

Other sites and services allow computer-crime victims themselves to get more directly involved in the war on cybercrime. One example is the Internet

Fraud Complaint Center (IFCC), created by the FBI and the National White Collar Crime Center (NWCCC): "A dedicated Web site located at http://www.ifccfbi.gov provides consumers and small businesses nationwide with the ability to file Internet fraud complaints online with the IFCC" (Lormel and Johnston, 2001, p.67):

> By facilitating the flow of information between law enforcement and victims of fraud, the IFCC streamlines the case initiation effort on behalf of both the victim and the law enforcement agencies. The key to the IFCC's success is its ability to relay timely and complete information to the appropriate local, state, and/or federal law enforcement agencies. With the IFCC, all levels of law enforcement receive the data they need to identify and address new fraud trends (p.68).

Hall (p.6) notes that when the IFCC went online in May 2000, it registered nearly 4,000 complaints in its first four days. Computers have also been of great assistance to organized crime, opening new avenues for illegal activity.

Organized Crime

Organized crime goes by many names—the mob, the syndicate, the rackets, the Mafia and La Cosa Nostra. A basic definition of **organized crime** is "a continuing criminal conspiracy, having an organized structure, fed by fear and corruption and motivated by greed" (Das, 1999, p.1). Albanese (2000, p.411) elaborates on this definition: "The consensus of investigators focuses on four primary elements: a continuing organization, an organization that operates rationally for profit, the use of force or threats, and the need for corruption to maintain immunity from law enforcement."

Organized crime is distinct from other forms of crime in that it is characterized by corruption and enforcement powers.

These features make organized crime especially threatening, not only to the police, but to our entire democratic process.

Organized crime is particularly challenging to law enforcement because of the numerous types of groups involved. The President's Commission on Organized Crime has identified 11 different groups: La Cosa Nostra (Italian), outlaw motorcycle gangs, prison gangs, Triads and Tongs (Chinese), Vietnamese gangs, Yakuza (Japanese), Marielitos (Cuban), Colombian cocaine rings, Irish, Russian, and Canadian. Albanese (p.413) notes:

> This curious mixture includes groups defined in terms of ethnic or national origin, those defined by the nature of their activity (i.e., cocaine rings), those defined by their geographic origin (i.e., prison gangs), and those defined by their means of transportation (i.e., motorcycle gangs). Such a haphazard approach to defining and describing organized crime does little to help make sense of its causes, current events, or how policies against organized crime should be directed.

Despite the various and distinct origins of organized crime groups, many of them participate in the same activities, including heavy involvement in gambling, drugs, prostitution, pornography, loansharking and infiltration of legitimate businesses—"virtually anything that offer[s] prospect of a high profit" (Das, p.3). For example, the La Cosa Nostra (LCN), the most well-known organized crime faction currently operating in the United States, is involved in drug trafficking, extortion, illegal gambling, money laundering, murder, obstruction of justice and a variety of financial fraud schemes (Das, p.3).

Russian organized crime (ROC) is becoming a growing threat in the United States and may present law enforcement with its toughest challenge yet: "The ROC syndicates conduct the most sophisticated criminal operations ever seen in the United States, based on their access to expertise in computer technology, encryption techniques and money-laundering facilities" (Zalisko, 2000, p.18). Furthermore, the trafficking in human beings (women and children sold as sex slaves and indentured household servants) has become a $6-billion-a-year enterprise for ROC and is flourishing in the United States (Zalisko, p.18). According to Finckenauer and Voronin (2001, p.26):

> The threat and use of violence is a defining characteristic of Russian organized crime in the United States. . . . The common use of violence is not surprising, since extortion and protection rackets are such a staple of Russian criminal activity. Contract murders, kidnappings, and business arson have all been employed by Russian organized crime. Arson is used against businesses that refuse to pay extortion money. . . .
>
> [ROC is also] extensively engaged in a broad array of frauds and scams, including health care fraud, insurance scams, stick frauds, antiquities swindles, forgery and fuel tax evasion schemes. Recently, for example, Russians have become the main purveyors of credit-card fraud in the United States.

Most organized crime groups have their hands in the drug trade: "Globally, drug trafficking is the economic mainstay of organized crime, [and] accounts for 40% of organized crime activity in the U.S. and for profits estimated at about $100 billion per year" (Das, p.3). An additional challenge for law enforcement is found in the partnering of different organizations for profit in illegal narcotics. O'Neal (2000, p.4) notes the LCN and ROC actively cooperate in domestic drug trafficking and:

> ROC groups have also formed alliances with Colombian drug traffickers to import cocaine into Russia, possibly transshipping through the United States. The two groups have traded Colombian drugs for Russian weapons. Further, Colombian drug traffickers have acquired Soviet-designed military aircraft for their drug-running operations.

Numerous strategies and methods have been proposed to combat organized crime (Das, pp.4–5):

- International cooperation—various countries, including the Netherlands, South Africa, the United States, Canada and Australia, are assigning officers to duty in foreign countries to strengthen international police cooperation.
- Interagency cooperation.
- Legislative initiatives—U.S. laws include the Omnibus Crime Control and Safe Streets Act and the Racketeer Influenced and Corrupt Organization (RICO) Statute, which allows for criminal forfeiture of property and is

considered the most sweeping statute yet passed by Congress to attack organized crime activity.

- Police use of community resources—opening lines of communication between the public and police.

Many contend the public and government play active roles in perpetuating organized crime and, in fact, are sometimes directly responsible for creating opportunities that allow such enterprises to thrive. Das (p.6) asserts that politicians and the people they serve must take an active stance against organized crime by discontinuing their associations with these entities:

> Organized crime is made possible by crooked politicians and crooked companies. . . . Organized crime would not exist without widespread public participation in prohibited activities and services. Nor would it exist if the interests controlling governments did not bring about the criminalization of activities and services desired by many. In the final analysis making a popular good or service illegal, the government creates a market vacuum which is filled by entrepreneurial criminals. Drugs provide an example of this. Governments have, in fact, created the market vacuums that were filled by entrepreneurial criminals, often with assistance of corrupt or corruptible government officials.

Yet another area of concern for law enforcement is the dramatic increase in bias or hate crimes.

Bias Crimes

"Generically," says Levin (1999, p.8), "*hate crime* refers to those criminal acts committed because of someone's actual or perceived membership in a particular group." According to the UCR for 2000 (p.58): "A **hate crime,** also known as a **bias crime,** is a criminal offense committed against a person, property, or society which is motivated, in whole or in part, by the offender's bias against a race, religion, disability, sexual orientation or ethnic/national origin." Hate crimes may also be seen as a form of **xenophobia,** the fear and hatred of strangers or foreigners.

Hate crimes may be motivated by bias against a person's race, religion, disability, sexual orientation or ethnicity.

FBI statistics indicate race is the most frequent motivation of hate crime, followed by religion, as shown in Figure 3.3. In fact racial prejudice motivated more than half of the 7,876 hate crime incidents reported to the FBI in 1999 (UCR, p.59). Furthermore, murders fueled by racial bias reached a five-year high in 1999 ("FBI: Racism Is . . .," 2001, p.7). These figures should be viewed with caution, however. A report by the Southern Poverty Law Center ("Hate Crime Statistics . . .," 2001, p.5) states: "The overall hate crime statistics are virtually useless. While the published hate crime totals have been running at about 8,000 a year, the real figure is probably closer to 50,000. And these numbers are critically important. Only when we know the level and nature of hate crime in the United

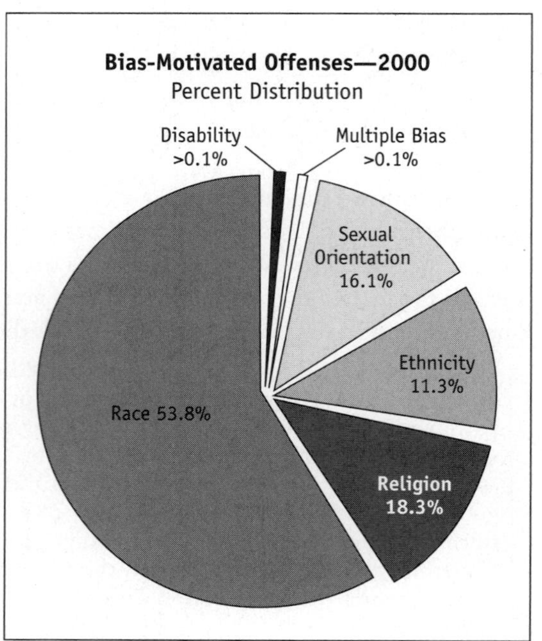

Source: FBI UCR, 2001.

Figure 3.3
Bias Motivation, 2000

States will we be able to allocate resources in an effective way to combat it." Petrosino (1999, p.22) goes beyond the statistics, stating:

> Hate crimes are despicable acts. Their toll only begins with the victim. Harm expands to the victim's family, group, and society itself. Its greatest cost is not only measured in property damages, medical expenses, or the loss of wages, but also in the depreciation of the human spirit in dignity, liberty, and security.

Hate crimes differ from other attacks on people or property in some important ways, as shown in Table 3.3. Paynter (2000, pp.52–53) explains the "overkill" and ripple effects associated with bias crime:

> The level of viciousness in a hate crime often rises above that of a similar crime where hate is not a motive. If there's a homicide, there may be 100 stab wounds, or the body may be mutilated or set on fire. . . .
>
> The vicious nature of such crimes traumatizes and terrorizes victims, if they survive the attacks. The victims' families may feel frustrated and powerless. Members of the community who share the victim's characteristics often feel vulnerable and victimized themselves. In addition, hate incidents and hate crimes, if unaddressed, can lead to community unrest.

While hate crimes may happen anywhere, the U.S. Department of Justice's Community Relations Service (CRS) reports that hate crimes are occurring with increasing frequency and more visibility and hostility on college and university campuses than in any other arena ("College Campuses Are . . .," 2000, p.11).

Offenses frequently involved in bias crimes include cross burning, swastika painting, bombing, hanging in effigy, disturbing a public meeting, graffiti, obscene letters or phone calls, or face-to-face oral abuse. As with other types of

Table 3.3
Hate-Based Crimes and Non–Hate-Based Crimes Compared

Characteristic	Non–Hate-Based Incidents	Hate-Based Incidents
Relationship of victim to perpetrator	Most assaults involve two people who know each other	Assaults tend to be "stranger" crimes
Number of perpetrators	Most assaults have one perpetrator and one victim	Involve an average of four assailants for each victim
Nature of the conflict	Tends to be even	Tends to be uneven—hate crime perpetrators often attack younger or weaker victims, or arm themselves and attack unarmed victims
Amount of physical damage inflicted	Not typically "excessive"	Extremely violent, with victims being three times more likely to require hospitalization than "normal" assault victims
Treatment of property	In most property crimes, something of value is taken	More likely that valuable property will be damaged or destroyed
Perpetrator's personal gain	Attacker settles a score or profits from the crime	In most, no personal score is settled and no profit is made
Location of crime	No place with any symbolic significance	Frequently occur in churches, synagogues, mosques, cemeteries, monuments, schools, camps and in or around the victim's home

Source: Adapted from Christina Bodinger-deUriarte. "Hate Crime: The Rise of Hate Crime on School Campuses." Research Bulletin No. 10 of Phi Delta Kappa, Center for Evaluation, Development, and Research, December 1991, p.2.

crimes, the Internet is being used by hate groups to build a sense of community through encrypted messages, chat rooms, e-mail communication and Web sites:

> Hate crimes and other bias-motivated incidents are not always physical. With the Internet growing on a daily basis, students have increasingly become the targets of e-mail propaganda sent by hate groups and other separatist organizations or by other students and even faculty. Thousands of students have been sent e-mail letters filled with threats, slurs and biased opinions that, because of the anonymity of the Internet, are often hard for officials to track and regulate ("College Campuses . . .," p.12).

One well-publicized crime of hate was the savage beating and death of Matthew Shepard, an openly gay student at the University of Wyoming. Just 21 years old, Shepard was brutally beaten, tied to a wooden fence miles out of town and left to die alone, allegedly by two men with strong anti-homosexual convictions. Another widely publicized hate crime was the murder of James Byrd, Jr., an African-American who was hitchhiking home. The three white men who picked him up did not give him a ride home, however, but instead took him to a wooded area where they beat him unconscious. They then chained him to the back of their truck and dragged him several miles, his right arm and head being torn from his body in the process. The assailants were linked to racist groups (Hohler, 1998).

One hate group is the Neo-Nazi Skinheads, youths with shaved heads or closely cropped hair, usually between the ages of 13 and 25 and typically male.

At a New Nationalist Socialist Party rally, skinheads celebrate Adolf Hitler's birthday. Like Hitler, Skinheads believe in the supremacy of the Aryan race and frequently engage in hate crimes against those not of that race.

© Bob Self/Silver Image

They sport Nazi insignia, tattoos and/or Satanic symbols and preach violence against African-Americans, Hispanics, Jews, Asians and homosexuals.

Passage of the Hate Crime Statistics Act of 1990 directed the U.S. Justice Department to collect bias-crime data nationwide. The program is voluntary, however, and no budgetary provisions were made. Many states have also passed legislation mandating the collection of bias-crime statistics. In addition the U.S. Department of Justice has created a hotline (1-800/347-HATE) that citizens can use to report bias crimes.

Dunbar (1999, p.64) notes: "Hate crime laws have resulted in the promulgation of additional sentencing options and penalty enhancements for convicted perpetrators." Currently, 40 of the 50 states, the District of Columbia and the federal government have laws allowing penalty enhancement for hate crimes (Vogel, 2000, p.3). Twenty-five states allow victims to bring civil suits against perpetrators. In most of these states, victims can sue for actual and punitive damages and obtain an injunction. Suits can be brought regardless of criminal proceedings, with the burden of proof being a preponderance of evidence (a lesser standard than in criminal proceedings). In some states if the offense is committed by a juvenile, the parents are liable up to $5,000.

The final area of criminal behavior to explore is ritualistic crime.

Ritualistic Crime

A **ritual** is a system of rites, a ceremonial act. Rituals are heavily linked to a belief system and may include symbols, artifacts, words, gestures, costumes and music. Whether this belief system is a formal religion or not, it is protected by the First Amendment right to worship as one wishes.

Rituals have a rich heritage. The Egyptians used amulets as good luck charms to ward off evil or to bring about good fortune. The Greeks practiced several forms of ritual, including hydromancy, similar to our wishing wells. They also put much faith in astrology and the signs of the zodiac. The Romans, too, practiced rituals, primarily fertility rites. Later in Europe and in the United States, witchcraft became a focus. In Europe more than 200,000 witches were killed for their beliefs.

All recognized religions have rituals meaningful to their members. Cults also use rituals to draw their members together. According to Szubin et al. (2000, p.16): "In sociological terms, a 'cult' may be defined as a movement that is foreign to the culture in which it lives." They point out that groups such as the Zen Buddhists are viewed by many Americans as "cults" but actually represent mainstream movements in other parts of the world. Consequently (p.17):

> Most scholars of religion avoid the word "cult" altogether because it carries with it a set of negative connotations. . . . These scholars instead refer to cults as "new religious movements" or "NRMs" because the majority of "cults" are young religious movements still in their first generation.

Satanic cults have one strong leader to whom all members give allegiance. Often the leader is worshipped as an anti-God—the embodiment of Satan and evil. Members are often youths who do not fit in with their peers and have no self-identity. In the cult they are accepted and given a feeling of belonging, worth and power. They are often influenced by heavy metal music and may dress in a punk style. Members of cults frequently wear pentagrams and inverted crosses. Dark clothing is common, as is self-mutilation, such as sticking safety pins through nipples. *Satanic rituals* commonly include robes (red or black), daggers, candles, altars and pentagrams. They often involve chanting, occur at night and are conducted in strict secrecy. None of this ritualistic activity is illegal and, as Szubin et al. (p.17) emphasize, the majority of NRMs stay within the boundaries of the law. Some, however, do not.

When the rituals of a group involve crimes, such as desecration of cemeteries, grave robbing, cruelty to animals, child sexual abuse and even murder, they become a problem for law enforcement. As noted by Los Angeles Police Department Investigator Patrick Metoyer, "We don't investigate warlocks, satanists, vampires, Jews, Catholics, or Protestants. We investigate *crime*."

A **ritualistic crime** is an unlawful act committed during a ceremony related to a belief system. It is the crime, *not* the belief system, that must be investigated.

Indicators of satanic or ritualistic involvement in a crime include inverted crosses, candles, altars, animal parts, colored salt, incense, such symbolism as 666 (referring to an anti-Christ), swastikas or books on the occult. Normal investigative techniques are not effective with ritualistic crime. Usually multiple victims and multiple suspects are involved, and often logic will not work.

Having examined the various classifications and types of crime law enforcement must handle, consider next the types of people involved in such crime and the factors contributing to their involvement.

Offenders—What Leads People to Commit Crime?

The reason people commit crime has been debated since crime was first defined. Some blame crime on the failings of the criminal justice system—understaffed police forces, lenient judges, overcrowded jails and prisons and overworked, burned-out probation and parole officers. Others blame society and the overwhelming absence of personal and community responsibility and accountability—abusive parents, permissive parents, inadequate schools and incompetent teachers, the decline of religion, media violence, drugs and high rates of unemployment.

Paradoxically, researchers at the John Jay College of Criminal Justice suggest incarceration may be another cause of crime:

> Crime, according to traditional theorists, is caused by three phenomena: poverty, ethnic heterogeneity and residential mobility. Current theorists also include single-parent families, structural density and urbanization as causes of crime. All of these factors are thought to increase social disorganization by decreasing social integration and informal social control, as well as increase isolation from economic and political forces. . . . Incarceration should also be included as a factor, [since] high incarceration rates produce high levels of residential mobility . . ., which weakens family and economic life, causing crime to increase ("Study Finds Incarceration . . .," 1999, p.11).

A detailed discussion of the causes of crime is beyond the scope of this text. Only the major theories are briefly discussed.

Theories of Criminality and Causes of Crime

The **classical theory,** developed by Italian criminologist Cesare Beccaria (1738–1794), holds that people are rational and responsible for their acts.

> The classical theory sees people as free agents with free will. People commit crimes because they want to.

A refinement to the classical theory is the *routine activity theory* developed by Lawrence Cohen and Marcus Felson, which states that the volume and distribution of predatory crime (where an offender tries to steal an object directly) correlates highly with three variables found in everyday American life:

1. The availability of suitable targets (homes/stores containing easily sold goods).
2. The absence of watchful guardians (homeowners, neighbors, friends, relatives, guards, security systems, etc.).

3. The presence of motivated offenders (unemployed individuals, drug abusers, etc.).

The intersection of these three variables increases the chances of a predatory crime occurring. This theory gives equal weight to the role of victim and offender. It also suggests that the opportunity for criminal action depends on the victim's lifestyle and behavior.

The classical theory of crime causation was called into question toward the end of the nineteenth century. Among the leading opponents was Cesare Lombroso (1835–1909), an Italian criminologist who developed the **positivist theory.** Lombroso's studies (1911) supported a biological causation for deviant behavior, suggesting that individuals who did not conform to society's laws and regulations were biologically inferior. *Biological theorists* hold that how a person acts is basically a result of heredity.

The positivist theory sees criminals as "victims of society" and of their own biological, sociological, cultural and physical environments.

Lombroso maintained that criminals are born with a predisposition to crime and need exceptionally favorable conditions in life to avoid criminal behavior. Building on Lombroso's idea that environmental influences affect criminal behavior, some scholars developed the positivist view based on the concept of **determinism.** Determinism regards crime as a consequence of many factors, including population density, economic status and the legal definition of crime. This multiple-factor causation theory brought the positivist view into direct conflict with the notion of free will.

The Influence of Biology

A medieval law states: "If two persons fall under suspicion of crime, the uglier or more deformed is to be regarded as more probably guilty." Such a law is based on a belief that criminals are born, not made. While we've come a long way in our understanding of the causes of crime since the Middle Ages, a person's biological makeup continues to be among those factors many believe are correlated with criminality:

> Studies indicate that vulnerability to antisocial behavior is partially a function of genetic and biological make-up which manifests during childhood as particular behavioral, cognitive and psychological traits. . . . Specifically, evidence is mounting to implicate dysfunctions of several chemical systems in the brain in sensation-seeking, impulsivity, negative affect and other cognitive and behavioral correlates of antisocial behavior (Fishbein, 1998, pp.1,3).

Biological functions and conditions that have been related to criminal behavior include such variables as brain tumors, disorders of the limbic system, endocrine abnormalities, chromosomal abnormalities and neurological dysfunction produced by the prenatal and postnatal experience of infants.

Adoption studies have lent support to the biological theory of criminal behavior. A fairly powerful argument can be made for a biological basis of criminality when it can be shown that the adopted-away children of criminal biological parents grow up to display criminal behavior, especially when the adoptive (nonbiological) parents are not themselves criminal.

A counterposition to the biological theory is the *behavioral/environmental theory,* which suggests that criminals are made, not born.

The Influence of the Environment

Many environmental factors have been identified as contributing to criminality, including poverty, unemployment, the disintegrating family and drug and alcohol abuse.

Poverty is a pervasive, persistent, devastating threat to many of our nation's families, particularly to youths. Poverty encompasses a host of problems, including overcrowded and unhealthy living conditions in unsafe, crime-ridden neighborhoods; inadequate schools; limited access to health care; and single and/or teen parenthood. Poverty was identified by the Census Bureau as one of six parameters that indicate a risk to children's welfare, the other parameters being absent parents, single-parent families, unwed mothers, parents who have not completed high school and welfare dependence.

Unemployment is intimately linked to poverty. Numerous studies suggest that a booming economy leads to decreased levels of unemployment, alleviating poverty and translating into a drop in crime:

> Starting in the mid-1990s, the United States has been experiencing a great economic boom. . . . Unemployment fell to levels that just a few years earlier most experts had thought impossible. . . .
>
> Over roughly the same period, the rate of crime reported in the FBI's Uniform Crime Reports (UCR) fell, while crime reported in the National Victimization Survey continued the downward trend begun in the 1970s. . . .
>
> The preponderance of studies, particularly the most recent econometric work, supports the claim that the booming economy helped reduce the crime rate (Freeman, 2001, pp.23–24).

The *family* is another strong environmental influence on criminal activity. As mentioned, the Census Bureau has identified unwed mothers and single-parent families as two risks to children's welfare. Sadly, many families serve as the training ground for violent behavior, perpetuating what has been termed the "cycle of violence." Studies show: "Being abused or neglected as a child increased the likelihood of arrest as a juvenile by 59 percent, as an adult by 28 percent, and for a violent crime by 30 percent" (Widom and Maxfield, 2001, p.1). In many violent homes, drug and alcohol abuse is a continual presence.

Drug and alcohol abuse, although arguably linked to an organic (biological) chemical disorder or imbalance, is considered a significant environmental factor in crime causation. The role drugs and alcohol play in crime can be viewed two ways: (1) drug and alcohol use physically alters individuals, lowering inhibitions and increasing confidence, which can then lead them to commit criminal acts (domestic abuse, rape, assault, drunk driving, etc.) or (2) a dependence on drugs and/or alcohol may lead a person to commit crime to support the addiction (robbery, burglary, etc.). The relationship between drugs and crime is summarized by Menard et al. (2001, pp.269–270):

> Crime typically is initiated before substance use . . . [however,] once crime and substance use are initiated, each appears to increase the likelihood of continuity of the other. . . . The most plausible conclusion is that drugs and crime are related by mutual causation: crime affects drug use and drug use affects crime.

Significant evidence links use of narcotics with criminality. Wilson (2000, p.1) reports: "An estimated 61,000 (16%) convicted jail inmates committed their offenses to get money for drugs. Two-thirds of convicted jail inmates were actively involved with drugs prior to their admission to jail." Furthermore: "About 138,000 (35.6%) convicted jail inmates were under the influence of drugs at the time of the offense." Other data indicate more than half of all inmates in state and federal prisons reported committing their current offenses under the influence of drugs or alcohol. According to Mumola (1999, p.2):

> A third of State and a fifth of Federal prisoners reported the influence of alcohol at the time of the offense. . . . For both State and Federal prisoners, the specific offenses most closely related to alcohol use at the time of the offense were violent ones—assault, murder, manslaughter, and sexual assault.

The Combination of Biology and Environment

Comparisons of groups of criminals with groups of noncriminals have failed to produce any single characteristic that absolutely distinguishes the two groups. However, a growing body of evidence suggests that the forces operating to stimulate criminal behavior may be a complex interaction between predisposing biological/genetic factors and certain environmental agents that trigger criminal tendencies.

It is likely that criminal behavior is the result of both heredity and life experiences.

Put simply, biological abnormalities in some people heighten their sensitivity to adverse environmental circumstances, making them more prone to antisocial behavior. This relationship between genes and the environment is often viewed as synergistic; the genes alone won't cause the behavior, nor will the environment alone. When they function together in a specific combination, however, the individual will display criminal responses.

Because the concepts of crime, delinquency and deviancy apply to such a wide range of behaviors, having in common only the fact that they have been declared illegal, no single causal explanation is possible. The complex interplay of factors leading to the commission of a crime are illustrated in Figures 3.4 and 3.5.

Career Criminals or Recidivists

Of major concern is the **chronic** or **career criminal**—a small group of offenders arrested five or more times as juveniles. Although most offenders "age out," chronic offenders continue a life of crime. Traditional programs aimed at rehabilitation have little effect on such criminals. Such an offender is also considered a *repeat offender* or **recidivist.**

Some refer to our criminal justice system as a revolving door, with criminals getting out of prison faster than the authorities can convict and incarcerate others. Often those who were released are involved in more crime and are right back in prison. The Violent Crime Control and Law Enforcement Act of 1994

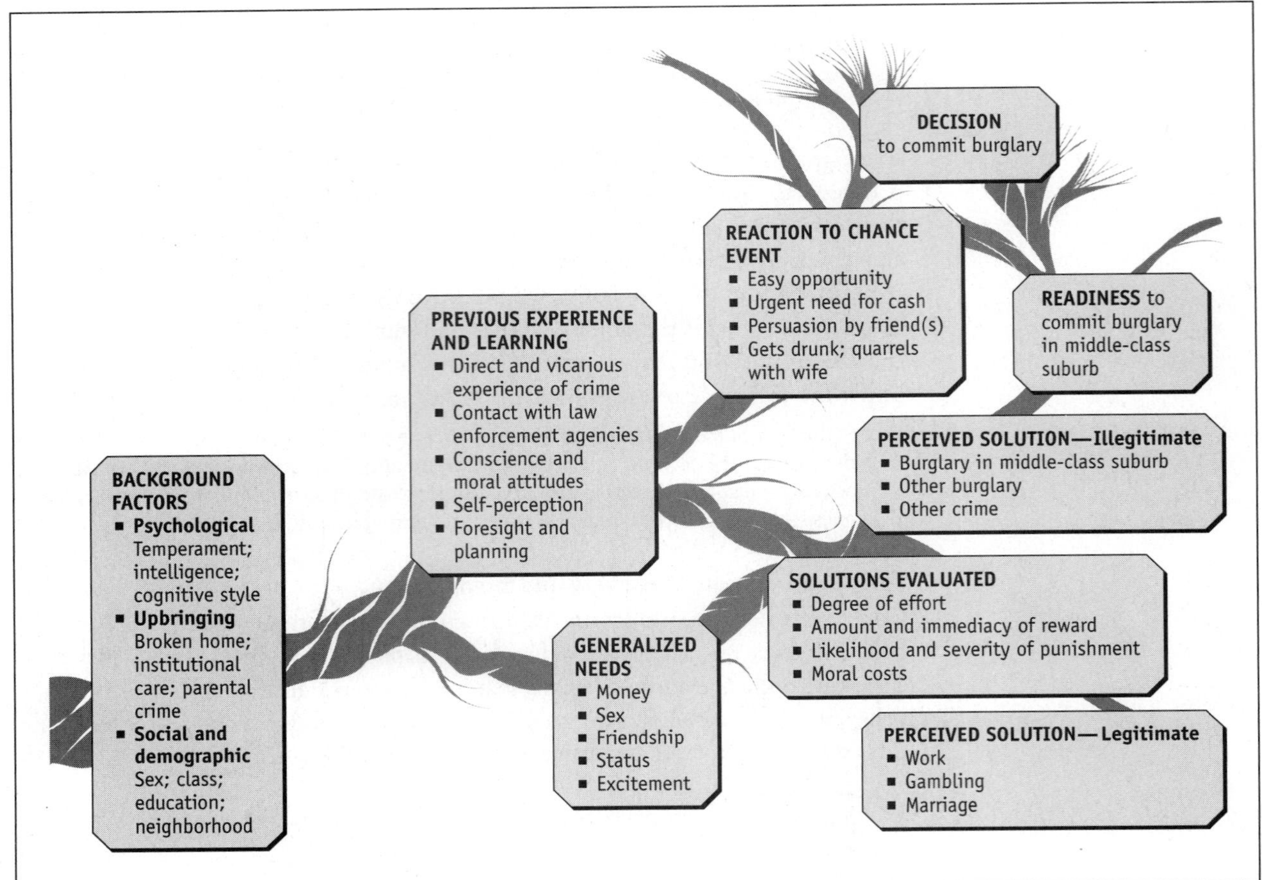

Figure 3.4
Criminal Involvement: The Decision to Get Involved in Crime

Source: Joel Samaha. *Criminal Justice*, 3rd ed. St. Paul, MN: West Publishing Company, 1994, pp.58–59. Reprinted by permission. All rights reserved.

reflects the desire to deal with recidivism and the perpetual revolving door, calling for "mandatory life imprisonment without possibility of parole for federal offenders with three or more convictions for serious violent felonies or drug-trafficking crimes." Some states, such as California, have enacted similar "three strikes and you're out" legislation.

In addition to targeting career criminals, the criminal justice system must focus attention on youths, especially juvenile delinquents, because delinquency is often the beginning for the career criminal.

Juvenile Offenders

State specifications as to the age of a juvenile vary, but most state statutes define a juvenile as an individual under the age of 16 or 18. Juvenile delinquency, therefore, is considered behavior by a person not of legal age that violates a local, state or federal law. Drowns and Hess (2000, p.516) define **delinquency** as "actions or conduct by a juvenile in violation of criminal law or constituting a status offense; an error or failure by a child or adolescent to conform to society's expectations of social order, where the child either resides or visits." A **delinquent** is "a child adjudicated to have violated a federal, state or local law; a minor who has done an illegal act or who has

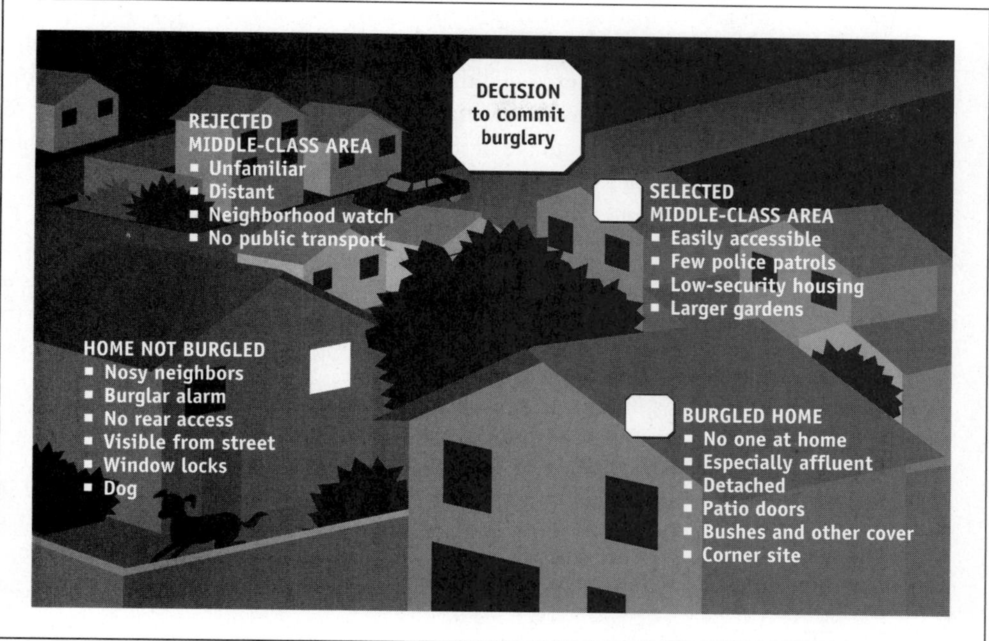

Figure 3.5
The Criminal Event: The Decision to Commit a Specific Burglary

Source: Joel Samaha. *Criminal Justice*, 3rd ed. St. Paul, MN: West Publishing Company, 1994, pp.58–59. Reprinted by permission.

been proven in court to have misbehaved seriously. A child may be found delinquent for a variety of behaviors not criminal for adults (status offenses)."

According to ten Bensel (n.d., p.41), national expert on child abuse and neglect, studies have shown that virtually "all violent juvenile delinquents have been abused children," that "all criminals at San Quentin prison . . . studied had violent upbringings as children" and that "all assassins . . . in the United States during the past 20 years had been victims of child abuse."

Juvenile delinquency presents a serious challenge with an enormous number of youths involved. Self-report studies indicate approximately 90 percent of all young people have committed at least one act for which they could be brought to juvenile court. However many of these offenses are minor (for example fighting and truancy), and state statutes often define juvenile delinquency so broadly that virtually all youngsters could be classified as delinquent.

The Children's Bureau estimates that one in every nine youths and one in every six male youths will be referred to juvenile court for a delinquent act (excluding traffic offenses) before his or her eighteenth birthday. Arrest statistics point out the severity of the problem: "In 1999, law enforcement agencies in the United States made an estimated 2.5 million arrests of persons under age 18" (Snyder, 2000, p.1). Although the number of juvenile arrests for murder declined between 1993 and 1999, and the juvenile arrest rates for burglary have declined substantially since 1980, juvenile arrests for curfew and loitering violations increased 113 percent between 1990 and 1999, while juvenile arrests for drug abuse violations increased 132 percent during the same time period (Snyder, p.1). Caution must be used when interpreting arrest statistics, however: "The juvenile proportion of arrests exceeded the juvenile proportion of crimes cleared by arrest in each offense category, reflecting the fact that juveniles are more likely to commit crimes in groups and are more likely to be arrested than are adults" (Snyder, p.2).

Status Offenders

A special category of offenses has been established for juveniles, designating certain actions as illegal for any person under the state's defined juvenile age of 16 or 18. These are **status offenses,** violations of the law applying to only those under legal age. They include absenting from home, truancy, drinking alcoholic beverages, smoking, violating curfew and incorrigibility.

Serious and Violent Offenders

The Office of Juvenile Justice and Delinquency Prevention (OJJDP) notes (*Serious and Violent Juvenile Offenders,* 1998, p.1): "Serious and violent juvenile (SVJ) offenders comprise a troubled and often dangerous population." They are responsible for a substantial and disproportionate part of the national crime problem.

Victims of Crime

Everyone expects law enforcement officers to know how to deal with criminals. Of equal importance, however, is officers' ability to deal with crime victims. This not only enhances the image of police officers as professionals but enhances communications that likely will result in officers' ability to obtain more crime-related information. Crime victims are often said to be the overlooked element of the criminal process: "Victims have been an invisible and forgotten part of the criminal justice system for too long. Today, they are emerging from the wilderness and claiming their rightful place" (Evans, 1998, p.68).

Kinds of Victims

Direct or **primary victims** of crime are those initially harmed by injury, death or loss of property as a result of crimes committed. When a violent crime occurs, the impact often goes further than the victim. Often the entire community suffers. **Indirect** or **secondary victims** of crime are all other community members who may be threatened or fearful as a result of the commission of crime. This can include family, relatives, friends, neighborhoods, the entire community and even police officers who must deal with the aftermath of violent crimes, such as battered children and grisly deaths.

If a small-town youth murders his entire family or opens fire in the neighborhood school, the community may go into shock. Everyone feels vulnerable. Fear sets in. Morale drops. Trust plummets. In addition convicted criminals sentenced to prison are financially supported by society while incarcerated. In short everyone pays the price as a victim of crime.

Victimization Facts—Who's at Risk?

In 2000 U.S. residents age 12 or older experienced nearly 26 million criminal victimizations. Of these 19.3 million were property crimes; 6.3 million were crimes of violence (rape, robbery and assault), and 0.3 million were personal thefts (Rennison, 2001, p.1).

Distinct demographic characteristics, called **risk factors,** influence the chance of being victimized. The degree of risk people face is affected by individual factors as well as household factors related to how and where they live.

Individual Risk Factors

Data from the NCVS indicate certain individuals are at greater risk than others: "Those most vulnerable to violent victimization in the past—males, teens, and blacks, for example—continued to be the most vulnerable in 2000" (Rennison, pp.6–7):

- *Gender:* Men are more likely than women to be victims of crime. In 2000, men experienced violent crime at a rate 42% greater than females, were robbed at rates 125% greater and were victims of aggravated assault at rates 159% greater than females. An exception is seen for rape and sexual assault, where females were victimized at rates significantly greater than males.
- *Age:* In general, the younger the person, the higher the rate of violent victimization, regardless of the type of violence considered. People ages 12 to 19 experienced overall violence at a higher rate than people in older categories.
- *Race:* Blacks are more likely to be victims of violent crime—especially aggravated assaults and robberies—than whites or people of "other races."
- *Marital Status:* The divorced or separated and the never married are more likely than the married or the widowed to be victims of crime. In 2000, people who had never married experienced violence at a rate about six times that of widowed people and four times that of married people.

Household Risk Factors

Certain types of households are more likely to experience criminal victimization than others. Included in the high-risk category are renters, households headed by younger people, households with annual incomes less than $7,500 and households in urban areas (Rennison, p.7):

- *Household Income:* In general, as income goes up, the risk of personal victimization goes down. In 2000, people in households with annual incomes of less than $7,500 experienced violence at rates significantly higher than those in every other income bracket.
- *Residence:* Those who live in urban areas suffer more victimizations than residents of suburban or rural areas. In 2000, urban residents experienced overall violence, robbery, aggravated assault, simple assault, rape and sexual assault at rates higher than suburban and rural residents. Suburban residents were robbed at a higher rate than rural residents, but rural residents had a slightly higher rate of rape and sexual assault than suburban residents.

Violent crime hits children, minorities and the poor hardest. Males are more often victimized than females. As income rises and as age increases, the victimization rate drops.

Beyond statistics several other factors enter into understanding victimization, including the relationship between the victim and offender, the use of weapons and how victims protect themselves—or attempt to do so.

Other Factors in Victimization

The Victim/Offender Relationship

When people worry about crime, they are most often worried about being attacked by strangers. This fear is often justified. With the exception of murder and rape, most violent crimes are committed by strangers. Males, African-Americans and young people face the greatest risk of violent crime by strangers and are victimized by violent strangers at an annual rate almost triple that of women. African-Americans are more than twice as likely as whites to be robbed by strangers.

The risk of robbery is less for older people, but this may be because many older people are no longer physically able to move about outside their homes, and many others may fear crime and, consequently, remain at home most of the time. Older people who are active and mobile may be at as much risk as the general population.

Women are more vulnerable than men to assaults by acquaintances and relatives, with two-thirds of all assaults on divorced and separated women committed by acquaintances and relatives. Spouses or former spouses committed only 5 percent of the assaults by single offenders. In almost three-fourths of spouse-versus-spouse assaults, the victim was divorced or separated at the time of the incident.

More than half of all homicides are committed by someone known to the victim. Further, victims and offenders are usually of the same race.

How Victims Protect Themselves

Victims of violent crime can protect themselves by returning physical force, by verbal response, by attracting attention, by nonviolent evasion or by brandishing a weapon. Rape victims are more likely to use force, try a verbal response or attract attention and are less likely than others to do nothing to protect themselves. In contrast robbery victims are least likely to try to talk themselves out of being victimized and most likely to do nothing.

Effects of Victimization

Victims of violent crimes often suffer from the effects of the victimization for the rest of their lives. Shootings, knifings, acid throwings or beatings are traumatic, with long-lasting physical, emotional and psychological damage to victims and their families. Victims may also suffer financially through the loss or destruction of property (including irreplaceable property with only sentimental value), time lost from work, medical costs and the introduction of security measures to prevent future victimization. The greatest effect of victimization, however, is often psychological.

Victims may suffer physical, economic and psychological harm that lasts their entire lives.

Fear of Victimization

Public opinion polls show that, while people do fear crime in general, they usually feel their own neighborhoods are relatively safe. If someone in the neighborhood is victimized, however, the entire neighborhood may feel much more vulnerable.

The people with the highest risk of being victimized, young males, do not express the greatest fear of victimization. Those who express the greatest fear of being victimized are women and the elderly, even though they are at lower risk than other groups. Whether they are at lower risk because they take measures to reduce their chances of being victimized is not known. If the elderly, for example, restrict their activities because they are afraid of becoming crime victims, this fear is, in itself, a sort of victimization.

The "Second Wound": Further Victimization by the Criminal Justice System

While feeling the impact of being victimized, many victims are subjected to a second victimization.

A second victimization may occur as a result of insensitivity on the part of those in the criminal justice system.

Police are trained extensively in dealing with criminals but do not receive much training in communicating with victims. Victims are often the only ones who can identify the offender and the property stolen in the crime. The victim's property may be held for months until introduced as evidence in the trial. The victim is often called to testify in a trial and subjected to severe cross-examination, more than the person charged with the crime, since the defendant is not required to take the witness stand.

The investigative and prosecution process may require a number of trips to the court or county attorney's office, which is not only an expense but requires time off from employment. Victims often complain that once they make their initial contribution to the investigation, they are not kept informed of the progress of the case. They often are not notified when the offender is released from custody or incarceration, preventing them from taking safety precautions.

Victims may also be victimized again by lack of release data and notification and by intimidation.

In one case a woman was brutally murdered by her former boyfriend, who had earlier been arrested and charged with her rape. However, he unexpectedly made bail, and two days after his release, the man ambushed her as she left work and shot her six times in the head at close range. She died instantly. No one had notified her, the police or the prosecutors in the case that the offender was out of jail.

One solution to this problem is the Victim Information and Notification Everyday (VINE) system that is spreading across the country, having already reached at least 300 communities in 26 states. The system is activated by calling a toll-free number and providing a prisoner's name or ID number. The user receives computerized information about where the prisoner is being held, the date of upcoming parole hearings and when the sentence expires. It also provides the phone number and address of the facility holding the prisoner.

Victims and witnesses are often further victimized by overt or covert intimidation, most commonly in gang and drug cases, as well as domestic violence cases. Intimidation may occur in the courtroom in the form of threatening looks or gestures or packing the courtroom with the defendant's friends. Such intimidation seriously hampers the efforts of law enforcement, prosecutors and the entire criminal justice system. One approach to countering such intimidation is to take a class of police cadets into courtrooms where intimidation is suspected.

Assisting Victims—Historical Overview

In 1965 California established the first crime victim compensation program. Since then, most states have established similar programs. In 1975 the first "Victim's Rights Week" was organized by the Philadelphia district attorney. In 1979 Frank G. Carrington, considered by many to be the father of the victims' rights movement, founded the Crime Victims' Legal Advocacy Institute, Inc.

Many support groups for victims of crime exist in each state and many municipalities or counties—rape crisis centers, family shelters, victims of crime groups, domestic violence groups, Mothers Against Drunk Drivers (MADD), the National Organization for Victim Assistance (NOVA) and other groups. Significant legislation has also been passed to assist crime victims.

The Crime Victims' Reparations Act

This act, passed in 1974, gives victims the right to be compensated for the cost of crimes, including medical and funeral costs, loss of income, counseling services and other expenses.

The Victim and Witness Protection Act of 1982

To help victims cope with the labyrinth of police, courts and corrections, the federal government passed the Victim and Witness Protection Act, mandating that the U.S. Attorney General develop procedures to assist victims and witnesses through this legal process. The act provides for victim impact statements (VIS) at sentencing and parole hearings, discussed in detail shortly.

The Crime Victims' Bill of Rights

In 1983 the Crime Victims' Bill of Rights was passed, recognizing for the first time the rights of victims to participate in criminal prosecutions. Until then, prosecutors were not obligated to inform victims about crucial decisions, such as plea bargain arrangements. Victims have acquired even more rights since then, including the opportunity to make a statement at the time of sentencing.

The Victims of Crime Act (VOCA) of 1984

This act established the Crime Victims' Fund, made up of federal criminal fines, penalties and bond forfeitures to support state victim compensation and local victim service programs. The fund provides grants to states for compensation to crime victims, crisis intervention, salaries of crime victim service personnel, child abuse and prevention, and victim assistance programs.

The Victim and Witness Protection Act of 1994

This act provides for compensation and other victim assistance from fines, penalties and forfeited bail bonds paid by convicted federal offenders. Courts often make restitution part of the sentence, depending on the circumstances and merits of each case.

Crime Victims' Rights

Every state has enacted laws that provide basic rights to crime victims, and over half the states have amended their constitutions to further protect the rights of crime victims. While these rights vary across the nation, most victims have the following rights (*Victims' Rights,* 1998):

- *The right to information* about the case as it progresses through the justice system
- *The right to notification* of many different types of justice proceedings
- *The right to participate* in court proceedings related to the offense
- *The right to be reasonably protected* from the accused offender
- *The right to information* about the conviction, sentencing, imprisonment and release of the offender
- *The right to receive restitution* from the offender

Victims may become involved in the criminal justice system during plea bargaining, during the trial and during sentencing.

Victim Participation

The two most common methods of victim participation in the criminal justice process are through the **victim impact statement** (VIS) and the **victim statement of opinion** (VSO). The VIS is an objective account of medical, financial and emotional injuries the victim suffered as a result of the crime. The details are typically provided to a probation officer, who then writes a summary report to include with the defendant's presenting packet. The report then passes to the judge, who may give it as much or as little consideration as he or she desires. The VSO, in contrast, is more subjective, allowing victims to tell the court their opinions as to what sentence a defendant should receive. The opinion may be presented verbally in court by the victim or delivered in a written statement to the judge. Nearly every state allows victim impact statements, and most states allow victim statements of opinion.

Victim Restitution

Four basic types of restitution programs are currently offered to victims:

1. Restitution components of victim assistance programs
2. Victim/offender reconciliation programs
3. Restitution employment programs
4. Restitution as a function of routine probation supervision

Victim Compensation Programs

Almost all states have established programs to assist crime victims and witnesses. Victim compensation programs supplement existing programs that help victims, such as rape crisis centers and prosecutors' victim assistance programs. All states compensate crime victims for medical expenses, mental health counseling and lost wages. In addition survivors of deceased victims may be compensated for funeral expenses and loss of support in all states. Most states have added drunk driving and domestic violence to their list of compensable crimes.

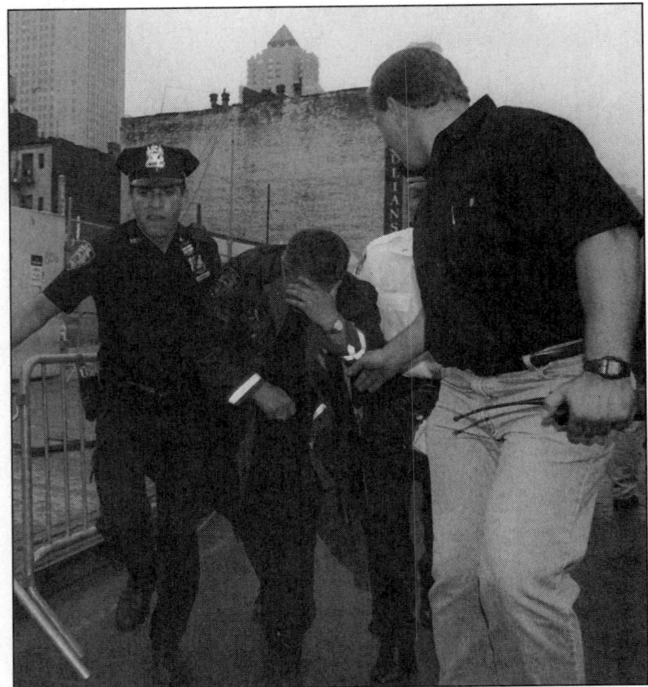

AP/Wide World Photos

An injured New York City police officer is assisted by colleagues during a protest by union members. Police barriers could not contain protestors who clogged Fifth Avenue blowing whistles, waving flags and chanting.

Victim/witness services may also be provided by non–criminal justice agencies, such as local or state departments of health or human services. In addition many private organizations have developed such programs as rape crisis centers. If a victim dies, payments may cover burial and related expenses, payable to dependent survivors. Often people injured while trying to prevent a crime or apprehend an offender (Good Samaritans) are also eligible for payment.

The Role of the Police

The first and all-important contact between the police and a victim is made during the preliminary investigation. Police officers must be realistic with victims. If a police agency has an "early case closure system," victims should be told that nothing further can be done unless additional information comes to light. Victims should be given the case number and a phone number to call if they should obtain more information about the crime.

Victims should be told of any assistance available to them, and if applicable, reminded to call their insurance companies. If victims need legal advice, police officers should advise them about the legal aid office. If a case continues under investigation or will go to court, police officers should maintain contact with victims (and witnesses). If property is recovered, it should be returned to victims as soon as possible. If a case goes to court, victims should be briefed as to their roles and should be kept updated.

Truthfulness and embellishment are problems for the police and prosecution, and, indeed, some complaints are false, motivated by revenge, jealousy, monetary gain or other reasons. The victim's reluctance to follow through with prosecution is also a problem for police and prosecuting attorneys, especially in cases where the victim knows the offender. The victim may wish to cooperate but may be a poor witness due to personal physical appearance, mental or emotional instability, fear of reprisal, passage of time or reluctance to testify in court. Robinson (2000, p.6) concludes:

> The rights of crime victims must be high on our list of law enforcement priorities. Unless we teach our police officers and first responders the skills of compassion and show that sensitivity and sympathy are important tools in their arsenal for peace and safety, victims will continue to be victims.

Police Officers as Victims

Police officers are not immune from being victimized. Officers are assaulted, robbed, burglarized and victimized in all the ways civilians are, including being killed. In 2000, 151 federal, state and local law enforcement officers were killed in the line of duty: "51 were shot to death, 47 died in automobile accidents, 20 were struck by automobiles while outside of their own vehicles, eight died in motorcycle accidents, seven were killed in aircraft accidents, and the remainder died of a variety of other causes" ("151 Law Enforcement Officers . . .," 2001, p.7). Brown and Langan (2001, p.iv) add: "Since 1976, an average of 79 police officers have been murdered each year in the line of duty. . . . The majority of police officers murdered by felons were killed while responding to disturbance calls (16%) or arrest situations (39%)."

The most common way police officers become victims, however, is as secondary victims, dealing with the pain of victims and with the distress of seeing the "bad guys" get off easy or out of prison early.

Summary

When people are victimized, they often do not report it to police. In fact one-half to two-thirds of all crimes are not reported to police. The most frequently used sources of information about crime are the media, official government statistics and self-reporting surveys. The crimes most frequently reported to police, the most serious crimes in the nation, are called Part I or Index Crimes. The eight Part I crimes are murder, aggravated assault causing serious bodily harm, forcible rape, robbery, burglary, larceny/theft, motor vehicle theft and arson. Other serious crimes include white-collar crime, computer-related crime, organized crime, bias or hate crime and ritualistic crime.

White-collar crime—occupational or business-related crime—includes fraud involving credit cards, checks, identity theft, securities, insurance, illegal competition and deceptive practices, as well as bankruptcy fraud, embezzlement and pilferage, bribes, kickbacks, payoffs and receiving stolen property. White-collar crime involves billions of dollars annually.

Of growing concern is white-collar, computer-related crime. Computer crimes are relatively easy to commit and difficult to detect. Most are committed by insiders, and most are not prosecuted. A white-collar crime distinct from other types of crimes is organized crime, which is characterized by corruption and enforcement powers. Hate crimes may be motivated by bias against a person's race, religion, ethnic group or sexual orientation. A ritualistic crime is an unlawful act committed during a ceremony related to a belief system. It is the crime, *not* the belief system, that must be investigated.

Crimes are committed by youths and adults. Why? Two fundamental philosophies exist. The classical theory sees people as free agents with free will. People commit crimes because they want to. The positivist theory, in contrast, sees criminals as "victims of society" and of their own biological, sociological, cultural and physical environments. It is likely that criminal behavior is the result of both heredity and life experiences. No definitive answer exists as to why people commit crimes. Of the theories set forth, several suggest a combination of sociological, psychological and biological factors.

A few criminals commit many crimes. Repeat offenders, juvenile and adult, are responsible for much of our crime. Juvenile delinquency is behavior by a person not of legal age that violates a local, state or federal law. Serious and violent juvenile offenders are responsible for a substantial and disproportionate part of the national crime problem.

Violent crime hits children, minorities and the poor hardest. Males are more often victimized than females. As income rises and as age increases, the victimization rate drops. Victims may suffer physical, economic and psychological harm that lasts for the rest of their lives. A second victimization may occur as a result of insensitivity on the part of those in the criminal justice system. Victims may also be victimized again by lack of release data and notification and by intimidation. Victims may become involved in the criminal justice system during plea bargaining, during the trial and during sentencing.

Discussion Questions

1. Why are some crimes divided into categories or degrees?
2. Would a law that made the reporting of all crimes to the police mandatory be a good deterrent to future criminal activity?
3. Should computer hackers pay a heavy penalty for their misdeeds?
4. Should additional penalties be imposed on people found guilty of committing bias crimes?
5. How long does one remain a criminal—until the crime has been "paid for" or for a lifetime?
6. Have you ever known an adult convicted of a crime? A juvenile? If so what was he or she like?
7. Does your state have victim compensation laws? If so how do they compare with those provided in other states?
8. Have you ever been victimized? Has a member of your family? A friend or neighbor? What were the effects?
9. Do you feel that in most cases the police in your area are sensitive to crime victims' needs?
10. Discuss the current differences between the rights of the criminal and the rights of the victim. Should there be changes in these rights?

InfoTrac *College Edition Assignment*

Use InfoTrac College Edition to help answer the Discussion Questions as appropriate.

- Use InfoTrac College Edition to find *hate groups,* and particularly note Robert Stacy McCain's brief article on hate groups. Compare his opinions with those of at least two others. Be prepared to share your perspective with the class.

Internet Assignments

- Using the key words *crime news,* bring up the category of crime news 2000. After reading about the various crimes, do you feel heinous crimes are on the increase?
- Select one topic covered in this chapter and research it using any of the Web sites listed in the resources on the book-specific Web site.

Book-Specific Web Site

The book-specific Web site at http://info.wadsworth.com/0534552803 hosts a variety of resources for students and instructors. Included are extended activities from each chapter in which students write a policy, use critical thinking skills to make choices in response to a given scenario, use InfoTrac College Edition with direct links to articles for participation in topical discussion forums, and analyze court cases using Web links for research. Many activities can be printed or emailed to instructors. Plus, cited cases with Web links, interactive key term FlashCards, PowerPoint presentations, chapter objectives, and an extensive collection of chapter-based Web links provide additional information and activities to include in the curriculum.

References

Albanese, Jay S. "The Causes of Organized Crime." *Journal of Contemporary Criminal Justice,* November 2000, pp.409–423.

Barry, Patricia. "Sept. 11 Terrorism Puts Spotlight on Identity Theft." *AARP Bulletin,* December 2001, p.25.

Bellah, John L. "Identity Theft: Ruining Credit and Creating Criminal Records." *Law and Order,* October 2001, pp.222–226.

Brown, Jodi M. and Langan, Patrick A. *Policing and Homicide, 1976–98: Justifiable Homicide by Police, Police Officers Murdered by Felons.* Bureau of Justice Statistics, March 2001. (NCJ 180987)

"College Campuses Are Easy Targets for Acts of Hate." *NCJA Justice Bulletin,* June 2000, pp.11–12.

Cornell, Susan E. "Cybercrime Summit." *Law and Order,* June 2001, pp.55–60.

Correia, Mark E. and Bowling, Craig. "Veering Toward Digital Disorder: Computer-Related Crime and Law Enforcement Preparedness." *Police Quarterly,* June 1999, pp.225–244.

Crime in the United States, 1999 Uniform Crime Reports. Washington, DC: Federal Bureau of Investigation, 2000.

"Crime Rate Declines According to BJS Survey; FBI's Crime Index Is Steady." *NCJA Justice Bulletin,* June 2001, pp.1, 5–6.

Das, Dilip. "Organized Crime: A World Perspective." *ACJS Today,* January/February 1999, pp.1, 3–7.

Dees, Tim. "Cyber Crime." *Law and Order,* May 2001, pp.27–28.

Drowns, Robert W. and Hess, Kären M. *Juvenile Justice,* 3rd ed. Belmont, CA: West/Wadsworth Publishing Company, 2000.

Dunbar, Edward. "Defensing the Indefensible: A Critique and Analysis of Psycholegal Defense Arguments of Hate Crime Perpetrators." *Journal of Contemporary Criminal Justice,* February 1999, pp.64–77.

Evans, Donald G. "Training Enhances Victim Services." *Corrections Today,* February 1998, p.68.

"FBI: Racism Is the Hate That's Driving Most Bias-Related Crime." *Law Enforcement News,* February 14, 2001, p.7.

"FBI's Crime Figures Dropping, but Improvement Is Slacking." *Criminal Justice Newsletter,* January 10, 2001, p.5.

Finckenauer, James O. and Voronin, Yuri A. *The Threat of Russian Organized Crime.* National Institute of Justice, June 2001. (NCJ 187085)

Fishbein, Diana. "Building Bridges." *ACJS Today,* September/October 1998, pp.1, 3–5.

Freeman, Richard B. "Does the Booming Economy Help Explain the Fall in Crime?" In *Perspectives on Crime and Justice: 1999–2000 Lecture Series,* National Institute of Justice, March 2001. (NCJ 184245)

Gest, Ted. *Crime and Politics: Big Government's Erratic Campaign for Law and Order.* Oxford University Press, 2001.

Goodman, Marc. "Making Computer Crime Count." *FBI Law Enforcement Bulletin,* August 2001, pp.10–17.

Hall, Dennis. "Make No Mistake: The Next 'War' Has Already Arrived." *Police,* July 2000, p.6.

"Hate Crime Statistics Are 'in Shambles,' Rights Group Says." *Criminal Justice Newsletter,* November 29, 2001, pp.5–6.

Hoffmann, John. "National Incident Based Reporting System: Still Far from 'National.'" *Law and Order,* January 2000, pp.31–34.

Hohler, B. "Klan Rally Bares Hatred, but Jasper Thwarts Violence." *The Boston Globe,* June 28, 1998, pp.A1, A16.

"House Passes Measure to Bar Child Abuse through the Internet." *Criminal Justice Newsletter,* May 15, 1998, p.5.

"Identity Theft Heads the FTC's Top Ten Consumer Fraud Complaints in 2001." *NCJA Justice Bulletin,* January 2002, pp.15–16.

"Information, Please: News Media and Police Squabble over Records Access." *Law Enforcement News,* February 14, 2001, pp.1, 6.

Johnston, Richard L. "The National Cybercrime Training Partnership: Helping Your Agency Keep Pace with Electronic Crime." *The Police Chief,* January 2002, pp.52–54.

Lawrence, Richard. "School Violence, the Media, and the ACJS." *ACJS Today,* May/June 2000, pp.1, 4–6.

Levin, Brian. "Hate Crimes." *Journal of Contemporary Criminal Justice,* February 1999, pp.6–21.

Lombroso, Cesare. *Crime: Its Causes and Remedies.* Montclair, NJ: Patterson Smith, 1968. Originally published in 1911.

Lormel, Dennis M. and Johnston, Richard L. "Internet Crime: Is Your Agency Ready to Respond?" *The Police Chief,* May 2001, pp.66–70.

Menard, Scott; Mihalic, Sharon; and Huizinga, David. "Drugs and Crime Revisited." *Justice Quarterly,* June 2001, pp.269–299.

Mumola, Christopher J. *Substance Abuse and Treatment, State and Federal Prisoners, 1997.* Bureau of Justice Statistics Special Report, January 1999. (NCJ 172871)

Neeley, DeQuendre. "New Name and Mission." *ASIS Dynamics,* March/April 2000, p.2.

"The New and Improved UCR—Is Anyone Paying Attention?" *Law Enforcement News,* September 15, 2000, pp.1, 8.

"151 Law Enforcement Officers Killed in Line of Duty in 2000." *Criminal Justice Newsletter,* January 10, 2001, p.7.

O'Neal, Scott. "Russian Organized Crime: A Criminal Hydra." *FBI Law Enforcement Bulletin,* May 2000, pp.1–5.

Paynter, Ronnie L. "Healing the Hate." *Law Enforcement Technology,* April 2000, pp.52–61.

Petrosino, Carolyn. "Connecting the Past to the Future: Hate Crime in America." *Journal of Contemporary Criminal Justice,* February 1999, pp.22–47.

Rataj, Tom. "Cybercrime Causes Chaos." *Law and Order,* June 2001, pp.43–46.

Rennison, Callie Marie. *Criminal Victimization 2000: Changes 1999–2000 with Trends 1993– 2000.* Bureau of Justice Statistics National Crime Victimization Survey, June 2001. (NCJ 187007)

Robinson, Michael D. "Seeking Justice for Victims of Crime." *The Police Chief,* September 2000, p.6.

Rusnell, Charles. "Cybercops." *Law and Order,* June 2001, pp.52–53.

Serious and Violent Juvenile Offenders. Washington, DC: Office of Juvenile Justice and Delinquency Prevention, May 1998. (NCJ 170027)

Snyder, Howard N. *Juvenile Arrests 1999.* OJJDP Juvenile Justice Bulletin, December 2000. (NCJ 185236)

"Study Finds Incarceration May Increase Crime." *NCJA Justice Bulletin,* September 1999, pp.11–12.

Szubin, Adam; Jensen, Carl J., III; and Gregg, Rod. "Interacting with 'Cults': A Policing Model." *FBI Law Enforcement Bulletin,* September 2000, pp.16–24.

ten Bensel, R. Testimony. Quoted in *Child at Risk,* 41. Office of Juvenile Justice and Delinquency Prevention. U.S. Department of Justice. Washington, DC: U.S. Government Printing Office (no date).

Victims' Rights: Right for America. Office of Victims of Crime, 1998.

Vogel, Brenda L. "Perceptions of Hate: The Extent to which a Motive of 'Hate' Influences Attitudes of Violent Crimes." *Journal of Crime and Justice,* Vol. 23, No. 2, 2000, pp.1–25.

Widom, Cathy S. and Maxfield, Michael G. *An Update on the "Cycle of Violence."* National Institute of Justice Research in Brief, February 2001. (NCJ 184894)

Wilson, Doris James. *Drug Use, Testing, and Treatment in Jails.* Bureau of Justice Special Report, May 2000. (NCJ 179999)

Zalisko, Walter. "Russian Organized Crime: The Foundation for Trafficking." *Police,* May 2000, pp.18–22.

Chapter 4

Contemporary Policing: An Overview

As a law enforcement officer, my fundamental duty is to serve the community; to safeguard lives and property; to protect the innocent against deception, the weak against oppression or intimidation and the peaceful against violence or disorder; and to respect the constitutional rights of all to liberty, equality and justice.

—Law Enforcement Code of Ethics

Do You Know?

- Why we have police?
- How police agencies relate to the people?
- What five traditional goals most law enforcement agencies set?
- What two concerns must be balanced by law enforcement?
- What two department organizational categories are?
- What functions are handled in administration?
- How officers receive their information?
- What the NCIC is?
- What types of records are typically used in law enforcement?
- Why centralization of records is encouraged?
- What is required by a data privacy act?
- What functions are handled in field service?
- What basic styles of policing have been identified?
- How the police image arises?

Can You Define?

administrative services
community policing
discretion
field services
image
police authority
roll call
styles
subculture
typologies

INTRODUCTION

A police funeral symbolizes six themes that illuminate the meanings of police in our contemporary society:

> First, the police, to many audiences, represent the presence of the civil body politic in everyday life—they symbolize the capacity of the state to intervene and the concern of the state for the affairs of its citizenry. To many they symbolize as well the continuity and integrity of the society by their visibility and attachment to traditional values of patriotism, honor, duty, and commitment. . . .
>
> Second, the mobilization in uniform of a large body of officers transmits messages about their mutual identification with the corporate body of police—it speaks to the reality of the occupation as formal social control. . . .
>
> Third, the police role conveys a sense of *sacredness* or awesome power that lies at the root of political order, and authority, the claims a state makes upon its people for deference to rules, laws, and norms. . . .
>
> Fourth, the police, and by inversion the death of a police officer, represent also the means by which the political authorities maintain the status quo. They act in the interests of the powerful and the authoritative against those without power and without access to the means to power. . . .
>
> Fifth, the police represent the capacity to deter citizens from committing acts that threaten the order they are believed to symbolize. The police are expected to deter crime, to deter immorality, to deter evil thoughts, or conspiracies to commit crimes. The loss of a police life can be seen as an indication of the vulnerability of the society, of the weakness of the sacred moral binding of the society, and of the reduced capacity to deter such acts. . . .
>
> Finally, this drama with its associate public media coverage indicates and reaffirms the centrality of formal social control in everyday life, and it provides a legitimate occasion for the dramatization of the palpable police presence (Manning, 1997, pp.20–23).

This chapter begins with a look at why we have police and what police do. Next is a discussion of how policing relates to the people, followed by the basic goals of policing and the organization of law enforcement agencies. Then the police culture is examined, as are the styles of police work. The chapter concludes with a discussion of the police image.

Why We Have Police

Why does a modern society such as ours need police? Think about that. Why might you call the police? What if a neighbor's barking dog kept you awake night after night and the owner ignored your complaints? You might sue him, but that would involve time and expense. You might consider shooting the dog, but that could get you sued. Society offers you another option: call the police. Police sociologist Egon Bittner (1974, p.30) says we have this option because situations occur in which "something-ought-not-to-be-happening-and-about-which-something-ought-to-be-done-NOW!"

In our society it is the police who have the authority to do something and to do it now. That something may involve the use of coercive force. In fact Bittner (1980) suggests that this capacity to use force is the core of the police role:

> In sum, the role of the police is to address all sorts of human problems when and insofar as their solutions do or may possibly require the use of force at the point of their occurrence. This lends homogeneity to such diverse procedures as catching a

AP/Wide World Photos

Police officers line the road from the Salem Baptist Church in McDonnough, Georgia, as other officers march alongside the funeral procession carrying the remains of Forest Park Police Officer Richard Cash. Representatives from over 100 law enforcement agencies from around the state attended the funeral service. Cash was shot during a traffic stop in Forest Park.

criminal, driving the mayor to the airport, evicting a drunk person from a bar, directing traffic, crowd control, taking care of lost children, administering medical first aid, and separating fighting relatives.

It is the police who can demand conformity to society's laws and expectations.

Police are necessary when coercion is required to enforce the laws.

The widespread stereotyped image of the police, however, commonly overemphasizes their role as "crime fighters," often to the exclusion of all others.

What Do Police Do?

What is it that makes the general public think of the law enforcement aspect of police work more often than the social service aspect, when approximately 90 percent of a police officer's time is spent in the social service function?

> The cover of a major city's annual police report dramatically shows two police officers reaching for their guns as they burst through the doors of a massive black and white police car which is screeching to a halt . . . the flashing red lights and screaming siren complete the illustration. A less dramatic scene on an inside page of the report shows a police officer talking to a grateful mother whose lost child was returned. Which one of these illustrations most accurately describes the police role? . . . The *New York Times* reports that policemen like to think of themselves as uniformed soldiers in an extremely dangerous war against crime . . . in fact the police are more social workers and administrators than crime fighters (Webster, n.d., p.94).

Most people have ideas about what the police do. According to Manning (p.27):

> "To police" means in the most general sense to control by political means the behavior and morality of the members of a politically organized unity. This sense

> of the word was derived early from the Greek word *polis,* meaning *city,* later roughly translated as *politics.* Policing in this sense means controlling, monitoring (in terms of correcting misguided behavior), tracking and altering, if required, public conduct.
>
> Policing also refers . . . to the tasks that people expect the police individually and in the aggregate to perform for them.

So are the police primarily crime fighters or preservers of the peace? The answer varies by department, but in most departments, the police serve all these functions. Where the emphasis is placed is increasingly influenced by the citizens within the jurisdiction. It is from them the police derive their power and to them that they are accountable.

Policing and the People

Police authority comes from the people—their laws and institutions. Although the Tenth Amendment reserves police power for state and local governments, these governments must adhere to the principles of the Constitution and the Bill of Rights as well as to federal and state statutes. Police agencies are not only part of their local community, they are part of state and federal government which, through legislation, provides their formal base of authority. Police are also part of the state and federal criminal justice system which, through the court, determines society's course in deterring lawbreakers and rehabilitating offenders.

Note in Figure 4.1 that the arrows between the citizens, governments and courts go two ways—citizens are not only governed by laws passed by the legislation, interpreted by the courts and enforced by the police; they also play a role in establishing laws by electing the representatives whose actions and decisions ultimately influence policing. To a large extent, the goals and priorities of a police agency are established by what the community wants. For example a community might want more patrols at night, stricter enforcement of traffic regulations during rush hour or reduced enforcement for certain violations such as speeding.

Priorities are often more influenced by the desires of the policed than by any other consideration. Because the success of policing depends heavily on public support, the citizens' wishes must be listened to and considered. Of interest is that one-third of the U.S. population is comprised of "baby boomers," who are generally conservative.

The people largely determine the goals of policing and give law enforcement agencies their authority to meet these goals. Citizen support is vital.

Because law enforcement is a highly visible representative of local government whose officers are on duty 24/7, people often call upon police for services that they are not specifically required to perform. Other agencies might be providing these services, but people do not know of them. For example if a woman seeks help in dealing with a drunken husband (he is not abusing her; he is just drunk), a drug counselor, minister or social worker might be the appropriate person to call. The woman, however, often does not know this. Because the

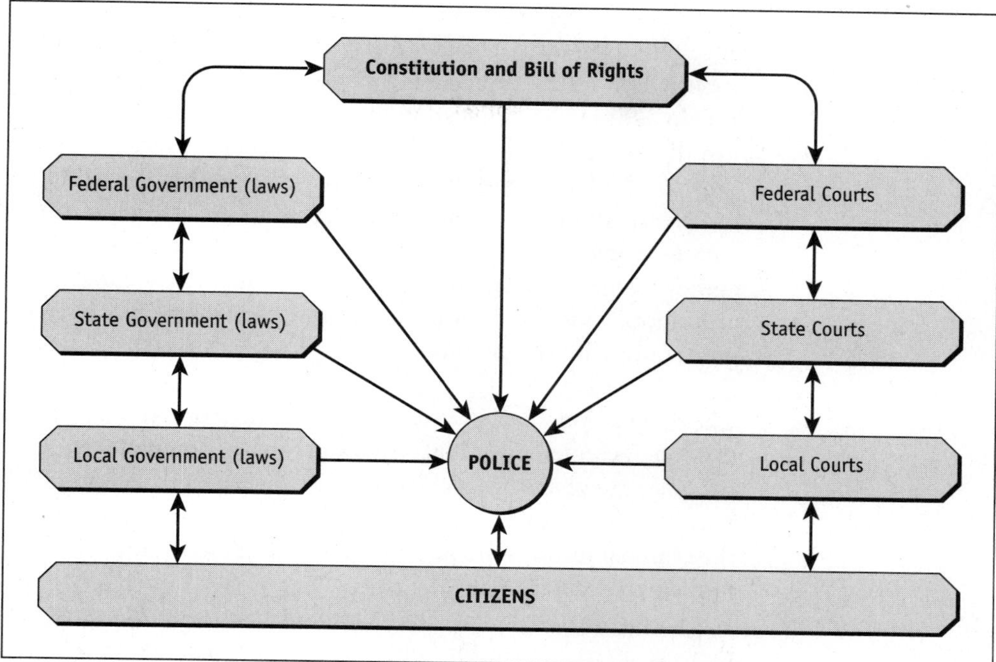

Figure 4.1
Sources of Police Authority

police agency's reactions to requests for help affect the amount of respect they receive and promote a cooperative relationship with the public, they usually respond as helpfully as possible, even when the matter is technically civil and outside their responsibility.

Traditional Goals of Policing

Because citizens have such a great influence on the goals of policing within the community, the goals of different police agencies vary. Traditionally, however, five basic goals have been established.

Historically, the basic goals of most police agencies are to:

1. Enforce laws.
2. Preserve the peace.
3. Prevent crimes.
4. Protect civil rights and civil liberties.
5. Provide services.

These goals often overlap. For example officers intervening in a fight may not only enforce a law by arresting a suspect for assault, they may also maintain order, prevent others from becoming involved in the fight, protect the civil rights and civil liberties of the suspect, the victim and the bystanders and provide emergency service to an injured victim.

Success or failure in meeting each goal directly affects the success or failure of fulfilling the other goals. Although five goals normally established by police are listed, in reality, policing is a single role comprised of numerous responsibilities. In addition any discussion of goals in law enforcement must consider the vast differences between small and large agencies, as well as between rural, suburban and urban departments. Small agencies, often located in rural or suburban areas, tend to have much less specialization, a closer relationship to the citizens being served and less diversity among those citizens and within the agency. Large agencies, often located in urban areas, are likely to have more specialization, a more distant relationship to the citizens being served and much greater diversity among those citizens.

Enforcing Laws

The designation *law enforcement agency* underscores the central importance of this long-accepted goal. Historically, enforcing laws has been a prime goal of policing. However this goal has become increasingly complex. Police not only must decide what laws to enforce, but they also must serve as an integral part of the criminal justice system, responsible for apprehending offenders and assisting in their prosecution.

Unfortunately, because police are in the closest contact with the public, they are often blamed for failures in the criminal justice system. For example an assault victim whose attacker is found innocent in court may feel resentment not only against the court but also against the department. The release of a suspect from custody for lack of sufficient evidence, the failure of a prosecutor to take a case to trial or the failure of the corrections system to reform a convict prior to parole or release all directly affect the public image of policing. The public image of policing is critical considering a large percentage of police work is in direct response to citizen complaints or reports. In fact public support may be the single most important factor in the total law enforcement effort.

Because each community and each state has numerous statutes and limited resources, full enforcement of all laws is never possible. Even if it were, it is questionable whether full enforcement would be in keeping with legislative intent or the people's wishes. **Discretion,** that is judgment, must be exercised as to which laws to enforce. Both the department and the public must accept that not all laws can be enforced at all times.

Each department must decide which reported crimes to actively investigate and to what degree, and which unreported crimes to seek out and to what degree. The law does not set priorities; it simply defines crimes, classifies them as felonies or misdemeanors and assesses penalties for them. The department sets its own priorities based on citizens' needs.

Usually departments concentrate law enforcement activities on serious crimes—those that pose the greatest threat to public safety and/or cause the greatest economic losses. From that point on, priorities are usually determined by past department experience, citizen wishes and expectations and available resources.

Preserving the Peace

Preserving the peace has also long been accepted by police as an important goal. They have the legal authority to arrest individuals for disturbing the peace or for disorderly conduct.

Police are often called to intervene in noncriminal conduct such as that which occurs at public events (crowd control), in social relations (domestic disputes) and in traffic control (parking, pedestrians) to maintain law and order. They often help people solve problems that they cannot cope with alone.

Often such problems, if unresolved, could result in crime. For example loud parties, unruly crowds or disputes between members of a family, business partners, landlord and tenant, or a businessperson and customer might result in bodily harm—assault. Studies indicate that domestic violence often leads to homicide.

A department's effectiveness in actually preserving the peace will largely be determined by public acceptance of this role. Often if police officers simply ask a landlord to allow an evicted tenant access to his or her apartment to retrieve personal possessions or asks the host of a loud party to turn down the stereo, this is enough. Mere police presence may reduce the possibility of a crime—at least temporarily. Here, as in enforcing laws, public support is vital.

Preventing Crime

Crime prevention is closely related to law enforcement and peace preservation. If the peace has been kept, crime has, in effect, been prevented. Crime prevention differs from peacekeeping and law enforcing in that it attempts to eliminate potentially dangerous or criminal situations. It is proactive.

If police are highly visible in a community, crimes may be prevented. For example, a routine patrol might not only discover a crime in progress, but it might also prevent crimes from being committed. This connection is extremely difficult to prove, however, because it is not known what crimes might have been committed if the police were not present.

Crime prevention activities often undertaken by police departments include working with juveniles, cooperating with probation and parole personnel, educating the public, instigating operation identification programs and providing visible evidence of police authority. In addition many community services often provided by police departments aid in crime prevention.

Just as police officers cannot be expected to enforce all the laws at all times, they cannot be expected to prevent all crimes from occurring. Klockars (1991, p.244) suggests: "The 'war on crime' is a war police not only cannot win, but cannot in any real sense fight. They cannot win it because it is simply not within their power to change those things—such as unemployment, the age distribution of the population, moral education, freedom, civil liberties, ambitions, and the social and economic opportunities to realize them—that influence the amount of crime in any society." Regarding these "quality-of-life" issues, recall Klockars stressed (p.250): "[The police] cannot control economic conditions, poverty, inequality; occupational opportunity, moral, religious, family, or secular education; or dramatic social, cultural, or political change. These are the 'big ticket' items in determining the amount and distribution of crime. Compared to them what police do or do not do matters very little."

A study of resident/police relations in poor urban communities revealed: "The degree of trust that residents have in police is considered to be the degree to which community members believe that the police will share their priorities, act competently, behave dependably, and treat them with respect" (Stoutland, 2001, p.227). However (p.241):

> Many community members were not convinced that the police shared all of their priorities. They saw the police as focusing too narrowly on crime reduction for the short term and not enough on overall quality-of-life issues. Furthermore, a few community members were convinced the police shared so few of their priorities that they were unwilling to cooperate with them and in general avoided contact.

This is where the idea of **community policing** comes from—the need for the police and the people in a community to work together as "coproducers of crime prevention" (Klockars, p.251). The citizens know what the community's problems are and how they might be solved. Citizens are on the front lines and know the pain of victimization. Community policing is the focus of Chapter 5.

Protecting Constitutional Rights

Not only are departments charged with enforcing laws, preventing crime and providing services, they are expected to do so as specified by the U.S. Constitution and Bill of Rights.

The first paragraph of the *Law Enforcement Code of Ethics* concludes with the statement that law enforcement officers have a fundamental duty "to respect the constitutional rights of all to liberty, equality and justice." As noted by the National Advisory Commission on Criminal Justice Standards and Goals (1973, p.9) a quarter century ago: "Any definition of the police role must acknowledge that the Constitution imposes restrictions on the power of the legislatures to prohibit protected conduct, and to some extent defines the limits of police authority in the enforcement of established laws."

The commission, however, goes on to state (p.9): "Concern for the constitutional rights of accused persons processed by the police has tended to obscure the fact that the police have an affirmative obligation to protect all persons in the free exercise of their rights. The police must provide safety for persons exercising their constitutional right to assemble, to speak freely, and to petition for redress of their grievances."

Police officers are independent decision makers and have both personal and positional power. One tool officers have is discretion. Right or wrong, officers are often guided by the seriousness of the law violation, who committed it, and the person's age, race and social class.

Many citizens are angered when a suspect's rights prevent prosecuting a case. They begin to doubt the criminal justice system. However, should these same people find themselves suspected of a crime, they would expect their rights to be fully protected. As Sir John Fortescue said: "Indeed, one would rather twenty guilty persons should escape the punishment of death than one innocent person should be executed." The United States must guarantee all citizens, even those perceived as unworthy of such protection, their constitutional rights, or there is danger of a police state.

The authority, goals and methods of the police must promote individual liberty, public safety and social justice. Protecting civil rights and civil liberties is perceived by some as the single most important goal of policing. As a case in point, the National Advisory Commission on Criminal Justice Standards and Goals states (p.9): "If the overall purposes of the police service in today's society were narrowed to a single objective, that objective would be to preserve the peace in a manner consistent with the freedoms secured by the Constitution."

These civil rights and civil liberties also extend to juveniles. Juveniles are subjected to a conglomeration of laws and restraints that do not apply to adults, called status offenses. For example, juveniles are often arrested for liquor law violations, curfew violations, absenting from home, truancy, smoking, incorrigibility and suspicion. Usually the police deal directly with status offenses, warning the youths or returning them to their parents unless the youth has been a habitual offender.

Concern for crime control must be balanced by concern for due process—a large challenge for law enforcement.

Providing Services

In addition to enforcing laws, preserving the peace, preventing crime and protecting civil rights and liberties, the police are often called on to provide additional services to their community. This role is acknowledged in the first sentence of the *Law Enforcement Code of Ethics:* "As a law enforcement officer, my fundamental duty is to serve the community." Many police departments have as their motto: "To Serve and Protect."

As society has become more complex, so have the types of service requested. Many new demands are made including giving information, directions and advice; counseling and referring; licensing and registering vehicles; intervening in domestic arguments; working with neglected children; rendering emergency medical or rescue services; dealing with alcoholics and the mentally ill; finding lost children; dealing with stray animals; and controlling traffic and crowds. In addition many police departments provide community education programs regarding crime, drugs, safety and the like.

Considerable disagreement exists regarding what type and amount of services the police should provide. They are often inappropriately asked to perform functions that might better be performed by another government agency—usually because they are the only government representatives available around the clock and because they have the resources and the authority to use force if necessary. However in many small cities and towns the police services provided (even though considered by some as inappropriate "social services") could not be provided by any other agency.

Many police departments offer referral services to direct people in need to the proper agency. For example in Washington, DC, the department uses a *Referral Handbook of Social Services* that indexes available governmental and private services by problem and agency. Police in Milwaukee, Wisconsin, have a comprehensive directory of almost 500 community agencies and organizations.

Of primary importance is that people who need help receive it; who provides the help is secondary. Because many people are likely to turn first to the police for help, however, the department must be prepared either to provide the help or to refer the person to an agency that can provide it.

Organization of the Department

Gaines and Cordner (1999, p.351) state: "Police departments are organizations, with missions, goals, structures, managers, workers, and clients. The top managers of police agencies are usually the ones held most accountable for the organization's effective performance and respectable public image." According to Gaines and Cordner, top law enforcement administrators have two sets of obligations:

- *Internal obligations*—concerned with running the organization: organizing, staffing, directing and controlling
- *External obligations*—concerned with the organization's "environment": dealing with important outside forces that affect the agency, such as politicians, the community, the media, judges, prosecutors and the like.

They also note that from the 1950s through the 1970s, police administration tended to emphasize internal obligations, whereas during the 1980s and 1990s the focus shifted to law enforcement's external obligations.

The nation's police departments vary greatly, from small, informally organized departments with few employees to highly organized metropolitan police departments with many subdivisions and thousands of employees. The specific organization of a police department is influenced by the department's size, location and the extent and type of crime with which it must deal. For example, small police departments often combine patrol, traffic, community services and investigative tasks in a single division; large police departments usually have separate divisions for each. A community with a major freeway running through its business section faces different problems than a community located on a coast or on a border between the United States and Canada or Mexico. Communities with large groups of minorities face different problems than those that are homogeneous. For some communities traffic control is a major problem; for others gambling, smuggling or racial unrest may be priorities.

Whatever an agency's size, the police organization seeks "strict accountability through a clear rank structure, military symbols and procedures, a rigid communicational hierarchy, and close supervision" (Manning, p.96). The chief of police oversees the operation of the entire department. Under the chief, depending on the size of the department, are captains, lieutenants, sergeants and police officers. Traditionally most departments have been structured in a militaristic pyramid, with the chief at the top, as depicted in Figure 4.2. Many departments are moving away from a tall hierarchy to a more flattened structure with fewer officers in supervisory positions, more officers in the patrol division and an emphasis on teamwork rather than on strict obedience to higher authority.

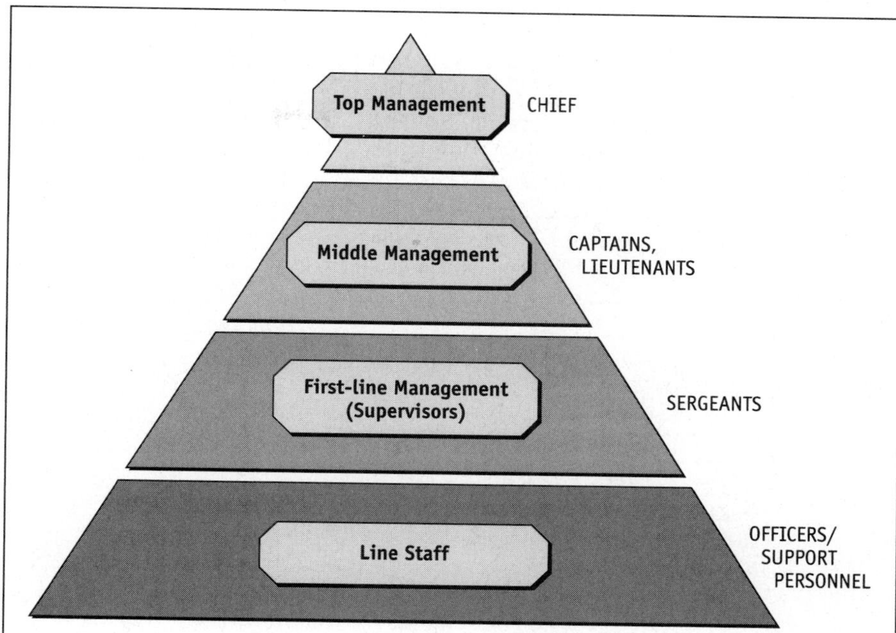

Figure 4.2
Typical Police Department Management Structure Pyramid

Another responsibility of the police chief is to coordinate the efforts of two primary groups—administrative and field services.

Most police departments are organized into two basic units: administrative services and field services. Tasks and personnel are assigned to one or the other.

Administrative services (also called staff or support services) include recruiting and training, planning and research, records and communications, and crime laboratories and facilities, including police headquarters and jail. Teamwork is essential within and between field services and administrative services. **Field services** (also called operations or line services) include patrol, traffic, community service and investigation. Whatever the size or configuration of the department, basic administrative and field services will be expected. The clear lines depicted in Figure 4.3 may become blurred as departments move to community policing and a team approach.

Administrative Services

Administrative services include communications and records, recruitment and training and provision of special facilities and services.

Administrative services are those functions that occur "behind the scenes," away from the front line of the officer in the field. These services include clerical and technical efforts to support and manage the information needed and generated by those in field services. Administrative services' two areas that most directly affect the efficient provision of field services are communications and records.

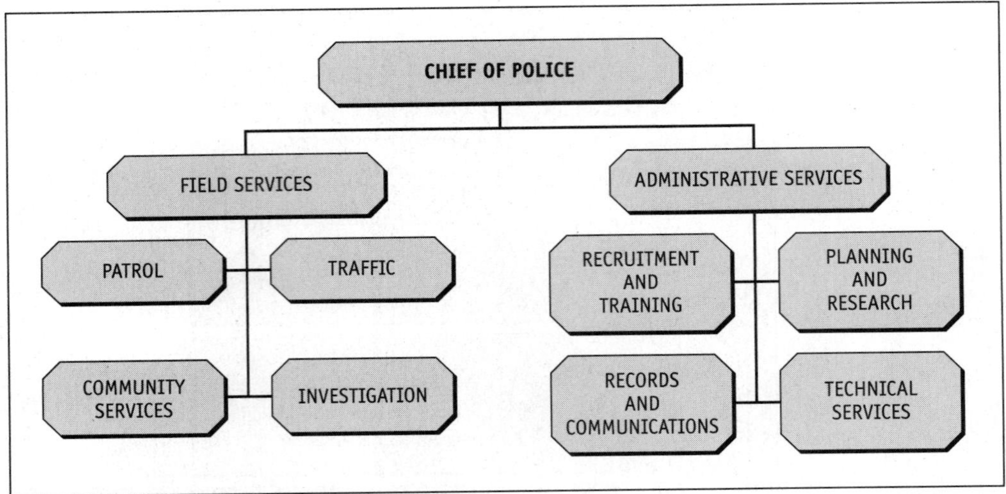

Figure 4.3
Typical Department Organization of Services

Communications

To properly serve the community, police officers must be kept currently and completely informed. They must know where and how much of each type of crime occurs. They also have to know what services are needed.

Current information is usually provided at roll call, by radio and phone and by computer.

Roll Call

One of the most important functions of the administrative division in its support of the other units is keeping members informed of daily police operations and providing administrative instructions, special assignments and tasks to be performed. This is usually done at a **roll call** session before the officers on the next shift "hit the street."

Up-to-date information is usually provided in a daily bulletin, which contains brief summaries of what has transpired in the previous 24 hours. Officers are given a synopsis of each complaint received and acted on, as well as descriptions of missing and/or wanted persons, stolen personal property and stolen autos.

Radio and Phone Communications

The information provided at roll call is continuously updated by radio or cell phone. Data are available to officers in patrol cars or carrying portable radios or cell phones. The introduction of the small, hand-carried police radio, cell phone and beeper have extended the communications system so that officers on foot may be reached to assist mobile patrol units and vice versa. This immediate communication has improved law enforcement officers' safety and provided bet-

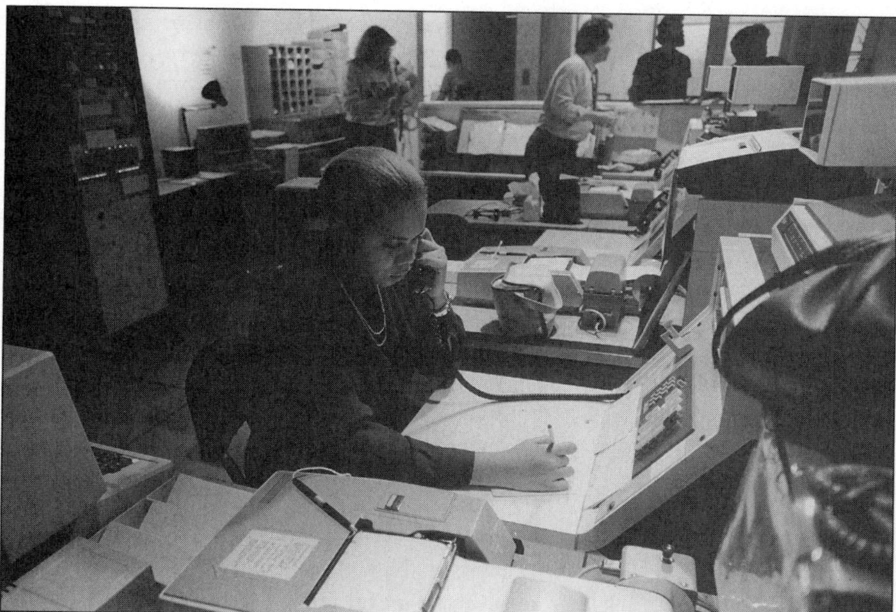

© Richard Bermack/Impact Visuals

Before giving calls to the dispatcher, some agencies have operators screen them to segregate informational calls from service calls.

ter allocation of resources. Radio transmission dependability has improved steadily over the years and has resulted in a great reduction in response time to calls for service or reported criminal activity.

Communication is the lifeline of the police department. The police dispatcher receives all citizens' requests for police service. In some instances the calls come directly to the dispatcher, who must act upon them and determine their priority. Some agencies have telephone operators screen the calls before giving them to the dispatcher to segregate informational calls from service calls.

Dispatchers are responsible for knowing what patrol vehicles are ready for assignment and dispatching them to requests for service. They may also have some records responsibility, for example making out the original incident complaint report containing the time the call was received, the time the patrol was dispatched, the time it arrived, the time it cleared and the disposition of the call. In addition, dispatchers handle walk-in complaints. Some may also monitor jails through a closed-circuit television hookup. Such a system exists in many smaller and medium-sized departments.

In larger agencies several dispatchers handle incoming calls and assign priority according to seriousness and availability of officers to respond. Larger agencies may also have direct and complete integration of police radio with regular telephone service. In this system any call to the police emergency number is automatically channeled to the dispatcher, who controls squad cars assigned to the area from which the caller is telephoning.

Many cities have a *911 system.* A person needing emergency police, fire or rescue service dials 911, and a central dispatching office receives the call directly. The eventual goal is to have 911 as the emergency number for police service in all U.S. cities. Our increasingly mobile society and advancing technology have affected how law enforcement receives communications from the public. Rogers (2001a, p.88) notes that 20 to 25 percent of all emergency calls to 911 are made from wireless phones, and that in 1999, 43 million cellular users dialed 911 for a distress call, which translates to 118,627 calls a day or 82 calls each minute.

In 1996, in response to the proliferation of cell phones and the public's increasing reliance on them to reach out for help, the Federal Communications Commission (FCC) issued a mandate for all wireless service providers to implement E911 technology, which uses geolocation capabilities to quickly trace a caller's location. When fully implemented, E911 service will require wireless carriers to identify the location of the caller within 125 meters at least two-thirds of the time. Thus, if a victim is carjacked and left on the street in an unfamiliar part of town, or is locked in the car's trunk and driven to unknown parts, armed with a cell phone they might be able to call 911 and have authorities pinpoint the victim's, and possibly the suspect's, location.

Computers

Computers have revolutionized law enforcement operations, including various administrative functions and communication avenues. Some systems facilitate officers' report writing. Many departments equip patrol cars with laptops that enable officers to write their reports in the field and send them directly to their departments, saving time and improving accuracy.

Computers have also brought tremendous benefits to the communication efforts of law enforcement, whether occurring within a department, between agencies and departments or with the community. Going online allows officers to access vital data and share information with other officers and managers, locally, nationally and even globally. Furthermore, the Internet provides a forum in which a department can communicate with the community, not only to give the public information about police activities and events but also to get information by soliciting leads from citizens to help in crime prevention and detection efforts.

An abundance of computer technology and programs have been implemented by law enforcement, and more are being developed all the time. Emphasizing the value of this technology, Kanable (2001, p.115) states: "To make smart decisions, law enforcement officers and managers need accurate information fast. . . . The use of information is appreciated as one of the most important things a department can do to control crime, disorder and fear." One data dissemination software program is SmartCOP, which makes real-time information available to the officer in the field, thereby providing improved officer safety, reduced response time, a possible solution to the racial profiling issue and interoperability.

Interoperability, or the capacity of various telecommunications and computing devices to "talk" to each other, has become an important issue because of the many companies independently producing PCs, mobile phones, pagers, printers, display monitors and other devices. In the absence of interoperability, these devices remain virtually isolated from each other, able to communicate only through the use of multiple proprietary, or product-specific, cables. Reliance on cable connections greatly limits a user's range of movement and decreases the portability of attached devices. An emerging technology designed to facilitate interoperability is Bluetooth, "a short-range wireless radio technology that makes it possible to transmit signals over short distances to connect telephones, computers and a range of other devices, without cabling or wires. It facilitates transmission of both voice and data in connections that are virtually instantaneous and secure, even when the devices are not within the line of sight" (Rogers, 2001b, p.83).

Bluetooth technology can be applied to obtain wireless connectivity to the Internet and enables one-to-one and one-to-many connections between a variety of digital devices, such as telephones, printers, fax machines, personal digital assistants (PDAs), desktop and laptop computers, keyboards and joysticks (Rogers, p.84). Such interoperability creates a *personal area network* (PAN) that allows all the devices a person is working with to interact without cables, thus enhancing freedom of movement. Rogers (p.86) notes: "An example of this type of personal area network for law enforcement officers would be in a vehicle. An officer's PAN might include a navigational tool that is voice-activated; a hands-free wireless headset for a mobile phone, pager or PDA; and an untethered mic for a video camera." A PAN might also include a wireless connection to a computer database.

One vital source of information for officers in the field is the FBI's online computerized National Crime Information Center (NCIC). In 1967 the FBI implemented this computerized crime information storage system dedicated to serving law enforcement and criminal justice agencies nationwide. Under this system each state has a number of computer terminals that interface with the FBI's main computer in Washington, DC. The computer contains records of stolen property, such as guns, autos and office machines and, in some cases, records of persons wanted on warrants. Hitt (2000, p.12) notes: "Since NCIC's inception in January 1967 transactions have gone from 2 million for that entire first year to approximately 2.5 million *a day* currently."

The National Crime Information Center gives all police agencies in the country access to the computerized files of the FBI.

The NCIC computer receives information from other federal law enforcement agencies and from state and local law enforcement agencies. The NCIC makes it possible for a law enforcement officer in Texas who stops a suspicious person or car from California to make an inquiry, in a matter of seconds, on the status of the individual and/or the car to the Washington NCIC terminal. The officer can be quickly informed if the car has been stolen or if an arrest warrant is outstanding on the person in the car.

In 1999, the FBI implemented a new generation of NCIC—NCIC 2000—to take up the challenge of meeting the ever-increasing demand for instant criminal justice information. Among the new capabilities of NCIC 2000 are:

> . . . the addition of image processing (i.e., mugshots, signatures, and identifying marks); automated single-finger fingerprint matching; and information linking, which provides the ability to associate logically related records across NCIC files for the same criminal or the same crime. . . . NCIC 2000 also automates functions that employees previously had to perform manually . . . [such as] online validation of records and [automatic collection of] statistics (Hitt, p.13).

The great volume of information contained in various state and federal computers is another aid to police officers in maintaining up-to-date records systems.

With the enormous amounts of information police departments must receive, transmit and be able to retrieve, an effective, efficient records system is imperative.

Records

The quality of records kept is directly related to the quality of communications and field services provided. To give proper direction, police agencies must have sound records systems as well as efficient communications systems. Police departments throughout the country vary in their reporting systems and their needs in management control and effective operational control. Their activities require keeping records not only of criminal activity but of all vital department activities.

Types of Records

Police records may be categorized as (1) administrative records, (2) arrest records, (3) identification records and (4) complaint records.

Administrative records include inventories of police equipment, personnel records, evaluation reports, department memorandums and all general information that reflects correspondence or services rendered. *Arrest records* contain information obtained from arrested persons when booked and information about the control and/or release of prisoners and court procedures. *Identification records* contain fingerprints, photographs and other descriptive data obtained from arrested persons.

Complaint records contain information related to complaints and reports received from citizens or other agencies, as well as any actions initiated by the police. Because police work is public business, it requires accurate documentation of complaints received and the action taken by officers. Complaints may be criminal or noncriminal; they may involve lost or damaged property, traffic accidents, medical emergencies or missing persons. Requests for police assistance may also involve robberies, murders, burglaries, vandalism, children playing in the streets or cats up trees.

Most police agencies have a procedure for recording complaint information on either forms or data processing cards. Initial complaint records are filled out on all complaints or requests for service received by the dispatcher or a police officer. Information on the initial complaint record normally shows the complainant, victim, address of each, type of complaint, time of day, day of week, the officer handling the complaint or request, the area of the community where it occurred, the disposition, whether there was an arrest and whether follow-up reports or further investigation is justified.

Benefits of Efficient Records Systems

An efficient records system is a vital management tool that aids in assessing department accomplishments, developing budget justifications, determining additional workforce needs, evaluating the performance of officers and assessing whether objectives and goals have been met.

Evaluation of carefully kept records will generally reflect needs in training, recruitment, public relations and allocation of resources, as well as general effectiveness. Management's continual or periodic evaluation of records for planning and research has allowed police agencies to provide better service to the public, and, in turn, they have gained greater public support.

Centralized, integrated, accurate systems of communication and records increase the effectiveness and efficiency of field services.

Privacy of Records

The most sensitive aspect of records on persons arrested is the possibility of including in the file unsubstantiated information that might be derogatory, incomplete or incorrect—information that disseminated to the wrong person could prove damaging and provide cause for a civil action against the police agency. In addition police agencies often tend to retain information longer than necessary.

The Department of Justice has issued regulations to assure that criminal history record information is collected, stored and disseminated in a way that ensures its completeness, integrity, accuracy and security while protecting individual privacy. The regulations apply to all state and local agencies and individuals collecting, storing or disseminating criminal history information either manually or by computer.

A data privacy act regulates the use of confidential and private information on individuals in the records, files and processes of a state and its political subdivisions.

Because states have been slow in passing privacy act legislation, a certain amount of confusion often occurs among those who try to abide by the Department of Justice regulations. The effect of some state legislation has been that in the absence of an emergency classification, almost all information or data a police agency has kept on individuals legally must be made available to anyone requesting it. This unfortunate situation has been avoided in other states.

Administrative services are vital to the efficient functioning of any police department, but they are a *support* for the field services.

Field Services

Sometimes field services are performed by one division, sometimes by separate divisions. They may be further specialized by the type of individual involved: juveniles, gamblers, prostitutes, burglars, drug dealers and so on; by specific geographic areas (beats); by specific times when demand for service is highest, for example holiday traffic; or by abnormal conditions, such as strikes and protests.

Field services include patrol, traffic, community services and investigation.

Traditionally police departments have been generalists. That is most of their personnel is assigned to patrol, and each officer is responsible for providing basic law enforcement services of all types to a specified geographic area. General patrol has been and is the backbone of police work in smaller departments. Larger departments tend to be more specialist oriented.

Patrol

Usually 60 to 70 percent of a department's police officers are assigned to patrol operations, providing continuous police service and high visibility of law enforcement. Tasks include crime prevention, response to calls for service, self-initiated activity and completing administrative functions. Although other divisions may have more prestige, patrol officers are the first and primary contact between the public and the criminal justice system. They not only initiate the criminal justice system, they strongly influence the public's perception of this system. The patrol function is discussed in detail in Chapter 6.

Traffic

Traffic may be a responsibility of patrol, or it may be a separate function. A well-rounded traffic program involves many activities designed to maintain order and safety on streets and highways. Traffic officers enforce traffic laws, direct and control traffic, provide directions and assistance to motorists, investigate motor vehicle crashes, provide emergency assistance at the scenes of crashes, gather information related to traffic and write reports.

The most frequent contact between the police and the noncriminal public is through traffic encounters. Consequently the opportunity for improving community relations by how traffic violations are handled must be considered. Although the traffic responsibilities of a police officer may not have the glamour of a criminal investigation, they are critical not only to the safety of the citizens but also to the police image. In addition many criminal arrests result from traffic stops, for example wanted persons and discovery of contraband. The traffic function is discussed in detail in Chapter 6.

Investigation

Although some investigations are carried out by patrol officers, the investigation services division (also known as the detective bureau) has the responsibility for follow-up investigation. The success of any criminal investigation relies on the cooperative, coordinated efforts of both the patrol and the investigative functions.

The primary responsibilities of the investigator are to make certain the crime scene is secure, interview witnesses and interrogate suspects, photograph and sketch the crime scene, obtain and identify evidence and record all facts related to the case for future reference. Investigation is discussed in detail in Chapter 7.

Community Service/Community Relations

In essence every action of police officers affects community relations—either positively or negatively. Many larger departments have separate community relations divisions or community service divisions to strengthen communication channels between the public and its police department and/or to stress public education programs and crime prevention programs. The importance of community relations and community service is emphasized throughout this text.

Specialized Officers

In addition to the basic divisions within police departments, larger departments frequently train officers to perform highly specialized tasks. Specialized officers may include evidence technicians, identification officers, intelligence officers, juvenile officers, vice officers, K-9-assisted officers and tactical forces officers. Specialized officers are discussed in Chapter 7.

The vast array of required general and specialized functions performed by police presents a special challenge in rural areas.

Rural Policing

Most rural departments have only one officer on duty who may be backed up by an off-duty officer, an on-call officer or a neighboring department, and this backup may be more than 30 minutes away. That makes rural policing potentially more dangerous. In addition, uniformed patrol officers in rural environments must be better prepared than their counterparts in urban environments who can defer to specialists when needed.

In some areas of the country, rural policing is performed by a sheriff responsible for a given county. Often the county sheriff is an elected office, making it accountable to the local community. In the majority of states, it is a constitutional office rather than an agency created by state statute, so it can be abolished only through constitutional amendment, and none of its powers or responsibilities may be changed by a county board.

The office of county sheriff has existed for hundreds of years, with roots in ninth century England. The sheriff's office has evolved into a multi-purpose agency with more diverse legal responsibilities than most local police departments, including providing correctional services (transporting prisoners and administering the county jail), providing court security through the assignment of bailiffs, processing judicial writs and court orders, seizing property claimed by the county, collecting county fees and taxes, and selling licenses and permits.

Not all county agencies are rural. Many urban counties also have sheriffs' departments. For example San Diego County includes the city of San Diego and ranks sixteenth in population of all U.S. metropolitan areas. The San Diego County Sheriff's Department has more than 3,000 members and 31 facilities located throughout the county.

Within larger departments, urban, suburban or rural, a subculture is likely to exist.

The Police Subculture

A **subculture** is any group demonstrating specific patterns of behavior that distinguish it from others within a society. Policing has been identified as a subculture commonly referred to as "The Blue Brotherhood." According to Paoline et al. (2000, p.576): "Police officers' occupational attitudes and values are shaped by a working environment characterized by uncertainty, danger, and coercive authority. Officers' adaptations to this environment form the basis for the police culture—a set of outlooks widely shared among officers. This is part of the conventional wisdom about police." Often departments attempt to influence the subculture through organizational socialization, as described by Manning (p.129): "*Organizational socialization* of members involves the adaptation of members' selves to organizational contingencies and to required team work."

Solar (1998, pp.22–23) stresses that: "Understanding cultural influences means understanding the history of an organization; the context in which events took place; the values and tendencies of the people involved, both current and former members; and other factors." According to Haught (1998, p.7): "An agency's true culture is its default setting. In other words the behavior that occurs when important people are visiting is not the department's 'culture,' but rather it's what takes place while conducting 'normal' business."

Police officers work nights and weekends; deal with highly confidential material that cannot be shared with friends; must enforce the law impartially, even when a friend violates a law; and frequently face public hostility, abuse, name calling and biased reporting in the media. A combination of these factors largely accounts for the existence of a "police culture." Gaffigan and McDonald (1997, p.30) itemize six beliefs commonly found within the police subculture:

1. The police are the only real crime fighters.
2. No one else understands the work of a police officer.
3. Loyalty counts more than anything.
4. It is impossible to win the war on crime without bending the rules.
5. The public is demanding and nonsupportive.
6. Working in patrol is the least desirable job in the police department.

Individuals who become police officers commonly lose their nonpolice friends within a few years. In addition to working different hours, they may make some of their friends uneasy, especially those who drink and drive or who habitually speed. Police officers' friends often do not understand some of the actions police are forced to take in fulfilling their responsibilities.

In addition to losing their nonpolice friends, officers may also come to realize that they are now a part of a group isolated from the rest of society—a fellowship united by risk, hardship and fear. Although officers are highly visible, they are set apart. They may be feared, disliked, hated or even assaulted by citizens. Thus they keep close ranks for protection and security. The closer they become, the more citizens fear and distrust them, leading to even tighter ranks, and so the cycle goes. The police become the "in group," and everyone else is the "out group." To a police officer the world consists of cops and civilians, or perhaps better phrased as cops versus civilians.

This "us versus them" attitude, fairly common in some departments, leads to defensiveness exhibited in such ways as reluctance to give up traditional police responsibilities (for example traffic control on state highways) or reluctance to explain their actions to citizens. Official police silence is sometimes necessary to protect the rights of others or to safeguard an investigation, but sometimes it is, in reality, a defensive response. The "us versus them" mentality may also foster an unofficial "blue wall of silence":

> A "Code of Silence" exists today in the law enforcement profession. Those who would suggest that some law enforcement officers today no longer hide behind the banner of loyalty are either naïve or concealing reality, contributing to the problem and enabling others to do the same. Some progress has been made in tearing down this age-old problem, but in many ways a police culture that exalts loyalty over integrity still exists (McErlain, 2001, p.87).

Furthermore, according to Trautman (2001, p.71): "The Us vs. Them mentality is usually present within the minds of those who participate in the code of silence. The code of silence and the Us vs. Them phenomenon often bond together."

Officers who isolate themselves from the community and from their non-police friends often develop a "one-track" life with the central focus being law enforcement. They may have few outside interests, devoting their attention to reading articles and watching programs related to law enforcement and socializing only with others in the law enforcement field.

The subculture of a department or agency can directly affect the styles of police work within it.

Styles of Policing

Many studies have looked at **styles** of policing and have classified these styles into clusters called **typologies.** Although few police officers fall completely into a single typology, most tend to exhibit several behaviors to place them into a specific typology.

Basic styles of policing include the following:

- Enforcer
- Crime fighter/zealot
- Social service agent
- Watchdog

The *enforcer* focuses on social order and keeping society safe. Enforcers are less concerned with individual rights and due process. Such officers are often critical of the Supreme Court, politicians, police administrators and minority interest groups. Enforcers have little time for minor violations of the law or for the social services aspect, seeing them as a waste of police time and resources. Officers of this typology are most likely to use excessive force.

The *crime fighter/zealot* is like an enforcer in that a primary goal is to keep society safe. These officers tend to deal with all laws and all offenders equally. The crime fighter/zealot is often relatively new, inexperienced or unable to see the gray areas associated with policing. Zealots are less critical of the social service aspects of policing than are enforcers.

The *social service agent* is more accepting of the social service roles and more attuned to due process. Such officers are often young, well educated and idealistic. Like the enforcer and the crime fighter, social service agents are also interested in protecting society but are more flexible in how this is approached.

The *watchdog* is on the opposite end of the spectrum from the enforcer. The watchdog is interested in maintaining the status quo, in not making waves. Watchdogs may ignore common violations, such as traffic offenses, and tolerate a certain amount of vice and gambling. They use the law more to maintain order than to regulate conduct. They also tend to judge the requirements of order differently depending on the group in which the infraction occurs.

Table 4.1 summarizes these typologies as described by three sources. No officer is purely one type or another, and an officer may change from one style to another depending on the situation. In any given department, it is likely that a variety of policing styles with some combination of the preceding typologies can be found. Policing style is greatly influenced by an officer's personality.

Table 4.1 The Typologies of Policing Styles

James Q. Wilson (1968)	Robert Pursley (1987)	Joseph Senna and Larry Siegel (1993)
Legalistic	Enforcer	Law enforcer
	Zealot	Crime fighter
Service style	Social service agent	Social agent
Watchdog	Watchdog	Watchdog

Stereotypes

The police deal daily with criminals, complainants and citizens who may be cursing, yelling, lying, spitting, fighting, drunk, high, angry, irrational, demanding, manipulative or cruel. Some officers' reactions to these daily encounters and the negative personality traits displayed may result in *all* officers being stereotyped as suspicious, cynical, indifferent, authoritarian, bigoted and brutal.

Suspicious

Police work requires an officer to be wary of people and situations that are out of the ordinary, for example a person with an umbrella on a sunny day or a person wearing sunglasses at midnight. Not only is keen observation critical to effective investigation and crime prevention, it is critical to self-defense. Danger is always possible in any situation. Police officers develop a perceptual shorthand to identify certain kinds of people as potential assailants, that is, officers come to recognize certain gestures, language and attire as a prelude to violence.

Cynical

Because police officers deal with criminals, they are constantly on guard against human faults. Officers see people at their worst. They know that people lie, cheat, steal, torture and kill. They deal with people who do not like police, who even hate them, and they feel the hatred. In addition they may see people they firmly believe to be guilty of a heinous crime freed by a legal technicality. This cynicism may also lead to paranoia.

Indifferent

When police officers are called to the scene of a homicide, they are expected to conduct a thorough, impartial investigation. Their objectivity may be perceived by grieving relatives of the victim as indifference or coldness. Officers must remain detached, however; one of the grieving relatives might well be the murderer. Further a certain amount of distancing is required to work with difficult situations.

Authoritarian

Effective law enforcement requires authority; authoritarianism comes with the job. Without authority and respect, an officer cannot effectively compel citizens of the community to obey the law. As noted by the French philosopher Pascal: "Justice without force is powerless; force without justice is tyrannical." The physical appearance of the police officer adds to this authoritarian image. The uniform, gun, baton and handcuffs project an image to which many people respond with uneasiness or even fear. However, this image projects the right of the police to exercise the lawful force of the state in serving and protecting as well as in enforcing laws. The difficulty arises when the power that comes with the position is transferred to "personal power."

Bigoted

Police are frequently victims of problems they have nothing to do with and over which they have no control. They are not to blame for the injustices suffered by minority groups: housing, educational and employment discrimination. Often, however, members of minority groups perceive the police as a symbol of the society that has denied them its privileges and benefits. Tension between minority groups and any representatives of "authority" has become almost a way of life in many parts of large cities. The minority group members vent their anger and frustration on the police, and some police come to feel anger and dislike for them.

Brutal

Sometimes force is required to subdue suspects. Unfortunately the crime-related aspects of a police officer's job are what frequently draw public attention. When police officers have to physically subdue a suspect, people notice. When they help people get into their locked cars, few notice.

Sometimes, however, more force is used than is required, crossing the line from justifiable force to police brutality. This, too, is easier to understand if one considers the other traits that often become part of the police "personality," particularly cynicism and authoritarianism. Police officers may use excessive force with a rapist if they believe that the probability is great that the rapist will never be brought to trial because of the prosecutor's policies on rape cases. They may also erroneously believe that violence is necessary to obtain respect from individuals who seem to respect nothing but force and power.

A study by Jesilow and Meyer (2001, p.109) examined how "public attitudes towards the police were affected by the incidents that swirled around Rodney King: the repeated television airings in 1991 of his beating by police officers, the subsequent acquittal of those officers for their actions and the urban violence that followed." They (p.117) suggest a notable difference in attitude between residents living in neighborhoods characterized by crime and disorder and college-educated residents who, as a group, live in "better" neighborhoods:

> In neighborhoods that had crime problems . . . the Rodney King affair probably had less impact. The residents remained concerned about law enforcement issues that were more central to their everyday experiences (e.g., catching whomever burglarized their homes). . . . The college educated seemed to be the group most affected by the King events. They probably watched the news reports and were familiar with and disgusted by the officers' behavior.

Perhaps the residents in the more challenged neighborhoods had simply become desensitized to police misconduct, having had more negative personal

Table 4.2
Police Actions Seen Negatively and Positively

Action by Officer	Negative Person	Positive Person
Steps in to stop a fight in a bar	Interference	Preserving the peace
Questions a rape victim	Indifferent, cold	Objective
Uses a baton to break up a violent mob	Brutal	Commanding respect
Steadily watches three youths on a corner	Suspicious	Observant

contacts with the police, while the more educated and affluent citizens were somewhat more naïve or idealistic about police officer conduct and, thus, more incensed when that image was shattered.

Indeed, the eyes of the beholder determine how a police officer's actions will be interpreted or described. Jesilow and Meyer (p.115) contend: "It makes some sense that those who have had a run in with the law might be more likely to criticize officer behavior following Rodney King. They have external validation for their complaints." Along these lines, a person who dislikes police officers will probably perceive a specific behavior negatively, whereas the same behavior might be perceived positively by one who has a high regard for police officers. Consider, for example, the actions listed in Table 4.2 and the way each is described by a person who feels negatively about the police and one who feels positively about the police.

Two conflicting views exist today as to why these traits might occur more often among police officers than in the general population. One view, the *unique traits viewpoint,* suggests policing attracts individuals who already possess these traits. The opposing view, the *socialization viewpoint,* suggests that the traits are developed by the experiences the officers have as they become socialized into their departments.

Despite the contention that the police personality may include negative traits, the public image of the police remains high.

The Police Image

Each police officer is an individual. Police officers are fathers, mothers, sons, daughters, uncles, aunts, coaches of Little League teams, church members and neighbors. As people they like to be liked, but often their profession requires that they take negative actions against those who break the law. As a result they are often criticized and berated for simply doing their jobs. Although police officers are individuals just like those in the community they have sworn to "serve and protect," their behavior is very public. It may simply be that they are extraordinarily visible ordinary people.

The public's **image** of the police varies greatly. Some see police officers as protectors; others see them as militaristic harassers. The sight of a police officer arouses feelings of respect, confidence and security in some citizens; fear, hostility and hatred in others; and indifference in yet others. According to Johnson (2001, p.27): "The police officer's uniform has a profound psychological impact on others." He (p.31) asserts: "The uniform of a police officer conveys the power and authority of the person wearing it. . . . Citizens in the presence of a person in a police uniform cooperate more and curb their illegal or deviant behaviors."

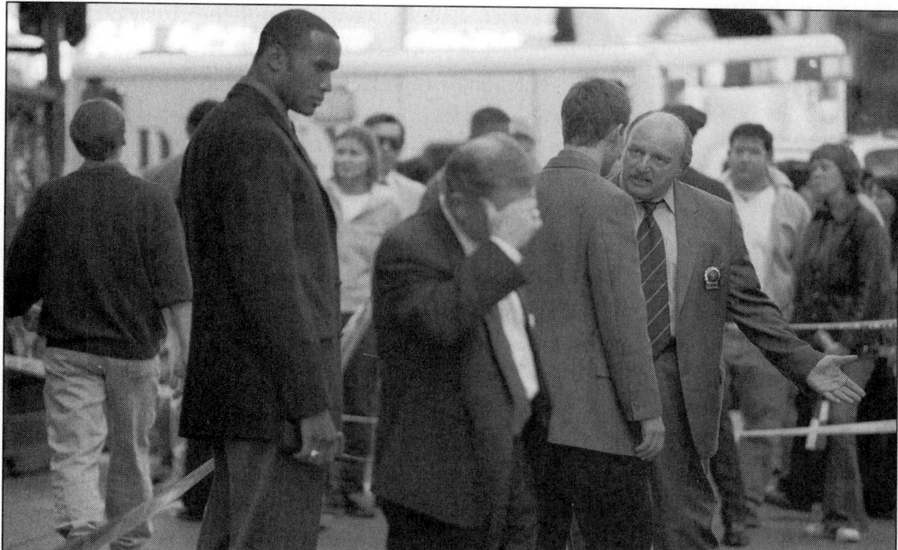

Photofest

In the popular television series NYPD Blue, Dennis Franz plays the hard-nosed Detective Sipowitz, a good example of a cop who often uses the ends to justify the means.

The image of the police officer often portrayed on television has not been helpful. The "Dirty Harry" tactics, with violence and disregard for civil rights, are often presented as the way police officers behave. The effects of television on both the police image and the fight against crime cannot be accurately measured. Certainly it has an impact. Hardly an hour passes without an illegal search, a coerced confession, police brutality and general violence dealt out by television police officers. Many modern police "heroes" are shown blatantly indulging in illegal and unconstitutional behavior, which in effect instills in the public the opinion that police misconduct is acceptable and, in fact, sometimes the only way to apprehend criminals. The same criticisms may be applied to our movies.

The police image results from the media portrayal of police officers and from everyday contacts between individual police officers and citizens.

In spite of what is written in books or portrayed on television and in movies, the abstraction called the "police image" is primarily the result of day-to-day contacts between police and citizens. Langan et al. (2001, p.1) report:

> In 1999 an estimated 43.8 million persons age 16 or older, about 21% of all persons of this age, had at least one face-to-face contact with a police officer. . . .
>
> The rate of police-citizen contact for whites was about 17% higher than for blacks and about 32% higher than for Hispanics. The rate of contact for males was about 20% higher than for females, and rates of contact varied inversely with age: those age 18 to 19 experienced a rate of contact 160% above that of those age 50 or older. . . .
>
> About half of all persons experiencing a contact with police indicated that the reason for the contact was a motor vehicle stop. . . .
>
> About 1 in 5 persons with a face-to-face contact with a police officer said that they had contacted the police to report a crime. . . .
>
> Overall, less than half of 1% of the population age 16 or older reported they had contact with police and were threatened with or actually experienced force during the contact.

It is the behavior of police officers at the patrol level rather than at the command level that is of greatest importance in establishing the police image. In turn the individual behavior of the police officer who creates the police image is the result of several factors, including length of service, the community served (ghetto or exclusive suburb), training and experience.

Factors Influencing Police Image

In addition to easily identifiable and predictable factors, such as experience, training and locality served, many subtle factors influence police behavior and image, including the nature of police work itself, the police officer's unique relation to the criminal justice system, a confusion of identity, the democratic nature of our society and the individual officer's personality.

The Nature of Police Work

Many demands are placed on police officers—they are under constant pressure and faced with rapidly changing conditions, sometimes life-threatening situations, with few guidelines and little supervision. They often must "play it by ear."

Police officers must interact with people from all walks of life who are involved in criminal and noncriminal activities and must use broad discretion in a wide variety of situations. They deal with crimes already committed and with people who are hurt, confused, angry and upset. Yet officers must remain neutral, calm and objective. They may appear indifferent or unsympathetic, but much like physicians, they cannot become personally involved and still do a professional job.

The image resulting from the nature of police work might easily be compared to the image of a football referee. It is readily accepted that referees are necessary to the game. Without them chaos would reign. Despite their importance, however, their image is often negative. No matter what call they make, a great many people are unhappy with them. They are usually perceived as being on the opponent's side. Defeats are often blamed on referees, but seldom is a referee given credit for a team's victory. It is often a thankless, sometimes dangerous job. Fans have tried to physically assault referees. They call them abusive names. It often makes one wonder what kind of person could work under such pressures.

Unique Relationship to the System

Another factor influencing the police image is the officers' relationship to the law. Although police officers are many people's first contacts with the criminal justice system, they often feel like outsiders in the judicial system. They may feel their investigation and apprehension of criminals is hampered by legal restrictions and that suspects have more rights than victims.

Although police officers are frequently blamed for unacceptable crime rates, their participation in the legal system is often minimized. They may be made to feel as if they were on trial during the court proceedings as the defense attorney cross-examines them. They are seldom included in any plea bargaining, and many defendants are found not guilty because of loopholes or legal technicalities. When a confessed robber is acquitted on a technicality or a known rapist is not brought to trial by the prosecutor, police officers may take this as a personal affront, as a criticism of their investigative expertise. Citizens of the community may also blame the police for the unsuccessful prosecution of a suspect. Legal technicalities may even result in the police officer being sued for false arrest.

Role Conflict

The role conflict faced by many police officers has a direct influence on the image projected. Many police officers feel they are law enforcement officers, not social workers. They did not create nor can they control the social problems that exist and that prompt numerous service calls. When they do respond to such calls, their help is often perceived as interference; they may be berated or even assaulted.

How the Public Really Feels about the Police

Despite individual complaints or even localized criticism about law enforcement, general public support of and confidence in the police appears solid and favorable. Results of a Gallup poll conducted from June 8–10, 2001, indicate the public held more confidence in the police than in the majority of other American institutions. The poll, which analyzed public confidence in 16 specific institutions, revealed that 57 percent of Americans have a great deal or quite a lot of confidence in the police, ranking them third after the military and the church/organized religion.

In another poll conducted October 11–14, 2001, to the question, "How much confidence do you have in the ability of the police to protect you from violent crime?" 25 percent responded "a great deal" and 41 percent responded "quite a lot." An August 29–September 5, 2000, poll asked, "How much respect do you have for the police in your area?" with 60 percent responding "a great deal" (www.Gallup.com/poll/indicators).

Summary

Police are necessary when coercion is required to enforce the laws. The people largely determine the goals of policing and give law enforcement agencies their authority to meet these goals. Citizen support is vital.

One primary goal of police agencies is to enforce laws and assist in prosecuting offenders. A second important goal is to preserve the peace. A third goal is crime prevention. A fourth goal is to protect citizens' constitutional rights. In seeking this goal, law enforcement faces the challenge of balancing the concern for crime control with the concern for due process. A fifth goal of police agencies is to provide services.

Most police departments are organized into two basic units: field services and administrative services. Tasks and personnel are assigned to one or the other. Administrative services provide support for field services and include communications and records, recruitment and training and provision of special facilities and services. Current information is usually provided at roll call, by radio and phone and by computer.

In addition to direct communication, police officers also rely upon information contained in various records depositories. The National Crime Information Center (NCIC) gives all police agencies in the country access to the computerized files of the FBI. Among the types of records the police officer may use are administrative, arrest, identification and complaint records. Centralization of local police agencies' records allows the various line functions to be coordinated.

Centralized, integrated, accurate systems of communication and records increase the effectiveness and efficiency of field services. Access to information is not always unlimited, however. A data privacy act regulates the use of confidential and private information on individuals in the records, files and processes of a state and its political subdivisions. Within the field services provided in a police department are patrol, traffic, community services and investigation. Sometimes these are specialized departments; sometimes the services are provided by a single department.

With the varying roles and responsibilities police officers have, it is not surprising that distinct styles of policing have developed. Four basic styles of policing are the enforcer, the crime fighter/zealot, the social service agent and the watchdog. The style of policing demonstrated by various officers contributes to their image. The police image results from the media portrayal of police officers and from everyday contacts between individual police officers and citizens.

Discussion Questions

1. How has communication between the officer in the field and headquarters changed in the last 100 years?
2. How have the responsibilities of police officers changed over time?
3. What services should police officers provide? Which are provided in your community?
4. What style of policing will you probably lean toward? Why?
5. Have you witnessed firsthand police discretion? Explain.
6. Do you feel police agencies and officers have too little, too much or just the right amount of discretion?
7. What is your image of the police? What do you believe your community thinks of the police?
8. Have you seen examples of unethical behavior in police work? Of actual corruption?
9. What do you see as the greatest challenge for police officers in the twenty-first century?
10. What effect, if any, did the September 11, 2001, terrorist attacks in America have on your image of the police? Do you think that event changed how our country views the efforts of law enforcement?

InfoTrac *College Edition Assignments*

Use InfoTrac College Edition to help answer the Discussion Questions as appropriate.

- Use InfoTrac College Edition to locate articles on *truancy*. Outline how communities are dealing with this problem. How are police assisting communities in addressing this problem? Be prepared to share your outline with the class.
- Use InfoTrac College Edition to compare the image of the police in the United States to that of the police in Singapore. Outline the main similarities and differences, and be prepared to share your findings with the class.
- The National Crime Information Center (NCIC) has a wealth of information. Use InfoTrac to find the NCIC and outline what it has to offer. Select one area of interest to explore and write a brief recap of what you learned. Be prepared to share your outline and recap with the class.

Internet Assignment

Use the Internet to search for *police culture*. Select a document that indicates how the police culture changes in or is affected by a multicultural society. Briefly outline the major changes, and be prepared to share your findings with the class.

Book-Specific Web Site

The book-specific Web site at http://info.wadsworth.com/0534552803 hosts a variety of resources for students and instructors. Included are extended activities from each chapter in which students write a policy, use critical thinking skills to make choices in response to a given scenario, use InfoTrac College Edition with direct links to articles for participation in topical discussion forums, and analyze court cases using Web links for research. Many activities can be printed or emailed to instructors. Plus, cited cases with Web links, interactive key term FlashCards, PowerPoint presentations, chapter objectives, and an extensive collection of chapter-based Web links provide additional information and activities to include in the curriculum.

References

Bittner, Egon. "Florence Nightingale in Pursuit of Willie Sutton: A Theory of Police." In *The Potential for Reform of Criminal Justice,* edited by H. Jacob. Beverly Hills, CA: Sage Publications, 1974, pp.17–44.

Bittner, Egon. *The Functions of Police in Modern Society.* Cambridge, MA: Oelseschlager, Gunn and Hain, 1980.

Gaffigan, Stephen J. and McDonald, Phyllis P. *Police Integrity: Public Service with Honor.* A Partnership between the National Institute of Justice and the Office of Community Oriented Police Services, January 1997.

Gaines, Larry K. and Cordner, Gary W. *Policing Perspectives: An Anthology.* Los Angeles: Roxbury Publishing Company, 1999.

Haught, Lunell. "Meaning, Resistance and Sabotage—Elements of a Police Culture." *Community Policing Exchange,* June 1998, p.7.

Hitt, Stephanie L. "NCIC 2000." *FBI Law Enforcement Bulletin,* July 2000, pp.12–15.

Jesilow, Paul and Meyer, Jon' A F. "The Effect of Police Misconduct on Public Attitudes: A Quasi-Experiment." *Journal of Crime and Justice,* Vol. 24, No. 1, 2001, pp.109–121.

Johnson, Richard R. "The Psychological Influence of the Police Uniform." *FBI Law Enforcement Bulletin,* March 2001, pp.27–32.

Kanable, Rebecca. "SmartCOP Helps Make Informed Decisions." *Law Enforcement Technology,* April 2001, pp.115–120.

Klockars, Carl B. "The Rhetoric of Community Policing." In *Community Policing: Rhetoric or Reality,* edited by J. R. Greene and S. D. Mastrofski. New York: Praeger Publishers, 1991.

Langan, Patrick A.; Greenfeld, Lawrence A.; Smith, Steven K.; Durose, Matthew R.; and Levin, David J. *Contacts between Police and the Public: Findings from the 1999 National Survey,* Washington, DC: Bureau of Justice Statistics, February 2001. (NCJ 184957)

Manning, Peter K. *Police Work: The Social Organization of Policing,* 2nd ed. Prospect Heights, IL: Waveland Press, Inc., 1997.

McErlain, Ed. "Acknowledging the Code of Silence." *Law and Order,* January 2001, p.87.

National Advisory Commission on Criminal Justice Standards and Goals. *The Police.* Washington, DC: U.S. Government Printing Office (LEAA Grant Number 72-DF-99-0002, and NI-72-0200), 1973.

Paoline, Eugene A., III; Myers, Stephanie M.; and Worden, Robert E. "Police Culture, Individualism, and Community Policing: Evidence from Two Police Departments." *Justice Quarterly,* September 2000, pp.575–605.

Rogers, Donna. "Drive for E911 Picks Up Speed." *Law Enforcement Technology,* March 2001a, pp.88–92.

Rogers, Donna. "The Truth about Bluetooth." *Law Enforcement Technology,* April 2001b, pp.82–90.

Solar, Patrick J. "Changing Organizational Culture: Monitoring and Developing Professional Officer Skills." *Law and Order,* May 1998, pp.22–27.

Stoutland, Sara E. "The Multiple Dimensions of Trust in Resident/Police Relations in Boston." *Journal of Research in Crime and Delinquency,* August 2001, pp.226–256.

Trautman, Neal. "Truth about Police Code of Silence Revealed." *Law and Order,* January 2001, pp.68–76.

Webster, J. A. "Police Task and Time Study." *Journal of Criminal Law, Criminology, and Police Science,* Vol. 61 (no date).

Chapter 5

Community Policing, Problem-Solving Policing and Service

The vocation of every man and woman is to serve other people.

—Leo Tolstoy

Do You Know?

- What community policing is?
- What the four major dimensions of community policing are?
- What the two critical elements of community policing are?
- What problem-oriented policing is?
- What four strategies are involved in the SARA model of problem-oriented policing?
- What community services a police department may provide its citizens?
- Who is ultimately responsible for successful police/community relations?
- What community programs have been developed for youths?
- What community crime prevention programs have been developed?
- How our population has changed in the past decades and how it is likely to continue to change?
- What special law enforcement challenges are presented by this changing population?

Can You Define?

American Dream
CPTED
de facto segregation
deinstitutionalization
demographers
ghetto
ghetto syndrome
heuristic
hot spots
integrated patrol
medical model
paradigm shift
SARA model
stereotype
target hardening

INTRODUCTION

Approaches to policing vary from jurisdiction to jurisdiction. Gaines and Cordner (1999, pp.119–120) suggest police agencies can choose from among four overarching strategies: professional crime fighting, strategic policing, problem-oriented policing and community policing. They note: "*Professional crime fighting* basically corresponds to policing as practiced since the 1960s: patrol cars spread throughout the jurisdiction, calls are handled as they come in, all crimes are followed up by detectives, etc." This strategy has been refined into *strategic policing* in some agencies as a more targeted approach, relying on directed patrol, proactive tactics and the like. *Problem-oriented policing* is somewhat similar to strategic policing but "takes a more analytical and multifaceted approach with less reliance on arrest and enforcement." *Community policing* takes this strategy as a "primary tactic, but its most distinctive feature is reliance on the community itself to exert informal social control in order to help reduce crime and disorder."

Crime control is a primary goal of each of the four strategies. The professional crime fighting strategy focuses on general deterrence based on maximum police car visibility. Strategic policing focuses on specific deterrence and incapacitation. Problem-oriented policing focuses on primary and secondary prevention, and the community policing strategy focuses on primary prevention but also relies on deterrence and incapacitation.

Seldom will only one of these strategies be evident within an agency, but one strategy usually predominates. This chapter examines the community policing and the problem-oriented policing strategies, as well as the vast array of community services an agency might be called upon to provide and the consumer-oriented approach being adopted by agencies throughout the country.

The chapter begins with community policing because the ramifications of the change from a professional model to a community-oriented model affect all aspects of police operations. Included within the discussion are the definitions currently applied to community policing, its historical roots, its four major dimensions, its key elements and the relationship between community policing and decreases in crime. This is followed by a discussion of problem-oriented policing, a vital component of community policing, including how it is defined and what it consists of. Next the role of community services and the importance of effective police-community relations are explored, including programs that have been implemented for youths and for crime prevention. The chapter concludes with a discussion of the challenges to community policing, including impediments to its implementation as well as the changing population to be served.

Community Policing Defined

Numerous definitions of community policing exist, but a common thread runs through them. Consider the following definitions:

> Community policing is an organization-wide philosophy and management approach that promotes community, government, and police partnerships; proactive problem solving; and community engagement to address the causes of

crime, fear of crime and other community issues (Upper Midwest Community Policing Institute, n.d.).

The essence of community policing is to return to the day when safety and security are participatory in nature and everyone assumes responsibility for the general health of their community—not just a select few, not just the local government administration, not just the safety forces, but absolutely everyone living in the community (Brown, 2001, p.56).

Chief David Bejarano: "It [community policing] is not a project. It's not a program. It's a culture" (Abshire and Paynter, 2000, p.56).

Community policing is . . . a belief that working together, the police and the community can accomplish what neither can accomplish alone (Miller and Hess, 2002, p.xix).

Community policing is a philosophy that stresses working proactively with citizens to prevent crime and to solve crime-related problems.

Community policing might be best understood by looking first at its historical roots, then the components of the philosophy and the four major dimensions it encompasses and, finally, its implementation, as well as impediments to implementation.

Historical Roots of Community Policing

While community policing is considered innovative, its central tenets of involvement with and responsiveness to the community are similar to the principles set forth by Sir Robert Peel in 1829 when he asserted that " . . . the police are the public and the public are the police." However as the police evolved in the United States, they grew farther apart from the public they served. Social distancing was enhanced by the advent of patrol cars to replace the traditional foot patrol.

Traditional police departments are insular organizations that respond to calls for service from behind the blue curtain. This insular, professional approach began to change in many agencies in the late 1970s and early 1980s. Gaines and Cordner (p.137) note: "Community policing has been around, as both a label and a specific police strategy, for about twenty years. It started out as a fuzzy notion about increasing police-citizen contact and reducing fear of crime, then settled into a period during which it was seen as having two primary components—problem solving and community engagement." This evolution is also described by Cordner (1999, p.137):

> In less than two decades, community policing has evolved from a few small foot patrol studies to the pre-eminent reform agenda of modern policing. With roots in such earlier developments as police-community relations, team policing, crime prevention, and the rediscovery of foot patrol, community policing has become . . . the dominant strategy of policing—so much so that the 100,000 new police officers funded by the 1994 Crime Bill must be engaged, by law, in community policing.

Community policing is viewed by many as a **paradigm shift** from the traditional, professional model of policing. Table 5.1 summarizes the differences between these two approaches to policing.

Table 5.1
Traditional vs. Community Policing: Questions and Answers

Question	Traditional	Community Policing
Who are the police?	A government agency principally responsible for law enforcement	Police are the public and the public are the police: the police officers are those who are paid to give full-time attention to the duties of every citizen
What is the relationship of the police force to other public service departments?	Priorities often conflict	The police are one department among many responsible for improving the quality of life
What is the role of the police?	Focusing on solving crimes	A broader problem-solving approach
How is police efficiency measured?	By detection and arrest rates	By the absence of crime and disorder
What are the highest priorities?	Crimes that are high value (e.g., bank robberies) and those involving violence	Whatever problems disturb the community most
What, specifically, do police deal with?	Incidents	Citizens' problems and concerns
What determines the effectiveness of police?	Response times	Public cooperation
What view do police take of service calls?	Deal with them only if there is no real police work to do	Vital function and great opportunity
What is professionalism?	Swift, effective response to serious crime	Keeping close to the community
What kind of intelligence is most important?	Crime intelligence (study of particular crimes or series of crimes)	Criminal intelligence (information about the activities of individuals or groups)
What is the essential nature of police accountability?	Highly centralized; governed by rules, regulations and policy directives; accountable to the law	Emphasis on local accountability to community needs
What is the role of headquarters?	To provide the necessary rules and policy directives	To instill organizational values
What is the role of the press liaison department?	To keep the "heat" off operational officers so they can get on with the job	To coordinate an essential channel of communication with the community
How do the police regard prosecutions?	As an important goal	As one tool among many

Source: M. K. Sparrow. "Implementing Community Policing." *Perspectives on Policing.* U.S. Department of Justice, National Institute of Justice, November 1988, pp. 8–9.

Status Today

Community policing has gained much support and momentum since its "reintroduction" in the 1970s and 1980s. The extensive growth in this policing philosophy is reported by Hickman and Reaves (2001, p.1):

> State and local law enforcement agencies had nearly 113,000 community policing officers or their equivalents during 1999, compared to about 21,000 in 1997. This included 91,000 local police officers in 1999, up from 16,000 in 1997.
>
> Sixty-four percent of local police departments serving 86% of all residents had full-time officers engaged in community policing activities during 1999, compared to 34% of departments serving 62% of residents in 1997.

They (p.1) further note an estimated 15,500 full-time sheriffs' deputies were assigned to community policing in 1999, compared to approximately 3,600 in 1997.

The Dimensions of Community Policing

It could be argued that the success of community policing depends on how clearly a community voices its concerns to the police and how well the police address or respond to such concerns. To examine such interactions and understand how this policing philosophy translates into practice, the concept of community policing can be dissected into specific dimensions. According to O'Shea (2000, p.389):

> Community-policing approaches police change from two dimensions, one administrative and the other political. The administrative aspects of community policing address structural and managerial issues, for example, decentralization, participatory management, and so on. The political dimension is somewhat less straightforward because it seeks to address the conditions of bureaucracy that conflict with democratic principles.

O'Shea (p.390) states: "The political dimension of community policing begins with the assumption that the police have become estranged from the public they serve." He suggests that in communities where the police fail to represent faithfully the interests and preferences of their constituency, the community policing effort is compromised.

Another view of community policing is presented by Cordner, who identifies four major dimensions of community policing and the most common developments within each dimension.

The four major dimensions of community policing are (1) philosophical, (2) strategic, (3) tactical and (4) organizational.

The philosophical dimension includes the major paradigm shift away from the professional model to a broader view of the police function. This dimension also recognizes the critical element of teamwork and a partnering philosophy—the citizens who serve as the eyes and ears that report crime and the police who then act to keep crime down. Together, they complement each other for the good of the community.

"The strategic dimension of community policing," says Cordner (p.139), "includes the key operational concepts that translate philosophy into action. These strategic concepts are the links between the broad ideas and beliefs that underlie community policing and the specific programs and practices by which it is implemented." This includes shifting the focus from time of day to geographic location and from a reactive, crime-fighting focus to a proactive, crime-prevention focus.

The third dimension, the tactical, gets down to the "nuts and bolts" of putting community policing into action. Most often an integral part of this dimension is a problem-solving approach stressing community involvement.

The organizational dimension traditionally is quasi-militaristic and authoritarian. According to Cordner (p.145): "Some aspects of traditional police organization structure seem more suited to routine, bureaucratic work than to the discretion and creativity required for COP." He notes that organizational restructuring associated with community policing includes:

- Decentralization—widening the designation of authority and responsibility so line officers can act more independently
- Flattening—reducing the number of hierarchical levels to improve communication and diminish bureaucracy

- Despecialization—reducing the number of specialized units, channeling more resources toward the direct delivery of police services to the public
- Teams—improving efficiency and effectiveness by pooling officer resources in groups
- Civilianization—replacing sworn personnel with nonsworn personnel to maximize cost effectiveness; reassigning sworn personnel to where they are most needed

Key Elements of Community Policing

McEwen (1998, p.13) lists six key elements of the Chicago Alternative Policing Strategy (CAPS) of community policing:

1. The entire department and the city were to be involved.
2. Officers were to have permanent beat assignments.
3. There was to be a serious commitment to training.
4. The community was to play a significant role in the program.
5. Policing was to be linked to the delivery of city services.
6. There was to be an emphasis on crime analysis.

Other key elements often present within agencies adopting community policing include decentralization of authority and structure, with police and citizens sharing power and being empowered to address community problems together.

The two critical key elements of community policing are partnerships and problem solving.

Partnerships

Partnerships are a cornerstone of community policing. Officers and their departments may team up with citizens, businesses, private policing enterprises and other law enforcement agencies to achieve their community policing objectives.

Police/public partnerships can be seen as existing on two levels. On a more passive level, the community assumes a compliant role and shows support for law and order by what they *don't* do—they don't interfere with routine police activities and they don't, themselves, engage in conduct that disrupts the public peace. Gehrand (2000, p.111) sums up this passive partnership: "No police department can control crime and disorder without the consent and voluntary compliance by the public."

On an active level, citizens step beyond their daily law-abiding lives and get directly involved in projects, programs and other specific efforts to enhance their community's safety. Cordner (p.143) suggests: "Participation of the community in its own protection is one of the central elements of community policing." Such participation may include neighborhood block watches, citizen crime patrols and youth-oriented educational and recreational programs. Citizens may respond independently or form groups, perhaps collaborating with the local police department.

However today's heterogeneous communities often foster differing and conflicting interests, which are sometimes represented by competing interest groups. Clashes may result between the elderly and the youths within a community, or between various ethnic and cultural groups within a neighborhood:

> Finding common interests around which to rally entire communities, or just identifying common interests on which to base police practices, can be very challenging and, at times, impossible. . . .
>
> Fortunately, nearly all citizens want to be safe from violence, want their property protected, and want some level of orderliness in their neighborhoods. Officers can usually find enough consensus in communities upon which to base cooperative efforts aimed at improving safety and public order (Cordner, pp.143–144).

The September 11, 2001, terrorist attacks on America, while unquestionably horrific and devastating, had a positive effect by bringing even the most diverse, fragmented communities together in ways rarely seen before. The government's appeal to the nation's public to become "soldiers" in the effort to preserve our American way of life and to be increasingly vigilant about activities occurring in their neighborhoods is a direct application of the community policing philosophy. Everyone is made to feel they have a part to play, an implicit responsibility, in keeping themselves, their communities and their country safe from harm.

Law enforcement can also partner with local businesses to help combat community problems. Broder (2001, p.A31) reports on the recently launched "CEOs for Cities," a consortium of business leaders, university presidents and mayors of both parties. He explains:

> "Partnership" is the key concept in the approach they are pushing, often built around community development corporations—locally led groups that leverage public and private funds into projects that upgrade housing, improve commercial and recreational facilities and organize neighborhoods to fight crime and demand better schools.

Herbert (2001, p.A23) adds that CEOs for Cities is "committed to the idea that vibrant cities are essential to the long-term health of the U.S. . . . [and contends] that the concentration of poverty in the cities, along with the related issues of racial isolation and social pathology, may well be the nation's number one problem."

Another partnership involves "The World's Largest Block Watch on Wheels"—Cab Watch. According to Haldar (2001, p.13): "Cab drivers in New York are eight times more likely than the average citizen to witness or be involved in crimes and emergencies." Taking advantage of the "sheer size, scope, and potential" of the city's taxi industry, Haldar explains:

> Cab Watch broadens the city's reach in law enforcement without spending a dime of tax money. With the help of the New York Police Department, Cab Watch trains cab drivers to report incidents and accidents without putting themselves or others at risk. Then, it outfits the drivers with 911-direct wireless phones, which are donated. . . .
>
> In the last two years, Cab Watch has expanded from a 50-driver pilot program to more than 1,700 drivers outfitted with wireless phones and ready to dial 911 on the spot. Drivers have alerted police to hundreds of incidents, helping to lead to the arrest of suspects in slayings, hit-and-runs, burglaries, assaults, even

> incidents of pick-pocketing. The cabbies' quick calls have also helped save lives in car accidents and building fires.

Various partnerships may be formed to tackle specific community crime problems. For example, in the City Heights area of San Diego, a neighborhood challenged by a very culturally diverse population, widespread poverty and a violent crime rate more than double the citywide average, local residents had identified drug-related crime and juvenile delinquency as their primary concerns. Partnering members of law enforcement with community members was considered a potential solution to these problems. As Stewart-Brown (2001, p.10) describes: "The City Heights Neighborhood Alliance, comprised of a team of police officers and civilian community organizers, set out to solve drug-related crimes in partnership with community residents and to provide residents with the knowledge and skills to solve their own neighborhood quality-of-life problems."

The community benefits from partnerships by a commitment to crime prevention, public scrutiny of police operations, accountability to the public, customized police service and involvement of community organizations. The police benefit by greater citizen support and increased respect, shared responsibility and greater job satisfaction.

Partnerships are also a focal point of the **medical model** sometimes used to explain the relationship between the police and the community. In medicine patients are primarily responsible for their own health, with physicians advising patients on how to be healthy, as well as assisting when health problems arise. So, too, in the community citizens are responsible for public safety and keeping their neighborhoods healthy, and they cannot expect the police to take sole responsibility for it. In this community wellness concept, the police and the public share responsibility for the causes of crime, the fear of crime and actual crime.

Another aspect of the medical model is an emphasis on prevention rather than cure, on being proactive rather than reactive and on treating causes rather than symptoms. The medical profession has found that rather than investing all its resources in curing disease, it is more effective to prevent disease in the first place. Such prevention requires the skill and expertise of the professional, as well as the willing, responsible cooperation of the patient. Harpold (2000, p.25) asserts:

> Preventive medicine also constitutes an important part of the police treatment methodology. The police should advocate crime prevention practices, such as Neighborhood Watch, in the communities they serve. While such programs do not make neighborhoods impervious to crime, they can create an internal support system that makes the community stronger in the fight against disease. They also help educate the public.
>
> Community education represents a crucial component in helping patients share responsibility for their own health as well as defining the legal boundaries for their behavior. Community policing should create citizens who are vigilant, not vigilantes.

Interestingly, one of the private-sector businesses that public law enforcement has begun forging partnerships with is private security. In years past, much competition and animosity existed between public and private police. Public law enforcement officers regarded private security personnel as police "wanna-be's," and those in the private sector considered public police officers trigger-happy, ego-inflated crime fighters who often held themselves to be above the law.

Recently, however, these two groups have put aside their differences to focus on their common goal of ensuring public safety. Seamon (1999, p.17) notes: "The past two decades have seen a dramatic expansion of private security worldwide, greatly outpacing the growth of public law enforcement." Recognizing the ever-tightening budget constraints placed on public law enforcement agencies, Paynter (2000, p.6) suggests: "Privatization of policing services appears to answer some of policing's present woes. By partnering with private organizations, law enforcement may be able to address the public's calls for increased policing services and better focus on its primary function, which is to combat crime." One such partnership exists in the Private Sector Liaison Committee (PSLC) founded by the International Association of Chiefs of Police (IACP) in 1986. The committee's stated mission was to "develop and implement cooperative strategies for the enhancement of public law enforcement and private sector relationships in the interest of the public good" (Seamon, p.17).

In addition to partnerships with a community's citizenry and private sector businesses, police departments may also partner with other public law enforcement agencies at various jurisdictional levels.

Cooperative Policing

In the effort to make policing at the community level a success, agencies must not overlook the importance of the services provided at the county, state and federal levels, the basis of *cooperative policing.* Erickson (1998, p.53) explains the significance of such cooperation among the levels of law enforcement:

> Through problem- or community-oriented policing, many communities have become extremely competent in dealing with problems within their geographic communities. They are hard-pressed, however, to address problems that are pushed into their communities by outside forces. Obvious examples include drug manufacturing and trafficking, transportation safety issues, auto theft rings, gambling and the interjurisdictional movement of street gangs.

Cooperative policing entails developing partnerships, not only among various agencies of law enforcement, but also among such agencies and the public they serve. According to Erickson (pp.54–55), cooperative policing is built upon a shared responsibility for safe communities, emphasizes effectiveness and excellence in police work and strives to balance enforcing the law with developing community approaches to problem solving. The citizen is the customer, and the community is more than just a geographic site. Erickson (p.59) concludes: "Cooperative policing is consistent with and complementary with local agencies' efforts at problem-oriented or community-oriented policing."

Community Policing, Partnerships and the Decrease in Crime

According to the Bureau of Justice Statistics National Crime Victimization Survey (NCVS), from 1999 to 2000 the violent crime rate declined 15 percent, reaching the lowest level in NCVS history, and property crime declined 10 percent, continuing a more than 20-year decline. Other data from the FBI's Uniform Crime Reports indicates the crime index rate fell for the ninth straight year in 2000, declining 3.3 percent from 1999, 18.9 percent from 1996 and 30.1 percent from 1991 (BJS Web site: www.ojp.usdoj.gov/bjs).

McGarrell, a criminal justice professor and director of Hudson's Crime Control Policy Center, states: "Most observers acknowledge that the national trend toward community policing has been a key catalyst in the decrease [in crime]" (Hall, 1998, p.6). According to McGarrell, three key elements supported by a strong community-police partnership are required for a sizeable decrease in crime to occur: (1) proactive enforcement—the police don't wait for an offense to occur, (2) crime prevention programs and (3) a strong sense of community (Hall, p.6).

Rogers (1998, p.43) reports: "There is a direct correlation between the number of officers on the street and the decline in crime." The decrease in crime, however, cannot all be attributed to community policing efforts. Quality-of-life issues, a robust economy and a population with greater numbers of elderly and fewer juveniles also contribute to lower crime rates. As one criminal justice scholar explained: "When you have a graying population and fewer teenagers, you tend to have less crime. You can almost trace the peaks and valleys to the number of teenagers" (Rogers, p.42).

Some have praised community policing efforts for their ability to reduce citizens' fear of crime. However, caution is needed when evaluating such results. Figure 5.1 presents the theoretical relationship between community policing and citizen fear of crime.

Acknowledging the impediments, criticisms and cautions concerning the community-oriented policing philosophy is a vital step in moving forward to

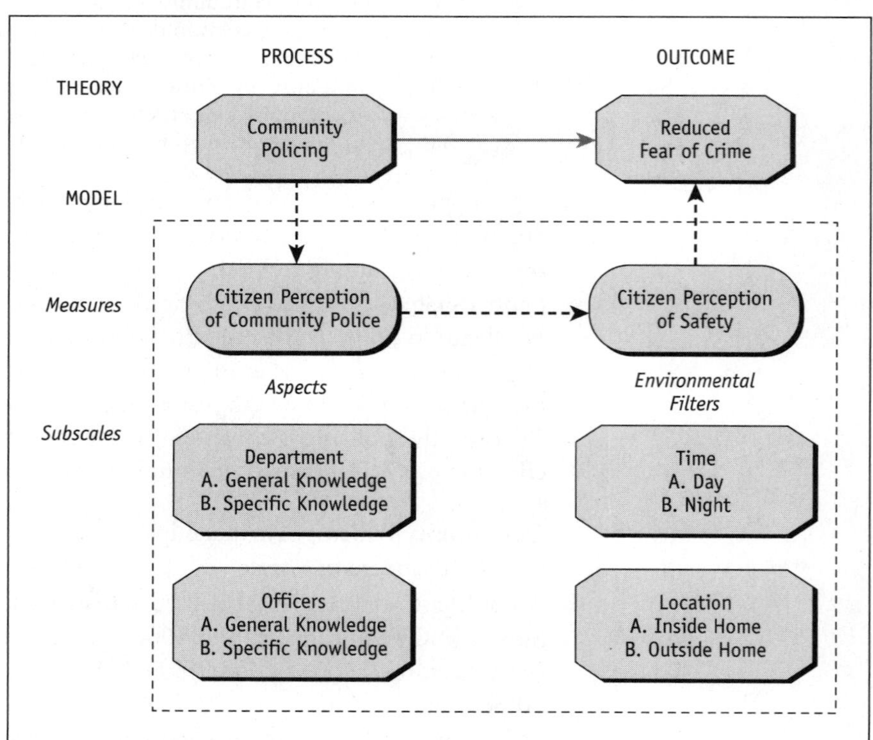

Figure 5.1
Theoretical Relationship between Community Policing and Fear of Crime and Model for Testing Theory

Source: A. Steven Dietz. "Evaluating Community Policing: Quality Police Service and Fear of Crime." *Policing: An International Journal of Police Strategy and Management,* Vol. 20, No. 1, 1997, p. 88. Reprinted by permission.

true police/community partnerships. Another vital step is to adopt a problem-oriented approach to policing, which is, again, proactive rather than reactive.

Problem-Oriented Policing and Problem Solving

Problem-oriented policing and community-oriented policing are sometimes equated. In fact, however, problem-oriented policing is an essential component of community policing. Its focus is on determining the underlying causes of problems, including crime, and identifying solutions. Goldstein, considered the "father of problem-oriented policing," makes the distinction between community-oriented and problem-oriented policing (Rosen, 1997, p.8):

> Community policing . . . is designed to place emphasis on one great need in policing, which is to engage the community, to emphasize the point that the job of social control essentially in our society depends upon networks other than the police, that the police can only facilitate those networks and support them. Problem-oriented policing, on the other hand, places the major emphasis on the need to reconceptualize what the police are doing more generally, to focus attention on the wide range of specific problems that police confront and to try to encourage a more analytical approach to those problems.

Miller and Hess (p.15) assert:

> Where traditionally policing has been *reactive,* responding to calls for service, community policing is *proactive,* anticipating problems and seeking solutions to them. The term *proactive* is beginning to take on an expanded definition. Not only is it taking on the meaning of anticipating problems, but it is also taking on . . . that of accountability and choosing a response rather than reacting the same way each time a similar situation occurs. Police are learning that you do not obtain different results by applying the same methods. In other words, to get different results, you need to apply different tactics.

In highlighting the benefit of problem solving and being proactive, Rahtz (2001, p.57) observes:

> The emphasis on solving problems is what separates our two styles of policing. Reactive Jack's day is dictated by the radio. Anyone in the community who picks up the phone and dials 911 has more control over Jack than his supervisor does. Jack's workday is not informed by any serious analysis of the problems on his beat. Instead, he runs willy-nilly where the radio calls lead. He handles the calls as quickly as possible, and in the time between radio runs he cruises about with little purpose waiting for the next dispatch. For a lot of cops, that is the sum total of police work.
>
> For beat officers tired of the merry-go-round of reactive policing, for cops looking for a more intelligent approach to police work, community policing emphasizing problem solving will be a godsend.

Many law enforcement agencies have now combined the operational strategies of community-oriented policing and problem solving (COPPS) to address a broad range of crime problems and the quality-of-life issues associated with them. Borrello (1998, p.24) elaborates: "COPPS is meant to be a partnership, a shared responsibility based on trust, to reduce crime, violence and fear in our neighborhoods. To many, it is the changing of policing in America."

Problem-oriented policing, a vital component of the community policing philosophy, requires that police move beyond a law enforcement perspective in seeking solutions to problems.

As noted by Goldstein (1990, p.2): "The dominant perspective of policing is heavily influenced by the primary method of control associated with the work—the authority to enforce the criminal law." He suggests that this view has "disproportionately influenced the operating practices, organization, training, and staffing of police agencies." It is like tunnel vision. Effective problem-oriented policing requires abandoning the "simplistic notion that the criminal law defines the police's role" and accepting that "policing consists of developing the most effective means for dealing with a multitude of troublesome situations." He suggests that "these means will often, but not always, include appropriate use of the criminal law."

Goldstein illustrates this change in perspective with the way the police have approached the drug problem, that is, with a law enforcement approach. Gradually the police and the public are coming to realize that this approach, arresting and prosecuting drug dealers, is ineffective. Goldstein contends:

> The challenge is to determine what use should be made by the police of the criminal law (given the difficulty of the process and limited resources); what other means are available to the police for dealing with the problem; and what the police (given their first-hand knowledge of the magnitude and complexity of the problem) should be urging others to do in responding to it.

Spelman and Eck (1987, p.2) explain that problem-oriented policing is the result of 20 years of research into police operations converging on three main themes:

1. *Increased effectiveness* by attacking underlying problems that give rise to incidents that consume patrol and detective time.
2. *Reliance on the expertise and creativity of line officers* to study problems carefully and develop innovative solutions.
3. *Closer involvement with the public* to make sure that the police are addressing the needs of citizens.

They note that problem-oriented policing uses four strategies, often referred to as the **SARA model.**

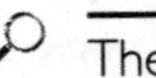

The four strategies of the SARA model of problem-oriented policing are:
1. **S**canning—grouping individual incidents into meaningful "problems."
2. **A**nalyzing—collecting information from all available sources (not just police data).
3. **R**esponding—selecting and implementing solutions.
4. **A**ssessing—evaluating the impact of the solution.

According to Martinez (1998, p.605): "Problem solving is the process of moving toward a goal when the path to that goal is uncertain." Making mistakes is a basic part of this process:

> There is no formula for true problem solving. If we know exactly how to get from point A to point B, then reaching point B does not involve problem solving. Think of problem solving as working your way through a maze. In negotiating a maze, you make your way toward your goal step by step, making some false moves

> but gradually moving closer toward the intended end point. What guides your choices? Perhaps a rule like this: choose the path that seems to result in *some* progress toward the goal. Such a rule is one example of a *heuristic.* A **heuristic** is a rule of thumb. It is a strategy that is powerful and general, but not absolutely guaranteed to work. Heuristics are crucial because they are *the* tools by which problems are solved [boldface added] (Martinez, p.606).

The Crime Triangle

One proposed tool to help law enforcement use problem solving to tackle crime is the crime triangle (Figure 5.2). The Minneapolis Police Department's Repeat Call Address Policing (RECAP) experiment used the crime triangle as part of its strategy. As explained by Buerger (1999, p.151): "Theoretically, the basis for the RECAP strategy lies in Cohen and Felson's Routine Activities Theory (1979), which proposes that crime occurs during the intersection, in time and space, of motivated offenders and suitable victims (or targets), under circumstances of absent or inadequate guardianship: a Crime Triangle similar to the fire triangle of fuel, heat, and oxygen. Crime was presumed amenable to suppression if any of the three legs of the triangle was removed, or neutralized."

As illustrated in the crime triangle, one critical element of crime is location. Criminal justice researchers and practitioners have only recently begun to shift their focus from *people* who commit crimes to *places* where offenses occur. One result of this shift has been the identification of **hot spots,** specific locations with high crime rates. (The term is borrowed from geology in describing areas

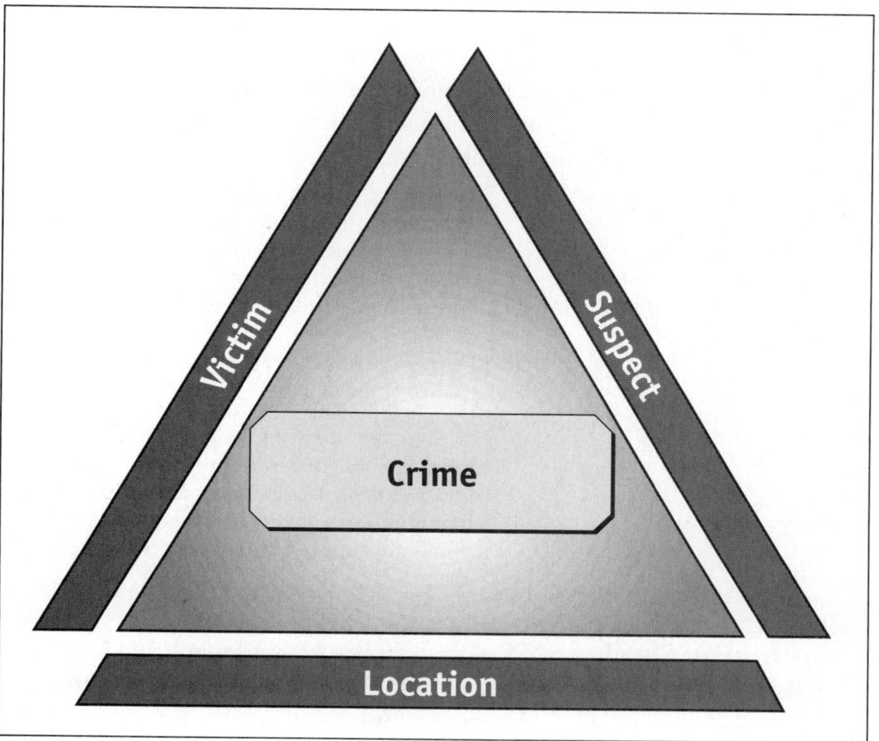

Figure 5.2
The Crime Triangle

where hot magma rises toward the earth's surface, creating the potential for volcanic eruption.) A hot spot may be a single address or intersection, a group of addresses in close proximity to each other or an entire block or more.

Borrowing a concept from ecology, Braiden (1998, p.8) proposes another way to view the significance of location in the problem-solving efforts of policing—"the hunt and the habitat":

> I can't think of two special-interest groups more philosophically opposed to each other than hunters and animal rights activists, yet there are two things they totally agree upon: The species will survive the hunt; it will not survive loss of its habitat.
>
> What can policing learn from this basic principle of nature? Well, if the ultimate goal is to eliminate the criminal species forever, surely the best way to do that is to eliminate the habitat that spawns and sustains that species. Structured as it is, the criminal justice system puts 95 percent of its resources into the hunt while the habitat is left almost untouched. We can never win working that way, because the habitat never stops supplying new customers for the hunt.

So what is law enforcement to do if they hope to sharpen their problem-solving skills and maximize the effectiveness of their efforts? Several long-term solutions have been suggested.

Long-Term Solutions

Continuing with the ecological analogies, communities may be seen as fertile environments, or gardens, able to produce nearly anything if the proper conditions are present. However, like most gardens, weeds (crime) inevitably crop up and need to be removed to allow the more desirable flowers (law-abiding citizens) the necessary room and resources to grow. The federal government's Weed and Seed program was intended to help "groom" communities, planting seeds to help rebuild urban neighborhoods and weeding out the elements of crime, but some have criticized that too much focus has been placed on weeding and not enough on seeding:

> The program has, indeed, helped some communities thin their gardens of people (and conditions) contributing to crime, disorder, and fear. It is the seeding that has been dubious. What if communities, with a helping hand from the police, really could incubate what anthropologist Jane Goodall calls the "roots and shoots"—people and institutions that make for a vibrant, ecologically sound garden (Geller, 1998, p.154)?

Returning to the analogy introduced by the medical model, Glensor and Peak (1998, p.2) assert:

> Like a patient requiring long-term care, neighborhoods plagued with problems require periodic attention to ensure a healthy environment is preserved. In recent years, a growing number of communities that developed and implemented successful community-oriented intervention strategies have wrestled with the problems of maintaining reduced crime levels after the initial intervention has taken place.

A Community Service Orientation

A key strategy of community policing is linking policing to the delivery of city services. Community service translates into customer service. If policing is viewed as a business, its product is service, and its customers are the citizens, businesses, organizations and agencies within its jurisdiction.

Taking a page from the business world, "customer oriented" means providing the best service possible; being courteous, honest, open and fair; treating each person as an individual, not as an inconvenience; listening and being responsive to what each person wants; keeping promises; knowing who to refer people to; and thanking people when they are helpful. Police officers should be "consumer friendly" as they serve and protect. The types of service provided by the police take a variety of forms.

Police departments may provide a wide variety of services including giving information, directions and advice; counseling and referring; licensing and registering vehicles; intervening in domestic arguments; working with neglected and/or abused children; rendering emergency medical or rescue services; dealing with alcoholics and the mentally ill; finding lost children; dealing with stray animals; controlling crowds; and providing community education programs on crime prevention, drug abuse, safety and the like.

Although some police departments have a separate division assigned the responsibilities of community service and some have made community service a responsibility of a patrol team, in reality, community service is a vital part of every police officer's job.

Preserving Community Peace and Safety

"To serve and protect" means different things to different agencies. The National Emergency Number Association (NENA) (2001) reports: "At the end of the 20th century, nearly 93% of the population of the United States was covered by some type of 9-1-1 service. Ninety-five percent of that coverage was Enhanced 9-1-1. Approximately 96% of the geographic US is covered by some type of 9-1-1." According to Burg (1998, p.1), while a majority of 911 calls are for law enforcement assistance, some calls are clearly not the result of a crisis: "People use 911 because it's there, it's handy and they know they'll get a response. They call in for the time of day and numerous other nonemergencies. We once received a 911 call from a woman because she hadn't received her Sunday paper!" Burg asks: "So where do we draw the line? What separates service from servitude? Running from call to call vs. community policing?" Burg's answer:

> I believe that it is essential that officers, in most instances, talk one-on-one with the complainant. . . . If the scenario is to "see the woman," and while you're assisting her in rehanging her drapes, she tells you about the strange glow from her neighbor's house each night, and in following up on that, you discover a marijuana hydroponics operation. . . .
>
> There is no question that we need to strike a balance between "to serve" and community policing. Both are beneficial.

Many citizens use 911 as a local hotline, a number to call to get the right number to call. To help handle the barrage of such calls, some police agencies are going online with Web sites for citizen information and input. The Los Angeles Police Department's Internet Web site:

> . . . directs users to more than half a dozen categories, including Visit Your Community, General Information, Get Involved and Saluting the Heroes.
>
> For those who dread a visit downtown to headquarters for any reason, whether to make a complaint, report a crime or give kudos to an effective officer, those

activities and more can now be done on line—and in a wide variety of languages, including Korean, Chinese and Spanish. More than a dozen hot line and resource telephone numbers are included, too, to report everything from gang violence to child abuse. Crime-related tips can even be submitted anonymously.

Under Frequently Asked Questions (FAQs), the site provides comprehensive answers to some of urban life's less pressing concerns—for example, how to get bulky trash items picked up and how to fight a traffic ticket. On the serious side, LAPDOnline guides users in how to view the state's sex offender index and how Megan's Law operates ("LAPD Unveils . . .," 1998, p.11).

Clearly, serving as a resource is one aspect of law enforcement's duty "to serve." As another part of their role to preserve the peace and safety of the public, police officers may be dispatched to handle calls regarding domestic violence, to intervene in disputes and disturbances, to quell civil disturbances and to maintain order in labor/management disputes and strikes.

Handling Domestic Disputes and Civil Disturbances

Thistlethwaite et al. (1998, p.388) state: "Domestic assault is the most common form of violence encountered by the police." According to some estimates, *family violence and domestic disputes* account for more than 40 percent of all violent crime calls to police (Strandberg, 1998b, p.32). Getz (1998a, pp.45–46) reports: "In all, domestic violence affects the lives of 8 to 15 million people in America when its impact on families is included in the equation. . . . It is a major cause of injury, disability, homelessness, addiction, attempted suicide, child abuse and physical and mental problems."

Paynter (1998, p.23) described the community effort needed in fighting domestic violence: "Successfully prosecuting domestic violence cases inherently depends on your department's ability to work with other agencies, from medical professionals to shelter advocates and social workers. . . . Support also needs to come in the form of both victim and batterer counseling. . . . Statistically, 70 percent of all batterers will beat their spouse again in the absence of counseling and other intervention." Furthermore (p.24): "Taking a proactive position vs. a reactive position toward domestic violence can lower recidivism and ultimately reduce domestic violence–related homicides."

Another common and often dangerous type of call made to the police department is for assistance in settling *disputes or quarrels,* for example bar fights. Often alcohol is involved in such situations. Tempers are short, and the potential for violence is ever present. The potential for disputes and disturbances exists in a variety of situations—parties to traffic crashes, young people blasting stereos and other incidents where hostility may arise. The fine line between obnoxious behavior that infringes on other people's peace and harmless antics that merely defy standards of "good behavior" is easily crossed. Neighborhood residents may be annoyed when teenagers hang out on the streets, and people walking down a city sidewalk may be disturbed by activists passing out political or religious fliers, yet the teenagers and activists each have a legal right to be doing what they are doing.

Civil disturbances and riots present another challenge to police in preserving community peace and safety. The civil disturbances on campuses throughout the country in the 1960s highlighted the role of the police in controlling such

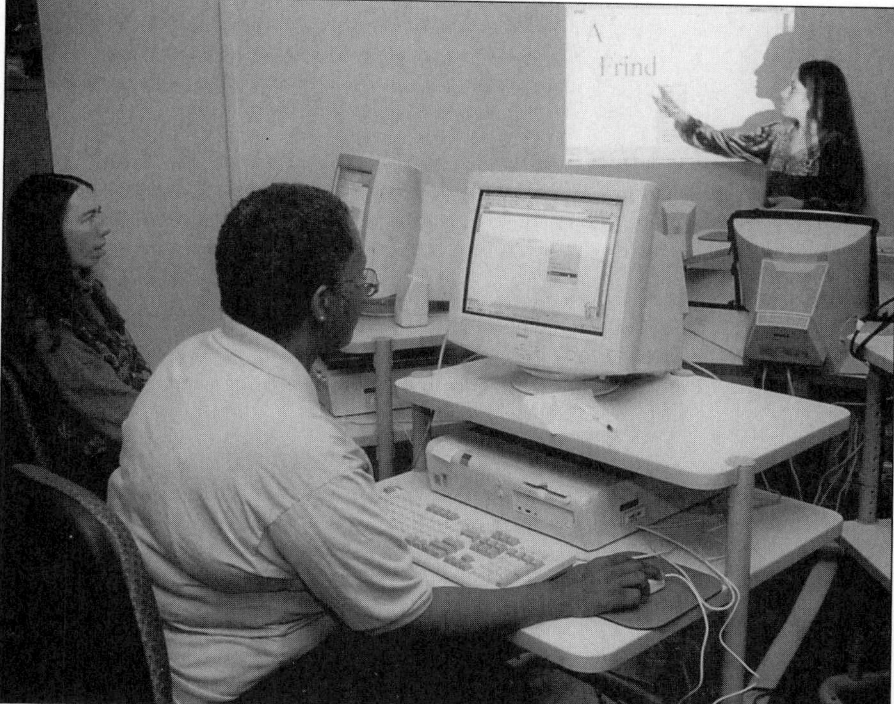

AP Photo/Anna Mia Davidson

At the Jubilee Women's Center in Seattle, a volunteer computer teacher demonstrates how spell check works for two women living in the transitional shelter. One of the women said she married too young, too poor and with too little education. Abused and with no money to pay Seattle's high rent, she found help from the Jubilee Women's Center where she can learn skills to make it on her own.

disturbances. Although civil disturbances are not as prevalent today, demonstrations continue throughout the country—for example antiwar protests, demonstrations against legislative decisions, demonstrations for or against abortion and protests against industries engaged in manufacturing war materials.

In dealing with civil disturbances, the primary responsibilities of police officers are to maintain order and to protect lives and assets. In the event of sit-in demonstrations, it may be necessary to forcibly remove participants. However, police must also be aware of citizens' constitutionally protected right to *peacefully* assemble. Only when the assembly is no longer peaceful do officers have the responsibility to intervene. Determining what constitutes peaceful assembly places a large amount of discretionary power in the hands of police officers.

Civil disturbances may escalate to even greater destructive riots than in Watts. Danaher (1998, p.17) recounts events following the University of Arizona men's basketball team's victory over the heavily favored Kentucky Wildcats at the NCAA finals on March 31, 1997:

> From the time the final game began at 5 P.M., until the final whistle, shortly after 10 P.M., the streets were deserted, the bars were packed but under control. . . .
>
> When the seconds ticked down to zero, a tremendous energy force was unleashed. The bars along Fourth Avenue erupted and the streets quickly began filling with thrilled and intoxicated fans. The pilot in the police helicopter reported thousands of college students on the move from their dorm rooms to the Fourth Avenue area only a few blocks away.
>
> Not helping matters were the media reports that evening, suggesting to fans that THE place to be was on Fourth Avenue. The officers in the area were quickly overwhelmed. . . .

Mark Richards/PhotoEdit

During civil disturbances or riots police are faced with not only controlling the crowds but protecting property. Here police capture looters during a riot and stand ready to protect the property from further looting.

> The media was everywhere with their television cameras and lights, only adding to the frenzy that was being whipped up by the growing crowd. . . .
>
> Just after 1 A.M., when the bars closed, the mood began to turn ugly on northern Fourth Avenue. A crowd of several hundred had gathered and began pelting officers and deputies with rocks and bottles. A contingent of SWAT officers and canine units were rushed to the area. The officers fought back with O.C. and C.S. gas. They deployed "stingball" grenades, Sage gun rounds, and more than 60 high-impact flex baton rounds fired from shotguns. The remnants of the disturbance were finally cleared by 2:30 in the morning.

Because seemingly insignificant events can turn ugly fast, Getz (1998b) asserts that agencies must be prepared for "anything" before anything happens. Consider what occurred in St. Petersburg, Florida, a city recognized as having one of the finest community policing programs in the country (p.86): "Who would have expected that a routine traffic stop would escalate into a white cop shooting a young black man and from there to the two separate riots that rocked the city in the Fall of 1996. . . . What the world saw on the nightly news was St. Petersburg in flames, police officers pinned down by automatic gunfire, stores being looted and a community torn asunder. A sniper attempted to shoot a police helicopter out of the sky."

Labor/management disputes and strikes may also threaten community peace and safety. Strikes are legal, but as with the right to assemble, the strike must be peaceful. If strikers physically restrict others from crossing the picket line, they are acting illegally, and the police may be called to intervene. In such instances police officers must remain neutral. Their only responsibility is to prevent violence and property damage or loss.

Providing Emergency Services

Patrol officers are often the first on the scene of a situation requiring emergency services. For example, at the scene of a traffic accident, police are responsible for providing first aid to any injured persons. They may also be called to help people who have been injured in other ways or who become seriously ill. Police officers should be thoroughly trained and certified in CPR and advanced first aid, including measures to stop bleeding and to deal with fractures, shock, burns and epileptic seizures.

Police officers may be required to transport to the nearest medical facility accident victims or gravely ill or injured people. In fact in some communities, the police department is the sole ambulance service, and patrol cars are specially equipped to serve as ambulances. This policy of providing ambulance service tends to make the public more appreciative of the police department and may foster citizen cooperation.

Natural disasters, such as floods, tornadoes, hurricanes, fires and earthquakes, can produce emergency conditions requiring police action. They may need to provide first aid to victims, provide crowd control and protect the property of those involved. Furthermore, many departments are also actively involved in search-and-rescue operations that may or may not be necessitated by natural disasters.

In some departments police and fire fighting are combined into a public safety department. In such instances police officers must be trained in fire suppression techniques. In departments where the police are not primarily responsible for fire suppression activities, they may still be the first to arrive at the scene of a fire and can lend valuable assistance to the firefighters.

If a bomb threat is made or a bomb is actually found, the police are usually the ones to be notified. In such instances their main responsibility is to assure the safety of those in the bomb's vicinity and to call in experts to actually dispose of the bomb. Frequently a bomb disposal unit of a military installation is called. Larger departments may have their own bomb disposal teams. In the event of an actual explosion, be it intentional or accidental, the police are usually responsible for crowd control and for investigating the incident.

The heroism of law enforcement officers was graphically illustrated in the September 11, 2001, attack on America when officers were rushing to the World Trade Center twin towers as citizens were rushing from it. Twenty-three New York City police officers and 37 Port Authority officers lost their lives in addition to 356 emergency rescue workers who also perished (NYPD Web site, Port Authority Web site and www.vwtcmemorial.com).

Other Community Services

Police departments may or may not provide several other services, depending on local policy, including helping to locate missing persons; investigating damage-to-property incidents; providing a lost and found; dealing with missing and stray animals; providing escort services; assisting people who have locked themselves out of their vehicles or homes; transporting civilians on official business; licensing handguns, parade permits and the like; inspecting buildings for adherence to fire codes, health codes and building codes; inspecting trucks' weights; and answering alarms, which can be a tremendous drain on a police department given the false-alarm problem.

Hundreds of programs have aided the police not only by improving law enforcement efforts but also by enhancing community relations. As police officers' knowledge of the community and its citizens increases, so does their effectiveness as law enforcement officers. Their street contacts and sources of information are also vastly improved. While community acceptance of crime-prevention programs depends on the overall effectiveness of all police operations, it is the individual police officer on the street who serves as the department's community relations officer. The officer's actions, demeanor, appearance and empathy translate into positive or negative community relations.

The police officer on the street is ultimately responsible for the success of police-community relations.

Community relations is a responsibility of both the police and citizens. The majority of police departments in the country have implemented some types of community-oriented programs, the most common being programs for youths, educational programs, block watch programs, special task units and foot or mounted patrol. Other community-oriented programs include block meetings, volunteer programs, business watch, storefront stations, victim contact programs, citizen surveys and community newsletters.

Youth Programs

The youths of our country are of critical importance.

Programs for youths may include PAL programs, school resource officers, McGruff, Explorer posts and the DARE program.

The PAL Program

Police Athletic League (PAL) programs have been in operation for more than 50 years. These programs were developed to give youths opportunities to interact with police officers in sports, providing positive alternative activities. In Portland, Oregon, the police department has adopted the program to deal with increasing gang violence and street sales of drugs. Sports in their program include boxing, wrestling, football, soccer, martial arts, basketball, racquetball, track and field, volleyball and speed and quickness training.

School Resource Officers

Girouard (2001, p.1) states: "Although research continues to show that schools are relatively safe places for children . . . the subject of school safety continues to concern families, school administrators, and communities." The response to this concern is not new; the first police-school liaison program was developed in Flint, Michigan, in 1958.

Atkinson (2001, p.55) asserts: "Demand for school resource officers (SROs) has increased dramatically with heightened public concern about school safety." Lavarello (2000, p.6) adds: "School-based policing programs are now one of the, if not THE, fastest growing areas of law enforcement!" The Omnibus Crime Control and Safe Streets Act of 1968 defines an SRO as "a career law enforcement officer, with sworn authority, deployed in community-oriented policing, and assigned by the employing police department or agency to work in collaboration with school and community-based organizations" (Girouard, p.1).

Atkinson notes that, as public safety specialists, SROs contribute daily to the safety and security of the schools in which they work: "Experience has taught that the presence of an SRO has a deterrent effect on illegal and disruptive behavior" (p.57). Additionally: "In a teaching capacity, an SRO can educate students about their rights and responsibilities according to the law" (Paynter, 1999, p.35).

Operation CleanSWEEP

One innovative response to school crime and violence is Operation CleanSWEEP (Success with Education/Enforcement Partnership), which treats students who've violated certain criminal codes on campus with a combination of retributive and rehabilitative measures. "In other words," Penrod (2001, p.64) explains, "they are both punished and given appropriate counseling to help them avoid problem behavior in the future." Paynter (p.65) continues:

> For many teens, Operation CleanSWEEP represents their first encounter with the notion of personal accountability, and they are meant to feel the sting of a reprimand to their actions. . . . Instead of suspending or expelling the student, the program keeps the offender in the classroom. This allows the student's education to proceed without interruption. . . .
>
> Operation CleanSWEEP is also made up of two other components: a security assessment that inspects schools for safety-related problems, and a speaker's bureau that provides participating campuses with presentations, demonstrations, and guest speakers on a wide variety of crime- and security-related issues.

McGruff

The "McGruff Takes a Bite Out of Crime" program began as a national media campaign using public service announcements from late 1979 to 1981. It was hoped that McGruff would become to crime prevention what Smokey the Bear was to fire prevention. The campaign's four major objectives were to:

- Change citizen feelings about crime and the criminal justice system, particularly feelings of frustration and hopelessness.
- Generate an individual sense of responsibility for reducing crime among citizens.

- Encourage citizens, working within their communities and with local law enforcement agencies, to take collective crime prevention action.
- Enhance existing crime prevention programs at the local, state and national levels.

Police Explorers

Police Explorers are senior Scouts (boys or girls) who volunteer time with a police department. Most departments require three to six months' probation and provide extensive training in personal conduct, first aid, police procedures, weapons familiarization, crime scene investigation, traffic control, radio procedures, interpersonal communication, criminal law and specialized police duties.

Giordano (2001, p.148) describes how one community recruited local teens already involved in the Explorer program to help curb speeding and other traffic problems through an effort called CAN ID (Cadets Assisting Neighborhoods to Identify Driving Violations):

> After a brief training in traffic monitoring practices, including the use of hand-held digital radar detectors, the students or cadets who sign up for CAN ID take to the streets in teams of two to watch for moving violations, which range . . . from "people who blow through stop signs" to those who ignore pedestrians in crosswalks. . . .
>
> The cadets, however, don't hand out tickets to delinquent drivers. Instead, they take their logs back to the department, where with the help of police officers, they run the plate numbers to identify the drivers. A warning letter is sent out to each of the motorists . . . [advising that] future violations will be documented.

DARE

The well-known Drug Abuse Resistance Education (DARE) program was developed jointly by the Los Angeles Police Department and the Los Angeles Unified School District. Its purpose is to teach elementary school children to "say no to drugs," to resist peer pressure to experiment with drugs and to find alternatives to drug use. DARE places police officers in schools to teach kids about self-esteem, the dangers of drugs and how to resist peer pressure to try them.

Evaluation of DARE programs has met with mixed reviews. Supporters of DARE point out that such programs bring millions of children into positive contact with police officers. Other advocates claim it may not be the *content* of the program so much as the *nature* of the program that makes it a success: "I do believe that the program's success can be measured in terms of the positive relationships it offers between the police department and the children we serve and, in turn, their families, the next generation of young adults and of course, our whole community" (Gruber, 1998, p.52).

Others, however, are more critical of the benefits, if any, offered by DARE programs. According to *Law Enforcement News* ("Truth, DARE . . .," 1998, p.1):

> A six-year study that tracked students who took Drug Abuse Awareness Education classes taught by police officers has concluded that the popular program has little effect in persuading youths to stay away from illegal drugs.
>
> The longitudinal study by Dennis P. Rosenbaum, chairman of the Criminal Justice Department at the University of Illinois at Chicago, tracked 1,800 students starting in the fifth and sixth grades, before they began taking DARE courses.

> About 1,100 students were still participating in the study six years later, by which time they were in high school. . . .
> The study found that DARE had little effect on preventing future drug use as the students got older, and in some cases, may have contributed to the likelihood of their involvement in drugs and alcohol.

Other Programs

Programs in the schools, such as lectures and videos about "Children and the Law," have aided police in their fight against vandalism and shoplifting. They reach a segment of society that represents future citizens, informing children of the crime problem in our society and how they might help reduce this problem.

The Beaufort (South Carolina) Police Department is involved in several youth-oriented policing efforts (Kanable, 2000, pp.36, 38). For example, during the summer, the department hosts a Saturday morning Movie Club for elementary school students. During the movie intermission, students are presented with public safety issues ranging from water safety to drug awareness. The Beaufort PD offers a mentoring program for at-risk elementary students, providing weekly one-on-one time for an officer to tutor a child or to simply discuss what kinds of problems the student might have. In the high school, the Beaufort PD teaches a student police academy as part of a leadership class.

In response to a disturbing increase in crimes involving weapons on local school campuses, the San Jose (California) Police Department developed the Safe Alternatives and Violence Education (SAVE) program. As of June 2000, 1,562 students and 1,618 parents had participated in SAVE, "a one-day, six hour class taught primarily by cops, during which the realities of violence as well as the consequences of and responsibilities for bad choices are discussed" ("Short-Term Youth Violence . . .," 2000, p.12). Students referred to the program were those caught with weapons, including knives, guns, brass knuckles and explosives, as well as those who'd been involved in fist fights or who had merely threatened violence. According to program officials, 84 percent of students who participated in SAVE remained violation free a year later, and 78 percent were violation free six years after the class.

The Reno (Nevada) Police Department has developed the Kid's Korner program, which focuses on strengthening ties with families living on the fringe of the community in temporary housing at the city's weekly motels ("Cops Fight Crime . . .," 2000, p.10). Through this "knock-and-talk" program, officers responding to calls at the motels have identified cases of child abuse, situations where parents could not locate their children and instances where youngsters were not registered for school. According to the Bureau of Justice Assistance (BJA): "Kid's Korner, with its emphasis on building positive relationships between law enforcement officers and the residents they serve, is an example of community policing at its finest."

In addition to community programs to help combat crime, many police departments have programs to promote safety and the general welfare of the public. Most such programs are aimed at children, such as bike safety programs.

Community Crime Prevention Programs

Many police departments have instituted programs aimed at preventing crime in the community.

Crime prevention programs include neighborhood or block watch programs, operation identification programs, home security, store security and automobile security.

Neighborhood or Block Watch Programs

Block watch programs instruct homeowners to form cooperative groups to deter burglaries and thefts when homeowners are away and to provide safe places for children who might be threatened on their way to or from school. Such neighborhood watch programs bring neighbors together in an effort to reduce the incidence of crime in their neighborhood. The program helps homeowners know their neighbors and their neighbors' daily routines. They are encouraged to report suspicious activities or persons in their neighborhood to the police.

With the cooperation and involvement of all citizens, such as sharing the responsibility of checking neighbors' homes when they are on vacation, the neighborhood is a safer place to live. Most programs emphasize that residents should *not* try to apprehend suspects, so programs do not create "vigilante" actions.

These citizen crime-reporting programs (CCRPs) are the most widely used police-community crime-prevention programs in the country. These groups serve as "eyes and ears" for the police. Signs stating that the neighborhood is involved in a CCRP are usually prominently displayed at curbside, as well as on the homes or apartments themselves. Often such programs lead to establishing property identification programs.

Operation Identification Programs

Police have also implemented operation identification programs in which citizens are loaned markers to identify their property with a permanent identification number. If these items are lost or stolen and recovered by the police, the identification number provides a method of identifying the rightful owner. If the items are found in the possession of a burglar or thief, the number can help police prosecute and convict the suspect. Stickers and decals are given to citizens so they can place warnings on their doors and windows to deter burglars from trying to steal that property (see Figure 5.3).

Home Security

Police officers may go to a citizen's home, evaluate its security and suggest methods for making the home a less inviting target for crime. Recommendations may be made to install deadbolt locks, improve lighting and so on. In some communities, a subsidy is available for making recommended changes.

Store Security

Police departments may also help store owners reduce losses from shoplifting by studying their stores and recommending action. Recommendations might include hiring store detectives; implementing educational campaigns; installing convex, wide-angle mirrors in isolated areas; installing closed-circuit television cameras or installing electronic systems using special magnetic or microwave-sensitive tags. The tags require a deactivating device or a special tool to remove

Figure 5.3
Operation I.D. Sticker

Source: Courtesy of Minnesota Crime Watch—Department of Public Safety.

them without damaging the merchandise. If a customer leaves an area of the store before a salesperson removes the tag or deactivates it, a sensor sounds an alarm, and store personnel apprehend and detain the suspect for the police.

Often crime prevention through environmental design **(CPTED)** is an integral part of these programs. Based on Oscar Newman's concept of "defensible space," CPTED uses access control, lighting and surveillance as key strategies of **target hardening,** that is, making it more difficult for crime to occur.

Automobile Security

Because of the vulnerability of autos to theft, many antitheft programs and devices have been introduced to make it more difficult for a person to steal a car and more difficult for that person to use or sell it without its stolen nature being detected.

Automobile manufacturers have contributed by making the ignition switch mechanism lock the steering wheel and by having a separate steering post lock key and door lock key. Some police agencies have placed on every parking meter a sticker asking, "Have you locked your car?" and provided dashboard stickers that remind motorists, "Have you taken your keys and locked your car?"

Some cities have encouraged used-car dealers to fence in their lots or chain their entrances and exits. Public education campaigns have also been instituted using newspaper, radio, television and placard publicity, as well as bumper stickers with slogans reminding motorists to lock their cars.

An innovative anti–auto-theft program using modern technology is the Lo-Jack Auto Recovery System (LARS), which uses a homing device installed in a customer's car that is automatically activated if the car is reported stolen.

A less expensive, less high-tech program is the Combat Auto Theft (CAT) program initiated in New York City in 1988. In this program a special decal is placed in the car's rear window. The police can stop any vehicle with this decal they see being driven between 1 A.M. and 5 A.M. without probable cause for the stop. In this voluntary program, car owners who normally do not operate their vehicles during these hours sign a consent form and are given the CAT decal to affix prominently on the inside of the car's rear window.

What Works/What Doesn't

According to Sherman et al. (1998, p.1), a systematic review of more than 500 scientific evaluations of crime prevention practices has led to the following conclusion: "Enough evidence is available . . . to create provisional lists of what works, what doesn't, and what's promising." The results of this review were presented in a 1997 report to Congress. Tables 5.2, 5.3 and 5.4 outline the findings.

Table 5.2
Crime Prevention Programs That Work

- **For infants:** Frequent home visits by nurses and other professionals
- **For preschoolers:** Classes with weekly home visits by preschool teachers
- **For delinquent and at-risk preadolescents:** Family therapy and parent training
- **For schools:**
  - —Organizational development for innovation
  - —Communication and reinforcement of clear, consistent norms
  - —Teaching of social competency skills
  - —Coaching of high-risk youth in "thinking skills"
- **For older male ex-offenders:** Vocational training
- **For rental housing with drug dealing:** Nuisance abatement action on landlords
- **For high-crime hot spots:** Extra police patrols
- **For high-risk repeat offenders:**
  - —Monitoring by specialized police units
  - —Incarceration
- **For domestic abusers who are employed:** On-scene arrests
- **For convicted offenders:** Rehabilitation programs with risk-focused treatments
- **For drug-using offenders in prison:** Therapeutic community treatment programs

Source: Lawrence W. Sherman et al. *Preventing Crime: What Works, What Doesn't, What's Promising.* National Institute of Justice Research in Brief, July 1998, p. 1.

Table 5.3
Crime Prevention Programs That Don't Work

- Gun "buyback" programs
- Community mobilization against crime in high-crime poverty areas
- Police counseling visits to homes of couples days after domestic violence incidents
- Counseling and peer counseling of students in schools
- Drug Abuse Resistance Education (DARE)
- Drug prevention classes focused on fear and other emotional appeals, including self-esteem
- School-based leisure-time enrichment programs
- Summer jobs or subsidized work programs for at-risk youth
- Short-term, nonresidential training programs for at-risk youth
- Diversion from court to job training as a condition of case dismissal
- Neighborhood watch programs organized with police
- Arrests of juveniles for minor offenses
- Arrests of unemployed suspects for domestic assault
- Increased arrests or raids on drug market locations
- Storefront police officers
- Police newsletters with local crime information
- Correctional boot camps using traditional military basic training
- "Scared Straight" programs whereby minor juvenile offenders visit adult prisons
- Shock probation, shock parole and split sentences adding jail time to probation or parole
- Home detention with electronic monitoring
- Intensive supervision on parole or probation (ISP)
- Rehabilitation programs using vague, unstructured counseling
- Residential programs for juvenile offenders using challenging experiences in rural settings

Source: Lawrence W. Sherman et al. *Preventing Crime: What Works, What Doesn't, What's Promising.* National Institute of Justice Research in Brief, July 1998, p. 7.

Table 5.4
Crime Prevention Programs That Are Promising

- **Proactive drunk driving arrests with breath testing** (may reduce accident deaths)
- **Community policing with meetings to set priorities** (may reduce perceptions of crime)
- **Police showing greater respect to arrested offenders** (may reduce repeat offending)
- **Polite field interrogations of suspicious persons** (may reduce street crime)
- **Mailing arrest warrants to domestic violence suspects who leave the scene before police arrive**
- **Higher numbers of police officers in cities** (may reduce crime generally)
- **Gang monitoring by community workers and probation and police officers**
- **Community-based mentoring by Big Brothers/Big Sisters of America** (may prevent drug abuse)
- **Community-based afterschool recreation programs** (may reduce local juvenile crime)
- **Battered women's shelters** (may help some women reduce repeat domestic violence)
- **"Schools within schools" that group students into smaller units** (may prevent crime)
- **Training or coaching in "thinking" skills for high-risk youth** (may prevent crime)
- **Building school capacity through organizational development** (may prevent substance abuse)
- **Improved classroom management and instructional techniques** (may reduce alcohol use)
- **Job Corps residential training programs for at-risk youth** (may reduce felonies)
- **Prison-based vocational education programs for adult inmates** (in federal prisons)
- **Moving urban public housing residents to suburban homes** (may reduce risk factors for crime)
- **Enterprise zones** (may reduce area unemployment, a risk factor for crime)
- **Two clerks in already-robbed convenience stores** (may reduce robbery)
- **Redesigned layout of retail stores** (may reduce shoplifting)
- **Improved training and management of bar and tavern staff** (may reduce violence, DUI)
- **Metal detectors** (may reduce skyjacking, weapon carrying in schools)
- **Street closures, barricades and rerouting** (may reduce violence, burglary)
- **"Target hardening"** (may reduce vandalism of parking meters and crime involving phones)
- **"Problem-solving" analysis unique to the crime situation at each location**
- **Proactive arrests for carrying concealed weapons** (may reduce gun crime)
- **Drug courts** (may reduce repeat offending)
- **Drug treatment in jails followed by urine testing in the community**
- **Intensive supervision and aftercare of juvenile offenders** (both minor and serious)
- **Fines for criminal acts**

Source: Lawrence W. Sherman et al. *Preventing Crime: What Works, What Doesn't, What's Promising.* National Institute of Justice Research in Brief, July 1998, p. 10.

Services and Programs That Implement Community Policing

The community policing movement has had a profound impact on community service, particularly on services in the "promising" category. Programs that have not succeeded have often been implemented in agencies whose approach was more traditional, where community policing was seen merely as a way of operating, not as an overall philosophy of policing. Providing services to a community is more complex now than in previous times.

Challenges to Community Policing

Despite the many advantages and benefits of community policing, its implementation is not without challenges. Critics and skeptics exist both internally, among officers and police managers, and externally, in the community at large. Furthermore, even when the community policing philosophy has the support of the department and the public, our increasingly diverse population presents an ever-expanding challenge to community policing efforts.

Resistance and Misguided Perceptions

Many officers have difficulty accepting or appreciating the community-oriented policing philosophy. Some wonder whether officers will or should readily accept the increased accountability that accompanies greater decision-making responsibilities. Others question the willingness of police administrators to embrace decentralization, to "loosen the reins" and empower officers with greater authority, responsibility and decision-making capabilities. These organizational impediments are some of the chief barriers to implementation.

Other challenges to implementation include community resistance, a concern that community-oriented policing is "soft" on crime and structural impediments involved with making the change from a reactive to a proactive policing mission. The impediment of limited resources is also a reality: how to simultaneously respond to calls for service, solve crimes and conduct activities involved with community policing. Another large obstacle is the difficulty of changing the police culture.

The perception that community policing goes against aggressive law enforcement practices is perhaps one of the most difficult impediments to overcome. No agency wishes to be perceived as "softies," and no community wants to place crime control and safety in the hands of "pushovers." However, the goals of community policing and aggressive enforcement are not mutually exclusive. The combination of these two elements has been termed **integrated patrol.**

Benefits of Community Policing to Officers

To help overcome doubts and misperceptions about the strength and virtue of the community policing philosophy, it is valuable to note studies that demonstrate that community policing benefits not only the community but the participating officers as well. Sherwood (2000, pp.208–209) asserts:

> The data do suggest that departments that make changes in their structure and function toward a more community-based system of policing are better positioned to bring about job enrichment. . . .
>
> Allowing officers to work regularly with neighborhood residents creates a natural work unit that will increase skill variety and task identity. Furthermore, by granting police officers the increased responsibility and authority to engage in proactive problem solving, managers enhance the vertical loading of the job and increase autonomy. Combining tasks into a more identifiable and complete piece of work to be performed by the officer also strengthens skill variety and task identity.

Such enhanced skill variety and task identity abilities are vitally important for community policing officers faced with serving and protecting an increasingly diverse population.

Serving and Protecting Our Increasingly Diverse Population

Our society has changed tremendously over the past decades, as have the challenges facing law enforcement. Technology has made the task easier, but the increasing diversity of our population has made it more difficult. In addition although poverty has always existed in the United States, the gap between those who live in poverty and those who are more affluent is widening. The **American Dream,** that anyone can succeed through hard work and sacrifice, is becoming much more difficult to attain, not only for members of minority groups but also for middle-class people of all ethnic and racial backgrounds. A college education, the traditional key to "getting ahead," is becoming prohibitively expensive for many youths. Jobs are harder to find. Many high-paying assembly line and factory jobs have been mechanized and computerized.

Our elderly population is increasing rapidly, as is our minority population. In addition hundreds of thousands of immigrants are pouring into the United States, a great many of whom speak no English. The homeless population is growing at an alarming rate, and the number of people with infectious diseases is also escalating. Each of these populations presents a challenge to police.

Our population is becoming older and has more minorities, more immigrants, more homeless people and more individuals with infectious diseases. In addition the gap between those who live in poverty and those who are more affluent is widening.

The Growing Elderly Population

Our elderly population is growing and will continue to do so. In 1996 the first wave of "baby boomers" turned 50. In the twenty-first century, the financial burden of caring for our elderly, the majority of whom are white, will fall to an increasing number of minority members who themselves may be struggling financially. Further, as the "graying of America" continues, more people with Alzheimer's disease will be in our communities, presenting an additional challenge to law enforcement. As Strandberg (1998a, p.46) notes:

> Alzheimer's . . . is one of the problems law enforcement faces more and more frequently across the country.
>
> Four million Americans have Alzheimer's disease. [It affects] one in 10 people over the age of 65 and one half of people over the age of 85. . . . It is estimated that 14 million Americans will have Alzheimer's disease by the middle of the [twenty-first] century unless a cure or prevention is found. . . .
>
> Law enforcement can't afford to ignore these numbers. It might be wandering, it might be shoplifting, it might be an emotionally charged confrontation—it can be any number of situations—and it might be Alzheimer's.

The Growing Minority Population

Demographers, individuals who study the characteristics of human populations, predict that in less than 100 years, white dominance of the United States will end. **De facto segregation** continues to keep many minorities trapped in decaying crime- and drug-riddled, inner-city neighborhoods. Of particular concern is that many minority members live in ghettos. A **ghetto** is an area of a city in which people of a specific ethnic or racial group live in poverty. The frustrations, sense of futility and failure experienced by those who live in ghettos have been described as the **ghetto syndrome**—a vicious cycle of poverty and welfare dependency leading to inability to go to college or prepare for a good-paying job, leading to lack of motivation, further unemployment, poverty and welfare dependency.

Adding to the growing minority population is the ever-increasing number of immigrants.

The Growing Immigrant Population

White Anglo-Saxons were not the original inhabitants of North America. Aside from Native Americans, the settlers of this country were all immigrants, primarily of European descent. In fact, Europeans constituted more than 80 percent of all immigrants throughout the nineteenth century and remained the primary "type" of immigrant until the 1960s. However, during the 1970s, nearly 4.5 million immigrants entered the United States, and more than 7 million arrived in the 1980s. At least 80 percent of these immigrants came from Latin America or Asia. From 1994 to 1997, between 700,000 and 900,000 immigrants became permanent U.S. residents each year, the overwhelming majority of whom came from Mexico and Asia ("Immigration," 2001).

Recent immigrants tend to cluster in specific areas, often in poor neighborhoods that have high crime rates. Consequently the tendency is to **stereotype** them as being involved in crime, when as often as not they are victims rather than perpetrators. The majority of immigrants are law-abiding, trying to build a new life and fit into our society.

Many immigrants speak no English and fear the authorities. They are very likely to become victims, particularly of violent crime. Compounding this problem is the fear and lack of respect many immigrants hold for authorities of law. This distrust and unfamiliarity with our customs can result in volatile situations. For example the commonly used arrest position of having a suspect kneel, back to the officer with hands clasped behind the head, is the position used for executions in Vietnam. Distrust of law enforcement often leads to another problem—failure to report crime and victimization.

Major challenges presented by immigrants are language barriers, unfamiliar customs and failure to report victimization.

In addition to problems of crime, problems also arise when others in the community believe the new immigrants are taking their jobs. For example, in St. Paul, Minnesota, blacks and whites have banded together to resist the competition from the influx of Hmongs.

Another challenge is that of the thousands of *illegal* immigrants entering the United States each year. These immigrants will avoid coming into contact with the police for fear of deportation. They are especially easy targets for those who would take advantage of them.

The Growing Homeless Population

The homeless problem can be found throughout the United States. Among the three million plus homeless people in the United States are veterans, the mentally ill, the physically disabled or chronically ill, the elderly, families, single parents, runaway children, alcoholics/drug abusers, immigrants and traditional tramps, hobos and transients. A large number of mentally ill people are homeless partially as the result of the **deinstitutionalization** policies of the mid-1960s and 1970s, by which hundreds of thousands of mentally ill patients were discharged from state psychiatric facilities. Where sleeping on the streets is illegal, what begins as a social problem becomes a law enforcement problem.

The public often pressures the police to "do something" about homeless people, yet often the only thing officers can do is persuade street people to move along. Until a homeless person breaks the law by panhandling, trespassing, breaking into buildings, shoplifting, dealing drugs or committing some other offense, police power to arrest that person is limited by statutes and laws.

The challenge in dealing with homeless people is to balance compassion for them with the public's right to be free from interference.

As with the newly arrived immigrants, homeless people are also a challenge to law enforcement because they are often victims. What limited possessions they have may be stolen. They may be assaulted, and they have no phone from which to call 911.

The Growing Number of Individuals with AIDS and Other Infectious Diseases

Heiskell and Tang (1998, p.34) report:

> While law enforcement officers have an extremely small chance of contracting a disease on the job, hardly a day passes that policing personnel do not come in contact with crime victims and suspects who are infected with diseases. Many times, officers may not even know that a certain individual they are dealing with has a disease—perhaps even a contagious one. Two diseases that should be of particular concern to police officers are AIDS and hepatitis B.

AIDS is a spectrum of reactions to the human immunodeficiency virus (HIV), which infects and destroys specific white blood cells, undermining the body's ability to fight infection. A person can be infected with HIV and remain symptom-free for years, but even without symptoms that person can transmit the virus to others.

The AIDS virus is most commonly transmitted by exposure to contaminated blood, semen and vaginal secretions, primarily through sexual intercourse and needle-sharing by intravenous drug users; from a mother to her fetus during pregnancy; and through infected blood transfusions. Fortunately the virus is fairly fragile outside the body and can be destroyed by heat, common household disinfectants, bleach and even by soap and water. Those at high risk of contracting HIV include intravenous drug users, homosexuals and individuals having sexual contacts with people in these groups, including prostitutes.

The growing number of individuals with AIDS is of concern to law enforcement. An estimated 40,000 new HIV infections occur in the United States each year. In 2000, between 800,000 and 900,000 U.S. residents were HIV-positive and another 300,000 had full-blown AIDS ("Acquired Immunodeficiency Syndrome," 2001).

Although the AIDS virus causes the greatest concern for most police officers, greater danger lies with tuberculosis (TB), hepatitis and meningitis. The hazards posed by infectious diseases can be avoided by not drinking, smoking, eating or chewing gum at a crime scene, and by wearing protective gloves.

The Growing Number of Individuals with Disabilities

An estimated 43 million people in the United States—more than one-sixth or 17 percent of our population—have physical or mental disabilities, making them the largest minority in the country. This includes the hearing impaired, the severely visually impaired, those who use wheelchairs and those with mental retardation.

With the passage of the Americans with Disabilities Act of 1990, more people with disabilities are in the mainstream. Title III of this act states: "No individual shall be discriminated against on the basis of disability in the full and equal enjoyment of the goods, services, facilities, privileges, advantages, or accommodations of any place of public accommodation." This affects every police agency in the country in that it must be made accessible to individuals with disabilities.

Further those in law enforcement must learn to distinguish between behaviors resulting from disabling conditions and those resulting from excessive alcohol use or the use of drugs. Among the disabling conditions that might be mistaken for inebriation or a drug high are epilepsy, diabetes, Alzheimer's disease, carbon monoxide poisoning, mental retardation or certain types of head injury. Again education and training are vital.

Consider the plight of a man at the airport to take a business trip who becomes disoriented and dizzy. He wanders around the airport for several hours, appearing intoxicated, asking everyone he sees in uniform for help or to call an ambulance. He is ignored, thought to be a drunk. Finally his condition deteriorates to the point he can't talk, so he shows his driver's license to a taxi driver who takes him home. He staggers to the front door and begins pounding on it. His wife, alarmed, thinks it's a prowler and calls the police. When they arrive they find him sprawled out on the ground "dead drunk" and place him under arrest. When his wife comes outside, she is horrified and says he must be ill. They take him to the hospital where he is diagnosed with a malignant brain tumor, causing his brain to swell, resulting in the *appearance* of intoxication. Such are the makings of lawsuits against police officers and their departments.

The Widening Gap between the Rich and Poor

Law enforcement must also be concerned with the dynamics of economics in this country because money, or lack of it, is often the basis for criminal activity. This widening gap and the increase in the number of people trying to exist below the poverty line translates into potentially more theft and the types of violence that accompany offenses motivated by economic gain.

A Final Note on Diversity

Although our varied population presents a challenge to policing, such diversity also bolsters the staying power of community policing. As Plummer (1999, p.99) contends: "Community policing implies appreciation for diversity in the way we look, think, and act, and our willingness to accept diversity as expressed in our communities." The mission statement of the St. Paul (Minnesota) Police Department, which reads, "The St. Paul Police Department will be more reflective of and more responsive to the community we serve," encapsulates this philosophy of respecting diversity:

> By "reflective," we mean that we will do our best to represent the diversity that exists in our community, in as many dimensions as we can, within the sworn and civilian population of the organization. By "responsive," we mean that we will establish communications with all our communities so that we understand their issues and concerns (Finney, 2000, p.4).

Plummer (pp.101–102) concludes: "Community policing is not a gimmick or shallow program. It is a mindset and philosophy fueled by inclusion, tolerance, and good old-fashioned police work."

Summary

Many law enforcement agencies are adopting community policing, a philosophy that stresses working proactively with citizens to prevent crime and to solve crime-related problems. The four major dimensions of community policing are (1) philosophical, (2) strategic, (3) tactical and (4) organizational. Two critical elements of community policing are partnerships and problem solving. Problem-oriented policing requires that police move beyond a law enforcement perspective in seeking solutions to problems. Problem-oriented policing (the SARA model) uses four strategies: (1) scanning—grouping individual incidents into meaningful "problems," (2) analyzing—collecting information from all available sources, (3) responding—selecting and implementing solutions and (4) assessing—evaluating the impact of the solution.

Community policing also promotes a community-service focus. Departments may provide a wide variety of services, including giving information, directions and advice; counseling and referring; licensing and registering vehicles; intervening in domestic arguments or in disputes and quarrels; working with neglected and/or abused children; rendering emergency medical or rescue services; dealing with alcoholics and the mentally ill; finding lost children; dealing with stray animals; controlling crowds; and providing community education programs on crime prevention, drug abuse, safety and the like. Such efforts are important, as the police officer on the street is ultimately responsible for the success of police-community relations.

Programs for youths may include PAL programs, school resource officers, McGruff, Explorer posts and the DARE program. Crime prevention programs include neighborhood or block watch programs, operation identification programs, home security, store security and automobile security.

Community policing requires much interaction with citizens, a particular challenge given the increasing diversity of our citizenry. Our population is becoming older and has more minorities, more immigrants, more homeless people and more individuals with infectious diseases. In addition the gap between those who live in poverty and those who are more affluent is widening. Major challenges presented by immigrants are language barriers, unfamiliar customs and failure to report victimization. The challenge in dealing with those who are homeless is to balance compassion for those "on the streets" with the public's right to be free from interference.

Discussion Questions

1. What community services are available in your community? Which are most important? Which might be frivolous? Are any necessary services not provided?
2. What do you feel are the greatest strengths of community policing?
3. What is the relationship of problem-oriented policing to community policing?
4. What basic similarities and differences exist between community policing and such systems as the tithing system?
5. Might community policing dilute the power and authority of the police?
6. Which "growing population" discussed in this chapter do you feel is the greatest challenge to law enforcement? Why?
7. Are community policing and problem solving important in your police department?
8. What do you see as the greatest impediment to implementing community policing? Problem-oriented policing?
9. Which position do you favor for dealing with the homeless: strict enforcement, benign neglect or somewhere in between?
10. What do you see as the greatest benefit of community policing and problem-oriented policing?

InfoTrac *College Edition Assignment*

Use InfoTrac College Edition to help answer the Discussion Questions as appropriate.

- Use InfoTrac College Edition to find "What Taxpayers Need to Know about COPS," an article describing the intentions of the Violent Crime Control Act of 1994 designed to reinforce community policing. List the results of this act, and be prepared to discuss your list with the class.

Internet Assignment

Use the search engine Google.com to find a number of community policing programs that failed. List them and comment on why they failed. Be prepared to share your comments with the class.

Book-Specific Web Site

The book-specific Web site at http://info.wadsworth.com/0534552803 hosts a variety of resources for students and instructors. Included are extended activities from each chapter in which students write a policy, use critical thinking skills to make choices in response to a given scenario, use InfoTrac College Edition with direct links to articles for participation in topical discussion forums, and analyze court cases using Web links for research. Many activities can be printed or emailed to instructors. Plus, cited cases with Web links, interactive key term FlashCards, PowerPoint presentations, chapter objectives, and an extensive collection of chapter-based Web links provide additional information and activities to include in the curriculum.

References

Abshire, Richard and Paynter, Ronnie L. "Putting the 'Community' in Community Policing." *Law Enforcement Technology,* October 2000, pp.50–58.

"Acquired Immunodeficiency Syndrome." Microsoft® Encarta® Online Encyclopedia 2001. http://encarta.msn.com

Atkinson, Anne J. "School Resource Officers: Making Schools Safer and More Effective." *The Police Chief,* March 2001, pp.55–63.

Borrello, Andrew J. "Community Oriented Policing: Is It Nonsense or Success?" *Police,* October 1998, pp.24–32.

Braiden, Chris. "Policing—The Hunt and the Habitat." *Law Enforcement News,* October 31, 1998, pp.8, 10.

Broder, David S. "Urban Renewal Even the GOP Could Love." *The Washington Post,* May 9, 2001, p.A31.

Brown, Jim. "Community Policing Reality Check." *Law and Order,* April 2001, pp.55–58.

Buerger, Michael E. "The Problems of Problem-Solving." In *Policing Perspectives: An Anthology,* edited by Larry K. Gaines and Gary W. Cordner. Los Angeles: Roxbury Publishing Company, 1999, pp.150–169.

Bureau of Justice Statistics Web site: http://www.ojp.usdoj.gov/bjs

Burg, Mike. "To Serve and Protect?" *Police,* December 1998, pp.1, 52.

"Cops Fight Crime by Investing in Kids." *Law Enforcement News,* September 15, 2000, p.10.

Cordner, Gary W. "Elements of Community Policing." In *Policing Perspectives: An Anthology,* edited by Larry K. Gaines and Gary W. Cordner. Los Angeles: Roxbury Publishing Company, 1999, pp.137–149.

Danaher, Kevin. "Genesis of a Sports Riot: When Celebratory Crowds Lose Control." *Police,* June 1998, pp.16–21.

Erickson, Lee C. "Cooperative Policing: Bridging the Gap of Community Policing." *The Police Chief,* July 1998, pp.53–59.

Finney, William K. "Providing Proper Police Service in the 21st Century." *Community Policing Exchange,* January/February 2000, p.4.

Gaines, Larry K. and Cordner, Gary W. *Policing Perspectives: An Anthology.* Los Angeles: Roxbury Publishing Company, 1999.

Gehrand, Keith. "University Policing and the Community." *Law and Order,* December 2000, pp.111–117.

Geller, William A. "As a Blade of Grass Cuts through Stone: Helping Rebuild Urban Neighborhoods through Unconventional Police-Community Partnerships." *Crime and Delinquency,* January 1998, pp.154–177.

Getz, Ronald J. "Largo Police Attack Domestic Violence." *Law and Order,* November 1998a, pp.44–50.

Getz, Ronald J. "Lessons Learned from the St. Petersburg Riots." *Law and Order,* May 1998b, pp.86–92.

Giordano, Alice. "Teen Drivers Turn into Speed Busters." *Law and Order,* July 2001, pp.148–149.

Girouard, Cathy. *School Resource Officer Training Program.* Washington, DC: Office of Juvenile Justice and Delinquency Prevention, Fact Sheet #05, March 2001. (FS-200105)

Glensor, Ronald W. and Peak, Kenneth. "Lasting Impact: Maintaining Neighborhood Order." *FBI Law Enforcement Bulletin,* March 1998, pp.1–7.

Goldstein, Herman. *Problem-Oriented Policing.* New York: McGraw-Hill, 1990.

Gruber, Charles A. "A Positive Evaluation of DARE." *Law and Order,* April 1998, p.52.

Haldar, Sujoy. "NYC Cabbies Extend Police Reach." *Community Links,* March 2001, p.13.

Hall, Dennis. "More Evidence to Enlist Your Town in the Fight against Crime." *Police,* June 1998, p.6.

Harpold, Joseph A. "A Medical Model for Community Policing." *FBI Law Enforcement Bulletin,* June 2000, pp.23–27.

Heiskell, Lawrence E. and Tang, David H. "AIDS and Hepatitis: What Are the Risks to Police Officers?" *Police,* January 1998, pp.34–36.

Herbert, Bob. "Championing Cities." *The New York Times,* April 26, 2001, p.A23.

Hickman, Matthew J. and Reaves, Brian A. *Community Policing in Local Police Departments, 1997 and 1999.* Washington, DC: Bureau of Justice Statistics Special Report, February 2001. (NCJ 184794)

"Immigration." Microsoft® Encarta® Online Encyclopedia 2001. http://encarta.msn.com

Kanable, Rebecca. "Community Policing at Its Best." *Law Enforcement Technology,* October 2000, pp.34–40.

"LAPD Unveils Its 'One-Stop Shopping' Web Site." *Law Enforcement News,* October 31, 1998, p.11.

Lavarello, Curtis. "School Based Policing: Specialized Training Will Ease Liability." *ASLET,* November/December 2000, pp.6, 51.

Martinez, Michael E. "What Is Problem Solving?" *Phi Delta Kappan,* April 1998, pp.605–609.

McEwen, Tom. "Chicago's Bold Experiment in Policing." *Law Enforcement News,* January 31, 1998, pp.13–14.

Miller, Linda S. and Hess, Kären M. *The Police in the Community: Strategies for the 21st Century,* 3rd ed. Belmont, CA: West/Wadsworth Publishing Company, 2002.

National Emergency Number Association. http://www.nena9-1-1.org, 2001.

O'Shea, Timothy C. "The Political Dimension of Community Policing: Belief Congruence between Police and Citizens." *Police Quarterly,* December 2000, pp.389–412.

Paynter, Ronnie L. "Breaking the Code of Silence." *Law Enforcement Technology,* June 1998, pp.20–24.

Paynter, Ronnie L. "Policing the Schools." *Law Enforcement Technology,* October 1999, pp.34–39.

Paynter, Ronnie L. "Privatization: Something to Think About?" *Law Enforcement Technology,* September 2000, p.6.

Penrod, Gary S. "Operation CleanSWEEP: The School Safety Program That Earned an A-Plus." *The Police Chief,* March 2001, pp.64–65.

Plummer, Larry C. "Community Policing: Thriving Because It Works." *Police Quarterly,* March 1999, pp.96–102.

Rahtz, Howard. *Community-Oriented Policing: A Handbook for Beat Cops and Supervisors.* Monsey, NY: Criminal Justice Press, 2001.

Rogers, Donna. "Community Policing and the Crime Rate." *Law Enforcement Technology,* October 1998, pp.42–44.

Rosen, Marie Simonetti. "A LEN Interview with Professor Herman Goldstein, the 'Father' of Problem-Oriented Policing." *Law Enforcement News,* February 14, 1997, pp.8–10.

Seamon, Thomas. "IACP's Private Sector Liaison Committee: Partners in Public Safety." *The Police Chief,* June 1999, pp.17–21.

Sherman, Lawrence W.; Gottfredson, Denise C.; MacKenzie, Doris L.; Eck, John; Reuter, Peter; and Bushway, Shawn D.

Preventing Crime: What Works, What Doesn't, What's Promising. National Institute of Justice Research in Brief, July 1998. (NCJ 171676)

Sherwood, Charles W. "Job Design, Community Policing, and Higher Eduction: A Tale of Two Cities." *Police Quarterly,* June 2000, pp.191–212.

"Short-Term Youth Violence Prevention Program Claims Long-Term Success." *NCJA Justice Bulletin,* June 2000, pp.12–13.

Spelman, W. and Eck, J. E. "Problem-Oriented Policing." Washington, DC: National Institute of Justice, January 1987.

Stewart-Brown, Recheal. "Community Mobilization: The Foundation for Community Policing." *FBI Law Enforcement Bulletin,* June 2001, pp.9–17.

Strandberg, Keith W. "Not Your Typical Suspect." *Law Enforcement Technology,* October 1998a, pp.46–50.

Strandberg, Keith W. "Reducing Family Violence." *Law Enforcement Technology,* January 1998b, pp.32–36.

Thistlethwaite, Amy; Wooldredge, John; and Gibbs, David. "Severity of Dispositions and Domestic Violence Recidivism." *Crime and Delinquency,* July 1998, pp.388–398.

"Truth, DARE and Consequences." *Law Enforcement News,* April 15, 1998, p.1.

Upper Midwest Community Policing Institute. "Community Policing Defined." No date.

Chapter 6

Patrol: The Backbone of Policing

The difference between the ordinary and the extraordinary is the little extra.
—Anonymous

Do You Know?

- What the primary responsibilities of patrol are?
- What other responsibilities may be assigned to patrol?
- How patrol has traditionally functioned? What changes might make it more effective?
- What directed patrol does?
- What methods of patrol may be used? Which are most effective?
- What type of shift and beat staffing often lessens the effectiveness of preventive patrol?
- What the primary goal of traffic law enforcement is?
- What the responsibilities of the traffic officer are?
- What the most basic causes of motor vehicle crashes are?
- What implied consent laws are?
- Why all uniformed officers should enforce traffic laws?

Can You Define?

aggressive patrol
cold crimes
differential response strategies
directed patrol
implied consent
incident-driven policing
racial profiling
random patrol
road rage
scofflaws
selective enforcement

INTRODUCTION

Patrol is the most vital component of police work. All other units are supplemental to this basic unit. Patrol can contribute to each of the common goals of police departments, including preserving the peace, protecting civil rights and civil liberties, enforcing the law, preventing crime and providing services. Unfortunately in many departments, patrol officers not only have the position with the least prestige, but they also are the lowest paid, the least consulted and the most taken for granted. Patrol officers strive to move "up."

Patrol is responsible for providing continuous police service and high-visibility law enforcement, thereby deterring crime and maintaining order.

In addition patrol officers must understand the federal, state and local laws they are sworn to uphold and use good judgment in enforcing them.

In recent years, our society has become more diverse, many social controls have broken down and information technology has proliferated, making the patrol function increasingly complex and critical to accomplishing the police department's mission. Most officers in a department are assigned to the patrol function, and most of a department's budget is usually spent here. Patrol officers have the closest contact with the public and have the most influence on how the public perceives the police in general. To those departments instituting community policing, the patrol is critical.

No matter what approach to patrol is used, the patrol function is the most visible form of police activity, and individual patrol officers represent the entire police department. The tasks they are expected to accomplish are almost overwhelming.

This chapter begins with a discussion of the responsibilities of the patrol officer and the types of patrol most frequently used. This is followed by a description of common methods of patrol and a brief description of the structure and management of patrol. Next, an important subset of patrol is described—the responsibilities of the traffic officer, including an in-depth look at the major responsibility of dealing with traffic crashes. Next the importance of crash reports and crash reconstruction is discussed. The chapter concludes with discussions of the relationship between traffic enforcement and the apprehension of criminals and how patrol and traffic enforcement support community policing.

Patrol Officer Responsibilities

Patrol officers' basic responsibilities in most police departments are to enforce laws, investigate crimes, prevent criminal activity and provide day-to-day police services to the community. The specific duties involved in fulfilling these responsibilities are varied and complex. The size of the department often dictates what functions are assigned to patrol.

Patrol officers may be responsible for:

- Assisting people.
- Enforcing laws.
- Investigating crimes.
- Keeping traffic moving.
- Maintaining order.
- Resolving conflicts.

As protectors patrol officers promote and preserve order, respond to requests for services and try to resolve conflicts between individuals and groups. As law enforcers the first duty of patrol officers is to protect constitutional guarantees (as described in Chapter 8); the second duty is to enforce federal, state and local statutes. Patrol officers not only encourage voluntary compliance with the law but also seek to reduce the opportunity for crimes to be committed.

Patrol officers also serve important traffic control functions, described later in this chapter, and important investigative functions, described in Chapter 7.

Finally patrol officers in any community are the most visible government representatives and are responsible for the safety and direction of hundreds of people each day.

Types of Patrol

Patrol is often categorized as either general or specialized. Both general and specialized patrol seek to deter crime and apprehend criminals, as well as to provide community satisfaction with the services provided by the police department. General patrol does so by providing rapid response to calls for service. Specialized patrol does so by focusing its efforts on already identified problems. Whether general or specialized patrol is used depends on the nature of the problem and the tactics required to deal with it most effectively.

General Patrol

General patrol is also referred to as preventive patrol, random patrol and routine patrol. The term *routine patrol* should not really be used, however, because there is nothing routine about it. The challenges of general patrol change constantly. The patrol officer may be pursuing an armed bank robber in the morning and rescuing a cat from a tree in the afternoon.

Traditionally patrol has been random, reactive, incident driven and focused on rapid response to calls.

These characteristics can be seen in the main activities officers engage in during a typical patrol shift: random/preventive patrol, self-initiated activities, calls for service, directed patrol and administrative duties.

Random/Preventive Patrol

Traditionally patrol officers begin their shifts on **random patrol** in squad cars in hopes of detecting (intercepting) crimes in progress, deterring crime by creating an illusion of police omnipresence or being in the area and able to respond to crime-in-progress calls rapidly. Preventive patrol is generally done by uniformed officers moving at random through an assigned area. Because officers usually decide for themselves what they will do while on preventive patrol, this time is sometimes referred to as "noncommitted" time. It comprises between 30 and 40 percent of patrol time, but it is often broken into small segments because of interruptions by self-initiated activities, service calls and administrative duties.

Often priorities for preventive patrol are identified and/or assigned during roll call. For example patrol officers may be told to watch for a known escaped criminal sighted in the area.

A serious challenge to random patrol began 30 years ago in the findings of the often-quoted Kansas City Experiment. Funded by a grant from the Police Foundation, the *Kansas City Preventive Patrol Experiment* of 1972 is often referred to as the most comprehensive study of routine preventive patrol ever undertaken. The basic design divided 15 beats in Kansas City into three different groups:

- Group 1 Reactive Beats—five beats in which no routine preventive patrol was used. Officers responded only to calls for service.

- Group 2 Control Beats—five beats maintained their normal level of routine preventive patrol.
- Group 3 Proactive Beats—five beats doubled or tripled the level of routine preventive patrol.

The results of the study were that decreasing or increasing routine preventive patrol as done in this experiment had no effect on crime, citizen fear of crime, community attitudes toward the police on delivering services, police response time or traffic crashes. Klockars (1983, p.130) asserted that the results of the Kansas City Patrol Experiment indicated that "it makes about as much sense to have police patrol routinely in cars to fight crime as it does to have firemen patrol routinely in fire trucks to fight fire."

Although the Kansas City study found no significant differences in the incidence of crime resulting from varying the *level* of patrol, the results might have been different if they had varied the *form* of the patrol. For example, would the outcome differ if patrol officers more aggressively probed individuals, places and circumstances, being *proactive* rather than *reactive,* directed rather than random? Studies conducted in Syracuse, San Diego and Houston found that patrol officers could expect to intercept fewer than 1 percent of street crimes, giving credence to the saying: "Random patrol produces random results."

Given that streetwise criminals study police patrol methods and select targets not likely to be detected, and given that many crimes are committed on the spur of the moment, particularly such violent crimes as murder and assault, and given that much crime is committed inside buildings, out of the patrols' sight, Goldstein (1990, p.35), the father of problem-oriented policing, suggests a different approach: "Focusing on the substantive, community problems that the police must handle . . . requires the police to go beyond taking satisfaction in the smooth operation of their organization; it requires that they extend their concern to dealing effectively with the problems that justify creating a police agency in the first instance." This approach could greatly affect the second area of patrol activity, self-initiated tasks.

Self-Initiated Tasks

Officer-initiated activities usually result from officers' observations while on preventive or directed patrol; that is they encounter situations that require their intervention. For example an officer may see a crime in progress and arrest the suspect. Usually, however, officer-initiated activities involve community relations or crime-prevention activities, such as citizen contacts or automobile and building checks. Officers may see a large crowd gathered and decide to break it up, thereby preventing a possible disturbance or even a riot. Or they may see a break in a store's security, take steps to correct it, and thus prevent a possible burglary later.

Officers are sometimes hesitant to get involved in community services and preventive activities because such duties make them unavailable for radio dispatches and interfere with their ability to respond rapidly to service calls. Handheld radios, beepers and cell phones have allowed patrol officers more freedom of movement and have allowed them to initiate more activity.

Too often little attention is paid to the officer's use of noncommitted time, which is commonly regarded as having no function other than to ensure that officers are available to quickly respond to service calls. Frequently noncrime service calls interrupt a patrol officer's self-initiated activity that could prevent or deter crime. Emphasis on rapid response to all service calls has sometimes retarded the development of productive patrol services. Obviously not all service calls require a rapid response.

Calls for Service

The two-way radio has made the service call an extremely important element of patrol. It has also made it necessary to prioritize calls. A radio dispatch almost always takes precedence over other patrol activities. For example if an officer has stopped a traffic violator (a self-initiated activity) and receives a call of an armed robbery in progress, most department policies require the officer to discontinue the contact with the motorist and answer the service call.

In most departments calls for service drive the department. This is known as **incident-driven policing.** Because 40 to 60 percent of patrol officers' time is spent responding to calls for service, the way police respond to such calls significantly affects every aspect of their function.

The response is usually reactive, incident driven and as rapid as possible. Given that fewer than 20 percent of dispatched calls for service involve crime and that of these 75 percent are **cold crimes** (discovered after the perpetrator has left the scene), such an approach is unlikely to make best use of police resources. Many departments have found that **differential response strategies,** suiting the response to the call, are much more effective.

Call-related factors to consider include the type of incident and when it happened, that is, how much time has elapsed since it occurred. An in-progress major personal injury incident would be viewed differently than a minor noncrime incident that occurred several hours ago.

Calls for service may be answered by either sworn or nonsworn officers. The response time and nature of the response may vary considerably, from an immediate on-site response, to an on-site response within an hour, to a response when time permits. The caller may need to arrange an appointment for an officer to respond, or the officer may simply telephone a response without ever meeting the caller face-to-face. If it is determined the call for service does not require the dispatch of an officer, either sworn or nonsworn, the complainant may be told to come to the department to file a complaint, asked to mail in a complaint or be referred to another agency altogether. Although police response time is often a cause of citizen complaints, if citizens know what to expect, complaints can be reduced.

In addition to the use of differentiated response strategies, patrol might also become more effective if it were less incident driven (reactive) and were, rather, more problem driven, as discussed in Chapter 5. The problem-oriented approach is often criticized as being unrealistic because it demands so much patrol officer time. However as Goldstein (p.152) suggests:

> The time now wasted between calls for help and in the limited number of self-initiated activities of officers can be put to better use. The value of many of the

specialized and permanent jobs (other than patrol) to which officers are currently assigned can be challenged, with reassignment to more useful work. Many hours can be saved by using different responses to problems. Alternatives to arrest, when feasible, can greatly reduce the inordinate amount of time commonly consumed in processing an arrest. Calls to the police can be screened more effectively and, where appropriate, handled by telephone or diverted to another unit of the department or to another agency.

Patrol might be more effective if it were proactive, directed and problem oriented and if it used differentiated response strategies.

Directed Patrol

Directed or **aggressive patrol** meshes well with problem-oriented policing and with community-oriented policing and focuses on high-crime areas or specific offense types.

Directed patrol uses crime statistics to plan shift and beat staffing, providing more coverage during times of peak criminal activity and in high-crime areas.

Swope (1999, p.79) states: "Aggressive, or proactive, patrol focuses on the prevention and detection of crime by investigating suspicious actions, events and behaviors. Officers purposefully engage, or have contact, with individuals behaving in a suspicious manner." Furthermore (p.82): "Aggressive patrol is apprehension oriented while community policing is prevention oriented. The reality is, apprehension is prevention."

Specific activities that qualify as "aggressive patrol" include field interrogation, aggressive traffic enforcement and detection of environmental anomalies, which are unusual activities that warrant further investigation. As Swope (p.81) asserts: "Criminal acts create environmental anomalies":

> At 1930 hours on a Saturday evening an officer notices a dry cleaner shop with its lights on and movement inside. The officer knows the shop always closes at 1700 hours on Saturdays. This is an environmental anomaly, it is unusual and needs to be investigated. . . . If an inquiry finds that the owner of the store is working late, the owner in all likelihood would be very pleased that the police were vigilant in protecting his business.

Swope also cautions: "The fact that an environmental anomaly takes place does not guarantee criminal activity."

A method that enhances the effectiveness of aggressive patrol is geographic permanence: "If officers are regularly assigned the same beat they get to know the normal activities of the community. This knowledge adds to an officer's ability to recognize what is unusual and requires some response" (Swope, p.81). Geographic permanence also fosters rapport between police and citizens, helping with the overall mission of community policing:

> Community policing adds to aggressive patrol in that officers get to know the law abiding residents of a community, mutually identify problems, receive information, and develop more focused responses. Community policing does not mean that police go soft on crime. Meeting with the community to explain aggressive patrol tactics can build consensus and facilitate understanding and acceptance of the tactic (Swope, p.82).

Administrative Duties

Administrative work includes preparing and maintaining the patrol vehicle, transporting prisoners and documents, writing reports and testifying in court. Efforts to make patrol more cost-effective have often been aimed at cutting time spent on administrative duties. Some departments have greatly reduced the time officers spend maintaining their vehicles. Other departments have drastically reduced the amount of paperwork required of patrol officers by allowing them to dictate reports, which secretaries then transcribe, or by using computer-generated reports.

The types of reports police officers frequently use include motor vehicle reports, vehicle recovery reports, offense reports, continuation reports, juvenile reports, missing persons reports, arrest/violation reports and record checks.

A Demanding Role

Whether general or specialized, the demands made on patrol officers are many. Patrol officers who are "swamped" responding to calls for service on a first-come, first-served basis have little or no time to perform in the other two major spheres of activity or to perform required administrative duties.

Methods of Patrol

Patrol officers in the United States were originally on foot or horseback. Bicycles were introduced in policing in Detroit in 1897 and automobiles in 1910. Airplanes were first used by the New York City Police Department in 1930. At that time daredevil pilots were flying all over the city, sometimes crashing in densely populated areas. The New York Airborne police unit was created to control reckless flying over the city. These means of patrol and others can be found in the twenty-first century.

Patrol can be accomplished by foot, automobile, motorcycle, bicycle, horseback, aircraft and boat. The most commonly used and most effective patrol is usually a combination of automobile and foot patrol.

Foot Patrol

The word *patrol* is derived from the French word *patrouiller,* which means, roughly, to travel on foot. Foot patrol, the oldest form of patrol, has the advantage of close citizen contact and is *proactive* rather than reactive. Its goal is to address neighborhood problems before they become crimes. Most effective in highly congested areas, foot patrol may help to deter burglary, robbery, purse snatching and muggings. Kelling (n.d., pp.2–3) reports the consistent findings of two foot patrol experiments:

- When foot patrol is added in neighborhoods, levels of fear decrease significantly.
- When foot patrol is withdrawn from neighborhoods, levels of fear increase significantly.
- Citizen satisfaction with police increases when foot patrol is added in neighborhoods.
- Police who patrol on foot have a greater appreciation for the values of neighborhood residents than police who patrol the same areas in automobiles.

- Police who patrol on foot have greater job satisfaction, less fear and higher morale than officers who patrol in automobiles.

The 1980s saw a significant trend back to foot patrol. In the 1990s it became almost synonymous with community policing. Foot patrol is relatively expensive and does limit the officer's ability to pursue suspects in vehicles and to get from one area to another rapidly. Used in conjunction with motorized patrol, foot patrol is highly effective. According to the National Neighborhood Foot Patrol Center, Michigan State University School of Criminal Justice (n.d.):

> Foot patrol is an exercise in communication—an attempt to develop rapport between the officer on the beat and the citizens he or she serves. Foot patrol officers constantly interact with the community. They instruct citizens in crime prevention techniques and link them to available governmental services. They are catalysts of neighborhood organizations.

The center notes that "motorized patrolling has proven ineffective in certain key areas. Crime rates continue to rise, and even in areas where they are not high, vagrants, abandoned cars, and groups of juveniles on the street create an impression that the environment is violent and uncontrollable." The center cites a series of experimental programs conducted by criminal justice researchers to see if a modified version of foot patrol could contribute to modern policing. The intent was not to replace motorized patrol but rather to provide a combination of foot and motorized patrol, capitalizing on the strengths of each.

Automobile Patrol

Automobile patrol offers the greatest mobility and flexibility and is usually the most cost-effective method of patrol. It allows wide coverage and rapid response to calls; the vehicle radio provides instant communications with headquarters. The automobile also provides a means of transporting special equipment and prisoners or suspects.

However, while patrolling in a vehicle, officers cannot pay as much attention to details they might see if they were on foot, such as a door ajar, a window broken or a security light out. The physical act of driving may draw attention away from such subtle signs that a crime may be in progress. Furthermore, research on the effectiveness of preventive patrol indicates that a crime prevented by a passing vehicle can be, and usually is, committed as soon as the police are gone. In effect police presence prevents street crime only if the police can be everywhere at once.

Modern patrol cars are greatly enhanced by technology. According to Campbell (1998a, p.39):

> Improved radio communications is just one of the many new technologies currently in use in patrol cars. . . .
>
> With more departments utilizing onboard computers in patrol cars, the software sector of the industry has also grown to meet new demands for mobile information systems. . . .
>
> A wireless data transmission system . . . eliminates the need to process information through a dispatcher. This allows the dispatcher to concentrate on other incoming calls and it provides officers in the field with the requested

> information in a matter of seconds. . . . A call is never broadcast over the air; it's wirelessly transmitted. This allows officers to have backup without alerting someone who might be monitoring a police scanner.

Another type of technology finding its way into patrol cars is the visual surveillance and imaging systems similar to those used by the military. Campbell (1998b, p.34) comments on the Night Cam surveillance gear: "Officers can conduct surveillance operations from more than one hundred yards away without using any illumination to betray their position. . . . The Night Cam, and other light amplification–based technology, is useful at night or in other low-light situations."

An additional type of visual technology being used by patrol is thermal imaging. States Campbell (1998b, pp.34–35): "Nightsight, a thermal imaging system . . . can be used 24 hours a day, under any conditions. . . . All objects, both animate and inanimate, emit and reflect electromagnetic radiation over a wide spectral band, although the vast majority of this radiation (other than visible light) can't be seen by the human eye. . . . In addition to body heat, Nightsight can also detect the heat images created by such things as a car engine, tire tracks and even a handprint." In one case a suspected drug dealer had tossed aside a bag of cocaine while fleeing police, leaving a "hot" handprint that Nightsight was able to detect. The evidence was recovered, and the suspect was apprehended.

A third type of video technology commonly used in patrol cars is the dashboard-mounted video camera. Campbell (1998b, p.35) notes: "It's part of the evolution of a police officer's standard equipment: nightstick to gun to radio to video camera."

One-Officer versus Two-Officer Squads

One factor of importance when using automobile patrol is whether to have one or two officers assigned per squad. Circumstances should determine whether a one-officer or a two-officer unit is more appropriate. The single-officer unit is the rule rather than the exception, and most incidents can be handled by one officer. If two officers are required, two one-officer units can be dispatched to the scene. Two-officer units should be restricted to those areas, shifts and types of activities most likely to threaten the officers' safety, for example during the evening or in high-crime areas.

The one-officer unit offers several advantages, including cost-effectiveness in that the same number of officers can patrol twice the area, with twice the mobility and with twice the power of observation. In addition officers working alone are generally more cautious in dangerous situations, recognizing that they have no backup. Officers working alone also are generally more attentive to patrol duties because they do not have a conversational partner. The expense of two cars compared to one, however, is a factor.

Police unions usually support two-officer patrol units and may include provisions for two-officer units in their contracts, jeopardizing management's ability to best use available resources and to make rational decisions about personnel deployment and scheduling. Consider the fact that of the 51 law enforcement officers feloniously killed in the line of duty during 2000, 39 were assigned to vehicle patrol. Of those killed while on vehicle patrol, 8 were assigned to two-officer vehicles and 31were assigned to one-officer vehicles. From 1991 to 2000, of the officers feloniously killed while on vehicle patrol, 83 were assigned to two-officer vehicles while 203 were assigned to one-officer vehicles (*Law Enforcement Officers* . . ., 2001, pp.4,32).

However as Johnson (1999, p.68) states: "Experiments by the Police Foundation using both types of unit staffing in a large city police department revealed that officers in two-officer units were more likely to be assaulted by a citizen, be injured in the line of duty, and have a suspect resist arrest. Studies that have looked at the frequency of assaults and injuries to patrol officers have upheld these findings that single-officer units tend to be safer." Johnson also notes other negatives associated with two-officer units include the fact that they have a higher rate of generating citizen complaints about both verbal and physical abuse against citizens.

Motorcycle Patrol

Motorcycle patrol has been a popular option for agencies throughout the country for many decades. In fact, according to Polan (2000, p.71): "Police motorcycle officers (PMOs) have patrolled our streets to enforce our traffic regulations since their introduction in Pittsburgh, Pa., almost 100 years ago." Motorcycles are used for traffic enforcement, escort and parade duty. In fact motorcycles and automobiles have dominated traffic enforcement for the past seven or eight decades. They can also enhance community relations: "It is at once a functional unit and a public relations tool—and it is both in all kinds of weather, as long as it is operated with caution and common sense" (Sharp, 1998, p.49).

Among the disadvantages of motorcycles are their relatively high cost to operate, their limited use in adverse weather and the hazards associated with riding them.

Bicycle Patrol

Bike patrols have been used since the early 1900s. Vonk (2000, p.26) notes: "Over the past 15 years, police bicycle patrols have become common in today's era of crime fighting and community policing." Strandberg (2001, p.102) adds: "Bike patrols are on the cutting-edge of community policing. Many cities have instituted these patrols, and their communities are better for it."

Bicycle patrol is sometimes used in parks and on beaches or in conjunction with stakeouts. According to Vonk (p.26):

> Police on bikes are found in large and small cities, on almost every college campus, and even on the federal level including the United States Military. Police cyclists have proven success in the areas of urban drug enforcement, public housing projects, surveillance, and community relations.

Bike units are ideal for patrolling small areas and for performing directed patrol assignments. They may even be used to cover small areas some distance apart, with departments mounting bike racks on patrol cars for officers to transport their bikes to various patrol sites. In addition to mobility, bicycles provide a "stealth factor" and an "element of surprise" because they can be ridden very quietly and do not attract attention. Furthermore: "Bike officers offer a more

Associated Press/AP

The Petersburg, Virginia, Bureau of Police formed a bicycle unit in 1993 to patrol some of the most crime-ridden areas of the city. Criminal activity decreased with roundups of street-level drug dealers. Why do you think bicycle patrols were effective in this situation?

visible presence, and bike patrols can police certain kinds of crime better than officers on foot or in a vehicle" (Strandberg, 2001, p.102).

Assignment to bicycle patrol requires physical conditioning. According to Bobit (1998, p.32): "Once thought of as 'sissy' duty, today, bicycle patrol officers must maintain above average physical condition and adhere to rigorous training and a strenuous regime." Hoffman (1998, p.55) adds: "Bike officers pedal an average of 15 to 25 miles a day; 85% of bike units surveyed operate night patrols, 50% operate year around, and 50% operate in the rain. More than 50% of the units have regularly scheduled maintenance programs for their bicycles and 75% of the departments surveyed require special training for bike officers. The average expense to operate a fully equipped bike is $1,000 and annual maintenance is about $100." To enhance the effectiveness of bicycle patrol, the addition of electric motors is being considered for the next generation of bike patrols:

> [The E-bike is] a police bike ready for action equipped with a 36-volt battery that can drive the bike up hills and push it up to 18 to 20 mph on a straightaway. . . .
>
> The police edition E-bike is not meant to be ridden on the motor throughout a shift, however. The bike is designed to be ridden like any police bike. The motor is there for a burst of speed to cover ground quickly and for a burst of power to get up a steep hill (Strandberg, 2001, pp.102–103).

Bicycle patrol remains very appealing to agencies, officers and the community. Bobit (p.35) reports: "Research conducted by several departments shows an increase in morale, health, and fitness among its bicycle patrol officers. . . . [As one officer says]: 'When the idea of bicycle detail surfaced, no one wanted to be on the unit. Now, it's a prime job and the position is in demand. Because bike officers rarely transfer to other units there is always a long waiting list.'"

Mounted officers are especially effective in situations requiring crowd control. Notice advanced protection given the horses.

Mounted Patrol

Mounted patrol evolved from military antecedents and comprises some of the oldest and most varied police units in the United States. In 1871 the New York City Police Department was one of the first agencies in the country to establish a mounted patrol unit (Wexler, 1998b, p.78). "Today," states Fine (2001, p.6), "more than 600 organized mounted patrol units form a visible pedestal and serve citizens throughout their jurisdiction."

Mounted patrols function in a variety of capacities, from community relations, to park and traffic patrol, to crowd and riot control, to crime prevention. Mounted patrols have also been used to assist in evidence searches at crime scenes, round up straying livestock, search for lost children in tall corn or grass and apprehend trespassers. Wexler (1998b, pp.78–79) states: "One of the primary responsibilities of the Mounted Unit is to control crowds during demonstrations and other occasions when pedestrian or vehicular traffic is particularly dense. An officer astride a 1,600-pound horse is indeed an omnipresent figure." According to one mounted patrol officer: "One horse and rider is equal to 10 foot patrolmen in a crowd control situation" (Strandberg, 1999, p.107).

Chief Deputy Benbow of the Sacramento County Sheriff's Department comments: "The malls love us, because when we appear, crime drops dramatically. And the reason is simple. We can see THEM, and they can see US" (Dangaard, 1998, p.88). And, as Strandberg (1999, p.106) points out: "Horses stand out, especially in the middle of a busy city. Citizens can't help but notice a horse, and that alone helps convey the message that the police are there and on the job."

Adds Frank Robinson, executive director of the Town Center Improvement District in Houston, Texas (Dangaard, p.89): "A friendly policeman on a horse can do more in five minutes to spread good will than any big-shot advertising campaign. It's a hands-on interaction with the Public . . . and people LOVE to pet horses!"

Although horses may be intimidating, one real danger to them is the drunken driver. In South Carolina, according to Smith (1999, p.72), a law has been passed making killing police horses a felony, just as if the animal was an officer.

Air Patrol

Air patrol is another highly effective form of patrol, especially when large geographic areas are involved, such as with a widespread search for a lost person, a downed plane or an escaped convict. A helicopter 500 feet in the air has 30 times the visual range of a unit on the ground, providing a patrol capacity equal to 15 squad cars. Furthermore a helicopter can arrive at a crime scene 5 to 10 times faster than street-level units. As one aviation unit commander states: "At night when your backup is many minutes away, it's a good feeling to hear those rotors and have the scene suddenly lit up" (Swager, 2000, p.40). He (p.42) continues: "In the last three years, we've gone from reactive to proactive, and our pilots seem to have the knack of being in the right place at the right time, monitoring patrol channels for the area they're in and maintaining really good working relationships with other units. You can ask the deputy on the street how he feels when he hears those rotors coming."

Wexler (1998a, pp.20–21) notes: "The rapid growth in the use of police helicopters nationwide took off in the late 1960s. . . . Today, there are more than 200 airborne law enforcement units throughout the nation. Every day they are up in the sky performing an astonishing number of crime-fighting and life-saving operations. Choppers are supporting officers on the ground, apprehending dangerous fugitives, rescuing, and even assisting in aerial firefighting." Helicopters and small aircraft are generally used in conjunction with police vehicles on the ground in criminal surveillance and in traffic control, not only to report tie-ups but to clock speeds and radio to ground units. Helicopters have also been used to rescue persons from tall buildings on fire and in other situations, such as floods. In addition air travel is a cost-effective means of transporting prisoners over long distances.

Helicopters, even when donated to an agency, are extremely expensive to maintain. A cost-effective alternative aircraft for law enforcement is the gyroplane, which carries a much lower operating cost, requires less training to fly and is generally safer in flight than a helicopter (Paynter, 1999, p.132). Other less conventional aerial conveyances have proven useful in law enforcement efforts. An unmanned aerial vehicle (UAV) named "Cypher" holds promise for law enforcement applications: "The Cypher UAV offers autonomous flight modes that include auto take-off and landing . . . [and] has great potential for law enforcement use in certain tactical situations. Some examples include: counter-narcotics, search and rescue, and surveillance" (Morrison, 1998, p.66).

Water Patrol

Water patrol is used extensively on our coasts to apprehend gun and narcotics smugglers. Inland, water patrols are used to control river and lake traffic. Water patrol units are very specialized and are used in relatively few cities in the

United States. In those cities with extensive coasts and other waterways, however, they are a vital part of patrol.

Watercraft range in size from personal watercraft, such as wave runners, to fully equipped 30-foot cruisers. Cost-effective inflatable equipment is also being used by some departments. Water patrols are used for routine enforcement of such things as vessels exceeding "no wake" speed limits, intoxicated operators and safety inspections, as well as search-and-rescue operations, emergency transportation in flooded areas, general surveillance and antismuggling operations. Huntington (1998, p.36) notes: "When TWA Flight 800 went down, the NYPD Police Harbor Unit suddenly found itself in the limelight. Playing a pivotal role in the recovery of bodies and wreckage throughout the ordeal, officers and boats of the NYPD Harbor Unit were featured on television news footage around the world."

Close ties can develop between a boating community and the marine agencies that patrol it. DeFranco (1999, p.71) states:

> Water cops serve a special population: boaters and nautical enthusiasts. . . . Typically their efforts concentrate on education and rescue, rather than ticket writing and arrests. Because so many groups of people must share limited bodies of water, boaters, swimmers, anglers and personal watercraft (PWC) users alike welcome the presence of these officers, who help ensure everyone has safe, equitable access to marine resources.

Special-Terrain Patrol

Some police departments may require special-purpose vehicles to patrol. For example areas that receive a lot of snow may have snowmobiles as part of their patrol fleet. These vehicles may be especially useful in rescue missions as well as on routine patrol. Police departments with miles of beaches or desert to patrol may use jeeps and dune buggies. Police departments in remote, rugged or mountainous parts of the country may use four-wheel-drive all-terrain vehicles (ATVs):

> ATVs are best suited to use in the dirt. With their fat, low-pressure floatation-type tires, they're practically unstoppable, whether deep sand or gumbo mud lies ahead. Small fallen trees or hills that would block normal police bikes—to say nothing of cruisers—are child's play for an ATV.
>
> These qualities allow ATV-mounted officers to patrol and respond quickly in rugged terrain that might otherwise demand helicopters or horses. The racks on ATVs can carry a substantial amount of support equipment as well (Kariya, 2000, p.38).

Combination Patrol

Combination patrol provides the most versatile approach to preventing or deterring crime and apprehending criminals. The combination used will depend not only on the size of the police department but also on the circumstances that arise. Table 6.1 summarizes the most common methods of patrol, their uses, advantages and disadvantages.

High Visibility versus Low Visibility

High-visibility patrol is often used in high-risk crime areas in hopes of deterring criminal activity. In addition high-visibility patrol gives citizens a sense of safety, justified or not. Types of high-visibility patrol include foot patrol, especially with a canine partner; mounted patrol; marked police car and motorcycle patrol; and helicopter patrol.

Table 6.1
Summary of Patrol Methods

Method	Uses	Advantages	Disadvantages
Foot	Highly congested areas Burglary, robbery, theft, purse snatching, mugging	Close citizen contact High visibility Develop informants	Relatively expensive Limited mobility
Automobile	Respond to service calls Provide traffic control Transport individuals, documents and equipment	Most economical Greatest mobility and flexibility Offers means of communication Provides means of transporting people, documents and equipment	Limited access to certain areas Limited citizen contact
Motorcycle	Same as automobile, except that it can't be used for transporting individuals and has limited equipment	Maneuverability in congested areas and areas restricted to automobiles	Inability to transport much equipment Not used during bad weather Hazardous to operator
Bicycle	Stakeouts Parks and beaches Congested areas	Quiet and unobtrusive	Limited speed Not used during bad weather Vulnerability of officer Physical exertion required
Mounted	Parks and bridle paths Crowd control Traffic control	Size and maneuverability of horse Build rapport with citizens	Expensive Limited carrying capacity Street litter
Air	Surveillance Traffic control Searches and rescues	Covers large areas easily	Expensive Noisy
Water	Deter smuggling Water traffic control Rescues	Access to activities occurring on water	Expensive
Special-terrain	Patrol unique areas inaccessible to other forms Rescue operations	Access to normally inaccessible areas	Limited use in some instances

Low-visibility patrol is often used to apprehend criminals engaged in targeted crimes. Many of the specialized patrol operations would fall into this category. Types of low-visibility patrol include unmarked police cars and bicycles.

The relative effectiveness of high-visibility and low-visibility patrol has not been determined. A combination of both high- and low-visibility patrol is often needed and most effective.

Structure and Management of Patrol

Traditionally patrol officers have been assigned a specific time and a specific geographic location or beat to patrol. The beats are set up to be of equal geographic size, yet such a structure poses obvious problems because the workload is not the same at all hours of the day or in all areas.

Equal shift and beat size staffing creates major problems and lessens the effectiveness of patrol during certain times and in certain areas.

Several attempts have been made to overcome the problems inherent in equal shift and beat size staffing. Some departments, usually larger ones, assign officers according to the demand for services, concentrating the officers' time where it is most needed, although union contracts sometimes make this difficult.

Crime mapping is also used to determine where patrol is most needed. Groff and La Vigne (2001, p.257) note: "Law enforcement officers and civilian crime analysts have been mapping crime with push pins and paper maps virtually since the time that police agencies were established." However: "The recent introduction of user-friendly, raster-based mapping software, designed primarily for environmental and planning purposes, offers new tools for examining and predicting crime and criminal behavior."

Geographic information systems (GIS) play a vital role in "data-driven decision-making" by enabling law enforcement to better use crime information and statistics to help guide policy and practice (La Vigne and Wartell, 2000, p.ix). According to Travis (1999, p.v): "Today about 13 percent of law enforcement agencies are using GIS regularly to analyze their crime problems, and we are certain to see this number increase significantly as more and more agencies begin using computerized crime mapping to identify and solve their crime problems." Emphasizing the value of GIS to officer effectiveness and safety, Harries (1999, pp.67–68) asserts:

> Officers who spend time on the streets are entitled to the most up-to-date and comprehensive data related to their patrol areas. These data should be easily accessible and user friendly. The most useful kind of information should focus on recent area history, with an emphasis on change. Effective policing emphasizes patterns, and mapping and understanding change are key to understanding these patterns.

Mapping can identify correlations between crime, demographics, societal issues and more, and can help departments deploy their resources more effectively. One police chief describes the impact mapping technology can have on targeting crime in a certain area (Rogers, 2001, p.65): "It's like if a health care professional said: 'Someone in this group has cancer. Let's give everyone chemotherapy.' That's how we have dispensed community resources in the past. Now we can tailor our response based on the community diagnosis." Rogers (2000, p.74) notes:

> Law enforcement has taken mapping a step further by employing . . . increasingly sophisticated programs in unexpected ways. Among these applications are traffic accident reconstruction, crime scene modeling, phone log displays and off-road maps. . . .
>
> Law enforcement is also increasing its reliance on freeware that works across departments or regions . . . [including] the Regional Crime Analysis Program (ReCAP). . . . Operating in conjunction with a department's existing records management system, GIS and multiple data mining tools, ReCAP has been shown to recognize subtle increases in criminal activity up to 3 months before it is noticed by experienced crime analysts. It also enables agencies to share records with other departments.

Rogers (2001, p.66) relates another example of how expanded mapping technology can help agencies better target problem areas and possibly predict where future incidents may occur by isolating patterns within patterns:

> In one case a young victim was beaten to death by a group of youth, in what the department called "a swarming." Several subsequent crimes were similar and officers soon realized they had a pattern of swarming. Using a tool called Vertical Mapper, which presents a 3D image, they overlaid public transportation and elementary and secondary schools with the locations of the beatings. They found these crimes were occurring after school and near certain schools and train stations.

The application of crime mapping technology continues to evolve. Ward (2000, p.133) notes: "Much has been written about the 'computer comparison statistics' system, abbreviated as COMPSTAT, that allows police to track crime incidents almost as soon as they occur—and about the role COMPSTAT has played in revolutionizing policing and transforming the organizational design and culture of the NYPD." Anderson (2001, p.9) reports nearly a third of the nation's larger police departments (those with 100 or more sworn officers) have implemented some form of Compstat and another quarter plan to do so. He explains:

> William Bratton, who was New York City's police commissioner from 1994 to 1996, is credited with developing Compstat along with his deputy commissioner, Jack Maple, in an effort to get control of the city's huge police force. . . . [Compstat] stressed four guiding principles: accurate, timely intelligence; rapid deployment; effective tactics; and relentless follow-up and assessment. . . .
>
> The spread of Compstat began as police from other cities visited New York and began setting up their own versions. Minneapolis, for example, created Codefor, based on the Compstat principles, and credits it with double-digit declines in homicides, aggravated assaults, robberies, burglaries and auto thefts from 1998 to 1999. . . .
>
> The appeal of the strategy extends beyond crime control. Information and accountability help police make better sense of their jobs. . . . [One officer] says that the sense of heightened focus and accountability is quickly felt at the patrol level. "I like it," he says. "The captain knows a lot more about what's going on in the district, and that increases the police officer's awareness of what's going on. Everyone is more informed."

In addition to focusing efforts on crime hot spots, another basic function of patrol officers is enforcing traffic laws. This duty is often met with mixed reaction from the community—favorably when the police stop neighborhood speeders and other "dangerous drivers," negatively when citizens themselves are the subjects of traffic stops.

Traffic Division

Traffic law enforcement, the most frequent contact between police and law-abiding citizens, is a critical responsibility of officers. In the United States the regulation of traffic and enforcement of related laws have existed for over a century. In 1901 Connecticut established the world's first speed statute limiting horseless carriage speeds to 12 mph in cities and 15 mph in rural areas.

The principal objectives of the traffic division are to obtain, through voluntary citizen compliance, the smoothest possible movement of vehicles and pedestrians consistent with safety and to reduce losses from crashes. Furthermore, because officers are on the streets so much of the time, they often are among the first to know of problems in the transportation system and can provide information as well as advice on overall system planning.

The primary goal of traffic law enforcement is to produce voluntary compliance with traffic laws while keeping traffic moving safely and smoothly.

Detecting traffic violations is no different for a patrol officer than detecting vandalism, auto theft, burglary or trespassing. The officers know general police methods; they appreciate the functions they have to perform while on patrol; and they know traffic laws and the department's traffic policies. A thorough knowledge of the department's overall traffic program, its objectives and operations, will make the patrol officers assigned to traffic responsibilities more effective.

Traffic officers may be responsible for enforcing traffic laws, directing and controlling traffic, providing directions and assistance to motorists, investigating motor vehicle crashes, providing emergency assistance at the scene of a crash, gathering information related to traffic and writing reports.

Enforcing Traffic Laws

Police officers seek the compliance of motorists and pedestrians with traffic laws and ordinances, as well as driver license regulations and orders, and they may issue warnings or citations to violators.

Speeding—most every one does it at one time or another, if not all the time, and many justify it as "just going with the flow of traffic." However speeding has become an increasing problem for law enforcement, as more cars travel the streets and people seem more in a hurry than ever before to get from point A to point B. In fact some don't even realize they're speeding until they see the flashing lights of the law in their rearview mirror. To combat the problem of leadfooted drivers, some agencies are using portable Speed Monitoring Awareness Radar Trailers (SMARTs) parked alongside the road. These trailers clock and digitally display motorists' speeds beneath a posted speed-limit sign in an effort to gain voluntary compliance with speed laws and reduce accidents.

A problem related to speeding is red-light running. Many people think they simply don't have a spare minute to spend sitting at an intersection. Furthermore traveling at 5 or 10 miles per hour, or more, over the posted speed limit makes stopping for red lights that much more difficult. However, the Insurance Institute for Highway Safety's Highway Loss Data Institute estimates more than 800 people die each year in crashes that involve red-light running, and more than 200,000 are injured in such crashes (www.hwysafety.org). Some jurisdictions are installing red-light cameras to help enforce traffic laws. These cameras photograph red-light runners, getting a shot of the license plate for identification, and typically stamp the date, time of day, time elapsed since the light turned red and the vehicle's speed. Kanable (2000, p.24) reports approximately 40 communities across the country use cameras to enforce traffic laws, and studies show such programs reduce red-light running by about 40 percent.

Once an officer has probable cause, whether it's having clocked a driver exceeding the posted speed limit, witnessing a red-light runner or some other traffic violation, a traffic stop can be made. Kalk (1998, p.36) cautions:

> There is no such thing as a routine traffic stop. Traffic stops are one of the most dangerous aspects of a police officer's job.
>
> When stopping a vehicle, a police officer has little knowledge of the facts and circumstances occurring in the life of the driver of the automobile or in the lives of the passengers in the automobile. The police officer does not know if the occupants of the motor vehicle have experienced a traumatic event during the day, are under the influence of alcohol or drugs, have weapons or have some type of motivation for wanting to injure or kill the police officer. Every traffic stop is unique.

A traffic stop often leads to a ticket being issued. According to Cox (1998, p.42): "Tickets cause police officers more trouble than virtually anything else they do, in large part because they underestimate the impact of this seemingly mundane duty. Traffic contacts are immeasurably more than simply spotting a violation and putting it on paper. On the contrary, interactions with traffic violators are highly complex psycho-dynamic situations." He notes (p.43): "Police officers frequently write tickets for the wrong reasons. The best reason to write tickets is to enhance the safety of the public, whether it's the driver you have stopped, other drivers, pedestrians, cyclists or any other users of the streets and sidewalks." His (p.43) advice to officers when pulling out their ticket books: "Bear in mind that the vast majority of people stopped for traffic violations are John and Jane Doe average citizens—hurried and busy people—just ordinary folks."

Some violators, however, are not just "average citizens"; they are serious traffic offenders. Anderson (2000, p.49) states: "Traffic fugitives may not always be pursued aggressively, perhaps because of a lack of resources or the mistaken belief that even serious traffic offenders are relatively harmless. In fact, their flaunting of the law endangers all of us and kills many people every year on our roads and highways. Thus, a proactive stance to bring these offenders to justice can reap many benefits for the community."

Police are sometimes accused of using the pretext of a traffic stop to execute another agenda, such as searching a vehicle or driver for drugs. The question: Is the temporary detention of a motorist who the police believe has committed a civil traffic violation constitutional under the Fourth Amendment if the officer, in fact, had some other law enforcement objective? The Supreme Court's decision, through its ruling in *Whren v. United States* (1996), is yes:

> The temporary detention of a motorist upon probable cause to believe he has violated the traffic laws does not violate the Fourth Amendment's prohibition against unreasonable seizures, even if a reasonable officer would not have stopped the motorist absent some additional law enforcement objective.

In other words, the test for the validity and constitutionality of a stop is not whether police officers "would have" made the stop but rather whether the officers "could have" made the stop. In *Whren,* the officers could have, and did, make a valid stop because the driver committed a traffic violation, even if the actual purpose for making the stop was to search for drugs. Consequently, the real purpose of a stop, even if ulterior, does not render the stop and subsequent search invalid if there was, in fact, a valid reason for the stop.

Directing and Controlling Traffic

Police officers frequently are called on to direct traffic flow, control parking, provide escorts and remove abandoned vehicles. They often are asked to assist in crowd control at major sporting events. They also are responsible for planning traffic routing, removing traffic hazards and assuring that emergency vehicles can move quickly through traffic.

In many jurisdictions officers and other responders en route to an emergency, such as ambulances or fire trucks, can control traffic lights to their favor, eliminating the need to slow or stop at a red light and preventing crashes that may occur when a squad car or other emergency vehicle passes through an intersection against the light. In these systems a frequency-coded signal is emitted from the approaching vehicle to a signal controller device on the traffic light, providing a green light to the emergency vehicle.

Other Responsibilities

Police officers *provide information and assistance* to motorists and pedestrians by patrolling, maintaining surveillance of traffic and the environment, conducting driver-vehicle road checks and being available when needed. Officers *investigate crashes,* including gathering facts at the scene and reconstructing the crash, and then report these facts as a basis for preventing crashes and providing objective evidence for citizens involved in civil settlements of crash losses. They may also prepare cases for court and appear as prosecution witnesses when there has been a violation, such as drunk driving. At a crash scene, the police officer may *assist crash victims* by administering first aid, transporting injured persons, protecting property in the victim's vehicle and arranging for towing of disabled vehicles.

Police officers *report* on crashes, violations, citations and arrests, the disposition of court actions, drivers' cumulative records, roadway and environmental defects and exceptional traffic congestion. The reports help the traffic engineer and traffic safety education agencies by providing information useful for their crash prevention programs and for planning for traffic movement or vehicle parking. Furthermore traffic-related records, including registration records, drivers' licenses, traffic citations and collision reports, may play an important role not only in traffic management but also in criminal investigations.

Sometimes police officers serve unofficially as the city's road inspectors as they discover problems in either road conditions or traffic flow. They may propose corrections to achieve safer, more effective motor vehicle and pedestrian travel and vehicle parking.

The Traffic Program

Violating traffic laws does not carry the social stigma attached to the violation of other laws, such as laws against murder and rape. Running a stoplight or speeding is not considered a crime, and people regularly and unconsciously violate laws designed to ensure safe use of the streets and highways. Recall the distinction between crimes that are *mala in se* (bad in themselves) and *mala prohibita* (bad because they are forbidden). Traffic laws are excellent examples of *mala prohibita* crimes.

A properly administered and executed police traffic law enforcement procedure is probably the most important component of the overall traffic program. If people obey the traffic laws, traffic is likely to flow more smoothly and safely, with fewer tie-ups and crashes. Effective traffic law enforcement usually consists of at least five major actions: (1) on-the-spot instructions to drivers and pedestrians, (2) verbal warnings, (3) written warnings with proper follow-up, (4) citations or summonses and (5) arrests. Traffic officers consider the circumstances of each incident and apply their discretion in determining which action is most appropriate.

The question inevitably arises as to how much enforcement is needed to control traffic and reduce crashes. This local issue must be determined for each jurisdiction; however a nationally approved guide, called the *Enforcement Index,* has been developed to assist in this determination.

Selective Traffic Law Enforcement

Because traffic violations occur every hour of every day, police departments cannot enforce all traffic regulations at all times. It is impossible to achieve 100 percent enforcement and almost always unwise to try to do so. Based on thorough investigations of crashes, summarization and careful analysis of the records, **selective enforcement** targets specific crashes and/or high-crash areas, such as excessive speed around a school yard or playground where young children are present. Adequate records are essential to the overall effectiveness of the selective enforcement program.

Selective enforcement is not only logical, it is practical because most police departments' limited workforces require them to spend time on violations that contribute to crashes. Enforcement personnel, such as officers on motorcycles or officers assigned to a radar unit, are usually the officers assigned to selective traffic enforcement. The officers' activity is directed to certain high-crash areas during certain days of the week and certain hours of the day or night.

Studies in city after city have proven a definite relationship between crashes and enforcement. In analyzing crash reports, one finds at the top of the list year after year the same traffic violations contributing to crashes and the same group of drivers being involved. Crashes are discussed later in the chapter.

Almost everyone has heard in exhaustive detail a friend's version of getting an "unfair" speeding ticket. The person will tell several people about it. In terms of quality and selective enforcement, this has the effect of informing the general public that the police are doing their job. Chermak et al. (2001, p.365) examined citizens' perceptions of aggressive traffic enforcement and report: "Overall the findings suggest that citizens strongly support aggressive traffic enforcement practices and that the implementation of such strategies does not reduce their support."

High-quality enforcement is not only supported by the public, it has an important effect on the would-be traffic violator. When the public is informed of the police department's enforcement program and it is understood and believed to be reasonable and fair, the public will usually accept and support it.

Racial Profiling

Margolis et al. (2000, p.18) state: "The issue of racial profiling is one of the most important issues facing law enforcement today. Racial profiling is a national focal point of the wider concerns about race relations in law enforcement." Ramirez et al. (2000, p.3) define **racial profiling** as "any police-initiated action that relies on the race, ethnicity, or national origin rather than the behavior of an individual or information that leads the police to a particular individual who has been identified as being, or having been, engaged in criminal activity." They note:

> Dedicated police officers and professional police practices have contributed to making our communities safer. The majority of police officers are hard-working public servants who perform a dangerous job with dedication and honor; however, the perception that some police officers are engaging in racial profiling has created resentment and distrust of the police, particularly in communities of color.

The problem of racial profiling has become so common that in Orange County, California, the phenomenon is being called DWA—"driving while Asian"; in El Paso, Texas, it's DWM—"driving while Mexican"; and nationwide the practice is called DWB—"driving while black." According to Scoville (2000, p.16): "While other types of profiling—such as the psychological profiling of serial killers and serial rapists practiced by the FBI—have been recognized and accepted as forensically viable, racial profiling stands alone as a vocational pariah." The dilemma for law enforcement is that race is one element of a complete profile and is commonly used in describing suspects. However, the courts have begun imposing legal curtailments on law enforcement's consideration of such characteristics: "Until recently, courts have said that race can be among the factors used in determining whether a suspect should be questioned, but the 9th Circuit Court of Appeals recently ruled against the practice" (Scoville, p.18).

A 1999 Gallup poll showed 81 percent of Americans disapprove of "racial profiling" as a law enforcement technique, and 59 percent believe it is a widespread police practice. A June 2000 Mark Penn poll echoed the earlier results and found that 75 percent of Americans consider "racial profiling" a problem, and 69 percent believe police should be prohibited from taking race into account when targeting people as suspects ("Overcoming the Perception . . .," 2001, p.94). Citing results from their study of contacts between the police and the public, Langan et al. (2001, p.2) report:

> In 1999 an estimated 10.3% of licensed drivers [19.3 million people] were pulled over by police one or more times in a traffic stop. . . . Blacks (12.3%) were more likely than whites (10.4%) to be stopped at least once, and blacks (3.0%) were more likely than whites (2.1%) to be stopped more than once. . . . During the traffic stop, police were more likely to carry out some type of search . . . on a black (11.0%) or Hispanic (11.3%) than a white (5.4%).

Interestingly, when examining data pertaining to the race of the officer involved in traffic stops, the study revealed that black drivers had a worse outcome than white drivers regardless of the officer's race, whether white or black (p.19). Smith and Petrocelli's (2001, p.4) study of police traffic stops involving drivers of different races and ethnic backgrounds found:

> Minority citizens in general, and African Americans in particular, were disproportionately stopped compared with their percentage in the driving-eligible population. However, they were searched no more frequently than Whites; in fact, Whites were significantly more likely than minorities to be the subjects of consent searches. Compared with Whites, and after controlling for variables, minority drivers were more likely to be warned, whereas Whites were more likely to be ticketed or arrested. Examining officer race as a predictor revealed White officers were no more likely than minority officers to stop, search, or arrest minority drivers.

For departments seeking accreditation by the Commission of Accreditation for Law Enforcement Agencies (CALEA), the prohibition of racial profiling has been added to its list of more than 400 standards:

> Agencies seeking accreditation will now be required to prohibit any traffic or field contact, asset seizure or forfeiture effort based on bias. . . .
>
> The accreditation standard concedes that profiling in itself can be a useful tool in law enforcement, but goes on to describe bias-based profiling as the selection of an individual based solely on race, ethnic background, sexual orientation, religion, and economic status, among other characteristics . . . [which] may lead to allegations of constitutional-rights violations, as well as undermining legitimate law enforcement efforts ("CALEA Takes Stand . . .," 2001, p.5).

Horne (2001, p.8) reports: "Measures dealing with racial profiling have been introduced in 24 states so far this [legislative] session, with 14 states taking some action. At this time, however, only one measure has been signed into law." Jurisdictions across the country place racial profiling among the top most important law enforcement issues, and they are striving to develop policies to address this concern:

> From the standpoint of professional law enforcers, there are two overarching reasons why we must ensure that racial and ethnic profiling is not substituted for reasonable suspicion in traffic stops and other law enforcement activities. First and foremost, it is the right thing to do. The Constitution must always come first in law enforcement. The ends do not necessarily justify the means, and we cannot take shortcuts with civil liberties. Second, law enforcement needs the public's trust in order to be successful in our mission. This includes the trust of people of all races, ethnic groups, religions, and political beliefs ("Policies Help Gain . . .," 2000, p.24).

Data analysis technology is available to help police managers make critical personnel and operational decisions in their efforts to prevent racial profiling: "The Police Foundation has announced that its Institute for Integrity, Leadership, and Professionalism in Policing has developed computer software for collecting and analyzing data on police officer–citizen contacts, including traffic stop data. The technology [is] called the Risk Analysis Management System and the Quality of Service Indicator" (www.policefoundation.org). Racial profiling is discussed further in Chapter 10 as an important issue facing police officers.

Public Education Programs

The police also strive to educate the public in traffic safety. Although education is not their primary responsibility, they often participate in local school programs, private safety organizations, local service clubs and state safety councils. The police know these programs are important and that they can contribute to the community good.

Traffic safety education, including wearing seat belts, also has high public relations value. An officer on the school grounds supervising the school crossing guards (patrols) or teaching kids bicycle safety contributes much to the police officers' image by reflecting their concern for the safety and welfare of the community's youths. Safety education, however, is a community responsibility, and community agencies should assume their share of work and not rely solely on the police department for the entire effort.

Traffic Crashes

Motor vehicle crashes are a leading cause of death for people ages 1 to 44. During the hour in which you read this chapter, there will be some 200 crashes resulting in injury and 5 resulting in death. Billions of dollars are lost annually through motor vehicle crashes, and the cost in human suffering and loss is impossible to estimate.

Most crashes involve factors relating to the driver, the vehicle and the road. The interaction of these factors often sets up a series of events that culminate in the mishap.

The basic causes of motor vehicle crashes are human faults, errors, violations and attitudes; road defects; and vehicle defects.

Good driving attitudes are more important than driving skills or knowledge, a fact frequently overlooked in driver education programs. Drivers who jump lanes, try to beat out others as they merge from cloverleafs, race, follow too closely or become angry and aggressive account for many of our serious motor vehicle crashes. Negative driver behavior, such as illegal and unsafe speed, failure to yield the right of way, crossing over the center line, driving in the wrong lane, driving while under the influence of alcohol or drugs and road rage, increases the number of crashes and causes traffic statistics to rise year after year.

Drinking and Drugs

In the early 1970s, law enforcement gave contacts with drunk drivers a low priority, preferring to avoid such encounters. However as Lundman (1998, p.527) notes: "Public attitudes, social movement organizations, and criminal justice laws regarding drunk driving have undergone significant changes in recent years." Data from the National Highway Traffic Safety Administration (NHTSA) indicates the number of people killed by drunken drivers in the United States increased in 2000 for the first time in five years ("Drunk Driving Deaths Up," 2001):

> Overall highway deaths increased slightly in 2000 to 41,812, up from 41,717 in 1999. . . . Forty percent of those, or 16,653, involved alcohol, up from 38 percent, or 15,976, the previous year. It is only the second time alcohol-related deaths have increased since 1986, when 24,045 people were killed.

Glasscock (2000, p.6) states: "Every 33 minutes, someone in this country dies in an alcohol-related crash." He further notes: "Impaired driving, both alcohol- and drug-related, is a leading cause of death for people under 30, and impaired drivers injure more than 300,000 people every year." Because so many fatal automobile crashes involve drivers who have been drinking alcohol, legislators and law enforcement agencies have tried to find a valid way to determine if drivers are under the influence of alcohol. In 1953 New York enacted the first implied consent statute.

Implied consent laws state that any person driving a motor vehicle is deemed to have consented to a chemical blood test of the alcohol content of his or her blood if arrested while intoxicated; refusal to take such a test can be introduced in court as evidence.

The alcohol content in a person's body can be determined through breath, urine or blood tests. The courts have held that this is *not* a violation of a person's Fifth Amendment privilege against self-incrimination. One of the first cases to test the constitutionality of forcibly taking blood from an arrested person was *Breithaupt v. Abram* (1957). In this case the conviction was upheld. Then in 1966, in the landmark case of *Schmerber v. California,* the issue was greatly clarified. The U.S. Supreme Court upheld the conviction and stressed that taking a blood sample was not a violation of the privilege against self-incrimination:

> We hold that the privilege protects an accused only from being compelled to testify against himself, or otherwise provide the state with evidence of a testimonial or communicative nature, and that the withdrawal of blood and use of analysis in question in this case did not involve compulsion to these ends.

The Court did caution that the blood sample should be taken by medical personnel in a medical environment. The Court also ruled that the blood test did not violate the Fourth Amendment even though there was no warrant. The Court reasoned that the blood-alcohol content might have dissipated if the officer had been required to obtain a warrant before ordering the test.

State statute often defines illegal levels of blood-alcohol concentration (BAC), with some states as low as .08 and others as high as .15, with the average at the .10 level. The National Institute on Alcohol Abuse and Alcoholism and the Clearinghouse on Alcohol Information state that a BAC level above .05 is described as "driving while impaired." Horne (p.8) reports:

> So far this [legislative] session, almost 30 states have considered legislation to lower the blood alcohol concentration (BAC) standard for drunk driving from 0.10 to 0.08 percent. Driving this large number of bills is a federal government mandate for tougher DWI legislation. [In the fall of 2000] President Clinton signed into law a measure that establishes a national 0.08 percent BAC standard for drunken driving. States that fail to comply with the national standard will lose 2 percent of their federal highway grants, starting in fiscal year 2004. That penalty increases to 5 percent in fiscal 2005, 6 percent in fiscal 2006, and 8 percent in fiscal 2007.

Blood-alcohol concentration can be influenced by many factors, including physiological differences, food consumption, the amount of ethanol ingested and the time elapsed between drinking and testing.

Sobriety Checkpoints

Many states use sobriety checkpoints to deter driving while under the influence of alcohol. In *Michigan Department of State Police v. Sitz* (1990), the Supreme Court ruled that "sobriety checkpoints are constitutional" because the states have a "substantial interest" in keeping intoxicated drivers off the roads and because the "measure of intrusion on motorists stopped at sobriety checkpoints is slight."

Safety for motorists and officers must be a primary consideration, including proper lighting, warning signs and clearly identifiable official vehicles and personnel. A neutral formula must be used to decide who to stop, for example every third car. Finally each motorist should be detained only long enough for officers to briefly question the driver and to look for signs of intoxication, such as the odor of an alcoholic beverage on the breath, slurred speech and glassy or bloodshot eyes.

Alcohol is not the only substance that may impair drivers. Drugs, whether legal over-the-counter prescription medications or illegal substances, can adversely affect a person's driving competency.

Drug Checkpoints

Citing the success and validity of sobriety checkpoints, some jurisdictions have tried implementing drug interdiction roadblocks as natural extensions of the acceptable DUI checkpoints. In 1998 the Indianapolis Police Department established a narcotics checkpoint under the following guidelines:

> Police stationed approximately 30 officers at each checkpoint and stopped a predetermined number of vehicles. At least one officer would approach each vehicle, advise the driver that he was being stopped briefly at a drug checkpoint, and ask to see a driver's license and registration. The officer would look for signs of impairment by the driver, and conduct an examination of the vehicle from the outside. A drug-detection dog would walk around the outside of the vehicle.
>
> The program guidelines advised officers that they could conduct a search only by consent or based on particularized suspicion. The officers were also instructed that the total duration of each stop was to be less than five minutes, unless there was a legal justification to conduct a search ("Supreme Court Strikes . . .," 2000, p.1).

Despite these guidelines, the U.S. Supreme Court, in *City of Indianapolis v. Edmond* (2000), ruled 6 to 3 that such narcotics interdiction roadblocks were unconstitutional and violated the Fourth Amendment's protections against unreasonable search and seizure. Makholm (2001) states: "The Court, over the dissents of Justices Rehnquist, Scalia, and Thomas, determined that the Indianapolis checkpoints were unconstitutional in that the purpose behind these checkpoints was indistinguishable from the 'general interest in crime control.'"

Occupant Restraints and Air Bags

According to National Highway Traffic Safety Administration studies, safety belts are 45 percent effective in preventing fatalities, 50 percent effective in preventing moderate-to-critical injuries, and 10 percent effective in preventing minor injuries. When safety belts are combined with air bags, injuries are reduced by 68 percent. Beginning in 1998 all new cars were required to have driver and passenger air bags along with safety belts, and effective 1999 light trucks were required to have them.

Aggressive Driving and Road Rage

A tailgater on the freeway veers into the next lane, puts the pedal to the metal to pass and then cuts back in front of the car it was once behind. The car now tailing speeds up so the two cars' bumpers nearly touch. Tempers flare, words fly, fingers flip. Both drivers wish they had a gun. Is this a case of aggressive driving or road rage? They are not the same. The National Highway Traffic Safety Administration (NHTSA) makes the distinction that aggressive driving is a traffic violation and **road rage** is a criminal offense, with aggressive driving often precipitating road rage incidents (*Aggressive Driving Enforcement . . .*, 2000).

One well-publicized incident of road rage began in February 2001 as a two-car fender-bender that led to a confrontation in which one driver hurled the other driver's dog into traffic to its death and then sped away. It ended five months later with the dog-throwing driver receiving the maximum sentence allowed for his actions—three years behind bars ("Man Gets 3 Years . . .," 2001, p.A6). The judge rejected the defendant's plea for leniency, saying it was a case of rage-induced violence and that he feared the defendant could harm someone in the future.

According to the NHTSA: "Aggressive driving has emerged as one of the leading safety hazards on U.S. highways and, according to several recent studies, is considered to be more dangerous than drunk driving or driving without seatbelts by many American drivers." Federal authorities estimate that in 1998, more than two million crashes and nearly 5,300 fatalities resulting from such crashes can be attributed to aggressive driving.

Common behaviors of aggressive drivers include tailgating, changing lanes unsafely, weaving in and out of traffic, exceeding speed limits, driving too fast for road conditions and ignoring traffic control devices such as stop lights and yield signs. A study by the American Automobile Association (AAA) found the most common reasons given for driving aggressively were lateness, slow traffic in the high-speed lane and frustration at traffic congestion (*Aggressive Driving Enforcement . . .*).

Responsibilities of the Officer Called to the Scene of a Crash

Frequently police officers are the first to arrive on the scene of a traffic crash who are equipped, trained and legally responsible for providing services—perhaps lifesaving services if they act quickly and effectively. In addition to rendering first aid to crash victims, police officers have several other duties to perform, such as protecting victims from further harm, reducing to the greatest extent possible the involvement of other cars as they arrive on the scene, summoning emergency services for victims and, if needed, towing services for the vehicles involved, protecting the victims' personal property, locating witnesses, securing evidence and in other ways investigating the crash and keeping traffic moving as though no crash had occurred.

Crash reports by police officers provide a guide for many other department activities. In addition a host of other agencies involved in traffic make use of the information in crash reports. Public information agencies, such as newspapers, television and radio disseminate information about traffic, traffic conditions, road conditions and crashes. Attorneys and the courts use crash reports to determine the facts about the crashes that result in lawsuits. The state motor vehicle department or state department of public safety, which has the power to suspend or revoke driver's licenses, also uses information contained in these reports. Legislative bodies in each state may rely on crash reports when they plan for providing funds, equipment and personnel to effectively enforce traffic safety programs and when they determine what laws must be passed to control traffic.

Traffic crash reports may be used by engineers, both federal and state, who research ways to improve highway systems and by the National Safety Council and state safety councils that compile statistics related to crashes: Who is having them? Where? When? How? The reports may be used by insurance companies that base their automobile insurance rates on the crash record of the community.

Crash reports serve as the basis of traffic law enforcement policy, crash prevention programs, traffic education, legislative reform of traffic laws, traffic engineering decisions and motor vehicle administrative decisions.

Crash Reconstruction

Crash reconstruction using videotape can establish the facts of crashes and help in lawsuits, insurance cases and vehicular criminal cases. In video reconstruction, scale models of the vehicles are used, often with a photo or video of the crash scene itself as the background. Speed calculations are made from the reporting officer's diagram and notes.

A plethora of computer software programs are also available to help crash investigators re-create the scene and determine some of the "unknowns," such as how fast the vehicles were traveling, if and how environmental elements factored into the crash and how stationary objects may have affected vehicle trajectory.

Traffic Enforcement and the Apprehension of Criminals

The standard traffic stop results in many arrests for more serious crimes. In fact as Hurley (1998, p.16) states: "Every officer should be encouraged to detect and apprehend those who commit traffic violations during their tour of duty. Statistics indicate that routine enforcement of traffic laws detects more criminal activity and results in more arrests than do investigative techniques." Georges (2000, p.53) adds: "As important as a reduction in traffic crashes is, traffic safety programs produce other important benefits. The largest of these is the detection and deterrence of crime. . . . A simple analysis demonstrates that many criminal offenders drive badly!" He concludes: "It has often been said that one of the best crime prevention tools is a police car making a traffic stop."

A case in point: Oklahoma state trooper Charles Hanger stopping Timothy McVeigh's car because it didn't have license plates. Trooper Hanger, unaware of the driver's involvement in the day's earlier terrorist bombing of the Alfred P. Murrah Building in Oklahoma City, cited McVeigh for, among other things, the absence of license tags and carrying a concealed gun. While McVeigh was sitting in a jail cell, being processed into the system for his offenses, investigators handling the immediate aftermath of the bombing were searching for suspects, including McVeigh. Their database search turned up a "hit," and the trooper was credited for apprehending, albeit unwittingly, a terrorist. McVeigh was later convicted and executed for his involvement in the bombing.

All uniformed officers should enforce traffic laws because of the potential for apprehending a felon.

Patrol and Community Policing

The support of patrol officers for community policing is vital. Some communities are making the patrol officer an integral part of the neighborhood. One inexpensive approach to integrating patrol officers into the neighborhood is found in Providence, Rhode Island, and Horry County, South Carolina, where McDonald's restaurants have provided reserved tables and telephone lines for officers to use. Signs reading "Police Work Station" are posted prominently. Weiss and Dresser (2001, p.117) note: "Small things like reclaiming shopping carts, removing drunks from park benches, discouraging panhandling and advocating street lighting can reduce a city's crime rate, allowing it to regain its ambiance and beauty." They describe how the city of St. Petersburg, Florida, approached the local crime problem from a community policing perspective.

"St. Pete" had been in seedy decline for many years, with a vacancy rate of 26 to 30 percent, until the implementation of the Downtown Deployment team in 1985. This unit patrols a seven-square-mile city center area from morning until bar closing time, focusing on the small things—the misdemeanor offenses—thus allowing police to "cut into the staging ground for larger crime." One of the methods used by this uniformed services task force is identifying local **scofflaws,** people who habitually violate the law. According to Weiss and Dresser (p.117): "By establishing a high profile and looking for scofflaw misdemeanors, the policy takes away the sense of lawlessness and discourages crime."

Another activity that has helped reduce neighborhood crime involves community policing officers teaching landlords how to screen tenants (p.117): "If the police learn of a crack pusher, they call the landlord who will evict the tenant and even return the security deposit. Now, crack houses are closed down within a couple of days. The police work with the people of a community, urging them to report violations."

The unit has also engaged the business community in the effort to lower crime and disorder, and "business groups are actively aiding the police in enforcing statutes and gaining convictions" (p.118). Through the ongoing, high-profile efforts of the downtown task force, an overall 25 percent reduction in downtown crime has been achieved, and the city is now considered a center for arts, culture, sports and entertainment.

Summary

Of all the operations performed by the police, patrol is the most vital. Patrol is responsible for providing continuous police service and high-visibility law enforcement, thereby deterring crime. In addition patrol officers may be responsible for assisting people, enforcing laws, investigating crimes, keeping traffic moving, maintaining order and resolving conflicts.

Traditionally patrol has been random, reactive, incident driven and focused on rapid response to calls. Patrol might be more effective if it were proactive, directed and problem oriented and if it used differentiated response strategies. Directed patrol uses crime statistics to plan shift and beat staffing, providing more coverage during times of peak criminal activity and in high-crime areas.

Patrol can be accomplished by foot, automobile, motorcycle, bicycle, horseback, aircraft and boat. The most commonly used and most effective patrol is usually a combination of automobile and foot patrol. Several factors are important in the structure and management of patrol. Equal shift and beat size staffing creates major problems and lessens the effectiveness of patrol during certain times and in certain areas.

Many hours are spent in traffic-related police work. The primary goal of traffic law enforcement is to produce voluntary compliance with traffic laws while keeping traffic moving safely and smoothly. Traffic officers have many responsibilities and specific tasks to perform. Traffic officers may be responsible for enforcing traffic laws, directing and controlling traffic, providing directions and assistance to motorists, investigating motor vehicle crashes, providing emergency assistance at the scene of a crash, gathering information related to traffic and writing reports.

However effective a traffic program may be, motor vehicle crashes will occur. The three basic causes of crashes are (1) human faults, errors, violations and attitudes, (2) road defects and (3) vehicle defects.

Alcohol is often involved in traffic crashes. In an effort to determine if a driver is intoxicated, legislatures have enacted implied consent laws. These laws state that any person driving a motor vehicle is deemed to have consented to a chemical test of the alcohol content of his or her blood if arrested while intoxicated; refusal to take such a test can be introduced in court as evidence.

All uniformed officers should enforce traffic laws because of the potential for apprehending a felon. The responsibilities of the patrol/traffic officer in a mobile society are numerous, demanding and vital.

Discussion Questions

1. What type of patrol is used in your community?
2. Why doesn't patrol have as much prestige as investigation?
3. Why is patrol considered a hazardous assignment by some and a boring assignment by others?
4. Which do you support, a one-officer or two-officer patrol unit? Why?
5. If you had your choice of patrol, what method would you select? Why?
6. What kind of traditional patrol do you feel is effective? Which of the suggested changes do you support?
7. Have you ever been involved in a traffic crash? How would you evaluate the performance of the officer(s) responding to the call?
8. What can the public do to make the traffic officer's job easier?
9. Does your state have a seat belt law? If so, when was it passed, and what kind of penalty does it impose?
10. When do you think police officers should issue warning tickets rather than citations for people who are speeding?

InfoTrac *College Edition Assignment*

Use InfoTrac College Edition to help answer the Discussion Questions as appropriate.

- Check *police patrol* on InfoTrac College Edition and note the Supreme Court case *Atwater v. City of Lago Vista* (arrest for minor traffic offenses). This case covers arrest, discretion and police punishment. It is historical and could be used as a guideline. Outline important points of the case, and be prepared to share and discuss your notes with the class.

 *Internet Assignment*

Go to http://www.ih2000.net/ira/copbook.htm and outline the article "Police on Patrol: The Other Side of the Story." This is a test of discretionary problems. Be prepared to discuss some of these problems with the class.

Book-Specific Web Site

The book-specific Web site at http://info.wadsworth.com/0534552803 hosts a variety of resources for students and instructors. Included are extended activities from each chapter in which students write a policy, use critical thinking skills to make choices in response to a given scenario, use InfoTrac College Edition with direct links to articles for participation in topical discussion forums, and analyze court cases using Web links for research. Many activities can be printed or emailed to instructors. Plus, cited cases with Web links, interactive key term FlashCards, PowerPoint presentations, chapter objectives, and an extensive collection of chapter-based Web links provide additional information and activities to include in the curriculum.

References

Aggressive Driving Enforcement: Strategies for Implementing Best Practices. National Highway Traffic Safety Administration, 2000. http://www.nhtsa.dot.gov/people/injury/enforce/aggressdrivers/aggenforce/

Anderson, David C. "Crime by the Numbers—Compstat Takes Off." *Law Enforcement News,* March 15, 2001, p.9.

Anderson, John Wesley. "Innovative Program Reels in Serious Traffic Offenders." *The Police Chief,* July 2000, pp.49–52.

Bobit, Bonnie. "Bicycle Patrols: Spinning Along a Road of Popularity." *Police,* February 1998, pp.32–35.

"CALEA Takes Stand on Racial Profiling." *Law Enforcement News,* April 15, 2001, p.5.

Campbell, Frank. "Patrolling Technology, Part 1." *Police,* February 1998a, p.39.

Campbell, Frank. "Patrolling Technology, Part 2." *Police,* April 1998b, pp.34–36.

Chermak, Steven; McGarrell, Edmund F.; and Weiss, Alexander. "Citizens' Perceptions of Aggressive Traffic Enforcement Strategies." *Justice Quarterly,* June 2001, pp.365–391.

Cox, J. Stephen. "Writing Traffic Tickets: A Very Non-Routine Event." *Law and Order,* May 1998, pp.42–46.

Dangaard, Colin. "Mounted Patrol Fills Niche." *Law and Order,* March 1998, pp.88–92.

DeFranco, Liz Martinez. "Patrolling the Water." *Law Enforcement Technology,* February 1999, pp.71–74.

"Drunk Driving Deaths Up." DeKalb Police STAR Team Web article, September 24, 2001. http://www.dekalbstarteam.com

Fine, John C. "Police on Horseback: A New Concept for an Old Idea." *FBI Law Enforcement Bulletin,* July 2001, pp.6–8.

Georges, William P. "Traffic Safety Strategies Yield Tangible Benefits." *The Police Chief,* July 2000, pp.53–54.

Glasscock, Bruce G. "National Drunk and Drugged Driving Prevention Month." *The Police Chief,* December 2000, p.6.

Goldstein, Herman. *Problem-Oriented Policing.* New York: McGraw-Hill, 1990.

Groff, Elizabeth R. and LaVigne, Nancy G. "Mapping an Opportunity Surface of Residential Burglary." *Journal of Research in Crime and Delinquency,* August 2001, pp.257–278.

Harries, Keith. *Mapping Crime, Principle and Practice.* Washington, DC: Institute of Justice, December 1999. (NCJ 178919)

Highway Loss Data Institute, Insurance Institute for Highway Safety. http://www.hwysafety.org

Hoffman, John. "Police Bike Association Looks to Future." *Law and Order,* April 1998, pp.54–56.

Horne, Jennifer. "State Legislatures Address Important Law Enforcement Issues." *The Police Chief,* June 2001, p.8.

Huntington, Roy. "Harbor Units: Beat May Be Different, but Goals Are Same." *Police,* February 1998, pp.36–38.

Hurley, James J. "Traffic Enforcement a Key to Crime Reduction." *Law and Order,* October 1998, pp.16–18.

Johnson, Richard. "The Advantages of Two-Officer Patrol Teams." *Law and Order,* January 1999, pp.68–70.

Kalk, Dan. "Taking Control of Traffic Stops." *Police,* May 1998, pp.36–37.

Kanable, Rebecca. "Red Light Runners." *Law Enforcement Technology,* September 2000, pp.24–28.

Kariya, Mark. "Rough Riding on an ATV." *Law Enforcement Technology,* September 2000, pp.38–42.

Kelling, George L. *Foot Patrol.* Washington, DC: National Institute of Justice, no date.

Klockars, Carl B. *Thinking about Police: Contemporary Readings.* New York: McGraw-Hill, 1983.

Langan, Patrick A.; Greenfeld, Lawrence A.; Smith, Steven K.; Durose, Matthew R.; and Levin, David J. *Contacts between Police and the Public: Findings from the 1999 National Survey.* Washington, DC: Bureau of Justice Statistics, February 2001. (NCJ 184957)

LaVigne, Nancy G. and Wartell, Julie. *Crime Mapping Case Studies: Successes in the Field,* Vol. 2, 2000.

Law Enforcement Officers Killed and Assaulted, 2000. Washington, DC: Federal Bureau of Investigation Uniform Crime Reports, 2001. http://www.fbi.gov/ucr/killed/00leoka.pdf

Lundman, Richard J. "City Police and Drunk Driving: Baseline Data." *Justice Quarterly,* September 1998, pp.527–546.

Makholm, John A. "Legal Lights." *The Law Enforcement Trainer,* January/February 2001.

"Man Gets 3 Years for Tossing Dog to Its Death." Associated Press, as reported in (Minneapolis/St. Paul) *Star Tribune,* July 14, 2001, p.A6.

Margolis, Jeremy; Watts, Darren; and Johnston, Iain. "Proactive Defense Strategies Can Minimize Risk." *The Police Chief,* July 2000, pp.18–23.

Morrison, Richard D. "Eye in the Sky." *Law Enforcement Technology,* June 1998, pp.66–68.

National Neighborhood Foot Patrol Center (pamphlet). East Lansing, MI: Michigan State University, no date.

"Overcoming the Perception of Racial Profiling." *Law and Order,* April 2001, pp.94–101.

Paynter, Ronnie L. "Gyroplanes: A Cost-Effective Alternative." *Law Enforcement Technology,* October 1999, pp.132–135.

Polan, Jim. "Motorcycle Operations Require Training." *Law and Order,* July 2000, pp.71–73.

The Police Foundation. http://www.policefoundation.org

"Policies Help Gain Public Trust." *The Police Chief,* July 2000, pp.24–29.

Ramirez, Deborah; McDevitt, Jack; and Farrell, Amy. *A Resource Guide on Racial Profiling Data Collection Systems: Promising Practices and Lessons Learned.* Washington, DC: Justice Department, November 2000. (NCJ 184768)

Rogers, Donna. "Mapping Covers New Ground." *Law Enforcement Technology,* July 2000, pp.74–78.

Rogers, Donna. "The Rap on Mapping." *Law Enforcement Technology,* June 2001, pp.64–68.

Scoville, Dean. "A View Askew: A Sideways Look at Racial Profiling." *Police,* August 2000, pp.16–23.

Sharp, Arthur G. "Coming Your Way: Motorcycles on Ice?" *Law and Order,* October 1998, pp.44–49.

Smith, Eileen Robinson. "Charleston's Mounted Patrol: An Integral Part of the Police Force." *Law and Order,* January 1999, pp.71–72.

Smith, Michael R. and Petrocelli, Matthew. "Racial Profiling? A Multivariate Analysis of Police Traffic Stop Data." *Police Quarterly,* March 2001, pp.4–27.

Strandberg, Keith W. "High on Horses." *Law Enforcement Technology,* October 1999, pp.106–108.

Strandberg, Keith W. "E-Bike Makes Biking a Breeze." *Law Enforcement Technology,* June 2001, pp.102–107.

"Supreme Court Strikes Down Drug Interdiction Roadblocks." *Criminal Justice Newsletter,* February 15, 2000, pp.1–2.

Swager, Brent. "Aviation Unit Cost-Effective." *Law and Order,* May 2000, pp.40–42.

Swope, Ross. "Aggressive Patrol: Forward to the Past." *Law and Order,* July 1999, pp.79–82.

Travis, Jeremy. "Foreword." In *Mapping Crime: Principle and Practice* by Keith Harries. Washington, DC: National Institute of Justice, December 1999, p.v. (NCJ 178919)

Vonk, Kathleen. "Riding a Mountain Bike on Patrol: A Training Issue?" *The Law Enforcement Trainer,* September/October 2000, pp.26–29, 38–39.

Ward, Thomas J. "Commissioners, Chiefs and COMPSTAT." *Law and Order,* July 2000, pp.133–137.

Weiss, Jim and Dresser, Mary. "Cleaning Up the City." *Law and Order,* June 2001, pp.117–118.

Wexler, Sanford. "Above All Else." *Law Enforcement Technology,* September 1998a, pp.20–24.

Wexler, Sanford. "Police Work Isn't Horseplay, Even for Horses." *Law Enforcement Technology,* October 1998b, pp.78–80.

Cases Cited

Breithaupt v. Abram, 352 U.S. 432 (1957)

City of Indianapolis v. Edmond, No.99-1080 (2000)

Michigan Department of State Police v. Sitz, 496 U.S. 444, 110 (1990)

Schmerber v. California, 384 U.S. 757 (1966)

Whren v. United States, 517 U.S. 806 (1996)

Chapter 7

Specialized Roles of Police

Knowledge is of two kinds. We know a subject ourselves, or we know where we can find information upon it.

—Samuel Johnson

Do You Know?

- What the primary characteristic of an effective investigator is?
- What the primary responsibilities of the investigator are?
- What questions investigators seek answers to?
- Why both sketches and photographs of a crime scene are usually needed?
- How investigators must deal with evidence?
- What DNA profiling is?
- What the three basic types of identification are?
- In what two areas intelligence units work?
- Why all officers are juvenile officers much of the time?
- In what areas vice officers become involved?
- What tactical forces officers are?
- How K-9s are used? In what categories they may be specifically trained?
- What types of law enforcement agencies are considered nontraditional?

Can You Define?

ballistics
biometrics
body language
chain of evidence
complainant
contamination
corroborate
cyanoacrylate
digitizing
discovery crimes
DNA profiling
empathy
evidence
field identification
follow-up investigation
forensic science
informant
interrogate
interview
involvement crimes
kinesics
latent fingerprints
modus operandi (M.O.)
nonverbal communication
perception
preliminary investigation
riflings
solvability factors
suppressible crimes
totality of circumstances
undercover
witness

INTRODUCTION

In addition to the general function of patrol, including traffic assignments, a number of specialized functions are also required of law enforcement personnel. Sometimes all the functions are performed by a single person—a formidable challenge. In large departments, however, separate divisions may exist for each specialized function. Some patrol officers receive special training to deal with specific problems, such as hostage and sniper situations, VIP protection, riot or crowd control, rescue operations and control of suppressible crimes.

Suppressible crimes are crimes that commonly occur in locations and under circumstances that give police officers a reasonable opportunity to deter or apprehend offenders. Included among suppressible crimes are robbery, burglary, car theft, assault and sex crimes. Such problems often involve a need for covert surveillance and decoys, tactics that cannot be used by uniformed patrol officers.

Specialized operations are often used to saturate particular areas or to stake out suspects and possible crime locations. Countermeasures to combat street crimes have included police decoys to catch criminals—one of the most cost-effective and productive apprehension methods available. Officers have posed as cab drivers, old women, truck drivers, money couriers, nuns and priests. They have infiltrated drug circles as undercover agents. Usually operating in high-crime areas, decoy officers are vulnerable to violence and injury. The results are considered worth the risk, however; an attack upon a decoy almost always results in the attacker's conviction.

This chapter begins with what is often considered the most glamorous aspect of policing—investigation. Next the specialized functions of profilers and intelligence officers are explored. This is followed by a discussion of juvenile officers, vice officers, tactical forces officers, K-9-assisted officers and reserve officers. The chapter concludes with a description of nontraditional officers, such as those found on transit lines and in parks and airports.

Investigation

To the general public, the term *criminal investigation* often brings to mind the detective as portrayed in novels, on the radio, in magazines and on television. The detective or investigator single-handedly digs out evidence, collects tips from informants, identifies criminals, tracks them down and brings them to justice. Investigation is a prestigious assignment.

In reality, however, as research has established, patrol officers are responsible for most arrests. Recall that aggressive traffic officers make more criminal arrests than detectives. In a great many departments throughout the country, the detective is a patrol officer—no special detective or investigative division exists. Throughout this chapter, when the term *investigator* is used, it may refer either to a patrol officer performing investigative duties or to a specialist. Investigators do *not* determine the suspects to be guilty; they remain objective in their investigation.

> A primary characteristic of an effective investigator is objectivity.

The investigator seeks the truth, not simply proof of the suspect's guilt. Article 10 of the *Canons of Police Ethics* (International Association of Chiefs of Police) states:

> The law enforcement officer shall be concerned equally in the prosecution of the wrongdoer and the defense of the innocent. He shall ascertain what constitutes evidence and shall present such evidence impartially and without malice. In so doing, he will ignore social, political, and all other distinctions among the persons involved, strengthening the tradition of the reliability and integrity of an officer's word.
>
> The law enforcement officer shall take special pains to increase his perception and skill of observation, mindful that in many situations his is the sole impartial testimony to the facts of a case.

The Preliminary Investigation

The **preliminary investigation** consists of actions performed immediately upon receiving a call to respond to the scene of a crime and is usually conducted by patrol officers.

The importance of response time has been debated. Traditionally, rapid response has been stressed, but this has been called into question. Some studies have found that arrests are seldom attributed to fast police response to reported serious crimes because about 75 percent of all serious crimes are **discovery crimes,** crimes uncovered after they have been committed. Only the remaining 25 percent, the **involvement crimes,** require rapid response.

According to Donofrio (2000, p.117): "Most crime scene investigators are familiar with Locard's Exchange Principle. In essence this principle dictates that if an individual comes in contact with an environment, both are changed in some ostensibly insignificant way. . . . In short, when coming in contact with an environment, individuals will both add to and take away from it." What are the implications of this principle to first responders at a crime scene? Donofrio (p.117) explains: "This [principle] is the savior as well as the nemesis of law enforcement. The suspect through this exchange leaves behind a potential gold mine of evidence. Conversely, this principle becomes the enemy of investigators when officers unknowingly take trace evidence away."

The National Institute of Justice's Technical Working Group on Crime Scene Investigation (2000, pp.11–17) has developed a guide for law enforcement that sets forth the following prioritization of efforts for first responders arriving at a crime scene:

1. *Initial Response/Receipt of Information*—The initial response to an incident shall be expeditious and methodical. The initial responding officer(s) shall promptly, yet cautiously, approach and enter crime scenes, remaining observant of any persons, vehicles, events, potential evidence, and environmental conditions.
2. *Safety Procedures*—The safety and physical well-being of officers and other individuals, in and around the crime scene, are the initial responding officer(s') first priority. The initial responding officer(s) arriving at the scene shall identify and control any dangerous situations or persons.
3. *Emergency Care*—After controlling any dangerous situations or persons, the initial responding officer(s') next responsibility is to ensure that medical attention is provided to injured persons while minimizing contamination of the scene.
4. *Secure and Control Persons at the Scene*—The initial responding officer(s) shall identify persons at the crime scene and control their movement.
5. *Boundaries: Identify, Establish, Protect, and Secure*—The initial responding officer(s) at the scene shall conduct an initial assessment to establish and control the crime scene(s) and its boundaries.

6. *Turn Over Control of the Scene and Brief Investigator(s) in Charge*—The scene briefing is the only opportunity for the next in command to obtain initial aspects of the crime scene prior to subsequent investigation.
7. *Document Actions and Observations*—Documentation must be maintained as a permanent record.

The preliminary investigation results are written in an incident report containing the basic facts about the crime, the crime scene and any suspects. Some cases are solved during this phase. For those that are not, the decision must be made as to whether to pursue the case. Usually this decision is based on **solvability factors,** that is, factors affecting the probability of successfully concluding the case, such as whether there are witnesses and/or physical evidence. If the solvability factors indicate the case might be successfully resolved, a follow-up investigation is conducted.

The Follow-Up Investigation

The **follow-up investigation** may be conducted by the investigative services division, sometimes also known as the detective bureau. Therefore successful investigation relies on cooperative, coordinated efforts of both the patrol and the investigative functions. In most smaller departments, the same officer handles both the preliminary and the follow-up investigations.

Investigative Responsibilities

The responsibilities of investigators are many and varied.

Investigative responsibilities include:
- Securing the crime scene.
- Recording all facts related to the case.
- Photographing, measuring and sketching the crime scene.
- Obtaining and identifying evidence.
- Protecting and storing evidence.
- Interviewing witnesses and interrogating suspects.
- Assisting in identifying suspects.

Securing the Crime Scene

Any area that contains evidence of criminal activity is considered a crime scene and must be secured to eliminate **contamination,** that is, the introduction of something foreign into the scene, moving items at the scene or removing evidence from it. The first officer on the scene must protect it from any change. This single responsibility may have far-reaching effects on solving the crime. Physical evidence must be properly protected to have legal and scientific validity.

Recording Relevant Information

Investigators record all necessary information by photographing, sketching and taking notes to be used later in a written report and testifying in court.

The investigator must obtain answers to the questions: Who? What? Where? When? How? and Why?

Answers to these questions are obtained by observation and by talking to witnesses, complainants and suspects, as discussed shortly. They are recorded in notes, photographs and sketches or are in the form of physical evidence.

Photographing, Measuring and Sketching the Crime Scene

The scene is usually photographed, measured and sketched. The photographs show the scene as it was found, taken in a series to tell a story. Close-up photographs of evidence, such as footprints, tire tracks and tool marks are also taken. In addition to traditional photography, other types of photography, such as ultraviolet, infrared and aerial are used. Videotaping has become increasingly common in recording a crime scene.

The digital camera has made photography much more efficient and cost-effective. The process, called **digitizing,** is being used by many agencies. Digital photography can enhance obscured fingerprints, record crime scenes and take mug shots. Digital photographs can also be enlarged or manipulated; for example a mug shot showing a criminal with long hair and a mustache can be manipulated to shorten the hair and to remove the mustache.

In addition to photographs, a sketch is usually made of the scene. Sketches can be selective and can also show entire areas, for example an entire layout of a home or business. The sketch need not be an artistic masterpiece as long as it includes all relevant details and is accurate and clear. (See Figure 7.1.)

Computer programs based mostly on computer-aided design (CAD) have made crime scene sketching much easier. According to Dees (2001, p.12): "Crime scene drawing software . . . [makes] it possible for anyone who can use a keyboard and mouse to produce a top-flight drawing. . . . CAD software makes it as easy to produce a true scale drawing as it is to produce a rough

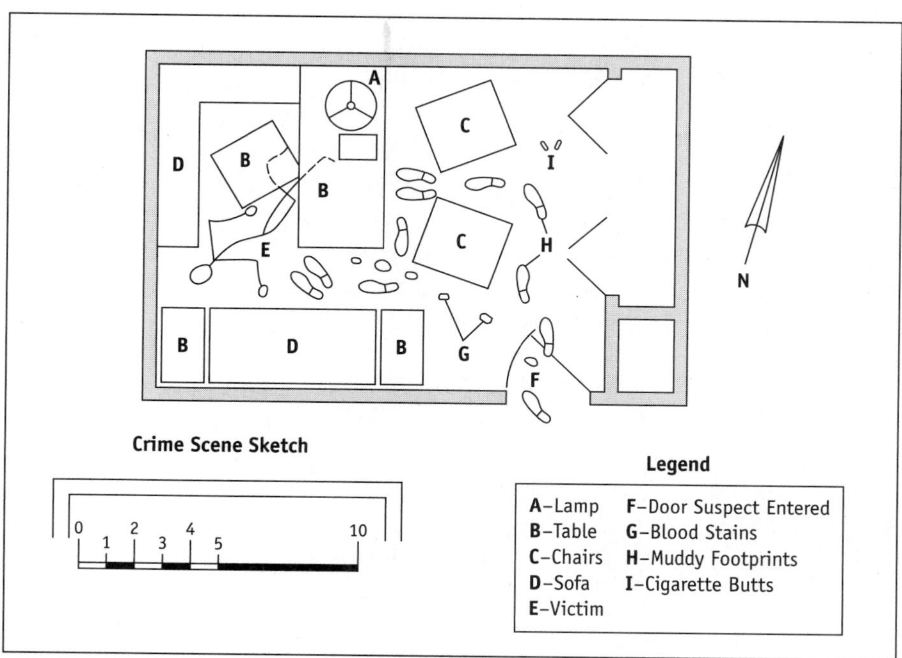

Figure 7.1
Crime Scene Sketch

Source: Wayne W. Bennett and Kären M. Hess. *Criminal Investigation,* 6th ed. Belmont, CA: Wadsworth Publishing Company, 2001, p.51. Reprinted by permission.

sketch, and there is no limit to the size of the 'paper' on which the drawing is displayed. . . . CAD software also allows for the creation of layers that include certain objects but omit others."

Both photographs and sketches are usually needed. The photographs include all details and can show items close up. Sketches can be selective and can show much larger areas.

Obtaining and Identifying Physical Evidence

A large part of an investigator's role centers around obtaining information and **evidence**–proof that a crime has been committed, as well as proof that a particular person (the suspect) committed the crime. All important decisions will revolve around the available evidence and how it was obtained.

Investigators recognize, collect, mark, preserve and transport physical evidence in sufficient quantity for analysis and without contamination.

The kind of evidence to be anticipated is often directly related to the type of crime committed. Scenes of *violent crimes* frequently contain such evidence as blood, hair, fibers, fingerprints, footprints and weapons. Scenes of property crimes are commonly characterized by forcible entry with tools leaving marks on doors, windows, safes, money chests, cash registers and desk drawers. Among the most common types of evidence found at the crime scene are fingerprints, blood, hair, fibers, documents, footprints or tire prints, tool fragments, tool marks, broken glass, paint, insulation from safes, bite marks, firearms and explosives.

Fingerprints are often found at crime scenes. **Latent fingerprints** are made by sweat or grease that oozes out of the pores from little wells under the ridges at the ends of the fingers. Fingerprint identification is an extremely important form of positive identification. *Identification officers* have specialized training in taking, identifying and filing fingerprints. They are skilled in using scanners and computers in their identification.

An important development in detecting and preserving fingerprints is the **cyanoacrylate,** or superglue, fuming process. When cyanoacrylate is heated, fumes are generated that adhere to fingerprints. This process can be used on items taken to a crime laboratory or items at the scene. Lighting can also help detect fingerprints and trace evidence: "The latest forensic light source, superglue chamber or finger powder processor can help crime scene units find what they're looking for" (Laska, 1998, p.120). Regarding the usefulness of barcodes and other identifying codes on items, Nyberg (1998, p.118) notes: "Now, investigators can use the numbers on almost anything to track the movement of an item, and hopefully find its intersection in the world with a victim or offender."

Individuality is not limited to a person's fingertips. Palmprints are now being recognized as valuable evidence when found at a crime scene; in fact, sometimes such prints are the only evidence. One crime lab associate director (Kanable, 2001, p.42) states: "If you process a large amount of evidence, about 25 to 30 percent of the latent impressions are going to be palmprints or partial palmprints." An officer of a company that manufactures and sells AFIS technology estimates 30 percent of cases have nothing but palms (Kanable, p.43).

But because palmprints can have 1,000 minutiae, or 8 to 12 times more minutiae than fingerprints, manual comparison of suspect palmprints is extremely tedious. However: "Palmprint technology is starting to catch up with fingerprint technology . . . [and] there may come a day when automated palmprint identification systems spread throughout the U.S. as AFIS technology did" (Kanable, p.42). The capability exists in many European countries, where palmprint technology is a requirement.

A specialized form of "fingerprinting" is DNA profiling. Deoxyribonucleic acid (DNA) is the basic building block comprising each person's genetic code. DNA is found in virtually every cell in a person's body, including blood, semen, hair and skin cells, and it provides a blueprint for the various characteristics that make each person unique. A person's distinctive DNA composition remains the same throughout life, making it a powerful investigative tool: "DNA evidence collected from a crime scene can link a suspect to a crime or eliminate one from suspicion in the same way that fingerprints are used" (Turman, 2001, p.1).

DNA profiling uses the material from which chromosomes are made to positively identify individuals. No two individuals, except identical twins, have the same DNA structure.

Although DNA profiling is expensive and very labor intensive, the implications for law enforcement are tremendous. To enhance DNA's evidentiary value to criminal investigations, a database similar in concept to AFIS has been developed. Known as CODIS, the FBI's Combined DNA Index System is an electronic national database and searching mechanism containing hundreds of thousands of DNA profiles obtained from evidence samples from unsolved crimes and from known offenders.

DNA evidence has also been used to free persons wrongly convicted of and imprisoned for serious crimes, such as rape or homicide: "As a result of DNA testing, more than 70 persons previously convicted of capital crimes and frequently having served long prison terms have been exonerated" (National Commission, 2000, p.1). In light of such findings, the National Commission on the Future of DNA Evidence was created in 1998 to examine the potential of such evidence and how the National Institute of Justice could encourage its most effective use as a crime fighting tool. Commission members include representatives from the prosecution, the defense bar, law enforcement, the scientific and medical communities, academia and victims' rights organizations.

One of the Commission's technology projections regarding the future of DNA evidence has direct applications to the officer or investigator in the field: "Within 10 years we expect portable, miniaturized instrumentation that will provide analysis at the crime scene with computer-linked remote analysis. This should permit rapid identification and, in particular, quick elimination of innocent suspects" (p.3). However, such technology will likely place law enforcement under further scrutiny regarding their competence in investigative techniques. Indeed, *People v. Simpson* (1995) made apparent the need for thorough, professional processing of a crime scene and the importance of focusing on proper evidence collection procedures rather than on the reliability of evidence.

Another type of evidence often found at crime scenes is a *firearm.* A firearm left at a crime scene may be traced to its owner through the serial number, the manufacturer's identification or the dealer who sold it. The firearm might also contain the suspect's fingerprints or other marks that could lead to identification.

The make of the weapon is usually determined by the **riflings,** spiral grooves cut into the gun's barrel during its manufacture. The riflings vary considerably from manufacturer to manufacturer. **Ballistics** deals with the motion of the bullet, *not* with identification of the weapon from which it was fired.

Protecting and Storing Evidence

All evidence collected is marked to identify who collected it. It is then packaged and placed in the evidence room until needed. If it is removed from the evidence room for any reason, strict check-out and check-in procedures are followed to maintain the **chain of evidence,** that is, documentation of who has had possession of the evidence from the time it was discovered and taken into custody until the present time.

Some agencies have established the position of *evidence technician.* The evidence technician is usually a patrol officer who has received extensive classroom and laboratory training in crime scene investigation. In departments that have small detective bureaus and relatively inexperienced officers, this position fills a notable void. The officer has not been relieved of regular patrol duties but may be called on to conduct crime scene investigations.

Interviewing and Interrogating

A large part of any investigation is talking with people to obtain information. The community-oriented philosophy of policing stresses the importance of communicating with citizens to identify problems and concerns. Investigators **interview** those with information about a crime. They talk with victims, witnesses and friends, coworkers, neighbors or immediate members of victims' and suspects' families. Investigators **interrogate** suspects, those they believe to be connected with a crime.

A **witness** is a person other than a suspect who has helpful information about a specific incident or a suspect. A witness may be a **complainant** (the person reporting the offense), an accuser, a victim, an observer of the incident, an expert, a scientific examiner of physical evidence or an **informant.** Beckwith and Burke (2000, p.109) note the merit in using informants to further criminal investigations: "Informants are, and have been, an important factor in many drug trafficking situations and have been aiding law enforcement for centuries. Because of the informant and the value of their information, many crimes that may have gone undetected have resulted in arrests." They also identify what motivates people to inform: "While an informant might receive money as a reward, most informants cooperate with law enforcement to receive a reduced sentence for a pending criminal matter. Other common motives include revenge, public safety, fear and perverse. Perverse refers to an informant offering an initial motive, while keeping the real motive secret."

Investigators may also interview scientific or expert witnesses for information about or interpretation of specific facts of a case. If the police intend to use such expert testimony in court, however, they must be aware of the Federal Rules of Evidence governing such witnesses. Scuro (2000, p.29) explains that various court decisions have set limits on the admissibility of expert witness testimony when presented in the form of opinions or inferences.

Experience has illustrated time and again that no two people will view the same situation in exactly the same way. How a witness describes what has happened is affected by many factors, some subjective (within the individual) and some objective (inherent in the situation). **Perception** of an incident is affected by the viewer's accuracy of observation, interpretation of what is seen and attention to the incident.

This perception factor greatly affects the usefulness of a witness's statement regarding a criminal event. As former Attorney General Janet Reno (1999) recognized: "Even the most honest and objective people can make mistakes in recalling and interpreting a witnessed event; it is the nature of human memory." Gillen and Thermer (2000, pp.52–53) assert: "Reliable memory retrieval by an eyewitness to a crime is . . . challenging when the event has occurred some time ago or has traumatized the witness or both. . . . Certain interviewing styles, too, can minimize the witness's ability to recall facts about the crime." A five-phase technique known as *the cognitive interview* is designed to elicit the maximum amount of reliable information from an eyewitness.

In applying this technique, it becomes the investigator's task to dispel the witness's anxiety and establish rapport. The investigator must become an active listener and lead the witness into an open-ended narration in which the context of the event is re-created and the witness is asked to give a narrative description of the event. The approach here is similar to what people do every day in trying to jog their memories; for example, you're sitting on the couch and have a thought, perhaps to get a nail clipper from the bathroom. But when you get to the bathroom, you can't remember what it was you came for. After a few frustrating moments trying to recall the object of your quest, you head back to the couch and suddenly it hits you—nail clipper! As Gillen and Thermer (p.54) explain, when you approached the couch, you returned to the context in which the nail clipper thought was created.

During the witness's narrative description, the investigator should avoid interrupting and should use pauses when the witness stops speaking. Gillen and Thermer (p.55) state: "By taking advantage of the power of the pause, the investigator is saying to the witness, tell me more." It is also important for investigators to have **empathy** or understanding of those they interview. This is not the same as sympathy. It simply means trying to see things from the other person's point of view.

A frequently overlooked but extremely important aspect of communication is what is conveyed beyond the words used. This includes both nonverbal communication and body language. **Nonverbal communication** includes everything but the actual words in a communication: tone, pitch, rate, inflection. A nervous person may speak rapidly in a high-pitched voice. Nonverbal communication also includes how a person is dressed. As noted by Miller and Hess (2002, p.152):

> The police communicate with the public most obviously through the uniform they wear, the way they wear it and the equipment they carry. . . . Wearing a uniform may be called the ultimate in *power dressing.* Uniforms are authoritative and professional and have an impact on the public's behavior.

Body language, also called **kinesics,** refers to messages conveyed by how a person moves. Consider, for example, the contrast between a person slouched in a chair and one sitting at rigid attention, or the person shuffling down the street and one running.

In such cases as robbery, assault or rape, eyewitness testimony of the victim or a witness may be all that is necessary for a conviction. It is always preferable, however, to have physical evidence to **corroborate** the eyewitness testimony, that is, to support or confirm the testimony. Many departments videotape interviews and interrogations.

Identifying Suspects

If officers do not witness a crime, eyewitness identification plays an important part in the arrest, as well as in the trial proceedings. Very specific questions and use of an identification diagram may aid witnesses in identifying suspects. Other information related to the suspect is also obtained: for example how the suspect left the scene—running, walking, in a vehicle—and in what direction.

If the witness knows the suspect, the investigator asks about the suspect's personal associates, habits and where he or she is likely to be found. Usually, however, the witness does not know the suspect. In such cases investigators must obtain identification in other ways.

The three basic types of identification are:

- Field identification.
- Photographic identification.
- Lineup identification.

Each type of identification is used in specific circumstances, and each must meet certain legal requirements to be admissible in court. Sometimes more than one type of identification is used.

Field identification is at-the-scene identification, made within a short time after a crime has been committed. Generally the suspect is returned to the crime scene for possible identification, or the witness may be taken to where the suspect is being held. Field identification is used when a suspect matches the description given by a witness and is apprehended close to the crime scene. The critical element in a field identification is time.

Field identification is based on a **totality of circumstances,** taking into consideration the witness's concentration on the suspect when the crime was committed, the accuracy of the description, the certainty at the time of the confrontation and the length of time between crime commission and the field identification. A reasonable basis for believing that immediate identification is needed must exist because the suspect does not have the right to have counsel present (*United States v. Ash, Jr.*, 1973).

Photographic identification is another option. Most people are familiar with the procedure of having victims and witnesses go through mug books in hopes of finding a picture of the person they saw commit a particular crime. This type of identification is time consuming and is profitable only if the suspect has a record.

Mug shots are not the only types of photographs used in suspect identification. Frequently officers know, or have a strong suspicion about, who committed a given crime. If the suspect is not in custody, or if it is not possible to conduct a fair lineup, officers may present photographs of people of similar general descriptions to victims or witnesses, who may identify the suspect from among the photographs.

A third option is a lineup, allowing witnesses to observe several individuals, one of whom is the suspect, to see if the witnesses can identify the suspect. A suspect may be asked to speak, walk, turn, assume a stance or make a gesture.

If for any reason a suspect refuses to cooperate in a lineup, photographic identification may be used. The suspect's refusal to participate may be used against him or her in court.

Another way to identify a suspect may be the **modus operandi** or **M.O.** Computer software is useful for managing large volumes of data in M.O. files.

The Use of Computers in Investigations

Computers are being used to identify fingerprints, track evidence, analyze evidence and aid in case investigation and management.

Fingerprints

One of the first uses of computers in law enforcement was to assist in identifying fingerprints. More and more departments are installing automated fingerprint identification systems (AFIS). A more recent use of computers in fingerprinting has been the introduction of **biometrics**—measuring physical characteristics, such as fingerprints or voice, by computer.

Evidence

A computerized evidence tracking system (ETS) can prevent countless problems. Many such systems are available. Often they incorporate barcodes, such as those used on merchandise in grocery stores.

Laboratory Analysis

The FBI Laboratory uses computers in most of its operations. Use of computers has greatly enhanced **forensic science,** that is, the study of evidence.

Case Management/Investigation

Sophisticated software packages have been developed to help with case management—receiving, processing, organizing and interrelating all aspects of information on a case. They can also keep track of ongoing progress in an investigation.

As discussed in detail in Chapter 6, computerized crime mapping technology has allowed even small agencies to get big city crime analysis.

The Internet

The Internet has revolutionized the way law enforcement gathers and shares information. Not only does the Internet provide access to unlimited general information, it also presents a forum in which a department can reach out to the community. With many households online, and more sure to follow, a department's Web page may post requests for tips regarding certain crimes, inform the public about local public safety issues and increase awareness of law enforcement activities and achievements.

Community Policing and Investigation

In many departments, the detective squad is seen as the "country club" unit, segregated from the other divisions. Investigators have a reputation of being "prima donnas," reluctant to seek help from or share information with officers in other units. Interaction with one another may be infrequent, even within the detective squad itself. Such a culture effectively isolates investigators from a sea of information held by other officers, resources that could be vital to solving a case.

In line with the community policing philosophy, investigators are now recognizing the benefits in developing partnerships with various community members as well as with other units in the department. This approach makes investigation more proactive and fosters problem solving among detectives. According to Singh (2001, p.4): "A shift to community-oriented investigations is an acknowledgement that crime is a complex phenomenon that requires a balanced response. Adopting a balanced approach means that detectives must collaborate better among themselves and with other community stakeholders." Partners that may be enlisted to enhance investigative efforts include the department's community policing unit, the crime prevention unit, crime victims and local businesses.

Singh (p.7) explains how such initiatives should not be thought of as "programs," which have a beginning and an end, but rather as cultural changes in the way police do their work. The intention of these initiatives is not to create a community investigation unit but "to create an entire department equipped to use problem solving in its everyday police work" (p.8).

Profilers

Since the first police investigation, detectives have focused on relatively superficial characteristics to identify suspects, such as height, weight, race, gender, age, accent, type of car driven, M.O., etc. While these descriptors remain valid and are still considered when searching for suspects, investigators have begun delving deeper into suspects' personalities, psyches, pathologies and resultant behaviors to develop more complete portraits of criminals. Lines (1999, p.49) states: "In 1984, the FBI began training U.S. federal agents and police officers in the techniques of criminal investigative analysis—commonly referred to as 'criminal profiling.'" Such profiles can and often do exist in the absence of any physical descriptors.

Eggers (1999, pp.242–243) notes: "The terms *psychological profiling, offender profiling, criminal profiling* or *criminal personality profiling* have become almost household words when the public hears about serial killers or unsolved murders in the mass media or in works of fiction." However, as Eggers (p.243) points out, such popular portrayals of profiling are inaccurate, promoting the myth that profiling is a magical skill. But as Cook and Hinman (1999, p.230) note, the criminal profiling technique is a combination of art and science: "In a make-believe world, [profilers] always get the villains, usually after face-to-face denouements. In the real world, profiling is not as dramatic, or as accurate. It depends on the profiler's ability to draw upon investigative experience, training in forensic and behavioral science, and empirically developed information about the characteristics of known offenders."

They (p.231) further explain: "Profilers study the evidence of the offender's activities with the victim and the offender's preparation and technical attention to details to develop a profile of the kind of person who is most likely to have committed the crime. When the profile is complete, the descriptors in it are compared to potential suspects as they are developed." According to Davis (1999, p.291): "The manner in which a violent crime is performed expresses the psychological pattern, makeup, and expression of the individual performing it. Criminal investigative analysis, or criminal personality profiling, examines and identifies the subtle habits, psychological traits and personality variables associated with criminal activity."

Intelligence Officers

Most large departments have an intelligence division whose top officer reports directly to the chief and whose activities are kept from the rest of the department. Intelligence units work in two areas.

Intelligence officers may be undercover officers investigating crime or internal affairs officers investigating officers within the department.

Undercover

The first area is **undercover** work—ongoing investigations into such criminal activity as illegal sale of guns, payoffs to police officers or politicians, major drug cases and organized crime activities. Undercover employees (UCEs) often work on cases in cooperation with county, state and federal investigators. Band and Sheehan (1999, p.1) state: "Undercover assignments come in many varieties. They include everything from short-term, buy-bust scenarios to longer-term investigations lasting months or years. The essence of all cases, however, remains the same. UCEs develop relationships and eventually betray them."

Given the nature of such assignments and their reliance on anonymity and obscurity, undercover intelligence officers do not wear uniforms or drive marked cars, and they may use assumed names and fictitious identities. To avoid identification problems, some large agencies use officers who have just graduated from rookie school because they are less known on the street. Strandberg (1998b, p.82) states: "Undercover operations are the ultimate method acting. The undercover officer has to look and act whatever part he or she is playing, but the stakes are much higher. The consequence of a bad performance isn't a bad review, it could be a matter of life or death."

One approach to undercover work is the sting operation, where police deceive criminals into openly committing illegal acts. Such operations, however, carry legal risks for law enforcement. Officers must adhere to department policies and procedures, and accurately document their activity, lest the undercover agents and the agency be accused of entrapment.

While undercover operations are often perceived as mysterious and glamorous assignments, physical dangers abound. Even the most cautious officers may find themselves unavoidably immersed in the violence that defines the criminal world, victims of assault, shootings and worse, sometimes at the hands of other officers who are unaware of their undercover status. Dumont (2000, p.103) asserts: "Undercover work is exciting, extremely useful, and dangerous—extremely dangerous. Dealing with criminals is dangerous on any level; posing as one to gain their confidence and ultimately expose them is many times more dangerous."

According to DeBlanc and Redman (2000, p.34): "Many narcotics officers and agents are seriously injured or killed each year while conducting mid and upper level undercover drug investigations." Dumont (p.105) adds: "Violence has become synonymous with the drug trade. This is partly attributed to the increased exposure to lengthy prison terms or the paranoia associated with sustained drug use." Sometimes the violence occurs suddenly, for no apparent reason: "An FBI agent, working undercover, was shot and killed for no explainable reason. Adding to the mystery was the fact that the assailant was also killed and, therefore, could not be interrogated as to why a drug deal that appeared to be proceeding according to plan ended in the death of a 16–year veteran of the FBI" (Dumont, p.105).

In addition to legal and physical dangers, undercover work can take its toll on officers' psyches, as Strandberg (1998b, p.82) notes: "Sometimes the psychological dangers can outweigh the physical dangers for undercover cops." Family and social relationships may suffer from such assignments, as officers are precluded from sharing what they're involved in with those closest to them. Intense, long-term operations may also lead to officer burnout, which may couple with complacency, causing an agent to lose focus, not pay attention to important details or misread a potentially threatening situation (Dumont, p.109). Furthermore many undercover officers find it difficult to return to routine police work once the covert operation is over, with some even turning to crime themselves.

Internal Affairs

The second area of intelligence work is investigating officers in the department. For example the intelligence unit may investigate a complaint of an officer drinking on duty, corruption or other activities considered conduct unbecoming an officer. Officers assigned to internal affairs (IA) are often quite unpopular with their peers, and other officers assisting IA investigators are frequently stigmatized and labeled "rats." Arnold (1999, p.43) states: "Oftentimes unfairly portrayed in television crime dramas and police novels, internal affairs investigators have become the pariahs of fictional law enforcement agencies. Unfortunately some officers in real-life police departments regard internal affairs investigators the same way." Nonetheless, internal affairs investigations, also called personnel complaint investigations, are an essential function of today's professional and ethical police agencies.

According to Arnold (p.43): "Simply stated, the job is to determine the facts. Supervisors must view each case as they would any other investigation, even though the 'crime' may be a violation of department rules and the 'suspect' is an employee." Klockars ("Who Polices the Police?" 2000, p.1) notes the challenge is to create "an environment in the police agency where assignment to IA is not regarded as a badge of betrayal but as a position of honor and responsibility."

Both the International Association of Chiefs of Police (IACP) and the Commission on Accreditation for Law Enforcement Agencies (CALEA) have developed policies and standards addressing the need for effective, efficient methods for receiving and processing all complaints of misconduct involving law enforcement personnel. One policy commonly implemented is the rotation of IA personnel, which helps obstruct corruption:

> With the emphasis on community policing in recent years, "new kinds of bedfellows" can develop between officers and those in the community. "There are always some people who want dirty cops, so you have to be rolling people in and out," [says Delattre].
>
> Having career officers in IA tends to create an out-and-out "us and them" situation in the rank-and-file, who believe investigators think they are all dirty and are trying to get ahead over their backs ("Who Polices the Police?" p.6).

Juvenile Officers

Police officers are often the first contact for youths in legal trouble. Therefore it is justifiable and logical to have juvenile police specialists. Because most juvenile work is informal and officer discretion plays a critical role, such as determining whether to release, refer or detain, juvenile officers must be chosen from the most qualified officers in the department. The usual flow of how police interact with youths in the juvenile justice system is illustrated in Figure 7.2.

> Because juveniles commit a disproportionate number of local crimes, all officers are juvenile officers much of the time. Also, the police usually are youths' initial contact with the juvenile justice system. They have broad discretion and may release juveniles to their parents, refer them to other agencies, place them in detention or refer them to a juvenile court.

Whether a juvenile is actually taken into custody usually depends on a number of factors, the most important of which is the seriousness of the offense. Other considerations include age, attitude, family situation, previous record and the attitudes of the school and the community. Figure 7.3 illustrates the discretionary decision points in police handling of juveniles. The probation department may or may not be part of a juvenile division.

The police may also be responsible for some specific services involving children, such as helping to locate missing or runaway children, conducting fingerprinting programs and investigating reports of neglected or abused children.

On October 12, 1982, President Ronald Reagan signed into law the Missing Children Act, requiring the attorney general to "acquire, collect and preserve

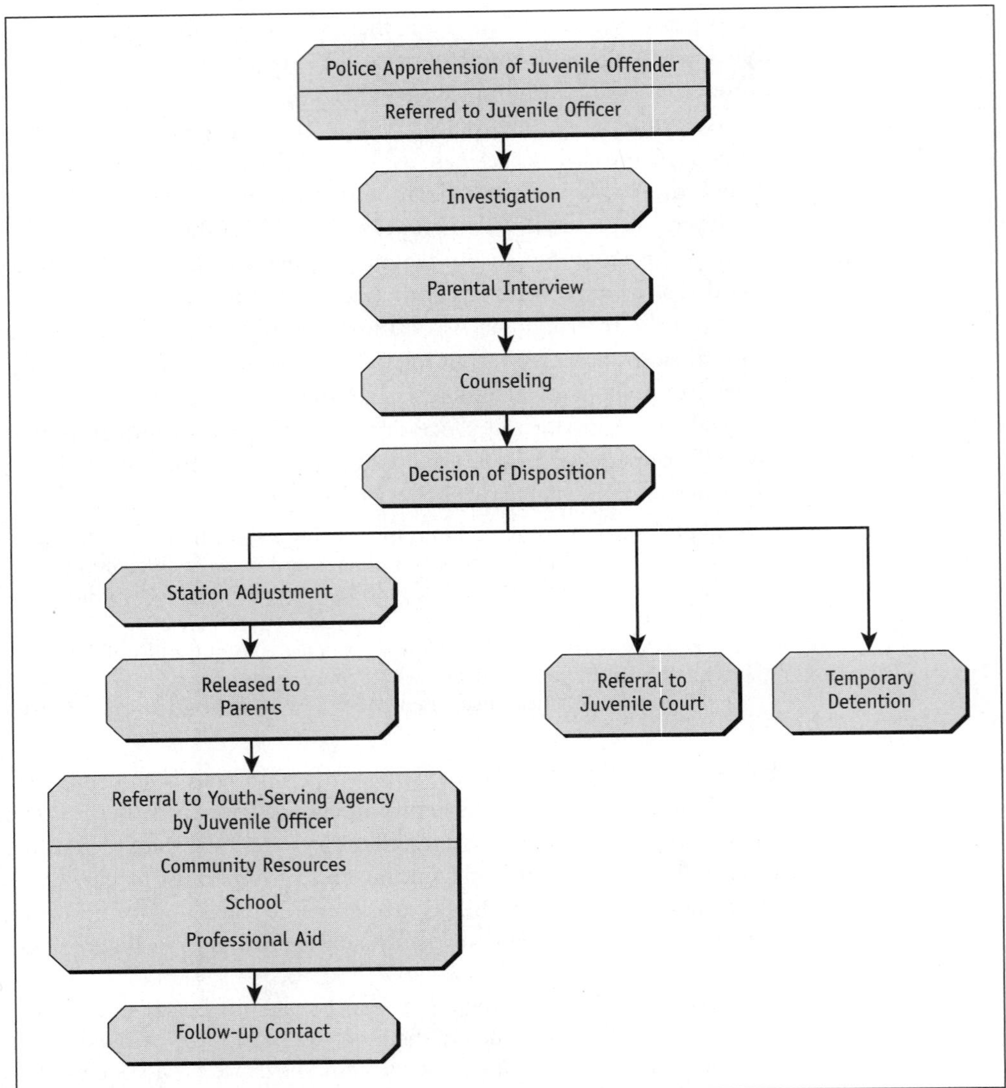

Source: Reprinted by permission of the International Association of Chiefs of Police.

Figure 7.2
Police Responsibility for Juveniles

any information which would assist in the location of any missing person (including children . . .) and provide confirmation as to any entry (into FBI records) for such a person to the parent, legal guardian or next of kin." While this law does not require that the FBI investigate the case, it does give parents, legal guardians or the next of kin access to the information in the FBI National Crime Information Center's (NCIC) Missing Person File.

Because of this law, it is important that children be fingerprinted. Many schools have instituted such a program in conjunction with the local police department. The same procedures used to search for a missing child might be used to locate a runaway child.

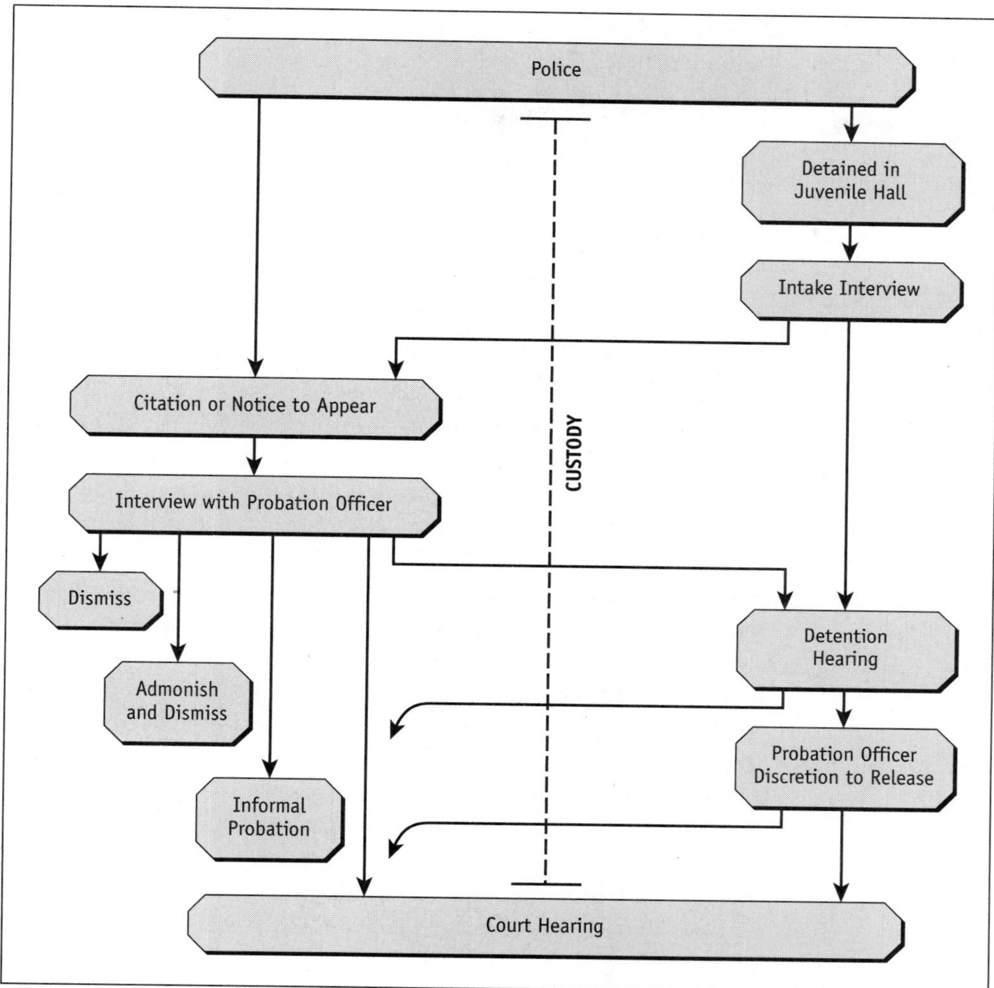

Source: Reprinted by permission of the International Association of Chiefs of Police.

Figure 7.3
Decision Points in Police Handling of Juveniles

Police are also called on to investigate reports of neglected or abused children. In most jurisdictions parental abuse or neglect of children is a crime, but jurisdictions vary in what constitutes abuse or neglect. Usually neglect includes failure to feed and clothe a child or provide adequate shelter.

A special type of juvenile officer is the school resource officer (SRO), discussed in detail in Chapter 5. Kanable (1999, p.68) asserts: "School personnel [and] law enforcement need to work together to secure the unique environment of schools." Many schools have turned to SROs to help address the problems of gang violence, drug use, property crime, assaults and other crimes committed on school grounds. Schuiteman (2000, p.77) notes: "SROs report success in reducing violence, preventing conflict, and improving school security." SROs are enhancing their effectiveness through specialized training in such areas as critical incident response, legal issues for SROs and school administrators, identifying adolescent drug use and bullying prevention and intervention (Schuiteman, p.74).

Like officers on the streets, officers in schools are now using Crime Prevention Through Environmental Design (CPTED) to identify, prevent and solve crime problems. According to Paynter (1998, p.60): "CPTED changes in a school might include adding lighting to a dark area on the school grounds or in the hallways, installing security gates or perimeter fencing, or trimming shrubs blocking windows and doorways around the school."

Vice Officers

Vice officers usually concentrate their efforts on illegal gambling, prostitution, pornography, narcotics and liquor violations.

Sometimes the work is coordinated with that of intelligence officers.

Vice problems vary from community to community. For example some areas of the country allow prostitution, but most do not. For areas where prostitution is illegal, it often seems to law enforcement as if they're fighting a losing battle. Strandberg (1998a, p.62) notes: "Prostitution is the world's oldest profession, and despite law enforcement's best efforts, all signs point to it getting older." To combat the problem, Strandberg (1998a, p.62) states: "Most departments use a mixture of investigative methods, including undercover operations, stings, landlord programs and sweeps." Some jurisdictions publish the names of people arrested for soliciting prostitutes in hopes of deterring the activity. For agencies that post their lists on the Web and can track the number of "hits," such pages are proving to be very popular sites. In St. Paul, Minnesota, for example, the police department's Web site had about 9,000 hits before they began posting the names of prostitution "customers." Now the site has registered 105,000 hits and counting, making it "by far the most popular page in the city's system," says St. Paul's Police Chief William Finney (Strandberg, 1998a, p.63).

Tactical Forces Officers

Tactical units supplement the patrol force and may operate selectively in high-crime areas. They may suppress burglaries, robberies or auto thefts. They may be used in hostage situations and where persons have barricaded themselves.

Special crime tactical forces are immediately available, flexible, mobile officers used to deploy against any emergency or crime problem.

To help combat the increasing aggressiveness of those outside the law, many agencies have turned to paramilitary policing, such as SWAT (Special Weapons and Tactics) teams. Some departments refer to their tactical units as Critical Incident Response Teams, Emergency Response Teams or Special Operations, but their functions are all the same. Paynter (2000, p.34) states: "The primary mission of any tactical team is containment and neutralization."

SWAT team members are highly trained in marksmanship, guerrilla tactics, patrolling, night operations, camouflage and concealment and use of chemical agents. They often participate in field exercises to develop discipline and team-

Miami Beach SWAT team members move into position in front of a houseboat on the Intracoastal waterway where an armed suspect had been discovered. SWAT team members are trained to contain and neutralize high-risk situations.

AP/Wide World Photos

work. Sanow (2000, p.55) explains: "A SWAT team is commonly made up of a series of two-man cells. The generic five-man team is made up of a point man or scout and his cover man, the team leader and his cover man, and the rear guard. This is generally the order in which the team stacks outside a door, moves down a hall or in the open." According to Strandberg (2000, p.31): "SWAT units are considered one of the elite units in law enforcement, and they recruit as such. SWAT teams around the country have little problem getting the people they need. Most units have waiting lists and are very picky about whom they choose."

Some have criticized the overemphasis on physical assault and combat techniques by tactical teams, yet such aggressive measures are becoming more necessary as today's street gangs and drug traffickers become better armed, stocking arsenals of semiautomatic and assault weapons that would make many law enforcement agencies envious. Glick (2000, p.42) addresses such criticism with the observation: "Police tactical teams have strict use of force rules and are rarely deployed in an offensive situation. Almost always, SWAT teams are called out for defensive purposes." He (p.44) reports that most SWAT incidents are resolved peaceably, without gunfire, and cites statistics from the National Tactical Officers Association (NTOA):

> Preliminary information gathered through September 1999 strongly indicates that SWAT saves lives. Of the 385 critical incidents reported, 341 [89%] were resolved

without shots fired after SWAT arrived. Critical incidents are those in which weapons are used, there are injuries to victims and/or officers, and there is a real threat to the health and welfare of a community.

In 195 [51%] of the critical incidents, the suspects were either arrested after a SWAT team made entry or surrendered to the tactical team under other circumstances.

Implementing a special operations unit may present a tricky balancing act for departments that are also committed to a community policing philosophy. When weighing the benefits of the community-oriented policing (COP) model against those of the paramilitary model, Robinson (2000, p.14) notes: "Most departments do not choose one model over the other, but instead try to do both. . . . The challenge for trainers is how to train officers to function effectively in both modes." In comparing the two models, Robinson (p.14) observes:

> Community-Oriented Policing grew out of public dissatisfaction with police forces that were perceived as "occupying armies" rather than public servants—and with police concerns about increasing calls for service. . . . [On the other hand] SWAT teams arose out of a different historical context and follow a very different model. Since the first SWAT team appeared in Los Angeles to combat the riots of the 1960s, the concept of specially equipped and trained tactical units to deal with high-risk situations has taken firm hold. . . .
>
> Policing under the COP model is multi-dimensional and proactive, depending heavily on officers' abilities to look at situations from a "big picture" perspective and to problem-solve creatively. . . . [On the other hand] SWAT teams are by definition reactive, and are deployed only for critical situations. . . . SWAT team call-ups are defined, one-time encounters that do not involve ongoing relationships with citizens. . . .
>
> To be effective in the COP model, officers need to be open and people-oriented, comfortable with being known as a person. They need to show individual initiative. . . . [On the other hand] SWAT teams depend on highly practiced teamwork, not individual initiative. . . . The uniforms and gear contribute to enhancing the team image and diminishing the individuality of the officers involved.

Robinson (p.15) notes: "In many ways the characteristics and activities that make effective neighborhood officers are the exact opposite of those that make effective SWAT team members. One might think that there could be no crossover. Few departments have the luxury, however, of being able to field a full-time SWAT team." Consequently, line officers in smaller and mid-sized departments, even in some large departments, may receive critical incident training so that, when called upon, they may function tactically.

K-9-Assisted Officers

According to Wallentine (1998, p.36): "Working police dogs have been around almost as long as society has needed law enforcement. Ancient Egyptians used dogs for keeping order. In Greece and Persia, dogs were equipped with sharply spiked collars to tear at the legs of horses bearing cavalry soldiers. When nineteenth-century Paris was faced with a gang problem, police dogs were set loose to disperse the gangs. The first organized K-9 unit in the United States began in 1907 in New York City."

An estimated 7,000 police K-9 teams were patrolling the nation in 1998. And while police service dog programs, unlike police officers, do not have any national reporting base, Russ Hess, national executive director of the United States Police Canine Association, Inc., observes there are more police K-9 units today than ever before and, in light of the events of September 11, 2001, we are likely to see a worldwide increase in the number and use of explosive detector dogs (2001).

> K-9s are used to detect concealed suspects, drugs, weapons and explosives; find evidence discarded by fleeing suspects; control crowds and break up fights; recover lost articles; and locate distressed persons and dead bodies.

Police dogs are often used in place of a second officer on automobile and foot patrols. Service K-9s can run down a suspect, jump barricades and maneuver through confined spaces more readily than a human officer, thereby significantly decreasing the risks to their two-legged counterparts. Today's police dog has intensive schooling with one officer—the dog's partner. Both spend many weeks under a special trainer and receive instruction specific to one of five general categories.

> K-9s may be specifically trained in search, attack and capture, drug detection, bomb detection and crime deterrence.

Some overlap and cross-training does occur, although rarely is one dog trained or expected to perform in all capacities. As Kanable (1998, p.57) explains: "Patrol dogs have about four to six months to study obedience, agility, aggression, tracking, searching, handler protection, apprehension under gunfire, apprehension without gunfire and recall. Detector dogs have about two months to learn how to discriminate scents and develop a nose for crime." A variety of detector scents are available to help train these K-9s, including narcotics (cocaine, heroin, LSD, marijuana), powder explosives, distressed bodies and cadaver scent.

Various breeds of dogs are used, but the most popular is the German shepherd. Greg Zipoy, head training officer for the Minneapolis, Minnesota, Police Department's K-9 unit, claims: "Obviously, these German shepherds are special dogs. They're real loyal, very protective of the handler, seem to be very aggressive, do good scent work and can accommodate the 20-below weather. Bloodhounds may be better for tracking, but for an all-around dog, it's hard to beat a German shepherd" (Levy, 1998, p.E1). To work the streets as a law enforcement "officer," it is vitally important that the canine possess an even temperament and a strong personality:

> The police dog is being held to a higher standard than ever before, just like their human counterparts in law enforcement. While dogs are still dogs with four paws and a wet nose, officers must answer to any complaint that is lodged regarding the actions of their canine partners. As a result, methods and equipment to train these animals are evolving as departments use costly, high-powered dogs with various areas of expertise ("The K-9 Technology . . .," 2000, p.116).

© Joel Gordon 2001

On Day 2 of the World Trade Center Disaster police and search and rescue dogs are on their way to "Ground Zero" in the WTC collapse restricted area in lower Manhattan. K-9s are effective helpers in the efforts to locate victims at disaster scenes.

The cost of training such dogs can be a major deterrent to small departments. While some agencies are fortunate enough to receive donated dogs, many must purchase their canines, which can be quite costly. Levy (p.E10) reports: "The German shepherds most desired for police work are valued at up to $3,500." Many agree that dogs are a bargain compared to the cost of human officers. Jim Nichols, national president of the United States Police Canine Association (USPCA), states: "The cost to work a dog at our agency is $.58 a day, and the dog doesn't draw any retirement."

Whatever the cost, the benefits of K-9 units are many. Rubin (1998, p.87) notes: "At one traffic stop, a K-9 named Schadow sniffed out 40 pounds of cocaine—street value $2.7 million—in a hidden compartment behind the dashboard. In a three-day period, Schadow and his handler seized $3.5 million in drugs." Detector dogs are also used in airports and on planes, in schools, in the workplace and at border checkpoints.

In addition to functioning in active crime fighting and prevention duties, K-9 units have helped in search and rescue (SAR) efforts to locate victims of bombings and plane crashes and are also used to enhance community relations.

Reserve Officers

Some departments have reserve units to help achieve departmental goals. Reserve officers, also called auxiliary police, patrol in uniform and are visible symbols of law enforcement, although they cannot write citations. Reserve officers also help in public education programs, informing the public about such things as drugs and bike safety and Operation Identification, in which valuables are marked for identification in case of theft. When a crime does occur, reserves can guard the crime scene while the officers continue with their routine or specialized patrol.

Volunteer reserve officers come from a variety of backgrounds and are driven by many different motivators. Weinblatt (2000, p.23) notes: "In some states . . . the cadre of recently recruited volunteers is almost exclusively made up of younger folks exploring a possible career in policing." The Los Angeles County Sheriff's Search and Rescue division has 110 noncompensated reserve deputies, 90 percent of whom are EMT trained. The New Mexico State Police's search and rescue division has more than 1,000 volunteers who conduct over 300 missions every year. According to the unit's director: "We have career volunteers with hundreds of missions under their belts; including bankers, attorneys and doctors. They are no strangers to responsibility" (Weinblatt, 1999, p.20).

Besides performing traditional street patrol, reserves may be found on bicycles, in the water and in the air. "Volunteer aviators may extend the resources of larger agencies. . . . Reserves have used their private life aviation related skills and certifications as pilots, observers and mechanics to create and maintain an airborne law enforcement presence" (Weinblatt, 1998, p.20).

While departments of all sizes across the country supplement their policing efforts with reserve officers, Weinblatt (2001, p.30) observes: "Reserves in the United States have a much larger presence in smaller, rural agencies . . . [which] have been forced to do more with less." The sheriff of Union County, North Carolina, acknowledges that volunteers engaged in search-and-rescue missions and other reserve activities are really "an extension of community policing. Through this partnership with the citizens, we have extended our reach into the community" (Weinblatt, 1999, p.20). Reserve officers are not always welcomed with open arms, however, and controversy often accompanies their use.

Nontraditional Agencies

According to Hall (1998, p.6): "Nearly 20,000 law enforcement agencies in America are what we'd term 'nontraditional' and are found across the country on campuses of universities, in parks, at airports, and on railroad, transit and subway lines, and elsewhere."

Nontraditional law enforcement agencies include transit police, airport police and park police.

Transit Police

Several large jurisdictions, such as New York City and San Francisco, as well as the federal railways, use transit police to augment traditional law enforcement efforts. According to Campbell (1998, p.15): "The four boroughs of New York

City—Manhattan, the Bronx, Brooklyn and Queens—are divided into 42 transit districts with 150 to 200 officers responsible for all the lines and stations within each district. . . . All patrol officers, including sergeants and lieutenants, are on foot." He notes that NYPD transit officers handle relatively little crime, spending more time on accidents, medical emergencies and riders trying to beat the fare, which is theft of service. Rapes are rare and murders nearly nonexistent. San Francisco's BART (Bay Area Rapid Transit) also has its own police department, with nearly 200 officers responsible for 95 miles of track running across four counties (Campbell, p.16).

The Amtrak Police Department, headquartered in Philadelphia and authorized by Congress in 1974, employs more than 300 sworn officers and several dozen civilians in 29 field offices nationwide: "Special units include a K-9 unit, a bicycle patrol unit and a criminal investigation unit. Amtrak officers have four main areas of responsibility: the stations, the trains, the railroad right of way and the maintenance facilities" (Campbell, p.17).

Airport Police

Most major metropolitan airports staff their own police departments, with responsibilities that include enforcing FAA regulations regarding aviation safety, protecting visiting dignitaries, handling medical emergencies, assisting stranded passengers and those experiencing vehicle trouble in the airport parking lots, dealing with ground transportation, controlling traffic, investigating accidents, responding to property crimes within the terminal, dealing with suspicious or abandoned luggage and packages, and maintaining security both inside and outside the terminal.

Some airport police departments are quite large, as the facility itself often constitutes "a city within a city." For example the Los Angeles International Airport (LAX) Police Bureau staffs approximately 350 people who are responsible for policing 3,600 acres of airport property (Campbell, p.18). Once officers complete police academy training, those assigned to LAX undergo an additional 16 weeks of training to learn such things as state and federal vehicle codes, the distinction between the various colored lights on the airfield and how to identify the different types of commercial passenger aircraft (p.18).

Park Police

The oldest federal uniformed law enforcement agency in the United States is the U.S. Park Police, established by order of President George Washington in 1791 to provide services in the public squares and reservations in the District of Columbia (Campbell, p.20). Park officers, or rangers, also patrol the various national parks throughout the country and perform a wide range of functions, including responding to accidents and campground mishaps, clearing "bear jams" that stop traffic and have park guests jumping out of their vehicles to take pictures, combating drug dealing and organized theft operations, and investigating crimes.

Park rangers must complete training in a broad range of topics to prepare for the variety of duties they must perform. Courses include wildlife management, wild-land and structural fire response, search and rescue, emergency medical services, underwater diving, boat operations, aviation safety, domestic violence, suicide intervention, physical fitness, firearms use and all areas of public safety (Gale and Stone, 1998, p.33).

Summary

A large part of an investigator's role centers around *objectively* obtaining and presenting information and evidence. Investigative responsibilities include securing the crime scene; recording all facts related to the case; photographing, measuring and sketching the crime scene; obtaining and identifying evidence; interviewing witnesses and interrogating suspects; and assisting in identifying suspects.

Investigators must obtain answers to the questions: Who? What? Where? When? How? and Why? Usually they must obtain both photographs and sketches because although photographs include all details and can show items close up, sketches can be selective and can show much larger areas.

A primary responsibility of investigators is to recognize, collect, mark, preserve and transport physical evidence in sufficient quantity for analysis and without contamination. DNA profiling uses the material from which chromosomes are made to positively identify individuals. No two individuals, except identical twins, have the same DNA structure.

If officers do not witness a crime, eyewitness identification plays an important part in the arrest, as well as in the trial proceedings. The three basic types of identification are field identification, photographic identification and lineup identification.

Most large departments have an intelligence division whose top officer reports directly to the chief and whose activities are kept from the rest of the department. Intelligence officers may be undercover officers investigating crime or internal affairs officers investigating officers within the department.

Because juveniles commit a disproportionate number of local crimes, all officers are juvenile officers much of the time. Larger departments often have several types of specialized officers. Vice officers usually concentrate their efforts on illegal gambling, prostitution, pornography, narcotics and liquor violations. Special crime tactical forces are immediately available, flexible, mobile officers deployed against any emergency or crime problem. K-9s have been used to detect concealed suspects, drugs, weapons and explosives; find evidence discarded by fleeing suspects; control crowds and break up fights; recover lost articles; and locate distressed persons and dead bodies. K-9s may be specifically trained in search, attack and capture, drug detection, bomb detection and crime deterrence.

In addition to traditional police departments, many areas of the country employ "nontraditional" law enforcement officers, including transit police, airport police and park police.

For more materials related to the content in this chapter, go to the *Introduction to Law Enforcement and Criminal Justice* Web site: http://info.wadsworth.com/wrobleski.

Discussion Questions

1. What are the goals of an investigating officer?
2. What does a preliminary investigation consist of?
3. What differences exist between a studio photographer and a crime scene photographer?
4. Why is DNA profiling not more commonly used in criminal investigations?
5. Why and how are computers being used in investigations?
6. Why would people not want to help put a stop to crime by being witnesses?
7. How do empathy and perception interact? Why are they important to an interviewer/interrogator?
8. Does your community have any of the nontraditional police agency types discussed? If so, what are they, how many sworn officers do they employ, and what are their main duties?
9. Do you believe nontraditional law enforcement officers receive less respect than their more traditional counterparts? If so, why might this be?
10. Should reserve officers have authority to write citations? Make arrests?

 InfoTrac *College Edition Assignment*

Use InfoTrac College Edition to help answer the Discussion Questions as appropriate.

- Using InfoTrac College Edition, find *criminal investigation.* Then find the article, "The Post-Columbo Era: How the Courts Killed Good Detective Work," discussing how laws limit methods of criminal investigation. Outline the article, and be prepared to share and discuss your outline with the class.

 *Internet Assignment*

Search for the keyword *undercover officer.* Find the article, "Undercover Police Work," and outline it. Again, be prepared to discuss your outline with the class.

 *Book-Specific Web Site*

The book-specific Web site at http://info.wadsworth.com/0534552803 hosts a variety of resources for students and instructors. Included are extended activities from each chapter in which students write a policy, use critical thinking skills to make choices in response to a given scenario, use InfoTrac College Edition with direct links to articles for participation in topical discussion forums, and analyze court cases using Web links for research. Many activities can be printed or emailed to instructors. Plus, cited cases with Web links, interactive key term FlashCards, PowerPoint presentations, chapter objectives, and an extensive collection of chapter-based Web links provide additional information and activities to include in the curriculum.

References

Arnold, Jon. "Internal Affairs Investigation Guidelines." *Law and Order,* May 1999, pp.43–46.

Band, Stephen R. and Sheehan, Donald C. "Managing Undercover Stress: The Supervisor's Role." *FBI Law Enforcement Bulletin,* February 1999, pp.1–6.

Beckwith, R. J. and Burke, Tod W. "Using Informants: Who Can Be Trusted?" *Law and Order,* August 2000, pp.109–110.

Campbell, Frank. "Traditional Values, Nontraditional Agencies." *Police,* March 1998, pp.14–21.

Cook, Patrick E. and Hinman, Dayle L. "Criminal Profiling: Science and Art." *Journal of Contemporary Criminal Justice,* August 1999, pp.230–241.

Davis, Joseph A. "Criminal Personality Profiling and Crime Scene Assessment." *Journal of Contemporary Criminal Justice,* August 1999, pp.291–301.

DeBlanc, Donald and Redman, Walter. "Officer Safety for Undercover Violence." *The Law Enforcement Trainer,* September/October 2000, pp.34–35.

Dees, Tim. "Crime Scene Drawing Programs." *Law and Order,* August 2001, pp.12–14.

Donofrio, Andrew W. "First Responder Duties." *Law and Order,* April 2000, pp.117–122.

Dumont, Lloyd F. "Minimizing Undercover Violence." *Law and Order,* October 2000, pp.103–109.

Eggers, Steven A. "Psychological Profiling: Past, Present, and Future." *Journal of Contemporary Criminal Justice,* August 1999, pp.242–261.

Gale, Rick and Stone, Rebecca. "Walking on the Wild Side: National Park Service Rangers at Yellowstone National Park." *Police,* December 1998, pp.32–33.

Gillen, Joseph J. and Thermer, Clifford E. "DNA-Based Exonerations Warrant a Reexamination of the Witness Interview Process." *The Police Chief,* December 2000, pp.52–57.

Glick, Larry. "The Paramilitary in SWAT—A Product of 'Parareportage.'" *Police,* April 2000, pp.42–44.

Hall, Dennis. "Let's Not Forget the Solid Work by 'Nontraditionals.'" *Police,* March 1998, p.6.

Hess, Russ. National Executive Director, United States Police Canine Association, Inc., Springboro, OH. Personal e-mail correspondence: December 4, 2001. uspcadir@aol.com

Kanable, Rebecca. "Training Is Nothing to Bark At." *Law Enforcement Technology,* November 1998, pp.56–58.

Kanable, Rebecca. "Patrolling the Schools." *Law Enforcement Technology,* September 1999, pp.68–73.

Kanable, Rebecca. "Palmprint Technology Catches Up to Fingerprint Technology." *Law Enforcement Technology,* March 2001, pp.42–45.

"The K-9 Technology and Training Evolution." *Law Enforcement Technology,* September 2000, pp.116–119.

Laska, Paul R. "Beyond Fishbowls." *Law Enforcement Technology,* October 1998, pp.120–122.

Levy, Paul. "Partners." (Minneapolis/St. Paul) *Star Tribune,* March 28, 1998, pp.E1, E10.

Lines, Kate. "Police Profilers." *The Police Chief,* September 1999, p.49.

Miller, Linda S. and Hess, Kären M. *The Police in the Community: Strategies for the 21st Century,* 3rd ed. Belmont, CA: West/Wadsworth Publishing Company, 2002.

National Commission on the Future of DNA Evidence. *The Future of Forensic DNA Testing: Predictions of the Research and Development Working Group.* Washington, DC: National Institute of Justice, November 2000. (NCJ 183697) http://www.ojp.usdoj.gov/nij/dna

Nyberg, Ramesh. "Cracking Barcodes and Finding Other Leads." *Law Enforcement Technology,* October 1998, pp.118–119.

Paynter, Ronnie L. "Safe Schools." *Law Enforcement Technology,* November 1998, pp.59–61.

Paynter, Ronnie L. "Gearing Up for SWAT." *Law Enforcement Technology,* March 2000, pp.34–39.

Reno, Janet. "Message from the Attorney General." *Eyewitness Evidence: A Guide for Law Enforcement.* Washington, DC: U.S. Justice Department, Office of Justice Programs, 1999.

Robinson, Patricia A. "Neighborhood Cops or Special Ops? Policing in the New Millennium." *The Law Enforcement Trainer,* March/April 2000, pp.14–16, 45.

Rubin, Hal. "K-9, an Officer's Best Friend." *Law and Order,* November 1998, pp.85–87.

Sanow, Ed. "A Basic SWAT School: The Bloomington, IN, Police Model." *Law and Order,* December 2000, pp.55–58.

Schuiteman, John G. "Early Returns Positive for Virginia's Model SRO Program." *The Police Chief,* November 2000, pp.74–77.

Scuro, Joseph E., Jr. "Evidence Rules Amendments." *Law and Order,* August 2000, pp.29–30.

Singh, David. "Community-Oriented Investigation at the North Miami Beach Police Department." *Practitioner Perspectives.* Washington, DC: Bureau of Justice Assistance, April 2001. (NCJ 185367)

Strandberg, Keith W. "Investigating Prostitution." *Law Enforcement Technology,* August 1998a, pp.62–65.

Strandberg, Keith W. "Walking in a Criminal's Shoes." *Law Enforcement Technology,* October 1998b, pp.82–84.

Strandberg, Keith W. "Building a Team." *Law Enforcement Technology,* March 2000, pp.30–32.

Technical Working Group on Crime Scene Investigation. *Crime Scene Investigation: A Guide for Law Enforcement.* Washington, DC: National Institute of Justice, January 2000. http://www.ojp.usdoj.gov/nij

Turman, Kathryn M. *Understanding DNA Evidence: A Guide for Victim Service Providers.* Washington, DC: Office for Victims of Crime, April 2001. (NCJ 185690)

Wallentine, Ken. "Dogs of War." *Police,* December 1998, pp.36–38.

Weinblatt, Richard B. "Reserve Expertise Makes Air Support a Reality." *Law and Order,* February 1998, p.20.

Weinblatt, Richard B. "Discovering a Valuable Asset: Reserve Search and Rescue Units." *Law and Order,* May 1999, pp.18–20.

Weinblatt, Richard B. "Shifting Motivations: Community Service Gives Ground to Aspiring Careerists." *Law and Order,* March 2000, pp.23–24.

Weinblatt, Richard B. "Reserves Aid Rural Counties." *Law and Order,* January 2001, pp.30–32.

"Who Polices the Police?" *Law Enforcement News,* March 31, 2000, pp.1,6.

Cases Cited

People v. Simpson, 23 (1995)

United States v. Ash, Jr., 413 U.S. 300 (1973)

Chapter 8

Policing within the Law

The patrol officer is the first interpreter of the law and in effect performs a quasi-judicial function. He makes the first attempt to match the reality of human conflict with the law; he determines whether to take no action, to advise, to warn, or to arrest; he determines whether he must apply physical force, perhaps sufficient to cause death. It is he who must discern the fine distinction between a civil and a criminal conflict, between merely unorthodox behavior and a crime, between a legitimate dissent and disturbance of the peace, between the truth and a lie. As the interpreter of the law, he recognizes that a decision to arrest is only the first step in the determination of guilt or innocence. He is guided by, and guardian of, the Constitution.

—Task Force on the Police

Do You Know?

- The major provisions of the Fourth Amendment?
- On what sources probable cause can be based?
- What basic principles underlie stop and frisk and what differences distinguish them?
- What significance the *Terry* case has in relation to the Fourth Amendment?
- What principal justifications are set forth by the courts for reasonable searches? What limitations are placed on them?
- What a search warrant is and what it must contain? What may be seized?
- How a warrantless search can be challenged?
- What authorities and restrictions are provided by the following cases: *Chimel? Carroll? Chambers? Coolidge? Maryland v. Wilson?*
- What special conditions apply to searches of vehicles?
- Whether open fields, abandoned property or trash can be searched without a warrant?
- Whether general searches are constitutional?
- What the authorities for lawful arrest are?
- When the Miranda warning must be given?
- What the public safety exception provides?

Can You Define?

administrative warrant
affidavit
arrest
circumstantial probable cause
consent
contraband
curtilage
custody
dual motive stop
emergency situations
entrapment
exigent circumstances
expertise
extenuating circumstances
eyewitness
field detention
field inquiry
forced entry
frisk
immediate control
in custody
inevitable discovery doctrine
informational probable cause
inspection warrant
instruments of a crime
lawful arrest
magistrate
mobility
nightcap warrants
nighttime search warrants
no-knock search warrant
observational probable cause
open fields doctrine
ordinary care
pat down
plain feel/touch doctrine
plain view
pretext stop
probable cause
protective sweep
public offenses
public safety exception
reasonable
reasonable search
reasonable seizure
search
search warrant
seizure
stop
stop and frisk
threshold inquiry
waiver
wingspan

INTRODUCTION

> Decency, security, and liberty alike demand that governmental officials shall be subjected to the same rules of conduct that are commands to the citizen. In a government of laws, existence of the government will be imperiled if it fails to observe the law scrupulously. Our government is the potent, the omni-present teacher. For good or ill, it teaches the whole people by its example. Crime is contagious. If the government becomes a lawbreaker, it breeds contempt for the law; it invites every man to become a law unto himself; it invites anarchy. To declare that in the administration of the criminal law the end justifies the means—to declare that the government may commit crimes in order to secure the conviction of a private criminal—would bring terrible retribution. Against this pernicious doctrine this court should resolutely set its face.

This synopsis was delivered by Supreme Court Justice Louis D. Brandeis in *Olmstead v. United States* (1928) and says, in effect, that government agents, including police officers, are subjected to certain restrictions in enforcing the laws. Those who are entrusted with the responsibility of protecting life and property must understand the principles of the federal and state constitutions and the duties that flow from their application, as well as the many laws and statutes that have been enacted. In short, police officers must know the law without the benefit of having gone to law school. Any violations of the law can result in evidence being disallowed under the Exclusionary Rule, as discussed in Chapter 2.

This chapter begins with a discussion of the Fourth Amendment, which governs searches and seizures. This is followed by explanations of sources of probable cause and the principle of stop and frisk. Next lawful searches are described, including the principal justifications for searching, gaining entrance, nighttime and no-knock search warrants, what may be seized, administrative warrants and warrantless searches. Also discussed under lawful searches are warrantless searches of vehicles, plain view searches, plain feel/touch searches and searching open fields, abandoned property and trash. The discussion of lawful searches concludes with a look at aerial searches, the inevitable discovery doctrine and limitations on searches.

Next lawful arrests are discussed, covering the elements of a criminal arrest, arrest warrants and arresting without a warrant, and concluding with a segment on protecting suspects' rights, including waiver of rights, the public safety exception, involuntary confessions and the issue of entrapment. The chapter concludes with a summary of the key cases presented.

The Fourth Amendment

> The right of the people to be secure in their persons, houses, papers, and effects, against unreasonable searches and seizures, shall not be violated, and no warrants shall issue, but upon probable cause, supported by oath or affirmation, and particularly describing the place to be searched, and the persons or things to be seized.

Arbitrary searches and/or seizures have no place in a democratic society. In fact colonial grievances against unreasonable searches and seizures, in part, led to the revolt against English authority. The Fourth Amendment of the Constitution guarantees the right of citizens to be secure from such arbitrary searches and seizures.

The constitutional standards for searches and seizures, including arrests, are contained in the Fourth Amendment, which requires that searches and seizures be reasonable and based on probable cause.

The terms *reasonable* and *probable cause* provide a very fine, but significant, weight to balance the scales of justice, which measure the conduct of all people. Without what is referred to as probable cause, the laws that govern us might easily become unbalanced, that is, too permissive or too restrictive.

The second part of the Fourth Amendment, called the "warrant clause," states: "No warrants shall issue but upon probable cause." In other words all warrants (search and arrest warrants) must be based on probable cause.

Reasonable

The rules for determining what constitutes a **reasonable search** or **reasonable seizure** result from interpretation of the first part of the Fourth Amendment, called the "reasonable search and seizure clause," which states, in part: "The right of the people to be secure in their persons, houses, papers, and effects, against unreasonable searches and seizures shall not be violated." **Reasonable** means sensible, justifiable, logical, based on reason.

Probable Cause

The concept of probable cause is one of the oldest and most important in criminal law, having existed for more than 2,000 years and occurring in both Roman law and the common law of England. **Probable cause** requires more than mere suspicion; it requires facts or proof that would lead a person of reasonable caution to believe a crime has been committed or that premises contain evidence of a crime.

In *Draper v. United States* (1959), the U.S. Supreme Court stated: "Probable cause exists where the facts and circumstances within their (the arresting officers') knowledge and of which they had reasonable trustworthy information are sufficient in themselves to warrant a man of reasonable caution in the belief that an offense has been or is being committed." *Smith v. United States* (1949) defines probable cause as: "The sum total of layers of information and the synthesis of what the police have heard, what they know, and what they observe as trained officers. We [the courts] weigh not individual layers but the laminated total."

Probable cause may be based on:
- Observation by officers.
- Expertise of officers.
- Circumstantial factors.
- Information communicated to officers.

Often more than one source is involved.

Observational Probable Cause

Observational probable cause is what officers see, hear or smell, that is, evidence presented directly to the senses. This is similar to eyewitness testimony and is the strongest form of probable cause. The courts have generally recognized certain types of events as being significant in determining probable cause.

Suspicious activities contribute to probable cause. For example a car being driven slowly can be suspicious when (1) the car has circled a block several times, (2) the people in the car are carefully observing a building, (3) the building is closed and (4) the building is located in a high-crime area. All four factors contribute to probable cause. *Familiar criminal patterns* also contribute to probable cause. A person's conduct can indicate a familiar pattern associated with the sale of stolen property or narcotics or of someone casing a building. Any one fact by itself may not be sufficient, but collectively they provide justification—probable cause.

Expertise and Circumstantial Probable Cause

Expertise and **circumstantial probable cause** are often tied to observational probable cause. Police officers' knowledge of criminal traits and their ability to "put the pieces together" may also contribute to probable cause. For example two police officers questioned two men seen driving from an alley at 2:00 A.M. The officers noted the license number and occupants' names and questioned the driver and passenger. The two men were allowed to continue, but a short time later, when the officers learned there had been a burglary in a nearby town, they forwarded the description of the car and its occupants to the local police who apprehended the suspects. A search of the vehicle revealed burglary tools, as well as the property taken in two burglaries.

In the original confrontation with the suspects, the two officers were not satisfied with the suspects' explanation of why they were in the alley at such an early hour, and even though they did not have sufficient evidence to establish probable cause for an arrest, their investigation of the suspicious circumstances eventually led to the suspects' arrests and convictions.

Informational Probable Cause

Informational probable cause covers a wide range of sources. In the case previously described, the information about the two suspects forwarded by the police to the nearby town constituted informational probable cause. The major categories of informational probable cause are official sources, victims of crimes, informants and witnesses.

Official sources include police bulletins, police broadcasts and roll-call information. This information can be relied upon because it is received through official police channels. As in any other case, the original source of the information must be reliable. For instance if police officers make an arrest based on information obtained from other police officers, the original officers may be required to testify about *their* source of information. It is that source that must establish probable cause. The source may be a victim of a crime, an informant or a witness. Complete and otherwise credible information from an **eyewitness,** based on personal knowledge, is generally sufficient to establish probable cause.

Stop and Frisk

One basic responsibility of police officers, and one heavily reliant on reasonableness and probable cause, is investigating suspicious behavior. Officers may simply talk to someone acting suspiciously and decide no crime seems to be in progress or about to be committed, or they may confirm their suspicions and investigate further. The simple act of stopping someone may lead to a **stop and frisk.** The stop is also called a **field inquiry** or **threshold inquiry.**

The basic legal considerations in a stop and frisk situation were set forth in the landmark U.S. Supreme Court decision *Terry v. Ohio* (1968). Detective McFadden, a veteran police officer with 39 years' experience, saw two men standing near a jewelry store. They seemed to be just talking to each other, but to McFadden, "they just didn't look right." Based on his experience, he suspected they were casing the store and were possibly armed. He watched for a while as the men went through the routine of walking around, looking into the store window, walking to the corner and returning to the original spot to talk with the other. A third man joined them, went inside the store for a moment and came back out. The routine continued.

Deciding to act, McFadden approached the three men and identified himself as a police officer. He asked for their names and then grabbed one of the men, later identified as John Terry, placing him between himself and the other two. McFadden made a quick pat down of Terry's outer clothing and felt what he thought might be a gun in Terry's coat pocket. It turned out to be a .38 caliber revolver; another gun was removed from the coat of a man named Chilton. Terry and Chilton were formally charged with carrying concealed weapons.

The defense lawyers argued the guns could not be used as evidence, claiming they were illegally seized. The trial judge, however, found both men guilty.

Terry and Chilton appealed their conviction to the U.S. Supreme Court, but before the Court's decision was handed down in 1968, Chilton had died. Therefore its review applied only to Terry.

The issue: Is it always unreasonable for a police officer to seize a person and conduct a limited search for weapons unless there is probable cause for arrest? Recognizing McFadden as a man of experience, training and knowledge, certainly "a man of reasonable caution," the Supreme Court answered "no," upholding the trial court verdict. The Court noted that McFadden, as a man of "**ordinary care** and prudence" (boldface added), had waited until he had strengthened his suspicions, making his move just prior to what he believed would be an armed robbery. He had to make a quick decision when he saw the three gathered at the store, and his actions were correct.

The Supreme Court *(Terry v. Ohio)* said there is a **seizure** whenever a police officer restrains an individual's freedom to walk away, and there is a search when an officer explores an individual's clothing even though it is called a "**pat down**" or "**frisk.**"

A **stop** is a seizure if physical force or a show of authority is used. A frisk is a search.

Although stopping and frisking fall short of an arrest, they are definitely forms of search and seizure. Police officers stop citizens daily, but most encounters cannot be considered "seizure of the person" because the officers do not restrain the individual's liberty. Defining the term *frisk,* however, leaves no other alternative than to consider it a search. As the Supreme Court *(Terry)* cautioned: "It is simply fantastic to urge that such a procedure, performed in public by a police officer, while the citizen stands helpless, perhaps facing a wall with his hands raised, is a 'petty indignity.' . . . It is a serious intrusion upon the sanctity of the person, which may inflict great indignity and arouse strong resentment, and it is not to be undertaken lightly." The Court gave its own definition of stop and frisk by calling it a "protective search for weapons."

Stop and frisk is a protective search for weapons in which the intrusion must be limited to a scope reasonably designed to discover guns, knives, clubs and other hidden instruments that may be used to assault a police officer or others. *Terry* established that the authority to stop and frisk is independent of the power to arrest. A stop is *not* an arrest, but it is a seizure within the meaning of the Fourth Amendment and, therefore, requires reasonableness.

Several key court cases have clarified when police can and cannot execute a lawful stop and frisk. The decision in *Florida v. J.L.* (2000) established: "Reasonable suspicion for an investigative stop does not arise from a mere anonymous tip" (Milazzo, 2000, p.11). In this case, police acted solely on a tip describing a man carrying a gun and, with no other reason to suspect the individual of criminal involvement, frisked the man. Although the frisk did yield a firearm and the man was charged with carrying a concealed weapon, Scuro (2000, p.14) notes: "In reviewing the case, the U.S. Supreme Court upheld

AP Photo/Jeff Klein

Stop and frisk is a protective search for weapons in which the intrusion must be limited to a scope reasonably designed to discover guns, knives, clubs and other hidden instruments that may be used to assault a police officer or others. A stop is not an arrest, but it is a seizure and therefore requires reasonableness.

lower court rulings that granted the trial court action to suppress the gun as evidence as a result of an unlawful search . . . [noting] reliance solely on an anonymous tip would create a vulnerability to pranks, grudges, and other unreliable information."

He (p.14) also states: "The Supreme Court's decision in *Florida v. J.L.* . . . has placed a greater burden on both agency and individual officer to go beyond information provided anonymously and to affirmatively and actively take steps to verify its reliability prior to taking action to frisk for weapons." Bulzomi (2000, p.31) suggests the stop and frisk might have been ruled reasonable *if* the tipster had provided predictive information in addition to the descriptive information: "An anonymous tip may be bolstered where it predicts the subject's future behavior, and police can corroborate that prediction through observation and investigation."

Another case that focused on the justification for a stop and frisk is *Illinois v. Wardlow* (2000): "The U.S. Supreme Court ruled . . . that a person's sudden flight upon seeing a police officer can be used to establish reasonable suspicion for a 'Terry-type' stop" (Harris, 2000, p.108). In this case, Wardlow was seen in a Chicago neighborhood known for drug activity, holding an opaque bag. When a group of police cars drove past him, he fled swiftly. The officers, acting on reasonable suspicion, pursued, stopped and frisked Wardlow, finding a loaded gun.

The trial court convicted Wardlow of possession of a firearm, but the appellate court overturned the conviction, stating the discovery of the gun was the result of an unjustified stop and frisk and, thus, that evidence should have been suppressed. The U.S. Supreme Court reversed, with Chief Justice Rehnquist writing: "Headlong flight—wherever it occurs—is the consummate act of evasion; it is not necessarily indicative of wrongdoing, but it is certainly suggestive of such." The Court noted the officers had based their reasonable suspicion on three facts, not just one—the suspect's flight, the location of the incident as a known drug area and the opaque bag in the suspect's hand. Basing reasonable suspicion on only one fact, such as the flight alone, is less likely to hold up if challenged in court: "Officers would do well to build strong cases by articulating all the facts that establish reasonable suspicion" (Harris, p.110).

Sobriety checkpoints, serving the broad social benefit of protecting motorists from drunk drivers, are a form of stop and have been declared constitutional, provided they are conducted fairly and do not pose a safety hazard (*Michigan Department of State Police v. Sitz,* 1990). Border checkpoints, aimed at containing illegal immigration at the border itself, also serve a broad social benefit and, as such, have been declared constitutional ("Vehicle Checkpoints for . . .," 2000, p.4).

Recall from Chapter 6, however, that drug checkpoints have been found to violate the Fourth Amendment. In *City of Indianapolis v. Edmond* (2000), the Supreme Court deemed drug interdiction roadblocks an unconstitutional means to a valid law enforcement end, with Justice O'Connor writing for the majority: "We cannot sanction stops justified only by the generalized and ever-present possibility that interrogation and inspection may reveal that any given motorist has committed some crime." Interpreting *Edmond* as an exception to the Fourth Amendment would set a precedent allowing authorities to construct roadblocks for almost any conceivable law enforcement purposes and permitting police to make such "intrusions . . . a routine part of American life" ("Supreme Court Strikes Down . . .," 2000, pp.1–2).

The courts have also upheld police officers' right to detain suspects with less than probable cause. Such **field detention** occurred in the case of *Michigan v. Summers* (1981) in which police officers arrived at Summers' home to execute a search warrant. They encountered Summers coming down the steps and asked him to let them in and wait while they conducted their search. They found narcotics in the basement and then searched Summers, finding heroin in his pocket. The court ruled that it was legal to require the suspect to reenter his house and remain there until evidence establishing probable cause was found.

More recently, in *Illinois v. McArthur* (2001), the Supreme Court ruled that police did not violate the Fourth Amendment when they detained a man outside his trailer home for several hours while officers sought a warrant to search the residence for drugs ("Brief Seizure of Premises . . .," 2001, p.13). McArthur's estranged wife, in the process of moving her belongings out of their home, informed police that her husband had "dope" hidden under a couch inside the home ("Supreme Court Allows . . .," 2001, p.130). When police knocked on the door, told McArthur what his wife had said, and asked for consent to search the home, McArthur refused. While one officer left to get a search warrant, McArthur stepped out of the house onto the porch. Suspecting McArthur would destroy the evidence if allowed back inside the trailer, police told McArthur he could not reenter the residence unless accompanied by an officer until the search warrant was obtained. Two hours later, the search warrant was acquired and police searched the trailer, finding less than 2.5 grams of marijuana ("Court Lets Police . . .," 2001, p.3).

The trial court suppressed the evidence as a result of an unlawful police seizure, but the U.S. Supreme Court, in an 8-to-1 ruling, reversed:

The Court determined that this search and seizure was "reasonable" in light of four conditions: (1) the police had "probable cause" to believe contraband was in the home; (2) the police had good reason to believe McArthur would destroy the contraband before they could return with a warrant; (3) the police made "reasonable efforts to reconcile their law enforcement needs with the demands of personal privacy," i.e., they did not search without a warrant, did not immediately arrest him, and did allow him some access to his home in the interim period; and (4) "the police imposed the restraint for a limited period of time, namely, two hours" (Makholm, 2001, p.13).

Lawful Searches

A **search,** in the context of the Fourth Amendment, involves governmental invasion of privacy. Searches are intended to obtain incriminating evidence. The questions most often asked by prosecutors and courts before admitting evidence are: Was the search justified and therefore legal? Was the arrest, if there was one, legal?

The principal justifications established by the courts for the right to search are when:

- A search warrant has been issued.
- No warrant has been issued
  - But consent to search was given.
  - But exigent circumstances exist.
  - Because there is no expectation of privacy and, thus, no requirement for a search warrant.

These circumstances are the preconditions for a reasonable, legal search.

Searches Conducted with a Search Warrant

A **search warrant** is an order issued by a judge, a **magistrate,** with jurisdiction in the area where the search is to be made. The Fourth Amendment states that warrants must particularly describe "the place to be searched and the persons or things to be seized." To get a search warrant, police officers must first prepare an **affidavit,** a written statement about a set of facts establishing probable cause to search. The officer then presents the affidavit to a magistrate and swears under oath that the statement is truthful. If the magistrate determines, based on the facts presented, that probable cause to search exists, a search warrant is issued. The warrant must contain the reasons for requesting the search warrant, the names of the persons presenting affidavits, what specifically is being sought and the signature of the judge issuing it.

Technically all searches are to be made under the authority of a search warrant issued by a magistrate. A search warrant is a judicial order, based on probable cause, directing a police officer to search for specific property, seize it and return it to the court. The search must be limited to the specific area and specific items delineated in the warrant.

What May Be Seized

A search warrant must clearly specify or describe the things to be seized. The prosecution must accept the burden of proof when items not specified in the warrant are seized. Such items can be seized if a reasonable relationship exists between the search and the seizure of materials not described—that is, they are similar in nature to the items described, they are related to the particular crime described or they are contraband. **Contraband** is anything illegal to own or have in possession, such as heroin or a machine gun. It is not necessary that the contraband be connected to the particular crime described in the search warrant.

Gaining Entrance

Police officers are usually required to announce their authority and purpose before entering a home. In *Wilson v. Arkansas* (1995), a unanimous Supreme Court held that, absent exigent circumstances, officers are required to "knock and announce" to meet the reasonableness requirements of the Fourth Amendment. The Court also stressed, however, that the "Fourth Amendment's flexible requirement of reasonableness should not be read to mandate a rigid rule of announcement that ignores countervailing law enforcement interests." Such interests include threats of physical harm to police, pursuit of recently escaped arrestees, and situations when there is reason to believe evidence would likely be destroyed if police announced their presence in advance (del Carmen and Walker, 2000, p.83).

Sometimes the suspect will not allow entrance, or there may be no one home. In such cases police officers may forcibly enter the house by breaking an inner or outer door or window. If the dwelling is an apartment, they could get a passkey from a caretaker, but this would still be considered a **forced entry.** Opening a closed but unlocked door or window is also considered a forced entry.

Officers must be aware of variations in state statutes regarding knock-and-announce rules and that courts in different jurisdictions have shown, through their rulings, divergent approaches to such requirements. For example, the Seventh Circuit Court has ruled that a failure to knock and announce does not require suppression of evidence if the target resists (*United States v. Espinoza,* 2001). Although the officers did knock and announce their presence once, with no immediate reply from the occupant, they waited only five seconds before using a battering ram to gain entrance to the premises ("Knock and Announce Required? . . .," 2001, pp.13–14). In contrast, the DC Court of Appeals has held that officers who disregard the knock-and-announce rule when serving a search warrant on an empty house, while the occupants are standing outside the premises "within earshot" of the officers, have violated statutory requirements, thus providing standing for the residents to move to suppress any evidence recovered inside (*District of Columbia v. Mancouso,* 2001).

Nighttime and No-Knock Search Warrants

A search warrant is normally issued to be served during daylight hours and requires the officers to knock and announce themselves. As just discussed, however, circumstances sometimes exist when these procedures could render the police less effective. In such instances special warrants may be issued. Two special types of search warrants, nighttime and no-knock, must be authorized by a judge as special provisions of a search warrant.

Nighttime search warrants (also called **nightcap warrants**) must state the reasons, based on facts, for fearing that unless the search is conducted at night the objects of the search might be lost, destroyed or removed. Justifications for a nighttime search include the imminent consumption or movement of drugs, or information that the drug trafficking occurs only at night and drugs are not likely to be found at the target location during the day. Other valid reasons include situations when the cover of darkness is essential to officer safety or circumstances when a nighttime search would be less intrusive than a daytime search, such as in a business open to the public during the day (Wallentine, 1998, p.39).

Unannounced entries to execute search warrants must receive prior judicial authorization. The **no-knock search warrant** is reserved for situations where the judge recognizes normal citizen cooperation is unlikely and that an announced entry may result in loss, destruction or removal of the objects of the search. For example surprise entries are often used in searches for narcotics and gambling equipment. In either instance the court usually acknowledges that evidence can easily be destroyed during the time required to give notice, demand admittance and accept denial of entry.

Administrative Warrants

An **administrative** or **inspection warrant** is issued by a court to regulate building, fire, plumbing, electrical, health, safety, labor or zoning codes if voluntary compliance cannot be obtained. It does not justify a police entry to make an arrest.

Public safety personnel may enter structures that are on fire to extinguish the blaze. After the fire has been extinguished, officials may remain a reasonable length of time to investigate the cause of the blaze (*Michigan v. Tyler,* 1978). After this time, if the police want to return to the scene to conduct an investigation into the cause of the fire, they may need an administrative warrant. Such warrants require an affidavit stating the location and legal description of the property; the purpose, area and time of the search; and the use of the building. Searches are limited to items specified in the warrant. Evidence found may be seized, but once officers leave after finding evidence, they must have a criminal warrant to return for a further search.

Searches Conducted without a Warrant

The courts have recognized certain situations and conditions in which officers may conduct a search without first obtaining a warrant. Warrantless searches are justified when consent to search is given, when exigent circumstances exist or when no right to privacy exists.

Search with Consent

In a search where **consent** is given, the consent must be free and voluntary. It cannot be given in response to a claim of lawful authority by the officer to conduct the search at the moment.

Consent must be free and voluntary, and the search must be limited to the area for which the consent is given.

As noted by the Maine Supreme Court in *State v. Barlow, Jr.* (1974): "It is a well established rule in the federal courts that a consent search is unreasonable under the Fourth Amendment if the consent was induced by deceit, trickery or misrepresentation of the officials making the search." A recognized exception to this general rule is when undercover operations are involved.

When a court is asked to determine if consent to search was "free and voluntary," it considers such things as the subject's age, background, mental condition and education. Officers must not show weapons when making the request, as the courts have considered such displays coercive. The number of officers involved should not be a factor if no aggressiveness is shown.

The time of day might also be a consideration. Officers should generally avoid seeking voluntary consent to search at night. In *Monroe v. Pape* (1961), Justice Frankfurter said: "Modern totalitarianisms have been a stark reminder, but did not newly teach, that the kicked-in door is the symbol of a rule of fear and violence fatal to institutions founded on respect for the integrity of man. . . . Searches of the dwelling house were the special object of this universal condemnation of official intrusion. Nighttime search was the evil in its most obnoxious form."

Perhaps most important is the way the request to search is made. It must be a request, not a command. Furthermore, the consent may be withdrawn at any time, requiring officers to end the search immediately.

Warrantless Searches under Exigent Circumstances

The implicit right to privacy contained within the Fourth Amendment provides the rationale to guide law enforcement in obtaining search warrants whenever possible. When police officers secure a search warrant, they receive an advance court decision that probable cause exists, therefore justifying an intrusion on a subject's privacy. However, there are situations when **exigent circumstances—emergency situations** or **extenuating circumstances**—exist to justify a degree of police infringement on personal privacy to achieve a legitimate and overriding law enforcement objective, such as securing public safety or the safety of the officer.

In situations where police officers believe they have established probable cause but have no time to secure a warrant, they can act without a warrant, but a defense lawyer can challenge the search's legality. Although a number of challenges can be raised, two occur most frequently.

When police officers conduct a warrantless search, they may be challenged on the basis that:

- Probable cause was not established—in other words, given the facts, a magistrate would not have issued a warrant.
- The officers did have time to secure a warrant and had no justification to act without one.

Courts have recognized there are times when exigent circumstances justify reasonable, yet warrantless, searches and seizures based on police officers' decisions. Such circumstances include (1) searches incidental to a lawful arrest, (2) searches of automobiles and other conveyances and (3) plain view and plain feel/touch situations.

Incidental to a Lawful Arrest In a search incidental to a **lawful arrest,** the search must be made simultaneously with the arrest and must be confined to the immediate vicinity of the arrest (*Chimel v. California,* 1969). In *Chimel,* officers went to the suspect's home with a warrant to arrest Ted Chimel on a charge of burglarizing a coin shop. After the officers were let in, they handed Chimel the arrest warrant and told him they wanted to "look around." Chimel objected but was told the officers had a right to search because it was a lawful arrest.

The officers opened kitchen cabinets, searched through hall and bedroom closets, looked behind furniture in every room and even searched the garage. (Prior to this case, the courts had accepted extensive searches incidental to an arrest.) On several occasions the officers had Mrs. Chimel open drawers and move contents so they could look for items removed in the burglary. The search took nearly an hour and turned up numerous stolen coins.

Chimel was convicted in a California court but appealed his burglary conviction on the grounds that the evidence—the coins—had been unconstitutionally seized. The U.S. Supreme Court studied the principle of search incidental to arrest and determined:

> When an arrest is made, it is reasonable for the arresting officer to search the person arrested in order to remove any weapons that the latter might seek to use in order to resist arrest or effect his escape.
>
> It is entirely reasonable for the arresting officer to search for and seize any evidence on the arrestee's person in order to prevent its concealment or destruction and the area from within which the arrestee might gain possession of a weapon or destructible evidence.

In the *Chimel* case, the Supreme Court specified that the area of search can include only the arrestee's person and the area within his or her immediate control. The Court defined **immediate control** as being that area within the person's reach, also called the person's **wingspan.**

Limitations on a search made incidental to an arrest are found in the *Chimel* Rule, which states that the area of the search must be within the immediate control of the suspect, that is, it must be within his or her reach.

The court noted that if an arrest is used as an excuse to conduct a thorough search, such as in the *Chimel* case, the police would have power to conduct "general searches," declared unconstitutional by the Fourth Amendment more than 200 years ago.

In addition to allowing a limited search of suspects and the area within their reach, the Supreme Court has also allowed the **protective sweep,** defined as "a quick and limited *search of premises,* incident to an arrest and conducted to protect police officers and or others" (*Maryland v. Buie,* 1989). A protective sweep might include quick checks of closets or behind doors to see if anyone who may pose a threat is present:

> A protective sweep is not the same as a search incident to arrest. . . . The search incident to arrest requires no additional justification beyond the lawful arrest; the protective sweep requires reasonable suspicion of danger. The search incident to arrest is intended to protect the arresting officer from the danger posed by the arrestee and to protect destructible evidence; the protective sweep

> protects the arresting officer from danger posed by unknown third parties (Colbridge, 1998, p.27).

The Fourth Amendment commands such sweeps be reasonable and limited in duration, lasting "no longer than necessary to dispel the suspicion of danger" (Colbridge, p.30).

Warrantless Searches of Automobiles and Other Conveyances Officers who conduct searches without a warrant must prove an emergency or extenuating circumstance existed that did not allow them time to secure a search warrant. Such circumstances often involve automobiles and other conveyances, and the rules of reasonableness are quite different. The courts have long recognized the need for separate exemptions from the requirement of obtaining a search warrant where **mobility,** the capability of being moved quickly and with relative ease, is at issue.

The precedent for a warrantless search of an automobile resulted from *Carroll v. United States* (1925), a case that occurred during Prohibition and involved bootlegging. Two undercover federal agents, posing as buyers, met with bootleggers George Carroll and John Kiro to discuss a transaction. Although the meeting seemed to go well and arrangements were made, the bootleggers became somewhat suspicious and backed out of the deal. The agents resumed their normal duty of watching a section of road known to be used by bootleggers. Within a week after their unsuccessful attempt to make the "buy," the agents recognized Carroll and Kiro driving by and gave chase, but eventually lost the car.

Two months later they again recognized Carroll's car and pursued, this time overtaking it. Having reason to believe the automobile contained bootleg liquor, the agents searched the car and found 68 bottles of whiskey and gin, most behind the seats' upholstery where the padding had been removed. The contraband was seized, and the two men were arrested.

Carroll and Kiro were charged with transporting intoxicating liquor and convicted in federal court. Carroll's appeal, taken to the U.S. Supreme Court, led to a landmark decision defining the rights and limitations for warrantless searches of vehicles. The agents' knowledge of the two men and their operation, combined with the recognition of Carroll's car and the belief it was being used to transport liquor, produced the probable cause necessary to justify a search.

The *Carroll* decision established that the right to search an automobile does not depend on the right to arrest the driver or an occupant. It depends on the officer's probable cause for believing (1) the automobile's contents violated the law and (2) the conveyance would be gone before a search warrant could be obtained.

The requirement of mobility is also present in *Chambers v. Maroney* (1970), which involved the armed robbery of a service station. The station attendant described to officers the two men who held guns on him, and two boys gave a description of a car they had seen the men in circling the block before the robbery and later speeding out of the area. Within an hour officers spotted the vehicle and identified the occupants as the men the three witnesses had described. Police stopped the car and arrested the men. Officers took the car to the police station and searched it, finding two revolvers and a glove filled with change stolen from the service station. The evidence was seized and later used to convict Chambers and the other man.

Chambers appealed, with the defense contending the search was illegal because it was not made simultaneously with the arrest. The defense was right; as a search incidental to an arrest, it would have been illegal. However the Court observed the same set of circumstances in relation to the warrantless search of a vehicle; the seizing officers had probable cause to believe the contents of the automobile violated the law. Therefore it was the right to search, not the right to arrest, that provided the officers with authority for their actions.

The Supreme Court added another opinion to *Chambers* when it held it was not unreasonable under the circumstances to take the vehicle to the police station to be searched. Based on the facts, there was probable cause to search, and because it was a fleeing target, the Chambers vehicle could have been searched on the spot where it stopped. The Court reasoned that probable cause still existed at the police station and so did the car's mobility.

Chambers established that a car may retain its mobility even though it is impounded.

A case that tested mobility requirements was *Coolidge v. New Hampshire* (1971), involving the disappearance of a 14-year-old girl. Her body was found eight days after she disappeared and revealed she had been shot. A neighbor's tip led police to E. H. Coolidge, whom officers admitted was fully cooperative, even to the point of agreeing to a polygraph examination. The examination was conducted several days after Coolidge was first questioned. During the next two and a half weeks, evidence against Coolidge began to accumulate. The evidence included what the prosecution said was the murder weapon, which officers had obtained from Mrs. Coolidge.

The arrest and search warrants based on this evidence, however, were drawn up and signed by the man who became chief prosecutor in the case. The search warrant specifically designated Coolidge's car, which was in the driveway in plain view of the house at the time of the arrest. Mrs. Coolidge was told she was not allowed to use the car, and it was impounded before other officers took Mrs. Coolidge to a relative's home. During the next 14 months, the car was searched three times, and vacuum sweepings from the car were introduced as evidence.

Coolidge was convicted of the girl's murder. He appealed, challenging the legality of the evidence seized from the car based on invalid warrants. With the warrants declared void and unable to prove the search of the car was incidental to an arrest, the prosecution was left with only the contention that the seizure of the car should be allowable based on the standards established by *Carroll* and *Chambers.*

The Court considered the principles of the *Coolidge* case and weighed them against those of the precedent cases. Because testimony from witnesses and from

Coolidge indicated that his car was at the murder scene, the Court accepted that probable cause to search had been established. However was there sufficient cause to fear that the automobile might be moved?

The Court said no. Coolidge could not have gained access to the automobile when the officers came to arrest him, and in fact, he had received sufficient warning that he was a prime suspect to have already fled. The only other adult occupant, Mrs. Coolidge, was driven to a relative's home by other officers who were with her after the vehicle was actually taken to the station.

Coolidge v. New Hampshire established that the rule of mobility cannot be applied unless there is actually a risk the vehicle will be moved.

Vehicles may also be searched without a warrant when they are used in committing felonies. Such **instruments of a crime** include getaway vehicles, as well as automobiles, trailers or similar conveyances used to hide or transport stolen items.

The right to search vehicles incidental to an arrest was upheld in *New York v. Belton* (1981), when the Supreme Court ruled that officers can search a vehicle's interior and all its contents if an occupant has been lawfully arrested and the vehicle search is subsequent to the arrest. *United States v. Ross* (1982) held that the police may search a car, including containers in the car, without a warrant as long as they have probable cause to believe contraband is somewhere in the car.

Florida v. Jimeno (1991) extended the *Ross* decision in examining whether a person's consent to a vehicle search allowed the searching officer to open a container in the vehicle. In this case a police officer overheard Jimeno, who was using a public phone, arranging what sounded like a drug deal. When Jimeno drove off, the officer followed him, saw him make an illegal right turn at a red light, and pulled him over. The officer explained why he had stopped the car and also said that he suspected there were narcotics in the car. He requested permission to search, which was granted. The officer found a brown sack on the passenger side front seat, opened it and found a kilogram of cocaine. Jimeno was arrested and convicted. The Supreme Court upheld the decision, stating: "A criminal suspect's Fourth Amendment right to be free from unreasonable searches is not violated when, after he gives police permission to search his automobile, they open a closed container found within the car that might reasonably hold the object of the search."

Finally *Colorado v. Bertine* (1987) ruled that police can inventory the contents of an impounded vehicle. Police often routinely inventory the contents of impounded vehicles to accurately record an arrestee's possessions so they may be safely returned at the appropriate time. If during such a routine inventory, police find contraband or evidence of a crime, it is admissible in court. In this case Bertine was arrested for drunk driving, and the van he was driving was impounded. During a routine inventory search, police found canisters of cash and drugs, which were admitted in evidence, and Bertine was convicted. On appeal the Supreme Court ruled that a warrant was not required because it was a routine inventory search.

A relatively new issue related to vehicle stops is the **pretext stop,** also called a **dual motive stop,** in which a vehicle is stopped for a traffic violation, but the intent is to search the vehicle for contraband or evidence of a crime. For example if an officer sees a driver whom he believes acts suspiciously, the officer may follow the car hoping the driver will violate a traffic law so the officer may lawfully stop the car and make an inquiry. This issue has come up in several state courts, and case law on this issue is building. As noted in *United States v. Millan* (1994), if an officer's original intent in stopping a vehicle is to "check it out" and not for a specific violation, any subsequent search will be illegal. In this case the officer made a pretext traffic stop for a cracked windshield, but his real intent was to search for narcotics.

However, the question of pretext stops was addressed again in *Whren v. United States* (1996) with a different outcome when the Supreme Court stated: "The temporary detention of a motorist upon probable cause to believe he has violated the traffic laws does not violate the Fourth Amendment's prohibition against unreasonable seizures, even if a reasonable officer would not have stopped the motorist absent some additional law enforcement objective." In effect, the validity and constitutionality of a stop does not depend on whether police officers "would have" made the stop but rather whether the officers "could have" made the stop. The real purpose of a stop, even if ulterior, does not render the stop and subsequent search invalid if there was, in fact, a valid reason for the stop, such as in this case traffic violations. The dangers of "routine" traffic stops are high. This danger increases when the vehicle has more than one occupant, as affirmed in *Maryland v. Wilson* (1997).

Maryland v. Wilson established that, given the likelihood of a traffic stop leading to either violence or the destruction of evidence when passengers are in the vehicle, officers may order passengers out of the car pending completion of the stop.

It was noted that passengers outside the vehicle are denied access to any weapons that might be inside the car. The Court also recognized the possibility of violence if a traffic stop reveals further evidence of a more serious crime.

Plain View and Plain Feel/Touch **Plain view** refers to evidence that is not concealed and is seen by an officer engaged in a lawful activity. Vision can be augmented with binoculars and flashlights, but it is not proper to move or pick up items without probable cause to believe the items are contraband.

Closely related to the plain view doctrine is the **plain feel/touch doctrine** used in several states. A pivotal case in the plain feel/touch doctrine is *Minnesota v. Dickerson* (1993). Two officers saw Dickerson leave a known crack house and, upon seeing their marked squad car, abruptly turn and walk in the opposite direction. This aroused the officers' suspicions, so they followed Dickerson into the alley and ordered him to stop and be patted down. They found no weapons, but they did find a suspicious small lump in Dickerson's jacket. Dickerson was arrested and charged with drug possession. The officer testified in court that during the pat down, he felt a small lump in Dickerson's front pocket and, after manipulating it with his fingers, determined it felt like a lump of crack cocaine but never thought it was a weapon. The trial court found the search to be legal under the Fourth Amendment, stating:

> To this Court, there is no distinction as to which sensory perception the officer uses to conclude the material is contraband. An experienced officer may rely upon his sense of smell in DUI stops or in recognizing the smell of burning marijuana in an automobile. . . . The sense of touch, grounded in experience and training, is as reliable as perceptions drawn from the other senses. "Plain feel," therefore, is no different than "plain view."

The Minnesota Supreme Court, however, overturned the conviction stating that the sense of touch is less immediate and less reliable than the sense of sight and is far more intrusive into the personal privacy that is at the core of the Fourth Amendment: "A frisk that goes beyond that allowed under *Terry* is not valid. In this case, the search went beyond the 'patdown search' allowed in *Terry* because the officer 'squeezed, slid, and otherwise manipulated the packet's content' before knowing it was cocaine" (del Carmen and Walker, p.37).

The U.S. Supreme Court granted review of *Dickerson* and upheld the ruling of the Minnesota Supreme Court that the cocaine seizure was invalid:

> This goes beyond *Terry,* which authorizes a patdown for only one purpose: officer safety. That was absent here because the officer admitted that what he felt was not a weapon. The Court's decision might have been different, however, had the officer testified that he knew it was not a weapon when he felt the lump, but that he had probable cause to believe—from his experience as a police officer and the circumstances of this case—that the lump was cocaine. If those were the circumstances, the seizure may have been valid, not under stop and frisk, but under probable cause (del Carmen and Walker, p.38).

This ruling is significant because it supports limited plain touch or plain feel probes during frisks and, if contraband is plainly felt by the officer in good faith, allows any discovered evidence to be admissible in court.

The Court has applied the *Dickerson* logic to extend to luggage searches, ruling that police can visually inspect a bus passenger's luggage but cannot squeeze or otherwise manipulate baggage to determine whether it contains contraband (*Bond v. United States,* 2000). Chief Justice Rehnquist stated: "A bus passenger fully expects that his bag may be handled. He does not expect that other bus passengers or bus employees will feel the bag in an exploratory manner." It is unlikely, particularly in the wake of the September 11, 2001, terrorist attacks, that the ruling will extend to air travel, where the public has a lesser degree of expectation of privacy because of security issues ("Court Slaps New . . .," 2000, p.9).

Warrantless Searches Where No Reasonable Expectation of Privacy Exists

In some situations, officers may lawfully conduct a warrantless search even in the absence of an incidental arrest or exigent circumstances, simply because the Fourth Amendment protection against unreasonable searches and seizure is not at issue—there is no reasonable expectation of privacy. The situations involve (1) workplace privacy; (2) open fields, abandoned property and trash; and (3) aerial searches.

Workplace Privacy The issue of workplace privacy and whether public employees have a reasonable expectation of privacy at their jobs is complex. It is generally held that employees' personal effects are subject to full Fourth Amendment protection, even within the workplace, and that searches of items such as purses, wallets, briefcases and personal mail require probable cause and a warrant. However, in *O'Connor v. Ortega* (1987), the Supreme Court, observing that facilities within government and other public agencies are generally shared by and accessible to many, ruled that a public employee's position, by its very nature, allows a degree of intrusion into privacy that would otherwise violate the Fourth Amendment. In *Ortega* the Court held that all an employer needs for a work-related intrusion to qualify as reasonable under the Fourth Amendment is a reasonable suspicion that the investigative search will uncover evidence of an employee's work-related misconduct. A workplace search is also justified if it serves a valid noninvestigatory, work-related purpose, such as retrieving a needed file.

One controversial area is whether employers have a right to monitor how employees use the company's computers, including tracking an employee's online activities. Can employers reprimand employees who use e-mail for personal use or who visit non–work-related Web sites during office hours?

Open Fields, Abandoned Property and Trash

If something is open to the public and therefore has no expectation of privacy, it is not protected by the Fourth Amendment. This includes open fields, abandoned property and trash.

The principles governing search and seizure of open fields and trash were established in *Hester v. United States* (1924). In this case police were investigating bootlegging operations and went to Hester's father's home. As police approached the residence, they saw a man identified as Henderson drive up to the house, so they hid. When Hester came out and gave Henderson a bottle, the police sounded an alarm. Hester ran to a car parked nearby, took out a gallon jug, and he and Henderson ran across an open field. One officer chased them. Hester dropped his jug, and it broke, but about half its contents remained. Henderson threw his bottle away. Police found another broken jar containing liquid that appeared to be illegal whiskey. The officers seized the jars, even though they had no search warrant, and arrested Hester who was convicted of concealing "distilled spirits." On appeal his lawyer contended that the officers conducted an illegal search and seizure. The Court disagreed, saying:

> It is obvious that even if there had been a trespass, the above testimony was not obtained by an illegal search and seizure. The defendant's own acts, and those of his associates, disclosed the jug, the jar and the bottle—and there was no seizure in the sense of the law when the officers examined the contents of each after it had been abandoned. . . .
>
> The special protection accorded by the Fourth Amendment to the people in their "persons, houses, papers, and effects," is not extended to the open fields.

The **open fields doctrine** holds that land beyond what is normally associated with use of that land, that is, undeveloped land, can be searched without a warrant. **Curtilage** is the term used to describe the portion of property generally associated with the common use of land, for example buildings, sheds, fenced-in areas and yards. A warrant is required to search the curtilage. In *Oliver v. United States* (1984), the Supreme Court described the curtilage as "the area to which extends the intimate activity associated with the 'sanctity of a man's home and the privacies of life.'" The courts have generally regarded driveways, walkways to a house's front door and unfenced front yards as areas commonly accessed by neighbors, visitors, postal carriers, delivery drivers, salespeople and other members of the public. As such, these areas receive a lower level of protection in issues of privacy, and courts have upheld police officers' right to enter onto a property's "public access" areas without a warrant.

In *United States v. Dunn* (1987), the Supreme Court specified four factors to consider in determining if an area is within a home's curtilage:

- The proximity of the area to the home.
- Whether the area is within the same enclosure as the home.
- The nature of the use to which the area is put.
- Measures taken by the home's occupant to protect the area from the view of passersby.

Oliver v. United States strengthened the open fields doctrine by ruling that "No Trespassing" signs and locked gates do not constitute a "reasonable expectation of privacy":

> The test of a reasonable expectation of privacy is not whether the individual attempts to conceal criminal activity, but whether the government's intrusion infringes upon the personal and societal values protected by the Fourth Amendment. Because open fields are accessible to the public and because fences or "No Trespassing" signs, etc. are not effective bars to public view of open fields, the expectation of privacy does not exist and police are justified in searching these areas without a warrant.

Once a person throws something away, the expectation of privacy is lost. *California v. Greenwood* (1988) established that garbage left outside the curtilage of a home for regular collection could be inspected: "Here we conclude that respondents exposed their garbage to the public sufficiently to defeat their claim to Fourth Amendment protection. It is common knowledge that plastic garbage bags left on or at the side of a public street are readily accessible to animals, children, scavengers, snoops, and other members of the public." If no expectation of privacy exists, Fourth Amendment protection does not exist either.

Some states, however, do not allow such searches. A New Jersey Court ruled 5–2 that garbage left on a curb is private property that police officials cannot search through without a warrant:

> Garbage reveals much that is personal. We do not find it unreasonable for people to want their garbage to remain private and to expect that it will remain private from the meddling of the state.
>
> A free and civilized society should comport itself with more decency [than to allow] police to pick and poke their way through garbage bags to peruse without cause the vestiges of a person's most private affairs.

This case illustrates how critical it is that police officers know not only the federal laws, but also the laws of their respective states, which often can be more restrictive than federal laws.

Aerial Searches Another area closely related to the plain view doctrine and the open fields doctrine is that of aerial searches. *California v. Ciraola* (1986) expanded the police's ability to "spy" on the criminal offenders. In this case police received a tip that marijuana was being grown in the defendant's backyard. The yard was surrounded by two fences, one six feet tall, the other ten feet tall. Since the height of the fences precluded visual observation from the ground, the officers decided to fly over the curtilage at an altitude of 1,000 feet to confirm that it contained marijuana plants. Based on this information, a search warrant was obtained and executed, and the evidence was used to convict Ciraola on drug charges. On appeal the Supreme Court found that the defendant's privacy had not been violated since officers traveling in a navigable airspace are not required to avert their eyes when passing over homes or yards.

In *Florida v. Riley* (1989), the Court expanded this ruling when it stated that police do not need a search warrant to conduct even low-altitude helicopter searches of private property.

Thermal Imaging

The subject of searches, as an applied law enforcement procedure, has received close scrutiny by the courts and remains, in the public eye, an avenue vulnerable to invasion of privacy by the government. When technology is added to the picture, public concern takes on more of a "Big Brother" uneasiness, especially when the technology is aimed at someone's home. An example of how advancing technology affects Fourth Amendment privacy issues is seen in *Kyllo v. United States* (2001), a case involving thermal imaging.

During the course of a drug investigation, a federal agent used a thermal imager to scan the exterior of the home of a man suspected of growing marijuana. The scan, conducted without a search warrant, revealed abnormally high amounts of heat coming from the home, relative to neighboring residences. Investigators believed this data, combined with previously developed information, provided probable cause to secure a search warrant for the property. The search revealed not only marijuana plants but also drug paraphernalia and weapons, and Kyllo was convicted of manufacturing marijuana.

Kyllo appealed, arguing that targeting his home with a thermal imager was an unreasonable Fourth Amendment search and that evidence garnered from the illegal search should be suppressed. At the Ninth Circuit Court of Appeals, the court held that a thermal scan of a residence is not a search under the Fourth Amendment and "that Kyllo had no actual (subjective) expectation of privacy in the 'waste heat' radiating from the surface of his home because he made no effort to conceal the emissions" (Colbridge, 2001, p.27). Reasoning that such technology did not reveal intimate details about the activities inside the home, the circuit court agreed with the lower court's analogizing "the level of intrusion associated with a thermal imaging device to that involved in warrantless aerial surveillance" ("Use of Thermal . . .," 2001, p.186).

Kyllo, however, came before the U.S. Supreme Court, which reversed the circuit court's ruling. In a 5-to-4 decision, the Supreme Court asserted that using a thermal imager to surveil a home is a search under the Fourth Amendment and, as such, requires a search warrant based on probable cause: "In *Kyllo v. United States,* the U.S. Supreme Court drew a bright line around the home and announced a rule that warrantless police use of technology stops at the front door" (Colbridge, p.31).

The Inevitable Discovery Doctrine

In *Nix v. Williams* (1984), the Supreme Court ruled that illegally obtained evidence may be admitted at trial if the prosecution can prove that the evidence would "inevitably" have been discovered by lawful means. Former Chief Justice Warren E. Burger wrote in the majority opinion: "Exclusion of physical evidence that would inevitably have been discovered adds nothing to either the integrity or fairness of a criminal trial." The point of the **inevitable discovery doctrine,** he said, was to put the police in the same, not a worse, position than they would have been in if no police error or misconduct occurred.

Limitations on Searches

After establishing the right to search, police officers must determine the limitations on that right—limitations imposed by law and interpreted by the courts.

The most important limitation imposed on any search is that the scope must be narrowed. General searches are unconstitutional.

Often what is found during a search provides the probable cause to make an arrest. As with searches, in an arrest the general rule is that a warrant is required.

Lawful Arrests

Laws of arrest are generally uniform in all 50 states and in federal criminal proceedings. Statutes throughout the United States generally define **arrest** as the taking of a person into custody by the actual restraint of the person or by his or her submission to the custody of the officer so that he or she may be held to answer for a public offense before a judge.

Elements of Criminal Arrest

Four elements of a criminal arrest are:

1. An *intent* by an officer to make an arrest
2. *Authority* to arrest
3. A *seizure* or *restraint*
4. An *understanding* by the person that he or she is being arrested

Arrest Warrants

All states have a statute authorizing law enforcement officers to make arrests, but the Constitution stipulates that lawful arrests require an arrest warrant. From a practical point of view, police officers should obtain arrest warrants to protect themselves against civil liability for false imprisonment, even if it is later determined the arrest was unjustified. Like a search warrant, an arrest warrant requires an affidavit stating the facts supporting probable cause and sworn to by the officer presenting the affidavit. The judge determines if probable cause exists and, if so, issues the warrant. The warrant itself must name the person to be arrested, the offense and the officer(s) directed to make the arrest. The warrant must be signed by an impartial judge.

Arrest without a Warrant

Police officers may make lawful arrests without a warrant for felonies or misdemeanors committed in their presence, called **public offenses,** or for felonies not committed in their presence if they have probable cause. They may not, however, enter a dwelling to arrest without a warrant.

In *People v. Ramey* (1976), the California Supreme Court ruled "the Fourth Amendment prohibits a warrantless entry into a dwelling to arrest in the absence of sufficient justification for the failure to obtain a warrant." In *Payton v. New York* (1980), the Supreme Court extended this decision to apply to all states. Since then, "dwelling" has been expanded to include temporary residences including motels and hotels, tents in public campgrounds and migrant farm housing on private property.

If, however, an emergency situation exists and officers have probable cause to believe a person has committed a crime, they may make a warrantless arrest. The courts will determine its legality. As Hendrie (1998, p.32) explains: "If police officers are in hot pursuit of a criminal suspect and chase that suspect into a house, most courts permit the officers to follow that suspect into the house to apprehend him. It is not required that the officers stop and obtain a warrant before entering the house; there is an emergency—they are in hot pursuit."

If there is probable cause and an emergency situation exists, an officer may make an arrest without a warrant. The courts will determine whether the arrest was lawful.

The Fourth Amendment was intended to protect citizens from unjust arrests. The courts must balance this protection against the justice system's charge to protect society against those who violate its laws.

An arrest is never to be taken lightly. It can change a person's life forever. Officer discretion is critical when arrest decisions are made. It is also vital that officers clearly differentiate between a simple stop and frisk situation and an arrest. Sometimes a stop and frisk situation leads to an arrest situation. Table 8.1 summarizes the important differences.

Right to Resist Arrest

Sometimes when an arrest is made, the person being arrested resists, and the officer must use force to make the arrest, an issue discussed in Chapter 10. It should be noted here, however: "American courts initially adopted the common law right to resist arrest and supported it strongly until the mid-twentieth century, when reformers portrayed the right as archaic and ill-advised. . . . The trend during the past 40 years has been to eliminate the right to resist arrest" (Hemmens and Levin, 2000, p.474).

Table 8.1
Stop and Arrest

	Stop	Arrest
Justification	Reasonable suspicion	Probable cause
Intent of officer	To resolve an ambiguous situation	To make a formal charge
Search	Possibly a "pat down" or frisk	Complete body search
Record	Minimal	Fingerprints, photographs and booking

As of October 2000, only 12 states allowed the right to resist arrest (pp.481–482). The decision of whether to continue or eliminate this right rests on the degree to which we value liberty rather than order: "Courts abrogating the common law rule have often asked the rhetorical question of whether our freedom from bodily restraint is really as precious as the avoidance of violence and maintenance of public order" (Hemmens and Levin, p.494).

While support for the right to resist arrest is diminishing, other more vital rights—due process rights—continue to define the legal process and how the police interact with suspects.

Protecting a Suspect's Rights

Before interrogating any suspect, police officers must give the Miranda warning, as established in *Miranda v. Arizona* (1966). The U.S. Supreme Court asserted that suspects must be informed of their rights to remain silent, to have counsel present, to a state-appointed counsel if they cannot afford one and to be warned that anything they say might be used against them in a court of law. Many investigators carry a card that contains the Miranda warning to be read before interrogating a suspect. (See Figure 8.1.)

On the evening of March 3, 1963, an 18-year-old girl was abducted and raped in Phoenix, Arizona. Ten days after the incident, Ernesto Miranda was arrested by Phoenix police, taken to police headquarters and put in a lineup. He was identified by the victim and shortly thereafter signed a confession admitting the offenses. Despite the defense attorney's objections to the statement, the trial court admitted the confession. Miranda was convicted and sentenced from 20 to 30 years on each count.

Miranda appealed on the grounds that he had not been advised of his constitutional rights under the Fifth Amendment. The Arizona Supreme Court ruled in 1965 that because Miranda had been previously arrested in California and Tennessee, he knowingly waived his rights under the Fifth and Sixth Amendments when he gave his confession to the Phoenix police. In 1966, upon appeal, the U.S. Supreme Court reversed the supreme court of Arizona in a 5–4 decision and set up precedent rules for police custodial interrogation. Chief Justice Warren stated: "The mere fact that he signed a statement which contained a typed-in clause stating that he had 'full knowledge of his "legal rights"' does not approach knowing the intelligent waiver required to relinquish constitutional rights."

The Miranda warning must be given to a suspect who is interrogated in police **custody,** that is, when the suspect is not free to leave.

Miranda Warning

1. You have the right to remain silent.
2. If you give up the right to remain silent, anything you say can and will be used against you in a court of law.
3. You have the right to speak with an attorney and to have the attorney present during questioning.
4. If you so desire and cannot afford one, an attorney will be appointed for you without charge before questioning.

Waiver

1. Do you understand each of these rights I have read to you?
2. Having these rights in mind, do you wish to give up your rights as I have explained them to you and talk to me now?

Figure 8.1
Miranda Warning Card

Two terms are key in this situation: *interrogated* and **in custody.** The circumstances involved in an interrogation and whether it requires a Miranda warning were expanded in *Oregon v. Mathiason* (1977) when the Court said:

> Any interview of one suspected of a crime by a police officer will have coercive aspects to it, simply by virtue of the fact that the police officer is part of a law enforcement system which may ultimately cause the suspect to be charged with a crime. But police officers are not required to administer Miranda warnings to everyone whom they question. Nor is the requirement of warnings to be imposed simply because the questioning takes place in the station house, or because the questioned person is one whom the police suspect. Miranda warnings are required only where there has been such a restriction on a person's freedom as to render him "in custody." It was that sort of coercive environment to which Miranda by its terms was made applicable, and to which it is limited.

Custodial interrogation takes place in two situations: (1) when a suspect is under arrest or (2) when a suspect is not under arrest, but is deprived of freedom in a significant way. Sometimes both terms, *interrogation* and *in custody,* are issues, as was the case in *United States v. Mesa* (1980). In this case the FBI had an arrest warrant for a suspect charged with shooting his common-law wife and his daughter. The armed suspect barricaded himself in a motel room. Using a bullhorn, police tried to persuade the suspect to come out, but he refused. Finally he agreed to talk with them by phone. The FBI recorded the conversation, which included some incriminating statements by the suspect. The suspect finally surrendered peacefully and was arrested. The district court disallowed the recorded phone statements as evidence, stating they were obtained in violation of the suspect's rights and that the Miranda warning should have been given. The circuit court of appeals reversed the decision.

Miranda warnings are not required if questioning witnesses, in "stop and frisk" cases, or before fingerprinting and/or photographing during the arrest or booking process. Police who conduct DUI stops and ask routine questions need not give the Miranda warning (*Pennsylvania v. Muniz,* 1990). In this case an officer stopped Muniz on suspicion of driving under the influence. The officer asked him to perform three field sobriety tests, which Muniz failed. Muniz explained his failure by saying he had been drinking. When the officer asked him to submit to a Breathalyzer test, Muniz refused, so the officer read him the Miranda warning. The entire procedure had been videotaped, which was admitted into evidence at trial. The court ruled that the procedures used and videotaping them did not violate Muniz's constitutional rights. These were considered "real or physical" evidence, in contrast to "testimonial" evidence which is protected by the Fifth Amendment against self-incrimination. del Carmen and Walker (p.206) note:

> The main issue is what kind of self-incriminating evidence is admissible in court. The rule is that the Fifth Amendment prohibition against self-incrimination (which is protected by the *Miranda* rule) prohibits only testimonial or communicative self-incrimination and does not prohibit physical self-incrimination. The asking of routine questions, the answers to which are slurred, and the videotaping of the proceedings were self-incriminatory, but such incrimination was physical; the *Miranda* warnings were, therefore, not needed and the evidence was admissible in court.

Another case significant to the protection of suspects' rights actually resulted in two separate trials with two different prosecutors, yet both trials involved the same defendant, Robert Williams, and the same case, the Christmas Eve disappearance and suspected homicide of a 10-year-old girl. During the investigation, police developed information leading to suspect Williams and obtained a warrant for his arrest. Williams eventually turned himself in to police in a town 160 miles from where the girl disappeared, and Williams' lawyer agreed to have police return the suspect to the case's city of origin.

All agreed that Williams would not be interrogated in any way during the long car trip. However, during the drive, aware that Williams possessed a strong religious faith, one officer said the following to Williams, in what has become known as the "Christian Burial Speech":

> I want to give you something to think about while we're traveling down the road. . . . It's going to be dark early this evening. They are predicting several inches of snow for tonight, and I feel that you yourself are the only person that knows where this little girl's body is, that you yourself have only been there once, and if you get snow on top of it, you yourself may be unable to find it. And since we will be going right past the area on the way [back], I feel that we could stop and locate the body, that the parents of this little girl should be entitled to a Christian burial for the little girl who was snatched away from them on Christmas Eve and murdered.

The detective said he wasn't looking for an answer but that he just wanted Williams to think about it as they drove. Shortly after, Williams directed the officers to the girl's body. The lower courts admitted Williams' damaging statements into evidence, but the Supreme Court in *Brewer v. Williams* (1977) reversed, holding that any statements made by Williams were inadmissible because the way they were elicited violated his constitutional right to counsel:

> The pressures on state executive and judicial officers charged with the administration of the criminal law are great, especially when the crime is murder and the victim a small child. But it is precisely the predictability of those pressures that makes imperative a resolute loyalty to the guarantees that the Constitution extends to us all.

The Court granted Williams a second trial with a different prosecutor (*Nix v. Williams,* 1984). Again, Williams' statements were suppressed, but the Court allowed the body to be admitted as evidence not because it was found through the improper questioning by police but because an independent search party would have eventually discovered it. This is the inevitable discovery rule discussed earlier.

Other types of situations may arise in which the need to give the Miranda warning is in question: "Miranda warnings should be given to any person prior to an initial interview by a polygraph examiner, prior to being interviewed by a probation or parole officer, [and] prior to a psychological or psychiatric evaluation. Any statements given in such situations in the absence of Miranda warnings will very likely be inadmissible" (Kalk, 1998, p.52).

The Miranda warning recently survived a challenge to its validity in *Dickerson v. United States* (2000). The case involved Charles Dickerson, who voluntarily confessed to several bank robberies and waived his rights in writing. At trial, the defendant moved to suppress his confession because he had waived his rights before being given the Miranda warning. The Federal District Court granted his motion to suppress, but the U.S. Court of Appeals reversed the decision, stating that the lower court had used the wrong standard in judging the confession's admissibility.

The higher court noted that two years after the Miranda decision, Congress enacted 18 U.S.C. § 3501, which effectively attempted to nullify the Supreme Court's decision in Miranda by changing the test for the admission of confessions in federal court from the stricter Miranda rule to the less stringent judicial standard of totality of circumstances. The appellate court interpreted that Miranda was not a "Constitutional Holding" and Congress's later law superceded Miranda. Makholm (2000, p.13) states: "Needless to say, the 1968 law was never enforced, or for that matter was even widely known by most street officers. So what we have in the Dickerson decision is the United States Supreme Court asserting its constitutional powers."

In *Dickerson,* the Court, by a 7-to-2 margin, refused to strike down *Miranda* and upheld it as a constitutional decision that cannot be overruled by an Act of Congress. The Court added it could find no compelling reason to overturn a 43-year-old decision that "has become embedded in routine police practice to the point where the warnings have become part of our national culture." The Court's ruling in *Dickerson* also struck down § 3501 as unconstitutional: "Experience suggests that the totality-of-the-circumstances test which § 3501 seeks to revive is more difficult than *Miranda* for law enforcement officers to conform to, and for courts to apply in a consistent manner."

Thus, the *Dickerson* decision affirmed the "bright line rule," stating that in any custodial interrogation where a confession is made by a suspect, the confession will be presumed involuntary and, therefore, inadmissible in court *unless* the police officer first provides the suspect with the four specific warnings spelled out in *Miranda.* Petrowski (2001, p.30) observes: "The critical impact of the *Dickerson* decision is that intentional violations of the requirements of *Miranda,* commonly known as questioning 'outside *Miranda,*' now may provide the basis for a lawsuit alleging a federal Constitutional violation."

Waiving the Right

Suspects can *waive* their rights against self-incrimination and talk to police officers, but the **waiver** must be voluntary and must be preceded by the *Miranda* warning. The suspect must fully understand what rights are being given up and the possible consequences. If after hearing a police officer read *Miranda,* suspects remain silent, this is *not* a waiver. To waive their rights, suspects must state, orally or in writing, that (1) they understand their rights and (2) they will voluntarily answer questions without a lawyer present. Kalk (p.50) notes officers are allowed to ask more than once if a suspect would like to waive their rights: "If a suspect chooses to exercise his right to remain silent, police officers are *permitted* to periodically ask the suspect if he has changed his mind and desires to permit questioning."

Special care must be taken with individuals who do not speak English well, who are under the influence of drugs or alcohol, who appear to be mentally retarded or who appear to be hampered mentally in any way. It is preferable to get the waiver in writing. Caplan (n.d., pp.9, 12, 14) suggests these interrogation guidelines:

- Officers should honor a juvenile suspect's request to speak to a parent or guardian before waiving his rights.
- In major felony cases, the notification of rights, the waiver and the subsequent questioning should be videotaped.
- Any direct request for counsel requires all questioning to end. A request to speak to someone other than an attorney, such as a parent, friend or even a probation officer, is not an assertion of the right to counsel.
- When a suspect attempts to reach an attorney but is not successful, most courts hold that he has asserted his right and cannot be questioned.

The Public Safety Exception

The **public safety exception** is an important consideration when discussing the *Miranda* decision. On June 12, 1984, in a landmark 5–4 decision in *New York v. Quarles,* the U.S. Supreme Court announced that in certain cases police may question suspects in custody without first advising them of their right not to incriminate themselves.

Writing for the Court's majority, Justice Rehnquist cited the Court's decision in *Michigan v. Tucker* (1974) and made the distinction that the Miranda warnings are "not themselves rights protected by constitution, but are measures to insure that the right against compulsory self-incrimination is protected. . . . On some facts there is a 'public safety' exception to the requirement that Miranda warnings be given before a suspect's answers may be admitted into evidence, and that the availability of that exception does not depend upon the motivation of the individual officers." Although the Court set forth the "public safety exception," no attempt was made to determine in what situations this exception might apply.

The public safety exception allows police officers to question suspects without first giving the Miranda warning if the information sought sufficiently affects the officer's and the public's safety.

In *Quarles,* a young woman stopped two police officers and said she had been raped. She described her rapist who, she said, had just entered a nearby supermarket armed with a gun. The officers located the suspect, Benjamin Quarles, and ordered him to stop, but Quarles ran, and the officers momentarily lost sight of him. When they apprehended and frisked him, the officers found an empty shoulder holster. When the officers asked Quarles where the gun was, he nodded toward some cartons and said, "The gun is over there." The officers retrieved the gun, arrested Quarles and read him his rights. Quarles waived his rights and answered questions.

At the trial the court ruled that the statement, "The gun is over there," and the subsequent discovery of the gun resulting from that statement were inadmissible at the defendant's trial. However, the Supreme Court, after reviewing the case, ruled that if Miranda warnings had deterred the response to the officer's question, the cost would have been more than just the loss of evidence, which might lead to a conviction. As long as the gun remained concealed in the store, it posed a danger to public safety.

The Court ruled that in this case the need to have the suspect talk took precedence over the requirement that the defendant be read his rights. The Court ruled that the material factor applying this public safety exception is whether a public threat could possibly be removed by the suspect making a statement. In this case the officer asked the question only to ensure his and the public's safety. He then gave the Miranda warning before continuing questioning. Numerous other court decisions have favored public and officer safety over the right of suspects to be immediately read their rights and have recognized that this reasonable precaution should not compromise the admissibility of evidence.

Involuntary Confessions

Arizona v. Fulminante (1991) established that the "harmless error" doctrine applies to cases involving the admissibility of involuntary confessions. In this case Fulminante was suspected of murdering his stepdaughter, but evidence was insufficient to charge him. Later he was arrested and jailed on a federal charge of possession of a firearm. While in prison a fellow inmate, Sarivola, a paid FBI informant, told Fulminante that the other inmates considered him a child killer and that if he would admit to the crime, Sarivola would protect him from the inmates. Fulminante did confess. When he was released from prison, he also confessed to Sarivola's wife.

Fulminante was charged with the murder, and at the trial his confession was challenged as being coerced and therefore excluded by the Fifth and Fourteenth Amendments. His confession to the wife was also challenged as "fruit" of the first confession. The confessions were admitted, however; and Fulminante was convicted and sentenced to death. On appeal the Arizona Supreme Court declared that Fulminante's confession was coerced because he feared for his safety and needed Sarivola to protect him.

The question then became, did allowing the confessions to be admitted into evidence harm the defendant's case or was it a "harmless error"? In this case a majority of the court said the error was not harmless. del Carmen and Walker (p.189) explain the significance of this finding:

> The practice by many appellate courts of automatically reversing any conviction involving the erroneous admission of a confession, regardless of the confession's

> significance, has now been replaced by the "harmless error" doctrine. Under this rule, reversal of conviction on appeal now involves two steps. The first step is determining whether the confession is voluntary. If it is involuntary, the second step is in order: determining whether the admission of such evidence by the trial court was "harmless error." If the admission constitutes "harmless error" (as determined by the appellate court), the conviction is affirmed. Conversely, if the error is harmful or if the prosecution fails to establish beyond reasonable doubt that the error is harmless (as in the *Fulminante* case), the conviction is reversed.

Entrapment

del Carmen and Walker (p.232) state: "**Entrapment** is a defense in criminal law that questions the propriety of police action. It is defined as the act of government officers or agents in inducing a person to commit a crime that is not contemplated by the person for the purpose of instituting a criminal prosecution against him or her" [emphasis added]. Many Supreme Court cases in which entrapment was at issue have led to rulings that help define the boundaries for law enforcement. In *Sorrells v. United States* (1932), the Court stated:

> Society is at war with the criminal classes, and the courts have uniformly held that in waging this warfare the forces of prevention and detection may use traps, decoys and deception to obtain evidence of the commission of a crime. Resort to such means does not render an indictment thereafter found a nullity nor call for the exclusion of evidence so procured. . . . Entrapment is the conception and planning of an offense by an officer, and his procurement of its commission by one who would not have perpetrated it except for the trickery, persuasion or fraud of the officer.

The Court's ruling in *Grossman v. State* (1969) helped delineate police conduct constituting entrapment to include appeals to sympathy, guarantees that the act is legal and inducements making the crime unusually attractive. The Court further defined entrapment in its ruling in *Sherman v. United States* (1958): "Entrapment occurs only when the criminal conduct was 'the product of the creative' activity of law-enforcement officials. To determine whether entrapment has been established, a line must be drawn between the trap for the unwary innocent and the trap for the unwary criminal."

The line between "unwary innocents" and "unwary criminals" was clarified in *United States v. Russell* (1973): "There are circumstances when the use of deceit is the only practicable law enforcement technique available. It is only when the government's deception actually implants the criminal design in the mind of the defendant that the defense of entrapment comes into play." The Court elaborated on this ruling in *Jacobson v. United States* (1992), when it held government has the burden of proving "beyond a reasonable doubt" the defendant's predisposition to commit the offense. If the government fails to prove predisposition, the defense wins on the presumption that the defendant is an "unwary innocent" instead of an "unwary criminal."

A Recap of the Landmark Cases

The challenge of policing within the law is formidable, but critical. Officers must know constitutional restrictions on their powers at both the federal and state levels. Although statutes vary from state to state, several generalizations usually apply. The most important of these are summarized in Table 8.2.

Table 8.2
Summary of Major Court Rulings Regarding the Fourth Amendment (Search and Seizure), Fifth Amendment (Self-Incrimination), Entrapment and Exclusions to These Clauses

Doctrine	Case Decision	Holding
Fourth Amendment		
Probable Cause	*Smith v. United States* (1949)	Probable cause is the sum total of layers of information and the synthesis of what the police have heard, what they know, and what they observe as trained officers. The courts weigh not the individual layers but the laminated total.
	Draper v. United States (1959)	Probable cause exists where the facts and circumstances within the arresting officers' knowledge are sufficient to warrant a person of reasonable caution in the belief that an offense has been or is being committed.
Stop and Frisk	*Terry v. Ohio* (1968)	The authority to stop and frisk is independent of the power to arrest. A stop is not an arrest, but it is a seizure within the meaning of the Fourth Amendment and therefore requires reasonableness.
	Florida v. J. L. (2000)	Reasonable suspicion for an investigative stop does not arise from a mere anonymous tip.
	Illinois v. Wardlow (2000)	A person's sudden flight upon seeing a police officer can be used to establish reasonable suspicion for a *Terry*-type stop.
Sobriety Checkpoints	*Michigan Department of State Police v. Sitz* (1990)	Sobriety checkpoints are a form of stop and are constitutional if they are conducted fairly and do not pose a safety hazard.
Drug Interdiction Roadblocks	*City of Indianapolis v. Edmond* (2000)	Narcotics checkpoints are unconstitutional and violate the Fourth Amendment's protections against unreasonable search and seizure in that their purpose is indistinguishable from the general interest in crime control.
Field Detention	*Michigan v. Summers* (1981)	Police officers may detain suspects with less than probable cause and may legally require suspects to reenter their houses and remain there until evidence establishing probable cause is found.
	Illinois v. McArthur (2001)	Police did not violate the Fourth Amendment when they detained a suspect outside his home for several hours while officers sought a warrant to search the premises for drugs.
Search with a Warrant—Gaining Entrance	*Wilson v. Arkansas* (1995)	Whether police "knock and announce" their presence before executing valid search warrants is part of the Fourth Amendment inquiry into the reasonableness of a search.
	United States v. Espinoza (2001)	A failure to knock and announce does not require suppression of evidence if the target resists.
	District of Columbia v. Mancouso (2001)	Officers who disregard the knock-and-announce rule while serving a search warrant on an empty house, even if the occupants are standing outside the premises "within earshot" of the officers, have violated statutory requirements, thus providing standing for the residents to move to suppress any evidence recovered inside.
Administrative Warrants	*Michigan v. Tyler* (1978)	Public safety personnel may enter structures that are on fire to extinguish the blaze, after which officials may remain a reasonable length of time to investigate the cause of the blaze.
Warrantless Search with Consent	*State v. Barlow, Jr.* (1974)	Consent must be free and voluntary, and the search must be limited to the area for which the consent is given.
Time of Day of Search	*Monroe v. Pape* (1961)	Officers should generally avoid seeking voluntary consent to search at night.

continued

Table 8.2
(Continued)

Doctrine	Case Decision	Holding
Fourth Amendment, *cont.*		
Search Incidental to Lawful Arrest	*Chimel v. California* (1969)	When making an arrest, it is reasonable for an officer to search the person arrested to remove any weapons the latter might use to resist arrest or effect an escape. The search must be made simultaneously with the arrest and must be confined to the area within the immediate control of the suspect—that is, within his or her reach (wingspan).
Protective Sweeps	*Maryland v. Buie* (1989)	A protective sweep is legal and protects the arresting officer from danger posed by unknown third parties. The duration of the sweep is limited and can last no longer than necessary to dispel the suspicion of danger.
Warrantless Searches of Vehicles	*Carroll v. United States* (1925)	The right to search a vehicle is not dependent on the right to arrest the driver or an occupant. It depends on the probable cause the officer has for believing (1) the vehicle's contents violate the law and (2) the conveyance would be gone before a search warrant could be obtained (mobility).
	Chambers v. Maroney (1970)	A car may retain its mobility even though it is impounded.
	Coolidge v. New Hampshire (1971)	The rule of mobility cannot be applied unless there is actually a risk that the vehicle will be moved.
	New York v. Belton (1981)	Officers can search a vehicle's interior and all its contents if an occupant has been lawfully arrested and the vehicle search is subsequent to the arrest.
	United States v. Ross (1982)	Police may search a car, including containers in the car, without a warrant as long as they have probable cause to believe contraband is in the car.
	Colorado v. Bertine (1987)	Police can inventory the contents of an impounded vehicle.
	Florida v. Jimeno (1991)	A criminal suspect's Fourth Amendment right to be free from unreasonable searches is not violated when, after he gives police permission to search his automobile, they open a closed container found within the car that might reasonably hold the object of the search.
Pretext/Dual Motive Traffic Stops	*United States v. Millan* (1994)	If an officer's original intent in stopping a vehicle is to "check it out" and not for a specific violation, any subsequent search will be illegal.
	Whren v. United States (1996)	The real purpose of a stop, even if ulterior, does not render the stop and subsequent search invalid if there was, in fact, a valid reason for the stop, such as a traffic violation.
Danger of Traffic Stops	*Maryland v. Wilson* (1997)	Given the likelihood of traffic stops leading to either violence or destruction of evidence when passengers are in the vehicle, officers making traffic stops may lawfully order all of a vehicle's occupants, including passengers, to get out of the car pending completion of the stop, extending a previous Court decision applicable only to drivers.
Plain Feel/Touch	*Minnesota v. Dickerson* (1993)	Supporting limited "plain touch" or "plain feel" probes in frisk situations, if contraband is plainly felt by the officer in good faith, what he finds will not be suppressed. Under the Plain Feel Doctrine, an officer must determine simultaneously that an item is not a weapon and is, in fact, contraband.
	Bond v. United States (2000)	Extended *Dickerson,* ruling police can visually inspect passengers' luggage but cannot squeeze or otherwise manipulate baggage to determine whether it contains contraband.

Table 8.2
(Continued)

Doctrine	Case Decision	Holding
Fourth Amendment, *cont.*		
Workplace Privacy	*O'Connor v. Ortega* (1987)	As a general rule, searches of employees' private property (purses, wallets, personal mail) in their workspaces are subject to full Fourth Amendment protection, requiring probable cause and a search warrant. But the nature of a public employee's position allows some intrusion into privacy. All an employer needs for a work-related intrusion to be "reasonable" under the Fourth Amendment is reasonable suspicion the search will reveal evidence of an employee's work-related misconduct or that the search is necessary for a noninvestigatory, work-related purpose, such as retrieving a needed file.
Open Fields, Abandoned Property and Trash	*Hester v. United States* (1924)	If something is open to the public and has no expectation of privacy, it is not protected by the Fourth Amendment.
Curtilage	*Oliver v. United States* (1984)	A warrant is required to search the curtilage, the area to which extends the intimate activity associated with the "sanctity of a man's home and the privacies of life." "No Trespassing" signs and locked gates do not constitute a reasonable expectation of privacy.
	United States v. Dunn (1987)	Four factors to consider in determining if an area is within a home's curtilage are (1) the proximity of the area to the home, (2) whether the area is within the same enclosure as the home, (3) the nature of the use to which the area is put and (4) measures taken by the home's occupant to protect the area from the view of passersby.
	California v. Greenwood (1988)	Garbage left outside the curtilage of a home for regular collection may be inspected without a warrant. If no expectation of privacy exists, Fourth Amendment protection does not exist either.
Aerial Searches	*California v. Ciraola* (1986)	A defendant's privacy is not violated when officers traveling in a navigable airspace observe illegal activity or contraband.
	Florida v. Riley (1989)	Expands *California v. Ciraola* by stating police do not need a search warrant to conduct even low-altitude helicopter searches of private property.
Thermal Imaging	*Kyllo v. United States* (2001)	Using a thermal imager to surveil a home is a search under the Fourth Amendment and, as such, requires a search warrant based on probable cause.
Inevitable Discovery Doctrine	*Nix v. Williams* (1984)	Illegally obtained evidence may be admitted at trial if the prosecution can prove the evidence would "inevitably" have been discovered by lawful means.
Arrest without a Warrant	*People v. Ramey* (1976)	The Fourth Amendment prohibits a warrantless entry into a dwelling to arrest in the absence of sufficient justification for the failure to obtain a warrant. (California Supreme Court)
	Payton v. New York (1980)	Extended *People v. Ramey* to apply to all states.
Fifth Amendment		
Self-Incrimination	*Miranda v. Arizona* (1966)	Before questioning, police must inform suspects in custody of their rights to remain silent, to have counsel present, to state-appointed counsel if they cannot afford their own attorney and to be warned that anything they say may be used against them in a court of law.

continued

Table 8.2
(Continued)

Doctrine	Case Decision	Holding
Fifth Amendment, *cont.*		
Self-Incrimination, *cont.*	*Oregon v. Mathiason* (1977)	Police are not required to give Miranda warnings to everyone whom they question, nor is the requirement imposed simply because questioning takes place in the station house or because the questioned person is one whom the police suspect. Miranda warnings are required only where there has been such a restriction on a person's freedom as to render him or her "in custody."
Custodial Interrogation	*United States v. Mesa* (1980)	Incriminating statements in a suspect's recorded conversation are not obtained in violation of the suspect's rights if the Miranda warning is not first given.
DUI Stops	*Pennsylvania v. Muniz* (1990)	Officers conducting DUI stops who ask routine questions do not need to give the Miranda warning.
Right to Counsel	*Brewer v. Williams* (1977)	A suspect's incriminating statements were inadmissible because the way they were elicited violated his constitutional right to counsel.
Constitutionality of *Miranda*	*Dickerson v. United States* (2000)	Affirmed *Miranda* as a constitutional decision that cannot be overruled by an Act of Congress and upheld the "bright line rule": any confession made during a custodial interrogation will be presumed involuntary and, thus, inadmissible *unless* the police officer first provides the suspect with the four specific warnings spelled out in *Miranda.*
Public Safety Exception	*Michigan v. Tucker* (1974)	Miranda warnings are not themselves rights protected by constitution, but are measures to ensure that the right against compulsory self-incrimination is protected. On some facts there is a "public safety" exception to the requirement that Miranda warnings be given before a suspect's answers may be admitted into evidence, and the availability of that exception does not depend upon the motivation of the individual officers.
	New York v. Quarles (1984)	The public safety exception allows police to question suspects without first giving the Miranda warning if the information sought sufficiently affects the officer's and the public's safety.
Involuntary Confessions (Harmless Error)	*Arizona v. Fulminante* (1991)	When involuntary confessions are admitted into evidence, the question is: "Did the allowance harm the defendant's case or was it a 'harmless error'"? If the error is harmful or if the prosecution fails to establish beyond reasonable doubt that the error is harmless, the confession is inadmissible and any conviction based on it must be reversed.
Entrapment	*Sorrells v. United States* (1932)	Law enforcement may use traps, decoys and deception to obtain evidence of the commission of a crime. Resort to such means does not render an indictment thereafter found a nullity nor call for the exclusion of evidence so procured.
	Grossman v. State (1969)	Police conduct constituting entrapment includes appeals to sympathy, guarantees that the act is legal and inducements making the crime unusually attractive.
	Sherman v. United States (1958)	Entrapment occurs only when the criminal conduct was "the product of the creative" activity of law enforcement officials.
	United States v. Russell (1973)	Only when government deception actually implants the criminal design in the mind of the defendant does the defense of entrapment come into play.
	Jacobson v. United States (1992)	Government has the burden of proving "beyond a reasonable doubt" the defendant's predisposition to commit an offense. Failing to prove such a predisposition, the defense wins on the presumption the defendant is an "unwary innocent" instead of an "unwary criminal."

Summary

The constitutional standards for searches and seizures, including arrests, are contained in the Fourth Amendment, which requires that searches and seizures be reasonable and be based on probable cause. Probable cause requires more than mere suspicion. It requires facts or proof that would lead a person of reasonable caution to believe a crime has been committed by a specific individual or that premises contain evidence of a crime. Probable cause may be founded on (1) observation, (2) expertise, (3) circumstantial factors and (4) information conveyed to the officers, including official sources, victims of crimes and informants.

Stop and frisk is a form of search and seizure and, as such, is governed by the intent of the Fourth Amendment. A stop is not an arrest, but it is a seizure if physical force or a show of authority is used. A frisk, however, is a search. Stop and frisk is a protective search for weapons in which the intrusion must be limited to a scope reasonably designed to discover guns, knives, clubs and other hidden instruments, which may be used to assault a police officer or others; it is not a search for evidence of a crime. *Terry* established that the authority to stop and frisk is independent of the power to arrest. A stop is *not* an arrest, but it is a seizure within the meaning of the Fourth Amendment and, therefore, requires reasonableness.

Reasonable searches must also meet the standards set forth in the Fourth Amendment. The principal justifications established by the courts for the right to search are (1) a search warrant has been issued, (2) no warrant has been issued but consent to search was given, (3) no warrant has been issued but exigent circumstances exist or (4) no warrant has been issued because there is no expectation of privacy and, thus, no requirement for a search warrant.

Technically all searches are to be made under the authority of a search warrant issued by a magistrate. A search warrant is a judicial order directing a police officer to search for specific property, seize it and return it to the court. The search must be limited to the specific area and specific items delineated in the warrant. Probable cause is required for issuance of all warrants.

Police officers may conduct a search without a warrant if consent is given, exigent circumstances are present or no reasonable expectation of privacy exists. The limitations to a search made with consent are that the consent must be free and voluntary, not in response to an implied right to search, and the scope must be limited to the area for which consent has been given. When police conduct a warrantless search under exigent circumstances, they may be challenged on the basis that probable cause was not established (i.e., a magistrate would not have issued a warrant) or that the officers had time to secure a warrant and had no justification to act without one. The limitations placed on searches incidental to lawful arrest come from *Chimel v. California,* which states that the scope of the search must be narrowed to the area within the suspect's immediate control—that is, it must be within his or her reach.

Special provisions have been made for warrantless searches of cars and other conveyances due to their mobility. The *Carroll* decision established that the right to search an automobile is not dependent on the right to arrest the driver or an occupant. It depends on the probable cause the officer has for believing (1) the automobile's contents violate the law and (2) the conveyance would be gone before a search warrant could be obtained. *Chambers* established that a car may retain its mobility even though impounded. *Coolidge* established that the rule of mobility cannot be applied unless there is actually a risk the vehicle will be moved. *Maryland v. Wilson* established that, given the likelihood of a traffic stop leading to either violence or the destruction of evidence when passengers are in the vehicle, officers may order passengers out of the vehicle pending completion of the stop.

If something is open to the public and, therefore, has no expectation of privacy, it is not protected by the Fourth Amendment. This includes open fields, abandoned property and trash. Even when the required conditions are met, certain limitations are placed on the search. The most important limitation imposed on any search is that the scope must be narrowed. General searches are unconstitutional.

U.S. citizens are also protected against unreasonable arrest (seizure) by the Fourth Amendment. The Fourth Amendment requires that arrests be made by having a magistrate issue an arrest warrant, but police officers may make an arrest without an arrest warrant in certain circumstances. For example if there is probable cause and an emergency situation exists, an officer may make an arrest without a warrant. The courts will determine whether the arrest was lawful.

The Miranda warning must be given to a suspect who is interrogated in police custody, that is when the suspect is not free to leave. The public safety exception allows officers to question suspects without first giving the Miranda warning if the information sought sufficiently affects the officer's and the public's safety.

For more materials related to the content in this chapter, go to the *Introduction to Law Enforcement and Criminal Justice* Web site: http://info.wadsworth.com/wrobleski.

Discussion Questions

1. In popular television programs, how are police officers portrayed in relation to their duty to protect citizens' Fourth Amendment rights?
2. Why are the police not given total freedom to help stop crime? Why are they not allowed to use evidence that clearly establishes a person's guilt, no matter how they obtained this evidence?
3. In a state where stop and frisk is legal, can a police officer be sued for stopping and frisking someone?
4. What are the most important factors in determining if and when an arrest occurred?
5. Must all elements of probable cause exist before a lawful arrest can be made?
6. Why is the presence of 10 officers not considered intimidation when a request to search is made?
7. Have you ever been involved in a search and seizure situation? How was it handled?
8. From what you have learned about search and seizure, do you feel the restrictions placed on police officers are reasonable?
9. Do you support the plain touch/feel doctrine? Why or why not?
10. Is it too easy for criminals to allege entrapment? How can officers protect against this?

InfoTrac *College Edition Assignment*

Use InfoTrac College Edition to help answer the Discussion Questions as appropriate.

- Use InfoTrac College Edition to search for articles on the *bright-line rule* and zero in on the *Fourth Amendment* and *traffic stops.* Describe the bright-line rules in conjunction with the totality-of-circumstances test. Be prepared to discuss your findings with the class.

Internet Assignment

Go to *Dickerson v. United States* (http://supct.law.cornell.edu/supct/html/99–5525.ZS.html) and review this Supreme Court case. Note the dissents of Justices Scalia and Thomas. Outline the arguments on both sides (majority rule versus dissenting opinions), and be prepared to discuss your findings with the class and which position you agree with.

Book-Specific Web Site

The book-specific Web site at http://info.wadsworth.com/0534552803 hosts a variety of resources for students and instructors. Included are extended activities from each chapter in which students write a policy, use critical thinking skills to make choices in response to a given scenario, use InfoTrac College Edition with direct links to articles for participation in topical discussion forums, and analyze court cases using Web links for research. Many activities can be printed or emailed to instructors. Plus, cited cases with Web links, interactive key term FlashCards, PowerPoint presentations, chapter objectives, and an extensive collection of chapter-based Web links provide additional information and activities to include in the curriculum.

References

"Brief Seizure of Premises to Obtain a Search Warrant Permissible under the Fourth Amendment." *NCJA Justice Bulletin,* March 2001, p.13.

Bulzomi, Michael J. "Anonymous Tips and Frisks: Determining Reasonable Suspicion." *FBI Law Enforcement Bulletin,* August 2000, pp.28–32.

Caplan, G. M. *Model Procedures for Police Interrogation.* Washington, DC: Police Executive Research Forum (no date).

Colbridge, Thomas D. "Protective Sweeps." *FBI Law Enforcement Bulletin,* July 1998, pp.25–32.

Colbridge, Thomas D. "*Kyllo v. United States:* Technology versus Individual Privacy." *FBI Law Enforcement Bulletin,* October 2001, pp.25–32.

"Court Lets Police Bar Suspect from House Pending Warrant." *Criminal Justice Newsletter,* February 26, 2001, pp.3–4.

"Court Slaps New Curb on Luggage Search." *Law Enforcement News,* April 30, 2000, p.9.

del Carmen, Rolando V. and Walker, Jeffery T. *Briefs of Leading Cases in Law Enforcement,* 4th ed. Cincinnati, OH: Anderson Publishing Co., 2000.

Harris, Wesley. "Running from the Law: Supreme Court Clarifies Authority to Chase Fleeing Suspects." *Law and Order,* June 2000, pp.108–110.

Hemmens, Craig and Levin, Daniel. "Resistance Is Futile: The Right to Resist Unlawful Arrest in an Era of Aggressive Policing." *Crime and Delinquency,* October 2000, pp.472–496.

Hendrie, Edward M. "Warrantless Entries to Arrest: Constitutional Considerations." *FBI Law Enforcement Bulletin,* September 1998, pp.25–32.

Kalk, Dan. "The Rights Stuff: Reviewing the Miranda Warnings." *Police,* October 1998, pp.50–52.

"Knock and Announce Required? Check Your State." *The Law Officers' Bulletin,* August 30, 2001, pp.13–14.

Makholm, John A. "Legal Lights: *Dickerson v. United States.*" *The Law Enforcement Trainer,* July/August 2000, p.13.

Makholm, John A. "Legal Lights: *Illinois v. McArthur.*" *The Law Enforcement Trainer,* May/June 2001, p.13.

Milazzo, Carl. "Stopping and Chasing, or Is It the Other Way Around?" *The Police Chief, June* 2000, p.11.

Petrowski, Thomas D. "*Miranda* Revisited: *Dickerson v. United States.*" *FBI Law Enforcement Bulletin,* August 2001, pp.25–32.

Scuro, Joseph E., Jr. "Supreme Court Reviews 'Stop and Frisk' Conduct." *Law and Order,* August 2000, pp.12–14.

"Supreme Court Allows Police to Ban Suspect from Home while Seeking Search Warrant." *The Law Officers' Bulletin,* March 29, 2001, pp.130–131.

"Supreme Court Strikes Down Drug Interdiction Roadblocks." *Criminal Justice Newsletter,* February 15, 2000, pp.1–2.

"Use of Thermal Imaging Devices a Search, High Court Holds." *The Law Officers' Bulletin,* April 26, 2001, pp.186–187.

"Vehicle Checkpoints for Drugs Violate the 4th Amendment." *NCJA Justice Bulletin,* November 2000, p.4.

Wallentine, Ken. "No-Knock and Nighttime Searches." *Police,* September 1998, pp.37–39.

Cases Cited

Arizona v. Fulminante, 499 U.S. 279 (1991)
Bond v. United States, 120 S.Ct. 1462 (2000)
Brewer v. Williams, 430 U.S. 387 (1977)
California v. Ciraola, 476 U.S. 207 (1986)
California v. Greenwood, 486 U.S. 35 (1988)
Carroll v. United States, 267 U.S. 132 (1925)
Chambers v. Maroney, 339 U.S. 42 (1970)
Chimel v. California, 395 U.S. 752 (1969)
City of Indianapolis v. Edmond, (No. 99-1030, decided November 28, 2000)
Colorado v. Bertine, 479 U.S. 367 (1987)
Coolidge v. New Hampshire, 403 U.S. 443 (1971)
Dickerson v. United States, 530 U.S. 428 (2000)
District of Columbia v. Mancouso, (D.C. No. 00-CT-544, 8/2/01)
Draper v. United States, 358 U.S. 307 (1959)
Florida v. Jimeno, 499 U.S. 934 (1991)
Florida v. J.L., 120 S.Ct. 1375 (2000)
Florida v. Riley, 109 S.Ct. 693, 44 CrL (1989)
Grossman v. State, 457 P.2d 226 (1969)
Hester v. United States, 265 U.S. 57, 44 (1924)
Illinois v. McArthur, 121 S.Ct. 946 (2001)
Illinois v. Wardlow, (No. 98-1036, decided January 12, 2000)
Jacobson v. United States, 503 U.S. 540 (1992)
Kyllo v. United States, 121 S.Ct. 2038 (2001)
Maryland v. Buie, 109 S.Ct. 2447 (1989)
Maryland v. Wilson, 117 S.Ct. 882 (1997)
Michigan Department of State Police v. Sitz, 496 S. Ct. 444 (1990)
Michigan v. Summers, 452 U.S. 692 (1981)
Michigan v. Tucker, 417 U.S. 433 (1974)
Michigan v. Tyler, 436 U.S. 499 (1978)
Minnesota v. Dickerson, 113 S.Ct. 2130 (1993)
Miranda v. Arizona, 384 U.S. 436 (1966)
Monroe v. Pape, 365 U.S. 167 (1961)
New York v. Belton, 453 U.S. 454 (1981)
New York v. Quarles, 104 S.Ct. 2626 (1984)
Nix v. Williams, 104 S.Ct. 2501 (1984)
O'Connor v. Ortega, 107 S.Ct. 1492 (1987)
Oliver v. United States, 466 U.S. 170 (1984)

Olmstead v. United States, 277 U.S. 438 (1928)
Oregon v. Mathiason, 429 U.S. 492, 332 (1977)
Payton v. New York, 445 U.S. 573, 586–589 (1980)
Pennsylvania v. Muniz, 496 U.S. 582 (1990)
People v. Ramey, 16 Cal.3d 263, 274–275 (1976)
Sherman v. United States, 356 U.S. 369 (1958)
Smith v. United States, 337 U.S. 137 (1949)
Sorrells v. United States, 287 U.S. 435 (1932)
State v. Barlow, Jr., 320 A.2d 895 (Me. 1974)
Terry v. Ohio, 392 U.S. 1 (1968)
United States v. Dunn, 480 U.S. 294, 301 (1987)
United States v. Espinoza, (7 Cir., No.00-3090, 7/11/01)
United States v. Mesa, 638 F. 2d 582 3d Cir. (1980)
United States v. Millan, 56 CrL 1057, 9th Cir. (1994)
United States v. Ross, 456 U.S. 798 (1982)
United States v. Russell, 411 U.S. 423 (1973)
Whren v. United States, 517 U.S. 806 (1996)
Wilson v. Arkansas, 115 S.Ct. 1914 (1995)

Chapter 9

Gangs, Drugs and Terrorism: Threats to Our National Security

Gangs are now spreading through our society like a violent plague.

—Jackson and McBride, LAPD

Drug use and the crime it generates are turning the American dream into a national nightmare for millions of Americans.

—Lee P. Brown

Tonight we are a country awakened to danger and called to defend freedom. Our grief has turned to anger, and anger to resolution. Whether we bring our enemies to justice, or bring justice to our enemies, justice will be done. . . . Our war on terror begins with al-Qaeda, but it does not end there. It will not end until every terrorist group of global reach has been found, stopped, and defeated.

—President George W. Bush in an address to Congress, September 20, 2001

Do You Know?

- What the distinguishing characteristics of gangs are?
- How gang members might be identified?
- What the most common reasons for joining gangs are?
- What factors contribute to the formation of a gang?
- What the most important risk factor is for becoming a gang member?
- What act made it illegal to sell or use certain narcotics and dangerous drugs?
- What exactly federal law prohibits in relation to narcotics and dangerous drugs?
- What the most commonly observed drugs on the street, in possession of users and seized in drug raids are and what the most frequent drug arrest is for?
- What the most widely abused drug in the United States is?
- If drug use and alcohol abuse are linked to crime?
- What approaches to the drug problem have been suggested?
- What common elements are found in most definitions of terrorism?
- How the FBI classifies terrorist acts?
- What the lead federal agencies in combating terrorism are?
- What the key to successfully combating terrorism is?
- What two concerns are associated with the current "war on terrorism"?

Can You Define?

amphetamines
barbiturates
bioterrorism
Bloods
broken-window theory
civil injunction
cocaine
corporate gangs
crack
Crips
cyberterrorism
dangerous drugs
deliriants
drug gangs
drug-defined offenses
drug-related offenses
eco-terrorism
flake
gang
graffiti
hallucinogens
hedonistic gangs
heroin
instrumental gangs
interdiction
marijuana
methamphetamine
monikers
mules
narcoterrorism
narcotics
nystagmus
organized gangs
party gangs
PCP
predatory gangs
rock
scavenger gangs
serious delinquent gangs
sinsemilla
social gangs
territorial gangs
terrorism
traditional gangs
turf
wannabes

INTRODUCTION

Drugs and gangs are often mentioned in the same sentence. McCorkle and Miethe (1998, p.41), for example, state: "The past decade has witnessed increasing concern about street gangs and their role in violent crime and drug trafficking." Likewise *Addressing Community Gang Problems* (1998, p.23) says: "The type of violence most commonly associated with gangs is a function of the illegal sale and distribution of drugs." However, *Addressing Community Gang Problems* concludes that the research on the relationships between gangs, drugs and violence is inconclusive, stating (p.22): "Whether one is examining drug use or drug selling, the relationship between gangs and drugs has not been clearly defined or understood. A number of gangs are involved in using and selling drugs, while others are involved in selling but prohibit use by gang members."

The latest "gangs" to threaten America and, in fact, the entire civilized world are terrorist groups, including the al-Qaeda network responsible for numerous attacks on American interests abroad as well as the September 11, 2001, tragedy on our own soil.

This chapter begins by discussing the threat of gangs. First gangs are defined and the various types of gangs that have developed in the United States are described, including various racial and ethnic gangs and the increasing presence of females in gangs. This is followed by a discussion of specific characteristics of gangs, including the gang subculture and how gang members might be identified. Next reasons for joining a gang are discussed. This first section of the chapter concludes with a look at problems in prosecuting gang members, various gang control strategies and the role drugs and drug addiction play in the world of gangs.

The link between gangs and drugs provides the transition into the next section—the threat of drugs. Discussion of this topic begins with a look at the various narcotics and other dangerous drugs under federal regulation regarding their prescription, distribution and possession. Next, alcohol, the most widely abused drug in the country, is discussed, followed by an examination of the links between crime and illicit drug and alcohol use. This section concludes by exploring the impact drug use and abuse have had on society and the various drug control strategies being used in the war on drugs, ranging from incarceration to legalization.

The final section of the chapter examines the most recent threat to the United States—terrorism—which was thrust to the top of our nation's priorities by the events of September 11, 2001. This section begins by defining terrorism, examining the various motivations for terrorism and identifying the types of terrorism. Next is a look at domestic and international terrorism, followed by a chronology of major terrorist events that have occurred around the world from the first century to the present. The events of the September 11 terrorist attacks on America are then covered, including possible answers to the questions Why did it happen? and Who is responsible? The chapter concludes by examining law enforcement's role in the national response to terrorism and efforts to detect, prepare for, prevent, protect against, respond to and recover from terrorist attacks.

The Threat of Gangs

Gangs have existed in nearly every civilization throughout recorded history. Street gangs probably started in our country in Los Angeles at about the turn of the last century. According to Miller (2001, p.iii):

> The last quarter of the 20th century was marked by significant growth in youth gang problems across the United States. In the 1970s, less than half the States reported youth gang problems, but by the late 1990s, every State and the District of Columbia reported youth gang activity. In the same period, the number of cities reporting youth gang problems mushroomed nearly tenfold—from fewer than 300 in the 1970's to more than 2,500 in 1998.

The states with the largest number of gang problem cities in 1998 were California (363), Illinois (261), Texas (156), Florida (125) and Ohio (86) (p.ix). Miller (p.x) explains that the regional location of gang cities changed radically during the three-decade period. In the 1970s, the West ranked highest in the reported number of gang cities, and the South ranked lowest. By 1998, the South ranked second, with a 33-fold increase in gang cities since the 1970s. In the late 1990s there were approximately 200 cities with populations of 100,000 or more, and every one of these large cities reported youth gang problems.

However, gang problems are by no means confined to large cities. There has been a striking increase in the growth of gang problems in the nation's smaller cities, towns and villages: "Contemporary gangs—variously known as youth or delinquent gangs and street or criminal gangs—have become a widespread threat to communities throughout the Nation. Once considered largely an urban phenomenon, gangs have increasingly emerged in smaller communities, presenting a challenge that severely restrains local resources" (*Addressing Community Gang Problems,* p.xiii).

Reasons for the striking increase include drugs, immigration, gang names and alliances, migration, government policies, female-headed households, and gang subculture and the media (Miller, p.x). Miller's report (p.x) concludes: "The data provide considerable support for a prediction that the rate of growth that prevailed during the later 1990's will decrease in the early 2000's and some support for a prediction that the actual number of gang localities in the United States will decrease." This prediction is supported by key findings of the *1998 National Youth Gang Survey* (2000):

- In 1998, 48 percent of all respondents experienced gang activity, down almost 3 percent from 1997 and about 5 percent from 1996.
- In 1998, there were an estimated 28,700 gangs and 780,200 gang members active in the United States (down from an estimated 30,500 gangs and 816,000 gang members in 1997 and 31,000 gangs and 846,000 gang members in 1996), a modest decrease of 7 and 8 percent, respectively.
- In 1998, most respondents (42 percent) believed their youth gang problem was "staying about the same," 28 percent believed the problem was "getting worse," and 30 percent believed it was "getting better."

Despite the decrease in the problem, gangs still pose a significant challenge to law enforcement as Valdez (2000c, p.32) suggests: "Understanding the culture of street gangs has become essential for most of us in the criminal justice profession. Street gangs and the associated crime has impacted the police, the courts, corrections and most importantly the quality of life for many Americans." Furthermore, the proliferation of gangs has fueled much of the increase in violent crime; as gangs have spread across the nation, so too has the violence. One reason for this is the easy availability of guns, including semi- and fully automatic assault rifles.

Gangs Defined

The Chicago Police Department (*Gang Awareness,* n.d., p.1) defines a gang as "a group which has an organizational structure, leadership and . . . exists or benefits substantially from the criminal activity of its members." A **gang** is a group of individuals with a recognized name and symbols who form an allegiance for a common purpose and engage in unlawful activity.

A definition commonly accepted by law enforcement is that a gang is any group gathering continuously to commit antisocial behavior. But as Esbensen et al. (2001, p.124) caution: "Obviously the definition used greatly affects the perceived magnitude of the gang problem. By restricting gang membership status to gangs that are involved in delinquent activity and have some level of organization, we reduce the size of the gang problem substantially." The threat of gangs is better understood and addressed by categorizing the different types of gangs.

Types of Gangs

Some common types of gangs are the *neighborhood gang* or "*crew,*" a small group of youths from the same neighborhood loosely banded together for fun; the *street gang,* usually larger and more organized; and the *prison gang,* comprised of incarcerated members who protect each other and distribute contraband within the correctional facility. Shelden et al. (2001, pp.37–38) describe the major types of gangs identified by various studies by different researchers nationwide:

- **Hedonistic/social gangs**—only moderate drug use and offending, involved mainly in using drugs and having a good time; little involvement in crime, especially violent crime.

- **Party gangs**—commonly called "party crews"; relatively high use and sale of drugs, but only one major form of delinquency—vandalism; may contain both genders or may be one gender; many have no specific dress style, but some dress in stylized clothing worn by street gang members, such as baseball caps and oversize clothing; some have tattoos and use hand signs; their flexible turf is called the "party scene"; crews compete over who throws the biggest party, with alcohol, marijuana, nitrous oxide, sex and music critical party elements.
- **Instrumental gangs**—main criminal activity is property crimes (most use drugs and alcohol but seldom sell drugs).
- **Predatory gangs**—heavily involved in serious crimes (robberies, muggings) and the abuse of addictive drugs such as crack cocaine; may engage in selling drugs but not in organized fashion.
- **Scavenger gangs**—loosely organized groups described as "urban survivors"; prey on the weak in inner cities; engage in rather petty crimes but sometimes violence, often just for fun; members have no greater bond than their impulsiveness and need to belong; lack goals and are low achievers; often illiterate with poor school performance.
- **Serious delinquent gangs**—heavy involvement in both serious and minor crimes, but much lower involvement in drug use and drug sales than party gangs.
- **Territorial gangs**—associated with a specific area or turf and, as a result, get involved in conflicts with other gangs over their respective turfs.
- **Organized/corporate gangs**—heavy involvement in all kinds of crime, heavy use and sale of drugs; may resemble major corporations, with separate divisions handling sales, marketing, discipline, and so on; discipline is strict, and promotion is based on merit.
- **Drug gangs**—smaller than other gangs; much more cohesive; focused on the drug business; strong, centralized leadership with market-defined roles.

Racial or Ethnic Gangs

Most gangs are racially or ethnically homogeneous, comprised of members who share the same language, cultural background and, frequently, heritage. The *1998 National Youth Gang Survey* (p.xv) reported that nationally in 1998, 46 percent of all gang members were Hispanic, 34 percent were African-American, 12 percent were Caucasian, 6 percent were Asian, and 2 percent were of another race/ethnicity.

Hispanic Gangs

Between 1910 and 1925, a great influx of immigrants arrived from Mexico. These immigrants tended to live with others from their native areas of Mexico, and rivalries developed that eventually resulted in the formation of gangs, such as Bunker Hill, Mara Villa and San Fernando. These Hispanic gangs lived in barrios that often could trace their heritage back several generations. They had a strong system of tradition and became known as **traditional gangs.**

The depression of the 1930s brought Latino families from Arizona, New Mexico and Texas to Los Angeles. They fragmented into groups, each claiming its own territory and forming such gangs as Happy Valley, HoyoSoto, Alpine Hazard and White Fence. In the 1960s freeway displacement drove families from the central city eastward, where they created more new gangs, such as Lomas and Bassett.

Today, Hispanic gangs are comprised of not only Chicanos, a term reserved for those from Mexico, but also Puerto Ricans, Cubans and individuals from various Central and South American countries. Despite the diversity within the Hispanic gang community as a whole, individual gangs tend to remain ethnically homogeneous. Furthermore, Valdez (2001b, p.49) notes Hispanic street gangs are the fastest-growing type of gang in the United States today.

African-American Gangs

African-American street gangs also existed in the Los Angeles area for many years. They began as groups of young high school "thugs" who extorted money from students and terrorized teachers. One gang, calling itself the Crips, had the reputation of being the toughest African-American gang in Los Angeles, so other gangs began incorporating the word "Crip" into their names. Although these gangs shared a common name, they were in reality independent, and rivalries developed. Shelden et al. (p.12) explain: "One group of African-American youths who lived on a street called Piru in Compton began to get together for protection from attacks by Crip sets. They called themselves the Compton Pirus and are believed to be the first gang to borrow the term *blood brothers* and apply it to their gang name." Thus began the division of African-American gangs into the **Crips** and the Non-Crips or **Bloods.**

Because African-American gangs have not existed as long as Hispanic gangs, they do not have generations of tradition and, consequently, are often referred to as "nontraditional" gangs.

Asian Gangs

In the early 1900s, secret fraternal organizations called the Tongs used boys called Wah Chings as lookouts. As the Tongs became more legitimate and established, they no longer needed the Wah Chings. The Wah Chings, however, refused to disband, taking up where the Tongs left off.

Although the Tongs are now primarily benevolent societies, when necessary they will resort to violence through the Wah Chings. Eventually differences developed within the Wah Chings, and they split into two groups, with the older members becoming known as Yu Li, while the younger members retained the name Wah Ching.

A member of the Yu Li named Joe Fong became disenchanted with the Yu Li and broke off into another gang called the Joe Fong gang or Joe Boys. The massacre at the Golden Dragon restaurant in 1967 occurred when the Joe Fong gang attacked the Wah Ching gang. All three gangs, the Wah Chings, Yu Lis and Joe Boys, exist today and have spread to most major cities of the United States and Canada.

As with Hispanic gangs, ethnic diversity exists among Asian gangs. For example, Vietnamese gangs, described by Krott (2001, p.100), are a "small, but noticeably vicious minority of the Vietnamese community." Says Krott: "Vietnamese gangs are well known for their mobility and the typical gang consists of males and females, usually runaways, 13 to 25 years old with a propensity towards violence. Vietnamese gangs are motivated by quick money, the immediate gratification of a desire for an affluent life style." Further: "They are survival criminals with no long-term goals, and no attachments or allegiances to anything except each other. These are some of the most violent criminals on the American streets." They prefer to hang out in malls, billiard halls, Asian restaurants and coffee shops, bowling alleys and parking lots.

A new breed of Asian gang identified is the home invaders, whose well-armed and well-organized members specialize in home robberies of other Asians. The targeting of Asian victims by Asian gang members is relatively common, because of a general unwillingness among the Asian community to report victimization to the police. For example Gustafson (1998, p.B1) reports: "The Asian Crips went on a 12-day rampage earlier this spring, repeatedly raping at least seven young Hmong girls as part of a gang initiation ritual. . . . Hmong gang members are well aware that rape victims are stigmatized in the Hmong community and reluctant to tell authorities what happened."

White Ethnic Gangs

White ethnic gangs are composed primarily of European American members. Neo-Nazi skinheads are perhaps the best known white ethnic gang, with members who are militantly racist and advocate white supremacy. The Aryan Youth Movement (AYM) and White Aryan Resistance (WAR) are groups also aligned by racism. White "Stoner" gangs emphasize the occult and satanic rituals. White ethnic gangs typically engage in hate crimes directed at other ethnic and religious groups and those with "alternative" lifestyles. They may attack blacks, Hispanics, Jews or homosexuals. According to Walker et al. (2000, pp.53–54): "Skinheads are unique in the sense that they use violence not to protect turf, protect a drug market, or commit robberies but rather 'for the explicit purpose of promoting political change by instilling fear in innocent people.'"

Other Types of Gangs

Filipino neighborhood street gangs are similar to Hispanic gangs and may gravitate toward Mexican gangs. The most common Filipino gangs are the Santanas, the Tabooes and Temple Street. The Korean community also has active gangs, the most well known being the Korean Killers. Furthermore it has been noted that Native-American gangs are also spreading throughout the country.

Valdez (2001a, p.46) describes outlaw motorcycle gangs as among the "most dynamic gangs worldwide," influencing the drug trade, and using extortion, white slavery and money laundering. He estimates there are more than 1,000 motorcycle gangs in the United States and Canada. They have become "prolific traders in the drug market," and, as Valdez (p.48) cautions: "Motorcycle gangs involved in meth trafficking are going to be organized and will exhibit a willingness to use violence to accomplish their objectives." While the image of the biker gang member remains one of a leather-and-denim rough-and-tough guy, the reality today is that many members of such gangs are well-educated, some holding college-level degrees in finance, business and law to improve the gang's profitability.

One of the newest forms of gangs developing across the country is the train gang, able to infiltrate any community through which railroad tracks pass:

> The leading gang goes by the name of Freight Train Riders of America (FTRA). In 1984, this organization was established by a group of ex-Vietnam veterans in Montana . . . [and] originally formed for the purpose of camaraderie. In 1987, the group formed an enforcement arm known as the "Goon Squad" or the "Goonies." This branch kept other members in line and victimized nonmembers. . . . [The FTRA] targeted non-member transients for their food, clothing and money as a means of survival (Howard and Burke, 1998, p.117).

While a majority of gangs remain ethnically or racially homogeneous and limited to members of the same gender, hybrid gangs are growing in number. Beginning in the early 1990s, it was noted some gangs in Southern California were admitting females and persons of other races as members. Valdez (2001b, p.49) affirms: "Hybrid gangs are encountered with increasing frequency. These gangs often have a mixed race or multi-ethnic membership which can include female members."

Females and Gangs

Females may be part of an entirely female gang, participants in a coed gang or auxiliary members of a predominantly male gang. A female gang may have a name affiliated with its male counterpart, such as the Vice Ladies (from the Vice Lords). These auxiliaries usually consist of sisters and girlfriends of the male gang members. The females often assist the male gang, serving as decoys for rival gang members, as lookouts during the commission of crimes or as carriers of weapons when a gang war is impending. They may also carry information in and out of prison and provide sexual favors (they are often drug dependent and physically abused).

According to Howell (1998, p.3), females' involvement in gangs may be increasing proportionally with male gang involvement, and while the most common female gangs are still auxiliary gangs, the number of independent female gangs is increasing. *Addressing Community Gang Problems* (p.14) adds: "Many female groups are no longer simply extensions of male gangs. Female gang members manage their own affairs, make their own decisions, and often engage in a system of norms that is similar to that of male gangs."

The *1998 National Youth Gang Survey* (p.xiv) reported that nationally in 1998, only 8 percent of gang members were female. Of all jurisdictions responding, 171 reported female-dominated (more than 50 percent female) gangs. Female-dominated gangs represented 1.76 percent of all gangs. Moore and Hagedorn (2001, p.3) note: "Surprisingly, female gangs are somewhat more likely to be found in small cities and rural areas than in large cities. Their ethnicity varies from one region to another, with African American gangs predominant in the Midwest and Northeast and Latina gangs predominant in the Southwest."

Esbensen and Winfree (1998, p.509) conclude: "The stereotype of the girl as sex object and limited participant in the gang's delinquent activity apparently requires reexamination."

Characteristics of Gangs

Five general characteristics are often associated with gangs.

Distinguishing characteristics of gangs include leadership, organization, associational patterns, domain identification and illegal activity.

Leadership

Gang leadership is usually quite well defined and may be one of three types: (1) key personality, (2) chain of command or (3) collective. In the key personality leadership gang, one gang member, often older than the others and from the ranks of the hard-core membership, is a strong, influential leader. He becomes a role model for other gang members.

In a gang with a chain-of-command form of leadership, the gang functions like a military unit or even a police department. Each member within the group has a specific rank, with authority going from the top down.

In a gang with a collective leadership style, leaders change depending on the gang activity. If the gang is planning a crime, the best criminal mind is leader. If they are planning an attack on a neighboring gang, the best fighter is leader.

Organization

Gangs tend to be quite formally organized. One common organizational element is age, with many gangs typically having two to four age divisions. Another common organizational element is location; two or more gangs may have localized versions of the same gang name, for example the Southside Warriors and the Tenth Street Warriors. Gangs also tend to have a hierarchical authority, as described under leadership. As Miller and Hess (2002, p.249) note:

> The hard-core members who hold leadership positions pose a threat to the community and the police because (1) they typically possess guns and other weapons, and (2) they tend to be aggressively anti-social and are encouraged to be so by the gang as long as their behavior does not violate gang rules or discipline.

In addition to hard-core members, most gangs have a *marginal membership*, a much larger group that surrounds the hard-core members. Hard-core members are recruited from the marginal membership:

> Hard-core street gang members have associates. The associate has a full knowledge of gang activities and often is involved in the same criminal acts as hard-core members. However, the commitment level of the associate member is different from that of the hard-core member. The hard-core member's life is the gang. The associate has another life. . . . [with] other people and things that he values more in life than the gang. . . .
>
> The associate member is less likely to directly participate in acts of violence, although he may have been present when they occur. He perceives himself as less criminally culpable than the others. As a result, he is more likely than the hard-core member to provide statements to law enforcement. . . .
>
> Peripheral members are the best sources of information. They are the younger kids that live in "the neighborhood." Although they are ripe for hard-core recruitment, they tend to live on the fringe of the gang and are least likely to be involved in heavy violence (Lanata, 1998, p.87).

Another term for those on the fringes of gangs are **wannabes**—youths who aspire to become gang members, who dress and talk like gang members but who have not yet been accepted by the gang. Gangs are also on the lookout for "potentials" or "could be's," that is youths with dysfunctional families, those failing in school, those in trouble with the law and those living in impoverished neighborhoods born into an environment of street gang activity. Figure 9.1 illustrates the typical progression of youths in becoming hard-core members. It is from this group that the leaders emerge. They are the oldest group members and usually have extensive criminal records. They expect unquestioned obedience from all gang members.

Gang organization may vary considerably from gang to gang and from region to region. For example: "The gangs from Chicago—the Gangster Disciples and The Latin Kings—are more highly organized than their San Diego counterparts on every measure. . . . San Diego gangs report no written rules,

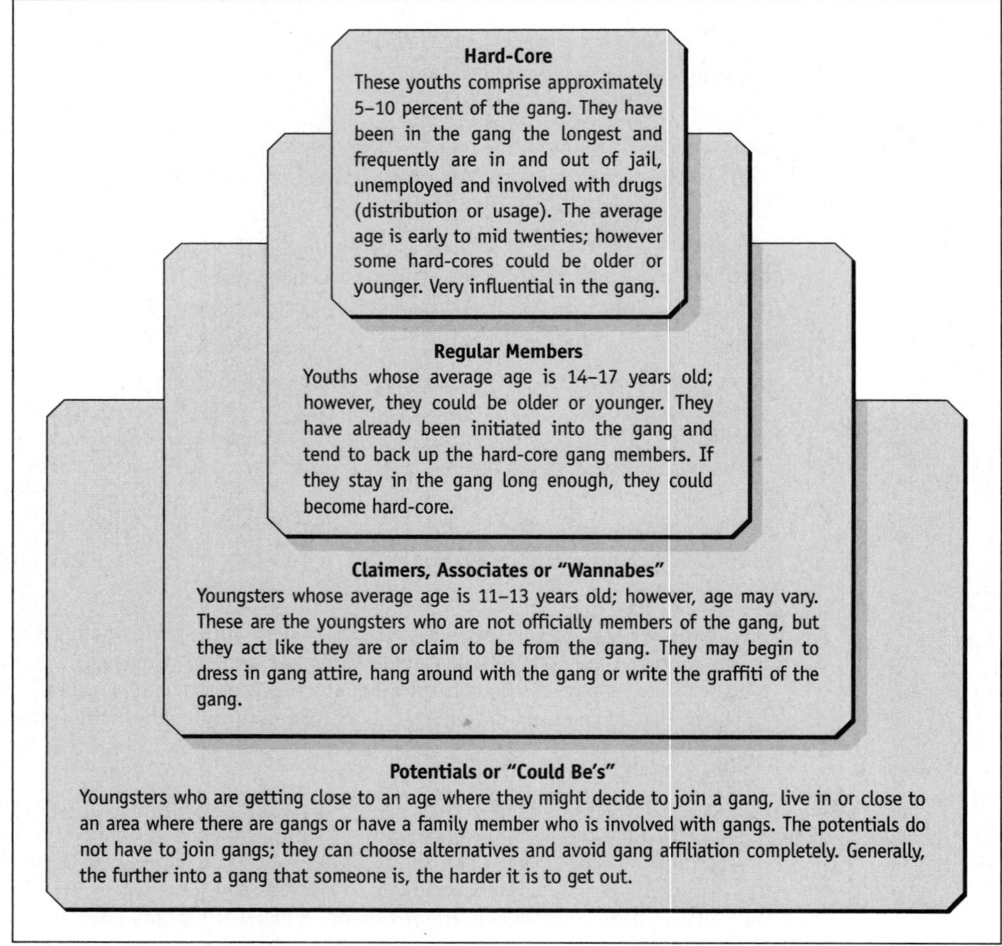

Hard-Core
These youths comprise approximately 5–10 percent of the gang. They have been in the gang the longest and frequently are in and out of jail, unemployed and involved with drugs (distribution or usage). The average age is early to mid twenties; however some hard-cores could be older or younger. Very influential in the gang.
Regular Members
Youths whose average age is 14–17 years old; however, they could be older or younger. They have already been initiated into the gang and tend to back up the hard-core gang members. If they stay in the gang long enough, they could become hard-core.
Claimers, Associates or "Wannabes"
Youngsters whose average age is 11–13 years old; however, age may vary. These are the youngsters who are not officially members of the gang, but they act like they are or claim to be from the gang. They may begin to dress in gang attire, hang around with the gang or write the graffiti of the gang.
Potentials or "Could Be's"
Youngsters who are getting close to an age where they might decide to join a gang, live in or close to an area where there are gangs or have a family member who is involved with gangs. The potentials do not have to join gangs; they can choose alternatives and avoid gang affiliation completely. Generally, the further into a gang that someone is, the harder it is to get out.

Figure 9.1
Progression into a Hard-Core Gang Member

Source: Robert W. Drowns and Kären M. Hess. *Juvenile Justice*, 3rd ed. Belmont, CA: West/Wadsworth Publishing Company, 2000, p.224.

few dues, and virtually no political activities. In Chicago, however, more than three-quarters of members reports these activities for their gang" (Decker et al., 1998, p.402).

The relationship of a gang to other gangs can also reveal the level of organization at which it functions. Decker et al. (p.416) assert:

> Relationships between gangs are important in attempting to determine whether gangs have come to resemble organized crime groups. Mutually reinforcing relationships built on instrumental concerns may indicate the evolution of street gangs from relatively disorganized groups to quasi-organized crime groups. . . .
>
> One measure of gang organization is a network of relationships between the gang and other groups. Such groups include businesses in the neighborhood, gangs in other cities, prison gangs, and other criminal enterprises that provide roles and opportunities for gangs and gang members.

Many street gangs have a prison affiliate, and vice versa. Decker et al. (p.419) state: "Because of their involvement in violence and drug sales, many gang members have been sent to prison in the last decade. Because prisons create the need for individual security and protection, they are perfect places for gangs to proliferate."

Associational Patterns

To many gang members, the gang is their life. Members become very close, with the gang, in many cases, taking the place of family, school and church. Loyalty, ego strength and camaraderie are all-important. An attack on a gang member is an attack on the entire gang.

Gangs often have specific criteria for membership and special initiation ceremonies. Some require that the person be "jumped in," that is, beaten, often severely, to test their courage and desire to become a member. Other gangs require new members to commit a crime or even to kill before they are fully admitted to the gang.

Domain Identification

Typically gangs stake out a geographic territory, or **turf,** as their domain. This may be a specific facility, such as a school, or it may be an entire neighborhood. If one gang trespasses on another gang's turf, gang violence is likely. Some gangs claim exclusive control over certain activities in an area, such as the right to collect fees from students for using the restrooms or "insurance" payments from local merchants in exchange for protection.

Criminal Activity

Research indicates that most gang members already were committing crimes before they joined a gang, but their delinquency rates increase dramatically after joining a gang ("Research Breaks Stereotypes . . .," 2000, p.2). The *1998 National Youth Gang Survey* (p.xv) key findings regarding gang and criminal activity included the following:

- Respondents were asked to estimate the proportion of youth gang members who engaged in certain specific types of serious and/or violent crimes. The percentage of respondents reporting involvement of "most or all" gang members was largest for drug sales (27 percent), followed by larceny/theft (17 percent), burglary/breaking and entering (13 percent), aggravated assault (12 percent), motor vehicle theft (11 percent) and robbery (3 percent).

- Nationwide, more than one-half (53 percent) of respondents said gang members in their jurisdiction used firearms in assault crimes "often" or "sometimes." Only 16 percent said their gang members did not use firearms in conjunction with assaults.
- One-third (34 percent) of all youth gangs were drug gangs (i.e., gangs organized specifically for the purpose of trafficking in drugs). Unexpectedly, drug gangs were most prevalent in rural counties, where 38 percent of the youth gangs were said to be drug gangs.

Gang-related crimes are typically violent, with vice, drug-related and property crimes comprising only one-fourth of the gang crimes reported. Data from an Ohio study reveals: "Gang members' criminal careers begin with property offenses (e.g., auto theft, burglary) and progress within 1.5 to 2 years to drug-related crimes and violent crime" (Huff, 1998, p.2).

A study by Esbensen et al. (1999) found that gang girls were very similar to gang boys in the types of illegal acts committed, although to a significantly lesser degree in number of incidents. They were not simply ancillary members, but rather: "They are involved in assaults, robberies, gang fights, and drug sales at substantial rates" (p.48). However, a significant difference between female and male gang members is that young women are much less likely to be victims of gang homicides (Miller and Decker, 2001, p.115). The vast majority of female gang homicide victims were not the intended targets of the attack. Miller and Decker (p.137) also report: "Young women used gender as a resource, both to accomplish gang crime and drug sales, and to temper their involvement in gang violence."

Violence is often used to send a message to other gangs. Howell (1998, p.11) states: "Gang-related drive-by shootings have increased in certain cities. Interestingly, killing is a secondary intent; promoting fear and intimidation among rival gangs is the primary motive." Violence may also be used against members within a gang if it is feared that a member will betray the gang's code of silence by talking to police.

Currey et al. (2001, p.1) report: "The overall number of youth gang homicides in U.S. cities declined during the 1990's, but trends varied in the early and later parts of the decade and by city. . . . Relatively few cities reported large numbers of gang homicides." Los Angeles and Chicago stand out among cities with the highest rates of gang homicide.

Gangs may also specialize in particular crimes, as Howell (1998, p.3) notes: "Certain offenses are related to different racial/ethnic youth gangs. African-American gangs are relatively more involved in drug offenses; Hispanic gangs, in "turf-related" violence; Asian and white gangs, in property crimes."

Other Gang Characteristics

Other characteristics may help identify gang members.

Gang members might be identified by their names, their symbols (clothing and tattoos) and how they communicate, including graffiti and sign language.

Names

Gang *names* vary from colorful and imaginative to straightforward. They commonly refer to localities, animals, royalty, rebellion, leaders or a combination. For example:

- Localities: Tenth Streeters, Southsiders, Alazones Courts, Johnstown Gang
- Animals: Tigers, Panthers, Cougars, Leopards, Cobras, Eagles, Hawks
- Royalty: Kings, Emperors, Lords, Knights, Barons, Dukes
- Rebellion: Rebels, Outlaws, Savages, Assassins
- Leader: Joey and Them Kids, Garcia's Boys
- Combination: West Side Warlords, Third Street Hawks, Spring Hill Savages

Individual gang members also often have colorful street names or **monikers.**

Symbols

Gang *symbols* are common. Clothing, in particular, can distinguish a particular gang. Sometimes "colors" are used to distinguish a gang. Gang members also use jerseys, T-shirts and jackets with emblems. However, some gangs, such as Asian gangs, seldom have a particular dress code, making identification difficult.

Tattoos are also used by some gangs, particularly outlaw motorcycle gangs and Hispanic gangs. African-American gang members seldom have tattoos.

Communications

Graffiti is a common form of communication used by gang members, frequently to stake out a gang's turf. Commonly called the "language of the street," Valdez (1998b, p.39) says of graffiti: "It can be used to mark off turf boundaries, be a way to give insults to rival gangs, act as a warning of impending death, list fallen comrades, announce the presence of a gang in a certain area of the city or show gang alliances." Defacing, erasing or substituting one gang's graffiti by a rival gang constitutes a challenge and usually results in violence and gang warfare:

> Much valuable information relative to police work may be gained from gang graffiti. For instance, one may be able to determine what gang is in control of a specific area by noting the frequency of the unchallenged graffiti. . . . Writing left unchanged reaffirms the gang's control. As one moves away from the center or core area of a gang's power and territory, the more rival graffiti and cross-outs are observed (*Street Gangs of Los Angeles County,* n.d.).

This Los Angeles White Paper also notes that African-American and Latino styles of graffiti are vastly different, with the African-American graffiti lacking the flair and attention to detail evidenced by the Latino gang graffiti. Much of the African-American gang wall writing is filled with profanity.

Mark Richards/PhotoEdit

Gang members communicate via graffiti and hand signals. They also often wear certain colors or items of clothing to identify themselves as members of a particular gang.

Graffiti artists, known as *taggers,* may act individually or be part of tag crews, which are separate from traditional street gangs. While the tagging phenomenon has been spreading across the United States since the early 1970s, it has also become an international issue. As the number of taggers and crews has grown, competition for "wall space" has increased. Once crews began placing their graffiti within turf claimed by traditional gangs, violent confrontations occurred, and taggers, once a relatively peaceful group, found themselves in need of protection from street-gang violence. As noted in *Addressing Community Gang Problems* (p.34): "The gap between taggers and gangs is being closed. . . . The larger a tagger crew, the more it begins to look and act like a street gang."

Another form of communication typical of gang members is hand signals. A person often uses these signs to indicate that he is with a specific gang.

Lists of criteria are often used to determine if an individual is a gang member. According to the Minnesota Gang Strike Force: "To be certified as a gang member, a person must meet at least three of the following 10 criteria" (Gustafson and Estrada, 1998, p.B7):

- Admits gang membership or association
- Observed to associate on a regular basis with known gang members
- Has tattoos indicating gang membership
- Wears symbols of gang membership
- Is photographed with known gang members

- Name is on a gang document, hit list or gang-related graffiti
- Identified as a gang member by a reliable source
- Arrested in the company of identified gang members or associates
- Corresponds with known gang members, or writes and/or receives correspondence about gang activity
- Writes about gangs on walls, books, paper, etc.

Miller and Hess (p.250) describe a typical gang member as "usually poor, a school dropout, unemployed and in trouble with the police." The *1998 National Youth Gang Survey* (p.xiv) reports that in 1998 respondents estimated that 60 percent of their gang members were adults (age 18 or older). This is a significant shift from 1996 when respondents estimated that exactly one-half of gang members were adults. Thus, it appears the youth gangs may be aging.

Stereotypes

While generalized descriptions and categorization of gangs and gang members help law enforcement deal with the gang problem, Howell (2000, pp.49–50) says studies have produced findings that contradict many of the traditional stereotypes of youth gangs:

- The gangs, drugs, and violence connection appears to apply more to adult drug and criminal gangs than to youth gangs.
- The seemingly intractable connection of gangs, drugs, and violence is not as strong among youth gangs as suggested by traditional stereotypes.
- It is not as difficult for adolescents to resist gang pressures as commonly believed. In most instances, adolescents can refuse to join gangs without reprisal.
- Gang members (especially marginal members) typically can leave the gang without serious consequences.
- At least in emerging gang areas, most adolescents do not remain in gangs for long periods, suggesting that members can be drawn away from gangs with attractive alternatives.
- Contemporary legends about gangs, especially initiation rites, are without scientific basis.
- Modern gangs make less use of symbols, including gang names, clothing and traditional initiation rites, than gangs of the past, and the meaning of their graffiti is sometimes murky or unclear.
- Drug franchising is not the principal driving force behind gang migration.

The Gang Subculture

Taken together, the many characteristics of gangs just described form a gang subculture. According to Miller and Hess (p.250): "A gang member's lifestyle is narrow and limited primarily to the gang and its activities. . . . Members develop fierce loyalty to their respective gang and become locked into the gang's lifestyle, values, attitudes and behavior, making it very difficult for a member to later break away from a gang."

Shelden et al. (p.61) state: "Youth gangs constitute a unique subculture in modern society. . . . They have their own unique set of values, norms, lifestyles, and beliefs." These values, norms, lifestyles and beliefs are often found in a gang code of behavior, which may include the requirement to always wear gang colors, to get a tattoo representing the gang, and, if arrested, to never reveal anything about the gang, as there is no lower life form than a "snitch."

Why People Join Gangs

Domash (2001, p.49) contends: "Why children join gangs is a complicated combination of social, political, family, educational and community factors." And, as Rowell (2000, p.35) notes: "Gangs grow because the gang provides kids with basic human needs. These include the need for security, love, friendship, acceptance, food, shelter, discipline, belonging, status, respect, identification, power and money."

The most frequently cited reason for people joining gangs is to *belong.* The close ties of gang members are a major motive for membership. Most gang members are underachievers who come from broken homes or homes with no strong male authority figure, and membership provides both psychological and physical security. According to Sidney J. Harris, nationally syndicated columnist: "Gangs make martyrs of losers. . . . Gang members tend to be chronic losers, who can accomplish nothing individually, or who live in so depressed an environment that only by banding together can they exercise any influence over their lives."

The most common reasons for joining a gang are for belonging, identity or recognition, protection, fellowship and brotherhood or from being intimidated to join.

According to Shelden et al. (p.157), the literature confirms that females become involved in gang life for generally the same reasons as males: "to meet basic human needs, such as belonging, self-esteem, protection, and a feeling of being a member of the family." They (p.157) say: "What emerges from a review of research on girl gangs is a portrait of young women who, just like their male counterparts, find themselves trapped in horrible social conditions, characterized by widespread poverty and racism." Moore and Hagedorn (p.3) add that the gang is often a refuge for young women victimized at home.

In our society of instant gratification, where happiness and success are often measured by the amount of money one has, it is hard to convince a youth who's making $1,000 a week guarding a crack house that he ought to be getting up at 4 A.M. every day to deliver newspapers. Shelden et al. have an entire chapter entitled: "Gangs in Context: Inequality in American Society," which states (p.208): "Under American capitalism, the 'free market' is largely a myth, and a 'surplus population' is constantly being created and reproduced. Most criminal activity of gang members is consistent with basic capitalist values, such as the law of supply and demand, the need to make money (profit), and the desire to accumulate consumer goods." They identify other factors contributing to the formation of gangs as changes in the labor market, the development of an underclass, and isolation in inner cities. They (p.208) conclude:

Unemployment, poverty, and general despair lead young people to seek out economic opportunities in the growing illegal marketplace, often done within the context of gangs.

Table 9.1
Theories Regarding Why Gangs Exist

Theory/Creator or Major Proponent	Premise
Social disorganization theory/Thrasher	Industrialization, urbanization and immigration break down institutional, community-based controls in certain areas. Local institutions in these areas (schools, families, churches) are too weak to give the people living there a "sense of community." Consequently, within such environments, conventional values are replaced by a subculture of criminal values and traditions that persist over time, regardless of who moves into or out of the area.
Strain theory/Merton	The lack of integration between culturally defined goals (professional success, wealth and status) and the legitimate, institutionalized means of achieving these goals imposes a strain on people, who may, as a result, react with deviant, criminal behavior. Thus, people at an economic disadvantage are motivated to engage in illegitimate activities (perhaps because of unavailability of jobs, lack of job skills, education, and other factors).
Cultural-deviance (subcultural) theory/Cohen	Working-class youths are ill-prepared for participation in middle-class institutions and, thus, become frustrated. This situation leads to reaction formation, in which the values of middle-class society are turned upside down. These values enable youths to gain status and improved financial standing through non-utilitarian, malicious, negative behavior.
Social learning theory/Sutherland	Youths become delinquent through association with other delinquents and also through contact with social values, beliefs and attitudes that support criminal/delinquent behavior.
Social bond (control) theory/Hirschi	Youths drift into gangs because of the limbo-like nature of adolescence—being suspended between childhood and adulthood, having greater expectations placed on them than when they were children, yet lacking the rights and privileges of adults. Proper socialization is essential at this critical juncture, which effectively "bonds" youths to society. What keeps people "in check" and away from deviant behavior is the social bond to society, especially the internalized norms of society.
Social development theory	Integrates social learning theory with control/bonding theory. The major cause of delinquency is a lack of bonding to family, school and prosocial peer groups coupled with the reinforcement of delinquent behavior. Looks at 17 risk factors (societal/cultural and individual/interpersonal) present before the onset of delinquency to determine whether, and to what extent, one is likely to become involved in persistent delinquent activity.
Labeling perspective	Youths who are simply "hanging out" together may be referred to as a gang often enough that they come to feel as if they are a gang.
Critical/Marxist perspectives	The capitalist political and economic system produces inequality. Those oppressed by capitalism engage in various types of crimes related to accommodation and resistance (predatory crime, personal crime) in an attempt to adapt to their disadvantaged positions and to resist the problems created by capitalist institutions.

Source: Robert W. Drowns and Kären M. Hess. *Juvenile Justice*, 3rd ed. Belmont, CA: West/Wadsworth Publishing Company, 2000, p.208. Adapted from Randall G. Shelden et al. *Youth Gangs in American Society*. Belmont, CA: Wadsworth Publishing Company, 1997, pp.28–49. Reprinted by permission.

Criminologists have proposed other theoretical reasons for why people join gangs, summarized in Table 9.1; however, an in-depth discussion of such theories is beyond the scope of this text. In addition to looking at *why* people join gangs, predisposing or risk factors should be considered.

Risk Factors

Shelden et al. (p.203) identify what they believe to be the most critical factor related to crime and delinquency:

> Nearly every criminologist agrees that the family is probably the most critical factor related to crime and delinquency. In fact, for over 50 years, research has shown that three or four key family-related factors best distinguish the habitual

delinquent from the rest of his or her peers. These factors include the affection of the parents toward the child (the lower the level of affection, the higher the rate of delinquency), the kind of discipline the parents use (those who use consistently harsh and physical discipline will produce the most habitual and violent delinquent), the prolonged absence of one or both parents (those from single-parent households are more likely to become delinquent), and the degree of supervision provided by the parents (the lesser the amount of supervision, the higher the rate of delinquency).

Family structure is probably the most important risk factor in the formation of a gang member.

Investigators have found certain common threads running through most families having hard-core gang members. The family is often a racial minority on some form of government assistance. It often lacks a male authority figure, or the male figure may be a criminal or drug addict and, therefore, a negative role model. Typically neither adult has more than an elementary school education. Children live with minimal adult supervision.

When one child first encounters law enforcement authorities, the dominant figure (usually the mother) makes excuses for the child, often accusing society. Thus children are taught early that they are not responsible for their actions and are shown how to transfer blame to society.

A second common family structure is one with two strong family leaders in a mother and father. Usually graduates from gangs themselves, they see little wrong with their children belonging to gangs. This is known as assembly-line production of gang members.

A third common family structure is where the parents are non-English speaking. The children tend to adapt rapidly to the American way of life and, in doing so, lose respect for their parents and the "old ways." They become experts at manipulating their parents, and the parents lose all control. Many of these structures overlap. Howell (1998, pp.6–7) summarizes the risk factors for youth gang membership (Table 9.2).

Prosecution Problems

McCorkle and Miethe (p.41) state: "The past decade has witnessed increasing concern about street gangs and their role in violent crime and drug trafficking. According to a recent national survey, more than 80 percent of prosecutors in large cities now acknowledge that gangs are a problem in their jurisdiction, that their numbers are growing, and that levels of gang-related violence are increasing."

Prosecution of gang-related crimes is often made difficult because victims and witnesses are reluctant to cooperate. One reason for the reluctance is a sense of futility in trying to rid an area of all gang activity—why bother getting involved and risk personal harm to put one gang away when another is poised to move right into the vacancy? For example Gustafson and Estrada (p.B1) report on the conviction of several key figures in the 6-0-Tre Crips gang, gang leader Robert G. (Buster) Jefferson and his half-brother Robert J. (Duddy) Jefferson: "Despite Duddy Jefferson's parting courtroom taunt—'We'll be back!'—the ruthlessly violent and frighteningly young 6-0-Tre gang has been crushed,

Table 9.2
Risk Factors Contributing to Youth Gang Membership

Domain	Risk Factors
Community	Social disorganization, including poverty and residential mobility Organized lower-class communities Underclass communities Presence of gangs in the neighborhood Availability of drugs in the neighborhood Availability of firearms Barriers to and lack of social and economic opportunities Lack of social capital Cultural norms supporting gang behavior Feeling unsafe in neighborhood; high crime Conflict with social control institutions
Family	Family disorganization, including broken homes and parental drug/alcohol abuse Troubled families, including incest, family violence, and drug addiction Family members in a gang Lack of adult male role models Lack of parental role models Low socioeconomic status Extreme economic deprivation, family management problems, parents with violent attitudes, sibling antisocial behavior
School	Academic failure Low educational aspirations, especially among females Negative labeling by teachers Trouble at school Few teacher role models Educational frustration Low commitment to school, low school attachment, high levels of antisocial behavior in school, low achievement test scores and identification as being learning disabled
Peer group	High commitment to delinquent peers Low commitment to positive peers Street socialization Gang members in class Friends who use drugs or who are gang members Friends who are drug distributors Interaction with delinquent peers
Individual	Prior delinquency Deviant attitudes Street smartness; toughness Defiant and individualistic character Fatalistic view of the world Aggression Proclivity for excitement and trouble *Locura* (acting in a daring, courageous, and especially crazy fashion in the face of adversity) Higher levels of normlessness in the context of family, peer group and school Social disabilities Illegal gun ownership Early or precocious sexual activity, especially among females Alcohol and drug use Drug trafficking Desire for group rewards, such as status, identity, self-esteem, companionship and protection Problem behaviors, hyperactivity, externalizing behaviors, drinking, lack of refusal skills and early sexual activity Victimization

Source: James C. Howell. *Youth Gangs: An Overview.* Washington, DC: Office of Juvenile Justice and Delinquency Prevention, August 1998, pp.6–7. (NCJ 167249)

authorities say. But if, instead, Jefferson had said: 'We'll be replaced,' gang cops and prosecutors grudgingly would have agreed."

Another reason for victim and witness reluctance is gang intimidation and fear of reprisal. Other obstacles to prosecution include uncertain victim and witness credibility, inadequate police reports and a lack of appropriate sanctions for juvenile gang members involved in criminal activities. In fact, some older gang members refer to their younger members as "minutemen" because if they do get "busted," they'll be out in a minute. Adults hire juveniles to run their drugs for them, knowing that if the juveniles get caught, not much will happen to them.

These challenges are among the many reasons innovative gang control strategies are being developed and put into practice.

Gang Control Strategies

Domash (2000, p.30) contends: "The first step in dealing with gangs is the acknowledgement of their presence in the community. Then, law enforcement must let it be known that it is not just a police problem; it is a community problem." As with many of the problems that plague society, partnerships are perhaps the best way to tackle the gang problem. Regarding the issue of youths, crime and the lure of gangs, Valdez (1998a, pp.86–87) concludes: "No single program can become the cure-all. . . . Collaborative partnerships that focus on five fundamental resources seem to have great short- and long-term impact":

1. *Ongoing relationships with caring adults,* such as parents, other caregivers, extended family members, neighbors, teachers and even probation and parole officers.
2. *Safe places and structured activities* that nurture youths' social skills, vocational interests and sense of civic responsibility.
3. *A healthy start,* making fundamental resources available from birth to age 20, to prepare youths not only for school but also for adulthood.
4. *Marketable skills through education,* providing a solid foundation in reading, writing, mathematics, science, technology and communications; cultivating thinking skills, creativity, decision making, problem solving and reasoning; developing positive attitudes, sense of responsibility, integrity, self-motivation and management. All to create "work ethic."
5. *Opportunities to serve,* providing service learning experiences that enhance self-esteem, a sense of personal confidence and social responsibility for others.

The Office of Juvenile Justice and Delinquency Prevention (OJJDP) reports that communities experiencing youth gang problems are implementing many different types of gang control strategies and activities: "Some are simple; others are complex. Examples include counseling programs, mentoring, recreational activities, outreach programs, court diversion, anti-gang sweeps, injunctions, special anti-gang statutes, and others that can be implemented as a part of a comprehensive community-wide approach or be implemented by themselves" (*Gang-Free Schools . . .,* 2000, p.6).

Both short- and long-term solutions are needed for dealing with gangs and gang violence. Short-term approaches would rely on law enforcement efforts, including stiffer penalties for hard-core gang members, and on special training for police, prosecutors and judges. Long-term solutions would emphasize preventive and community-based counseling for both gang members and their parents. The criminal justice system, a host of social service agencies, schools and the community at large all play an important role in addressing the gang problem.

Spergel and Curry (1990) studied strategies being used to deal with the gang problem and identified four basic approaches: (1) community organization, (2) social intervention, (3) opportunities provision and (4) suppression or law enforcement efforts. Although the study is dated, the findings still apply. These four approaches remain the basic areas being used.

Shelden et al. (p.243) identify four components of the criminal justice system that deal with the gang problem: (1) law enforcement, (2) prosecution, (3) courts and (4) corrections. They note: "Law enforcement represents society's first line of defense against crime. Consequently, law enforcement is the first segment of the criminal justice system that responds to the youth gang dilemma." Shelden et al. (p.263) conclude: "Current practices of law enforcement are not only ineffective in their attempt to suppress gangs but they may indeed perpetuate youth gangs."

In addition, according to Shelden et al., prosecutors have a tremendous amount of discretionary power and can be quite political when dealing with gang members. The courts, in contrast, continue to have their options decreased when dealing with gang members as the result of established guidelines jurists must follow. And finally, Shelden et al. (p.264) suggest that many politicians and legislative bodies have taken a "get tough on crime" stance, and this has often included gangs. They conclude: "Variables such as economic deprivation, racism, and segregation are sometimes neutralized by references to family values and individualism in political rhetoric. . . . The legal response [including all four components] demonstrates that practitioners, with few exceptions, *do not listen to gang members.*"

Table 9.3 summarizes law enforcement strategies used and their perceived effectiveness. The most frequently used strategies were in-state information exchanges, local agency operational coordination and selected violations. Judged most effective were suppression efforts, street sweeps and crime prevention efforts (Howell, 2000, p.46). In *Youth Gang Programs and Strategies,* Howell (p.65) concludes:

> Despite recent progress in preventing involvement in gangs during childhood and adolescence and in reducing serious and violent gang crime, the complexity of the youth gang problem defies an easy solution or single strategy. Current knowledge about which programs are effective in preventing and reducing youth gang problems is limited. The most effective program model will likely prove to be a combination of prevention, intervention and suppression strategies integrated in a collaborative approach, supported by a management information system, and validated by rigorous evaluation. Communities across the country are undertaking collaborative efforts to deal with youth gangs.

Police Gang Units

The United States has seen a dramatic increase in specialized gang units in the last 15 years, most of which have been established to gather intelligence on gangs (Katz et al., 2000, p.413). According to a study by Katz (2001, p.37), among large agencies with 100 or more sworn officers, special gang units existed

Table 9.3
Law Enforcement Strategies and Perceived Effectiveness*

Strategy	Used	Judged Effective (if used)
Some or a Lot of Use		
Targeting entry points	14%	17%
Gang laws	40	19
Selected violations	76	42
Out-of-state information exchange	53	16
In-state information exchange	90	17
In-city information exchange	55	18
Federal agency operational coordination	40	16
State agency operational coordination	50	13
Local agency operational coordination	78	16
Community collaboration	64	54
Any Use		
Street sweeps	40%	62%
Other suppression tactics	44	63
Crime prevention activities	15	56

*Percentage of cities, $n = 211$. The number of cities responding to each question varied slightly.

Source: From James C. Howell. *Youth Gang Programs and Strategies.* Washington, DC: OJJDP, August 2000, p.46. (NCJ 171154)

in 56 percent of all municipal police departments, 50 percent of all sheriff's departments, 43 percent of all county police agencies and 20 percent of all state law enforcement agencies. These findings suggest an estimate of 360 police gang units in the United States.

Gang expert Valdez (2000b, p.54) asserts that full-service gang units should use prevention, suppression and intervention to combat the gang problem. Suppression involves a collaboration among police, probation and prosecution, targeting the most active gang members and leaders. Intervention is aimed at gang members who want out of the gang. Intervention goals include giving the gang member the option of finishing high school or obtaining a GED, having tattoos removed, being given the option of gainful employment and being given legal assistance. Prevention efforts include conflict resolution efforts and peer counseling.

Fritsch et al. (1999, p.122) report on the Dallas Police Department's anti-gang initiative, begun in 1996 and designed to reduce gang violence:

> Five defined target areas that were home to seven of the city's most violent gangs received overtime-funded officers to implement several different enforcement strategies. The strategies included saturation patrol and aggressive curfew and truancy enforcement. . . . The findings indicated that aggressive curfew and truancy enforcement led to significant reductions in gang violence, whereas simple saturation patrol did not.

Injunctions and Legislation

Sometimes communities pass legislation, such as loitering ordinances, or take other legal measures, including injunctions, to bring gang problems under control. A **civil injunction** is a court order prohibiting a person or group from engaging in certain activities. However, injunctions and ordinances may be challenged as unconstitutional violations of the freedom of speech, the right of association and due process rights if they do not clearly delineate how officers may apply such orders.

For example, Chicago passed a gang congregation ordinance to combat the problems created by the city's street gangs. During the three years following passage of the ordinance, Chicago police officers issued over 89,000 dispersal orders and arrested more than 42,000 people (Schofield, 1999, p.30). However, in *City of Chicago v. Morales* (1999), the Supreme Court struck down the ordinance as unconstitutional because its vague wording failed to provide adequate standards to guide police discretion. The lesson here is that any civil injunctions a city passes must be clear in what officers can and cannot do when they observe what they believe to be gang members congregating in public places.

Tougher legislation is also being used as a gang control approach. Because some gangs use their younger members to commit serious crimes, relying on the more lenient juvenile sentencing laws, some jurisdictions have allowed courts to raise the penalties for teenagers convicted of gang-related offenses.

While injunctions, ordinances and legislation offer ways to help communities handle problems associated with gangs, they also raise serious issues regarding how to balance public safety with individual rights.

Computers

In the war against gangs, information and intelligence are vital. Indeed as Morrison (1998, p.74) asserts: "Criminal intelligence information is an important part of any heads-up police agency. As a direct result, most gang units pay close attention to seemingly tiny details for their intelligence sources. Unfortunately, since no nationwide central database exists on gangs, each individual agency, unit or state has to maintain its own records."

Some states are taking advantage of the ever-expanding network of on-line computer services to enhance information sharing. For example, a national database called RISS-GANGS is a partnership involving more than 4,500 federal, state and local law enforcement agencies, used to track and share gang intelligence (Valdez, 1999, p.54). Another computer technology used to track gangs is the General Reporting, Evaluation and Tracking (G.R.E.A.T.) system—a combination hot sheet, mug book and file cabinet ("A G.R.E.A.T. Program . . .," 1999).

In addition, many street gangs have Web sites law enforcement can monitor to learn about upcoming events, times and meeting places. According to "Underworld dot.coms" (2001, p.7): "Tens of thousands of gang-related sites have been posted over the past few years."

School Safety

Schools are one area where gang suppression efforts have been focused. According to the *1998 National Youth Gang Survey,* 40 percent of youth gang members in the United States are estimated to be under age 17. Presumably, most of these youths are still in school (Moore and Cook, 1999). The percentage of public school students who reported the presence of gangs in their schools nearly doubled from 17 percent in 1989 to 31 percent in 1995 (Kaufman et al., 1999).

Approximately two-thirds of these gang members are reportedly involved in violence, drug sales or gun-carrying (*Gang-Free Schools* . . ., p.6).

Trump (1998) lists several warning signs schools might use as gang identifiers: graffiti, colors, tattoos, initiations, hand signs, language and behavior such as sudden changes in behavior or secret meetings. Dill (1998, p.22) adds the following indicators: an increasing number of violent, racially based incidents; an increasing rate of absenteeism with crimes in the community increasingly committed by truants; and students carrying beepers, cell phones or pagers, which suggest that drugs are available in or around the school. Dill (p.22) asserts: "When a school has a gang problem, teachers and principals need ongoing technical assistance. They must learn how to avoid a show-down that pits student against teacher or student against principal in a bid for peer approval."

Preliminary results of a current OJJDP and National Institute of Justice study examining how schools are responding to the youth gang problem show that, on average, schools that report the presence of gangs have as many as 14 different anti-gang activities under way (*Gang-Free Schools* . . ., p.6).

Drug Addiction

Returning to the connection between drugs and gangs, many believe the fight against gangs will be in vain unless equal efforts are made at wiping out drug use. According to Valdez (2000a, p.53): "Nationally, many street gangs are getting involved in drug sales, and younger gang members are selling drugs. . . . The drug business and nonviolent, gang-related crime fuel a partnership between street gang members who were once rivals."

Gustafson and Estrada (p.B7) report: "Authorities . . . say the drug addiction problem that feeds the gangs' drug trade needs to be addressed." As one prosecutor notes: "Until we reduce the demand, we're never going to effectively wipe out the trade. All the interdiction and enforcement in the world isn't going to have enough of an effect as long as people want these drugs" (Gustafson and Estrada, p.B7).

The Threat of Drugs

American history is filled with drug use, including alcohol and tobacco. As the early settlers moved west, one of the first buildings in each frontier town was a saloon. Cocaine use was also common by the 1880s. At the beginning of the twentieth century, cocaine was the drug of choice, said to cure everything from indigestion to toothaches. It was added to flavor soft drinks like Coca-Cola.

In 1909 a presidential commission reported to President Theodore Roosevelt that cocaine was a hazard, leading to loss of livelihoods and lives. As the public became increasingly aware of the hazards posed by cocaine and other drugs, it pressed for legislation against use of such drugs.

In 1914 the federal government passed the Harrison Narcotics Act, which made the sale or use of certain drugs illegal.

In 1920 every state required its students to learn about narcotics' effects. In 1937 under President Franklin Delano Roosevelt, marijuana became the last drug to be banned. For a quarter of a century, the drug problem lay dormant.

Then came the 1960s, a time of youthful rebellion, of Haight Ashbury and the flower children, a time to protest the Vietnam War. A whole culture had as its theme: tune in, turn on and drop out—often through marijuana and LSD. By the 1970s marijuana had been tried by an estimated 40 percent of 18- to 21-year-olds and was being used by many soldiers fighting in Vietnam. Many other soldiers turned to heroin. At the same time, an estimated half million Americans began using heroin back in the States. The drug culture peaked in the mid-1970s, bringing with it the emergence of heavy cocaine use.

The United States became the most drug-pervaded nation in the world, with marijuana leading the way. The 1980s saw a turnaround in drug use, with celebrities advocating, "It's not cool to do drugs," and "Just say no to drugs." At the same time, however, other advertisements suggested that alcohol and smoking are where the "fun is." The United States remains a culture of pill poppers. In fact, according to Ericson (2001, p.1): "Research has long shown that the abuse of alcohol, tobacco and illicit drugs is the single most serious health problem in the United States, straining the health care system, burdening the economy and contributing to the health problems and death of millions of Americans every year." Glasscock (2001a, p.7) cites the following statistics on the drug problem:

- In 1999 an estimated 14.8 million Americans were current users of illicit drugs.
- In 2000 the use of Ecstasy by 12th graders rose 46 percent.
- There were 11,651 drug-related deaths in 40 U.S. metropolitan areas in 2000, and cocaine was the most mentioned drug.

Ericson (p.1) adds: "By the eighth grade, 52 percent of adolescents have consumed alcohol, 41 percent have smoked cigarettes, and 20 percent have used marijuana. By the 12th grade, about 80 percent have used alcohol, 63 percent have smoked cigarettes, and 49 percent have used marijuana."

Narcotics, Marijuana and Other Dangerous Drugs

The Controlled Substances Act (CSA) of 1984 placed all federally regulated substances into one of five schedules based on the substance's effects, medical use, potential for abuse, and safety or dependence liability. Drugs in Schedule I have the highest potential for abuse, unpredictable effects and no generally accepted medical use. Schedule I drugs include heroin, LSD, GHB and marijuana. At the other end of the scale, Schedule V drugs have the lowest potential for abuse, may lead to limited physical or psychological dependence and have many accepted medical uses. Drugs in this category include Lomotil, Robitussin A-C and over-the-counter or prescription drugs containing codeine. Drugs falling between these two extremes include the Schedule II substances of morphine, PCP, cocaine and methamphetamine; Schedule III substances such as anabolic steroids, codeine and some barbiturates; and Schedule IV substances including Valium, Xanax and Rohypnol.

Narcotics are drugs that produce sleep, lethargy or relief of pain and include heroin, cocaine and crack. Other **dangerous drugs** are addicting, mind-altering drugs, such as marijuana, depressants, stimulants and hallucinogens.

Methamphetamine and "club drugs" such as Ecstasy, GHB and Rohypnol are included in this category.

In most states narcotics and other dangerous drugs may not be used or sold without a prescription. Federal law prohibits sale or distribution not covered by prescription, but it does *not* prohibit possession for personal use.

Narcotics

Prohibited narcotics include heroin, cocaine and crack.

Heroin

Heroin, a commonly abused narcotic, is synthesized from morphine and is up to 10 times more potent. Heroin is physically addictive and expensive. It causes an easing of fears, followed by euphoria and finally stupor. While this drug can be smoked, snorted or eaten, injecting is the most common route of heroin administration (*Pulse Check,* 2001, p.13). Snorting, however, is reportedly on the rise (p.10). "Heroin appears to present an equal opportunity problem to all racial/ethnic groups" (p.12) but, "unlike race/ethnicity, socioeconomic status (SES) seems to play a major role in the groups of people most likely to use heroin . . . with the largest group of users . . . in the lower SES category" (p.13). *Pulse Check* (p.7) also reports: "During 2000, heroin was perceived as the most serious drug problem by . . . 26 percent of responding sources. . . . It ranked second only to cocaine."

Cocaine

Cocaine hydrochloride is a central nervous system stimulant narcotic derived from the South American coca bush. Peru and Bolivia are now the main sources of cocaine. Cultivation of the bush is legal in these countries, with most of the product sold to flavor soft drinks and for medical uses. Cocaine smuggling is big business, run primarily by Colombians. They often are assisted by tourists and students, called **mules.** Larger quantities are brought in by professional smugglers, often using private planes and boats. However, according to law enforcement sources, powder cocaine sellers are not often cited as affiliated with trafficking organizations, instead being more commonly mentioned as affiliated with gangs (*Pulse Check,* p.35).

Cocaine may be inhaled or injected, producing euphoria, excitation, anxiety, a sense of increased muscular strength, talkativeness and reduced feelings of fatigue. The pupils often become dilated, and the heart rate and blood pressure usually increase. Physical dependence on cocaine is possible, and psychological dependence can be extreme. Nationwide, most powder cocaine users are in their thirties or older (p.30). As with heroin users, powder cocaine users are found equally among all races and ethnicities. But unlike heroin users, the majority of powder cocaine users are in the middle SES category (p.31).

Rock, one form of cocaine, looks somewhat like rock sugar candy. Its purity varies from 70 to 80 percent. **Flake,** a more refined form of cocaine, comes in flat crystals and is approximately 95 percent pure. Another variation of cocaine widely available in communities throughout the country is crack.

Crack

Crack is a form of cocaine usually sprinkled on a marijuana or tobacco cigarette or mixed with marijuana or tobacco and then smoked in a pipe. Some jurisdictions have reported unusual practices in the administration of crack, including snorting it or dissolving it in lemon juice or vinegar and then injecting it (*Pulse Check,* p.30).

Crack produces the same intense rush and euphoria that cocaine does but at a greatly reduced cost. According to *Pulse Check* (p.23): "In most cities, baking soda is the standard ingredient added to powder cocaine to make crack, as cited by law enforcement sources." However, sources across the nation also mentioned many other adulterants, including sugar, lidocaine, brake fluid, rat poison, vitamin B-12, Benadryl, Novocaine, Anbesol and "anything white."

Pellet-size chunks of crack are often sold in small glass or plastic vials, film canisters or small zippered baggies, with prices much lower than for a similar amount of cocaine. Because of its low price, crack has been called the "equal opportunity drug," with crack-using populations predominantly in the lower SES category (*Pulse Check,* p.28). Nationally, race, gender and age differences among crack users appear fairly constant, with blacks, males and older adults (30 years and older) accounting for the largest proportions of crack users (pp.27–28). Street-level crack dealers, on the other hand, tend to be young adults, age 18–30 (p.34). Law enforcement sources report crack sellers are seldom affiliated with trafficking organizations but often involved in gangs (p.33). Furthermore, crack use among sellers is common, as is violence, including homicide, strong-arm tactics with other dealers and turf wars (p.34). Strong (2001, p.58) contends: "The transportation, distribution, abuse and criminal activity related to powdered crack cocaine constitute the greatest drug threat to the United States."

Marijuana

"**Marijuana** is the most widely available and abused illegal drug in the United States" [emphasis added] (Strong, p.58). It is almost certainly the most socially accepted illegal drug; legislation lessening penalties for its use has frequently been proposed. Although it has been known for nearly 5,000 years, it is one of the least understood, yet most versatile, of all natural drugs.

Marijuana, derived from the cannabis plant, is a hardy weed adaptable to most climates. It still grows wild in many parts of the United States and can survive in extremely adverse conditions. The marijuana plant is distinctive, resembling a poinsettia. It grows at a phenomenal rate from a seedling to a 20-foot plant in one year. The leaves are then picked and dried in the sun, a stove or even a clothes dryer. Many domestic marijuana growers are switching from outdoor to indoor cultivation. According to *Pulse Check* (pp.40–41): "The most common variety of marijuana is locally produced commercial grade. . . . Mexican commercial grade is the second most common variety. . . . **Sinsemilla,** or the seedless homegrown variety of marijuana, is the third most common type of marijuana available. . . . One of the least commonly reported marijuana varieties is British Columbian ('BC bud')" [emphasis added].

Marijuana is frequently used in the form of cigarettes, called joints, which have a distinctive odor. They are often smoked with the aid of a holder, called a roach holder or alligator clip. When smoked, marijuana's psychoactive ingredients enter the bloodstream quickly, causing rapid onset of symptoms. The drug's effects on the user's mood and thinking vary widely, depending on the marijuana's strength and the amount used, as well as the social setting and the anticipated effects. The drug usually takes effect in about 15 minutes, and effects last from two to four hours. "Social" doses of one or two cigarettes may cause an increased sense of well-being; initial restlessness and hilarity followed by a dreamy, carefree state of relaxation; alteration of sensory perceptions including expansion of space and time; a more vivid sense of touch, sight, smell, taste and sound; a feeling of hunger, especially a craving for sweets; and subtle changes in thought formation and expression.

Marijuana users span all ages, although adolescent users typically outnumber the young adult and older adult user groups (*Pulse Check,* p.43). The marijuana problem cuts across all racial/ethnic groups and knows no socioeconomic bounds (p.44). In addition: "More so than other drug users, marijuana users reside 'everywhere'— . . . inner-city, other urban, suburban, and rural places of residence" (p.44). According to Bennett and Hess (2001, p.496): "Whether marijuana abusers progress to hard narcotics or other controlled substances has not been totally researched. The vast majority of hard-narcotics users once used marijuana, but how many marijuana users proceed to hard drugs is unknown."

Street-level marijuana sellers are most commonly independent dealers, although biker gangs, street gangs and Mexican cartels have also been reported as sellers. While the ages of street-level marijuana sellers vary widely, ranging from 10 to 65 years, most law enforcement sources report adolescents and young adults predominate among marijuana sellers (p.47). Most marijuana is sold on the street, although homes and nightclubs are other common venues. It is also sold in schools and has reportedly been distributed in hospitals (p.47). Furthermore, most law enforcement sources report that marijuana sellers are usually users but are seldom involved in violence (p.47).

Other Dangerous Drugs

Depressants (Barbiturates)

Depressants, or **barbiturates,** are sedatives taken orally as a small tablet or capsule to induce sleep or to relieve tension. Small amounts of barbiturates make the user relaxed, sociable and good-humored. Heavy doses cause sluggishness, depression, deep sleep or coma. A barbiturate addict often shows symptoms of drunkenness: speech becomes slurred and indistinct, physical coordination is impaired, and mental and emotional instability occurs. Many barbiturate addicts are quarrelsome and have a "short fuse." Overdoses are common and frequently cause intentional or accidental death.

Stimulants (Amphetamines)

Stimulants, or **amphetamines,** are taken orally as a tablet or capsule, or intravenously, to reduce appetite and/or relieve mental depression. They are often taken by truck drivers, salespeople, college students and businesspeople who want to stay awake for long periods and by people who want to lose weight. Normal doses produce wakefulness, increased alertness and initiative, and hyperactivity. Large doses produce exaggerated feelings of confidence, power and well-being.

Heavy users may exhibit restlessness, nervousness, hand tremors, pupil dilation, mouth dryness and excessive perspiration. They may be talkative and experience delusions and/or hallucinations. Although small doses may produce cheerfulness and an unusual increase in activity, heavy and prolonged use may produce symptoms resembling paranoid schizophrenia. Handling this deviant behavior has always been a source of concern and danger for law enforcement officers.

One stimulant posing a major problem for law enforcement is **methamphetamine,** or "meth," also known as *speed, ice* and *crystal.* Like cocaine, meth is a potent central nervous system stimulant that the Drug Enforcement Administration (DEA) calls "a dangerous, sometimes lethal and unpredictable drug" (www.dea.gov, 2001). Meth is typically a white, odorless, bitter-tasting powder that easily dissolves in water. It can be smoked, snorted, injected or taken orally. Crystal meth is smoked in a manner similar to crack cocaine, but the euphoric effect of smoking ice lasts longer than that of smoking crack. Methamphetamine use frequently results in violent and erratic behavior in users. High doses or chronic use have been associated with increased nervousness, irritability and paranoia. Withdrawal from high doses produces severe depression.

Historically, suppliers of methamphetamine in the United States were outlaw motorcycle gangs and other independent trafficking groups. Although motorcycle gangs continue to produce meth and control a share of the market, Mexico-based trafficking groups entered the illicit meth market in 1995 and now dominate the trade in the United States. The majority of the meth made and distributed by Mexico-based organizations is produced within the United States, particularly in California and other western states. Recently, there has been a dramatic increase in the number of methamphetamine laboratories operating in certain states, such as Kansas, Missouri, Oklahoma and Arkansas.

The *1999 National Household Survey on Drug Abuse* estimated that 9.4 million Americans had tried meth, a marked increase from the 1994 estimate of 3.8 million. In addition the *1999 Monitoring the Future* survey found 4.8 percent of high school seniors reported having used the drug, compared to 2.7 percent in 1990 (www.dea.gov). *Pulse Check* (pp.50–51) adds that most meth users are young adults, white, male and of middle to lower SES. Furthermore (p.51): "The drug is a particular problem within the gay communities . . . [because it] is perceived by users as a 'health aid' to combat chronic fatigue associated with HIV."

Hallucinogens

Hallucinogens may produce distortion, intensify sensory perception and lessen the ability to discriminate between fact and fantasy. The unpredictable mental effects include illusions, panic, psychotic or antisocial behavior and impulses toward violence and self-destruction. Recent data indicates a rise in hallucinogen use.

Probably the best-known hallucinogen is LSD, which gets its name from the colorless, odorless substance lysergic acid diethylamide from which it is made. Although hallucinogens are usually taken orally as a tablet or capsule, their physical characteristics allow them to be disguised as various commonly used powders or liquids. LSD has been found on chewing gum, hard candy, crackers, vitamin pills, aspirin, blotting paper and postage stamps.

Another hallucinogen, **PCP** (phencyclidine), was developed as an anesthetic and is still used as such by veterinarians. It appeared in San Francisco in the 1960s and was called the "Peace Pill." As its use spread across the country, it was called by various other names, including angel dust, mist, zoom, superweed and angel weed.

Symptoms of PCP intoxication vary greatly from person to person, depending on the dosage, previous use and how it was ingested. A symptom almost always present in PCP intoxication is **nystagmus,** an uncontrolled bouncing or jerking of the eyeball when the intoxicated person looks to the extreme right or left, and up or down.

The chronic PCP user may experience emotional difficulties, such as chronic depression, paranoia, auditory hallucinations, anxiety and confusion. Social isolation and personality change may occur after extended use. Another possible effect of PCP intoxication is preoccupation with death. There is often a feeling of being out of the body and having a lack of sensory perception, resembling the experience of death itself. Many chronic users attempt suicide.

Much of the concern over the widespread use of PCP is the drug's ability to produce bizarre, sometimes tragic *aggressive, violent behavior.* Users often have hallucinations and disturbed thought patterns that may produce panic, which triggers aberrant or aggressive behavior. Police officers have been injured attempting to subdue a person under the influence of PCP. Overwhelming evidence shows that some users "freaked out" on PCP exhibit *superhuman strength* while showing aggression. One explanation is that the mind completely controls the body and causes users to believe the hallucinations are real. The adrenalin flows, and they fight desperately for survival using any method to escape the terror. The superhuman strength is also directly related to the drug's analgesic qualities under which users feel little or no pain.

"Club Drugs"

LSD and meth have also fallen into a growing category of drugs called "club drugs," named for their emerging presence in nightclub and rave settings. Other substances included in this group are Ecstasy, GHB, Rohypnol, ketamine and nitrous oxide.

Perhaps the most prolific club drug currently attracting law enforcement's attention is *MDMA* (3, 4-Methylenedioxymethamphetamine), also called *Ecstasy,* Adam, XTC, hug, beans and love drug. MDMA is a synthetic, psychoactive drug with both stimulant (amphetamine-like) and hallucinogenic (LSD-like) properties that create feelings of emotional closeness to others and break down any personal communication barriers that may exist. "Found at raves, concerts, bars, clubs, in schools of all levels and on the streets, Ecstasy is used by a large array of people" (Streit, 2001, p.24). In addition, according to Streit (p.25): "When on the drug, a user's energy levels go through the roof. 'You can dance, talk, drink, whatever, all night long,' says a user." However: "Within the four to six hours this drug lasts, a person may become confused or depressed, and feel anxiety, sleeplessness, drug craving or paranoia." *Pulse Check* (p.60) reports: "Ecstasy sellers, like ecstasy users, are predominantly white, male, middle-class young adults, whose ages range from 14 to 32 years." Most Ecstasy dealers also use the drug.

MDMA comes in tablet or capsule form and is almost always taken orally, although it can be snorted or dissolved in water and injected. Its chemical structure is similar to mescaline and methamphetamine—other synthetic drugs known to cause brain damage. In fact, brain imaging research in humans shows MDMA causes injury to the brain by affecting neurons that use serotonin, a chemical that plays a direct role in regulating mood, aggression, sexual activity, sleep and sensitivity to pain (www.dea.gov).

GHB, or gamma hydroxybutyrate, is a central nervous system depressant commonly sold as an odorless, colorless liquid in water bottles or as a powder mixed with beverages (*Pulse Check,* p.56). The DEA notes: "Although GHB was originally considered a safe and 'natural' food supplement and was sold in health food stores, the medical community soon became aware that it caused overdoses and other health problems," including unconsciousness, seizures, severe respiratory depression and coma. Abused by high school and college students and rave party attendees for its euphoric and hallucinatory properties, GHB is often combined with alcohol to magnify its intoxicating effect. Several cases have documented the use of GHB to commit sexual assault. In 1990, the Food and Drug Administration (FDA) issued an advisory declaring GHB unsafe and illicit except under FDA-approved, physician-supervised protocols. In March 2000, GHB was placed in Schedule I of the CSA (www.dea.gov). Club drug sales on the Internet are mentioned primarily in conjunction with GHB (*Pulse Check,* p.62).

Rohypnol (flunitrazepam), also called roofies or the "date rape" drug, is not approved for medical use in the United States but is legally prescribed in over 50 other countries. It is widely available in Mexico, Colombia and Europe and is used to treat insomnia and as a pre-anesthetic. Due to international treaty obligations, it has been placed in Schedule IV of the CSA. Rohypnol's effects include sedation, muscle relaxation and reduction in anxiety. Its sedative effects are approximately 7 to 10 times more potent than those of Valium. It is also fast-acting, with effects appearing 15 to 20 minutes after administration and typically lasting four to six hours. Because Rohypnol causes partial amnesia, users often cannot remember events that occurred while they were under the influence of the drug. This effect is particularly dangerous when the drug is used to commit a sexual assault because victims may not be able to clearly recall the assault, the assailant or the events surrounding the assault. Furthermore, Rohypnol impairs cognitive and psychomotor functions affecting reaction time and driving skill and, when used in combination with alcohol, can present a significant public safety hazard on the road (www.dea.gov).

Ketamine, sometimes referred to as "K" or "special K," is used primarily in the veterinary field as an anesthetic but also presents hallucinogenic and dissociative properties when used by humans (*Pulse Check,* p.56). Typical users and sellers are white middle-class youths, with distributors acquiring their product through veterinary office break-ins and pharmacy diversion (p.62). As with the other club drugs, ketamine is used at raves, nightclubs, private parties and in private residences.

Nitrous oxide, often referred to as "laughing gas," is an inhalant and a common propellant ingredient in many products. It is most typically used by white, suburban adolescents at raves and outdoor concerts (*Pulse Check,* p.62). Inhalants are alternatively called deliriants.

Deliriants

Deliriants are volatile chemicals that generally produce a "high" and loss of inhibition similar to that produced by alcohol. According to the DEA, deliriants, or inhalants, "are a chemically diverse group of psychoactive substances composed of organic solvents and volatile substances commonly found in more than 1,000 common household products, such as glues, hair spray, air fresheners, lighter fluid, and paint products. While not regulated under the Controlled Substances Act, many states have placed restrictions on the sale of these products to minors."

Although technically neither narcotics nor dangerous drugs, deliriants may be a prime cause of psychological dependency among young people. Deliriants may be sniffed or inhaled either directly from a container or "huffed" from a paper or plastic bag or cloth held close to the face. The DEA notes: "Once inhaled, the extensive capillary surface of the lungs allows rapid absorption of the substance. . . . Entry into the brain is so fast that the effects of inhalation can resemble the intensity of effects produced by intravenous injection of other psychoactive drugs."

The inhalant high is usually followed by depression. Users may also experience headaches, wheezing, nausea, slurred speech, diminished motor coordination and distortion in perceptions of time and space. A characteristic redness or irritation called "glue sniffer's rash" commonly occurs around the nostrils and lips. Sniffing highly concentrated amounts of solvent or aerosol chemicals can directly induce heart failure and death, or may act more slowly to create a number of chronic and often irreversible health problems, include hearing loss, brain and central nervous system damage, bone marrow damage, liver and kidney damage, and blood oxygen depletion (www.dea.gov).

Inhalant abuse is shockingly common among children and adolescents. Findings from the *1999 Monitoring the Future* study reveal that by the time students reach the eighth grade, 5 percent will be using inhalants monthly, and 19.7 percent will have used inhalants at least once in their lifetime. Because inhalants are readily available, inexpensive and easy to conceal, they are increasingly popular with young people and are, for many, one of the first substances abused (www.dea.gov).

Although the various narcotics and other dangerous drugs produce different effects, they have certain common factors: (1) they are mind altering, (2) they may become addicting—either physically or psychologically and (3) overdosage may result in convulsions and death.

The most commonly observed drugs on the street, in possession of users and seized in drug raids are heroin, opium, morphine, codeine, cocaine, crack and marijuana. Arrest for possession or use of marijuana is the most frequent drug arrest.

According to the *National Drug Threat Assessment 2001: The Domestic Perspective,* national demand indicators show continuing overall stability in cocaine, methamphetamine, heroin and marijuana use.

Alcohol

Many don't think of it as such, but alcohol is a drug. Although drinking alcohol is legal, laws have been established that regulate the age at which it becomes legal to drink, as well as the amount a person can drink and then operate a vehicle. The widespread abuse of alcohol is partly due to its legality but also to its social acceptance. Many people, although they know it's wrong and illegal, continue to drive after drinking. Drunk drivers are a life-threatening menace to themselves and others. Furthermore alcohol is the drug of choice among teenagers.

Alcohol, a depressant, is the most widely abused drug in the United States.

Alcohol is often a factor in accidents and crime—traffic fatalities, pedestrian accidents, home accidents, fire deaths, drownings, skiing accidents, boating fatalities, murders, assaults, rapes, sex crimes against children, domestic violence and suicides. According to Heiskell (2000, p.62): "Nearly 100,000 Americans die each year as a result of alcohol abuse. Alcohol is a factor in more than half of the nation's homicides, suicides and traffic accidents. It also plays a significant role in many domestic and social problems."

Alcohol use is clearly linked to criminal activity.

A study by the Harvard School of Public Health found that college students who frequently engaged in binge drinking were far more likely to experience alcohol-related problems than students who drank alcohol but did not binge drink. The study defined binge drinking as consuming at least five drinks in a row for men and at least four in a row for women two weeks before the survey. According to the study, approximately 44 percent of students were binge drinkers in 1999, the same rate as in 1993 ("Harvard Study Reveals . . .," 2000, pp.4–5).

Researchers have found that children of alcoholics are 70 percent more likely than children of nonalcoholics to abuse drugs and alcohol at some point in their lives. Many children under age 12 say they learned to drink or do drugs

AP/Wide World Photos

North Carolina officers participate in a roadblock on a Saturday night to check for drunk drivers as part of the state's "Booze It and Lose It" campaign. Sixty-nine people were charged with DUI, and six vehicles were seized.

from older brothers and sisters. During adolescence, fitting in is extremely important to teens. They are self-conscious and uncertain as to just who they are. Using alcohol and drugs helps anxious, awkward youths escape from a frightening world and gives them the illusion of membership, energy and confidence. Unfortunately many "innocent" drug users become involved in crime.

Illicit Drug Abuse and Crime

The relationship between illicit drugs and crime is complex: "Drugs and drug-using behavior are linked to crime in many ways. It is a crime to use, possess, manufacture or distribute illegal drugs. In addition the effects of drug-related behavior—violence as the effect of drug use, robberies to get money to buy drugs, violence against rival traffickers—influence society daily" (*Drug Treatment in the Criminal Justice System,* 2001, p.1).

Some acts involving drugs are illegal and are termed *systemic,* or **drug-defined offenses** in which violent crime occurs as a part of the drug business or culture. Examples of these offenses include marijuana cultivation, methamphetamine production and cocaine distribution. Other acts involve offenses in which the *effect* of the drug or the *need* for the drug is a contributing factor. These are called **drug-related offenses,** examples of which might include a user high on PCP who becomes violent and commits an assault because of the drug's pharmacologic effects, or an addict stealing to get money to buy drugs. Finally the *interaction* of drugs, crime and those involved with the drug culture may come into play, as when drug users and other deviants are exposed to situations that encourage crime, when criminal opportunities arise because of a drug user's contact with illegal markets and other offenders, or when offenders exchange criminal knowledge and learn criminal skills from each other.

The National Institute of Justice (NIJ) has implemented a Drug Use Forecasting (DUF) system to detect and track drug-use trends among people arrested for serious crimes. In this voluntary program, arrestees in several major cities are interviewed four times a year and asked to provide urine specimens, which are tested for illicit drugs. Initial tests showed a high level of drug use among the arrestees, with 50 to 80 percent of those arrested for serious crimes testing positive. The research also showed that criminals commit four to six times as much crime when they are actively using drugs as they do when they are drug free. According to the NIJ, most of those tested were charged with street crimes, such as burglary, grand larceny and assault. The most frequently found drugs were marijuana, cocaine, heroin, PCP and amphetamines.

Clearly, illicit drug use is linked to criminal activity.

Incarcerated adults and youths report high levels of drug use. Among those incarcerated for violent crimes, one-third of state prisoners and more than one-third of the incarcerated youths said they had been under the influence of an illegal drug at the time of their offense. In addition major drug use (cocaine, heroin, PCP, LSD and methadone) is related to the number of prior convictions for state prisoners: the greater the use of major drugs, the more prior convictions the inmate was likely to report.

Farabee et al. (2001, p.196) reported on the Drug Abuse Treatment Outcome Studies, which sampled over 7,000 clients in substance abuse treatment programs. They note: "The order of initiation of addiction and criminal careers was significantly related to participation in certain types of crimes, with those beginning criminal careers after beginning their addiction careers being more likely to engage exclusively in victimless than in predatory crimes." Weisburd and Mazerolle (2000, p.331) studied the relationship between street-level drug hot spots and crime and disorder problems in Jersey City, New Jersey. They found: "Drug hot spot areas include a disproportionate share of arrests and calls for police service not only for drug-related crime but for crime and disorder more generally. . . . The findings support the idea of a spatial link between street-level drug hot spot activity, disorder and serious crime."

Drugs and guns have also been linked. When crack became a major drug of choice, those recruited to distribute it were mainly youths. Fearing for their safety because they often carried large quantities of money, these youths also carried guns. Youths are apt to resort to violence to settle arguments rather than resolving disputes verbally. When guns are available, the outcome can be deadly.

Alcohol Abuse and Crime

Alcohol is often a significant factor in crime and other social problems. Belenko et al. (1998, p.84) report: "Alcohol is more closely associated with murder, rape, assault, and child and spousal abuse than any illegal drug." Alcohol abuse was common among criminals tested under the DUF system, with more than one-third of all prison inmates indicating they drank heavily. According to Greenfeld (1998, p.iii): "Nearly 4 in 10 violent victimizations involve use of alcohol [and] about 4 in 10 fatal motor vehicle accidents are alcohol-involved." Furthermore: "One-fifth (21 percent) of state prison inmates incarcerated for violent crimes were under the influence of alcohol—and no other substance—when they committed their crimes. In comparison, only 3 percent of violent offenders in state prison were under the influence of cocaine or crack alone when they committed their crimes, and only 1 percent were under the influence of heroin alone" (Belenko et al., pp.84–85).

Drugs and Society

Drugs affect not only the individual users but also society. State governments spent $81.3 billion on services to deal with alcohol and other drug problems in 1998, surpassing state spending on Medicaid or transportation and equaling the amount spent on higher education that year. Of the $81.3 billion spent, only $3 billion went to research, prevention and treatment of substance abuse ("Substance Abuse Costs . . .," 2001, p.5).

Although drug abusers may claim it is their right to do whatever they want with their own bodies, the results of such actions have serious implications for society. Users no longer control what they think, say or do and often pose a threat to others. According to Robinson (2000, p.7): "Drug-related illness, death and crime cost Americans almost $67 billion a year in health care, extra law enforcement, car crashes, crime and lost productivity due to drug use. International studies have shown that each dollar spent on drug prevention results in a savings of seven dollars that would otherwise be spent on treatment."

An estimated 50 percent of intravenous drug abusers are infected with HIV. Intravenous drug abusers comprise 17 percent of AIDS victims and, among new reported cases of AIDS, approximately one-third were intravenous drug abusers. According to the Centers for Disease Control (AIDS Policy and Law, n.d.): "Researchers now see intravenous drug abuse as the major vehicle for the AIDS virus to be spread to the general public." States have enacted more than 600 pieces of AIDS-related legislation dealing with employment, health care, insurance liability and criminal conduct. Some states are applying criminal punishment to those who knowingly spread HIV.

The costs of illicit drug use are high, and not only in financial terms. As noted by *The National Drug Control Strategy* (1998, p.1):

> Drug abuse impairs rational thinking and the potential for a full, productive life. Drug abuse, drug trafficking, and their consequences destroy personal liberty and the well-being of communities. Drugs drain the physical, intellectual, spiritual, and moral strength of America. Crime, violence, workplace accidents, family misery, drug-exposed children, and addiction are only part of the price imposed on society. Drug abuse spawns global criminal syndicates and bankrolls those who sell drugs to young people. Illegal drugs indiscriminately destroy old and young, men and women from all racial and ethnic groups and every walk of life. No person or group is immune.

Gondles (1998, p.6) adds: "The human toll is overpowering. Forget the lost productivity; forget the waste of man or woman; forget the financial impact of treatment or criminal justice costs. Remember just one thing—heartache. . . . Drug usage and drug addiction suck the very life out of our society. They drain us of our most important asset—our kids."

Drug Control

According to *The National Drug Control Strategy* (p.2): "Our nation's domestic challenge is to reduce illegal drug use and its criminal, health, and economic consequences while protecting individual liberty and the rule of law." The Office of National Drug Control Policy (ONDCP) has set forth clear goals to control drugs in this country. Its action plan is based on two basic rights of all citizens: the right to feel safe in one's home and community and the right to have one's children learn, grow and prosper in a safe and drug-free school and neighborhood. To meet its goals, specific drug-control strategies have been implemented (Figure 9.2).

The drug problem might be approached with the following methods:

- Crime control
- Punishment
- Rehabilitation
- Prevention
- Legalization

Crime Control

Crime control includes source control at the international level, interdiction at the national level and enforcement at the local level.

Source Control

According to Luitweiler (1998, p.41): "The most popular illegal drugs consumed in the States have historically been grown and manufactured *outside* the country." With the reigning drug lords living and working far from the scenes of their crimes, U.S. law enforcement faces a difficult challenge in controlling these sources of illegal drugs. Ronderos (1998, pp.384–385) states: "International drug dealing is a crime that involves the coordinated actions of different individuals in various jurisdictions. . . . Enforcement of the majority of illegal drugs requires some degree of cooperation and enforcement assistance between the supply-and-demand and the production-and-consumption countries."

Some drug sources have the open support of their national governments, with export of drug-related crops bringing substantial revenue to the countries. An example is opium production, the prevention of which, as Kaplan (n.d.) notes, would require controlling poppy cultivation and international cooperation. It is anticipated that the fall of the Taliban regime in Afghanistan and the de facto end to its national ban on poppy cultivation will return the country to its prior status as one of the world's leading opium producers, providing much-needed economic relief for struggling poppy farmers but adding to the global supply of drugs. Such regionally sanctioned drug sources are very difficult, if not impossible, to control.

International drug rings also pose a significant challenge to U.S. law enforcement. For example DEA agents have identified a Bangkok heroin cartel that is as powerful as the notorious Medellin and Cali Colombian rings. Difficulties in prosecuting the cartel include Thailand's reluctance to crack down on drug trafficking and the ingenious smuggling used by the cartel. In fact, some narcotics

Figure 9.2
Overview of Drug-Control Strategies

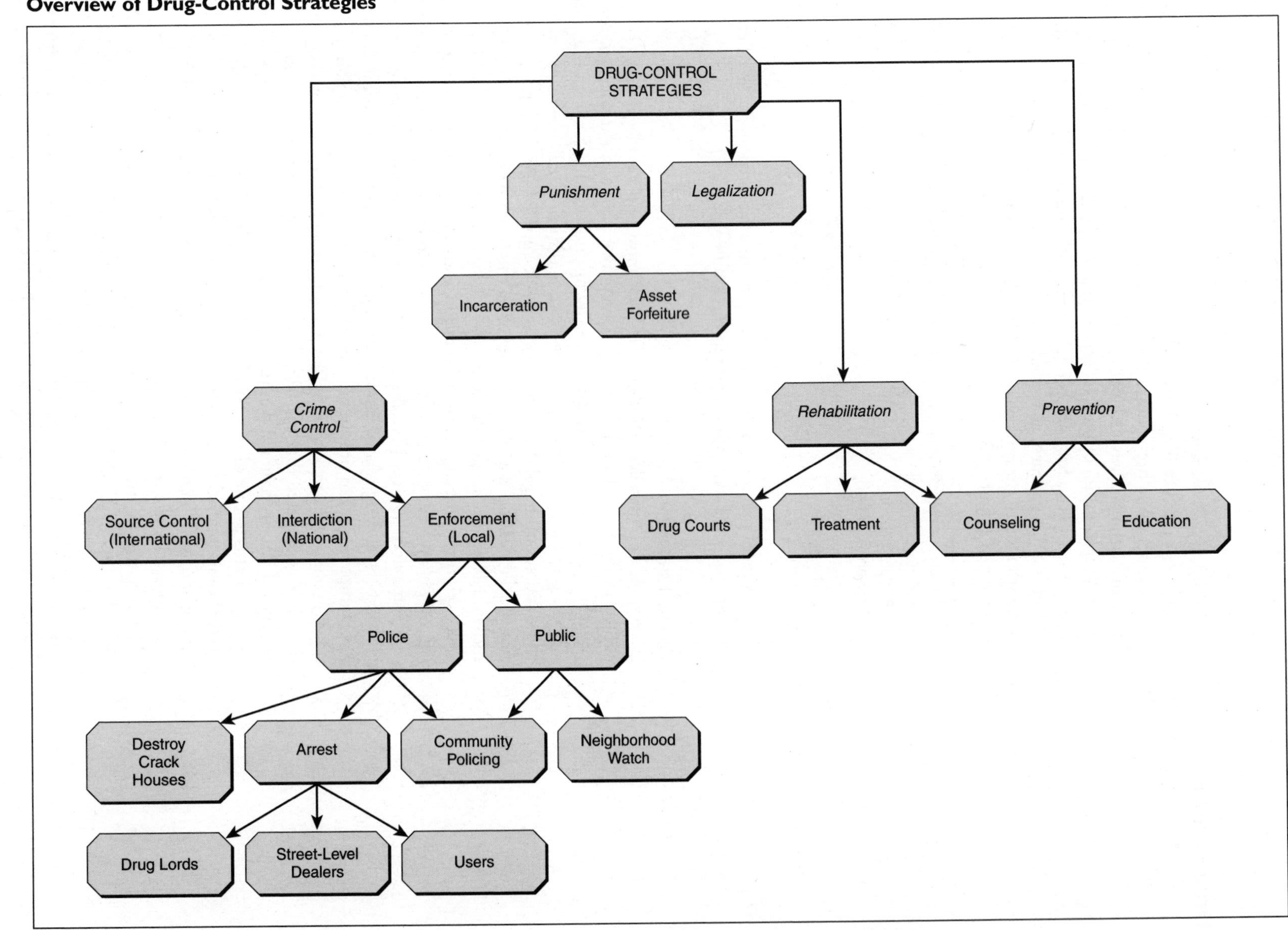

kingpins are virtually ignored by the government of the country in which they reside, whether out of intimidation and fear or because they have formed clandestine partnerships with such drug lords to profit from the business.

While the U.S. government cannot dictate how a foreign government should handle its resident drug lords, it can impose legislation aimed at preventing individuals and organizations from conducting illegal narcotics business within our national borders and prosecuting those who do or attempt to do so. The Foreign Narcotics Kingpin Designation Act requires federal officials to compile an annual list of suspected drug kingpins and take steps to freeze their U.S. assets and bar them from entering the country. It also subjects anyone who knowingly does business with drug kingpins to criminal penalties ("The Administration Names . . .," 2001, p.4).

After international drug sources have been addressed, the focus narrows in on ways to keep the drugs that are produced from getting into our country.

Interdiction

Interdiction is cutting off or destroying a line of communication—in the case of drug control, halting the flow of drugs into the United States. Constantine (1998, p.24) states: "Although the criminal organizations responsible for most of the drugs in the United States are based in foreign countries, they operate across all international and jurisdictional boundaries. Their command and control structure in the United States directs the networks and gangs responsible for drug distribution throughout the country." American drug users pay drug traffickers an estimated $140 billion a year. Some dealers hand out free drug samples to hook new buyers. Illegal drugs, from marijuana to cocaine, are readily available. Luitweiler (p.41) comments on interdiction and the growing worldwide drug trade:

> Over the past few years, drug gangs' capabilities have become far more threatening, as two new factors have emboldened international drug lords.
>
> First, political and economic barriers have been lowered . . . encouraging the free flow of people and products across international borders. . . .
>
> A second factor is drug traffickers' easy access to sophisticated communications technology, including fax machines, pagers, cell phones, personal communications systems and networks that are frequently changed to evade law enforcement.

Preventing smuggling is difficult given the United States' more than 12,000 miles of coastline. Kaplan suggests, for example, that the total heroin requirement of all American addicts for an entire year is probably less than 10 tons, yet 100 million tons of freight come into the United States yearly, and more than 200 million people cross American borders yearly.

Once drugs pass into our country, the focus narrows further, turning to enforcement.

Enforcement

The Drug Enforcement Administration (DEA) is the federal agency charged with enforcing our nation's drug laws. In 1992 the DEA was assigned to develop a system to help federal, state and local law enforcement agencies to investigate drug trafficking organizations, and in October 1997, the National Drug Pointer Index (NDPIX) became operational across the United States. As Constantine (p.25) notes: "Such a system would prevent duplication of effort, facilitate information sharing and, most importantly, prevent dangerous situations for law enforcement officers in the field."

One approach to handling the drug problem is to attack street-level drug markets. However, street drug rings can be quite sophisticated, with a kingpin purchasing narcotics from foreign smugglers. Under the kingpin are leaders who oversee drug packaging and distribution. Runners take the drugs to the street sellers. Lookouts can earn several hundred dollars a day just watching for the police. Enforcers, as the name implies, carry out the kingpin's orders, including killing people who get in the way of drug trafficking.

Nonetheless, as Strandberg (1998b, p.62) notes: "Street level drug trade is important for law enforcement because it is how U.S. customers buy their drugs. . . . Going after the buyer is a change in orientation for many police departments. . . . The action of street corner drug enforcement is to make that corner as police-dangerous for the buyer as it is for the seller." Another approach to the drug problem is to simply bulldoze known crack houses.

Punishment

Another way to handle the drug problem is to punish those involved in selling or using drugs, either through community service, incarceration or via asset forfeiture, in hopes such sanctions will deter future criminal behavior.

Community Service

For youthful first-time drug offenders, some communities are "taking a kinder, gentler approach," calling for teenagers to sit down with parents or lawyers and work out a punishment that fits the crime. Said one chief: "I would rather take these first-time offenders and work their fannies off during community service" ("Taking a Different Road . . .," 2001, p.5). The community service would preferably be done alongside a police officer.

Incarceration

Spending time behind bars has been a consequence of illegal activity for thousands of years. During the 1970s, many citizens and legislators advocated a "get tough" approach to the growing drug use crisis, viewing imprisonment of drug offenders as the best solution to the problem: "Since the introduction of mandatory drug sentencing laws during the 1970s, millions of substance abusers have been apprehended, processed, convicted and incarcerated by the nation's criminal justice system" (Weekes, 1998, p.8).

However, this nondiscretionary sentencing policy has filled our nation's correctional institutions with drug offenders, leaving less room for what many consider the "real " criminals—murderers, rapists and other violent offenders. Klug (2000, p.32) reports: "There are almost as many inmates imprisoned for drug offenses today—458,131—as the entire U.S. prison population in 1980—474,368. . . . Since 1980, the number of violent offenders entering prison has doubled, while the number of nonviolent inmates has tripled and the number of persons imprisoned for drug offenses has increased 11-fold." Furthermore: "It will cost states, counties and the federal government more than $9 billion this year to incarcerate drug offenders" (Klug, p.32).

With our correctional facilities overflowing, and the increasing number of violent offenders requiring prison space, courts have become more reluctant to incarcerate drug offenders. Adding to this reluctance is the growing body of evidence that tougher sentencing laws have not had much impact on reducing criminality in most drug offenders. According to a Bureau of Justice Statistics report, of those offenders charged in 1999 with a drug offense, approximately 65 percent had been arrested previously. Twenty-eight percent of these offenders had been previously arrested five or more times ("Drug Cases and Sentences . . .," 2001, p.13).

Given the many shortcomings of incarceration as an effective punishment for drug offenders, another solution gaining popularity is asset forfeiture.

Asset Forfeiture

Asset forfeiture was introduced in the United States through passage of the Racketeer Influenced and Corrupt Organization (RICO) Act in 1970 and the Continuing Criminal Enterprises Act in 1984. The Asset Forfeiture Program, enacted in 1984, allows the Justice Department to share seized assets with state and local law enforcement agencies that participate in the investigations and arrests. Kash (1998, p.56) explains:

> One of the best weapons law enforcement has in the war on drugs is its capability to seize and forfeit assets that have been used to violate the laws of the United States. The oft-cited 1974 U.S. Supreme Court case, *Calero-Toledo vs. Pearson Yacht Leasing Club,* defined "forfeiture" as "the taking by the government of property illegally used or acquired without compensating the owner."

This type of response is intended to deprive drug offenders of "ill-gotten gain," material possessions and wealth obtained through the sale or distribution of illegal drugs. Such forfeitures have included a recording studio, a Chevrolet dealership, a one-thousand-acre plantation, a horse farm with 210 Appaloosas, including a stallion worth $1.5 million, luxury homes, cars, boats and planes.

Two key cases in the 1990s set a stronger foundation for issues involving forfeiture. In *United States v. Ursery* (1996), the Court held that civil forfeiture does not constitute double jeopardy, under the rationale that the prohibition against double jeopardy applies only if both proceedings are criminal and not when one is civil. In *United States v. Bajakajian* (1998), the Court held that the Eighth Amendment does apply in civil forfeitures. In this case the offense was failing to make a report to customs agents when taking more than $10,000 out of the country. The Court ruled that the forfeiture of $357,144 was grossly disproportionate to the offense and required Bajakajian to forfeit only $15,000.

Rehabilitation

Another approach taken with criminals for many centuries has been that of rehabilitation, attempting to change offenders' behavior—to "cure" them—so they no longer wish to engage in unlawful activities. Today rehabilitation of drug and alcohol offenders is a major focus of many communities, social service

SEIZED
FROM A
DRUG
DEALER

© Joel Gordon

The Asset Forfeiture Program allows the Justice Department to share seized assets with state and local law enforcement agencies when they participated in the investigations and arrests. Many police departments and sheriff's departments use seized vehicles to convey a message to drug dealers and the public.

agencies, medical establishments and law enforcement agencies. Rehabilitation may be accomplished through drug courts, treatment programs and counseling.

Drug Courts

Drug courts are one attempt to deal with the drug problem and its resultant prison overcrowding. Since the first drug court began in 1989, almost 200,000 defendants have been placed in such courts across the nation (Wallentine, 2000, p.54). A study by the Vera Institute of Justice (*Do Drug Courts Save . . .*, 2000) found: "There is substantial evidence that drug courts have been successful in reducing the recidivism rates of low-level criminal offenders with drug abuse problems, while easing pressure on overcrowded jails." Huddleston (1998, p.98) suggests the following reason for the success of drug courts:

> Drug courts differ significantly from previous attempts to manage and rehabilitate drug-using offenders. Rather than relying upon fragmented criminal justice and treatment systems, drug courts bring the full weight of all intervenors to bear, forcing the defendant to address his or her underlying substance abuse problem. The judge, prosecutor, defense counsel, substance abuse treatment specialist, probation officer, law enforcement officer, correctional officer, educational and vocational experts, and community leaders create a unified system.

Several studies indicate that drug courts have higher retention rates, lower recidivism rates and are more cost effective than traditional drug treatment programs ("First Decade of Drug . . .," 2000, p.10). According to a Drug Court Clearinghouse and Technical Assistance Project, felons are not only required to become clean and sober, they also must earn a GED, obtain and maintain employment, be able to pay their debts, such as child support and drug court fees, and have a sponsor who helps them assimilate back into the community

(*Looking at a Decade of Drug Courts,* 1998). Another common requirement of drug courts is for offenders to submit to regular drug screens through urinalysis.

However, as Miethe et al. (2000, p.522) report: "Risks of recidivism for drug court participants are significantly higher than comparable offenders processed outside drug court. . . . The drug court is actually more stigmatizing than conventional courts and is not reintegrative enough in its orientation toward punishment."

Drug courts are discussed further in Chapter 12.

Treatment

As noted by Maxwell (2000, p.542): "During the past decade, court-ordered diversion and treatment procedures have proliferated in response to the problems of court congestion and prison overcrowding. Underlying these court orders are stiff sanctions that are often used to threaten offenders to comply with the court's mandate." Belenko et al. (p.86) state: "Research in recent years indicates that well-designed prison-based treatment can reduce post-release criminality and drug and alcohol relapse." However (p.85): "In state and federal prisons, the gap between available substance abuse treatment—and inmate participation—and the need for such treatment and participation is enormous and widening. An estimated . . . 70 to 85 percent of inmates need some level of substance abuse treatment."

Some have placed the onus of treating addicted offenders squarely on the shoulders of criminal justice. According to *Treatment Alternatives for Safe Communities Reports* ("New Drug Use . . .," 1998, p.4): "Treatment . . . must begin as soon as the addiction is identified and must continue throughout the criminal justice process."

Therapeutic communities have evolved into a successful treatment model for drug-addicted offenders. States Lipton (1998, p.106): "Historically, the term 'therapeutic community' (TC) has been used for several different forms of treatment—sanctuaries, residential group homes and even special schools—and for several different conditions, including mental illness, drug abuse and alcoholism." Lipton (p.106) says common therapeutic goals include getting past denial; changing attitudes toward offending, specifically toward one's primary offense; building morality; victim awareness, contrition and understanding of effects on victims; and relapse prevention.

Innovative attempts have been made at treating drug users, with the goal not necessarily the curing of drug addiction but the removal of the need to commit crime to get funds with which to buy drugs. For example under a two-market approach, drugs are supplied to addicts at clinics or other types of health facilities but are not available for nonaddicts. In Britain heroin is provided to addicts at clinics specifically set up for that purpose. In more recent years, however, they have switched to methadone, a synthetic opiate, as a maintenance drug.

One difficulty with sentencing offenders to treatment rather than prison is that often law enforcement officers see this as being soft on crime. As one officer stated: "Why should cops work so hard to arrest drug users if they're just going to get treatment anyway?" (Snyder, 2001, p.52).

Counseling

A common element of drug treatment programs is counseling focused on trying to understand the cause(s) of the addictive or criminal behavior. Addressing these underlying causes can result in changes that eliminate the need to "escape" into drugs or alcohol. The counseling of drug addicts is becoming more of a science as more is learned ("New Drug Use . . .," p.1): "As our understanding of the psychologies of the addiction-driven mind increases, the realization has come that treatment models must address multiple social environments." In other words addiction doesn't simply end with incarceration—it stays with addicted offenders whether they are on the streets, in court, behind bars or released to community supervision. Counseling may also be used proactively as a prevention strategy for those at risk of using and becoming addicted to drugs and/or alcohol.

Prevention

Prevention attempts to stop drug use before it starts. Belenko et al. (p.88) claim: "Prevention is the first line of defense against drug- and alcohol-related crime. . . . Since most addicts begin using drugs while they are teens, efforts to give youngsters the will and skill to not initiate drug or alcohol use are critical to keeping them out of the criminal justice system." The most common avenue taken with this strategy is education.

Education

The place to begin alleviating the problem of criminality is with our youths. It is vital to steer our nation's youths away from the devastation caused by drug use. In fact, the first goal of the 1998 National Drug Control Strategy is to educate and enable America's youths to reject illegal drugs, as well as alcohol and tobacco.

Educating youths about the dangers of drug use has become a common tool in the overall strategy to fight the drug problem. Chapter 5 discussed some youth programs currently operating in this capacity, such as Police Athletic Leagues and the DARE program.

The DARE (Drug Abuse Resistance Education) program has strong advocates such as Schennum (2001, p.103): "At present, it is refreshing to see DARE is still alive and effective. Today DARE is taught in more than 80% of all U.S. school districts, benefiting over 26 million students. DARE is an excellent program to assist parents and society as a whole in the fight against the influences of drugs, alcohol and tobacco on children and young adults." However, research has not substantiated these claims. *Law Enforcement News* ("Truth, DARE & Consequences . . .," 2001, p.1) reports on a University of Illinois study that tracked 1,800 students over six years and found that by the end of high school, any impact of the program had worn off. In fact, an increase in drug use was detected in suburban students who had gone through the DARE program. Similar findings were reported by a 10-year University of Kentucky study.

In response to these findings, DARE has revised its curriculum. As noted by Brown (2001, p.76): "The new program was developed in 1999 after the U.S. Departments of Education and Justice brought researchers and DARE officials together to resolve the ongoing controversy about the ineffectiveness of DARE." One key change is that the revised version of DARE will use police officers more as facilitators and less as instructors, helping children explore their own beliefs about drugs and develop their skills in asserting themselves and refusing drugs ("Drug Abuse Resistance Education . . .," 2001, p.2).

Public media campaigns have also focused on educating teens and preteens on the realities of drug use—how smoking causes bad breath and makes hair stink, or how getting drunk can become embarrassing if it leads to vomiting or having parents revoke driving privileges.

"Operation Broken Windows"

Another strategy used to prevent crime from moving into a community or to drive out crime that has already crept in is based on the **broken-window theory**—that if a window is broken in a building and is left unrepaired, it will signal that no one cares and that more damage can be caused without fear of punishment. It is an open invitation to crime. Strategies used to repair "broken windows" have included undercover operations, a uniformed police presence, a crackdown on trafficking by assigning K-9 units to local bus stations, and attention to social conditions: cutting the grass, removing the trash, repairing or installing streetlights and inspecting buildings for code violations.

Community mobilization can be a valuable asset in the effort to control drug use. Greenberg (2001, p.9) suggests: "The problem of substance abuse, including alcohol, is enormous. An entirely new corps of police professional is needed to serve as 'drug control specialists.'" He further asserts: "The regular and systematic use of auxiliary [volunteer] police personnel would appear to be a natural component of a community policing anti-drug strategy."

Simonson (2001, p.1) describes another approach emphasizing citizen cooperation: the drug-free communities support program. In June 1997, the Drug Free Communities Act became law. This act is "a catalyst for increased citizen participation in efforts to reduce substance use among youth, and it provides community anti-drug coalitions with much-needed funds to carry out their important missions." Through this program, an estimated $143.5 million will be authorized to support the program over five years. The two major goals of the Drug-Free Communities Support Program are (1) to reduce substance abuse among youths and, over time, adults and (2) to establish and strengthen community collaboration, including working with federal, state, local and tribal governments and private nonprofit agencies.

Legalization

Legalization of drugs has been a topic of debate in the United States since the passage of the Harrison Narcotics Act in 1914. Some advocate making marijuana and other drugs legal, just as alcohol is, claiming this would reduce the cost of maintaining a drug habit and, consequently, reduce the amount of crime committed to obtain money to support the habit.

Legalization proponents say the prohibition on drug use has resulted in enormous profits for drug dealers, jail overcrowding and urban terrorization by gangs. Opponents, however, claim legalization will provide a "green light" for drug use, leading to addiction and, consequently, to increases in crime.

Arguments for Legalization

Proponents of drug legalization provide the following arguments:

- Costs. Dollars now spent on enforcement could be used for education and treatment.
- Organized crime. Legalization would eliminate the drug lords' major source of funds.
- Revenues. Taxes on drugs, like taxes on alcohol and tobacco, could be used to finance treatment programs.

Citizens in some communities have already voiced their opinion on the legalization issue. Sanders and Constantine (1998, p.23) point out: "On November 5, 1996, voters changed the complexion of the debate forever. Proposals were passed in California and Arizona that made 'medical marijuana' available in California, and all Schedule I drugs available by prescription in Arizona."

As one chief commented, off the record: "It's not politically correct to say this, but I think many chiefs agree with me when I say this whole Drug War thing is a continued waste of money and law enforcement resources. We should think about decriminalizing a lot of this stuff and getting government control of it like we did with alcohol, because drug use is not going to go away. We've proven that we can't stop it" (Hall, 1998, p.6).

Many believe the way some drug users are currently treated—incarcerated and criminalized for no other reason than that they use drugs—is leading our nation on a downward spiral toward the status of a prison state. Weekes (p.8) asserts: "I believe countless lives are being compromised by the nation's approach toward drugs, not only through the criminalization of drug users, but also through the correctional system's inability to successfully work with those for whom substance abuse is a criminogenic factor, to assist them in successfully gaining control over their drug use behavior."

Arguments against Legalization

Those opposed to legalization of drugs give the following reasons for their objection:

- Increased drug use and addiction. Inexpensive, widely available drugs would increase addiction.
- Increased crime. Because of the proven link between drug use and crime, more drug users/addicts would lead to increased levels of crime.
- Medical costs. Health costs of drug abuse would increase.
- Social values. Legalizing drugs would make them socially acceptable.

According to Robinson (p.7): "Drug abuse is more than just a law enforcement problem. It is a public safety and public health problem. Drug legalization will lead to increased crime, reduce economic productivity, increase the burden on an already strained health care system, endanger those traveling on our roadways, and, most tragically, send a message to our children that drug use is acceptable." Moody (1998, p.6) states:

> One of the more outrageous yet ludicrous issues the United States is facing is that of drug legalization. At a time when the federal and state governments are moving to enact legislation that would severely regulate the tobacco industry because of the danger smoking poses to public health, the fact that anyone with any intelligence could seriously consider legalizing drugs seems preposterous. Yet that is exactly the situation we find ourselves in today.

Barry McCaffrey, director of the Office of National Drug Control Policy (ONDCP) and generally known as the "Drug Czar," has said: "We have suggested that treatment and prevention won't work unless America keeps a high social disapproval rate of drugs. These drugs ought to be against the law, and police ought to rigorously uphold the law. We are very skeptical about decriminalization. The more people that try these drugs, the more who will get addicted and commit crimes" (Strandberg, 1998a, p.54).

Nylén, head of the Swedish National Criminal Investigation Department, has examined Sweden's legalization experiment regarding nonmedical drug use and has reached the following conclusions (1998, p.35): "The bottom line is that the tendency to use drugs is based on social, cultural and psychological factors, as well as the individual assessment of the risks involved in using drugs. If it is easy to have access to drugs, and if society is permissive in its attitude, the number of addicts, crime and violence will increase."

The Need for a Combined Effort

The Counterdrug Technology Assessment Center (CTAC) within the Office of National Drug Control Policy is the central counterdrug enforcement research and development organization of the United States. According to the Executive Summary of the National Drug Control Strategy 2000 Annual Report (p.iii):

> In reducing the demand for illicit drugs, CTAC has worked in conjunction with the National Institute on Drug Abuse to provide the most advanced facilities to the nation's premier teams of medical researchers working on the underlying causes of substance abuse, dependence and addiction. . . .
>
> The R&D efforts are heavily concentrated in the areas of brain imaging technology and the development of catalytic antibodies, therapeutic drug assessment, treatment effectiveness, juvenile diversion from the criminal justice system and studies of the use of banned substances in intercollegiate and Olympic sports.
>
> The goals of the CTAC cover the basic range of options available to combat drugs:
>
> - Educate and enable America's youths to reject illegal drugs as well as alcohol and tobacco.
> - Increase the safety of America's citizens by substantially reducing drug-related crime and violence.
> - Reduce health and social costs to the public of illegal drug use.
> - Shield America's air, land and sea frontiers from the drug threat.
> - Break foreign and domestic drug sources of supply.

Abshire (1998, p.39) states: "Maybe it's time to . . . start thinking of [the drug trade] as the business it is. A business that involves social and public health issues, a business whose profits and losses are measured in lives." He also notes the need to invest in treatment as much as enforcement (p.36): "Supply and demand are the two horns of our drug dilemma. . . . Focusing on the supply side of the equation without giving the demand side equal time simply doesn't make any sense. It's not good business."

Leshner (1998, p.6) advocates viewing drug abuse and addiction as public health problems: "Understanding addiction as a brain disease explains in part why historic policy strategies focusing solely on the social or criminal justice aspects of drug use and addiction have been unsuccessful." This perspective is also evident in *The National Drug Control Strategy,* which states (1998, pp.3–4):

> The metaphor of a 'war on drugs' is misleading. Although wars are expected to end, drug control is a continuous challenge. . . .
>
> Cancer is a more appropriate metaphor for the nation's drug problem. Dealing with cancer is a long-term proposition. It requires the mobilization of support mechanisms—medical, educational, and societal—to check the spread of the disease and improve the prognosis. The symptoms of the illness must be managed while the root cause is attacked. The key to reducing both drug abuse and cancer is prevention coupled with treatment.

The "war on drugs" has been a top priority for the past decade; however, on September 11, 2001, as a result of the terrorist attacks on America, this priority changed. The war on drugs, at least for the moment, has taken a backseat to the new war on terrorism, as both the FBI and the U.S. Customs Service have made terrorism their top priority. Commissioner of Customs Bonner stated: "The battle against terrorism is and will be the highest priority for the U.S. Customs Service" ("Terrorism Fight Is Top Priority . . .," 2001).

The Threat of Terrorism

"Although not new to the United States, the threat of terrorism is changing and becoming more deadly. Over the last several years, the FBI has noted a new trend in terrorism within the United States that involves a transition from more numerous low-level incidents to less frequent but more destructive attacks, with a goal to produce mass casualties and attract intense media coverage" (Lewis, Jr., 1999, p.3).

Analyses of Gallup Polls over the past few years reveal that the American public has been significantly affected by recent terrorist events. For example, in a poll conducted January 10–14, 2001, respondents were asked, "What do you think is the most important problem facing the country today?" The question was open-ended, meaning respondents were not given a list and asked to pick one, but instead were allowed to respond with whatever came to mind. In this poll, ethics and morality topped the chart of most important problems (13 percent), followed by education (12 percent), crime/violence (9 percent) and dissatisfaction with the government (9 percent). No responses of "terrorism" were noted (Newport, 2001). However, in a November 8–11, 2001, poll that asked the same open-ended question, 37 percent of respondents stated terrorism was the country's most important problem, with concerns about the economy in general a distant second (16 percent) and fear of war (13 percent) coming in third (Jones, 2001).

Similarly, in an April 7–9, 2000, poll that asked "How worried are you that you or someone in your family will become a victim of terrorism?", 4 percent responded "very worried," 20 percent were "somewhat worried," and 75 percent were "not too worried" or "not worried at all." A September 11, 2001, poll, however, yielded vastly different results: 23 percent were "very worried," 35 percent were "somewhat worried," 24 percent were "not too worried," 16 percent were "not worried at all," and 1 percent reported knowing a victim of terrorism (Jones).

Law enforcement has necessarily been called on to respond to the threat of terrorism and to help quell the public's heightened state of alarm by restoring peace and security to our free country. The attorney general, John Ashcroft, has also announced plans for "a wartime reorganization and mobilization of the nation's justice and law enforcement resources" to meet the new "first and overriding" priority for the Justice Department: preventing additional terrorist attacks on America ("Ashcroft Announces Plan . . .," 2001, p.1).

Terrorism Defined

No single definition of terrorism is universally accepted because, as The Terrorism Research Center notes: "One man's terrorist is another's freedom fighter." The Center defines **terrorism** as "the use of force or violence against persons or property in violation of the criminal laws of the United States for purposes of intimidation, coercion or ransom." This is similar to the FBI's definition: "Terrorism is the unlawful use of force or violence against persons or property to intimidate or coerce a government, the civilian population, or any segment thereof, in furtherance of political or social objectives." The U.S. Code Title 22 defines terrorism as the "premeditated, politically motivated violence perpetrated against non-combatant targets by subnational groups or clandestine agents, usually intended to influence an audience." A more graphic definition is provided by James Poland: "Terrorism is the premeditated, deliberate, systematic murder, mayhem, and threatening of the innocent to create fear and intimidation in order to gain a political or tactical advantage."

Most definitions of terrorism have common elements, including the systematic use of physical violence, either actual or threatened, against noncombatants to create a climate of fear to cause some religious, political or social change.

Motivation for Terrorism

Most terrorist acts result from dissatisfaction with a religious, political or social system or policy and an inability to change it through acceptable, nonviolent means. Religious motives are seen in Islamic extremism. Political motives include such elements as the Red Army Faction. Social motives are seen in single-issue groups such as antiabortion groups. As Rehm and Rehm (2000, p.39) suggest: "Terrorists are trying to effect change in favor of a cause, be it social, environmental, religious, or political. They are often not interested in escaping and hiding in the community. They are waging war against society and do not count casualties or destruction as loss."

Types of Terrorism

Terrorism comes in many forms, including eco-terrorism, cyberterrorism, narcoterrorism and bioterrorism. **Eco-terrorism** seeks to "inflict economic damage to those who profit from the destruction of the natural environment" (Vallee, 2001, p.40). One such group is the Earth Liberation Front (ELF), often working with the Animal Liberation Front (ALF). Arson is a favorite weapon, responsible for tens of millions of dollars of property damage, including a U.S. Department of Agriculture building, a U.S. Forest Service ranger station and a Colorado ski resort. The group claims responsibility for releasing 5,000 mink from a Michigan fur farm, 600 wild horses from an Oregon corral and burning the Michigan State University's genetic engineering research offices. In 2000 they claimed responsibility for torching a $2 million home in Colorado. Between 1980 and 1999 in the United States eco-terrorists committed at least 100 acts of destruction, causing approximately $42.8 million in damages (Nilson and Burke, 2002, p.1).

Cyberterrorism is defined by the FBI as "terrorism that initiates, or threatens to initiate, the exploitation of or attack on information systems." Damage to our critical computer systems can put our safety and our national security in jeopardy.

Narcoterrorism includes hiring terrorists to protect the drug cartels as well as the sale and distribution of drugs by these cartels. Narcoterrorism was used by the Medellin cartel when it hired the M–19 organization to assassinate 12 Columbian Supreme Court justices. It should be noted, however, that some experts, including DEA and FBI agents, feel narcoterrorism is nonexistent. Drug traffickers are economically, not ideologically, motivated.

Bioterrorism involves such biological weapons of mass destruction (WMD) as anthrax, botulism and smallpox. The government classifies not only biological weapons, but also nuclear and chemical weapons as WMDs. Martinez, unit chief of the FBI's Weapons of Mass Destruction Operations, says: "The advances in biotechnology, the open-source literature and the availability of the materials have made producing a bio-weapon a viable concern" (Strandberg, 2001, p.89). Some experts suggest that bioterrorism is the third most likely terrorist act to occur. Incendiary devices and explosives are most likely to be used because they are easy to make. Chemical devices are next in likelihood because the raw materials are easy to get and easy to use.

The Central Intelligence Agency reports that at least 10 countries are believed to have or be conducting research on biological agents to be used as WMDs (Jones, 1999, p.42). As Lesce (1999, p.96) notes: "Because of our population concentrations and our mobility as individuals, we are especially vulnerable to a biological attack." He (p.95) reports that during late 1998 and 1999 several anthrax hoaxes occurred in various locations in the United States with almost 200 such hoaxes in 1998.

In October 2001, however, the threat became reality, when a photo editor in Florida died from inhalation anthrax. Several weeks later, anthrax-laced letters had been delivered to several major media networks and numerous government offices around Washington, DC. Environmental sampling also indicated massive amounts of anthrax spores at several post offices and mailroom facilities. As this text goes to press, there have been 18 confirmed cases of anthrax, including four fatalities, thousands of Americans who may have been exposed remain on antibiotics, and the Environmental Protection Agency (EPA) is facing difficulties in clearing the Hart Senate Office Building of all anthrax spores.

While no cases of anthrax have been linked to the September 11 terrorist attacks or the al-Qaeda network considered responsible for them, the incidents are regarded as terrorism, perhaps domestic in origin, and are being investigated as crimes. Despite the, as yet, relatively unsuccessful mass infection of Americans with anthrax, Rohen (2000, p.7) cautions: "WMD threats to the United States do exist. The only questions that remain are when and where the attacks will occur."

Classification of Terrorist Acts

The FBI categorizes terrorism in the United States as domestic or international terrorism.

Domestic Terrorism

The 1995 bombing of the Alfred P. Murrah Federal Building in Oklahoma City and the pipe bomb explosions in Centennial Olympic Park during the 1996 Summer Olympic Games highlight the threat of domestic terrorists. According to Lewis, Jr. (p.5): "Domestic terrorism involves groups or individuals who operate without foreign direction entirely within the United States and target elements of the U.S. government or citizens." They represent extreme right- or left-wing and special interest beliefs. Many are antigovernment, anti-taxation and engage in survivalist training to perpetuate a white, Christian nation.

The right-wing militia or patriot movement is a law enforcement concern because of the potential for violence and criminal behavior. As Morrison (1999, p.18) suggests: "Although membership in a militia organization is not illegal in the United States, it would be foolish to overlook the signs of violence exhibited by these organizations. Stockpiling firearms, ammo and other weapons is a clear indication that these groups are serious about using violence to promote their ideals." Some states have passed legislation limiting militias, including types of training they can undergo.

International Terrorism

International terrorism is foreign-based or directed by countries or groups outside the United States against the United States. The FBI divides international terrorism into three categories. The first threat is foreign state sponsors of international terrorism using terrorism as a tool of foreign policy, for example Iraq, Libya and Afghanistan. The second threat is formalized terrorist groups such as Lebanese Hezballah, Egyptian Al-Gamm's Al-Islamiyya, Palestinian HAMAS and Osama (alternately Usama) bin Laden's al-Qaeda. The third threat comes from loosely affiliated international radical extremists who have a variety of identities and travel freely in the United States, unknown to law enforcement or the government.

A Brief Chronology of Terrorism—Past to Present

Terrorism dates back to at least the first century when the Zealots, a Jewish sect, fought against Roman occupation of what is now Israel. In twelfth century Iran, a group of Shiite Muslims committed terrorist acts against religious and political leaders of Sunni Islam. Through the eighteenth century most terrorist movements were based on religious beliefs. However, the word *terrorism* first appeared during the French Revolution (1789–1799) when revolutionaries who seized power in France used violence against their enemies. Their period of rule was called the Reign of Terror (Bassiouni, 2001).

During the nineteenth century, and into the twentieth, terrorist movements continued to be politically based. In the 1930s Germany's Adolf Hitler, Italy's Benito Mussolini and the Soviet Union's Joseph Stalin all used terrorism to discourage opposition to their governments. In 1945 conflict between Arab nations and Israel resulted in waves of terrorism throughout the Middle East. Since 1960 Palestinian groups have carried out acts of terrorism to establish an independent Palestinian state.

In the United States, during the late 1800s and 1900s, the Ku Klux Klan advocated violence to terrorize blacks and their sympathizers. And from 1978 to 1995, the anarchist and terrorist known as the Unabomber, using homemade bombs either mailed or planted, killed 3 people and wounded 23 others. Arrested in 1996, Theodore Kaczynski claimed allegiance to radical environmentalists and those opposed to the effects of industrialization and technology, targeting university professors, computer professionals and corporate executives.

The United States' support of Israel resulted in several acts of terrorism against Americans by Palestinian radicals or supporters, including the 1983 attack by Shiite Muslim suicide bombers on the U.S. embassy in Beirut, Lebanon and on the U.S. Marine barracks in Beirut, killing nearly 300, mostly Americans. In 1988 a bomb destroyed Pan American Flight 103 over Scotland, killing 259, including 189 Americans, and two Libyan terrorists were later charged with the act. One was found guilty of murdering the 259 passengers and crew "while acting in furtherance of the purposes of . . . Libyan Intelligence Services," representing "a victory for the international effort to hold terrorists accountable for their crimes" (*Patterns of Global Terrorism-2000*). The court concluded it had insufficient evidence against the second suspect.

In the late 1980s the Animal Liberation Front used arson to terrorize in Davis, California; Tucson, Arizona; and Lubbock, Texas, and in 1990 the Popular Liberation Party used arson and bombs in Puerto Rico. Islamic radicals used a crude bomb made with agricultural fertilizer in a 1993 attack on the World Trade Center in New York that killed 6, injured nearly 1,000 and caused an estimated $600 million in damage. This blatant, foreign-sponsored terrorism was viewed with alarm and disbelief, yet because the towers still stood, Americans went on with life with a suppressed sense of invulnerability, and the fear of terrorism faded rapidly.

Then in 1995 a 4,800-pound truck bomb exploded in front of the Alfred P. Murrah Federal Building in Oklahoma City, killing 168 and injuring 500. Not only was this the deadliest terrorist attack the United States had ever endured up to that day, it was carried out by two Americans, Timothy McVeigh and Terry Nichols, both espousing the beliefs of a right-wing militia. The United States now faced the threat of both domestic and international terrorism. That same year the derailment of an Amtrak train in an Arizona desert was linked to terrorists.

In 1996 another truck bomb destroyed a barracks housing American military personnel in Dhahran, Saudi Arabia, killing 19 servicemen. In 1998 two U.S. embassies in East Africa were bombed, killing more than 200 people, including 12 Americans. Twenty-two people were charged with the crime. At the end of 2000, one had pled guilty to conspiring in the attacks, five were in custody in New York awaiting trial, three were in England awaiting extradition to the United States, and thirteen were fugitives, including Osama bin Laden (*Patterns of Global Terrorism-2000*). As noted by Rogers (2000, p.84): "Usama Bin Laden is on the FBI's 10 Most Wanted List wanted in connection with the August 7, 1998 bombings of U.S. Embassies in Dar Es Salaam, Tanzania, and Nairobi, Kenya. . . . Usama Bin Laden represents a new breed of terrorist, capable of anything from biological warfare to spreading a computer virus."

Terrorism continued into the twenty-first century, and on October 12, 2000, 17 sailors died when two suicide bombers attacked the USS Cole while it was refueling in the Yemeni port of Aden. Then came September 11, 2001, the worst terrorist attack in the history of the United States, when terrorists hijacked four commercial airliners shortly after their take-offs, while they still carried great amounts of fuel. Two of the planes were crashed into the twin towers of the World Trade Center in New York, leaving 4,815 people missing and 417 confirmed dead, including the 157 passengers aboard Flight 11 and Flight 175. An hour later Flight 77 crashed into the Pentagon, leaving 189 believed dead, including everyone on board. Soon after that, another hijacked airliner presumed to be en route to either the White House or U.S. Capitol building crashed into a rural area in Pennsylvania, killing 44 aboard Flight 93 ("Lost But Not Forgotten," 2001). Among those missing or confirmed dead were 311 firefighters and 65 police officers ("IACP Response . . .," 2001, p.14).

September 11, 2001

"September 11, 2001 will go down as the bloodiest day in U.S. history with more deaths than the 4,000 plus who died in one day at Antietam or the 2,400 who died at Pearl Harbor" (Hackett, 2001, p.9). The Terrorism Research Center declared: "The attack of September 11 will be the precipitating moment of a new kind of war that will define a new century. This war will be fought in shadows, and the adversary will continue to target the innocent and defenseless." The Center outlined the effects of this attack:

> The President of the United States made it very clear in his September 20th speech to the Congress, the nation, and the world, that this threat has not achieved its objectives of fear. Rather, it has galvanized the United States into action. The U.S. now sees a national security threat raised to an unprecedented level. However, the U.S. also sees an opportunity to solidify international support and national unity to combat this threat. . . .
>
> This threat is not directed solely against the United States—it is a threat directed against all countries that seek freedom, peace, and stability. The world's response to terrorism will change not only international efforts with respect to terrorism; it will change geopolitics as countries take sides and see mutual interests where few were apparent before. . . .
>
> Adversaries of the United States will increasingly avoid direct confrontation with American interests. They will attack the soft underbelly of American society.

> They will exploit the benefits of a free society and remind the world of the risks that come with liberty, of the price of freedom. They will try to lessen the luster of America, but they will only succeed in fueling the flame of inspiration and opportunity the U.S. offers to people of the world. In their attempt to diminish the American spirit, they will find the best of what America and her allies have to offer, coming right at them.

Indeed, the horrific events of September 11 pulled together and unified the American people in a way most had never seen. Patriotism was suddenly popular again—Wal-Mart alone sold 88,000 American flags on September 12. Thousands of volunteers helped search for victims and donated blood and money. New York Governor George Pataki ordered nearly 3,000 National Guard troops and 200 state troopers into New York City, and an estimated 300 search-and-rescue dogs were flown in with their handlers from dozens of agencies ("A New 'Date . . .,'" 2001).

Why Did It Happen?

In 1996 the FBI established a Counterterrorism Center to combat terrorism. Also in 1996 the Antiterrorism and Effective Death Penalty Act was passed, including several specific measures aimed at terrorism. It enhanced the federal government's power to deny visas to individuals belonging to terrorist groups and simplified the process for deporting aliens convicted of crimes.

In 1999 then–FBI Director Louis Freeh announced, "Our No. 1 priority is the prevention of terrorism" (Rogers, p.86). The FBI added a new Counterterrorism Division with four subunits: the International Terrorism Section, the Domestic Terrorism Section, the National Infrastructure Protection Center and the National Domestic Preparedness Office. But this was not enough to avert the tragic events of September 11. As Anderson (2001, p.4) states: "Unthinkable is a word that describes the recent terrorist attacks. Many other words—gut-wrenching sadness and bitter anger, dull shock and utter disbelief—also come to mind. How could it happen? And who? And why? Definitely why?"

For one thing, U.S. immigration policies make it relatively easy for terrorists to enter the country and move freely within it. In fact, several people with connections to Osama bin Laden's al-Qaeda group received pilot training in the United States. In addition, Vincent (2001, p.26) contends that the terrorists took advantage of two major holes in the U.S. aviation security system: (1) a system fault in the FAA's Computer Assisted Passenger Profile System (CAPPS) and (2) in its permissiveness in allowing knives and small cutting instruments on board planes. Both American and United Airlines used the CAPPS system which should have singled out some, perhaps all, of the hijackers. But the security measures applied only to checked baggage. No process was in place to notify screeners at screening points when a person met the CAPPS profile. As Vincent notes: "The hijackers probably did not know that this hole existed, but they did know that knives with less than four-inch blades were permitted."

In addition, those doing the screening are usually undertrained, underpaid and tired, many having to work two jobs to support themselves. To maintain the steady flow of hurried travelers trying to make their flights, screeners are instructed to spend only three to six seconds on each item passing through x-ray. Any distractions make this task more difficult.

Who Is Responsible?

The FBI, lead agency investigating the attacks, has undertaken what Attorney General John Ashcroft describes as "the largest investigation in the history of the United States, probably in the history of the world" ("September 11 Terrorism . . .," 2001, p.1). Approximately 4,000 FBI agents and 3,000 support personnel were assigned to the case nationwide, and by early October, the FBI was handling more than a quarter-million potential leads and tips. It has sent 18,000 law enforcement agencies a list of more than 190 witnesses, suspects and others they want to interview and, in the two months following the attack, the Justice Department had arrested more than 1,000 people suspected of having links to terrorist groups ("Ashcroft Announces Plan . . .," p.2).

The United States government, with concurrence from Britain and other United Nations member countries, believes it has an airtight case against bin Laden and several other suspects. Although no direct evidence links bin Laden with drug trafficking, ample evidence implicates the Afghanistan Taliban government, which provided sanctuary and other aid to bin Laden, in receiving much of its funding from the opium trade.

On November 13, 2001, the *Washington Post* reported that Britain would release more evidence implicating bin Laden in the September 11 attacks. The new dossier, updating charges laid out by Prime Minister Tony Blair on Oct. 4, relies heavily on bin Laden's statements made in videotapes since military strikes began in Afghanistan ("Britain to Release More Evidence . . .," 2001, p.A13). In one videotape bin Laden is reportedly shown saying the September 11 hijackers were "blessed by Allah to destroy America's economic and military landmarks." He is also quoted as saying, "Yes, we kill their innocents, and this is legal religiously and logically." Another video shows bin Laden talking with associates in a relaxed atmosphere, reveling in the success of the deadly attacks and bragging he'd known about them beforehand. Saying the attacks "benefited Islam greatly," bin Laden expressed pleasure that the destruction had exceeded his expectations. Although the media have been urged to use restraint in broadcasting statements by bin Laden, his statements are now so extreme, they have value for the antiterrorism coalition.

The U.S. Response—Detect, Prepare, Prevent, Protect, Respond and Recover

In addition to an intense investigation, the United States initiated military action against Afghanistan after the Taliban government repeatedly refused to turn over Osama bin Laden. In addition, security was heightened at U.S. airports and throughout the country. As Sanow (2001, p.4) cautions: "While this is the boldest, least expected and most costly terrorist attack on U.S. soil, it is not the first and will not be the last."

In September, Attorney General Ashcroft announced that every U.S. attorney was establishing an antiterrorism task force to be conduits for information about suspected terrorists between federal and local agencies ("U.S. Antiterrorism Organization . . .," 2001, p.7). On October 8, 2001, President Bush signed Executive Order 13228 establishing the Office of Homeland Security to be headed by Governor Tom Ridge. The mission of the new office is "to develop and coordinate the implementation of a comprehensive national strategy to secure the United States from terrorist threats or attacks" ("President Signs Homeland . . .," 2001, p.8). As noted by Rohen (2001, p.148): "Command and control of a terrorist threat or incident is a critical emergency management function that demands an integrated and unified framework for the preparation and execution of plans and order."

At the federal level, the FBI is the lead agency for responding to acts of domestic terrorism. The Federal Emergency Management Agency (FEMA) is the lead agency for consequence management (after an attack). The Office of Homeland Security serves in a broad capacity, facilitating collaboration between local and federal law enforcement to develop a national strategy to detect, prepare for, prevent, protect against, respond to and recover from terrorist attacks within the United States.

In addition, the Office for Victims of Crime (OVC) has available the Terrorism and International Victims Unit (TIVU) to help victims of terrorism and mass violence (*Terrorism and International Victims Unit,* 2002). This organization provides training and technical assistance to first responders. It provided support to Oklahoma City in 1995 following the bombing of the Alfred P. Murrah Federal Building. After the attack on America September 11, 2001, TIVU played a key role in OVC's response to victims and their families in New York.

The importance of partnerships between law enforcement agencies at all levels cannot be overstated as they apply to the war on terrorism:

- Every act of terrorism occurring within the United States remains local in nature. . . . The FBI's activities cannot succeed without cooperation and assistance from local law enforcement agencies (Bodrero, 1999, p.13).
- Municipalities must work with the federal government in fighting terrorism; federal agencies cannot do the job alone. . . . The basis for any effective counter-terrorism effort is intelligence (Parks and Curreri, 2000, p.61).
- Local officers will be a critical element in the overall success of incident and containment since they will have the data on the area, offenders and early activities (Rehm and Rehm, p.40).
- The nation is embarking upon a new and vigorous fight against terrorism, and local police agencies must be full partners in these efforts (Wexler, 2001a, p.1).

The key to combating terrorism lies with the local police and the intelligence they can provide to federal authorities.

Indeed, as Wexler (2001b, p.1) asserts, success in this war will "require an improved relationship between local and federal law enforcement with respect to intelligence sharing and target hardening. . . . If we are to truly mount a major preemptive offensive then this relationship must evolve to one that recognizes the significant role of both local and federal agencies working collaboratively, sharing intelligence and developing joint strategies."

In October, Glasscock (2001b), president of the International Association of Chiefs of Police, sent a letter to the membership, which began:

> The United States has begun air and group strikes against the Taliban in Afghanistan, taking the war against terrorism home to its instigators.
>
> But the war against terrorism isn't limited to actions overseas, or even restricted to military actions. The fight against terrorism begins in our own back yards—our own communities, our own neighborhoods—and police chiefs need to prepare themselves, their officers, and their communities—the people they've sworn to protect—against terrorism.

On October 26, 2001, President Bush signed into law the Uniting and Strengthening America by Providing Appropriate Tools Required to Intercept and Obstruct Terrorism (USA PATRIOT) Act, giving police unprecedented ability to search, seize, detain or eavesdrop in their pursuit of possible terrorists, saying: "This government will enforce this law with all the urgency of a nation at war." Bush asserted that the nation had little choice but to update surveillance procedures "written in the era of rotary telephones" to combat today's sophisticated terrorists ("Bush Signs Law . . .," 2001, p.A17). The law expands the FBI's wiretapping and electronic surveillance authority and allows nationwide jurisdiction for search warrants and electronic surveillance devices, including legal expansion of those devices to e-mail and the Internet.

In defending the viability and constitutionality of "roving wiretaps," Attorney General Ashcroft stated: "We are not asking the law to expand, just to grow as technology grows. . . . Terrorist organizations have increasingly used technology to facilitate their criminal acts and hide their communications from law enforcement. Terrorists are trained to change cell phones frequently, to route e-mail through different Internet computers in order to defeat surveillance" ("Congress Debates Terror . . .," 2001, p.3).

The PATRIOT Act also includes money laundering provisions and sets strong penalties for anyone who harbors or finances terrorists. Senate Banking Committee Chairman Paul Sarbanes calls the PATRIOT bill the most significant money laundering legislation "since money laundering was first made a crime" in 1986, adding: "Osama bin Laden may have boasted 'Al-Quaeda includes modern, educated youth who are as aware of the cracks inside the Western financial system as they are aware of the lines in their hands,' but with [the PATRIOT legislation], we are sealing up those cracks" ("Congress Debates Terror . . .," p.3).

The PATRIOT Act also establishes new punishments for possessing biological weapons. Further, it makes it a federal crime to commit an act of terrorism against a mass transit system.

Civil libertarians, however, are concerned that valued American freedoms will be sacrificed in the interest of national safety. For example, the Justice Department has issued a new regulation giving itself the authority to monitor inmate-attorney communications if "reasonable suspicion" exists that inmates are using such communications to further or facilitate acts of terrorism ("Justice

Dept. Moves . . .," 2001, p.2). However, criminal defense lawyers and members of the American Civil Liberties Union (ACLU) have protested the regulation, saying it effectively eliminates the Sixth Amendment right to counsel because, under codes of professional responsibility, attorneys cannot communicate with clients if confidentiality is not assured. The ACLU has vowed to monitor police actions closely to see that freedoms protected under the Constitution are not jeopardized.

Another concern is that some Americans may retaliate against innocent people of Middle Eastern descent, many of whom were either born in the United States or are naturalized citizens. For example, in October 2001 four Iraqi passengers were asked to get off a plane because the other passengers were uncomfortable with their presence.

Two concerns related to the "war on terrorism" are that civil liberties may be jeopardized and that people of Middle Eastern descent may be discriminated against or become victims of hate crimes.

We must remember the Japanese internment camps during World War II and make sure we do not repeat that mistake. As one police officer said on the Internet:

> I want to remind all of you that those residents of our neighborhoods who are Muslim share in the horror of Tuesday's events. They too are our American brothers and sisters. They were our neighbors and friends when we went to sleep on Monday night and the events of Tuesday morning did not change that. They are still our neighbors and friends today. . . . Our fears and sadness and anger are theirs as well, but they must also have a fear all their own, a fear of how they will now be perceived and treated. Let us show them that we will not be ruled by fear and anger, but instead by compassion. . . . We are still a land of many cultures, a land founded on idealistic principles that has always tried to welcome any who come to her shores. That's what we do here in America. . . . Should we choose to forget who we are as Americans, the terrorists win. They shall not win.

Summary

A major threat facing our nation today is gangs. Distinguishing characteristics of gangs include leadership, organization, associational patterns, domain identification and illegal activity. Gang members might also be identified by their names, their symbols (clothing and tattoos) and how they communicate, including graffiti and sign language. The most common reasons for joining a gang are for belonging, identity or recognition, protection, fellowship and brotherhood or from being intimidated to join. Unemployment, poverty and general despair lead young people to seek out economic opportunities in the growing illegal marketplace, often within the context of gangs. However, family structure is probably the most important risk factor in formation of a gang member. Many believe the fight against gangs will be in vain unless equal efforts are made at wiping out drug use.

Drug use and abuse pose another serious threat to our nation. In 1914 the federal government passed the Harrison Narcotics Act, which made the sale or use of certain drugs illegal, including narcotics and other dangerous drugs. In most states narcotics and other dangerous drugs may not be used or sold without a prescription. Federal law prohibits sale or distribution not covered by prescription, but it does not prohibit possession for personal use. The most commonly observed drugs on the street, in possession of users and seized in drug raids are heroin, opium, morphine, codeine, cocaine, crack and marijuana. Arrest for possession or use of marijuana is the most frequent drug arrest. Although legal, alcohol, a depressant, is the most widely abused drug in the United States. Alcohol use is clearly linked to criminal activity, as is illicit drug use. The drug problem might be approached by crime control, punishment, rehabilitation, prevention or legalization. The "war on drugs" has been a top priority for the past decade; however, on September 11, 2001, this priority changed, and the war on drugs, at least for the moment, has taken a backseat to the new war on terrorism.

The threat of terrorism has become a reality in America. Most definitions of terrorism have common elements, including the systematic use of physical violence, either actual or threatened, against noncombatants to create a climate of fear to cause some religious, political or social change. The FBI classifies terroristic acts as either domestic or international. It is the lead agency for responding to terrorism. The Federal Emergency Management Agency (FEMA) is the lead agency for consequence management (after an attack). The Office of Homeland Security facilitates collaboration between local and federal law enforcement to develop a national strategy to detect, prepare for, prevent, protect against, respond to and recover from terrorist attacks within the United States. The key to combating terrorism lies with the local police and the intelligence they can provide to federal authorities. Two concerns related to the "war on terrorism" are that civil liberties may be jeopardized and that people of Middle Eastern descent may be discriminated against or become victims of hate crimes.

Discussion Questions

1. Do you think the gang problem is as serious as authorities claim?
2. Are there gangs in your area? If so, in what criminal activities are they involved?
3. What do you think might be done to reduce the gang problem? Is a hard or soft approach to gang activity the best approach to curtail criminal activity?
4. Which drugs pose the greatest problem for law enforcement?
5. If drugs were legalized, would law enforcement agencies benefit?
6. Should alcohol be banned in the United States?
7. What is the best approach to combat drugs?
8. Which is the greater threat—domestic or international terrorism? Why?
9. Does your police department have a counter-terrorism strategy in place? If so, what?
10. What type of terrorist attack would you fear most? Why?

InfoTrac *College Edition Assignment*

Use InfoTrac College Edition to help answer the Discussion Questions as appropriate.

- Use InfoTrac College Edition to research *alcohol* and *teen drinking.* Find and take the alcohol self-test. Did any of the results surprise you? If you feel comfortable doing so, be prepared to share your results with the class.

Internet Assignments

Select two assignments to complete.

- Search for the key words *youth gangs.* Locate information on gangs in the United States and in foreign countries. Outline the similarities and differences between these gangs. Be prepared to discuss your findings with the class.
- Go to www.whitehousedrugpolicy.gov and outline the *president's drug policy.* Be prepared to share and discuss your outline with the class.

or

- Go to www.whitehousedrugpolicy.gov/drugfact/pulsechk/midyear2000/midyear2000.pdf for more current data on *drug use* to update your text. Be prepared to share with the class the updated data you found.
- Go to www.zonezero.com/exposiciones/fotografos/rodriguez for a photographic history of *gang life* seen from the street. Take notes on this photo essay, and be prepared to share your notes with the class.

- Go to the Web sites of the DEA (www.dea.gov), the FBI (www.fbi.gov), the Department of Justice (www.usdoj.gov) and the Department of the Treasury (www.ustreas.gov) and note how the different agencies are addressing the issue of *terrorism.* How do their focuses differ? Be prepared to share your findings with the class.
- Search for *USA PATRIOT Act* (2001). List specific applications of the Act to law enforcement practices and explain how they might differ from conventional practices. Do you believe the phrase "extraordinary times demand extraordinary measures" justifies "bending the rules," so to speak, in the war on terrorism? In other words, do the ends justify the means? Should law enforcement be permitted to use roving wiretaps and breach privileged inmate-attorney communications in the name of national security, or is this the beginning of the end of our civil liberties? Be prepared to discuss your answers with the class.
- Go to www.policeforum.org and find "Local Law Enforcement's Role in Preventing and Responding to Terrorism." Read and outline the article. Be prepared to share your outline with the class.

 Book-Specific Web Site

The book-specific Web site at http://info.wadsworth.com/0534552803 hosts a variety of resources for students and instructors. Included are extended activities from each chapter in which students write a policy, use critical thinking skills to make choices in response to a given scenario, use InfoTrac College Edition with direct links to articles for participation in topical discussion forums, and analyze court cases using Web links for research. Many activities can be printed or emailed to instructors. Plus, cited cases with Web links, interactive key term FlashCards, PowerPoint presentations, chapter objectives, and an extensive collection of chapter-based Web links provide additional information and activities to include in the curriculum.

References

Abshire, Richard. "Treatment vs. Enforcement: The American Drug Dilemma." *Law Enforcement Technology,* May 1998, pp.32–39.

Addressing Community Gang Problems: A Practical Guide. Washington, DC: Bureau of Justice Assistance, 1998.

"The Administration Names Additional Foreign Drug Kingpins." *NCJA Justice Bulletin,* June 2001, pp.4–5.

AIDS Policy and Law (letter to "Executives"). Washington, DC: Buraff Publications, a division of The Bureau of National Affairs, Inc. (no date).

Anderson, Larry. "The Next Challenge: Defining the Industry's Post-Catastrophic Role." *Access Control & Security Systems,* October 2001, p.4.

"Ashcroft Announces Plan for DOJ 'Wartime Reorganization.'" *Criminal Justice Newsletter,* November 14, 2001, pp.1–2.

Bassiouni, M. Cherif. "Terrorism." *World Book Online Americas Edition.* http://www.aolsvc.worldbook.aol.com/wbol/wbPage/na/ar/co/551940, October 9, 2001.

Belenko, Steven; Peugh, Jordon; Califano, Joseph A., Jr.; Usdansky, Margaret; and Foster, Susan E. "Substance Abuse and the Prison Population: A Three-Year Study by Columbia University Reveals Widespread Substance Abuse Among Offender Population." *Corrections Today,* October 1998, pp.82–89, 154.

Bennett, Wayne W. and Hess, Kären M. *Criminal Investigation,* 6th ed. Belmont, CA: West/Wadsworth Publishing Company, 2001.

Bodrero, D. Douglas. "Confronting Terrorism on the State and Local Level." *FBI Law Enforcement Bulletin,* March 1999, pp.11–18.

"Britain to Release More Evidence Implicating Bin Laden in Attacks." *Washington Post,* as reported in the (Minneapolis/St. Paul) *Star Tribune,* November 13, 2001, p.A13.

Brown, Cynthia. "DARE Officials, Responding to Critics, Come Up with New Program." *American Police Beat,* April 2001, p.76.

"Bush Signs Law that Expands Police Powers." Associated Press, as reported in the (Minneapolis/St. Paul) *Star Tribune,* October 27, 2001, p.A17.

"Congress Debates Terror Bill's Effects on Criminal Justice." *Criminal Justice Newsletter,* October 30, 2001, pp.1–4.

Constantine, Thomas A. "NDPIX: The National Drug Pointer Index." *The Police Chief,* April 1998, pp.24–30.

Currey, G. David; Maxson, Cheryl L.; and Howell, James C. *Youth Gang Homicides in the 1990's.* Washington, DC: OJJDP Fact Sheet #03, March 2001. (FS-200103)

Decker, Scott H.; Bynum, Tim; and Weisel, Deborah. "A Tale of Two Cities: Gangs as Organized Crime Groups." *Justice Quarterly,* September 1998, pp.395–425.

Dill, Vicky Schreiber. *A Peaceable School.* Bloomington, IN: Phi Delta Kappa Educational Foundation, 1998.

Do Drug Courts Save Jail and Prison Beds? New York: Vera Institute of Justice, 2000. Available at www.vera.org/ssc

Domash, Shelly Feuer. "Youth Gangs in America: A National Problem Evading Easy Solutions." *Police,* June 2000, pp.22–30.

Domash, Shelly Feuer. "Stolen Dreams." *Police,* June 2001, pp.46–51.

"Drug Abuse Resistance Education Plans Test of a New Curriculum." *Criminal Justice Newsletter,* February 26, 2001, pp.2–3.

"Drug Cases and Sentences Increased Significantly, BJS Reports." *NCJA Justice Bulletin,* September 2001, p.13. Available at http://www,ojp.usdoj.gov/bjs/abstract/fdo99.htm

Drug Treatment in the Criminal Justice System. Washington, DC: ONDCP Drug Policy Information Clearinghouse Fact Sheet, March 2001. (NCJ 181857)

Ericson, Nels. *Substance Abuse: The Nation's Number One Health Problem.* Washington, DC: OJJDP Fact Sheet #17, May 2001. (FS-200117)

Esbensen, Finn-Aage; Deschenes, E. P.; and Winfree, L. Thomas, Jr. "Differences between Gang Girls and Gang Boys." *Youth and Society,* Vol. 31, 1999, pp.27–53.

Esbensen, Finn-Aage and Winfree, L. Thomas, Jr. "Race and Gender Differences between Gang and Nongang Youths: Results from a Multisite Survey." *Justice Quarterly,* September 1998, pp.505–525.

Esbensen, Finn-Aage; Winfree, L. Thomas, Jr.; He, Ni; and Taylor, Terrance J. "Youth Gangs and Definitional Issues: When Is a Gang a Gang, and Why Does It Matter?" *Crime & Delinquency,* January 2001, pp.105–130.

Farabee, David; Joshi, Vandana; and Anglin, M. Douglas. "Addiction Careers and Criminal Specialization." *Crime & Delinquency,* April 2001, pp.196–220.

"First Decade of Drug Courts Show Positive Results." *NCJA Justice Bulletin,* July 2000, pp.10–11.

Fritsch, Eric J.; Caeti, Tory J.; and Taylor, Robert W. "Gang Suppression through Saturation Patrol, Aggressive Curfew, and Truancy Enforcement: A Quasi-Experimental Test of the Dallas Anti-Gang Initiative." *Crime and Delinquency,* January 1999, pp.122–139.

Gang Awareness. Chicago: City of Chicago, Department of Human Services, no date.

Gang-Free Schools and Communities Initiative. Washington, DC: Office of Juvenile Justice and Delinquency Prevention, 2000.

Glasscock, Bruce D. "The Global Menace of Drugs." *The Police Chief,* June 2001a, p.7.

Glasscock, Bruce D. Letter to IACP Colleagues, October 16, 2001b.

Gondles, James A. "Human Heartache: The Other Side of Drugs." *Corrections Today,* October 1998, p.6.

"A G.R.E.A.T. Program: Stopping Gang Violence before It Starts." *Law and Order,* February 1999, pp.73–74.

Greenberg, Martin A. "A Drug Strategy for the New Millennium." *Law Enforcement News,* September 28, 2001, pp.9–10.

Greenfeld, Lawrence A. *Alcohol and Crime.* Washington, DC: Bureau of Justice Statistics, April 1998. (NCJ 168632)

Gustafson, Paul. "Authorities Crack Down on Asian Gang Accused of Raping Hmong Girls." (Minneapolis/St. Paul) *Star Tribune,* June 7, 1998, pp.B1, B9.

Gustafson, Paul and Estrada, Herón Márquez. "Convictions Merely Dented Gang Activity." (Minneapolis/St. Paul) *Star Tribune,* August 9, 1998, pp.B1, B7.

Hackett, Frank A. "The Horror and the Heroes." *The Law Enforcement Trainer,* September/October 2001, p.9.

Hall, Dennis. "Drug War Talk Sounds Tough but Who Is Really Winning?" *Police,* January 1998, p.6.

"Harvard Study Reveals that College Binge Drinking Continues to Be a Problem." *NCJA Justice Bulletin,* 2000, pp.4–5.

Heiskell, Lawrence. "Alcoholism: Equal Opportunity Disease." *Police,* June 2000, p.62.

Howard, Christine and Burke, Tod. "Train Gangs Today: Another Threat to Law Enforcement." *Law and Order,* October 1998, pp.117–120.

Howell, James C. *Youth Gangs: An Overview.* Washington, DC: Office of Juvenile Justice and Delinquency Prevention, August 1998. (NCJ 167249)

Howell, James C. *Youth Gang Programs and Strategies.* Washington, DC: National Youth Gang Center, August 2000. (NCJ 171154)

Huddleston, C. West. "Drug Courts and Jail-Based Treatment." *Corrections Today,* October 1998, pp.98–101.

Huff, C. Ronald. *Comparing the Criminal Behavior of Youth Gangs and At-Risk Youths.* Washington, DC: National Institute of Justice Research in Brief, October 1998. (NCJ 172852)

"IACP Response to the September 11 Terrorist Attacks." *The Police Chief,* October 2001, pp.14, 182–184.

Jones, Jeffrey M. "The Impact of the Attacks on America." *Gallup News Service,* September 25, 2001. www.gallup.com

Jones, Tony L. "Weapons of Mass Protection." *Police,* December 1999, pp.42–45.

"Justice Dept. Moves to Monitor Inmate-Attorney Communications." *Criminal Justice Newsletter,* November 14, 2001, pp.2–3.

Kaplan, J. *Heroin.* Washington, DC: National Institute of Justice, Crime File Study Guide. U.S. Department of Justice, no date. (NCJ 97225)

Kash, Douglas A. "The Federal Forfeiture Adoption Option." *Police,* November 1998, pp.56–59.

Katz, Charles M. "The Establishment of a Police Gang Unit: An Examination of Organizational and Environmental Factors." *Criminology,* February 2001, pp.37–74.

Katz, Charles M.; Webb, Vincent J.; and Schaffer, David R. "The Validity of Police Gang Intelligence Lists: Examining Differences in Delinquency between Documented Gang Members and Nondocumented Delinquent Youth." *Police Quarterly,* December 2000, pp.413–437.

Kaufman, P.; Chen, X.; Choy, S. P.; Ruddy, S. A.; Miller, A. K.; Chandler, K. A.; Chapman, C. D.; Rand, M. R.; and Klaus,

P. *Indicators of School Crime and Safety, 1999.* Washington, DC: Bureau of Justice Statistics, 1999.

Klug, Elizabeth. "Inter Alia." *Corrections Compendium,* September 2000, p.32.

Krott, Rob. "Vietnamese Gangs in America." *Law and Order,* May 2001, pp.100–194.

Lanata, John. "Identifying and Interviewing Gang Members." *Law Enforcement Technology,* October 1998, pp.86–93.

Lesce, Tony. "Protecting Critical Infrastructures." *Law and Order,* September 1999, pp.95–98.

Leshner, Alan I. "Addiction Is a Brain Disease—and It Matters." *National Institute of Justice Journal,* October 1998, pp.2–6.

Lewis, John F., Jr. "Fighting Terrorism in the 21 Century." *FBI Law Enforcement Bulletin,* March 1999, pp.3–10.

Lipton, Douglas S. "Therapeutic Communities: History, Effectiveness and Prospects." *Corrections Today,* October 1998, pp.106–109, 146.

Looking at a Decade of Drug Courts. Washington, DC: Drug Court Clearinghouse and Technical Assistance Project, 1998.

"Lost But Not Forgotten." *USA Today,* October 8, 2001.

Luitweiler, David M. "International Cooperation Key to Success in Drug Wars." *The Police Chief,* September 1998, pp.41–46.

Maxwell, Sheila Royce. "Sanction Threats in Court-Ordered Programs: Examining Their Effects on Offenders Mandated into Drug Treatment." *Crime & Delinquency,* October 2000, pp.542–568.

McCorkle, Richard C. and Miethe, Terance D. "The Political and Organizational Response to Gangs: An Examination of a 'Moral Panic' in Nevada." *Justice Quarterly,* March 1998, pp.41–64.

Miethe, Terance D.; Lu, Hong; and Reese, Erin. "Reintegrative Shaming and Recidivism Risks in Drug Court: Explanations for Some Unexpected Findings." *Crime & Delinquency,* October 2000, pp.522–541.

Miller, Jody and Decker, Scott H. "Young Women and Gang Violence: Gender, Street Offending, and Violent Victimization in Gangs." *Justice Quarterly,* March 2001, pp.115–140.

Miller, Linda S. and Hess, Kären M. *The Police in the Community: Strategies for the 21st Century,* 3rd ed. Belmont, CA: West/Wadsworth Publishing Company, 2002.

Miller, Walter B. *The Growth of Youth Gang Problems in the United States: 1970–98.* Washington, DC: Office of Juvenile Justice and Delinquency Prevention, April 2001. (NCJ 181868)

Moody, Bobby D. "Staying Focused on the Dangers of Drugs." *The Police Chief,* June 1998, p.6.

Moore, Joan and Hagedorn, John. *Female Gangs: A Focus on Research.* Washington, DC: OJJDP Juvenile Justice Bulletin, March 2001. (NCJ 186159)

Moore, John P. and Cook, I. *Highlights of the 1998 National Youth Gang Survey.* Fact Sheet. Washington, DC: Office of Justice Programs, Office of Juvenile Justice and Delinquency Prevention, 1999.

Morrison, Richard. "Gangnet Helps Laptop Cops Snag Gang Bangers." *Law Enforcement Technology,* June 1998, pp.74–80.

Morrison, Richard. "Domestic Terrorism: How Real Is the Threat?" *Law Enforcement Technology,* January 1999, pp.18–19.

National Drug Control Strategy, 1998: A Ten Year Plan. Washington, DC: Office of National Drug Control Policy, 1998. (NCJ 168639)

National Drug Control Strategy—2000 Annual Report. Washington, DC: Office of National Drug Control Policy, 2000. (NCJ 180083)

National Drug Threat Assessment 2001: The Domestic Perspective. Johnstown, PA: National Drug Intelligence Center, 2001.

"A New 'Date Which Will Live in Infamy.'" *Law Enforcement News,* September 15, 2001, pp.1, 12.

"New Drug Use Statistics Prompt Need for Effective Treatment Alternatives." *Treatment Alternatives for Safe Communities (TASC) Reports,* Spring 1998, pp.1, 4.

Newport, Frank. "Morality, Education, Crime, Dissatisfaction with Government Head List of Most Important Problems Facing Country Today." *Gallup News Service,* February 5, 2001. www.gallup.com

Nilson, Chad and Burke, Tod. "Environmental Extremists and the Eco-Terrorism Movement." *ACJS Today,* January/February 2002, pp.1–6.

1998 National Youth Gang Survey. Washington, DC: National Youth Gang Center, November 2000. (NCJ 183109)

Nylén, Lars. "Legalizing Non-Medical Drug Use: The Swedish Experience." *The Police Chief,* February 1998, pp.32–35.

Parks, Bernard C. and Curreri, Joseph. "Terrorism and the Municipal Police Department." *The Police Chief,* March 2000, pp.61–63.

Patterns of Global Terrorism-2000. Office of the Coordinator for Counterterrorism, U.S. Department of State, April 2001. http://www.state.gov/s/ct/rl.../index.cfm?docid=2420&CFNoCache=TRUE&printfriendly=tru

"President Signs Homeland Security EO and Ridge Sworn In as Its Director." *NCJA Justice Bulletin,* October 2001, pp.8–10.

Pulse Check: National Trends in Drug Abuse. Washington, DC: Office of National Drug Control Policy, 2001.

Rehm, M. K. and Rehm, W. R. "Terrorism Preparedness Calls for Proactive Approach." *The Police Chief,* December 2000, pp.38–43.

"Research Breaks Stereotypes about Youth Gang Membership." *Criminal Justice Newsletter,* February 1, 2000, pp.2–3.

Robinson, Michael D. "Fighting Drug Legalization." *The Police Chief,* June 2000, p.7.

Rogers, Donna. "FBI Adds New Division to Prevent and Combat Terrorism." *Law Enforcement Technology,* May 2000, pp.84–88.

Rohen, Gary J. "Exercise 'Baseline' Training for Terrorism." *FBI Law Enforcement Bulletin,* January 2000, pp.1–7.

Rohen, Gary J. "WMD Response." *The Police Chief,* October 2001, pp.148–163.

Ronderos, Juan G. "Transnational Drugs Law Enforcement: The Problem of Jurisdiction and Criminal Law." *Journal of Contemporary Criminal Justice,* November 1998, pp.384–397.

Rowell, James D. "Kids' Needs and the Attraction of Gangs." *Police,* June 2000, p.35.

Sanders, Darrell and Constantine, Thomas A. "A Police Chief's Guide to the Legalization Issue." *The Police Chief,* February 1998, pp.23–30.

Sanow, Ed. "WTC: Where We Go from Here." *Law and Order,* October 2001, p.4.

Schennum, Tim. "Unfair Rap for DARE." *Law and Order,* August 2001, p.103.

Schofield, Daniel L. "Gang Congregation Ordinance: Supreme Court Invalidation." *FBI Law Enforcement Bulletin,* September 1999, pp.28–32.

"September 11 Terrorism Brings Changes in Law Enforcement." *Criminal Justice Newsletter,* October 15, 2001, pp.1–3.

Shelden, Randall G.; Tracy, Sharon K.; and Brown, William B. *Youth Gangs in American Society,* 2nd ed. Belmont, CA: Wadsworth Publishing Company, 2001.

Simonson, James M. *The Drug-Free Communities Support Program.* Washington, DC: OJJDP Fact Sheet #08, April 2001. (FS-200108)

Snyder, Nina. "Decriminalization of Dope Cases." *Police,* May 2001, pp.52–55.

Spergel, I. A. and Curry, G. D. "Strategies and Perceived Agency Effectiveness in Dealing with the Youth Gang." In *Gangs in America* by C. Ronald Huff, 1990.

Strandberg, Keith W. "Interview with Barry R. McCaffrey." *Law Enforcement Technology,* May 1998a, pp.54–55.

Strandberg, Keith W. "Waging War on the Street." *Law Enforcement Technology,* September 1998b, pp.62–66.

Strandberg, Keith. "Bioterrorism: A Real or Imagined Threat?" *Law Enforcement Technology,* June 2001, pp.88–97.

Street Gangs of Los Angeles County: A White Paper. No date.

Streit, Corinne. "The Increasingly Popular Club Drug: Ecstasy." *Law Enforcement Technology,* May 2001, pp.24–28.

Strong, Ronald L. "The National Drug Intelligence Center: Assessing the Drug Threat." *The Police Chief,* May 2001, pp.55–60.

"Substance Abuse Costs States $81 Billion Annually." *NCJA Justice Bulletin,* March 2001, pp.5–6.

"Taking a Different Road with First-Time Drug Violators." *Law Enforcement News,* February 28, 2001, p.5.

Terrorism and International Victims Unit. OVC Fact Sheet, January 2002. (FS-000276)

"Terrorism Fight Is Top Priority, Customs Commissioner Says." *Drug Enforcement Report,* Vol. 16, No. 24, 2001, p.1.

The Terrorism Research Center. http://www.terrorism.com/index.html

Trump, K. S. *Practical School Security Basic Guidelines for Safe and Secure Schools.* Thousand Oaks, CA: Corwin Press/Sage Publications, Inc., 1998.

"Truth, DARE & Consequences: Anti-Drug Program Officials Say Curriculum Needs a Makeover." *Law Enforcement News,* February 28, 2001, pp.1, 10.

"Underworld Dot-Coms: Gangs Staking Out Turf in Cyberspace." *Law Enforcement News,* October 31, 2001, p.7.

"U.S. Antiterrorism Organization Under Review; New Laws Being Considered." *NCJA Justice Bulletin,* September 2001, pp.1, 7–10.

Valdez, Al. "America's Promise a Possible Solution." *Police,* August 1998a, pp.84–87.

Valdez, Al. "Interpreting That Writing on the Wall." *Police,* April 1998b, pp.39–40.

Valdez, Al. "Using Technology in the War against Gangs." *Police,* July 1999, pp.52–54.

Valdez, Al. "Looking at a Year of Developments." *Police,* December 2000a, pp.53–55.

Valdez, Al. "Put Full-Service Gang Units to Work." *Police,* June 2000b, pp.54–55.

Valdez, Al. "Trying to Work Gangs: It's All about History, Infrastructure and, Today, Even the Internet." *Police,* June 2000c, pp.32–41.

Valdez, Al. "Biker Gangs: Crime on Wheels." *Police,* January 2001a, pp.46–48.

Valdez, Al. "East to West Gang Trends." *Police,* February 2001b, pp.49–50.

Vallee, Sarah. "Slash and Burn." *American Police Beat,* March 2001, pp.1, 40.

Vincent, Billie H. "What Went Wrong?" *Access Control & Security Systems,* October 2001, pp.1, 26–27.

Walker, Samuel; Spohn, Cassia; and DeLone, Miriam. *The Color of Justice: Race, Ethnicity, and Crime in America,* 2nd ed. Belmont, CA: Wadsworth Publishing Company, 2000.

Wallentine, Ken. "Drug Courts: A Change in Tactics." *Police,* April 2000, pp.54–56.

Weekes, John R. "America's War on Drugs: Unprecedented Success or Casualty of Failed Policy?" *Corrections Today,* October 1998, p.8.

Weisburd, David and Mazerolle, Lorraine Green. "Crime and Disorder in Drug Hot Spots: Implications for Theory and Practice in Policing." *Police Quarterly,* September 2000, pp.331–349.

Wexler, Chuck. *Local Law Enforcement's Role in Preventing and Responding to Terrorism.* Washington, DC: Police Executive Research Forum, October 2001a.

Wexler, Chuck. "Terrorism and Local Law Enforcement." *Subject to Debate,* September 2001b, pp.1–2, 4, 6, 11.

Cases Cited

Calero-Toledo v. Pearson Yacht Leasing Club, (1974)
City of Chicago v. Morales, 119 S.Ct. 18494 (1999)
United States v. Bajakajian, 524 U.S. 321 (1998)
United States v. Ursery, 518 U.S. 267 (1996)

Chapter 10

Issues Concerning Police Conduct

No one is compelled to choose the profession of a police officer, but having chosen it, everyone is obliged to perform its duties and live up to the high standards of its requirements.

—Calvin Coolidge

Do You Know?

- Whether police discretion is positive or negative?
- Whether minorities' encounters with police are proportional to their numbers in the general population? Whether discrimination or disparity may account for any disproportionality?
- When force should or should not be used?
- If use of deadly force is justifiable?
- The effectiveness or safety level of high-speed police pursuits?
- Whether civil liability is of much concern for modern police agencies and officers?
- What constitutes police corruption and whether it is common?
- What three areas can enhance police integrity and reduce corruption?

Can You Define?

corruption
deadly force
discrimination
ethics
excessive force
exculpatory evidence
force
homophobia
integrity
less-lethal force
liability
litigaphobia
pursuit
reasonable force

INTRODUCTION

Policing has several vital issues facing it in the twenty-first century. Some have existed for decades; others are relatively new. Each "Do You Know" presents more than facts—they present major issues that face policing because the questions have no correct answers. They are controversial. Notice also that some subjects, such as discretion, have been introduced earlier. The challenge of policing is stressed by Gaines and Cordner (1999, p.397) who say:

> Consider such issues as high-speed pursuits, use of physical fitness and intelligence tests in hiring, requirements that police officers have college degrees, increasing cultural diversity in the work force and in society, computer crime, gangs, domestic and international terrorism, the globalization of organized crime, police aid to developing democracies and so on. Because police organizations keep changing, technological developments occur more and more swiftly, and society keeps evolving, there should never be a shortage of new and interesting problems facing police or police administration.

This text has already covered some of these topics. This chapter focuses on issues related to how officers police—how they behave on the job—beginning with a discussion of police discretion. Next is a look at discrimination in enforcing the law based on a subject's gender, class or race. The critical issue of racial profiling is then examined, followed by discussions on use of force, police pursuits and civil liability issues associated with specific police conduct. The chapter concludes with a look at the issues of officer corruption, ethics and integrity.

Discretion

Discretion has been a theme throughout this text. Just as citizens can decide to obey the laws or not, police agencies and their officers can decide which offenses to actively seek to control and which offenses to simply ignore, which services to provide and at what level.

Police discretion is the freedom of an agency or individual officer to choose to act or not. Whether such discretion is positive or negative is an issue.

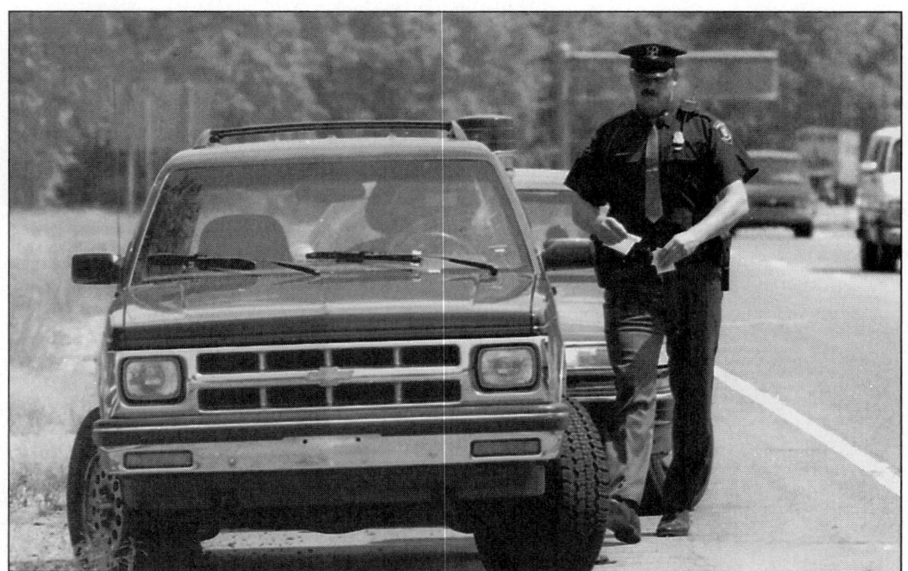

Richard Sheinwald/AP/Wide World Photos

The person receiving this traffic citation might be inclined to believe that this officer's discretion is not good. He may feel officers should be spending their time chasing "real criminals."

Any speeder who has talked a traffic officer out of issuing a ticket probably thinks police discretion is good. The person who receives a ticket, however, probably thinks the officer has erred in spending time chasing speeders rather than catching criminals.

Ramirez et al. (2000, pp.9–10) suggest that discretion can be viewed on a continuum from low to high. Low-discretion situations include those involving executing a search or arrest warrant, acting on a citizen complaint or seeing an obvious violation of the law, for example, a motorist going 10 miles over the posted speed limit, running a red light or driving recklessly. The officer usually need not ponder what action to take. High-discretion situations, in contrast, are much less clear cut, for example, failing to signal a lane change or perhaps even speeding to get to the hospital where a family member has just been brought to the emergency room. It is the high-discretion stops that invite both intentional and unintentional abuses.

As noted, one of the most important discretionary options police officers have is whether to arrest someone or not. If that decision is to arrest, then the discretionary power of the prosecutor comes into play, as summarized in Table 10.1.

The ability to use discretion is, indeed, a vital element of contemporary American policing and is at the heart of the issues discussed in this chapter. So, too, would any discussion of discretion be incomplete without recognizing the awesome power of citizen discretion. The less serious a crime is to the public, the less pressure is placed on police for enforcement. In addition, the wishes of complainants greatly influence police selective enforcement, often more than any other factor.

Police discretion is often at the center of issues involving discrimination, racial profiling, use of force and pursuit.

Discrimination in Policing: Gender, Class and Race Issues

"The guarantee to all persons of equal protection under the law is one of the most fundamental principles of our democratic society" (Gist, 2000, p.iii). When officers fail to treat equals equally because of economic status, race, religion, sex or age biases, discrimination occurs. Miller and Hess (2002, p.148) define **discrimination** as "showing a preference in treating individuals or groups

Table 10.1
Opportunities for Discretion

These Criminal Justice Officials	Must Often Decide Whether or Not or How to
Police	Enforce specific laws Investigate specific crimes Search people, vicinities, buildings Arrest or detain people
Prosecutors	File charges or petitions for adjudication Seek indictments Drop cases Reduce charges

Source: *Report to the Nation on Crime and Justice*. U.S. Department of Justice. Bureau of Justice Statistics, March 1988, pp.56–60.

or failing to treat equals equally. Some male traffic officers, for example, are known to issue warnings to females who violate traffic laws and to issue tickets to males for the same violation."

Gender Issues

The differential treatment of men and women by police is seldom raised as an issue. Why is it that so many more men than women are arrested and incarcerated? Do women commit fewer crimes, or are they given preferential treatment? No research has addressed this issue.

A gender-related issue that lacks much research is that of police attitudes toward gay individuals. Friction between the police and the gay community has been reported since the 1960s. Olivero and Murataya (2001, p.271) note: "Homicide in the gay community is a significant problem, with few law enforcement programs willing to address these problems. Moreover, those in the gay community are subject to assaults based solely upon their sexual orientation. . . . Currently there are calls for better police services for the gay community. This includes both better protection of gays and hiring members of the gay community as police officers."

What limited research is available has suggested police officers hold higher levels of **homophobia** than other sectors of society, that is, they are fearful of gays and lesbians (Olivero and Murataya). Based on such data, a line might then be drawn connecting officers who are homophobic to greater instances of discriminatory policing. Such officers may even engage in discrimination unconsciously. Of course, the research has not explored the issue this far, and such correlations remain pure speculation.

Class Issues

Another area receiving limited attention is discriminatory policing based on a person's economic level. Almost half a century ago, in *Griffin v. Illinois* (1956), Justice Hugo Black declared: "There can be no equal justice where the kind of trial a man gets depends on the amount of money he has." To many people, the O. J. Simpson double murder trial was a blatant example of unlimited financial resources being able to "buy" a not guilty verdict.

At the law enforcement level, those who are poor are much more likely to come to the attention of the police simply because they are on the streets more than those who are not poor. Many are homeless, and some of their behaviors, such as sleeping on park benches, have been made illegal, changing a social problem into a law enforcement problem.

Many poor people ride buses or trains—frequent targets of police sweeps for drugs. In West Palm Beach, bus sweeps over a 13–month period netted 300 pounds of cocaine, 800 pounds of marijuana, 24 handguns and 75 suspected drug "mules" (Cole, 1999, p.16). In one case a 28-year-old black man, Terrance Bostick, on his way from Miami to Atlanta, was asleep on a bus that had stopped in Ft. Lauderdale. Police officers boarded to work the bus looking for drugs. Wearing raid jackets with the Broward County Sheriff's Office insignia and displaying badges, one holding a gun, the officers awakened Bostick and asked to search his bag. Bostick agreed, and the officers found a pound of cocaine. Had Bostick been traveling in a private vehicle instead of a public transit vehicle, it is much more likely his illicit drugs would have gone undiscovered.

Bostick was convicted, and on appeal the case found its way to the Florida Supreme Court, which overturned the conviction. His lawyer argued that given the circumstances, most reasonable people would not feel free to ignore the police's request. Further, no reasonable person would agree to allowing a search of a bag containing cocaine. The case then went to the U.S. Supreme Court, which overturned the Florida Supreme Court decision. Cole (p.19) explains:

> The mere fact that they [the officers] had boarded the bus en route, were standing over him, blocking his exit, displaying badges and a gun and directing questions at him was not enough.
>
> The consequence of *Florida v. Bostick* [1991] is that police are free to engage in dragnet-like searches of buses and trains, in settings where it is extremely difficult for any citizen to refuse to cooperate.

And if a poor person does have a vehicle, it is often in need of repair, resulting in the person being ticketed for faulty equipment. Unfortunately, as Cox (2001, p.64) suggests: "Poverty is correlated with race and vehicle equipment violations so it can be expected that some police departments will disproportionately stop minority drivers for a lack of proper equipment."

Racial Issues

Walker et al. (2000, p.87) assert this country has a long history of conflict between the police and minorities and cite various studies supporting the existence of arrest discrimination.

> Racial and ethnic minorities are arrested, stopped and questioned, and shot and killed by the police out of all proportion to their representation in the population. There is much controversy over whether study results indicate a pattern of systematic *discrimination* or a *disparity* that is related to other factors such as involvement in crime (Walker et al., pp.87, 99).

In a discussion entitled "The Color of Reasonable Suspicion and Quality-of-life Policing," Cole (pp.41–42) gets readers thinking:

> In 1993, Reverend Jesse Jackson told a Chicago audience, "There is nothing more painful to me at this stage in my life than to walk down the street and hear footsteps and start thinking about robbery—then look around and see somebody white and feel relieved. Jackson is not alone. . . . As Professor Jody Armour has put it, "it is unrealistic to dispute the depressing conclusion that, for many Americans, crime has a black face."
>
> If this is true of a majority of Americans, is there any reason to believe that it is less true of American police officers? A police officer who considers the racial makeup of the prison population might rationally conclude that blacks are more likely to commit crime than whites. . . . But that it may be rational does not make it right.

Discrimination based on a person's race has come to the forefront of policing in the issue of racial profiling.

Racial Profiling

"Racial profiling continues to be one of the most critical issues facing law enforcement" (Meek, 2001, p.91). Racial profiling is defined by Ramirez et al. (p.3) as "any police-initiated action that relies on the race, ethnicity, or national origin rather than the behavior of an individual or information that leads the police to a particular individual who has been identified as being, or having been, engaged in criminal activity." According to the National Criminal Justice Association ("The Racial Profiling . . .," 2001, pp.8, 13):

> Racial profiling is a hot button issue for law enforcement today. Extensive media coverage of alleged use of racial profiling by police officers has not only caused many to believe the practice is deeply rooted, it has also helped to tarnish the minority community's trust in law enforcement. . . .
>
> Law enforcement officials say that honest discussion on the issue of racial profiling cannot take place without acknowledging that police officers are under tremendous pressure to crack down on drug use and trafficking. In addition, according to several federal intelligence reports, minority groups do, in fact, dominate cocaine and marijuana trafficking and often transport narcotics on highways.

In an address to a joint session of Congress on February 27, 2001, the sole criminal justice issue addressed by President Bush was racial profiling: "Too many of our citizens have cause to doubt our nation's justice, when the law points a finger of suspicion at groups instead of individuals. All our citizens are created equal, and must be treated equally" ("Bush and Ashcroft Announce . . .," 2001, pp.2–3). The president called on Attorney General Ashcroft to address this issue. At a press conference two days later, Ashcroft stated that racial profiling causes "a compound fracture" in the criminal justice system, hurting the victim and "injuring the trust that communities need to have in order to participate in law enforcement." Jaeger (2001, p.6) notes the American Civil Liberties Union (ACLU) has also taken up the cause, launching a Web site to raise awareness of racial profiling and to fight the practice (www.aclu.org/profiling).

The Police Executive Research Forum (PERF) surveyed more than 1,000 agency executives nationwide, reviewed materials of over 250 agencies, reviewed published literature and conferred with subject matter experts to generate a report on the issue of racial profiling, which concluded: "According to recent national surveys, the majority of white, as well as black, Americans say that racial profiling is widespread in the United States today" (Fridell et al., 2001, p.3). The report replaces the term *racial profiling* with *racially biased policing,* stating that use of the word *profiling* creates confusion about an "otherwise legitimate policing term." As Labbe (2001, p.25) insists: "Police have a mandate to battle crime. They use the tools they know work and profiling is one of them."

It is hoped use of the term *racially biased policing* will eliminate such criticism. According to the introduction to the PERF report (p.1):

> American policing is facing a tremendous challenge—a wide-spread perception that the police are routinely guilty of bias in how they treat racial minorities. This comes at a time when crime rates have fallen almost everywhere in recent years, and when the police might otherwise be celebrating their contribution to reducing crime and creating safe communities. Instead, the police find themselves baffled and defensive. . . .
>
> We believe that the vast majority of law enforcement in this country are hard-working men and women who are committed to serving all members of our communities with equity and dignity. Yet the challenges of addressing racially

> biased policing, and perceptions thereof, clearly indicate that police must do more to address the concerns of minority citizens.

Labbe (p.37) says the nation's war on drugs is the number one culprit behind accusations of racial profiling and quotes the director of the Criminal Justice Center for the National Center for Policy Analysis as saying: "It's an unpleasant fact that blacks are disproportionately involved in the drug trade. Cops aren't out to get blacks so much as to get drug dealers, creating collateral damage for black motorists." Labbe concludes: "To allow political correctness to disarm police of an important law enforcement tool on the grounds of unfounded claims of racism is criminal." The dilemma facing police when considering a subject's race is explained well by Ramirez et al. (p.3): "There is almost uniform consensus on two corollary principles . . . : police may not use racial or ethnic stereotypes as factors in selecting whom to stop-and-search, and police may use race or ethnicity to determine whether a person matches a specific description of a particular suspect."

The more recent war on terrorism has again highlighted the conflict law enforcement faces when using race to identify criminal suspects. Nislow (2001, p.11) contends: "After years of enduring harsh criticism and suspicion from the public for alleged racial profiling practices, law enforcement in the aftermath of the World Trade Center disaster has suddenly found itself on the high road, as some who once considered the practice taboo are now eager for police to bend the rules when it comes to Middle Easterners." To illustrate, a *Los Angeles Times* poll conducted shortly after September 11, 2001, showed 68 percent of respondents favored law enforcement "randomly stopping people who may fit the profile of suspected terrorists."

Yet, despite the pronounced shift in the public's apparent tolerance for profiling, police remain bound by the Constitution and the requisite cause for making a stop. According to one scholar: "You can't say all of a sudden that the wrongness of making stops based purely on ethnicity, race, color or age isn't true anymore. It's still true" (Nislow, p.11). A police chief contends: "We are a nation under attack at the moment, and we are preparing for war, but the values of a police department don't change" (Nislow, p.11). Another police administrator asserts: "Racial profiling has never been right, and it's not right now. There is no circumstance where you do away with someone's individual rights, because that leads to chaos" (Nislow, p.11).

In PERF's model policy for responding to race-based policing, consideration of Arab ethnicity is acceptable within the context of current circumstances as long as reasonable suspicion and probable cause exist (Nislow, p.11):

> Along a continuum of approaches, the policy goes a step beyond the more restrictive suspect-specific approach, which says race and ethnicity can be used only when police have a particular description. . . .
>
> [The PERF policy] "would allow you to take into consideration [that] we've just had terrorism, every person involved was of Middle Eastern descent, we don't know who we're looking for but we have some key behavioral cues and we know these people are overwhelmingly Middle Eastern."

In the PERF report foreword, Wexler (2001, pp.x–xi) outlines the three themes behind the recommendations made: "First, racially biased policing is at its core a human rights issue . . . antithetical to democratic policing. . . . Second, racially biased policing is not solely a 'law enforcement problem,' but rather a problem that can be solved only through police-citizen partnerships based on mutual trust and respect." The final theme, and the reason underlying publication of the report, is that "police personnel around the country want to respond effectively to local and national concerns regarding racially biased policing."

In October, 2001, the Supreme Court refused to hear the only remaining case docketed for the year concerning an equal protection claim in a case where police officers stop persons based primarily on racial or ethnic descriptions, in effect, upholding the ruling of the U.S. Court of Appeals for the Second Circuit in *Brown v. City of Oneonta.* As Spector (2002, p.10) explains: "The court held that where law enforcement officials possess a description of a criminal suspect that consists primarily of the suspect's race and gender, and where they do not have other evidence of discriminatory intent, they can act on the basis of that description without violating the Equal Protection Clause of the Fourteenth Amendment."

The court noted that subjecting officers to an equal protection strict-scrutiny analysis in making investigative detentions or arrests could hinder police work. Officers fearful of personal liability might fail to act when they are expected to. The court held: "Police work, as we know it, would be impaired and the safety of all citizens compromised. . . . The most vulnerable and isolated would be harmed the most. And, if police effectiveness is hobbled by special racial rules, residents of inner cities would be harmed most of all."

One way departments are approaching the problem is through data collection, and more than a dozen states have legislation requiring law enforcement agencies to record data on traffic stops (Carrick, 2001, p.79). However, as Rivera (2001, p.85) cautions: "The broadest issue with data collection is one that is often missed: collection is simply a process focusing on a symptom and not a solution to the problem. Data collection is a crucial first step in the right direction." Furthermore, data collection and *effective analysis* can be costly. In addition, all policies and procedures and all training materials should be reviewed for bias. And citizens should be involved in both the review and the data collection and analysis.

Closely related to the issue of racially biased policing is the perception that police use force more often with minorities than with whites. Indeed, the issue of police use of force on any citizen can become an issue.

Use of Force—When Is It Excessive?

English philosopher Herbert Spencer proclaimed in 1851: "Policemen are soldiers who act alone; soldiers are policemen who act in unison." As solitary soldiers the police are justified in using force when required to control crime and keep the peace in our society. Lathrop (2000, p.19) notes: "Use of force has become an ever-increasing area of concern for law enforcement professionals and the public they serve." The IACP defines **force** as "that amount of effort required by police to compel compliance from an unwilling subject" (*Police Use of Force . . .*, 2001, p.1).

If there is no resistance, no force should be used.

The IACP's model policy on police use of force states (IACP, 1995, p.1):

> This department recognizes and respects the value and special integrity of each human life. In vesting police officers with the lawful authority to use force to protect the public welfare, a careful balancing of all human interests is required. Therefore, it is the policy of this department that police officers shall use only that force that is reasonably necessary to bring an incident under control, while protecting the lives of the officer or another.

Langan et al. (2001, p.2) note that force includes contacts in which police officers pushed, grabbed, kicked or hit a citizen. Hitting is defined as striking with a hand or an object held in the officer's hand. Force also includes police dog bites, unconsciousness-rendering holds, handcuffs and leg restraints, chemical agents (pepper spray, Cap-Stun), electrical devices (Taser) and a firearm pointed in a citizen's direction or the threat to carry out any of these types of force. It goes without saying that the killing of a subject by an officer is the most extreme use of police force.

The IACP (*Police Use of Force . . .*, p.i) reports: "Police used force at a rate of 3.61 times per 10,000 calls-for-service. This translates to a rate of use of force of 0.0361%. Expressed another way, police did not use force 99.9639% of the time." According to this report (p.ii), from 1999 to 2000 the most common force used by officers was physical force, followed by chemical force and then impact. Arrests were the most frequent circumstance in which force was used, followed by disturbances, as shown in Figure 10.1. The IACP (p.iv) also notes that, from 1995 to 2000, 8,148 reported incidents included racial descriptors for both the involved officers and subjects, of which:

- 44 percent involved white officers using force on African-American subjects.
- 39 percent involved white officers using force on white subjects.
- 7 percent involved African-American officers using force on African-American subjects.
- 3.4 percent involved African-American officers using force on white subjects.

In certain situations, such as in disciplining children, performing investigatory stops and acting in self-defense or in defense of property, laws have been developed to help define use of force boundaries. For example when force is used for self-protection, four elements must be established for a defendant to successfully claim to have acted in self-defense (Territo et al., 1998, p.465):

- The belief that the force used was necessary for the defendant's own protection.

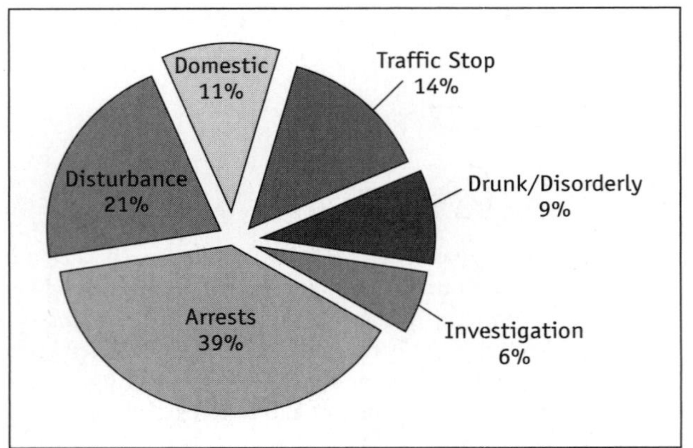

Figure 10.1
Percent of Officer Use of Force by Circumstance of Encounter (1999–2000)

Source: *Police Use of Force in America 2001*. Alexandria, VA: International Association of Chiefs of Police, 2001, p.iii. Reprinted by permission.

- The belief that the threat of harm was imminent.
- Proof that the threatened harm was unlawful.
- The force used by the defendant must have been reasonable.

According to the IACP (p.iv): "Subject intoxication appears to be a substantial predictor of police use of force during traffic stops. . . . 46% of all use of force incidents occurred where the subject was intoxicated or under the influence of drugs." The IACP (p.18) also found that officers with a college education tended to use less force of all types than officers with only a high school education.

Use of force exists along a continuum that officers may move up or down, depending on the situation or the "totality of circumstances."

The Use of Force Continuum

Connor (1991, p.30) notes that the amount of force used can be placed on a continuum: no force—used with a cooperative person; to ordinary force—used with a person who is resisting; to extraordinary force—used with a person who is assaultive. One use of force continuum is shown in Figure 10.2.

The Use of Force Model currently used by the Federal Law Enforcement Training Center (FLETC) closely parallels Connor's continuum (Nowicki, 2001b, p.35). The first level is the Compliant Level where the subject is cooperative. At the second level (Resistive Passive), no physical energy is expended by the subject, but the subject does not follow the officer's commands. The third level (Resistive Active) is where the subject expends energy to actively resist the arrest, for example grabbing hold of something and refusing to let go. The fourth level is the Assaultive (Bodily Harm) Level, where the subject physically attacks the officer or others. The fifth level is the Assaultive (Serious Bodily Harm or Death) Level where officers believe serious bodily injury or death is threatened.

As Rogers (2001, p.82) stresses: "Agencies need to have a continuum and officers need to be able to articulate it." Concurring, Lathrop (p.17) notes:

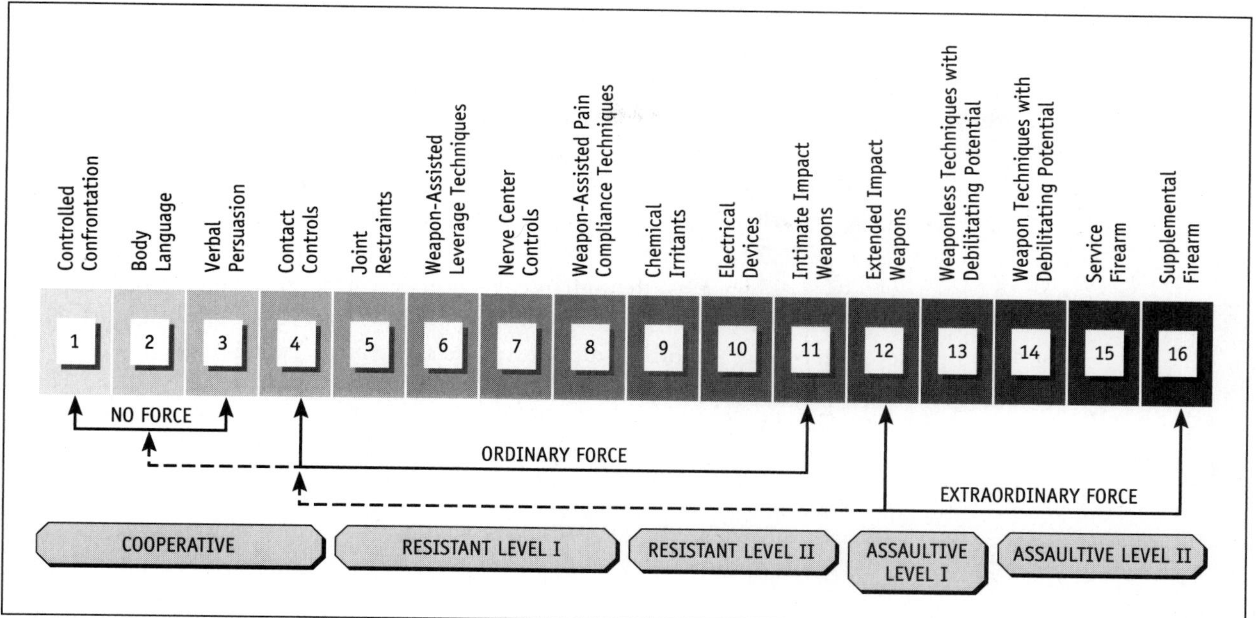

Figure 10.2
Use of Force Continuum

Source: Adapted from G. Connor. "Use of Force Continuum: Phase II." *Law and Order,* March 1991, p.30. Reprinted by permission of *Law and Order* Magazine.

"Many different types of a force option continuum exist. Every law enforcement agency should establish one that fits their needs and use it as part of the review process." He stresses: "Officers must use only the level and amount of force reasonably necessary to accomplish a law enforcement objective."

Reasonable Force

What constitutes **reasonable force** is established in *Graham v. Connor* (1989). In this case Graham, a diabetic, asked a friend to drive him to a store for some orange juice to counteract an insulin reaction. The friend agreed, but when Graham entered the store, he saw a long checkout line and, concerned about the delay, hurried out of the store to ask the friend to take him someplace else. Officer Connor, seeing Graham hastily enter and leave the store, grew suspicious and followed their car. Half a mile from the store, Connor made an investigative stop. Although the friend told Connor that Graham was simply suffering from a "sugar reaction," the officer ordered the two men to wait while he found out what, if anything, had happened at the store. When the officer returned to his patrol car to request backup, Graham got out of the car and passed out on the curb.

Moments later a number of other officers arrived on the scene. One officer rolled Graham over on the sidewalk and cuffed his hands tightly behind his back, ignoring the friend's pleas to get Graham some sugar. Several officers then lifted Graham up, carried him over to the friend's car, and placed him face down on its hood. Regaining consciousness, Graham asked the officers to check his wallet for a diabetic decal. One officer told him to "Shut up" and shoved

Graham's face against the hood of the car. Four officers grabbed Graham and threw him headfirst into the police car. Another friend of Graham's brought some orange juice to the car, but the officers refused to let him have it. Finally Officer Connor received a report that Graham had done nothing wrong at the store, and the officers drove him home and released him.

During this encounter Graham sustained a broken foot, cuts on his wrists, a bruised forehead and an injured shoulder. He also claimed to have developed a loud, permanent ringing in his right ear. Graham filed a lawsuit under 42 U.S.C. §1983 against the individual officers involved in the incident, alleging they had used excessive force in making the investigatory stop. The Court, however, ruled that the officer did not use excessive force, explaining:

> The calculus of reasonableness must embody allowance for the fact that police officers are often forced to make split-second judgments—in circumstances that are tense, uncertain, and rapidly evolving—about the amount of force that is necessary in a particular situation. . . . The reasonableness of a particular use of force must be judged from the perspective of a reasonable officer on the scene, rather than with the 20/20 vision of hindsight.

According to del Carmen and Walker (2001, p.174): "This case gives police officers a 'break' in civil liability cases involving the use of force . . . [by recognizing] that police officers often make split-second judgments in situations that involve their own lives and must, therefore, be judged in the context of 'a reasonable officer at the scene.' This is a test most police officers welcome."

Less-Lethal Force

As law enforcement technology expands, a wider variety of response options are becoming available to officers. For instances where an increased level of force is necessary but deadly force is too extreme, there are now a variety of **less-lethal force** alternatives. Common less-lethal options include Mace, CN and CS tear gas, oleoresin capsicum (OC) pepper spray, the Taser, projectile launchers and specialty impact munitions such as beanbags and flexible baton rounds, designed to deliver blunt trauma.

According to Heal (2000, p.76): "At present, the most common [less-lethal weapons] are kinetic-dependent devices. These devices employ kinetic energy, almost always in the form of a projectile, to inflict sufficient pain to cause compliance. They take the form of lead shot-filled pads (commonly called 'beanbags' or 'stun bags'), fin-stabilized rubber projectiles, hard rubber pellets, wooden dowels, and even liquid-filled bladders. They are fundamentally the same as their lethal counterparts but are simply bigger, softer and slower." Says Heal (2001, p.93): "When compared to the historical evolution of lethal munitions, the less lethal munitions in use today are the functional equivalent to the blunderbuss age: short-range, inaccurate and awkward." Nonetheless, use of these projectiles, commonly called extended range, impact munitions, continues to grow. According to James (2001, p.17): "The twelve-gauge pump shotgun and 'bean bag' round is the most common less-lethal system on the streets of America today."

Chemical agents such as CS and CN (tear gas) are less-lethal weapons effective for crowd control. Another effective chemical agent is OC (oleoresin capsicum) or pepper spray. According to Nowicki (2001a, p.28), it is effective in 80 to 90 percent of the situations in which it is used. OC can be delivered as a cone-shaped spray, a fogger, a stream, a splatter stream or foam. In many departments' force options, pepper spray is allowed when verbal commands are ineffective, even before control holds and impact weapons are suggested. Wallentine (2000, p.52) reports: "In the few legal decisions to consider this policy, courts find no fault with using OC to gain compliance when verbal commands fail." Current efforts to increase airline security include arming sky marshals with pepper ball guns that incapacitate a subject yet, unlike conventional bullets, will not puncture the plane's fuselage.

Capture nets are yet another less-lethal option, but they are difficult to deploy inside buildings or if a suspect is near a wall or other obstacle. In addition, once a suspect is ensnared, handcuffing and searching are difficult if not impossible.

A popular less-lethal weapon that has been in use for over 25 years is the stun gun, now called an electronic immobilization device (EID). One commonly used EID is the Taser, an acronym for Thomas A. Swift Electric Rifle (named after Tom Swift in the popular children's adventure series of the 1920s and 1930s). As Nielsen (2001, p.57) explains:

> Tasers are conducted energy weapons that fire a cartridge with two small probes (darts) that are connected to the weapon by high-voltage, insulated wire. When the probes contact the target, they transmit very short duration, high energy, electrical pulses along the wires to overwhelm the sensory nervous system, stunning the target. . . .
>
> Recognizing that even a single failure to stop is one failure too many, Taser International set out in early 1996 to create a less-lethal system that can stop focused combatants. The ADVANCED TASER was the result. . . .
>
> The 18 to 26 watt T-Waves cause an immediate, uncontrollable contraction of the muscle tissue. They're capable of physically debilitating the subject regardless of his mental focus or pain tolerance. . . .
>
> The accuracy of the advanced Taser is excellent. . . . In all cases, there has been virtual 100% instant incapacitation when the advanced Taser has been employed within its intended design parameters.

According to Jones (2001, p.70), the courts have approved use of this technology: "In *Caldwell v. Moore* the court evaluated evidence and ruled EID technology is less-lethal, non-injurious and represents a 'safety factor for all involved in comparison to hands-on tactics.'" And as Sanow (2001, p.4) contends: "Electronic force holds the greatest amount of technological promise for the future to halt violent conflicts with the least chance of injury to anyone."

A review of the effectiveness of less-than-lethal (LTL) force in suicide-by-cop incidents conducted by Homant and Kennedy (2000, pp.166–167) showed "a clear superiority of outcome associated with two LTL force approaches, instrumental and physical." The death rate for those in the combined LTL force categories was 55.6 percent compared to 89.2 percent in the negotiation and comparison categories combined. They found that the most successful tactic was physical force, generally wrestling the subject to the ground. However, this tactic also placed the officer at the highest level of risk.

K-9s as Less-Lethal Force

Dogs have been of tremendous help to law enforcement officers in locating and apprehending criminal suspects. This use, however, often requires the dog to apply force, at the handler's command, on the suspect and thus falls under the Fourth Amendment's requirement of reasonableness. As noted by Smith (2000, p.36), several court decisions around the country have indicated that law enforcement–trained K-9s are to be considered a less-lethal alternative—and safer—means of applying force.

In *Mendoza v. Block* (1994), the court ruled that the specific circumstances of a situation determine if the use of a K-9 is reasonable. For example, it is reasonable to send a K-9 after a fleeing suspect if that subject is believed to be armed and has ignored an officer's warning that a dog will be used unless the suspect surrenders. It is not reasonable, however, to sic a K-9 on a suspect who has fully surrendered or is already under complete control.

In *Robinette v. Barnes* (1988), where claims of unlawful use of deadly force were made after a suspect died as the result of a dog bite, the court held: "We do not dispute the fact that trained police dogs can appear to be dangerous, threatening animals. The dogs' ability to aid law enforcement would be minimal if they did not possess this trait. However, the mere recognition that a law enforcement tool is dangerous does not suffice as proof that the tool is an instrument of deadly force."

Less-Lethal Can Still Be Lethal

Debate has centered over the terminology applied to these weapons—should they be called *less-than-lethal, less-lethal, defensive, intermediate* or something else? Some use-of-force experts prefer the term *less-lethal* to *less-than-lethal* because of liability implications and misrepresentation of a weapon's lethality. Dorsch (2001, p.102) explains the dilemma such weapons pose for police: "If less lethal means are used, the officer can be sued; if an officer has less lethal ammunition but chooses not to use it, he can be sued." Borrello (2000, p.60) suggests the problem lies in the terminology: "What does 'less-lethal' mean? How can someone be less dead? Sarcasm aside, 'less-lethal' should mean that a weapon is lethal, just less lethal than another weapon, such as a firearm." He (p.61) notes: "These terms [*less-lethal* and *less-than-lethal*] create a trap for police officers and the agencies they serve and can be used for them or against them depending on the spin that can be attached in a litigation situation."

His (p.64) solution: "Use terminology that does not label or predict what the weapon will do in terms of lethality. Let the use of the weapon be dictated by the law, by training, by cutting edge policy and by the restraint and assessment of the officers who use the weapon." Borrello suggests so-called less-lethal weapons be called defensive weapons or intermediate weapons: "A defensive weapon can be anything used to protect an officer's life and an intermediate weapon's use can have any result dependent on its use by the officer."

Whatever term is used, it must be recognized that many of these alternatives *can* inadvertently cause death. While officers acknowledge the fatal possibilities that may accompany use of less-lethal force, there are times when officers are justified in using force they *know* will likely result in a subject's death.

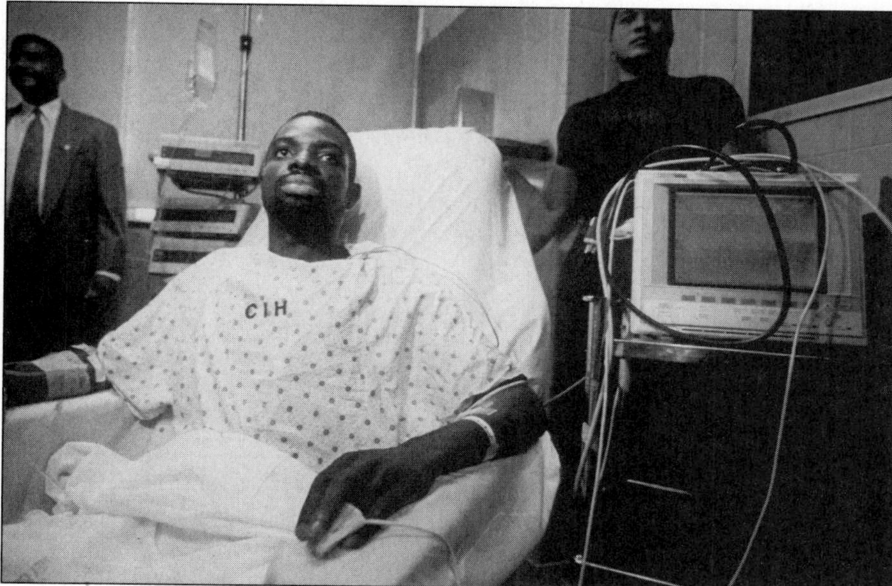

Photo by Stephen Ferry/Getty Images

Abner Louima received an $8.7 million settlement from New York City. Louima was arrested in a brawl outside a Brooklyn nightclub in 1997 and taken to the 70th Precinct stationhouse where Officer Volpe sodomized Louima with a broomstick. Louima sued for $155 million, claiming that officers conspired to create a "wall of silence and lies to obstruct justice."

Deadly Force

Authority of law enforcement officers to use deadly force is an awesome responsibility. When considering the justifiable use of **deadly force,** two interrelated rights are important: the legal right to use such force and the moral right compelling the officer to do so.

State legislators have generally given the police very broad discretion in this area, with most politicians fearful of being labeled as "soft on criminals" if they did otherwise. Many state statutes authorize use of deadly force to prevent commission of a felony. Yet, to balance the legal and moral rights involved, several states have adopted penal codes that do not rely solely on a crime being classified as a felony. They focus instead on the danger the suspect poses to the officer and society.

Justification for use of deadly force must consider not only the legal right, but also the need to apprehend the suspect compared to the arresting officer's safety and the value of human life.

A landmark Supreme Court ruling, *Tennessee v. Garner* (1985), bars police from shooting to kill fleeing felons unless there is an imminent danger to life. This ruling invalidated state laws (passed in almost half the states) that allowed police officers to use deadly force to prevent the escape of a suspected felon.

The case involved a 1974 incident in which a Memphis police officer shot and killed an unarmed 15-year-old boy fleeing from the police after having stolen $10 in money and jewelry from an unoccupied home. The officer testified that he shot the boy to prevent him from escaping. He had been trained to do so, and Tennessee law permitted him to do so. The Supreme Court ruled that the Tennessee "fleeing felon" statute was unconstitutional because it authorized use of deadly force against unarmed fleeing suspects who posed no threat to

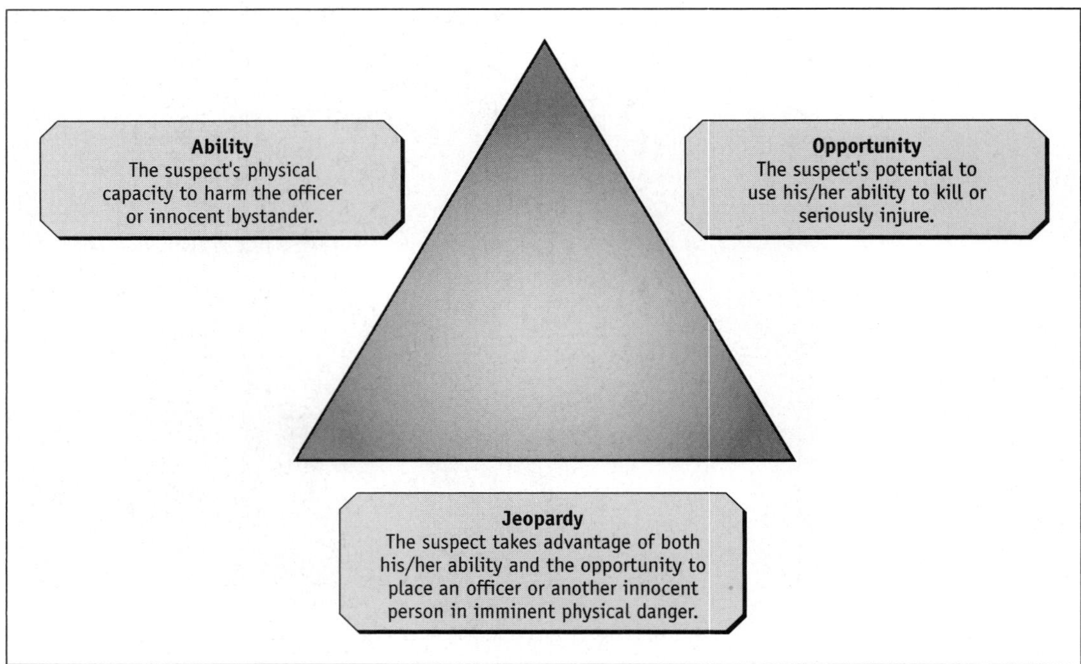

Figure 10.3
Decision Model: Deadly Force Triangle

Source: Dean T. Olson. "Improving Deadly Force Decision Making." *FBI Law Enforcement Bulletin*, February 1998, p.4. Reprinted by permission.

the officer or third parties. In effect, taking a life is a "seizure," which the Fourth Amendment states must be reasonable.

Olson (1998, p.1) notes: "As one of the most liability-prone activities in law enforcement, deadly force decision making tops the list of training priorities for many agencies." He (p.2) continues: "The deadly force triangle is a decision model designed to enhance an officer's ability to respond to a deadly force encounter while remaining within legal and policy parameters. The three sides of an equilateral triangle represent three factors—ability, opportunity, and jeopardy. All three factors must be present to justify deadly force." The deadly force decision model is illustrated in Figure 10.3. A summary of the law on the use of force is given in Table 10.2.

The amount of force police departments use and condone directly affects the public's attitudes toward the police. Excessive use of force has been a chronic complaint of minorities, particularly in the 1960s and the 1980s.

Excessive Force

The IACP (*Police Use of Force,* p.1) defines **excessive force** as "the application of an amount and/or frequency of force greater than that required to compel compliance from a willing or unwilling subject." According to their study excessive force was used only 0.42 percent of the time; excessive force was not used in 99.583 percent of all reported cases.

The IACP reports that from 1990 to 1999, men accounted for 80 percent of patrol officers but accounted for 95 percent of use-of-force settlements over $100,000 (Lonsway, 2001, pp.110–111). Women accounted for 20 percent of

Table 10.2
Summary of the Law on the Use of Force

Situation	Less-Than-Deadly Force	Deadly Force
In self-defense or in the defense of others	"The use of (reasonable) force upon or toward another person is justified when the actor (reasonably) believes that such force is immediately necessary for the purpose of protecting himself or herself (or another) against the use of unlawful force by such other person on the present occasion."[a]	"The use of deadly force is not justified . . . unless such force is necessary to protect . . . against death, serious bodily harm, kidnapping, or sexual intercourse compelled by force or threat."[b]
In the defense of property	"Only such degree of force or threat thereof may intentionally be used as the actor reasonably believes is necessary to prevent or terminate the interference."[c]	Under the old common law, deadly force could be used in the defense of property. All states now forbid the use of intentional deadly force in the defense of property.
To apprehend a person who has committed a crime	"When an officer is making or attempting to make an arrest for a criminal offense, he is acting for the protection of public interest and is permitted even a greater latitude than when he acts in self-defense, and he is not liable unless the means which he uses are clearly excessive."[d]	*Misdemeanor:* NEVER *Fleeing Felon:* Deadly force could be used when officers "have probable cause . . . to believe that the suspect (has committed a felony and) poses a threat to the safety of the officers or a danger to the community if left at large." *Tennessee v. Garner*
To stop a person for investigate purposes when only "reasonable suspicion" exists	Only such force that is reasonable and necessary under the circumstances that then exist	NEVER
Disciplining children (corporal punishment)	Only parents and other people having a status of *in loco parentis* to a child may use reasonable force "reasonably believed to be necessary for (the child's) proper control, training, or education."[e] Other persons (such as strangers or neighbors) may not discipline a child.	NEVER

[a]Sections 3.04(1) and 3.05(1) of the Model Penal Code.
[b]Section 3.04(2)(b) of the Model Penal Code.
[c]Section 939.49(1) of the Wisconsin Statutes.
[d]Restatement of Torts, Section 132(a).
[e]Restatement of Torts, Section 147(2), as quoted by the U.S. Supreme Court in *Ingraham v. Wright,* 429 U.S. 975,97 S.Ct. 481 (1976).
Source: Thomas J. Gardner and Terry M. Anderson. *Criminal Law, Principles and Cases,* 7th ed. Copyright by Wadsworth Publishing Company, 2000, p.127. Reprinted by permission.

the patrol officers but for only 5 percent of the settlements. Put another way, the ratio of male to female officers on patrol was 4:1, while the ratio of payouts for excessive force was about 19:1. Lonsway (p.111) concludes: "Female officers are not reluctant to use force, but they are not nearly as likely to be involved in the use of excessive force."

The U.S. Department of Justice has released a checklist for use in allegations of excessive use of force, noting that years of good policing practices and community trust can be jeopardized by a single act of, or perception of, police excessive use of force (EUF). The immediate steps to be taken are:

- Provide information promptly.
- Get an investigation underway promptly.

- Enlist the community's help and support.
- Anticipate and plan for the announcement of the results of the investigation.

One controversial type of force used by police is pursuit, which may result in injury or death for fleeing suspects, pursuing officers and/or innocent bystanders. In fact: "The role of vehicle pursuits in law enforcement ranks with police use of force as one of the most hotly debated public safety issues of our time" (Kerlikowske, 2000, p.vii).

Police Pursuits

According to Nugent et al. (n.d., p.iv): "Police throughout the country engage in hundreds of high-speed automobile chases every day. Enough of these result in serious property damage, personal injury, and death to make police pursuit a major public concern." They (p.1) define **pursuit** as: "An active attempt by a law enforcement officer on duty in a patrol car to apprehend one or more occupants of a moving motor vehicle, providing the driver of such vehicle is aware of the attempt and is resisting apprehension by maintaining or increasing his speed or by ignoring the law enforcement officer's attempt to stop him." Alpert et al. (2000, p.167) define pursuit more concisely as "a multistage process by which a police officer initiates a vehicular stop and a driver resists the order to stop, increases speed or takes evasive action, and/or refuses to stop."

While these definitions limit pursuits to actions involving vehicles and, indeed, most people think of high-speed vehicle chases when they hear a pursuit is in progress, the majority of "pursuits" are on foot. As Bohrer et al. (2000, p.10) point out: "Pursuing fleeing suspects constitutes a basic function of law enforcement officers. Because officers do this activity every day, they often become complacent about the dangers inherent in chasing suspects on foot and develop a false sense of security." They note: "A significant number of officers assaulted during foot pursuits had no plan of action other than arresting the suspect." Few departments have policies on foot pursuits and even fewer train in this area, instead focusing primarily on the execution and hazards of high-speed vehicle pursuit and whether such a pursuit should even be initiated.

To Pursue or Not to Pursue

The basic dilemma of pursuits is whether the benefits of potential apprehension outweigh the risks posed to police officers, the public and the suspects. According to a National Law Enforcement and Corrections Technology Center (NLECTC) bulletin, over 72 percent of police pursuits resulted in the successful apprehension of suspects. However, collisions occur in 32 percent of police pursuits. Twenty percent of the collisions result in property damage, 13 percent result in personal injury, and 1.2 percent involve a fatality. About 70 percent of all pursuit-related injuries and fatalities involve occupants in the pursued vehicle, 14 percent involve law enforcement and 15 percent involve innocent people (Paynter, 2000, p.144).

High-speed pursuits are both effective and dangerous.

Because of the high probability of damage to property and people not connected with the pursuit, many advocate discontinuing a policy of police pursuit. According to Alpert (1998, p.358): "Because most offenders are apprehended through hardhearted police investigations, many suspects who flee the police can be caught later without the risks of a high-speed pursuit." Others, however, contend that police pursuit serves a vital purpose, arguing that if lawbreakers knew they could simply drive away and the police wouldn't pursue, why would anyone ever stop? Many believe that with proper policies and increased officer training, pursuits should be allowed to continue.

To better understand the real benefits and risks of police pursuits, the Police Executive Research Forum (PERF) undertook a study that included prior research, a literature review and a national survey. Their report, *Police Pursuits: What We Know* (Alpert et al., p.1), begins: "Police pursuit driving is one of the most controversial topics in law enforcement today. Since the 1960s, researchers have focused on two juxtaposing positions in this debate—first, support for pursuit because of the need to enforce laws and apprehend violators, and second, opposition to pursuit because of the risk to public safety."

Their report includes the following findings and recommendations based on their research:

- The public overwhelmingly supports pursuits for serious crimes. This support echoes the results of earlier public opinion research on pursuit driving.
- Officers are conducting pursuits in a uniform pattern and making the same types of decisions.
- The more police cars that are involved in a pursuit, the more likely it will result in an accident.
- Three aspects of pursuit are agreed upon by law enforcement: (1) pursuits are dangerous, (2) pursuits must be controlled, and (3) involvement in a pursuit increases the participants' adrenaline and excitement.
- Increased excitement and adrenaline are likely to negatively affect driving decisions, are likely to impair the ability to drive tactically or intelligently, and are likely to affect what takes place after the pursuit has terminated and officers are physically apprehending suspects.
- The percentage of officers willing to pursue increase as the seriousness of the crime increases.
- The majority of officers said suspects flee because they have something to hide, but suspect data shows most offenders flee because they are under the influence of drugs or alcohol.
- Because police officers have discretion over the action that leads to a pursuit, the execution of a pursuit plan depends on the officers' attitudes, as well as their support for department policy.
- Nearly all the agencies (91 percent) reported having written policies governing pursuit situations. Nearly half reported having modified their pursuit policy within the past two years. Most of those (87 percent) had made the policy more restrictive.

Pursuit Policies

"First and foremost in the basics of vehicle pursuit," says Rayburn (2000, p.47), "is to have a good established policy that is well developed." Van Blaricom (1998, p.48) asserts: "There can be no doubt that high-speed pursuit is deadly force in just another form and should be treated the same from both a policy and practice perspective." As might be expected, pursuit policies range from a total ban on them to allowing officers complete discretion. Most policies suggest that factors to be considered include the offense, traffic conditions and weather conditions.

Many departments' pursuit policies include use of a pursuit continuum, similar to those established for use of force. Wisconsin, for example, has the following pursuit continuum (Wilczak, 2000, p.27):

- Presence: Marked squad
- Dialog: Emergency lights, siren, communication with dispatch
- Control: Multiple units, use of tire puncture strips/barricades
- Intermediate: Pursuit immobilization techniques, boxing-in, roadblocks (allowing for an escape route)
- Deadly Force: Pursuit immobilization techniques, roadblocks (complete blockage), ramming, shooting from a moving vehicle

Figure 10.4 illustrates another type of pursuit continuum going from simply trailing a suspect vehicle to ramming and use of firearms, depending on the known threat posed by the suspect as indicated by the behavior observed. Notice that "disengage as an option" is always present along the continuum. Such continuums make sense considering a large number of pursuits result from minor traffic law violations. Despite the possibility of such pursuits ending in a collision, the fact also remains that many pursuits result in the arrest of a felon.

Many pursuit policies use situational elements as the determining criteria in whether to initiate a pursuit, differentiating between serious offenses where officers have little or no discretion and a sworn duty to act and minor offenses where pursuit may be more discretionary. Wright and McCarthy (1998, p.52) identify these two classes of pursuit as imperative (Class I) and elective (Class II), the differences between which are explained in Figure 10.5.

Agencies often employ technology to make high-speed pursuits safer or eliminate them altogether. The most popular options are spike strips (tire-puncturing devices) and retractable barrier strips that can be remotely deployed so as to affect only the subject's vehicle. Strandberg (1998) also notes other technology that may reduce the risks of high-speed pursuits, including GPS tracking systems, aircraft intervention, vehicle-to-vehicle communication technology and traffic light warning systems to shut down traffic in an intersection through which the pursuit might pass. A major challenge, however, is that such technology must be designed for immediate deployment because: "More than half of the traffic accidents that occur during high-speed police pursuits happen during the first two minutes of the pursuit" ("Study: Spike Strips . . .," 1998, p.24).

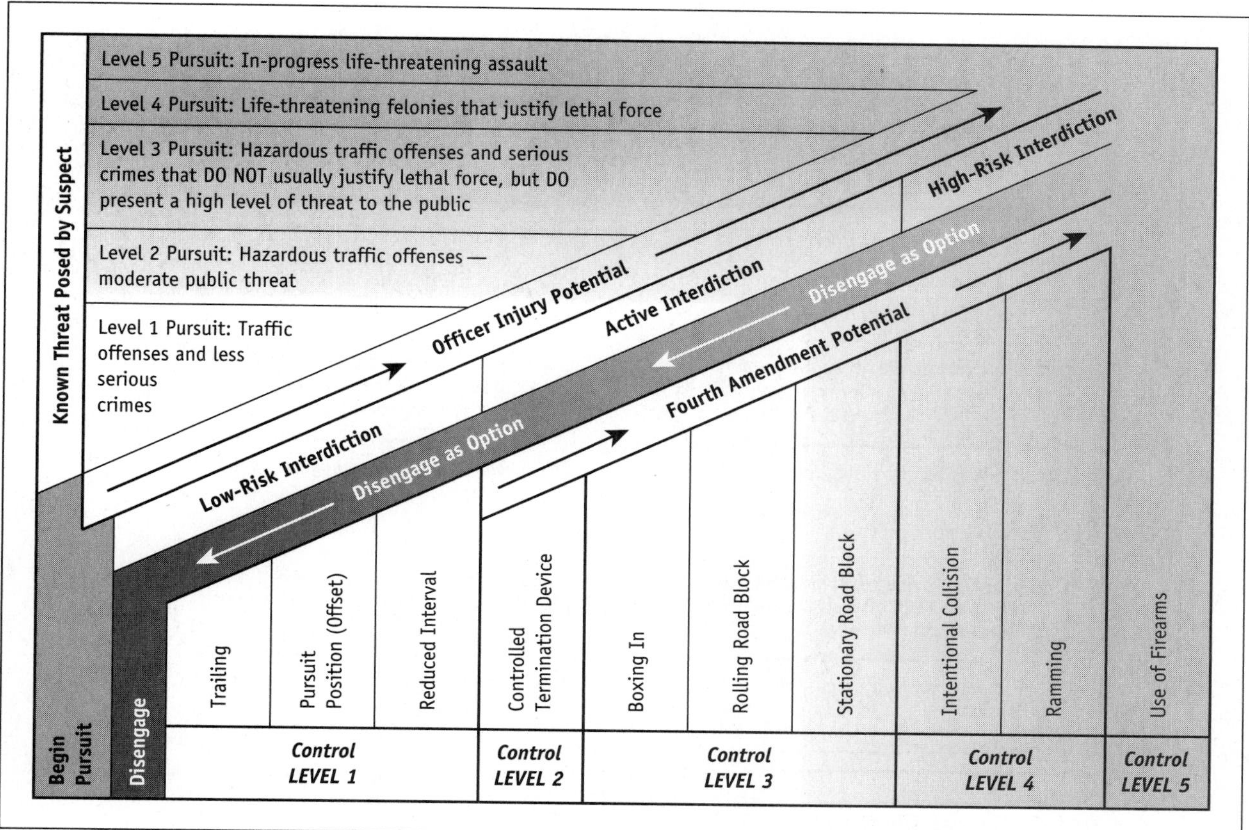

Figure 10.4
Pursuit Management Continuum

Source: Steven D. Ashley. "Pursuit Management: Implementing a Control Continuum." *Law and Order*, December 1994, p.60. Reprinted by permission.

In addition to sound pursuit policies, departments must provide training in use of the policy as well as in executing it. Without such training, departments increase their vulnerability to lawsuits.

Liability in Police Pursuits

Because so many police vehicle pursuits end in crashes, and some in fatalities, lawsuits are inevitable. Departments can, however, minimize the risk of lawsuits by creating a pursuit policy that balances the need to apprehend offenders in the interest of justice with the need to protect citizens from the risks associated with such pursuits (Pipes and Pape, 2001, p.16). Departments must also know what limitations and allowances state and federal statutes provide. For example, *Galas v. McKee* (1986) held that police pursuits were allowed to capture traffic violators. More recently, *County of Sacramento v. Lewis* (1998) set the standard for liability in police pursuits.

In the latter case 16-year-old Philip Lewis was a passenger on a motorcycle driven by 18-year-old Brian Willard. When Willard committed a traffic violation, a Sacramento County sheriff's deputy tried to stop the motorcycle, but the

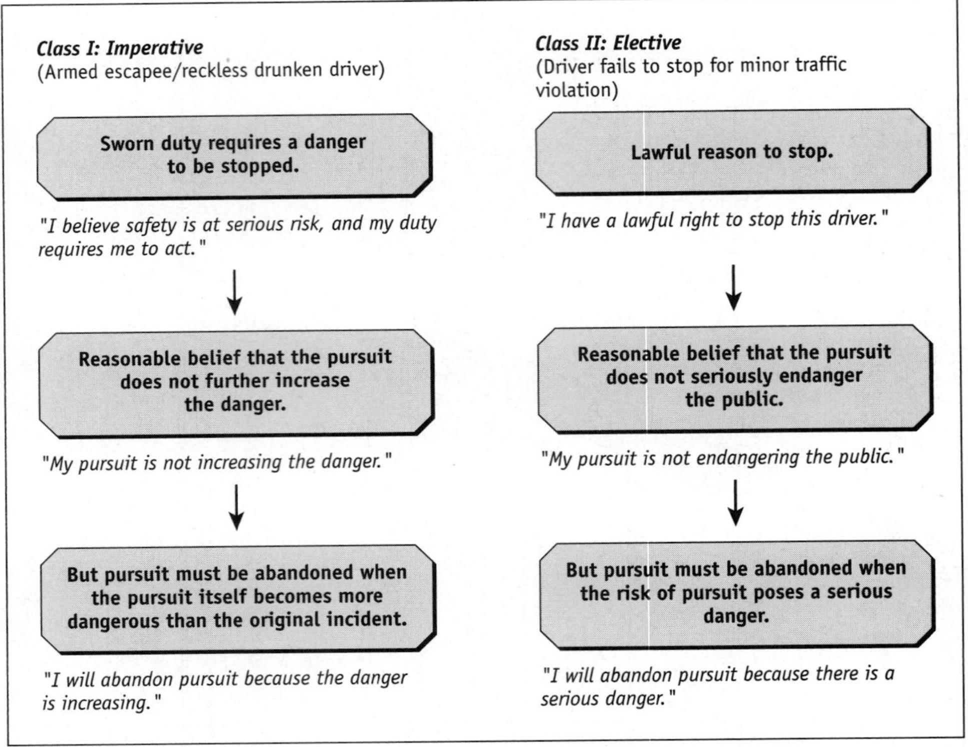

Class I: Imperative
(Armed escapee/reckless drunken driver)
Sworn duty requires a danger to be stopped.
"I believe safety is at serious risk, and my duty requires me to act."
Reasonable belief that the pursuit does not further increase the danger.
"My pursuit is not increasing the danger."
But pursuit must be abandoned when the pursuit itself becomes more dangerous than the original incident.
"I will abandon pursuit because the danger is increasing."
Class II: Elective
(Driver fails to stop for minor traffic violation)
Lawful reason to stop.
"I have a lawful right to stop this driver."
Reasonable belief that the pursuit does not seriously endanger the public.
"My pursuit is not endangering the public."
But pursuit must be abandoned when the risk of pursuit poses a serious danger.
"I will abandon pursuit because there is a serious danger."

Figure 10.5
Imperative vs. Elective Police Pursuit

Source: Phil Wright and Les McCarthy. "Why Do We Make Pursuit Policies?" *The Police Chief,* July 1998, p.52. Reprinted by permission. Copyright held by The International Association of Chiefs of Police, Inc. Further reproduction without express written permission is prohibited.

driver sped away. The deputy followed, and during the pursuit, the chase reached speeds of up to 100 miles per hour. The pursuit ended when the motorcycle tipped over and Lewis was struck and killed by the patrol car. The 9th Circuit Court ruled that the deputy was liable for Lewis's death by showing "deliberate indifference to, or reckless disregard for, a person's right to life and personal security."

The Supreme Court, however, overturned this ruling and held: "Only conduct that shows an intent on the part of the officer to cause harm unrelated to the legitimate object of making the arrest will meet the test of shocking and arbitrary conduct actionable as a deprivation of substantive due process." As a result of *Lewis,* "In high-speed vehicle pursuit cases, liability in Section 1983 cases ensues only if the conduct of the officer 'shocks the conscience.' The lower standard of 'deliberate indifference' does not apply" (del Carmen and Walker, p.270).

Ferrell (1998, p.12) states: "For almost half a century, the Supreme Court has applied a 'shocks-the-conscience' test to analyze claims similar to the one made in this case, and the Court considers *Rochin v. California* (1952) to be the benchmark case explaining this standard. . . . In the years between *Rochin* and *Lewis,* the Court explained that conduct that 'shocks the conscience' is conduct so brutal and offensive that it does not comport with traditional ideas of fair play and decency." Through this ruling, the Supreme Court "properly recognizes that law enforcement officers are not the ones who are to blame for police pursuits, and therefore, should not be held liable for accidents that result from them" ("Reaction to Supreme Court Ruling . . .," 1998, p.5). The president of the National Fraternal Order of Police echoed: "This death, while tragic, is not the fault of the officer, but that of the driver of the motorcycle who chose to endanger his own life, and the officers pursuing him" ("Reaction to Supreme Court Ruling . . .," p.5).

Fulton (1998, p.1) cautions: "Although the recent Supreme Court decision was a favorable ruling for the police this time, everyone in our industry should be adequately prepared to defend the next case with adequate policies, training and supervision." Scuro (1999, p.76) adds: "The Court decision does not preclude civil litigation involving high-speed chases from being pursued under state statutes for wrongful death or under an existing state tort claims act."

Civil Liability

As discussed, many aspects of police work (e.g., use of force, high-speed pursuits) leave officers and their departments vulnerable to possible lawsuits. Searches and arrests have the potential for lawsuits, as do failures to investigate or arrest. According to a survey by Vaughn et al. (2001), the most common allegations in lawsuits involved excessive use of force, false arrest or imprisonment, or unlawful searches/seizures. Slightly more than one-half of the police chiefs surveyed thought that police did not excessively or irrationally fear civil litigation, but a similar percentage indicated that lawsuits or the threat of litigation made it more difficult for police to do their job. Seventy-six percent believed that most lawsuits against police were frivolous.

Soto (1998, p.99) states: "**Liability** is defined by law as a legal obligation incurred for an injury suffered/complained which results from failure to conduct a specific task/activity within a given standard" [boldface added]. As discussed in Chapter 2, the U.S. Constitution and the Bill of Rights define the civil rights and civil liberties guaranteed each citizen by the government. Other civil rights protections with specific relevance to law enforcement are granted under 42 U.S.C. § 1983.

Civil liability suits, however, have not always been an issue for law enforcement. As Scuro (1998, pp.98–99) notes: "Until 1978, a public entity was not a 'person' who could abuse official power and authority to deprive constitutionally protected civil rights or act in a conspiracy to violate otherwise constitutionally protected rights. This changed in 1978 when the Supreme Court decided *Monell.*" This case and several subsequent cases effectively removed the absolute sovereign immunity previously enjoyed by governmental entities and their employees.

Today concern for civil liability is quite evident in law enforcement agencies' policies and practices.

"Lawsuit paranoia" has also been called **litigaphobia,** or the fear of litigation. Fear of being sued can cause confusion regarding which action to take in a given situation—the "damned if you do, damned if you don't" dilemma. As an example, for a while citizens in need of lifesaving assistance were filing and winning lawsuits against those who responded to their needs for injuries sustained during the assistance or other more ludicrous reasons. So people grew reluctant to "get involved," and lawsuits were then filed for failure to assist. To protect well-intentioned assistants, Good Samaritan laws were passed that required a showing of gross, wanton or willful negligence.

A police duty more commonly the subject of lawsuits is making arrests. High-risk warrantless arrest situations include drunk and disorderly arrests, escalating to excessive force claims and arrests under pro-arrest domestic violence statutes. In contrast is the officer sued for failing to arrest. This most often occurs when an officer fails to arrest an intoxicated driver.

The leading case in this area of "ministerial duties" is *Irwin v. Town of Ware* (1992). In this case an officer pulled over a vehicle that had "peeled out" of a bar's parking lot. The officer had the car's occupant get out, and an eyewitness said the driver was unsteady, holding his head and then holding onto the door. No sobriety tests were done, and the driver was sent on his way. Ten minutes later he was involved in a head-on collision that killed Misty Irwin. The court said the decision to arrest was not up to the officer. Because the state had enacted a statute authorizing police to arrest drunk drivers, this was their sworn duty.

The concept of "public duty" was reaffirmed in *Carleton v. Town of Framingham* (1993). In this case an officer talked with an obviously drunken person in a store. He waited until the driver got into his car and drove off before attempting to stop and arrest him. The driver did not stop and was involved in a head-on collision. Citing *Irwin* the court said the officer had a duty "to enforce the statutes with respect to intoxicated operators of motor vehicles and could anticipate that his failure to take action to remove the drunk driver from the highway could result in immediate and foreseeable physical injury to a member of the public."

Investigative procedure is another area of police work commonly brought up in lawsuits. Spector (1998, p.12) notes: "Almost every investigation requires officers to decide what evidence should be included in prosecutor reports and warrant applications, and what evidence should be put aside." Newbold (2001, p.10) notes: "The landmark case of *Brady v. Maryland* (1968) places on a prosecutor an affirmative constitutional duty to disclose **exculpatory evidence** (favorable to the accused) to a defendant" [bold added]: "We now hold that the suppression of evidence by the prosecution of evidence favorable to an accused upon request violates due process where the evidence is material either to guilt or to punishment, irrespective of the good faith or bad faith of the prosecution." Spector (p.12) cautions:

> Leaving out exculpatory evidence may lead to liability for false arrest, malicious prosecution, and illegal search and seizure claims. To support such liability claims, a plaintiff must show that the affiant knowingly and deliberately, or with reckless disregard for the truth, omitted facts that are material or necessary to a finding of probable cause [*Franks v. Delaware,* 1978].

The constitutional protections extended to police officers while performing their duties "under color of law" were affirmed in *Saucier v. Katz* (2001). According to Makholm (2001, p.57): "It is mildly ironic that 'saucier' is defined, at least in part, as 'impossible to repress or control' . . . for military police officer Donald Saucier apparently was able to do just that, i.e., control and arrest the plaintiff/protestor Elliot M. Katz." Katz, president of Defense of Animals, during an appearance by then Vice-President Gore, attempted to confront Gore with a banner that read: "Please Keep Animal Torture Out of Our National Parks." The military police, charged with keeping protestors at bay had been alerted to the probable presence of Katz, and Officer Saucier and a sergeant picked Katz up and delivered him to a military vehicle. Katz claimed he was "thrown" into the vehicle and had to catch himself to avoid being injured. Katz filed an excessive force suit against Saucier. The District Court denied Saucier qualified immunity, and at the Ninth Circuit of Appeals, Saucier fared no better. However, the Supreme Court overturned the Ninth Circuit Court's holding.

The Supreme Court held that courts must take a two-step approach: The first inquiry must be whether a constitutional right would have been violated on the facts alleged; second, assuming the violation is established, the question whether the right was clearly established must be considered on a more specific level. The Court explained that the privilege of qualified immunity is "an immunity from suit rather than a mere defense to liability; and like an absolute immunity, it is effectively lost if a case is erroneously permitted to go to trial. . . . We repeatedly have stressed the importance of resolving immunity questions at the earliest possible stage in litigation." In other words, the court is to resolve the issue of qualified immunity early and not put an officer through an entire trial.

Officer ignorance and disrespect for diversity may also lead to civil lawsuits. According to Rosenbaum (2001, p.68) chances of a lawsuit increase when officers fail to understand those who are different from themselves—different race, culture or background. They also increase when officers deal with persons with mental illness. Cultural awareness courses and sensitivity training are among the many ways departments can reduce officers' civil liability.

Reducing Civil Liability

So what can an agency and its officers do to reduce the risk of being named in a civil suit? When police chiefs were asked what steps could prevent lawsuits, the most frequent answers were treating people fairly, better training, better supervision, better screening and early identification of problem officers—in that order (Martinelli and Pollock, 2000, p.55).

To help with the increasing tangle of legal issues, many police agencies now employ part- or full-time legal advisors: "The legal advisor must ensure that policies not only meet appropriate legal standards, but are practical enough so as to allow officers the ability to perform their tasks while reducing the risk of liability" ("The Police Legal Advisor . . .," 1998, p.139). It is also noted (p.138): "The duties a police legal advisor may perform are as diverse and wide-ranging as the law-related needs of police agencies and officers. There is no standard job description for a police legal advisor; it will vary based on the size and needs of the police department and the objectives of the police chief."

While many departments cannot afford permanent, in-house legal counsel, it is vital that they development a sound working relationship with such an advisor: "Access to a specially trained police attorney helps ensure increased effectiveness in law enforcement by improving policy and decision making. Securing the services of a police legal advisor will often pay off in increased effectiveness and efficiency, as well as in greatly reduced liability exposure for the agency" ("The Police Legal Advisor . . .," p.144).

Another way departments are reducing civil liability is by modifying administrative policy decisions. A study by Worrall (1998) asked: "Do police administrators influence trends in litigation?" The answer he found—yes: "Most informative was the apparent relationship between civil liability and commitment to community-oriented policing [COP]. . . . The analysis here presents some initial evidence to support the notion that COP affects civil litigation in a favorable way" (pp.308–309).

As discussed in Chapter 5, community policing takes a proactive approach to combating crime and other problems that plague a community by encouraging and supporting partnerships between law enforcement agencies and officers and the citizens and organizations within the community they serve. This fundamental shift in policing philosophy is still resisted by some agency administrators, who are skeptical about the effectiveness and benefits of such an approach. However as Worrall suggests (p.309): "Perhaps conceiving of COP's implications for police departments from a different perspective—in this case, a liability perspective—can help to alleviate skepticism and quell uncertainties about what lies ahead for policing."

While agencies and their officers continue to struggle with the question "Is it legal?" another question often posed is "Is it ethical?"

Corruption, Ethics and Integrity—Where to Draw the Line

"More nationwide research was conducted on police corruption and integrity during the last five years than was completed throughout the preceding century. In spite of these advancements, scandals flourish and corruption continues to undermine America's trust in policing" (Trautman, 2001, p.91).

Swope (2001, pp.80–81) chronicles the commissions assigned to examine police corruption, beginning with the 1890s Lexow Commission and Mazet Commission and the 1910s Curan Committee to handle corruption in the New York City Police Department. The 1931 Wickersham Commission report documented corruption and brutality in the criminal justice system throughout the United States. The 1960s Knapp Commission again uncovered bribery and kickbacks throughout the NYPD. In 1974 the Philadelphia police were accused of engaging in criminal practices throughout the force. In the 1980s more than 70 Miami police officers were arrested for serious acts of corruption.

In 1993 the Mollen Commission report again found large-scale corruption in the NYPD including extortion, bribery and theft. From 1993 to 1995 more than 50 New Orleans police officers were arrested, indicted or convicted on charges including rape, aggravated battery, drug trafficking and murder. The Christopher Commission, investigating the Los Angeles Police Department after the Rodney King beating, found that significant numbers of LAPD officers "repetitively use excessive force against the public and persistently ignore the written guidelines of the department regarding force." In the late 1990s the Rampart Commission again found serious problems within the LAPD.

As Fuller (2001, p.6) notes: "The police service in this country is more closely scrutinized and subject to more uninformed, biased criticism than any other occupational group, with the possible exception of presidential candidates." Because of this close scrutiny, it is imperative that officers avoid corruption. However, as John Crew, director of the Police Practices Project of the American Civil Liberties Union (ACLU) says: "It [corruption] exists, but it's not just evil people—it's well-intentioned people in an atmosphere where it takes an almost superhuman effort to do the right thing" (Strandberg, 2000, p.98).

What Constitutes Corruption?

Rothlein (2000, p.68) observes: "While examples of police corruption vary greatly in kind and degree, they all have key elements in common: The conduct is prohibited by law or rule. It involves misuse of position. And the conduct involves a reward or personal gain to the officer." He (p.72) cautions: "Corruption is a corrosive element that will spread like rust if it is not contained and eliminated." Carter (1999, p.311) states: "Police corruption includes a wide variety of prohibited behaviors—either crimes or departmental rule violations—committed under the auspices of a police officer's position."

Police **corruption** occurs when an officer misuses authority for personal gain. It includes accepting gratuities and bribes as well as committing theft or burglary. The most common and extensive type of corruption is accepting small gratuities or tips.

Although discounts and free service are usually not considered important, cash payments to police officers are quite another matter. It is a serious issue when an officer accepts an outright bribe to refrain from making an arrest or imposing a fine. Another form of extremely serious police corruption occurs when officers appropriate material or money that comes into their possession in the line of duty, for example detectives dividing their "scores" of narcotics and cash, sometimes amounting to thousands of dollars, or property being taken from the property room and then mysteriously "disappearing."

The Knapp Commission, in its 1972 investigation of corruption among New York City police, distinguished between "grass eaters" and "meat eaters," with the grass eaters being officers who passively accepted gratuities offered to them, in contrast to the meat eaters who aggressively solicited payments. The commission also discovered another problem—officers who were not directly involved in corruptive practices but who tolerated or ignored such activities by their colleagues, thereby allowing an environment of corruption to flourish. According to Crew (ACLU): "If corruption is defined broadly as law enforcement officers willing to turn the other way or keep the code of silence, then corruption is a huge problem. Some would argue that it is the No. 1 barrier to achieving lasting improvements in police-community relationships, especially in communities of color where the misconduct has been more prevalent" (Strandberg, 2000, p.100). Corruption may also go beyond the motive of personal gain, as noted by Gaines and Cordner (p.299):

> Because police officers are granted substantial authority plus wide discretion in use of that authority, ethical issues and dilemmas arise in the course of police work. Sometimes the issues concern personal gain—should an officer accept free coffee? . . .
>
> Other ethical issues have less to do with personal gain and more to do with the means and ends of policing . . . for example, lying in court to obtain a conviction, creating a nonexistent informant to obtain a search warrant, or using physical coercion to encourage a suspect to confess.

According to Adcox (2000, p.19): "The tendency of police officers to place ends over means is not new. There is ample historical evidence to suggest that similar police values, beliefs and practices have existed since the inauguration of modern policing in the United States. History has shown that some police officers have come to value results over duty and principle, and the standard measurement of good police work has become goal achievement, with all else being secondary." He (p.27) further notes:

> As the only governmental entity granted awesome coercive authority, it is imperative that police officers exercise their power responsibly and ethically. The cynicism and stress caused by the many conflicting loyalties and expectations of modern policing can, however, cloud the honorable intentions of even the best police officer. When officers are confronted with the really "bad guys," there are strong temptations to take advantage of the powers entrusted and the discretion granted. . . .
>
> It takes individual moral courage and strong ethical principles to resist the "ends justifying means" pitfall.

This tendency to place ends over means is one reason corruption can arise and perpetuate, but the problem is much more complex.

The Corruption Continuum

Just as with the use of force and pursuits, a continuum exists to describe the transition from honest to corrupt cop. Gilmartin and Harris (1998, p.25) call it the "continuum of compromise"; O. W. Wilson referred to it as "the slippery slope hypothesis." Strandberg (2000, p.100) explains: "Corruption takes on many forms, and something seemingly insignificant can put an officer on a slippery slope, leading to major crimes." Gilmartin and Harris (p.25) add: "The transformation from an idealistic, highly ethical officer into a self-serving individual who believes 'if we don't look out for ourselves who will?' is a subtle process that usually occurs before the officer knows what has happened." They also assert (p.26): "Most officers will travel down and up the continuum numerous times during their careers." This progression is illustrated in Figure 10.6.

Lying by police officers may be quite minor or can be deadly serious. Perjury, a criminal offense, is seen by many officers who have traveled down the continuum of compromise as a legitimate way to fight slippery criminals who

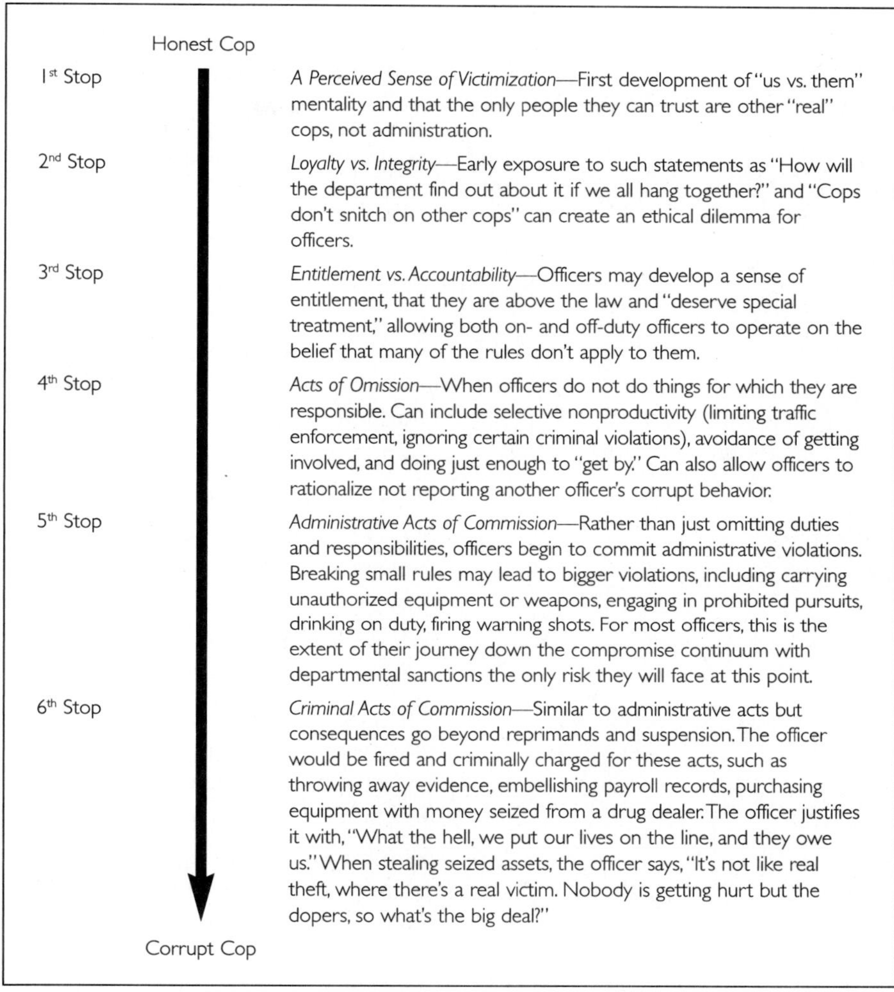

Honest Cop
1st Stop
A Perceived Sense of Victimization—First development of "us vs. them" mentality and that the only people they can trust are other "real" cops, not administration.
2nd Stop
Loyalty vs. Integrity—Early exposure to such statements as "How will the department find out about it if we all hang together?" and "Cops don't snitch on other cops" can create an ethical dilemma for officers.
3rd Stop
Entitlement vs. Accountability—Officers may develop a sense of entitlement, that they are above the law and "deserve special treatment," allowing both on- and off-duty officers to operate on the belief that many of the rules don't apply to them.
4th Stop
Acts of Omission—When officers do not do things for which they are responsible. Can include selective nonproductivity (limiting traffic enforcement, ignoring certain criminal violations), avoidance of getting involved, and doing just enough to "get by." Can also allow officers to rationalize not reporting another officer's corrupt behavior.
5th Stop
Administrative Acts of Commission—Rather than just omitting duties and responsibilities, officers begin to commit administrative violations. Breaking small rules may lead to bigger violations, including carrying unauthorized equipment or weapons, engaging in prohibited pursuits, drinking on duty, firing warning shots. For most officers, this is the extent of their journey down the compromise continuum with departmental sanctions the only risk they will face at this point.
6th Stop
Criminal Acts of Commission—Similar to administrative acts but consequences go beyond reprimands and suspension. The officer would be fired and criminally charged for these acts, such as throwing away evidence, embellishing payroll records, purchasing equipment with money seized from a drug dealer. The officer justifies it with, "What the hell, we put our lives on the line, and they owe us." When stealing seized assets, the officer says, "It's not like real theft, where there's a real victim. Nobody is getting hurt but the dopers, so what's the big deal?"
Corrupt Cop

Source: Adapted from Kevin M. Gilmartin and John J. Harris. "The Continuum of Compromise." *The Police Chief,* January 1998, pp.25–28.

Figure 10.6
The Continuum of Compromise

hire even more slippery lawyers. Some openly admit that lying in court by officers, referred to as "testilying," is a common and significant police issue. The impact of a single lie may be far-reaching. Schofield (1998, p.28) asserts: "Public trust is undermined whenever officers lie or remain silent when questioned about law enforcement matters." Officers' readiness to lie or remain silent is one measure of their integrity, or lack thereof.

How Corruption Arises and Perpetuates

In examining how police learn about ethics, Sherman (1999, p.301) states:

> Every occupation has a learning process (usually called "socialization") to which its new members are subjected. The socialization process functions to make most "rookies" in the occupation adopt the prevailing rules, values, and attitudes of their senior colleagues in the occupation. Very often, some of the existing informal

> rules and attitudes are at odds with the formal rules and attitudes society as a whole expects members of the occupation to follow. . . .
>
> Police officers . . . may be taught how to commit perjury in court to insure that their arrests lead to convictions, or how to lie in disciplinary investigations to protect their colleagues. They may be taught how to shake people down, or how to beat people up. Or they may be fortunate enough to go to work in an agency or with a group of older officers, in which none of these violations of official rules is ever suggested to them.

Other things officers may be taught include (Sherman, pp.305–306):

1. *Discretion A:* Decisions about whether to enforce the law, in any but the most serious cases, should be guided by both what the law says and who the suspect is.
2. *Discretion B:* Disrespect for police authority is a serious offense that should always be punished with an arrest or the use of force.
3. *Force:* Police officers should never hesitate to use physical or deadly force against people who "deserve it," or where it can be an effective way of solving a crime.
4. *Due Process:* Due process is only a means of protecting criminals at the expense of the law abiding and should be ignored whenever it is safe to do so.
5. *Truth:* Lying and deception are an essential part of the police job, and even perjury should be used if it is necessary to protect yourself or get a conviction on a "bad guy."
6. *Time:* You cannot go fast enough to chase a car thief or traffic violator, nor slow enough to get to a "garbage" call; and when there are no calls for service, your time is your own.
7. *Rewards:* Police do very dangerous work for low wages, so it is proper to take any extra rewards the public want to give them, like free meals, Christmas gifts, or even regular monthly payments (in some cities) for special treatment.
8. *Loyalty:* The paramount duty is to protect your fellow officers at all costs, as they would protect you, even though you may have to risk your own career or your own life to do it.

In addition to these socialization influences, other elements act to create and perpetuate officer corruption, such as officer personality and ego, police unions and lack of ethical guidance by police administration.

Sometimes corruption is the result of personality. Green (2001, p.87) describes four basic types of individuals: (1) the person of good character, (2) the person who has excellent self-control, (3) the person who is uncontrolled and (4) the person who is criminal or of evil character. The fourth type of person probably would not be hired by an agency with sound selection practices. It is the third type of individual, the one lacking self-control, who is most likely to become corrupt. If only one or two individuals in a department are corrupt, they are sometimes referred to as a "few rotten apples." And, as Rothlein (p.70) suggests: "Failure to investigate and expose a few 'bad apples' may allow them to spoil the whole barrel." As Swope (2001, p.80) notes: "It is the unethical breeding environment of the barrel that generates the major difficulties. It is the barrel, the culture of the police organizations, that can cause the root shaking scandals that periodically face some police organizations."

Police corruption may arise from officers thinking they are "above the law." As Thompson (2001, p.77) notes: "The American public readily understands and recognizes that the police are entitled to special privileges and exceptions relative to obeying the laws. Police officers are allowed to exceed the speed limits and violate traffic controls in the interest of law enforcement. They are allowed to carry concealed weapons, and they often own or have access to weaponry that is prohibited or at least greatly restricted to private citizens." Unfortunately, says Thompson: "Early in the indoctrination into policing, some officers receive the message that they are special and they are above the law." Thompson (p.79) stresses: "Equality under the law is the foundation of American criminal justice. If law enforcement officers believe they are above the law, then this subverts the very essence of law enforcement and criminal justice in our society."

Another reason corruption can perpetuate, according to Diop Kamau, executive director of the nonprofit Police Complaint Center, is the unions: "There's an abuse-denial misconduct pattern. Police unions are out of control. They want police protected in any and all circumstances. . . . Even with clear evidence of problems, police unions claim they're being picked on and treated unfairly by the media" (Pederson, 2001, p.139).

Corruption may also arise and perpetuate because departments fail to emphasize ethical behavior.

How Police Learn about Ethics

Ethics involves moral behavior, doing what is considered right and just. In contrast: "Unethical behavior is the result of a conscious decision-making process to abuse one's authority while in a position of public trust" (Byers, 2000, p.7). According to Swope (2001, p.83): "An officer's behavior is influenced more directly by the actions or lack of actions in response to ethical shortcomings of his superiors than by the states' directives or written ethical code of an organization."

Police managers may provide ethical leadership by helping officers develop their ethical decision-making skills. Campion (1998, p.3) notes:

> To help guide his officers, one lieutenant suggested his team follow this six-step process when faced with making an ethical decision:
>
> 1. Determine if the potential action or decision is legal.
> 2. Decide on the best solution for the greatest number of people.
> 3. Consider what would happen if the action you are about to engage in becomes a universal standard.
> 4. Think about how you would feel if your actions were made public. Would you be proud?
> 5. Follow the Golden Rule: "Do unto others as you would have them do unto you." Would you be happy with the decision if its outcomes were directed toward you?
> 6. Obtain a second opinion from a friend who is not vested in the outcome.

The International Association of Chiefs of Police has developed a code of ethics and "Police Code of Conduct" to guide police administrators and officers through the ethical standards expected. They include the primary responsibilities of a police officer, how the duties are to be performed, use of discretion, use of force, confidentiality, integrity, cooperation with other police officers and agencies, personal-professional capabilities and even private life. The Law Enforcement Code of Ethics is given in Appendix A.

The Importance of Police Integrity and Core Virtues

The National Institute of Justice and Office of Community Oriented Policing (*Police Integrity* . . ., 1997, p.86) note: "**Integrity**—as it applies to police service—is a series of concepts and beliefs that, combined, provide structure to an agency's operation and officers' professional and personal ethics. These concepts and beliefs include, but are not limited to, honesty, honor, morality, allegiance, principled behavior, and dedication to mission."

Avoiding bad behavior is not the same as having integrity any more than avoiding grammatical errors can make one a Pulitzer prize–winning author. Having integrity is more than simply playing by the rules. To develop officers with integrity, police departments need not only a formal code of ethics but also a statement of core values. Consider, for example, the El Paso Police Department's Code of Values (Adcox, p.24):

- We respect life.
- We revere the truth.
- We enforce the law.
- We seek community partnerships.
- We honor our police power.
- We conduct ourselves with dignity.

Swope (1998, p.37) states: "Police officers fall into the same bell curve as the general population. There are some officers with few core virtues, many with some and a few with many. The level of integrity in a police department depends on the influence exerted by those on the lower and upper portions of the bell curve."

A study funded by the National Institute of Justice surveyed over 3,000 officers from 30 police departments around the country to measure a department's "culture of integrity." Officers were asked to examine 11 common scenarios of police misconduct and then indicate if they would report the behavior ("How Do You Rate? . . .," 2000, p.6). It found that the more serious the transgression was perceived to be, the more willing officers were to report a colleague and to believe severe discipline appropriate:

> The four scenarios that were not considered major transgressions by officers included the off-duty operation of an outside security business, receiving free meals, accepting free holiday gifts, and the cover-up of a police drunken-driving accident.
>
> The intermediate level of misconduct, according to officers, included the use of excessive force on a car thief following a foot pursuit, a supervisor who offers time

off during holidays in exchange for a tune-up on her personal vehicle and accepting free drinks in return for ignoring a late bar closing.

The three remaining scenarios involved misconduct regarded as very serious, including accepting a cash bribe, stealing money from a found wallet and stealing a watch from a crime scene.

The study concluded that one of the most important indicators of integrity is the willingness of officers to report abuses and that in departments with a very strong environment of integrity, there's a willingness to discipline even low-level misconduct.

Many internal and external forces interact to influence police integrity. The dynamics of these forces are illustrated in Figure 10.7. Given the wide variety of

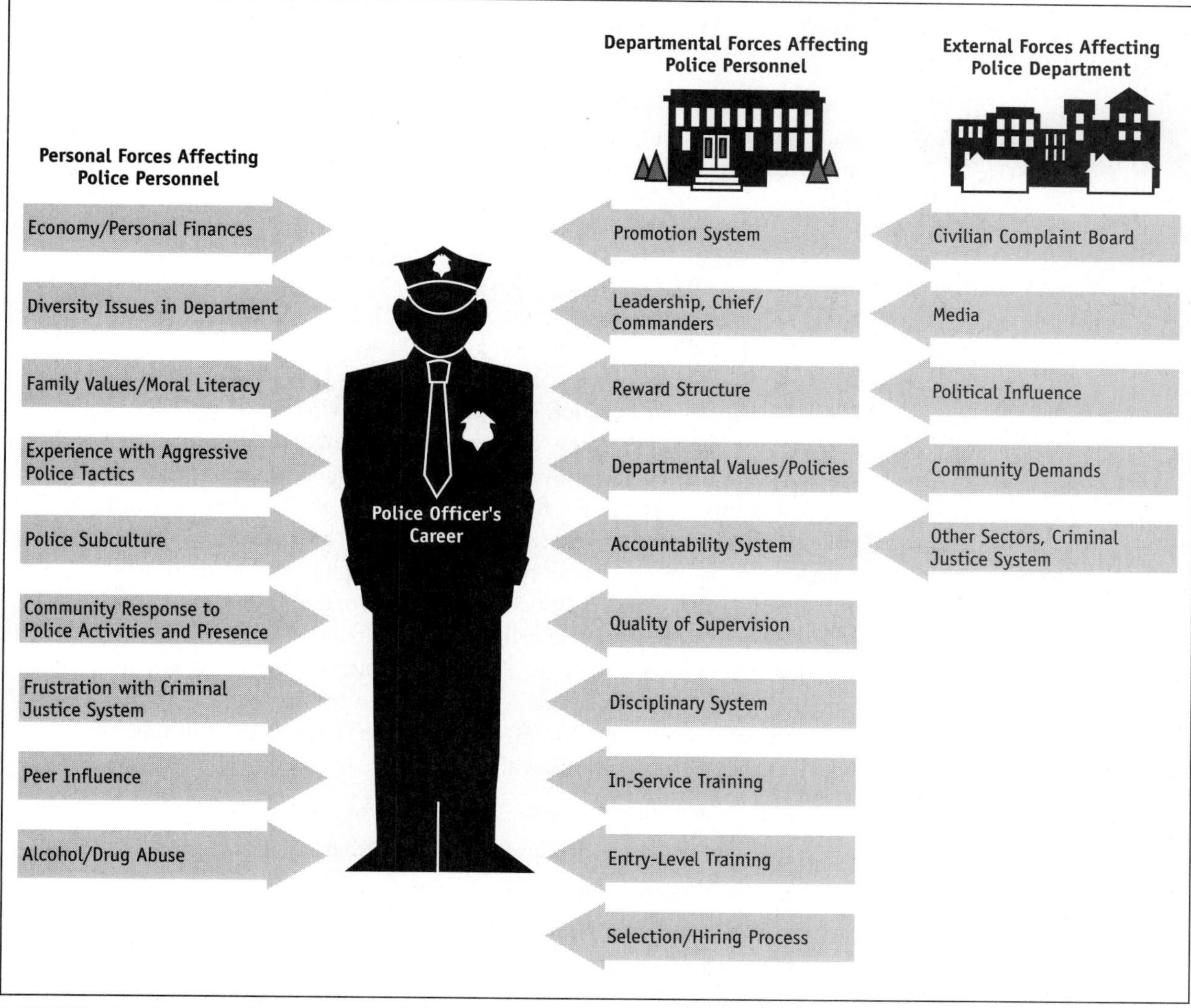

Source: *Police Integrity: Public Service with Honor.* Washington, DC: National Institute of Justice, January 1997, p.92.

Figure 10.7
Dynamics of Police Integrity

forces influencing officer integrity, the challenge of building an ethical police department has never been greater.

Building an Ethical Department

For administrators struggling to build an ethical department, it may come as small consolation to know that while corruption has been a persistent problem in American policing, it is not a unique phenomenon, nor is it one that can ever be beaten down completely and permanently. According to Carter (p.311):

> The corruption of police officers is a problem which spans cultures, countries and generations in that it is based in human weaknesses and motivations. Because even the lowest ranking police officer can exercise wide power and because there are people who want to take advantage of that power, the threat of corruption is inevitable. Administrators must recognize that no matter how aggressively the problem is controlled, investigated and penalized, there will always be someone in the organization who becomes susceptible to corruptive influences.

While acknowledging that corrupt officer behavior will likely never be eradicated entirely, administrators must not stop trying to achieve an ethical department. To help in this effort, administrators should focus on three areas to enhance police integrity.

Three areas in which to enhance police integrity and reduce corruption are:

- The applicant selection process
- Consistent reinforcement of values
- Anticorruption posture of checks and balances

In the applicant selection process, prior behavior, arrest records, drug use and integrity must be aggressively researched. Consistent reinforcement of values is also vital. Department personnel should regularly discuss and analyze conduct standards to strengthen their understanding of and commitment to such principles. Management's most important task is to create an environment in which every police officer can perform with integrity and professionalism. In an anticorruption posture of checks and balances, management can reinforce integrity, detect corruption and limit the opportunity for wrongdoing. The chief sets the level of integrity for the entire department. Supervisors provide leadership and guidance when needed.

McCarthy (2000, pp.36–43) suggests seven steps to prevent unethical behavior and develop officers with integrity:

1. Recruit with great care.
2. Establish appropriate policies and put them in writing.
3. Adopt a good employee evaluation process.
4. Make sure your sergeants share management's values and philosophies.
5. Develop operational controls.
6. Perform regular anticorruption inspections and audits.
7. Implant ethics and integrity training into every training activity.

McNeff (2001, p.10) also stresses: "In today's police environment, the incorporation of ethics into all aspects of police agency training and operations may yield wide-ranging benefits, including reduced exposure to liability." Rothlein (p.70) provides short- and long-term goals for reducing corruption within a department: Short term—change behavior by heightening the risk of detection and reducing opportunity and temptation. Long term—develop a value system and high ethical standard within the agency and manage the culture of the department.

Many departments are establishing early warning systems (EWS). As Arnold (2001, p.85) states: "Proactive approaches must be explored and expanded where some type of intervention is introduced prior to misconduct." Examples of early warning signs include poor performance, hostility and anger, unnecessary risk-taking, increases in use of force and insubordinate conduct. Arnold (p.86) stresses: "EWS must be developed and utilized to their utmost in order to identify those employees who have the potential for future misconduct. Quality intervention steps must be taken to modify and hopefully eliminate problem behavior. Efforts spent on these endeavors can have a lasting positive impact on an agency, its members and the communities it serves."

As departments seek to build ethical departments and officers with integrity, the newly organized National Commission on Law Enforcement Integrity may be of help. Information about this commission may be found at www.policeintegrity.org.

Summary

Policing has several vital issues facing it in the twenty-first century. Some have existed for decades, others are relatively new, and most are quite controversial. One of the most controversial issues surrounds police discretion, the freedom of an agency or individual officer to choose whether or not to act. If such discretion is positive or negative is an issue.

Closely related to discretion is the issue of discrimination versus disparity. Minorities are arrested, stopped and questioned, and shot and killed by the police out of proportion to their representation in the population. There is much controversy over whether study results indicate a pattern of systematic *discrimination* or a *disparity* related to other factors such as involvement in crime.

Use of force has been an issue of increasing concern for police agencies. When making an arrest, if there is no resistance, no force should be used. Justification for use of deadly force must consider not only the legal right, but also the need to apprehend the suspect compared to the arresting officer's safety and the value of human life.

One form of use of force is the police pursuit. High-speed pursuits are both effective and dangerous. They also raise serious liability issues. Today concern for civil liability is quite evident in law enforcement agencies' policies and practices.

The issues of corruption, ethics and integrity are also of concern. Police corruption occurs when an officer misuses authority for personal gain. It includes accepting gratuities and bribes as well as committing theft or burglary. The most common and extensive type of corruption is accepting small gratuities or tips. Three areas in which to enhance police integrity and reduce corruption are the applicant selection process, consistent reinforcement of values and an anticorruption posture of checks and balances.

Discussion Questions

1. Are police officers allowed too much discretion?
2. Do you see any problems with use of force continuums or pursuit continuums?
3. Should officers and their departments be shielded from civil liability as was previously allowed for under "sovereign immunity?" Why or why not?
4. What roles can K-9s assume in dealing with fleeing suspects?
5. Do you believe the phrase "excessive force" has different meanings to different people in the criminal justice system? If so, why?
6. Do you believe racial profiling is occurring in your police department? Your state? Give reasons for your answer.
7. Do you think chemical agents are appropriate to use in dealing with uncooperative, violent suspects?
8. Do police pursuits fulfill a vital purpose?
9. What is the most important characteristic of police integrity?
10. How prevalent do you think corruption is in law enforcement agencies?

InfoTrac *College Edition Assignment*

Use InfoTrac College Edition to help answer the Discussion Questions as appropriate.

- Use InfoTrac College Edition to research *police pursuits.* Notice the many cases reviewed, how they initially started, how they ended and what implications the court decisions had on liability. Many standards are recommended in dealing with police pursuits. Outline these and pick one standard you feel could be the best with the least officer liability. Be prepared to share your selection and reasoning with the class.

Internet Assignments

- Use the Internet to research *corruption in law enforcement.* Note the many uncomplimentary articles. Do these articles give you the idea there is another side to some police officers? Explain.
- Download *Racially Biased Policing* at www.PoliceForum.org and outline one chapter. Be prepared to share your outline with the class.

Book-Specific Web Site

The book-specific Web site at http://info.wadsworth.com/0534552803 hosts a variety of resources for students and instructors. Included are extended activities from each chapter in which students write a policy, use critical thinking skills to make choices in response to a given scenario, use InfoTrac College Edition with direct links to articles for participation in topical discussion forums, and analyze court cases using Web links for research. Many activities can be printed or emailed to instructors. Plus, cited cases with Web links, interactive key term FlashCards, PowerPoint presentations, chapter objectives, and an extensive collection of chapter-based Web links provide additional information and activities to include in the curriculum.

References

Adcox, Ken. "Doing Bad Things for Good Reasons." *The Police Chief,* January 2000, pp.16–27.

Alpert, Geoffrey P. "A Factorial Analysis of Police Pursuit Driving Decisions: A Research Note." *Justice Quarterly,* June 1998, pp.347–359.

Alpert, Geoffrey P.; Kenney, Dennis Jay; Dunham, Roger G.; and Smith, William C. *Police Pursuits: What We Know.* Washington, DC: Police Executive Research Forum, 2000.

Arnold, Jon. "Early Misconduct Detection." *Law and Order,* August 2001, pp.80–86.

Bohrer, Shannon; Davis, Edward F.; and Garrity, Thomas J., Jr. "Establishing a Foot Pursuit Policy: Running into Danger." *FBI Law Enforcement Bulletin,* May 2000, pp.10–15.

Borrello, Andrew. "The Terminology Trap: Non-lethal, Less-than-lethal, Less-lethal or Lethal?" *The Law Enforcement Trainer,* August 2000, pp.60–66.

"Bush and Ashcroft Announce Racial Profiling Initiative." *Criminal Justice Newsletter,* March 14, 2001, pp.2–4.

Byers, Bryan. "Ethics and Criminal Justice: Some Observations on Police Misconduct." *ACJS Today,* September/October 2000, pp.1, 4–8.

Campion, Michael A. "Good Character, Good Policing—Then and Now." *Community Policing Exchange,* March/April 1998, p.3.

Carrick, Grady. "A Police Response to Racial Profiling." *Law and Order,* October 2001, pp.79–82.

Carter, David L. "Drug Use and Drug-Related Corruption of Police Officers." In *Policing Perspectives: An Anthology,* edited by Larry K. Gaines and Gary W. Cordner. Los Angeles: Roxbury Publishing Company, 1999, pp.311–323.

Cole, David. *No Equal Justice: Race and Class in the American Criminal Justice System.* New York: The New Press, 1999.

Connor, G. "Use of Force Continuum: Phase II." *Law and Order,* March 1991, pp.30–35.

Cox, Stephen M. "Racial Profiling: Refuting Concerns about Collecting Race Data on Traffic Stops." *Law and Order,* October 2001, pp.61–65.

del Carmen, Rolando V. and Walker, Jeffery T. *Briefs of Leading Cases in Law Enforcement,* 4th ed. Cincinnati, OH: Anderson Publishing Company, 2001.

Dorsch, Don. "Opened Door for Lawyers, Burden for Officers." *Law and Order,* September 2001, p.102.

Ferrell, Craig E. "Police Pursuits: The Supreme Court Has Set the Standard." *The Police Chief,* August 1998, pp.11–12.

Fridell, Lorie; Lunney, Robert; Diamond, Drew; and Kubu, Bruce with Scott, Michael and Laing, Colleen. *Racially Biased Policing: A Principled Response.* Washington, DC: Police Executive Research Forum, 2001. Available on the Internet at www.policeforum.org

Fuller, John J. "Street Cop Ethics." *The Law Enforcement Trainer,* May/June 2001, pp.6–7.

Fulton, Roger V. "Editor's Notes." *Knight News for Law Enforcement and Security Professionals,* July–September 1998, p.1.

Gaines, Larry K. and Cordner, Gary W. *Policing Perspectives: An Anthology.* Los Angeles: Roxbury Publishing Company, 1999.

Gilmartin, Kevin M. and Harris, John J. "The Continuum of Compromise." *The Police Chief,* January 1998, pp.25–28.

Gist, Nancy E. "Foreword." In *A Resource Guide on Racial Profiling Data Collection Systems: Promising Practices and Lessons Learned* (monograph) by Deborah Ramirez, Jack McDevitt and Amy Farrell. Washington, DC: NCJ, November 2000. (NCJ 184768)

Green, Don. "Calculating Ethics." *Law and Order,* August 2001, pp.87–90.

Heal, Sid. "The Push for Less Lethal." *Law Enforcement Technology,* November 2000, pp.72–79.

Heal, Sid. "An Evaluation of Less Lethal." *Law and Order,* September 2001, pp.88–93.

Homant, Robert J. and Kennedy, Daniel B. "Effectiveness of Less than Lethal Force in Suicide-by-Cop Incidents." *Police Quarterly,* June 2000, pp.153–171.

"How Do You Rate? The Secret to Measuring a Department's 'Culture of Integrity.'" *Law Enforcement News,* October 15, 2000, pp.1, 6.

International Association of Chiefs of Police. *Model Policy: Use of Force.* Alexandria, VA: IACP, 1995.

Jaeger, Sandy. "DWB." *Security Technology & Design,* June 2001, pp.6, 69.

James, Steve. "Impact in the Field." *Police,* July 2001, pp.16–20.

Jones, Tony. "Electronic Immobilization Devices." *Law Enforcement Technology,* October 2001, pp.70–75.

Kerlikowske, Gil. "Foreword." In *Police Pursuits: What We Know,* by Geoffrey P. Alpert et al. Washington, DC: Police Executive Research Forum, 2000.

Labbe, J. R. "Get It Straight! Profiling Is Not Racism." *American Police Beat,* October 2001, pp.25, 37.

Langan, Patrick A.; Greenfeld, Lawrence A.; Smith, Steven K.; Durose, Matthew R.; and Levin, David J. *Contacts between Police and the Public. Findings from the 1999 National Survey.* Washington, DC: Bureau of Justice Statistics, February 2001. (NCJ 184957)

Lathrop, Sam W. "Reviewing Use of Force: A Systematic Approach." *FBI Law Enforcement Bulletin,* October 2000, pp.10–20.

Lonsway, Kim and the Law and Order Staff. "First Topic: Police Women and the Use-of-Force." *Law and Order,* July 2001, pp.109–114.

Makholm, John A. "Legal Lights." *The Law Enforcement Trainer,* November/December 2001, p.57.

Martinelli, Thomas J. and Pollock, Joycelyn M. "Law Enforcement Ethics, Lawsuits, and Liability: Defusing Deliberate Indifference." *The Police Chief,* October 2000, pp.52–67.

McCarthy, Robert M. "Steps Chiefs Can Take to Prevent Unethical Behavior." *The Police Chief,* October 2000, pp.36–43.

McNeff, Michael. "One Agency's Effort to Reduce Liability Risk through Emphasis on Ethics." *The Police Chief,* August 2001, p.10.

Meek, James Gordon. "Confronting Biased Enforcement Claims." *Law and Order,* October 2001, pp.91–96.

Miller, Linda S. and Hess, Kären M. *The Police in the Community: Strategies for the 21st Century,* 3rd ed. Belmont, CA: West/Wadsworth Publishing Company, 2002.

Newbold, Mark. "Officer Liability for Failure to Disclose Exculpatory Evidence." *The Police Chief,* May 2001, pp.10–13.

Nielsen, Eugene. "The Advanced Taser." *Law and Order,* May 2001, pp.57–62.

Nislow, Jennifer. "Are Americans Ready to Buy Into Racial Profiling?" *Law Enforcement News,* October 15, 2001, p.11.

Nowicki, Ed. "OC Spray Update." *Law and Order,* June 2001a, pp.28–29.

Nowicki, Ed. "Use of Force Options." *Law and Order,* February 2001b, pp.35–37.

Nugent, Hugh; Connors, Edward F., III; McEwen, J. Thomas; and Mayo, Lou. *Restrictive Policies for High-Speed Police Pursuits.* Washington, DC: National Institute of Justice, no date. (NCJ 122025)

Olivero, J. Michael and Murataya, Rodrigo. "Homophobia and University Law Enforcement Students." *Journal of Criminal Justice Education,* Fall 2001, pp.271–281.

Olson, Dean T. "Improving Deadly Force Decision Making." *FBI Law Enforcement Bulletin,* February 1998, pp.1–9.

Paynter, Ronnie L. "Ticking Time Bombs on the Road." *Law Enforcement Technology,* October 2000, pp.144–150.

Pedersen, Dorothy. "Rising Above Corruption." *Law Enforcement Technology,* October 2001, pp.136–142.

Pipes, Chris and Pape, Dominick. "Police Pursuits and Civil Liability." *FBI Law Enforcement Bulletin,* July 2001, pp.16–21.

Police Integrity: Public Service with Honor. National Institute of Justice and the Office of Community Oriented Policing Services, January 1997. (NCJ 163811)

"The Police Legal Advisor: The Importance of the Advisor's Role." *The Police Chief,* October 1998, pp.138–144.

Police Use of Force in America 2001. Alexandria, VA: International Association of Chiefs of Police, 2001.

"The Racial Profiling Controversy in America." *NCJA Justice Bulletin,* April 2001, pp.8, 13–15.

Ramirez, Deborah; McDevitt, Jack; and Farrell, Amy. *A Resource Guide on Racial Profiling Data Collection Systems: Promising Practices and Lessons Learned* (monograph). Washington, DC: NCJ, November 2000. (NCJ 184768)

Rayburn, Michael. "Pursuits: Getting Back to Basics." *Police,* September 2000, pp.47–48.

"Reaction to Supreme Court Ruling on Pursuits Is Upbeat—But Tempered." *Law Enforcement News,* May 31, 1998, p.5.

Rivera, Richard G. "Nine Ways to Prevent Racial Profiling." *Law and Order,* October 2001, pp.85–88.

Rogers, Donna. "Use of Force." *Law Enforcement Technology,* March 2001, pp.82–86.

Rosenbaum, Steven H. "Patterns and Practices of Police Misconduct." *Law and Order,* October 2001, pp.67–71.

Rothlein, Steve. "Fostering Integrity in Policing: A Corruption Prevention Strategy." *The Police Chief,* October 2000, pp.68–76.

Sanow, Ed. "Impact and Electronic Force." *Law and Order,* September 2001, p.4.

Schofield, Daniel L. "Ensuring Officer Integrity and Accountability: Recent Court Decisions." *FBI Law Enforcement Bulletin,* August 1998, pp.28–32.

Scuro, Joseph E., Jr. "Federal Civil Rights Update." *Law and Order,* June 1998, pp.98–101.

Scuro, Joseph E., Jr. "Supreme Court Update: Greater Immunity for Officers Involved in Pursuits." *Law and Order,* January 1999, pp.75–76.

Sherman, Lawrence. "Learning Police Ethics." In *Policing Perspectives: An Anthology,* edited by Larry K. Gaines and Gary W. Cordner. Los Angeles: Roxbury Publishing Company, 1999, pp.301–310.

Smith, Brad. "Police Service Dogs: The Unheralded Training Tool." *Police,* January 2000, pp.36–39.

Soto, Javier. "Avoiding the Teeth of Liability." *Law and Order,* August 1998, pp.99–104.

Spector, Elliot B. "Liability for Failure to Disclose Exculpatory Information." *The Police Chief,* April 1998, pp.12–14.

Spector, Elliot B. "Stopping Suspects Based on Racial and Ethnic Descriptions." *The Police Chief,* January 2002, pp.10–12.

Strandberg, Keith W. "Pursuit at High Speeds." *Law Enforcement Technology,* September 1998, pp.50–54.

Strandberg, Keith W. "Light Dawns on the Dark Side: Corruption." *Law Enforcement Technology,* July 2000, pp.98–104.

"Study: Spike Strips Effectively End Chase." *Law Enforcement Technology,* December 1998, p.24.

Swope, Ross E. "The Core-Virtue Bell Curve." *The Police Chief,* January 1998, pp.37–38.

Swope, Ross. "Bad Apples or Bad Barrel?" *Law and Order,* January 2001, pp.80–85.

Territo, Leonard; Halstead, James B.; and Bromley, Max L. *Crime and Justice in America: A Human Perspective,* 5th ed. Boston: Butterworth-Heinemann, 1998.

Thompson, David. "Above the Law?" *Law and Order,* January 2001, pp.77–79.

Trautman, Nel. "National Commission on Law Enforcement Integrity." *Law and Order,* August, 2001, pp.91–93.

Van Blaricom, D. P. "He Flees—To Pursue or Not to Pursue: That Is the Question." *Police,* November 1998, pp.46–49.

Vaughn, Michael S.; Cooper, Tab W.; and del Carmen, Rolando V. "Does Threat of Lawsuits Detract From or Improve Police Work? Assessing Legal Liabilities in Law Enforcement: Police Chiefs' Views." *Crime and Delinquency,* Vol. 47, No. 1, 2001.

Walker, Samuel; Spohn, Cassia; and DeLone, Miriam. *The Color of Justice: Race, Ethnicity, and Crime in America,* 2nd ed. Belmont, CA: Wadsworth Publishing Company, 2000.

Wallentine, Ken. "Pepper Spray as a Use of Force." *Police,* October 2000, pp.52–55.

Wexler, Chuck. "Foreword." In *Racially Biased Policing: A Principled Response* by Lorie Fridell et al. Washington, DC: Police Executive Research Forum, 2001, pp.ix–xi.

Wilczak, Thomas J. "Pursuits: Don't Let Them Get Away on Us." *The Law Enforcement Trainer,* March/April 2000, pp.26–27.

Worrall, John L. "Administrative Determinants of Civil Liability Lawsuits Against Municipal Police Departments: An Exploratory Analysis." *Crime and Delinquency,* April 1998, pp.295–313.

Wright, Phil and McCarthy, Les. "Why Do We Make Pursuit Policies?" *The Police Chief,* July 1998, p.52.

Cases Cited

Brady v. Maryland, 373 U.S. 89 (1968)
Brown v. City of Oneonta, 221 F.3d 329 (2nd Cir. 2000), *cert. denied,* 122 S.Ct.44 (2001)
Carleton v. Town of Framingham, 615 N.E.2d 588 (Mass. App. Ct. 1993)
County of Sacramento v. Lewis, 523 U.S. 833 (1998)
Florida v. Bostick, 501 U.S. 429 (1991)
Franks v. Delaware, 438 U.S. 154 (1978)
Galas v. McKee, 801 F.2d 200 (1986)
Graham v. Connor, 490 U.S. 386, 396 (1989)
Griffin v. Illinois, 351 U.S. 12 (1956)
Irwin v. Town of Ware, 467 N.E.2d (1992)
Mendoza v. Block, 27 F.3d 1357 (9th Cir. 1994)
Monell v. Dept. of Social Services of the City of New York, 436 U.S. 658 (1978)
Robinette v. Barnes, 854 F.2d 909 (6th Cir. 1988)
Rochin v. California, 342 U.S. 165 (1952)
Saucier v. Katz, 121 S.Ct. 2151 (2001)
Tennessee v. Garner, 471 U.S. 1 (1985)

Chapter 11

Departmental Issues

No great advance has ever been made without controversy.
—Lyman Beecher

Do You Know?

- What qualities are essential for good police officers?
- What the benefits of racially balanced and integrated police departments are?
- What advantages exist for law enforcement agencies that hire and retain more women?
- What steps are involved in officer selection?
- What basic requirements officer candidates must meet?
- Whether a college education is required of most police officer candidates?
- If police officers are required to live in the same community in which they work?
- What most physical fitness tests are like?
- What information is sought during interviews?
- What occurs during the background investigation?
- What is most important in the medical examination?
- What legal considerations in hiring practices are mandated by the Equal Employment Opportunity Act and the Americans with Disabilities Act?
- What the length and purpose of probation are?
- How stressful police work may be?
- Whether civilian review boards are positive or negative?
- How prevalent police unionization is?
- How public and private law enforcement differ?
- Whether moonlighting is accepted?
- If accreditation for law enforcement is worth the time and expense?
- If law enforcement is a profession?

Can You Define?

accreditation
affirmative action
bona fide occupational qualification (BFOQ)
burnout
civilian review
civilian review board
credentialing
moonlighting
multiple hurdle procedure
posttraumatic stress disorder (PTSD)
privatization
reverse discrimination
sexual harassment
situational testing
stress
union
union shop

INTRODUCTION

For years society has sought more effective law enforcement and a criminal justice system to meet its needs. At the same time criminologists, psychologists, sociologists, police practitioners and scientists have worked to solve America's crime problem. Despite some disillusionment and cynicism, progress has been made, and the future offers hope.

The most visible signs of progress in the vast criminal justice system have been in the field of law enforcement, and the most notable advancement in this field has been the professionalization of the police officer. This is, in part, because 80 to 90 percent of most police agencies' budgets are allocated for personnel, and therefore they are demanding higher quality performance from them. This is sometimes difficult to obtain, however, because most police departments are understaffed. The attrition rate throughout the United States—approximately 100,000 officers per year—compounds this problem and creates a constant demand for training.

An equally important force behind the professionalization of the police officer is the realization that to a large degree the future of law enforcement, its success or failure, is contingent on its police officers' quality and effectiveness, their status in the community and their ability to serve its residents. Women and members of minority groups are now considered necessary and valuable members in most departments. Although members of minority groups and women have had a long, difficult battle in achieving equal employment rights, today excellent opportunities exist for all who are interested in a law enforcement career.

This chapter begins with some suggestions on how to evaluate and select a law enforcement agency for employment. This is followed by a look at recruiting and selection and the federal guidelines and regulations affecting employment, including the Equal Employment Opportunity Act, affirmative action initiatives and the Americans with Disabilities Act. After examining who is selected and how, the chapter turns to what happens next, typically probation and training. The importance of retaining officers is discussed, including how factors such as salary, benefits, promotional opportunities, stress and burnout affect officer retention. This is followed by a look at several "hot button" topics in law enforcement—some controversial, some that police agencies seem eager to bring to the public's attention, and others that agencies prefer to handle discreetly in hopes of avoiding publicity—including civilian review boards, sexual harassment, unions, privatization, moonlighting and accreditation. The chapter concludes with a discussion of law enforcement as a profession.

Evaluating and Selecting an Agency for Employment

Before an agency can screen and select an officer candidate, the candidate must first select the agency. This is done by researching the available options, assessing one's own professional goals and then evaluating and selecting specific agencies to apply to. Several factors are important to those seeking employment in law enforcement, including, but not limited to, the advantages and disadvantages of the following:

- Employment with municipal, county, state or federal agencies
- Working in a small, medium or large agency

- Working in an environment with a high rate of crime versus an environment with little crime and, therefore, limited police enforcement activity
- Working in a community where one was raised or currently resides

Other factors to consider include the salary, pension and fringe benefits; the opportunities to work varied assignments in the broad spectrum of law enforcement; and the potential for promotion. What are the agency's current needs? Is there a hiring freeze? Does it have serious budget constraints?

Often, interested applicants may request a fact sheet containing a brief job description, the salary range and fringe benefits, and an application either in person at the department, over the phone or online. They may also be notified of the time and location of the next written examination.

How does a law enforcement candidate find an open position to evaluate? If the law enforcement agencies in the area are progressive, they will have a successful recruiting program. Many departments also recruit online by posting job openings on their Web sites.

While all departments seek "the best" candidates to hire, they must first specify which characteristics are most important. Finding individuals qualified to become police officers is no easy task. Recruiting, screening and selecting candidates is a continuous, critical function of all police agencies.

The Recruiting Process

Clark (1998a, p.1) notes that departments across the country are facing a mass exodus of retiring officers who began their careers during the late 1960s and early 1970s. Some departments are already beginning to feel the pinch of not having enough applicants to replace the growing number of officers who are leaving. Butterfield (2001, p.1) states: "Police departments in cities across the nation are facing what some call a personnel crisis, with the number of recruits at record lows." *Law Enforcement News* ("Coast to Coast . . .," 2000, p.1) also reports: "A double-edged sword hangs over police departments. While some cannot attract enough applicants to make up rates of attrition that are expected to become significant over the next few years, others are seeing their officers jump ship for what they perceive to be a better working environment."

Among the reasons given are the relatively low starting pay, competition among departments and, as Bratton (2001, p.32) suggests "the intense scrutiny and criticism for corruption, racial profiling, racial insensitivity, brutality, unresponsiveness to community concerns and professional incompetence." A survey of professional police recruiters from around the country found that low entry-level salaries and candidates' inability to pass the written police entrance exam were the two biggest recruitment problems (Brandon and Lippman, 2000, p.37).

In addition to falling numbers of recruits, departments face other recruiting problems. One is the need for recruits "who see policing as a calling, not just a job; who see the community as a partner, not as the problem; and who can be trusted to enforce the law without violating it themselves." Tate (2000, p.78) calls it the "recruitment dilemma: Finding that ideal police recruit, one who seeks a long-term career as one of society's peacekeepers, is increasingly difficult." In addition, as Olson (2001, p.2) notes: "The real challenge we are facing is not just finding the most qualified candidates, but at the same time attracting a much more diverse workforce."

Desired Qualities of Law Enforcement Officers

If citizens were asked what traits they felt were desirable in police officers, their responses might go something like this: police officers should be able to work under pressure, to accept direction, to express themselves orally and in writing. They should have self-respect and the ability to command respect from others. They should use good judgment; and they should be considerate, compassionate, dependable, enthusiastic, fair, flexible, honest, humble, industrious, intelligent, logical, motivated, neat, observant, physically fit, prompt, resourceful, self-assured, stable, tactful, warm and willing to listen and to accept change. Furthermore, with our society becoming increasingly diverse, the ideal officer would be able to police without bias or discrimination and be sensitive to the needs and concerns of various populations within a community. Unfortunately, no one has all these traits, but the more of these traits police officers have, the more likely they are to be effective in dealing with not only the citizens of the community but lawbreakers as well.

Nowicki (1999, pp.45–46) says: "Certain qualities are imperative for entry-level police officers, such as honesty, ethics and moral character." In addition, he identifies 12 traits of "highly effective police officers: enthusiasm, good communication skills, good judgment, sense of humor, creative, self-motivated, knows the job and the system, self-confidence, courage, understand discretion, tenacious, and have a thirst for knowledge."

For those departments implementing community policing, Lord and Schoeps (2000, p.173) studied the desired attributes of community-oriented, problem-solving police officers and identified 22 attributes they consider critical for effective COPPS officers: "These attributes emphasize problem solving; decision making; and the ability to gain new knowledge, technology, procedures and laws."

In most states law enforcement candidates must also be U.S. citizens and must meet rigorous physical and personal qualifications. Personal qualities, such as honesty, good judgment and a sense of responsibility, are especially important.

Qualities of a good police officer include reliability, leadership, judgment, persuasiveness, communication skills, initiative, integrity, honesty, ego control, intelligence, sensitivity and problem-solving ability.

Finding Qualified Applicants

Most departments recruit through traditional avenues such as handouts, media advertisements (newspapers, radio, TV), job fairs and visits to colleges. Kanable (2001, p.66) suggests: "Advertising in two or three local papers might not be enough. Advertising in a newspaper with circulation throughout the state, ethnic newspapers and law enforcement publications or newsletters might help." In addition, many agencies use their Web sites to provide information about the agency, job opportunities, how to apply and the like. The IACP has a job Web site, www.iacppolicejobs.com, where departments list job openings for a fee. Job searches, however, are free.

Some departments are focusing on recruiting second-career officers. For example a recent rookie class in the Appleton (Wisconsin) Police Department included a car salesman, a former teacher, a juvenile counselor, a dental technician, a nurse, a paramedic, a businessman and an assistant district attorney. Byrne (1998, pp.183–184) notes that departments such as Appleton, who are interested in finding problem-solvers with good people skills, "like recruiting people into police work as a second career [because of] the maturity and stability they bring with them. The older recruits have generally developed a level of maturity that is seldom seen in 21-year-old rookies right out of college, who have little experience outside of a classroom setting."

Nevertheless colleges remain a fundamental source of police recruits. One way departments are avoiding the obstacle of recruiting inexperienced college graduates is by accessing participants in the College Law Enforcement Program Internship. Although specific programs vary, student interns are generally placed with an agency and must complete a certain number of credit hours per term. Leach (1998, p.59) notes the mutual benefits of internship programs: "Interns get the opportunity to view an agency from the inside and the agency gets to see a prospective employee in a law enforcement setting."

Whichever avenues an agency selects for recruiting officer candidates, the target audience should be diverse.

Recruiting Minorities

To gain the community's general confidence and acceptance, police departments seek personnel to represent the community. An integrated department helps reduce stereotyping and prejudice. John Firman, research coordinator for the IACP, says: "A diverse department is a department with a much stronger capacity to understand issues and respond effectively to those issues." He adds: "A diverse department is a creative and dynamic department" (Streit, 2001, p.70).

Minority officers provide a department with an understanding of minority groups, their languages and their subcultures, all with practical benefits to successful law enforcement. For example a police officer who speaks Spanish can help to prevent conflicts between the police and the community's Spanish-speaking residents. A minority officer may also have insight into a particular population's cultural or behavioral idiosyncracies, such as the reluctance of those in the Asian community to report victimization to the police.

A racially balanced and integrated police department fosters community relations and increases police effectiveness.

Although many minorities view police as the "enemy" and would never consider joining their ranks, others view law enforcement as a way to a better life. An African-American police lieutenant from Atlanta explains why he became a police officer: "You got out of my neighborhood without ending up dead or in prison by either becoming a minister or a cop. I always fell asleep in church so I decided to become a cop."

Another issue related to minority officers is where they should be assigned. Many believe that minority neighborhoods should be policed by officers of the same background. Others, however, view this as a form of segregation.

In addition to minorities, another group gaining representation in law enforcement is women.

Recruiting Women

Strandberg (2000, p.76) observes: "Today, you'd be hard-pressed to find a medium- to large-sized department that didn't have female officers throughout the chain of command." He (p.81) states: "Women can be found in every capacity of law enforcement from bicycle patrol to SWAT teams to leadership roles, such as police chief or sheriff." In addition, according to Greene (2000, p.230): "During the past 25 years, the representation and advancement to leadership positions of Black female officers have increased." That's the good news.

The bad news, as reported by Gold (2000, p.159) is that overall, the increase of women in law enforcement has grown "a meager 5.3 percent from 1990 to 1999." Although women have been patrol officers in the United States for more than 30 years, they make up only 11.6 percent of officers nationwide ("Rank Objections," 1998, p.1). Furthermore, a study by the National Center for Women and Policing revealed women hold only 7.4 percent of top command positions (chiefs, deputy chiefs, commanders and captains), and women of color hold only 2.4 percent of top commands. Neubauer (1998, p.6) adds that, although the number of women in law enforcement is growing and progressing through the ranks, studies also show:

- Many departments lack strategies for recruiting women.
- Women officers still face bias from male officers.
- Sexual harassment still occurs in many departments.
- Women officers may face gender discrimination and a "glass ceiling" that inhibits advancement.

Regarding the promotional hurdles female officers commonly face, Kranda (1998, p.54) states: "For many agencies, attracting women to the applicant pool is not terribly difficult. The challenge lies in retaining those highly qualified women in whom the agencies have made significant investments during the recruiting process." *Recruiting and Retaining Women* (2001, pp.22–27) lists six advantages for law enforcement agencies that hire and retain more women based on research:

- Female officers are proven to be as competent as their male counterparts.
- Female officers are less likely to use excessive force.
- Female officers can help implement community-oriented policing.
- More female officers will improve law enforcement's response to violence against women.
- Increasing the presence of female officers reduces problems of sex discrimination and harassment within an agency.

- The presence of women can bring about beneficial changes in policy for all officers.

Studies show that women perform as well as men in police work, are less apt to use excessive force, can help implement community-oriented policing and can improve an agency's response to violence against women. In addition, an increased female presence among officers can reduce problems of sex discrimination and harassment and foster policy changes that benefit all officers.

Despite the many benefits women officers bring to law enforcement, they still are not accepted in many departments. The growing presence of females in a traditionally male-dominated profession has undoubtedly led to conflict between the genders. Miller (1998, p.156) states:

> Traditional policing, as a masculine paramilitary organization, has rejected feminine virtues and voices—almost seeing them as contagion that would contaminate the police image of the aloof professional or the macho crime fighter. The criminal justice and legal system overall is viewed by many as operating with a uniquely masculine voice—a detached and impersonal one that emphasizes the rational above the relational.

Miller (p.157) also asserts: "With the advent of a new genre of policing—community policing—feminine constructs . . . have been reintroduced. . . . To be accepted by police, however, these feminine traits must be appropriated as masculine traits and reshaped to appear powerful and desirable."

So what can departments do to improve their recruitment efforts? Prussel and Lonsway (2001, p.95) state: "Women go on-line in massive numbers, especially when they are searching for career opportunities. To attract these potential applicants, it is important that law enforcement agencies develop a 'woman-friendly' Web site." In addition, Lonsway (2001, p.16) says police need to dismantle their "warrior image" which is often so important in the selection process. The emphasis on upper body strength often washes out qualified candidates, especially women, despite the fact that a survey of law enforcement agencies found physical ability to be the *least* important of ten dimensions of "being a successful peace officer." The highest-ranking characteristic was integrity.

The Selection Process

The person wanting to become a police officer must usually go through several steps in the selection process, called the **multiple hurdle procedure.** Although procedures differ greatly from agency to agency, several elements are common to most selection processes.

Police officer selection usually includes:

- A formal application
- A written examination
- A physical fitness test
- A psychological examination
- An interview
- A background investigation
- A medical examination

The order in which these steps occur may vary from department to department. Figure 11.1 illustrates a typical selection process. Failure at any point in the selection process may disqualify a candidate.

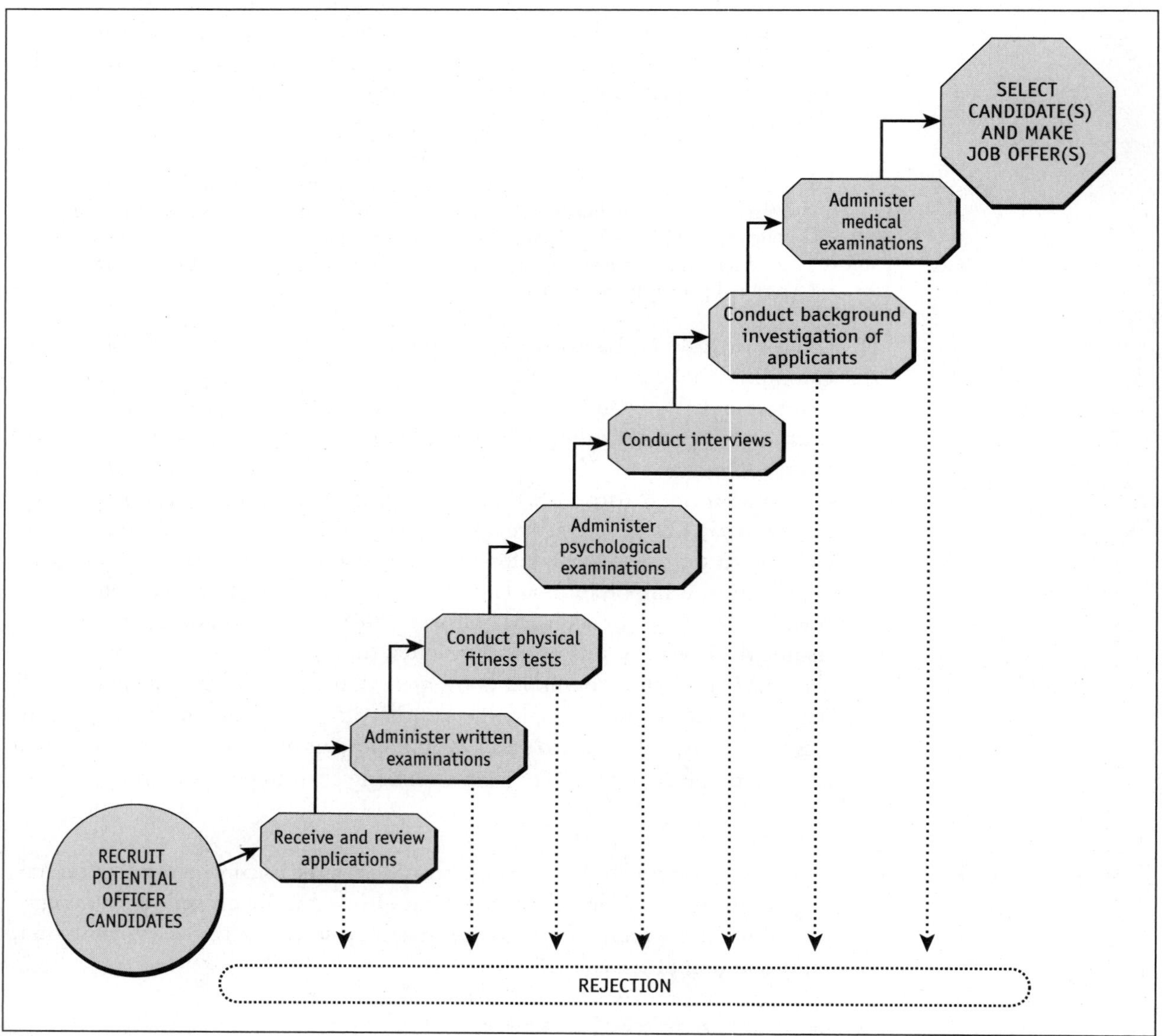

Figure 11.1
Typical Selection Process

Source: Adapted from J. Scott Harr and Kären M. Hess. *Seeking Employment in Criminal Justice and Related Fields,* 4th ed. Wadsworth Publishing Company, 2003, p. 176. Reprinted by permission. All rights reserved.

The Formal Application—Basic Requirements to Become a Police Officer

Usually a police officer candidate completes a formal application, which includes driving record; any criminal record; visual acuity; physical, emotional and mental condition; and education. Most police agencies and civil service commissions accept applications even when no openings are listed. The application is placed on file, and when an examination is to be conducted, the applicant is notified by mail or phone.

Most agencies require that a police officer:

- Be a U.S. citizen.
- Have or be eligible for a driver's license in the state.
- Not have been convicted of a felony.

Requirements related to education and residency are also frequently stated.

Education

Educational requirements for officers have long been a source of controversy in law enforcement. Opinions differ greatly as to how much education a police officer candidate should have or how much should be a prerequisite for advancement.

Most police agencies require a minimum of a high-school education or equivalency certificate, and some require a two- or four-year degree. Many police agencies are now requiring some college education for employment and/or promotion. Whether such education helps officers perform better has not been documented.

The basic issue is, *Does more "formal" education make for better police officers?* The topic has even been the source of litigation. For example in *Davis v. City of Dallas* (1978), the department's requirement that applicants have completed 45 semester hours of college credit with a "C" average was challenged. In this case the court ruled in favor of the police department:

> The City introduced evidence which supports the educational requirement. Numerous nationwide studies have examined the problem of setting the education requirement for police departments with favorable conclusions. A college education as a condition of hiring as a police officer has been recommended by the National Commission on Law Observance in 1931; by the President's Commission on Law Enforcement and Commission on Intergovernmental Relations in 1971; by the American Bar Association in 1972; and by the National Advisory Commission on Criminal Justice Standards and Goals in 1973. Defendant's experts established the relationship between college education and performance of police officers. A study by one expert relied upon factual data from two large metropolitan areas that took two years to complete, showing significantly higher performance rates by college-educated officers. A persuasive point was made that a high-school diploma today does not represent the same level of achievement which it represented 10 years ago.

Michelson et al. (1999, p.15) report: "Research has demonstrated that college-educated officers outperform their less educated counterparts in a number of critical areas, including communication skills, public relations, report writing, analytical skills, decision-making, adaptability to change and overall performance." In addition, they note: "Federal courts have recognized college education as a bona fide occupational qualification."

Proponents of higher education for officers contend college-educated officers are less biased, less authoritarian and less likely to use force than non–college-educated officers. Advocates of advanced learning also believe college-educated officers hone their ability to flexibly handle difficult situations and develop an increased empathy and tolerance for minorities and persons with different lifestyles and ideologies. Completing occupation-specific courses provides a more complete understanding of the "big picture" of the criminal justice system and a better appreciation for the prosecutorial, courts and correction roles. Furthermore the entire college experience allows time for the individual to mature and develop a general sense of responsibility.

Educational standards appear to be higher yet for police managers. According to a survey of police chiefs in medium-to-large jurisdictions ("More Specialization for CJ Grad Programs," 1998, p.7), 87 percent have bachelor's degrees and approximately half have master's, doctoral or law degrees: "The overwhelming majority of chiefs said they held degrees in criminology, criminal justice, justice administration, public policy, political science and government."

Despite all the supposed advantages, many contend that good officers could be lost if educational levels are set too high. Critics of a college education requirement assert college graduates would be unlikely to seek employment in law enforcement, particularly women and minority college graduates, which would undermine the progress being made in recruiting them.

Some police chiefs believe that too much education makes social service officers of personnel who ought to be fighting crime in the streets. Others feel that to require a degreed officer to perform such mundane tasks as issuing traffic tickets and parking tickets, making money runs and carding juveniles in liquor stores is demeaning. These opponents contend that such routine tasks soon diminish the highly educated officer's interest in law enforcement, which leads to greater job dissatisfaction, increasing turnover rates and higher hostility levels toward non–college-educated officers.

Critics of required higher education assert the skills effective officers need can be learned only on the street, not in a classroom. In a similar vein, Molden (1999, p.21) cautions: "Education, per se, does not a good cop make. First find a good cop, then educate him and you will probably have a better cop."

All controversy aside, the trend in today's law enforcement agencies appears to be supportive of high education standards for officers.

Residency Requirements

Over the years cities and municipalities have waived residency requirements to obtain better candidates. Though residency is still generally not required, some cities are again beginning to accept only candidates who reside within their boundaries.

It is always preferred and sometimes required that police officers live in the community they serve.

Sometimes compromises have been made whereby candidates are given one year to move into the community they serve. City and municipal politicians feel that by living in the community, a police officer becomes more closely identified with that community and more sensitive to its crime problems and more readily participates in community activities.

Local residency is particularly important for departments instituting community policing. In addition politicians' self-interests dictate that their police officers live in the community so they can contribute their fair share of taxes. Some officers, however, may not be able to afford the cost of housing in the community they serve.

The Written Examination

Some departments use a civil service examination. Others use examinations designed specifically for their department. In either case the examinations do not usually test knowledge of police work or procedures but rather various abilities and aptitudes. Their primary function is to screen out those who lack the "basic material" to be a police officer.

Written examinations are usually in multiple-choice format and last two to three hours. They may test spelling, grammar and mathematical ability. They may also test reasoning ability, problem solving, reading comprehension, interpersonal communications skills or ability to process information.

Critics, however, claim written exams can't measure common sense and penalize those who do not test well. Such tests may also inadvertently "weed out" candidates who possess other valuable skills that cannot be measured on paper. Another downside to written exams is the potential for adverse impacts against minority applicants and those for whom English is not their primary language.

Most written examinations are a straight pass/fail situation, serving as an entry into the next phase of the selection process. Some agencies, however, factor in the score on this examination into their final selection decision. Many reference books and study guides are available to help candidates prepare to take written examinations in law enforcement. Those candidates who do well on the written test go on to physical fitness testing.

Physical Fitness Tests

Eighty percent of police departments require physical fitness tests of applicants (Decicco, 2000, p.3). Physical fitness tests determine a candidate's coordination and muscular strength and ascertain whether the candidate is in good physical condition. The type of test varies with police agencies throughout the country.

A candidate may be required to run a designated number of yards and while doing so hurdle a three-foot barrier, crawl under a 24-inch bar, climb over a four- or six-foot wall with both hands on top of the wall and sprint the remaining distance—all within a designated time monitored by a police officer with a stopwatch. Candidates may also be required to climb ropes or fire ladders and do chin-ups or push-ups. Other variations of the physical fitness test may be required, but usually only a minimum of strenuous activity is obligatory. Figure 11.2 illustrates the physical fitness course used at the Criminal Justice Institute of Broward Community College in Ft. Lauderdale, Florida.

Physical fitness tests evaluate a candidate's coordination, speed and strength. The most common physical fitness tests are similar to military obstacle courses, which must be completed in a designated time.

Physical fitness tests are necessary because they simulate what an officer may have to do on the street—jumping over a fence, climbing a wall or chasing

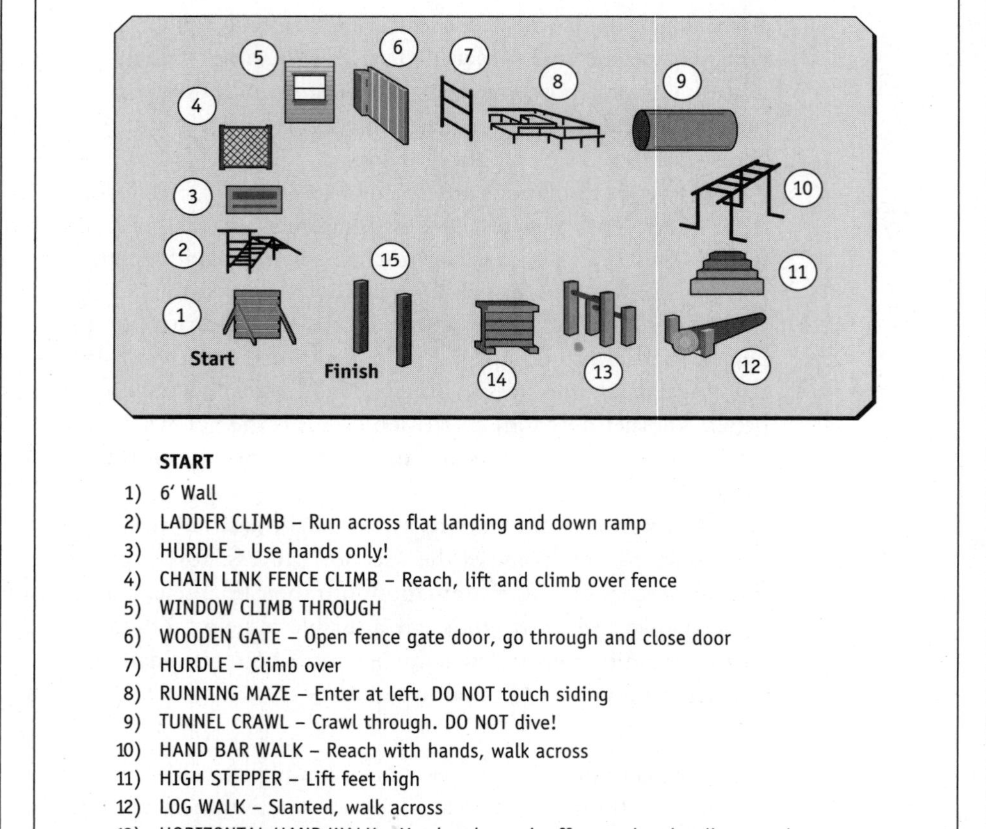

START

1) 6' Wall
2) LADDER CLIMB – Run across flat landing and down ramp
3) HURDLE – Use hands only!
4) CHAIN LINK FENCE CLIMB – Reach, lift and climb over fence
5) WINDOW CLIMB THROUGH
6) WOODEN GATE – Open fence gate door, go through and close door
7) HURDLE – Climb over
8) RUNNING MAZE – Enter at left. DO NOT touch siding
9) TUNNEL CRAWL – Crawl through. DO NOT dive!
10) HAND BAR WALK – Reach with hands, walk across
11) HIGH STEPPER – Lift feet high
12) LOG WALK – Slanted, walk across
13) HORIZONTAL HAND WALK – Use hands, push off ground and walk across bars
14) SHORT WALL – Jump up and over
15) POLE RUN – Run to your right, go $1^1/_2$ times around. DO NOT touch poles!

FINISH

Figure 11.2
Physical Fitness Course

Source: Criminal Justice Institute, Broward Community College, Ft. Lauderdale, FL. Reprinted by permission.

someone through backyards or streets. Candidates who are considerably overweight rarely pass the physical fitness test.

Candidates can prepare for the physical fitness test through a regular system of workouts. Running is an excellent general conditioner because it develops endurance and strengthens the legs. Sit-ups, leg-lift exercises, push-ups and lifting light weights are also helpful. Like knowledge, physical fitness does not develop overnight; it develops gradually over an extended period.

Psychological Testing

Psychological tests are administered to determine if the person is emotionally suited for a career in law enforcement. Employers use psychological tests to learn about the applicant's present state of mind, what is important to that person and how that person is likely to respond to certain stimuli. According to Curran (1998, p.88): "The selection of law enforcement personnel who exhibit stable emotional and behavioral functioning has become critical to law enforcement agencies. Excessive-force complaints, community policing initiatives and allegations of negligent hiring have demonstrated to personnel managers that hiring decisions must take into account the psychological characteristics of an applicant."

Psychological tests commonly used during officer selection include the Minnesota Multiphasic Personality Inventory—2 (MMPI-2), the California Psychological Inventory (CPI), the Myers-Briggs Type Indicator™, the Watson-Glaser Critical Thinking Appraisal and the Strong Interest Inventory. The IACP recommends: "Pre-employment psychological assessments should be used as one component of the overall selection process . . . [and] only licensed or certified psychologists trained and experienced in psychological test interpretation and law enforcement psychological assessment techniques should conduct screening for public safety agencies" ("Pre-Employment Psychological Evaluation . . .," 1998, p.95).

The Interview

The interviewing board usually consists of three to five skilled interviewers knowledgeable in their fields. They may be staff officers from the agency doing the hiring or from other agencies, psychologists, sociologists or representatives of a community service organization. The entire interviewing board may consist of members of a police or civil service commission. In smaller jurisdictions oral boards are sometimes replaced by an interview with the mayor, a member of the city council or the chief of police.

Interviews are used to evaluate an applicant's appearance, alertness, communication ability, social adaptability, judgment, emotional stability, and interest in and suitability for the job.

Interviews, whether structured or unstructured, are designed to elicit answers revealing the candidates' personalities and suitability for police work, *not* to determine their technical knowledge in the police field. Candidates should be prepared to answer questions such as:

- Why do you want to be a police officer?
- What have you done to prepare for a career in law enforcement?

- What do you believe are the causes of crime?
- How do you feel about community policing?
- What is the last book you have read?
- What was your favorite subject in school?
- When did you last get drunk?
- Why did you select this department to apply to?

Interviews also test a candidate's ability to use good judgment in specific situations. For example:

- A person is standing on the corner making a speech regarding the overthrow of the government. He is drawing a crowd, and a certain amount of animosity is being shown toward the speaker, indicating future trouble. How would you handle this situation?
- You are working radar and you clock the mayor going 39 mph in a 30 mph zone. How would you handle this situation?

The interview usually lasts about 30 minutes. The same questions are asked each candidate to allow comparison of answers. After the interview, each candidate's qualifications are evaluated and the candidate is given an overall rating, which is combined with the scores of the other examinations to yield a composite (total) score.

The Background Investigation

The applicant's background is a critical factor, and the background investigation serves two vital purposes: (1) it examines and verifies the past work and educational record of the candidate, and (2) it determines if anything in the candidate's background might make him or her unsuitable for police work. As Nelson (2000, p.88) stresses, the background investigation should never go shortchanged—"if for no other reason than to prevent a wrongful hiring lawsuit in the future."

Fuss et al. (1998, p.170) contend: "A thorough background investigation can make the difference between putting a qualified individual on the streets to protect and serve society or sending an unqualified individual who can cause harm to himself, society and the department that hires him." They (p.172) add: "Through litigation, society can hold a department liable for hiring an unqualified applicant, turning him loose on the streets and thus exposing himself and others to danger. This can be avoided through proper and thorough background investigations." The extensiveness of the background investigation is limited only by the number of candidates being investigated and time available.

Normally all information given by the applicant on the personal history sheet must be verified. Birth and age records are verified through vital statistics, and driving records are verified through the driver's license bureau. Adverse driving records containing drunken driving, driving after suspension or revocation of license, or a consistent pattern of moving violations may cause disqualification.

Candidates are fingerprinted, and the prints are sent to the FBI to determine if the candidate has a criminal record. The candidate's criminal record is also checked on the local and state levels, usually through fingerprints, name and date of birth. Juvenile records are normally discounted unless a person has committed a heinous crime.

Ironically because of the transient nature of our population, persons wanted on warrants in one part of the country have applied for a police officer's position in another part of the country. The criminal record check has sometimes resulted in their apprehension.

Military records are usually checked to verify service and eligibility under the veteran's preference acts of some states. The check also determines if the candidate was involved in any court-martials or disciplinary actions.

All personal and professional references listed on the history sheet are interviewed. Interviewing of references is sometimes criticized because candidates obviously will list only those who see them favorably; however these references may lead to others who know the candidates and have a different view of them. When candidates list out-of-town references, letters or questionnaires are usually mailed.

Previous employers are contacted to determine the applicant's work record. An inability to hold continuous employment may indicate trouble getting along with supervisors. A high absentee rate may indicate lack of interest or initiative or health problems.

The financial status of the candidate is also determined, usually through a credit records check. Those whose expenditures exceed their total incomes may be candidates for bankruptcy or bribery. Good credit indicates the person can live within his or her means and possesses self-control. The candidate may be required to submit a financial statement.

Educational records from high school, college and any other schools attended are usually checked through personal contact. The education record may indicate interests, achievements, accomplishments and social lifestyle while attending school. The scholastic record reflects not only intelligence but also study habits. Any degrees, certificates of achievement or awards are usually noted.

Polygraph examinations are growing in popularity as tools to verify information from background investigations, with approximately 56 percent of police departments currently using this test (Decicco, p.5). Although some states have banned use for pre-employment purposes, where it is used to screen police candidates, it is necessary to determine why it is being given. Some departments use the polygraph extensively, especially if they have many transient applicants from other parts of the country. Some agencies use it to determine if the candidate has ever engaged in criminal activity and was ever apprehended. Some want to know if the candidate has any sexually deviant behaviors. Others use it to verify the information the candidate has given on the application and history sheet.

The background investigation includes:

- Verification of all information on the application and history sheet.
- Check on driving record.
- Fingerprinting and a check on any criminal record.
- Check on military records.
- Interviews with personal references, acquaintances, past employers, neighbors and teachers.
- Check on financial status.
- Check on past performances at schools and previous jobs.

Testing or Assessment Centers

Some police departments use a testing or assessment center in the selection process, also called **situational testing.** Used by corporate America for over six decades, assessment centers were first accessed by law enforcement agencies during the mid-1980s to help with promotional decisions. Today such testing centers offer many benefits to agencies selecting and promoting law enforcement personnel.

Decicco (p.5) differentiates between an assessment center, which is a place, and an assessment center approach, which is "a method that supplements the traditional assessment and selection procedures with situational exercises designed to simulate actual police officer responsibilities and working conditions." He (p.6) states: "The courts have encouraged the use of assessment centers as the most fair and job-related method of assessing police officer candidates." Oliver (1998, p.9) notes:

> The real potential for growth in use of the assessment center method in law enforcement's current environment lies in our search for the prototype police officer. He or she is customer-service–oriented, is a team player, has high moral and ethical standards, has good written and oral communication skills, appreciates human diversity, has a positive attitude, and is a problem solver possessing good decision-making skills. The entry-level assessment center can evaluate these skills, knowledge and abilities.

Hutton and Sampson (1999, p.79) describe the four major areas most assessment center approaches examine: managing tasks, managing people, managing information and communication skills.

The Medical Examination

Medical requirements vary from jurisdiction to jurisdiction, but the purpose is the same. With the current emphasis on health care, more importance is placed on the medical examination. Citizens, concerned that police officers may retire early because of poor health, are demanding physically fit officer candidates. The medical standards usually include a variety of factors with some—vision, hearing and the cardiovascular-respiratory system—being more important than others.

Good eyesight is of great importance. Candidates who wear glasses that correct their vision to 20/20 can qualify in most departments. Likewise candidates who wear hearing aids that correct their hearing to meet the agency's requirements can qualify.

Because of job stress and the hypertension that often accompanies it, the cardiovascular system is thoroughly checked. The respiratory and cardiovascular systems play a critical role in fitness. To a great degree, endurance, the ability to continue exertion over a prolonged time, is directly related to the capacity of the cardiovascular-respiratory system to deliver oxygen to the muscles.

Vision, hearing and the cardiovascular-respiratory system are of prime importance in the medical examination.

Other medical factors often tested are the ratio of total cholesterol to HDL cholesterol (which identifies cardiovascular risk factors), blood pressure, smoking status, drug use and blood sugar level for diabetes. A physician who feels a candidate has a functional or organic disorder may recommend disqualification.

The Final Result

After all required tests are completed, they are analyzed, and a composite score is given for each candidate. A list is made of eligible candidates, and they are called as openings occur. Some larger police departments keep their eligibility lists one to two years, depending on civil service requirements or other requirements mandated by states or municipalities.

Federal Guidelines and Regulations

The basic rule of thumb is that all requirements must be clearly job related. A **bona fide occupational qualification (BFOQ)** is one that is reasonably necessary to perform the job. It may, on the surface, appear to be discrimination. For example in law enforcement, applicants may be required to have normal or correctable-to-normal hearing and vision because these attributes are required to perform the job.

Equal Employment Opportunity Act

In 1964 Congress enacted the Omnibus Civil Rights Law, of which Title VII concerned employment opportunities and prohibited discrimination based on sex, race, color, religion or national origin. The law also established the Equal Employment Opportunity Commission (EEOC) as its administrator. This law affected only private business, not state and local governments, and therefore had little impact on police agency practices.

However, in 1972 Congress passed the Equal Employment Opportunity Act, which modified Title VII to include state and local units of government. This law was passed because six years after the EEOC published guidelines for employment and promotion testing, few state or local central personnel selection agencies had taken positive steps to meet the guidelines.

The 1972 Equal Employment Opportunity Act prohibits discrimination due to sex, race, color, religion or national origin in employment of any kind, public or private, local, state or federal.

The EEOC legislation restricts the type of information that can be gathered from job applicants and requires all questions posed to applicants to be relevant to the job for which the applicant is applying. The following information cannot be asked about on application forms or during interviews: race or color, religion, national origin, age, marital status or ages of children, or if the person has ever been arrested. Applicants may be asked if they have ever been convicted of a crime and, if so, when and where it took place. Questions about education and experience are largely unrestricted.

Affirmative Action

The Affirmative Action Amendment (signed by President Nixon in 1973) further strengthened the power of the EEOC. **Affirmative action** refers to special endeavors by employers (including law enforcement agencies) to recruit, hire, retain and promote minority group members and to eliminate past and present employment discrimination. According to Walker et al. (2000, p.113): "The most controversial aspect of employment discrimination is the policy of affirmative action. The Office of Federal Contract Compliance defines affirmative action as 'results-oriented actions [taken] to ensure equal employment opportunity [which may include] goals to correct under-utilization . . . [and] backpay, retroactive seniority, makeup goals and timetables.'"

Affirmative action is more than simply not discriminating during hiring—it is actively favoring women and minorities. While the increases in the number of women and minorities in law enforcement agencies across the country are to be applauded, problems still exist. Sometimes these advancements are made at the expense of others—most notably white males. This is referred to as **reverse discrimination**—giving preferential treatment in hiring and promoting to women and minorities to the detriment of white males.

This issue has separated whites from minorities, men from women and the advocates of affirmative action from those who believe in a strict "merit" principle for employment and advancement. The majority position has been summarized as a concern that for every deserving minority group member who is provided a job or promotion through preferential quotas, a deserving, and often more qualified, nonminority person is deprived of a job or promotion. A growing number of majority member workers are complaining bitterly about their own civil rights being abridged, and some are filing reverse discrimination suits in court. Such suits, however, are not always easily won. In fact, the courts themselves have been deeply divided over the constitutionality of the reverse discrimination that some believe is implicit in minority quotas and double standards.

Frequently those who might be beneficiaries of affirmative action do not welcome it, as noted by a 20-year female sergeant who is Hispanic and one-quarter Navajo (Oglesby, 2002):

> When I joined the Los Angeles County Sheriff's Department in 1981, there was no significant demand for affirmative action; everyone was hired on merit and ability. Today, some 20 years later, those endorsing affirmative action are overlooking the fact that all citizens have the right to be protected and served by the best possible teachers, police officers, firefighters, doctors and other professionals. When we merely turn the tables on discrimination from one group to another, we defy all logic and common sense. When I am told that I as a female Hispanic must be entitled to affirmative action, which is preferential treatment, I become deeply insulted for the following reasons:
>
> - The assumption is that I am incompetent and inferior to white males, therefore rendering me incapable of succeeding on my own merit.
> - That assumption is degrading and undermines my morale and incentive to compete. Without that incentive, I will be less capable of

competing with others in the future as that preferential treatment can easily become an addictive crutch.
- My peers will not respect me because they will assume that I have accomplished everything through means of affirmative action.
- The public will have less respect for me for the same reasons.
- Therefore, if my peers and the public don't respect me, how can I respect myself? Or, the reverse, if I don't fully respect myself, why should anyone else respect me?
- As long as we have affirmative action, women and minorities will not get the respect they deserve.
- You don't eliminate discrimination by practicing discrimination.

While charges of reverse discrimination seem to struggle through the courts, the constitutionality of court-imposed quotas appears to find judicial favor, and the fact remains that affirmative action has played a great role in the increasing number of minorities and women in law enforcement.

Americans with Disabilities Act

Further complicating the selection and employment process is the Americans with Disabilities Act (ADA), which President Bush signed into law in July 1990. The purpose of this civil rights law is to guarantee equal opportunity to jobs for qualified individuals with disabilities.

The Americans with Disabilities Act (ADA) of 1990 prohibits discrimination in employment based on a disability.

Colbridge (2000b, p.28) explains: "For purposes of the ADA, disability means having a physical or mental impairment that substantially limits one or more major life activities, having a record of such an impairment, or being regarded as having such an impairment." Conditions excluded from protection, however, include current use of illegal drugs, compulsive gambling, kleptomania, pyromania, sexual behavior disorders and dysfunctions, pedophilia, voyeurism, exhibitionism and psychological disorders caused by current use of illegal drugs.

During the application process, the ADA prohibits employers from asking any questions or conducting any medical examinations that would identify applicants with disabilities or the nature and extent of such disabilities. Tests for use of illegal drugs are not considered medical examinations under ADA. However, as Scuro (2001, p.31) notes: "In the decade of the ADA's existence and practical application in this country, there are still no uniform standards to be applied when addressing the daily personnel issues that are a part of the routine operations of both a public sector law enforcement agency or private sector corporation."

Employers can ask pre-employment questions about the applicants' ability to perform essential, job-related tasks. Colbridge (2000a, p.30) notes: "Courts have upheld employers' decisions to not hire people with disabilities who lacked . . . qualifications . . . essential to the performance of the job." Such qualifications include firing a weapon, making forcible arrests and driving. He suggests: "Taking the time to meticulously identify these essential functions prior to advertising open positions can save time and money if a claim under the ADA arises." Colbridge (2000c, p.20) also notes: "Employers are not required to change the essential functions of a job in order to accommodate a person's disability."

Further, as Litchford (2000, p.15) says: "The courts have held that the ADA does not prohibit officers from taking enforcement action [against individuals with disabilities], including use of force, necessary to protect officer or public safety."

Probation and Training

According to Kaminsky (2001, p.32): "The avowed purpose of the probationary period is to provide some protection to an organization while it determines whether or not the new employee is all that the organization hoped they would be when hired." It is expected that during this period training would be comprehensive and on-going. "As we begin the 21st century," say Birzer and Tannehill (2001, p.233), "the need for more and improved police training is gathering increasing momentum." They stress:

> There is an obvious need for police officers to acquire knowledge of the latest legal decisions, technological advances, and tactical developments in the field, and to remain proficient in a number of job-related skills. There is also an urgent need for police officers who are skilled communicators and decision makers, who are capable of helping citizens identify and solve problems in their communities, and who possess effective mediation and conflict-resolution skills.

Unfortunately, many departments stress the physical aspects of policing and weapons without emphasizing that communication is usually an officer's most valuable weapon.

Some states have mandated that recruits must be given from 240 to 400 hours of police training within one year of employment. Coincidentally one year is also usually the length of time the officers are placed on probation.

> The probationary period is a trial period, usually one year, during which the officer is observed while obtaining training and applying this training on the streets.

Police officers may obtain their training in a state police academy, a city academy or a specialized rookie school. The basic training of police officers varies with each jurisdiction and its needs, but most officers will be trained in constitutional law, laws of arrest, search and seizure and in the various requests for service, such as accident investigation, crisis intervention and first aid.

While in training, recruits may be required to return to the department and spend a specified number of hours on street patrol. Some jurisdictions alternate their training periods every two weeks, allowing an officer to apply on the street what was learned in basic recruit school.

While on the street, the recruits ride with a field training officer or FTO, usually a sergeant, who monitors their movements and helps them apply principles learned in rookie school. While in school the officers are evaluated and tested by their instructors, who periodically send progress reports to the chief. After completing training they continue to ride with one or more training offi-

Michael Newman/PhotoEdit

These cadets are receiving military-type drill instruction at a training site. Physical training is a central part of the six-month to one-year probationary period common in most police departments.

cers who evaluate their street performance. Following successful completion of the probationary period, they are full-fledged police officers. After probation some states license the person to be a police officer. Legislatures in many states have adopted standards for police officers that must be met to satisfy the state's training requirements for licensing.

States have also mandated a certain amount of in-service training to keep the license current. Many of these in-service training requirements revolve around the behavioral sciences to give police officers a better understanding of the entire criminal justice system. Guest speakers from the corrections system, the court system and on many occasions from minority groups present their philosophy and objectives to police officers.

Preparatory police academies have been proposed as an alternative approach to law enforcement recruitment and training. Other training opportunities include national scholarship programs similar to the military's Reserve Officer Training Corps (ROTC). Wexler (1998, p.52) notes how the federally funded program, called Police Corps, aims to put better-educated police officers on patrol: "The 1994 federal anti-crime law appropriated $10 million to six states to develop police training programs. . . . College graduates who agree to serve four years in a participating police department will be reimbursed up to $30,000 in education costs."

Failure to Train

The ground rules for failure to train were initially established by the Supreme Court in *City of Canton v. Harris* (1989). In this case the Court held that inadequacy of officer training could serve as the basis of a Section 1983 liability only where the failure to train was the result of the "deliberate indifference to the rights" of the persons with whom the officer comes into contact. The Court's decision in this case, according to Spector (2001, p.75) left departments with "a lot of wiggle room and avenues to escape liability for failure to train."

However, the rather amorphous "deliberate indifference" standard has been replaced by the ruling in *Brown v. Bryan* (2000) in which the Supreme Court refused to consider the county's appeal concerning municipal liability for failure to train. As Risher (2001, p.10) explains: "The court held that a municipality may be liable for the inadequate training and misconduct of just one officer. . . . Any misstep by an officer that results in injury may lead to a failure-to-train claim."

Spector (p.73) notes: "Now, plaintiffs' attorneys will take the effort to plow through individual defendant officer's training records to find some deficiency related to their client's claimed injury, and if they want to spend a few bucks they'll hire some expert to identify these training deficiencies." He (p.77) notes that in *Brown,* the sheriff testified he didn't have sufficient funds to conduct training. The county ended up paying $642,300 for the failure-to-train claim.

Retention

Recruiting, selecting and training new officers is expensive and time consuming. Therefore it is essential that agencies retain their officers. Among the factors to consider—in addition to the personal satisfaction of the job and good working conditions—are salary and benefits, opportunities for promotion and the ability to avoid stress and burnout.

Salary and Benefits

Salaries among police departments in the country have little uniformity. A variety of factors influence a police officer's salary, such as the community's ability to pay, the cost of living in the area and the prevailing wages of similar police departments in surrounding areas.

Normally position-classification plans are implemented under a personnel ordinance or department rule book. Steps on the salary scale are established in each position classification. New recruits start at the bottom of the salary scale and receive increment raises after six months and each succeeding year until they reach their maximum salary, usually after three to five years. They obtain more salary only if granted a cost-of-living raise; however a promotion to the next rank would bring them into a higher salary bracket. Sergeants, lieutenants, captains and chiefs all have minimum and maximum starting levels, with the top salary usually reached after three years in the position.

To compensate those who do not attain a rank during their police careers, many police departments have adopted longevity plans whereby nonranking officers receive a certain percentage more of their salaries after the tenth year, the fifteenth year and so on. This seniority system has been attacked, however, on the grounds that it discourages initiative and further education.

When salary schedules are formulated, such fringe benefits as hospitalization and dental plans, insurance, vacation, sick leave and holidays are all considered. Police officers' indirect benefits from their employers are estimated to be approximately 33 percent, comparable to what business and industry currently allow their employees. In addition to the more common benefits of paid holidays and vacations, personal and family sick leave, and medical and dental insurance, other benefits a department might provide include a uniform and clothing allowance, child care, life insurance, disability insurance, hospitalization insurance, workman's compensation, military leave, deferred compensation, college incentive pay, tuition reimbursement, retirement fund, pension plan and credit union.

Policies vary regarding how to pay officers for overtime on the job, going to court while on duty, attending required training sessions while off duty and being called back to duty in an emergency. Some departments pay overtime; others give compensatory time off.

Police departments may belong to unions that bargain for them. Usually all conditions of employment are clearly spelled out in their contracts.

Promotional Opportunities

According to Garner (1998, p.24): "Probably the only thing consistent about the ways law enforcement agencies test for promotion is the inconsistency of the testing process from one department to the next." He notes: "Some departments rely solely on an eligibility list determined by candidates' scores on a written test. Others rely on assessment centers, oral boards or a combination of the two, while yet others combine some mixture of written and oral testing procedures. Whatever the nature of the examination process, the agency is attempting to rank order its promotional candidates in their ability to solve factual, issue-based and hypothetical problems and scenarios."

While the nature of the testing and evaluation depends, in part, on the rank level involved in the promotion, Bernstein (1998, p.67) adds: "The Assessment Center method of testing has become common for police ranks from Sergeant to Chief."

Stress and Burnout

No discussion of retention would be complete without recognizing the highly stressful nature of this profession. Police officers deal with crisis daily, usually that of someone else. Sometimes, however, the demands of the roles and how they are expected to be performed create enough stress to put police officers themselves into a crisis situation.

A police officer's job is highly stressful and may result in a personal crisis for the officer.

Dr. Hans Selye (1907–1982), known as the "father of the stress field," first defined **stress** as the nonspecific response of the body to any demand placed on it. He later said stress was simply the wear and tear caused by living. Volpe (2000, p.183) defines stress as "a physical, chemical or emotional factor that causes bodily or mental tension resulting from factors that tend to alter an existing equilibrium."

Stress can be either positive or negative. In ancient China the symbol for stress had two written characters—one for opportunity and one for danger. In fact the excitement/stress of police work is one important reason people enter the profession. Unfortunately much of the stress experienced by police officers and, indeed, the general population, is negative.

Stress may also be acute or chronic. Acute stress is temporary and often positive. It keeps a person alert and focused. Chronic stress, in contrast, is continuous and can be debilitating. Thompson (1999, p.109) perceives stress as primarily chronic, stating: "Stress is the product of an entire lifestyle, not an isolated incident. Someone once said that the only way to rid the body of stress was to die."

Everyone experiences stressors in their lives. Bennett and Hess (2001, p.437) observe: "Some common stress producers of daily living are changing relationships, a lifestyle inconsistent with values (too committed), money problems (credit-card debt, poor investments), loss of self-esteem (falling behind professionally, accepting others' expectations), and fatigue or illness (poor diet, lack of sleep or lack of exercise)." Police officers may experience any of these in addition to stressors unique to the profession. Kanable (1999, p.79) explains:

> Law enforcement offices are different from others in society in their work environment [in that it] is very negative, they have "burst stress" (they go from calm to high activity and pressure in one "burst"), they must constantly control their emotions, they don't work 9 to 5—they work shifts, they wear uniforms to distinguish them from society (this also can separate them from society), they work in a quasi-military structured institution and there are laws to follow and no gray areas.

Aaron (2000, p.438) identifies other stressors unique to law enforcement: "Unlike members of most other professions, police officers encounter experiences of physical danger, including the threat of serious injury or death to themselves, and exposure to others who have been seriously injured, killed, or otherwise traumatized. In addition, they are exposed to a number of organizational stressors that include negative public perception of police, perceived lack of departmental support, and interface with the judicial system." Reese (2001, p.14) adds: "Police officers can and often do become *vicarious victims*—stressed, altered, and in some cases destroyed by the crimes they investigate."

While shift work and pursuing armed suspects are relatively visible occupational hazards of policing, law enforcement is filled with many other "hidden stressors." One such insidious stressor is isolation—long hours spent alone on patrol, set apart from the rest of society by a uniform, and being held to a higher, almost nonhuman, standard than the general public. Adding to this sense of isolation is the daily interaction with the "criminal element" and routine exposure to the worst of the human condition—violence, death, pain, loss, poverty, drug addiction and lies, lies, lies. Over time, the effects of such stressors may spill over into officers' personal lives, leading them to distrust even their own family and friends.

Another hidden stressor is the unspoken, perhaps subconscious, double standard many citizens hold regarding the law, their personal freedoms and the responsibilities of the police. Examples of some of the mixed messages officers receive from the public include: "Stop those crazy drivers from speeding through my neighborhood. But you'd better not give me a ticket for rushing home." Or "Get tough on drunk drivers—they should have the book thrown at them. But I know I'm competent to drive after a night of bar-hopping with my friends." Or "Keep us safe. But don't invade our privacy."

If the stresses become great enough, officers may burn out. Being aware of and reducing stressors can prevent officer **burnout,** which Hawkins (2001, p.343) describes as "a syndrome of emotional exhaustion, depersonalization, and reduced personal accomplishment." According to Bennett and Hess (p.452): "Burnout occurs when someone is exhausted or is listless because of overwork or stress. Burnout results from long-term, unmediated stress. . . . Those most likely to experience burnout are those who are initially most committed. You cannot burn out if you have never been on fire."

Strategies for reducing stress and avoiding burnout including physical exercise, proper nutrition, adequate sleep, social outlets, relaxation techniques and time management. Many police departments are recognizing the hazards of stress for their officers and are taking steps to reduce or eliminate the causes over which they have control.

Another negative result of stress related to traumatic incidents is **posttraumatic stress disorder (PTSD).** Kates (2001, p.30) notes the distinction between posttraumatic stress and posttraumatic stress *disorder,* saying the difference lies in the symptoms:

> Posttraumatic stress may include some PTSD symptoms such as nightmares and flashbacks, but it also features symptoms like depression, eating disorders, heavy drinking and gambling, which are not part of PTSD's roster of reactions. Posttraumatic stress symptoms are generally short-lived, unlike PTSD's symptoms. . . .
>
> To be diagnosed with PTSD, candidates must meet two specific criteria. . . . [1] a person has experienced or witnessed a traumatic event that involves actual or threatened death or serious injury. . . . [and 2] the person has responded with intense fear, helplessness or despair. These reactions pave the way for PTSD to be set in motion. . . .
>
> You could sum up PTSD simply by saying that it consists of three clusters or groupings of symptoms. Those groupings are called reliving, avoidance and arousal [which he describes as difficulty concentrating and falling or staying asleep, overreacting to situations and being overly alert].

Kates (p.31) says that officers with PTSD experience "days and nights teeming with nightmares, cold sweats, tears and misery unimaginable to most."

In addition to such negative conditions as burnout and PTSD, as Mulroy (2000, p.67) contends: "Stress is now documented to cause performance levels to decline. Long-term stress is not only destructive, but may be fatal in police work." It can cause serious physical problems such as heart problems, and it can even lead to suicide.

Stress can have adverse effects on police behavior which may, in turn, lead to citizen complaints being filed against an officer or the agency. The complaint review process may occur internally by police department personnel or may be overseen by a civilian review board, which is another stressor in and of itself.

Civilian Review Boards—Can Police "Police" Themselves?

A **civilian review board** consists of citizens who meet to review complaints filed against the police department or against individual officers. The use and benefits of **civilian review** remains highly controversial.

Although civilian review boards have been used since the mid-1950s, administrators today still resist such "interference by outsiders." Many police chiefs say their jobs are tough enough without having civilian review boards constantly looking over their shoulders. Police leaders insist that only police officers can understand and judge the actions of other officers and that civilian oversight diminishes police morale and impedes officer performance. Finn (2000, p.23) suggests: "Basically, most agencies have opposed citizen oversight because they feel that oversight procedures represent outside interference, oversight staff lack experience with and understanding of police work, and oversight processes are unfair."

However many local officials worry that justice may not be served if the police judge each other: "Surveys found that one-half of all Americans do not believe the police can investigate other police officers in an unbiased manner. As a result, politicians and community groups push for the use of civilian oversight committees and civilian review boards to handle citizen complaints. For the past decade, over one-half of major city police departments include some type of civilian involvement when handling citizen complaints" (Johnson, 1998, p.4). According to Finn (p.26): "Despite serious reservations about citizen oversight, many law enforcement administrators have identified several ways that such systems can benefit police agencies. These include bettering an agency's image with the community, enhancing an agency's ability to police itself, and most important, improving an agency's policies and procedures."

Although community residents appear to prefer citizen review over internal police investigation, dissatisfaction remains high, and the heralded benefits remain disputed. As Johnson (p.4) reports: "Citizens in communities with a civilian review system do not appear to have more confidence in the manner in which departments handle citizen complaints. Studies analyzing several different civilian review systems revealed that citizens felt just as unsatisfied when a civilian review board handled their complaints as when the police handled their complaints."

Although citizen review boards are empowered only to recommend disciplinary actions, not to impose sanctions, many such as Walker ("Civilian Review Needs . . .," 1998, p.10) assert: "The accountability of police is enhanced by having citizen input in the complaint process."

An alternative to civilian review boards, a civilian ombudsman, has been used successfully in Boise, Idaho. As Boatman (2001, p.219) explains, a community ombudsman provides a liaison between police and residents and makes policy recommendations to the police, mayor and city council. The result: "The presence of a community ombudsman has seen minor complaints against police officers nearly double, but serious complaints have been cut in half" (p.220). Boatman concludes: "For the review process to work, it can be neither window dressing nor adversarial. Both the independence of the ombudsman and the ultimate responsibility and authority of the chief must be preserved."

Sexual Harassment

Sexual harassment has become an issue of concern because of the rising number of women in law enforcement and the resistance to change by many officers from the "old school" in the traditionally male-dominated occupation. In addition the number of sexual harassment cases has been increasing, and the monetary awards have been sometimes shocking. For example two ex-Long Beach policewomen were awarded $3.1 million in damages for sexual harassment. In 1997, state and federal losses from sexual harassment suits were $189 million and $267 million respectively (Carlan and Byxbe, 2000, p.124).

Sexual harassment is prohibited by Title VII of the 1964 Civil Rights Act, which states: "It is unlawful for any employer to discriminate against any individual with respect to his compensation, terms, conditions or privileges of employment, because of such individual's race, color, religion, sex, or national origin." Most state laws also prohibit sexual harassment.

The federal government defines **sexual harassment** as "unwelcome sexual advances, requests for sexual favors, and other verbal or physical conduct of a sexual nature" ("Preventing Sexual Harassment," n.d., p.1). The courts have classified unlawful sexual harassment as either *quid pro quo* harassment or *hostile environment* harassment:

> The quid pro quo type of sexual harassment . . . involve[s] a supervisor's demand for sexual favors from an employee in return for a job benefit. Most courts agree that such conduct constitutes discrimination in the terms or conditions of employment in violation of Title VII. . . .
>
> With hostile-environment harassment, the courts have generally agreed that an employer is liable for hostile environment (whether created by co-employees or by supervisors) only if the offensive conduct was sufficiently severe or pervasive to alter the terms and conditions of employment, and the employer knew, or should have known, about the offensive conduct (Byrd, 1998, p.147).

Pederson (2001, p.128) reports on a Florida study of 3,000 policewomen in which 69 percent claimed to have been sexually harassed on the job. Forty percent said it occurred daily. The most common offenses were jokes, comments, cartoons, calendars and verbal harassment. And, as expected, male officers initiated the vast majority of harassing behavior.

Many female officers are reluctant to report sexual harassment, well aware of the common perception among male officers that women are overly sensitive and prone to emotionalism. For females who have struggled to overcome this stereotype, filing a sexual harassment complaint means risking further alienation by their peers. According to Fuss and Snowden (2000, p.71): "Few people report sexual harassment and, of those who do, few feel the matter was resolved to their satisfaction." Thus, remaining silent is often seen as the lesser of two evils.

Harrington, director of the National Center for Women and Policing, explains what happens to an officer who files a complaint: "Offensive remarks may be made at roll call. There may be severe retaliation. Other officers may refuse to speak to her or refuse to cover her when she calls for help" (Pederson, p.130). Carlan and Byxbe (p.124) contend: "Harm caused by sexual harassment is often extreme. It can include humiliation, loss of dignity, psychological—and sometimes physical—injury, and damage to professional reputations and careers."

Although extensive evidence exists that sexual harassment has permeated even the most professional police agencies, administrators remain reluctant to acknowledge its presence and often exhibit surprisingly cavalier attitudes toward the problem. Carlan and Byxbe (p.124) report: "A recent survey indicated that 34 percent of law enforcement agencies in the United States have no written sexual harassment policy, and fewer than a quarter said they would promptly investigate a filed complaint. The failure to adopt a proactive and aggressive policy to eliminate sexual harassment is clearly a liability gamble."

Preventing sexual harassment from occurring is the best strategy for handling the issue, and, as Pederson (p.128) asserts: "Creating awareness of sexual harassment is the first step toward preventing it." Carlan and Byxbe stress: "Administrators are encouraged to have a written policy that sets forth the steps necessary to prevent sexual harassment from occurring. This policy should clearly communicate to all employees that sexual harassment will not be tolerated." In addition, says Bland (2000, p.64), the policy needs to be disseminated, complaints have to be investigated, remedial action should be taken as appropriate, and finally, all employees must be adequately trained.

Webster (1997, p.10) notes a twist in the problem of sexual harassment—according to the Equal Employment Opportunity Commission (EEOC), same-sex sexual harassment is also actionable. The EEOC Compliance Manual states that "the victim does not have to be of the opposite sex from the harasser. Since sexual harassment is a form of sex discrimination, the crucial inquiry is whether the harasser treats a member or members of one sex differently from members of the other sex." The Supreme Court ruling in *Oncale v. Sundowner Offshore Services, Inc.* (1997) expanded the definition of illegal same-sex harassment:

> Some courts have said same-sex harassment is barred only in the case of a gay supervisor making advances to a male underling.
>
> Disagreeing, [Justice] Scalia noted that harassment sometimes reflects a "general hostility" to another sex, not sexual attraction. For example, some men do not like working with women. If they harass them, their conduct is illegal, he said, even though sexual desire is not involved. The same holds true for same-sex harassment, he said ("Same-Sex Harassment . . .," 1998, p.A17).

Consequently, all officers, males and females alike, must protect their interests and help eradicate sexual harassment that threatens to undermine the effectiveness of policing. Another way in which officers seek to protect their interests is by establishing police labor unions and other local employee organizations.

Unions

During the early part of the twentieth century, police officers joined social groups, societies and clubs. Initially these groups centered their activities around social events and benevolent endeavors. In some instances these groups have functioned viably and contributed not only to their members' welfare but to department morale. In other departments these organizations have served as a vehicle for departmental dissidents to promote their own welfare and to create conflict.

"A **union,** in the broadest context, is any group authorized to represent the members of the law enforcement agency in negotiating such matters as wages, fringe benefits and other conditions of employment" (Bennett and Hess, p.226). A **union shop** is an agency where people must belong to or join the union to be hired.

Most police officers are currently members of local employee organizations and are not directly enrolled in a national labor union.

Unions are strongest in the northeast and on the west coast. The International Union of Police Associations (IUPA) began in 1978 as the only union exclusively designed for law enforcement personnel and, as of June 2001, there were 4,000 police unions in the United States with 225,000 sworn law enforcement members and 11,000 retired members. Bennett and Hess (p.227) observe: "Strong feelings for and against unions are common in the general public and among those in law enforcement. For many law enforcement agencies, unions are a positive force; for others, they create problems and dissension; and in yet others, they are nonexistent."

One common objection to unions is the tactics commonly employed, including slowdowns, "sickouts" and strikes. Although it is usually illegal for most public employees to strike, strikes by law enforcement officers have occurred in San Francisco, Tucson and Oklahoma City. Some of the strikes lasted only a few days, but others lasted weeks. In some cases strikers lost their jobs, but in others they obtained raises.

Other objections raised against unions include the fear that the law enforcement administrators and public officials who unionized police employees could abuse their collective bargaining power and that specific aspects of administration, such as transfers and promotions, could become bound up in arbitration and grievance procedures. Many administrators see the union as interfering with their leadership and with the officers in the ranks. In addition police unions have resisted changes in law enforcement organizations and techniques that affect their membership. For example the unions have opposed attempts to shift from two-person to one-person patrol cars. Unions have also objected to efforts to hire civilians in clerical positions, and they have resisted affirmative action efforts, seeking to maintain the status quo rather than to increase recruitment of women and minorities.

One highly debated issue related to union membership is who should belong. What ranks should be included? Should managers and supervisors belong to the same union as patrol officers? Another topic of concern to unions and their members is the growing presence of private police forces.

Privatization of Criminal Justice

Privatization refers to the practice of having nonsworn personnel, often private security officers, perform tasks traditionally performed by police officers. Private security forces include guards, patrols, investigators, armed couriers, central alarm respondents and consultants. Private security agencies and their officers perform many of the same functions as police and other government law enforcement agencies and their officers: they control entrances and exits to facilities; promote safety and security inside government buildings, courthouses and airports; safeguard equipment, valuables and confidential material; prevent and report fires and other property damage; and patrol restricted areas. Businesses and educational, industrial and commercial organizations often hire private security guards to protect their premises and investments. In addition, police agencies commonly subcontract with private companies and labs for evidence testing, fingerprint and handwriting analysis, and applicant screening.

There are, however, important differences between private security officers and police officers. Police officers are salaried with public funds, responsible to a chief of police and, ultimately, accountable to the community's citizens. Technically they are on duty 24 hours a day and have full authority to uphold the law, including the authority to make arrests and to carry a concealed weapon. Still police officers cannot be everywhere. Therefore many businesses and organizations have elected to hire special protection.

Basically two different types of private security may be hired: private patrols and on-site security officers. As the name implies, private patrols operate both on and off the premises of their employers and may check several customers' properties periodically during a specified time period. On-site security officers, however, stay on the property to safeguard the premises at all times. Another distinction exists between security officers employed by large industrial firms and night guards employed by small firms. The former are usually carefully screened, well paid and trained to perform specific duties. In contrast night guards are often retired from a regular job (sometimes as police officers), need only temporary work or are simply supplementing a regular income by taking on a second job.

Private security officers differ from police officers in that private security officers are salaried with private funds, are responsible to an employer and have limited authority extending to only the premises they are hired to guard. Security officers have no authority to carry concealed weapons and, unless deputized, have no authority to make arrests except as a citizen's arrest. Furthermore, their uniform and badge must not closely resemble that of a regular police officer.

Anderson (1999, p.4) suggests: "Sometimes the gap between the private security industry and the public law enforcement sector seems hopelessly wide, but if you look closely you can see it narrowing. Issues separate the two groups, but their overall goal—the protection of people and property—is proving to be a strong unifying force." According to Green (1998, p.95): "Partnerships between private security and public law enforcement have evolved beyond the traditional concept of private security supplementing police in street patrols. Private security professionals are now teaming up with local, state, and federal law enforcement to investigate past crimes and develop cooperative programs to prevent future incidents."

Many benefits to law enforcement may be realized through partnering with private security. While usually complementing law enforcement efforts, private security officers can assist in responding to burglar alarms, investigating internal theft and economic crimes, protecting VIPs and executives, moving hazardous materials, and controlling crowds and traffic for public events. Private policing, or privatization, also has an advantage in that security officers are not bound by many constraints public police officers are, such as having to give the Miranda warning to suspects. Furthermore private sector development of police stations, sheriffs' stations and jails is being advocated as an option for replacing outdated facilities.

Some police departments hire out full-time sworn officers to private enterprises for a fee. In other cases, police officers find part-time, supplemental employment on their own, sometimes against the preference or policy of their department.

Moonlighting

Moonlighting, working at a part-time job while fulfilling the obligations of a full-time position, has been a source of controversy in the police field for many years and falls within a gray area some departments prefer to avoid. Sharp (1999, p.82) observes: "There may be nothing closer to a 'Don't ask, don't tell' policy in law enforcement than the subject of off-duty employment for officers. As a recent survey indicated, for the most part administrators tolerate off-duty employment, but they are not enthralled with it."

Moonlighting is controversial and is handled differently from one department to the next.

Most police departments restrict the type of work that can be done and the number of hours an officer can work while off duty. Some cities allow their police officers to work off duty in only police-related areas; others allow them to work in only non–police-related areas. While allowing police officers to work off duty has definite advantages, disadvantages also exist and most cities and municipalities have developed policies that place limits on the officer's off-duty time. Policies on moonlighting address issues such as how to obtain permission for off-duty work, what types of off-duty jobs are not permitted and the like. Policies must also adhere to the Fair Labor Standards Act (FLSA) rules concerning moonlighting officers and the conditions attached to dual employment, joint employment, "special detail" work and "volunteer" work (Chamberlain, 1998).

Weinblatt (1999, p.84) notes: "Few chiefs or politicians will ban off-duty employment. The officers want it, and businesses want it." In fact, in many communities, the demand for off-duty officers has often outstripped the supply. The potential revenue for police departments that hire out their officers for private duty has enabled this approach to find favor among agencies traditionally opposed to moonlighting ("A Cop to Call . . .," 1998, p.5):

> Ending decades of opposition to the idea of its police officers being made available for private detail, the New York City Police Department has started a Paid Detail Program in which private groups or individuals can hire an officer to provide security at parties, meetings and other gatherings. . . .
>
> All potential "clients" will be scrutinized by the NYPD, and officers who participate will be rotated so they won't develop ties to a particular employer. Those with poor job records or who face criminal investigation or pending disciplinary action may not participate.

Standards regarding secondary employment of police officers are among the 439 standards outlined by CALEA for agencies seeking accreditation.

Accreditation

The Commission on Accreditation for Law Enforcement Agencies (CALEA) was formed in 1979 to develop a set of law enforcement standards and to establish and administer an **accreditation** process through which law enforcement agencies could demonstrate *voluntarily* that they meet professionally recognized criteria for excellence in management and service delivery. The commission is the combined effort of the International Association of Chiefs of Police (IACP), the National Organization of Black Law Enforcement Executives (NOBLE), the National Sheriffs' Association (NSA) and the Police Executive Research Forum (PERF). Members of these four organizations direct approximately 80 percent of the law enforcement community in the United States ("About CALEA," 2002).

The Commission on Accreditation for Law Enforcement Agencies was formed to develop professional standards and to administer a voluntary accreditation process, although controversy exists over the value of such accreditation.

The CALEA standards address nine major law enforcement subjects: (1) role, responsibilities and relationships with other agencies; (2) organization, management and administration; (3) personnel structure; (4) personnel process; (5) operations; (6) operational support; (7) traffic operations; (8) prisoner and court-related activities; and (9) auxiliary and technical services. The goals of these standards are to help law enforcement agencies (1) strengthen crime prevention and control capabilities, (2) formalize essential management procedures, (3) establish fair and nondiscriminatory personnel practices, (4) improve service delivery, (5) solidify interagency cooperation and coordination and (6) boost citizen and staff confidence in the agency ("The Standards," 2001).

CALEA's accreditation process consists of five phases: (1) the application, (2) self-assessment, (3) on-site assessment, (4) commission review and (5) maintaining compliance and re-accreditation. Any "legally constituted governmental entities having mandated responsibilities to enforce laws and having personnel with general or special law enforcement powers" are eligible to apply. As of September 1999, the number of accredited agencies in the United States was 534, between 3 and 5 percent of all agencies in the country (Sharp, 2000, p.93). And as of October 2001, 228,751 law enforcement and public safety professionals were members of organizations already accredited/certified by CALEA or were in the self-assessment phase ("It's a Fact," 2001).

Supporters of national accreditation contend it is one way to elevate law enforcement to a professional status and to assure that certain standards are met. Sylvester Daughtry, Jr., executive director of CALEA, has asserted: "Our standards are recognized by the courts as the prevailing professional standards that law enforcement agencies should adhere to" (Clark, 1998b, p.8). For agencies willing to meet the challenge, accreditation may provide the following benefits:

- A set of clear, written policies and procedures so every employee knows what's expected
- Assurance that department operations are consistent with current professional standards
- Greater accountability within the agency and higher morale
- Improved management/union relations

- Enhanced defense against citizen complaints and lawsuits and reduced litigation costs
- Controlled liability insurance costs and discounts from insurance carriers
- Increased professionalism, an enhanced reputation for the department and greater community advocacy
- Increased support of government officials bolstered by their confidence in the agency's ability to operate efficiently and meet community needs
- Greater justification for resource and budget requests
- A proven management system of written directives, sound training, clearly defined lines of authority, and routine reports that support decision making and resource allocation
- A better managed agency

As noted by Sharp (2000, p.95) a study by the Intergovernmental Risk Management Agency found that the number of [liability] claims per 100 officers is reduced by 17 percent in frequency and 35 percent in severity when agencies are accredited by CALEA. In fact, CALEA states: "Many agencies report a decline in legal actions against them, once they become accredited" ("Benefits of Accreditation," 2001). Says Sharp (p.94): "Fewer liability claims against a department translates into money savings. When you compare those savings to the costs of accreditation, the overall figures might mean that law enforcement agencies save money in the long run."

Despite these potential benefits, accreditation does have critics. A pool of randomly selected law enforcement agencies indicated five major arguments against accreditation: (1) too expensive, (2) too time-consuming, (3) dubious benefits, (4) hard to justify to community government and (5) department administration does not believe in it (Sharp, p.92). Table 11.1 summarizes the results of a survey of law enforcement administrators on the perceived benefits of accreditation.

Table 11.1
Perceived Benefits of Accreditation

Statement	Agreed	Disagreed	Unsure
Accreditation is more a status symbol or public relations tool than it is a valuable process.	53%	21%	26%
Accreditation has an appreciable impact on how well an agency performs.	54%	31%	15%
Accreditation does establish accountability within the office.	60%	28%	12%
Accreditation establishes uniformity in service delivery.	44%	32%	24%
Accreditation promotes efficient and effective administration and deployment of personnel.	36%	32%	32%
Accreditation provides stronger defense against lawsuits.	44%	40%	16%
Accreditation improves employee morale.*	24%	32%	44%

*Most significant finding

Source: Adapted from Arthur G. Sharp. "Accreditation: Fad or Fixture?" *Law and Order,* March 2000, p.93.

While criticism of the accreditation process is not new, and controversy has surrounded such standards from the start, much of the debate in recent years has centered on whether these standards facilitate or inhibit the implementation of community policing. CALEA presents a compelling argument in support of the facilitation of community policing through accreditation and how the two processes complement each other ("Community Policing," 2001):

> Implementing community policing requires the kind of dynamic and multifaceted process that accreditation encourages . . . a process that involves every component of the department and every facet of the community and local government . . . a process that fosters employee and citizen advice and counsel . . . and, a strategy designed to stimulate dialogue and feedback.
>
> Earning accredited status and implementing community policing can galvanize community support for a law enforcement agency. It can turn interagency cooperation into coordination and community apathy into collaboration. Community participation is an integral part of the self-assessment that marks the beginning of an agency's efforts toward accreditation.
>
> The commentary of standard 45.2.1 (Community Relations) further highlights the importance of community participation: "Law enforcement agencies should establish direct contacts with the community served. Without grassroots community support, successful enforcement of many laws may be difficult, if not impossible. Input from the community can also help ensure that agency policies accurately reflect the needs of the community."
>
> The accreditation self-assessment process provides many opportunities to institutionalize community policing. For example, preparing compliance documentation for . . . "Law Enforcement Role and Authority" . . . offers a chance for agencies to study and redefine their mission, statement of ethics and values, and vision of policing. This is also a logical time to take stock of the community's collective vision and opinions. . . . [Other parts] of the standards manual address organization, management, and administrative issues. While working on these standards, law enforcement agencies can consider such community policing precepts as decentralized authority and flattened organizational hierarchies. . . .
>
> Has the agency achieved diversity in the workplace? Do recruit and in-service training classes develop community policing skills such as effective communication with members of various ethnic and racial groups? Do the agency's performance evaluation criteria include community policing factors like community mobilization skills, group facilitation, problem-solving, and referral skills? . . . These questions deal with the standards [covering the subject of] "The Personnel Process." . . .
>
> Finally, not only do the accreditation standards help weave community policing into an agency's internal fabric, they also provide a way to integrate such objectives into external service-delivery. Key community policing objectives that can be applied when working on standards related to law enforcement operations, operations support, and communications are:
>
> - enhancing the role and authority of patrol officers;
> - improving analysis and information management; and
> - managing calls-for-service.
>
> In the Community Policing Consortium's monograph, *Understanding Community Policing: A Framework for Action,* CALEA's four founders advise that: "Community policing cannot be established through a mere modification of existing policy; profound changes must occur on every level and in every area of a police agency from patrol officer to chief executive, and from training to

technology. A commitment to community policing must guide every decision and every action of the department."

There is no reason why accreditation's strategic planning process cannot be used to facilitate community policing and meaningful change in a law enforcement agency. The preceding discussion clearly underscores this conclusion. But if further evidence is needed, consider the common bonds of community policing and accreditation:

- both require citizen and local government support;
- both encourage productive change in service-delivery strategies; and
- both require a leadership style that takes advantage of agency and community resources to institute value-driven rather than rule-driven management.

Accreditation requires law enforcement agencies to document their policies. Community policing requires agencies to engage the community in a process of evaluating what ought to be documented. Both ask participants to take a critical look at the status quo.

In addition to CALEA standards, other approaches to accountability in law enforcement are being proposed. According to Hoffmann (1998, p.59): "The Office of Law Enforcement Standards at the National Institute of Standards and Technology in Gaithersburg, Maryland, is conducting research to create standards that will impact law enforcement operations today and in years to come."

Another approach being used to ensure accountability is police **credentialing,** whereby individual police officers are evaluated by the National Law Enforcement Credentialing Board (NLECB). Hill (1999, p.40) explains: "The NLECB assesses specific law enforcement standards in much the same way that CALEA evaluates law enforcement agencies, with one significant difference: the subjects of these evaluations are *individual law enforcement officers."*

Credentialing has become the latest tool for officers and agencies wishing to enhance their professionalism.

Police Professionalism

Throughout this text policing has been referred to as a profession; however whether law enforcement technically qualifies as a profession is controversial. Part of the problem is that definitions of professionalism vary. To some, *professional* means simply an important job or one who gets paid, as opposed to an *amateur.* Others identify a profession as possessing certain markers, including (Capps, 1998, p.15):

- A consensus by customers regarding the profession's product or service
- A specialized body of knowledge and skills usually attained through extensive training and education
- Certification or accreditation through a professional organization
- An orientation toward clients or service
- A primary objective other than profit
- Use of an esoteric language
- Development of symbols, artifacts and journals
- Considerable discretion given to members

Sociologists, however, have identified certain elements that qualify an occupation as a profession.

Sociological Elements of Professionalism

The three key elements of professionalism are (1) specialized knowledge, (2) autonomy and (3) a service ideal.

Specialized Knowledge

The time when someone could walk into a police department, fill out an application and be hired is gone in most parts of the country. Many departments now require a two-year college degree, and some require a four-year degree. In addition to a college degree, many departments require that applicants complete skills training. As noted, most larger departments also have their own rookie schools or academies where new police officers learn what is expected in a particular agency. As technology advances and as criminals become more sophisticated, more knowledge and training can be expected to be required.

Autonomy

Professional autonomy refers to the ability to control entrance into the profession, to define the content of the knowledge to be obtained and to be responsible for self-monitoring and disciplining. In addition the autonomy of a profession is usually authorized by the power of the state; for example physicians, dentists, lawyers and teachers are licensed by the state. These professions are, in effect, legalized monopolies.

Law enforcement does fit the criterion of professional autonomy in that requirements to be a police officer are usually set by the legislature. The growth in the number of Peace Officers Standards and Training (POST) boards throughout the country to oversee the profession attests to this fact.

A Service Ideal

The third element of a profession, the service ideal, requires that members of the profession follow a formal code of ethics and be committed to serving the community. In this area police officers qualify as professionals, provided the department stresses the public servant aspects of police work.

Five I's of Police Professionalism

Some definitions of professionalism overlap with the preceding three elements and work well when applied to law enforcement. Griffin (1998) lists five elements of professionalism that policing, perhaps more than many other lines of work, expects and, in fact, requires of its employees:

- Integrity—few work environments in our country can equal the demands placed on police officers for individual character and moral integrity.
- Intellect—law enforcement is as intellectually demanding as any endeavor in our society.
- Industry—work habits that are results-oriented as opposed to activity-driven, heavy on follow-through and the realization that work is simply applied effort.

- Initiative—action is an essential ingredient. Law enforcement professionals can no longer afford to associate the concept of initiative with writing a citation or completing a field interview. These activities must be seen as mere steps in the implementation of a long-range plan.
- Impact—everyone has met the officer who can arrive on the scene, quickly evaluate the circumstances, and immediately begin orchestrating a resolution. Much of this skill is based on the personal quality of positive impact, characterized by a presence of confidence, competence and a positive attitude.

The Final Analysis—Does Law Enforcement Qualify?

Law enforcement continues striving for recognition as a profession. According to Yates (1999, p.7): "Increased training, stricter hiring requirements, and official removal procedures for unqualified officers are all elements of the peace officer professionalization movement. . . . Over the past quarter century, Peace Officer Standards and Training (POST) organizations or councils have played an active role in the police professionalization movement." From 1984 to 1997 the average nationwide basic recruit training requirement increased from 351.25 hours to 456 (Yates, p.11).

However: "Despite this positive development, in most states, the minimum education requirement to enter law enforcement has gone unchanged for decades. Although a college degree requirement has been advocated since the 1967 President's Commission, no states currently meet this goal" (Yates, p.11). Some states, such as Wisconsin and Minnesota, do require a two-year associate's degree to enter law enforcement, a step in the right direction.

Michelson et al. (p.15) point to the lack of a standard curriculum among colleges and universities offering degrees in law enforcement and criminal justice, calling this void "the missing link to police professionalism." They argue: "Police leaders have had a minimal role in defining their professional educational core" and urge: "Academic institutions must reach out to the police community to establish a national consensus on a curriculum of choice."

Summary

The future success (or failure) of our criminal justice system, especially our law enforcement system, depends in large part on the quality and effectiveness of our police officers. Therefore valid recruitment, screening, testing and selection procedures must be used to assure that only well-qualified candidates are hired. Qualities of a good police officer include reliability, leadership, judgment, persuasiveness, communication skills, initiative, integrity, honesty, ego control, intelligence, sensitivity and problem-solving ability. Individuals possessing such skills are sought through a careful selection procedure.

Agencies are also seeking to hire more minorities and women. A racially balanced and integrated police department fosters community relations and increases police effectiveness. Studies show that women perform as well as men in police work, are less apt to use excessive force, can help implement community-oriented policing and can improve an agency's response to violence against women. In addition, an increased female presence among officers can reduce problems of sex discrimination and harassment and foster policy changes that benefit all officers.

Police officer selection usually includes a formal application, a written examination, a physical fitness test, a psychological examination, an interview, a thorough background investigation and a medical examination. Most agencies require that a police officer candidate be a U.S. citizen, have or be eligible for a driver's license in the state and not have been convicted of a felony. Additional requirements may specify educational level and residency in the community served. Most police agencies require a minimum of a high school education or equivalency certificate, and some require a two- or four-year degree. Many police agencies are now requiring some college education for employment and/or promotion. Whether such education helps the officers perform better has not been documented. Regarding residency, it is always preferred and sometimes required that police officers live in the community they serve.

Since fitness is an important quality of law enforcement officers, physical fitness tests are used to evaluate a candidate's coordination, speed and strength. The most common physical fitness tests are similar to military obstacle courses, which must be completed in a designated time. The candidate also undergoes an oral interview to evaluate appearance, alertness, communication ability, social adaptability, judgment, emotional stability, and interest in and suitability for the job. The background investigation includes verification of all information on the application and history sheet; a check on driving record; fingerprinting and a check on any criminal record; a check on military records; interviews with personal references, acquaintances, past employers, neighbors and teachers; a check on financial status; and a check on past performances at schools and previous jobs. Finally, a medical examination is conducted to assess the candidate's vision, hearing and cardiovascular-respiratory system.

In addition to local and state requirements for recruitment and selection of police officers, certain federal guidelines and regulations must be met. Most important are the 1972 Equal Employment Opportunity Act, which prohibits discrimination due to sex, race, color, religion or national origin in employment of any kind, public or private, local, state or federal; and the Americans with Disabilities Act (ADA), which prohibits discrimination in employment based on a disability.

Once candidates have passed all tests in the selection process, they usually enter a one-year probationary period during which they are observed while obtaining training and while applying this training on the streets.

All police officers are subjected to the hazards of police work, and all are expected to fulfill the responsibilities of the job. Nevertheless, a police officer's job is highly stressful and may result in a personal crisis for the officer. Stress can have adverse effects on police behavior that may, in turn, lead to citizen complaints being filed against an officer or agency.

To help assure ethical behavior—individually and departmentally—some communities have established civilian review boards. A civilian review board consists of citizens who meet to review complaints filed against the police department or against individual officers. The use and benefits of civilian review remain highly controversial. Whether police officers should be unionized remains another controversial issue. Most police officers are currently members of local employee organizations and are not directly enrolled in a national labor union.

Controversy also surrounds the privatization of criminal justice responsibilities. Privatization refers to the practice of having nonsworn personnel, often private security officers, perform tasks traditionally performed by police officers. Private security officers differ from police officers in that private security officers are salaried with private funds, are responsible to an employer and have limited authority extending only to the premises they are hired to guard. Security officers have no authority to carry concealed weapons and, unless deputized, have no authority to make arrests except as a citizen's arrest. Furthermore, their uniform and badge must not closely resemble that of a regular police officer. Many agencies permit their officers to moonlight in private security and other fields. Moonlighting is controversial and is handled differently from one department to the next.

The issues of accreditation and police professionalism are additional topics of controversy. The Commission on Accreditation for Law Enforcement Agencies was formed to develop professional standards and to administer a voluntary accreditation process, although controversy exists over the value of such accreditation. Many question whether policing qualifies as a profession. The three key elements of professionalism are (1) specialized knowledge, (2) autonomy and (3) a service ideal.

Discussion Questions

1. What is the most common reason for rejection during the selection process?
2. What employment opportunities in law enforcement are available locally? In your county? Your state?
3. What are some societal factors interfering with police work?
4. How important do you think it is for officers to live in the community in which they work?
5. How much education do police officers need?
6. Does private policing represent a threat to public policing?
7. Do you favor or oppose civilian review boards? State your reasons.
8. Is sexual harassment a serious problem for police departments?
9. Do you support or oppose accreditation of police departments? Why?
10. Do you consider law enforcement a profession? What about the entire criminal justice field?

InfoTrac *College Edition Assignment*

Use InfoTrac College Edition to help answer the Discussion Questions as appropriate.

- Use InfoTrac College Edition to search for *police civilian review boards* and note the variety of approaches used to investigate police action. After reviewing some of the information, what is your opinion of these boards? Are they useful or not? Be prepared to discuss your view with the class.

Internet Assignments

- Using the keywords *police stress,* research the reasons law enforcement officers become stressed. Do any of them surprise you? What, if any, suggestions are given to prevent or reduce such stress? Be prepared to share your findings with the class.
- Go to the Web site of a law enforcement department and find starting salary and benefit figures for an officer *with* a college degree and one *without* a degree. Bring your data to class and calculate a mean (average) and median figure for the departments surveyed.

Book-Specific Web Site

The book-specific Web site at http://info.wadsworth.com/0534552803 hosts a variety of resources for students and instructors. Included are extended activities from each chapter in which students write a policy, use critical thinking skills to make choices in response to a given scenario, use InfoTrac College Edition with direct links to articles for participation in topical discussion forums, and analyze court cases using Web links for research. Many activities can be printed or emailed to instructors. Plus, cited cases with Web links, interactive key term FlashCards, PowerPoint presentations, chapter objectives, and an extensive collection of chapter-based Web links provide additional information and activities to include in the curriculum.

References

Aaron, Jeffrey D. "Stress and Coping in Police Officers." *Police Quarterly,* December 2000, pp.438–450.

"About CALEA." *CALEA Online,* January 4, 2002. www.calea.org/newweb/AboutUs

Anderson, Larry. "Partnering with the Public Sector." *Security Management,* August 1999, p.4.

"Benefits of Accreditation." *CALEA Online,* November 29, 2001. www.calea.org/newweb/accreditation

Bennett, Wayne W. and Hess, Kären M. *Management and Supervision in Law Enforcement,* 3rd ed. Belmont, CA: Wadsworth Publishing Company, 2001.

Bernstein, Jeff. "Preparing for Promotion." *Law and Order,* February 1998, pp.67–68.

Birzer, Michael L. and Tannehill, Ronald. "A More Effective Training Approach for Contemporary Policing." *Police Quarterly,* June 2001, pp.233–252.

Bland, Timothy S. "Get a Handle on Harassment." *Security Management,* January 2000, pp.62–67.

Boatman, Robert. "Monitoring the Police: The Civilian Ombudsman as a Community Liaison." *Law and Order,* October 2001, pp.219–220.

Brandon, Harry and Lippman, Barry. "Surfing for Success: Using the Web to Improve Recruitment." *The Police Chief,* November 2000, pp.37–41.

Bratton, William J. "Recruitment Crisis Gains Momentum." *American Police Beat,* October 2001, pp.1, 32.

Butterfield, Fox. "City Police Work Losing Its Appeal and Its Veterans." *The New York Times,* July 30, 2001, pp.1, A12.

Byrd, Edwin H., III. "Title VII and Employer Liability." *The Police Chief,* October 1998, pp.145–150.

Byrne, Edward C. "Recruiting Second-Career Officers." *Law and Order,* October 1998, pp.183–186.

Capps, Larry E. "CPR: Career-Saving Advice for Police Officers." *FBI Law Enforcement Bulletin,* July 1998, pp.14–18.

Carlan, Philip E. and Byxbe, Ferris R. "Managing Sexual Harassment Liability: A Guide for Police Administrators." *The Police Chief,* October 2000, pp.124–129.

Chamberlain, Jeffrey. "Moonlighting and the Fair Labor Standards Act." *Police,* March 1998, pp.38–39.

"Civilian Review Needs a More Proactive Stance." *Law Enforcement News,* November 15, 1998, p.10.

Clark, Jacob R. "Is Anybody Out There? Stiff Competition for Recruits Fuels Agencies' Personnel Woes." *Law Enforcement News,* April 30, 1998a, pp.1, 6.

Clark, Jacob R. "A LEN Interview with Sylvester Daughtry, Jr., Chairman of the Commission on Accreditation for Law Enforcement Agencies." *Law Enforcement News,* June 15/30, 1998b, pp.8–11.

"Coast to Coast, Good Police Recruits Just Keep Getting Harder to Find." *Law Enforcement News,* May 15/31, 2000, pp.1, 15.

Colbridge, Thomas D. "The Americans with Disabilities Act." *FBI Law Enforcement Bulletin,* September 2000a, pp.26–31.

Colbridge, Thomas D. "Defining Disability under the Americans with Disabilities Act." *FBI Law Enforcement Bulletin,* October 2000b, pp.28–32.

Colbridge, Thomas D. "Prohibited Discrimination under the Americans with Disabilities Act." *FBI Law Enforcement Bulletin,* December 2000c, pp.14–21.

"A Cop to Call Your Very Own." *Law Enforcement News,* July/August 1998, p.5.

Curran, Stephen F. "Pre-Employment Psychological Evaluation of Law Enforcement Applicants." *The Police Chief,* October 1998, pp.88–94.

Decicco, David A. "Police Officer Candidate Assessment and Selection." *FBI Law Enforcement Bulletin,* December 2000, pp.1–6.

Finn, Peter. "Getting Along with Citizen Oversight." *FBI Law Enforcement Bulletin,* August 2000, pp.22–27.

Fuss, Timothy L.; McSheehy, Brendan; and Snowden, Lynne. "Under Investigation: The Importance of Background Investigations in North Carolina." *The Police Chief,* April 1998, pp.169–172.

Fuss, Timothy L. and Snowden, Lynne L. "Surveying Sexual Harassment in the Law Enforcement Workplace." *The Police Chief,* June 2000, pp.63–72.

Garner, Gerald W. "Are You Ready for Promotion?" *Police,* July 1998, pp.22–24, 28.

Gold, Marion E. "The Progress of Women in Policing." *Law and Order,* June 2000, pp.159–161.

Green, David R. "Joining Forces against Crime." *Security Management,* May 1998, pp.95–98.

Greene, Helen Taylor. "Black Females in Law Enforcement." *Journal of Contemporary Criminal Justice,* May 2000, pp.230–239.

Griffin, Neal C. "The Five I's of Police Professionalism: A Model for Front-Line Leadership." *The Police Chief,* November 1998, pp.24–31.

Hawkins, Homer C. "Police Officer Burnout: A Partial Replication of Maslach's Burnout Inventory." *Police Quarterly,* September 2001, pp.343–360.

Hill, Steven J. "The Significance of Police Credentialing." *Police,* March 1999, pp.40–42.

Hoffmann, John. "National Institute of Standards and Technology: Setting Goals for the Future of Law Enforcement." *Law and Order,* June 1998, pp.59–60.

Hutton, Glenn and Sampson, Fraser. "The Assessment of Potential and the Potential of Assessment." *The Police Chief,* August 1999, pp.79–83.

"It's a Fact." *CALEA Update,* Issue 77, October 2001. www.calea.org/newweb/newsletter

Johnson, Richard R. "Citizen Complaints: What the Police Should Know." *FBI Law Enforcement Bulletin,* December 1998, pp.1–5.

Kaminsky, Glenn F. "Effective Utilization of the Probationary Period." *The Law Enforcement Trainer,* March/April 2001, pp.32–33.

Kanable, Rebecca. "Under the Gun." *Law Enforcement Technology,* July 1999, pp.78–82.

Kanable, Rebecca. "Strategies for Recruiting the Nation's Finest." *Law Enforcement Technology,* February 2001, pp.64–68.

Kates, Allen R. "Posttraumatic Stress Disorder: Hoax or Reality?" *The Associate,* January/February 2001, pp.29–31.

Kranda, April H. "Women in Policing: The Importance of Mentoring." *The Police Chief,* October 1998, pp.54–56.

Leach, Tad. "College Internship: An Aid to Recruitment." *Law and Order,* May 1998, pp.57–59.

Litchford, Jody M. "ADA Decisions Provide Guidance for Enforcement Activities." *The Police Chief,* August 2000, pp.15–17.

Lonsway, Kimberly A. "The Role of Women in Community Policing: Dismantling the Warrior Image." *Community Links,* September 2001, pp.16–17.

Lord, Vivian B. and Schoeps, Nancy. "Identifying Psychological Attributes of Community-Oriented, Problem-Solving Police Officers." *Police Quarterly,* June 2000, pp.172–190.

Michelson, G. Kelly; Heidingsfield, Michael J.; and Garrett, Dennis A. "The Missing Link to Police Professionalism." *Law Enforcement News,* October 31, 1999, pp.15–16.

Miller, Susan L. "Rocking the Rank and File." *Journal of Contemporary Criminal Justice,* May 1998, pp.156–172.

Molden, Jack B. "College Degrees for Police Applicants." *Law and Order,* January 1999, pp.21–22.

"More Specialization for CJ Grad Programs." *Law Enforcement News,* April 30, 1998, p.7.

Mulroy, Darrell E. "Stress: How It Contributes to Poor Performance." *Law and Order,* September 2000, pp.67–68.

Nelson, Kurt K. "A Tale of Two Cities: A Comparison of Background Investigations." *Law and Order,* May 2000, pp.85–88.

Neubauer, Ronald S. "The Future of Women in Policing." *The Police Chief,* December 1998, p.6.

Nowicki, Ed. "12 Traits of Highly Effective Police Officers." *Law and Order,* October 1999, pp.45–46.

Oglesby, Denise Chavez. Statement regarding affirmative action written for this text and updated in 2002.

Oliver, Patrick. "The Assessment Center Method: Not Just for Promotions Anymore." *Subject to Debate,* March/April 1998, pp.8–10.

Olson, Robert K. "Recruiting the Officers of the Future." *Subject to Debate,* August 2001, pp.2, 5.

Pederson, Dorothy. "Sexual Harassment: Is the Atmosphere Right for It in Your Precinct?" *Law Enforcement Technology,* October 2001, pp.128–134.

"Pre-Employment Psychological Evaluation Services Guidelines." *The Police Chief,* October 1998, p.95.

"Preventing Sexual Harassment." St. Paul, MN: Equal Opportunity Division, Department of Human Relations, no date.

Prussel, Deborah and Lonsway, Kimberly A. "Recruiting Women Police Officers." *Law and Order,* July 2001, pp.91–96.

"Rank Objections." *Law Enforcement News,* May 15, 1998, pp.1, 10.

Recruiting and Retaining Women: A Self-Assessment Guide for Law Enforcement. Los Angeles: National Center for Women and Policing, 2001. Available at www.ncjrs.org, site of the National Criminal Justice Reference Service.

Reese, James T. "6 Keys to Stress-Free Living." *The Associate,* January/February 2001, pp.14–17.

Risher, Julie A. "Police Liability for Failure to Train." *The Police Chief,* July 2001, p.10.

"Same-Sex Harassment Ruled Illegal." (Minneapolis/St. Paul) *Star Tribune,* March 5, 1998, pp.A1, A17.

Scuro, Joseph E., Jr. "The Americans with Disabilities Act in the 21st Century." *Law and Order,* February 2001, pp.31–33.

Sharp, Arthur. "Off-Duty Employment: More Headaches for Police Administrators." *Law and Order,* December 1999, pp.82–87.

Sharp, Arthur G. "Accreditation: Fad or Fixture?" *Law and Order,* March 2000, pp.92–98.

Spector, Elliot. "Emerging Legal Standards for Failure to Train." *Law and Order,* October 2001, pp.73–77.

"The Standards." *CALEA Online,* November 29, 2001. www.calea.org/newweb/accreditation

Strandberg, Keith. "Breaking through the 'Brass' Ceiling." *Law Enforcement Technology,* June 2000, pp.76–82.

Streit, Corinne. "Recruiting Minority Officers." *Law Enforcement Technology,* February 2001, pp.70–75.

Tate, Hugh. "The Recruitment Dilemma." *Law and Order,* May 2000, pp.78–82.

Thompson, Mike. "Avoiding the 'Killer in the Shadows.'" *Law and Order,* August 1999, pp.107–110.

Volpe, J. F. "A Guide to Effective Stress Management." *Law and Order,* October 2000, pp.183–188.

Walker, Samuel; Spohn, Cassia; and DeLone, Miriam. *The Color of Justice: Race, Ethnicity, and Crime in America,* 2nd ed. Belmont, CA: Wadsworth Publishing Company, 2000.

Webster, Stephanie H. "An Old Problem with a New Twist: Same-Sex Sexual Harassment." *The Police Chief,* December 1997, pp.10–12.

Weinblatt, Richard B. "Managing Off-Duty Jobs: A Clear Policy Is the Key to Success." *Law and Order,* November 1999, pp.84–88.

Wexler, Sanford. "College Graduates Committed to Community." *Law Enforcement Technology,* October 1998, pp.52–53.

Yates, Jennifer. "Police Professionalism: Issues in Peace Officer Standards and Training Councils." *Police Forum,* April 1999, pp.7–15.

Cases Cited

Brown v. Bryan, 219 F.3d 450 (5th Cir.2000)

City of Canton v. Harris, 489 U.S. 378 (1989)

Davis v. City of Dallas (1978)

Oncale v. Sundowner Offshore Services, Inc., 95 F.3d 56 (5th Cir. 1996), *cert. granted* 117 S.Ct. 2430 (1997)

Chapter 12

Courts and Corrections: Law Enforcement's Partners in the Justice System

Justice is truth in action.
—Disraeli

Do You Know?

- How the police aid the criminal justice process?
- What the typical hierarchy is within the state court system? The federal court system?
- How juvenile court differs from adult court?
- What was established by the *Kent, Gault, Winship* and *McKeiver* decisions?
- What the adversary system requires?
- What the critical criminal justice stages are?
- What purpose a preliminary hearing serves?
- What some alternatives to trial are?
- How the defense attorney may attempt to discredit the testimony of a police officer?
- What the purposes of corrections are?
- What correctional alternatives are being used in the United States?
- How jail differs from prison?
- What two philosophies are evident in U.S. prisons?
- How parole differs from probation?

Can You Define?

adjudicate
adversary system
appeal
appellate jurisdiction
arraignment
assembly-line justice
booked
boot camp
change of venue
charge
community justice
community service
complaint
corrections
court of last resort
cross-examination
day fines
day reporting centers (DRCs)
deterrence
discovery process
diversion
dual system
electronic monitoring (EM)
forfeiture
furloughs
general deterrence
halfway houses
house arrest
hung jury
incapacitation
incarceration
intensive supervision programs (ISPs)
intermediate sanctions
jail
judicial review
judicial waiver
jurisdiction
landmark decision
no bill
nolo contendere
original jurisdiction
parole
petition
plea bargaining
preliminary hearing

preponderance of the evidence
presumption of innocence
prison
pro bono work
probation
reasonable doubt
recidivism
rehabilitation
residential community corrections
restitution
restitution center
restorative justice
retribution
R.P.R.d
shock incarceration
specific deterrence
standing mute
venue
voir dire
writ of certiorari
writ of habeas corpus

INTRODUCTION

Our system of criminal justice has three interrelated components staffed by more than one million people: *law enforcement,* the *courts* and *corrections.* Each component and its personnel contribute to the criminal justice *process,* a well-defined legal continuum through which every offender may pass from detection and investigation of the criminal act; to arrest and accusation; to trial, conviction, sentencing and possibly incarceration; to eventual release. This process is illustrated in Figure 12.1. According to Territo et al. (1998, p.18):

> The agents of the Criminal Justice System—police, prosecutors, courts and corrections—are the main participants in the fight against crime. The police are responsible for detecting and apprehending people who violate the criminal law; prosecutors decide whether circumstances warrant prosecution; the courts decide guilt or innocence and sentence those who are convicted or plead guilty; the corrections component carries out the sentence of the court. The administration of justice sounds neat, orderly and systematic. Unfortunately, it is none of these things—least of all, systematic.

One reason for the lack of order within the justice system is that all the officials within the system can exercise discretion. Police officers' use of discre-

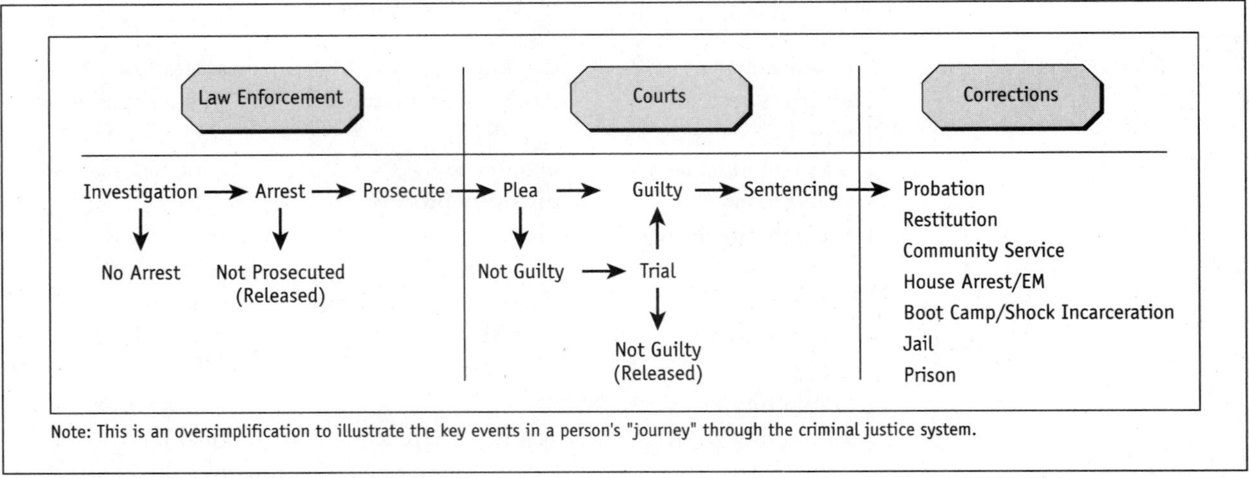

Figure 12.1
Criminal Justice System Overview

tion has been a theme throughout this text. However, prosecutors, judges, correctional officials and paroling authorities also have discretion, as shown in Table 12.1.

This chapter begins with a brief discussion of community justice and the role of the police as gatekeepers to the criminal justice system. This is followed by an overview of the court systems in the United States, including state court systems, the federal court system, the Supreme Court and several specialized courts. Next the adversary system and its key players—the defendant, the prosecutor, the defense attorney and the judge—are introduced. This is followed by a description of the critical stages in the criminal justice system. Because not all cases result in a court trial, alternatives to such a trial are discussed next, including diversion and plea bargaining. This is followed by a description of the typical trial. The discussion of courts concludes with an explanation of sentencing alternatives and case review and appeal.

The second part of the chapter focuses on corrections, beginning with a discussion of the purposes of corrections and an examination of the correctional alternatives available, including probation, a host of intermediate sanctions and incarceration. Next parole and community-based reintegration programs are described, followed by a look at recidivism and the highly controversial issue of the death penalty versus life without parole. The chapter concludes with a discussion of restorative justice and the role of the police in community corrections.

Community Justice

Just as the community policing philosophy is gaining the acceptance of police departments across the country, community justice is also finding its advocates. And like community policing, **community justice** is about "creating new relationships both within the justice system and with stakeholders in the community such as residents, merchants, churches, and schools, and testing new and

Table 12.1
Opportunities for Discretion

These Criminal Justice Officials	Must Often Decide Whether or Not or How to
Prosecutors	File charges or petitions for adjudication Seek indictments Drop cases Reduce charges
Judges or magistrates	Set bail or conditions for release Accept pleas Determine delinquency Dismiss charges Impose sentence Invoke probation
Correctional officials	Assign to type of correctional facility Award privileges Punish for disciplinary infractions
Paroling authority	Determine date and conditions of parole Revoke parole

Source: *Report to the Nation on Crime and Justice.* U.S. Department of Justice, Bureau of Justice Statistics, March 1988, pp.56–60.

aggressive approaches to public safety rather than merely responding to crime" (Feinblatt et al., 2001, p.1). Also, like community policing, community justice has at its core partnerships and problem solving, as evidenced by the six central goals of:

- Restoring the community.
- Bridging the gap between communities and courts.
- Knitting together a fractured criminal justice system.
- Helping offenders deal with problems that lead to crime.
- Providing the courts with better information.
- Building a courthouse that fosters these ambitions (Feinblatt et al.).

Community justice initiatives often start because citizens are dissatisfied with the criminal justice system, viewing it as slow, formal and unable to cope with matters, especially low-level offenses, that need rapid and informal attention: "If community justice is to be created, two things must happen: The criminal justice system's relation to the community must be realigned, and community members must work to create civility" (*Community Justice in Rural America . . .*, 2001, pp.9–12).

The Police as Gatekeepers to the Criminal Justice System

The police are the most visible element of the criminal justice system and play an integral role in its process. The criminal codes that guide police officers in enforcing laws are not a set of specific instructions. They are only rough maps of the territory in which police officers work. Regardless of how sketchy or complete the officers' education or experience, in reality they are interpreters of the law, holding enormous discretionary power, and may function as judge and jury at the start of every case. For example police officers who stop a person for speeding make a judicial decision when they give out a ticket. They might simply warn the next offender. By shooting and killing a fleeing felon who is likely to kill someone while trying to escape, the police officer delivers a capital penalty for a crime that may otherwise have netted probation or a prison term.

The importance of quality police work in getting a case to and through court becomes even more apparent when considering the sheer volume of cases handled by the justice system annually. According to Neubauer (1999, p.17): "Every year approximately 14 million persons are arrested by the police, 3 million for felonies and the rest for misdemeanors. Because of the large volume, overworked officials are often more interested in moving the steady stream of cases than in individually weighing each case on the scales of justice." This tendency has been referred to as **assembly-line justice,** which Neubauer defines as: "The operation of any segment of the criminal justice system in which excessive workload results in decisions being made with such speed and impersonality that defendants are treated as objects to be processed rather than as individuals."

Police officers aid the criminal justice process by (1) making arrests, (2) obtaining information and evidence, (3) writing reports, (4) identifying suspects and witnesses and (5) providing testimony in court.

Errors in any of these roles may seriously damage a case or even prevent a conviction. Police officers must become familiar with our courts, as well as each step of the criminal justice process, so they can intelligently bring about desired results.

The Court System

U.S. courts operate within a highly structured framework that may vary greatly from state to state. Many dualities exist within this framework, the most obvious being the **dual system** of state and federal courts.

Another duality within the courts is their **jurisdiction,** which does not refer to a geographic area but rather to a court's authority to try a case or to hear an appeal, the duality being that of *original* versus *appellate* jurisdiction. A court with **original jurisdiction** has the authority to try cases, whereas a court with **appellate jurisdiction** has the authority to hear an **appeal** to set aside a conviction. In some cases, a court has both types of jurisdiction, for example the U.S. Supreme Court.

A court with authority to try cases is often called a *trial* court, and because such courts are often the first to record the proceedings, they are also referred to as *courts of record.* A **court of last resort** refers to the highest court to which a case may be appealed.

Yet another duality is that of civil and criminal law, discussed in Chapter 2.

The State Court System

Each state's constitution and statutory law establish its courts' structure. Consequently great variety exists in the types of courts established, the names by which they are known and the number of levels in the hierarchy.

The hierarchy at the state level often goes up from courts of special or limited jurisdiction called justice of the peace (J.P.) courts, to trial courts or original and general jurisdiction courts (including probate court, municipal court, county court, circuit court, district court and superior court), to intermediate appellate courts, to the state supreme court.

Most cases originate in a municipal or county court, and it is in such courts that most law enforcement officers are called upon to testify. Although municipalities and counties are self-governed and have their own courts, they need to comply with state and federal laws. In some states cases may be appealed to an intermediate appellate court. In every state the state supreme court is the court of last resort at this level. Figure 12.2 illustrates the state court system. Cases may progress beyond this point, however, into the federal court system.

The Federal Court System

Within the federal court system a further duality exists: constitutional courts and legislative courts. The constitutional courts include the U.S. Supreme Court, as well as "such inferior Courts as the Congress may from time to time ordain and establish" (Article III, Section 1). These inferior courts include the courts of appeals, the district courts and numerous specialized courts. Legislative courts are lower in the hierarchy and include trial courts in the U.S. territories, specialized courts and the Military Court of Appeals.

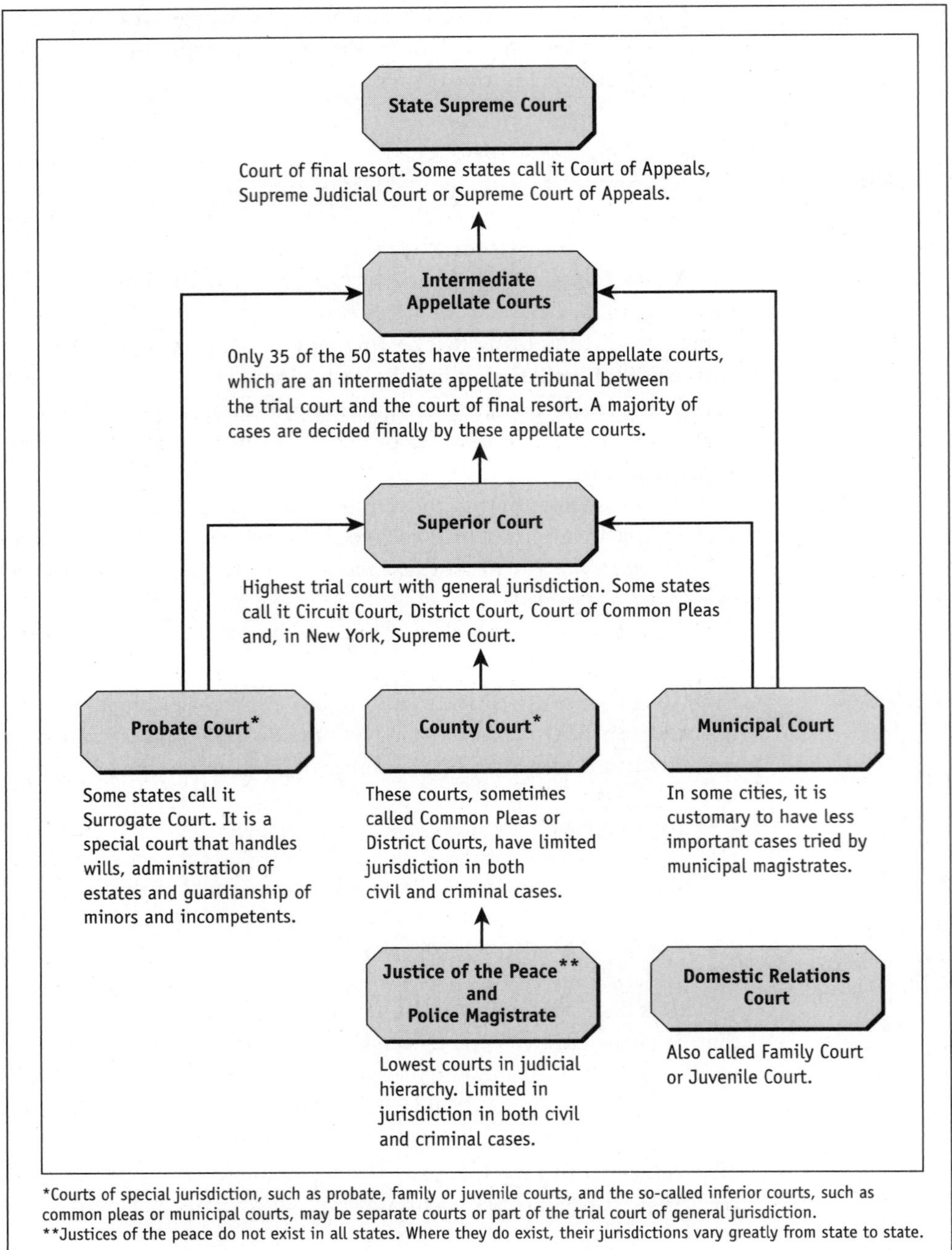

State Supreme Court
Court of final resort. Some states call it Court of Appeals, Supreme Judicial Court or Supreme Court of Appeals.
Intermediate Appellate Courts
Only 35 of the 50 states have intermediate appellate courts, which are an intermediate appellate tribunal between the trial court and the court of final resort. A majority of cases are decided finally by these appellate courts.
Superior Court
Highest trial court with general jurisdiction. Some states call it Circuit Court, District Court, Court of Common Pleas and, in New York, Supreme Court.
Probate Court*
Some states call it Surrogate Court. It is a special court that handles wills, administration of estates and guardianship of minors and incompetents.
County Court*
These courts, sometimes called Common Pleas or District Courts, have limited jurisdiction in both civil and criminal cases.
Municipal Court
In some cities, it is customary to have less important cases tried by municipal magistrates.
Justice of the Peace** and Police Magistrate
Lowest courts in judicial hierarchy. Limited in jurisdiction in both civil and criminal cases.
Domestic Relations Court
Also called Family Court or Juvenile Court.
*Courts of special jurisdiction, such as probate, family or juvenile courts, and the so-called inferior courts, such as common pleas or municipal courts, may be separate courts or part of the trial court of general jurisdiction.
**Justices of the peace do not exist in all states. Where they do exist, their jurisdictions vary greatly from state to state.

Figure 12.2
State Judicial System

Source: American Bar Association, *Law and the Courts.* Chicago: American Bar Association, 1974, p.20. Updated information provided by West Publishing Company.

J. J. Senna and L. J. Siegel. *Introduction to Criminal Justice*, 7th ed. St. Paul, MN: West Publishing Company, 1996, p.387. Reprinted by permission.

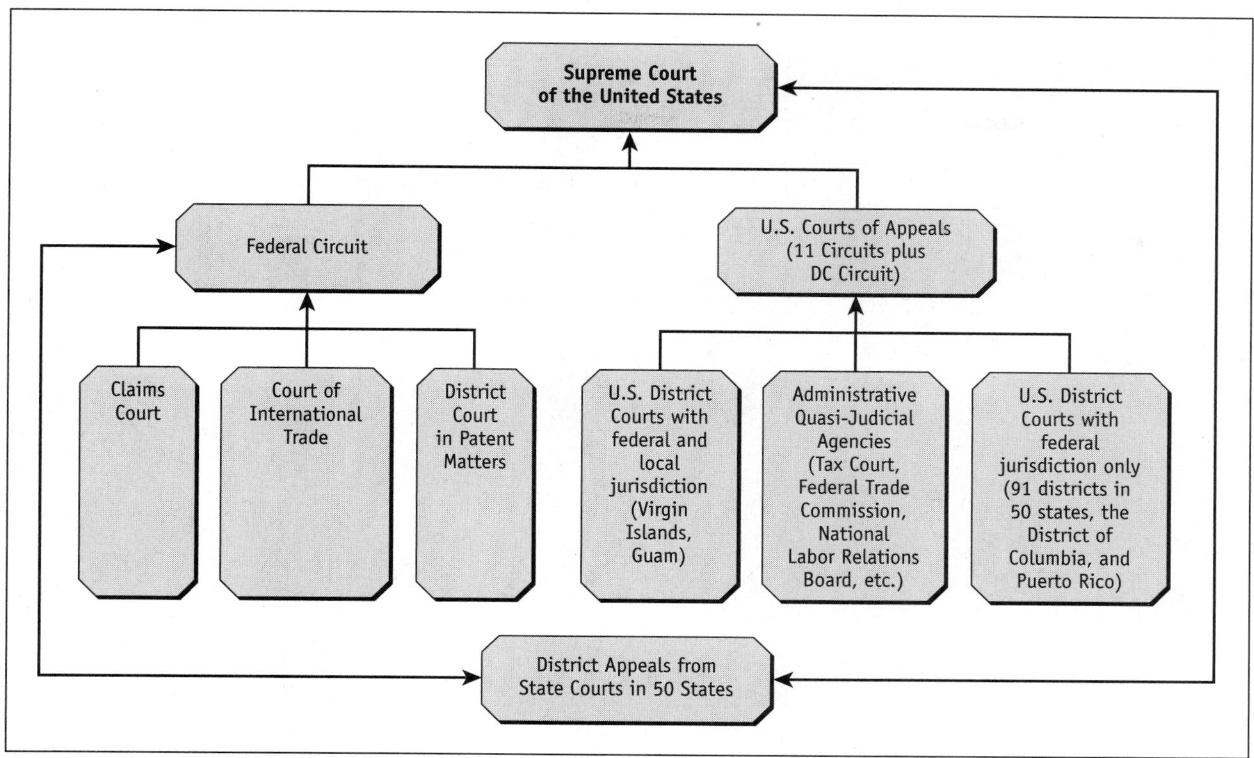

Figure 12.3
Federal Judicial System

Source: American Bar Association, *Law and the Courts.* Chicago: American Bar Association, 1974, p.21. Updated information provided by the Federal Courts Improvement Act of 1982 and West Publishing Company.

Source: J. J. Senna and L. J. Siegel. *Introduction to Criminal Justice,* 7th ed. St. Paul: West Publishing Company, 1996, p.21. Reprinted by permission. All rights reserved.

The federal court system is three tiered: district courts, appellate courts and the U.S. Supreme Court.

The three-tiered federal court system is illustrated in Figure 12.3. Furthermore, as illustrated in Figure 12.4, the federal court system is organized into districts and circuits. A state may be divided into federal districts (91 districts in 50 states), and several states may fall within a circuit (11 circuits plus a DC circuit).

The Supreme Court

The U.S. Supreme Court is presided over by nine justices appointed by the president of the United States, subject to Senate confirmation. The president also appoints a chief justice, who assigns the cases to the other justices. Most have been lawyers and are from the upper class and have been white, male, Protestant and graduates of prestigious universities. More than half were judges before their appointments.

The first black Supreme Court justice was Thurgood Marshall, appointed in 1967. He served until 1991. Sandra D. O'Connor was the first woman Supreme Court justice appointed in 1981. Table 12.2 displays the composition of the current Supreme Court.

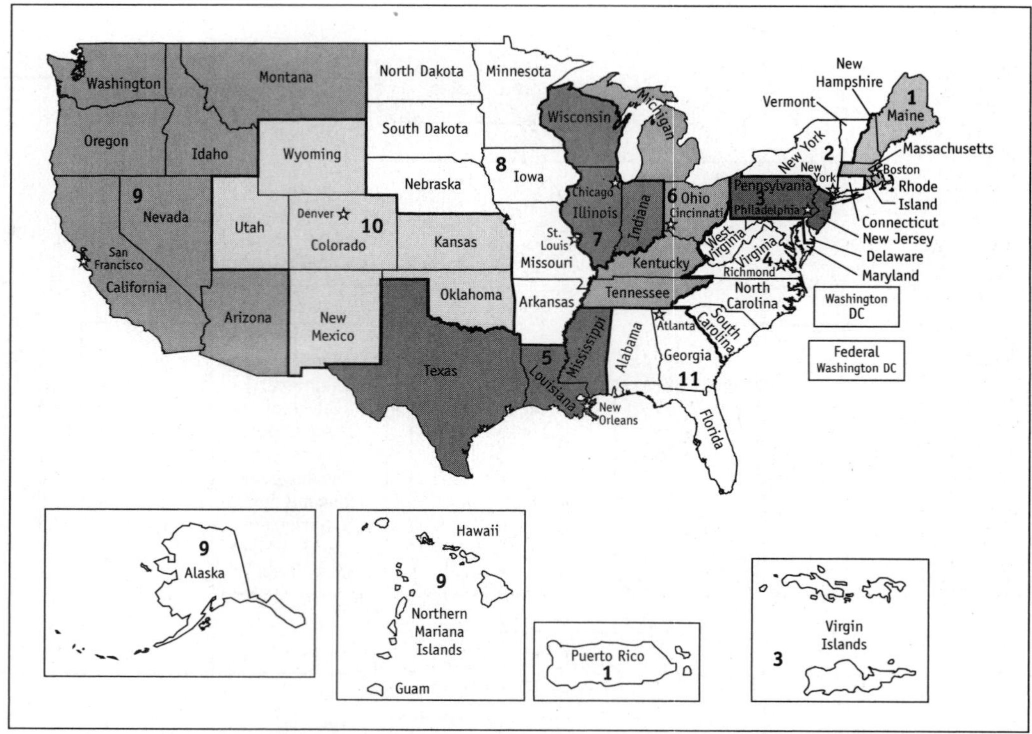

Source: West Publishing Company.

Figure 12.4
The Federal Judicial Circuits

Table 12.2
Supreme Court Justices in Order of Seniority

Name	Year of Birth	Home State	Year of Appointment	President	Senate Vote
William Rehnquist*	1924	Arizona	1971	Nixon	65-33
John Paul Stevens	1920	Illinois	1975	Ford	78-0
Sandra Day O'Connor	1930	Arizona	1981	Reagan	99-0
Antonin Scalia	1936	New York	1986	Reagan	98-0
Anthony Kennedy	1936	California	1988	Reagan	97-0
David Souter	1940	New Hampshire	1990	Bush	90-9
Clarence Thomas	1948	Georgia	1991	Bush	52-48
Ruth Bader Ginsburg	1933	New York	1993	Clinton	96-3
Stephen Breyer	1938	Massachusetts	1994	Clinton	87-9

*William Rehnquist was promoted from associate justice to chief justice in 1986.

Source: David W. Neubauer, *America's Courts and the Criminal Justice System*, 6th ed. Copyright © 1999 by West/Wadsworth Publishing Company, p.457. Reprinted by permission.

The Constitution established tenure for "life on good behavior." Therefore, the only way to remove a justice is through impeachment unless voluntary retirement can be obtained. When the Supreme Court decides to hear a case, it grants a **writ of certiorari,** which is a request for a transcript of the proceedings of the case for review. When the Supreme Court rules on a case, the ruling becomes precedent, commonly referred to as a **landmark decision,** that must be honored by all lower courts. The use of precedent in the legal system gives the Supreme Court power to influence and mold the everyday operating procedures of the police.

Specialized Courts

Specialized courts have developed to address specific criminal justice cases. It is hoped these alternatives to the traditional courtroom will dispense more equitable justice as applied to particular issues. Among the specialized courts are community courts, tribal courts, drug courts and juvenile courts.

Community Courts

One recent alternative to the traditional courtroom is the community court. As Feinblatt et al. (p.81) state: "Community courts are neighborhood-based courts that use the power of the justice system to solve local problems. These courts seek to play an active role in the life of their neighborhoods, galvanizing local resources and creating new partnerships with community groups, government agencies, and social service providers." According to Feinblatt et al. (p.7):

> To be effective a community court must address the needs of the court system's most important constituency: the people who live and work in neighborhoods affected by crime. To address these needs, a community court must ask a new set of questions. What can a court do to solve neighborhood problems? What can courts bring to the table beyond their coercive power and symbolic presence? And what roles can community residents, businesses, and service providers play in improving justice?

Tribal Courts

A court system often overlooked is the tribal court, operated under the Department of the Interior. Neubauer (p.72) states: "In 1789 Congress designated Native American tribes as foreign nations to enable the government to sign land and boundary treaties with them." This also allowed reservations to devise their own "governments," including organizations and processes to handle legal matters. The Indian Reorganization Act of 1934 further encouraged self-government by developing tribal constitutions and forming various government entities, including courts. According to Neubauer (p.73), there are 248 tribal courts, both civil and criminal, operating in 27 states. They hear cases pertaining to Native American law that affect both Native Americans and non–Native Americans living or operating a business within the jurisdiction of a Native American government.

Drug Courts

Treatment-based drug courts are relatively new. By providing drug treatment to offenders as soon as they enter the court system, instead of waiting until they have passed into the correctional component of criminal justice, drug courts have taken quite a different path from traditional court processes. "Since the first drug court was established in 1989 in Dade County, Florida, drug courts have significantly changed how judicial systems handle drug users and those who commit criminal offenses while using drugs" ("Drug Courts," 2001, p.18).

Drug courts are community-based courts designed to reflect community concerns and priorities, access community resources and seek community participation and support. Although the structure, scope and target populations of drug courts vary from one jurisdiction to another, the goals remain the same: to reduce recidivism and substance abuse and rehabilitate participants:

> Drug courts take drug offenders from traditional, adversarial courts and place them in drug courts where they can receive more appropriate treatment. Such courts try to establish an environment that the participant can understand—a system in which clear choices are presented and individuals are encouraged to take control of their own recovery. Participants undergo a long-term treatment and counseling program complete with sanctions, court appearances, and incentives. Participants who successfully complete a drug court program may be rewarded by dismissed charges, shortened sentences, or reduced penalties. Most importantly, though, graduating participants gain the necessary tools to rebuild their lives ("Drug Courts," p.18).

Senjo and Leip (2001) assert: "Drug treatment courts have grown in popularity, thanks in part to favorable program evaluations." One such evaluation conducted at the Columbia University (NY) Center for Addiction and Substance Abuse found that drug courts provide "the most comprehensive supervision and control of offenders' drug use behavior while they are on probation and living in our communities" ("Ten Years of Drug Courts," 1999, p.7).

The National Association of Drug Court Professionals (NADCP) reports that the field has grown to include over 600 drug courts in operation or the planning stages ("Ten Years of Drug Courts," p.6). In addition: "Drug courts have also spurred the evolution of such other community-based court programs as domestic violence courts, DUI courts, juvenile and family drug courts, neighborhood courts, and even 'deadbeat dad' courts" ("Drug Courts," p.18).

Juvenile Courts

Historically juvenile courts are informal, private, nonadversary systems that stress rehabilitation rather than punishment of youths.

Juvenile courts try to secure care and guidance for each minor under the court's jurisdiction. Laws relating to juveniles try to preserve and strengthen family ties whenever possible, removing minors from parental custody only when the minor's welfare or safety or protection of the public cannot be adequately safeguarded without such removal. Juvenile court also has jurisdiction over neglected and dependent children and over those who encourage, cause or contribute to a child's delinquency.

Juvenile courts vary from state to state, but most begin with some sort of intake, which usually begins as a **petition**—a document alleging a juvenile is a delinquent, status offender or dependent and asking the court to assume jurisdiction of the child. It is the formal process for bringing a matter before the juvenile court. Often the petition originates with a law enforcement agency, but

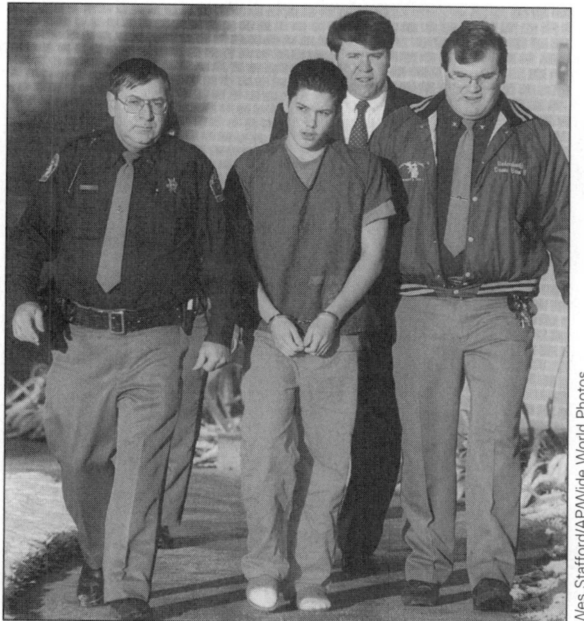

Arenac County Sheriff's officers escort T. J. James Tremble, 15, to court in Standish, Michigan, for sentencing in the shooting deaths of Peter and Ruth Stanley. Though most cases involving juvenile offenders are tried in the juvenile court system, Tremble was tried as an adult. He received two consecutive life terms.

Wes Stafford/AP/Wide World Photos

it can come from another source. The intake or initial screening is usually controlled and supervised by the juvenile court.

At the *adjudication hearing,* considered to be part of the preliminary hearing, the youth is questioned about the alleged offense. If the evidence is insufficient, the petition may be dismissed. If enough evidence exists that the child is delinquent, a court date is set for the *disposition hearing.*

At the disposition hearing, the judge has several alternatives. Based on the findings of the investigation, the judge may place the youth on probation or in a foster home, release the child to the parents, commit the child to an institution or make the child a ward of the court.

Serious juvenile offenders may be committed to mental institutions, reformatories, prisons, and county and state schools for delinquents. Some cities, such as New York and Chicago, have set up youth courts that are adult courts using the philosophy of juvenile courts. These youth courts usually confine their hearings to misdemeanors. The usual sequence of events within the juvenile court is illustrated in Figure 12.5.

Due Process Rights of Juveniles

Recall that before 1960, juveniles had no due process rights. To save them, children could be brought into court "without any process at all" *(Commonwealth v. Fisher).* In 1956 the landmark federal case of *Shioutakon v. District of Columbia* resulted in drastic changes in the juvenile justice system, when the courts established the role of legal counsel in juvenile court. If juveniles were to have their liberty taken away, such juveniles had the right to a lawyer in court. Several other landmark cases followed.

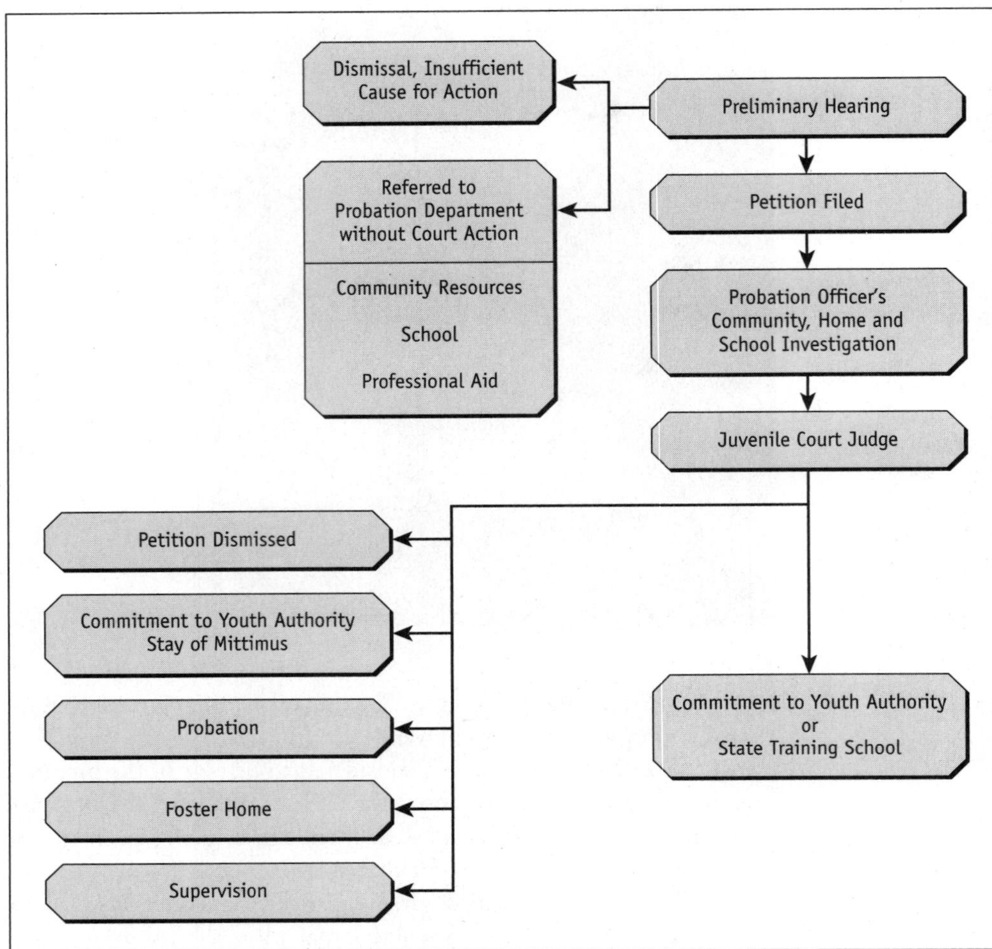

Source: Reprinted by permission of the International Association of Chiefs of Police.

Figure 12.5
Juvenile Court Responsibility

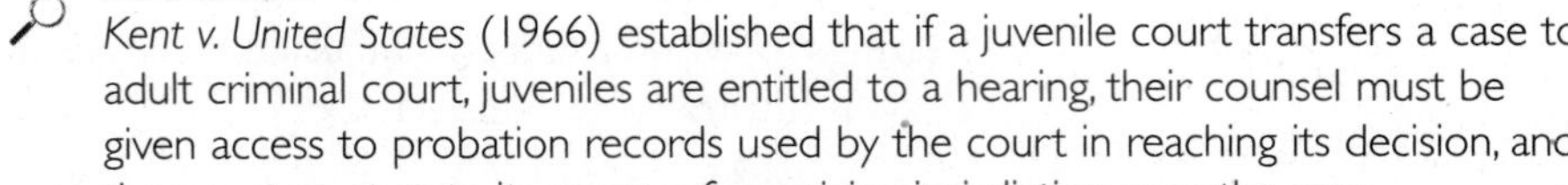
Kent v. United States (1966) established that if a juvenile court transfers a case to adult criminal court, juveniles are entitled to a hearing, their counsel must be given access to probation records used by the court in reaching its decision, and the court must state its reasons for waiving jurisdiction over the case.

In the appendix to the *Kent* decision, the Supreme Court established the following criteria for states to decide whether juveniles should be transferred to adult criminal courts for trial:

- The seriousness of the offense and whether the community's protection requires waiver
- Whether the offense was committed in an aggressive, violent, premeditated or willful manner

- Whether the offense was against persons or against property, greater weight being given to offenses against persons
- The desirability of trial and disposition of the offense in one court when the juvenile's associates in the alleged offense are adults who will be charged with crimes in the adult court
- The sophistication and maturity of the juvenile as determined by consideration of his or her home, environmental situation, emotional attitude and pattern of living
- The juvenile's record and previous history

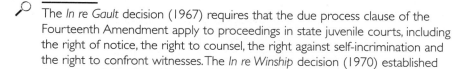

The *In re Gault* decision (1967) requires that the due process clause of the Fourteenth Amendment apply to proceedings in state juvenile courts, including the right of notice, the right to counsel, the right against self-incrimination and the right to confront witnesses. The *In re Winship* decision (1970) established that a juvenile defendant must be found guilty beyond a reasonable doubt.

However, not all of the Court's decisions favored the expansion of juveniles' due process rights. In 1971 the progress toward establishing due process for youths was slowed by the ruling in *McKeiver v. Pennsylvania.*

McKeiver v. Pennsylvania (1971) established that a jury trial is not a constitutional right of juveniles.

The juvenile justice system seeks to balance the informal, protective emphasis of the *parens patriae* doctrine with the constitutional rights of juveniles charged with crimes. In *Breed v. Jones* (1975), the court ruled on the issue of double jeopardy in juvenile cases. Breed was 17 years old when arrested for armed robbery, and a juvenile petition alleging armed robbery was filed. After taking testimony the judge sustained the petition. At a subsequent disposition hearing, however, the judge ruled that the respondent was not "amenable to the care, treatment and training program available through the facilities of the juvenile court" and ordered Breed prosecuted as an adult. Breed was subsequently found guilty of armed robbery in superior court. In its decision the Supreme Court held that "the prosecution of respondent in Superior Court, after an adjudicatory proceeding in Juvenile Court, violated the Double Jeopardy Clause of the Fifth Amendment."

Waiver to Adult Court

When juveniles commit a series of serious crimes or a single particularly violent crime, juvenile courts can **adjudicate** or judge them as adults. Such juveniles are then charged and required to appear in adult criminal court. The age at which youths come under the jurisdiction of the criminal courts varies from state to state, ranging from age 16 to 19.

All states allow juveniles to be tried as adults in criminal courts under certain circumstances, and in some instances a juvenile case may *not* be filed in juvenile court. The most common transfer provision is a **judicial waiver,** where the juvenile court waives its jurisdiction and transfers the case to criminal court (the procedure is also known as *binding over, transferring,* or *certifying* juvenile cases to criminal courts).

Several states also have judicial waiver allowing juvenile court judges to transfer cases based on a juvenile's age, type of offense, prior record and dangerousness. This discretionary power is also granted to prosecutors in several states.

Juvenile Drug Courts

Like the adult court, the juvenile court also has a drug court component. According to Cooper (2001, p.1): "Juvenile drug courts are intensive treatment programs that provide specialized services for drug-involved youth and their families." Cooper (p.1) notes since their inception in 1995, more than 140 juvenile drug courts have been established in the United States, and more than 125 are currently being planned. She (p.13) concludes: "Measured by indicators such as recidivism, drug use, and educational achievement, juvenile drug courts appear to hold significant promise."

Another approach to dealing with juveniles who enter into the juvenile justice system is the Teen Court Program.

Teen Court Programs

Teen Courts, also called Youth Courts and Peer Courts, are designed to address a variety of youthful problem behaviors, such as underage drinking, substance abuse, truancy and related offenses. The goal is to help youths to pursue a path leading to their becoming more responsible, productive citizens. Goodwin et al. (n.d., p.49) describe the Teen Court Program as a "community-based intervention/prevention program designed to provide an alternative response for the juvenile justice system for first-time, nonviolent, misdemeanor juvenile offenders, in which community youth determine the appropriate sanctions for the offender. The program will hold youthful offenders accountable and provide educational services to offenders and youth volunteers in an effort to promote long-term behavioral change that leads to enhanced public safety."

Harrison et al. (2001) describe the most common arguments for and against teen courts: "Proponents of the teen court model believe that it delivers benefits on several fronts: holding teens accountable; instilling respect for the judicial system (law-related education); and providing restorative justice. Critics argue that teen courts promote net-widening by targeting the least serious juvenile court referrals which would otherwise receive minimal dispositions." They also report that successful teen court participation was associated with lower recidivism: "Youths who completed teen court had significantly lower recidivism rates (23%) than youths who were referred to but did not complete the program (32%)."

Having looked at the organizational structures of our various court systems, next turn your attention to a concept on which our entire criminal justice system rests: the adversary system.

The Adversary System

Our criminal justice system is based on an **adversary system**—the accuser versus the accused.

Our adversary criminal justice system requires the accuser to prove beyond a reasonable doubt to a judge or jury that the accused is guilty of a specified crime.

Presumption of innocence means that the accused is assumed innocent until proof to the contrary is clearly established. On the side of the accused is the defendant and the defense attorney. On the side of the accuser is the citizen (or victim), the prosecutor and the police officer. They bear the burden of proof.

An impartial judge or jury hears both sides of the controversy and then reaches a decision as to whether the accuser has proven the accused guilty beyond a **reasonable doubt,** explained as: "The state of mind of jurors when they do not feel a moral certainty about the truth of the charges and when the evidence does not exclude every other reasonable hypothesis except that the defendant is guilty as charged" (Neubauer, p.521). Reasonable doubt is a more stringent evidentiary standard than that required in a civil trial, where a mere **preponderance of the evidence** is standard. This standard simply means it is more likely than not, based on the bulk of the evidence, that the plaintiff's version of the case holds up. Table 12.3 illustrates the various evidentiary standards of proof or degrees of certainty required in varying circumstances.

Table 12.3
Evidentiary Standards of Proofs—Degrees of Certainty

Standard	Definition	Where Used
Absolute certainty	No possibility of error; 100 percent certainty	Not used in civil or criminal law
Beyond reasonable doubt; moral certainty	Conclusive and complete proof, without leaving any reasonable doubt as to the guilt of the defendant; allowing the defendant the benefit of any possibility of innocence	Criminal trial
Clear and convincing evidence	Prevailing and persuasive to the trier of fact	Civil commitments, insanity defense
Preponderance of evidence	Greater weight of evidence in terms of credibility; more convincing than an opposite point of view	Civil trial
Probable cause	U.S. constitutional standard for arrest and search warrants, requiring existence of facts sufficient to warrant that a crime has been committed	Arrest, preliminary hearing, motions
Sufficient evidence	Adequate evidence to reverse a trial court	Appellate review
Reasonable suspicion	Rational, reasonable belief that facts warrant investigation of a crime on less than probable cause	Police investigations
Less than probable cause	Mere suspicion; less than reasonable to conclude criminal activity exists	Prudent police investigation where safety of an officer or others is endangered

Source: J. J. Senna and L. J. Siegel. *Introduction to Criminal Justice,* 9th ed. Belmont, CA: Wadsworth Publishing Company, 2002, p.391. Reprinted by permission.

The Defendant

Everyone, including a person suspected of committing a crime, has certain rights that must be protected at all stages of the criminal justice process. Defendants have all the rights set forth in the Bill of Rights. They may waive these rights, but if they do, the waiver should be in writing because proof of the waiver is up to the police officer or the prosecution. The police officer must be able to show that all rights have been respected and that all required procedures have been complied with.

The Fifth Amendment guarantees due process: notice of a hearing, full information regarding the charges made, the opportunity to present evidence before an impartial judge or jury and the right to refrain from self-incrimination. The Sixth Amendment establishes the requirements for criminal trials, including the right to a speedy public trial by an impartial jury and the right to have a lawyer. The Eighth Amendment forbids excessive bail and implies the right to such bail in most instances.

Because our system uses an adversary process to seek out basic truths, the right to counsel is fundamental. In *Faretta v. California* (1975), however, the Supreme Court held that the Sixth Amendment guarantees self-representation in a criminal case, but before the court can allow such self-representation, defendants must intelligently and knowingly waive their rights to the assistance of counsel.

The purpose of the right to counsel is to protect the accused from a conviction that may result from ignorance of legal and constitutional rights. Although defendants in all criminal cases have basic constitutional rights, often they do not know how to protect them. The right to counsel is indispensable to their understanding of their other rights under the Constitution.

The criminal justice system is sometimes criticized when a defendant is found not guilty because of a technicality. Even though a person confesses to a hideous crime, if he or she was not first told of his or her rights and allowed to have a lawyer present during questioning, the confession is not legal. As noted by the Supreme Court in *Escobedo v. Illinois* (1964):

> No system of criminal justice can or should survive if it comes to depend for its continued effectiveness on the citizens' abdication through unawareness of their constitutional rights. No system worth preserving should have a fear that if an accused is permitted to consult with a lawyer, he will become aware of and exercise these rights. If the exercise of constitutional rights will thwart the effectiveness of a system of law enforcement, then there is something very wrong with that system.

During the past several decades, many landmark decisions of the Supreme Court have extended the rights of individuals accused of a crime to have counsel at government expense if they cannot afford to hire their own lawyers. In *Powell v. Alabama* (1932), the Supreme Court ruled that in a capital case, the court must assign indigent defendants counsel as part of the due process of the law. The Court reaffirmed this right to counsel in *Johnson v. Zerbst* (1938), ruling that an indigent defendant charged with a *federal* crime had the right to be furnished with counsel. In *Betts v. Brady* (1942), the Supreme Court ruled that an indigent charged in a *state* court had *no* right to appointed counsel unless charged with a capital crime. In the famous *Gideon v. Wainwright* case (1963), the Supreme Court overruled *Betts v. Brady* and unanimously held that state courts must appoint counsel for indigent defendants in noncapital as well as capital cases.

Expanding on the "fairness" doctrine in *Argersinger v. Hamlin* (1972), the Supreme Court ruled that all defendants in court who face the possibility of a jail sentence are entitled to legal counsel and that if the accused cannot afford counsel, the state must provide one.

The Prosecutor

A prosecutor is an official elected to exercise leadership in representing the government and, hence, the people in the criminal justice system. Prosecutors may be city, county, state, commonwealth or district attorneys or solicitors. They are usually elected to a two- or four-year term at the state level. At the federal level, they are appointed by the president.

As the legal representatives of the people and law enforcement, prosecutors are responsible to the people who elected them. They determine law enforcement priorities and are key in determining how much, how little and what types of crimes the public will tolerate. They serve the public interest and consider the public's need to feel secure, its sense of how justice should be carried out and the community's attitude toward certain crimes. Sometimes a case becomes so well publicized that the prosecutor is forced to "do something about it" or face defeat in the next election.

Prosecutors are also the legal advisors for police officers; they decide what cases should be prosecuted and how. They rely heavily on police officers' input in determining if a case should be brought to court. Often, however, misunderstanding and even ill will results when a prosecutor refuses a police officer's request for a complaint because of insufficient evidence or some violation of a criminal procedure, such as an illegal arrest. Plea bargaining may also cause ill will between a prosecutor and a police officer.

Because both police officers and prosecutors are striving for the same end—justice—they should be familiar with each other's problems. Police officers, for example, should understand what the prosecutor can and cannot do, which types of cases are worth prosecuting and the need for and advantages of plea bargaining in certain situations. Prosecutors, on the other hand, should be sensitive to the police officers' objections to legal technicalities and excessive paperwork and should include police officers in plea bargaining when possible or, at the least, inform them when such bargaining has occurred.

Prosecutors may reject or dismiss a criminal case for many reasons, including lack of sufficient evidence linking the defendant to the offense; the offense not serving the interest of justice, such as a claim of $13 in property damage; problems with witnesses, such as a reluctance or failure to appear in court; and due process problems such as illegal searches or seizures and failure to Mirandize the defendant before questioning. Prosecutors may also determine the case would be best handled through pretrial diversion, such as a first-time drug offender successfully completing a drug treatment program.

Prosecutors perform one other critical function in the criminal justice process. They are responsible for protecting the rights of all involved, including the suspect. In essence they have a dual responsibility. On the one hand, they are the leaders in the law enforcement community, the elected representatives of the public and the legal advisors to the police. On the other hand, they are expected to protect the rights of persons accused of crimes. In *Berger v. United States* (1935), Justice Sutherland defined the prosecutor's responsibility as being "the representative not of an ordinary party to a controversy, but of a sovereignty whose obligation to govern impartially is as compelling as its obligation to govern at all; and whose interest, therefore, in a criminal prosecution is not that it shall win a case, but that justice shall be done."

Community Prosecution

Some prosecutors are also teaming up with citizens in the overall community justice movement. As Boland (1998, p.51) explains: "Community prosecution is a local political response to the public safety demands of neighborhoods as expressed in highly concrete terms by citizens who live in them."

As with community policing, community prosecution is not a program but rather a process dedicated to generating flexible solutions and responses to the various needs and problems faced by individual neighborhoods. Swope has referred to community prosecution as the "missing link" and states: "The police are only the gatekeepers [to the justice system], and the law enforcement effort really has no teeth without the support of the prosecutor. . . . Community policing can never reach its full potential without the inclusion of the prosecutor as a full partner, joining the police and neighborhood residents" (2001, p.11).

Swope (2000, p.114) suggests: "Community prosecution parallels community policing in important ways. Cliff Keenan, chief of the Community Prosecution Section, describes it as a philosophy. It is a nontraditional approach to prosecution, just as community policing is a nontraditional approach to policing. Community prosecution recognizes differences in neighborhoods and provides customized service. Community prosecution forms partnerships with the citizens and the police." This collaboration is also stressed by Boland (2001, p.38): "Because effective crime control is a joint effort, prosecutors need to ask other key actors, most importantly citizens and police, what they think they are getting from community prosecution. The best answers to these questions lie not in citywide random surveys, but in the police beats where the crime issue is defined in terms that are specific and concrete."

The Defense Attorney

The defense attorney represents the accused in court. Lawyers who represent the accused have the same duties and obligations whether privately retained, serving as a legal aid in the system or appointed by the court. They investigate the circumstances of the cases and explore facts relevant to their clients' guilt or innocence. They try to uncover evidence for their clients' defenses and organize the cases to present in court.

The majority of criminal cases are assigned to public defenders or to a few private lawyers who handle such cases. Public defenders are full- and part-time lawyers hired by the state or county government to represent people who cannot afford to hire a lawyer. Many lawyers donate time to represent the indigent, called ***pro bono* work.** Many others, however, are reluctant to do so.

Not all cities have public defenders. In smaller cities courts may appoint lawyers to represent poor people charged with crimes. In other cities the duty may be rotated among all lawyers practicing in the area as part of their professional obligation to society.

Although the role of the defense attorney has been glamorized by television series, criminal law is not emphasized in law school, which instead concentrates on business, property and tax law. Part of the reason for this is that clients are usually poor. In addition the public generally has little sympathy for criminals and even less for a lawyer who "gets the criminal off."

Community Public Defense

The community justice movement has also included innovations in neighborhood-focused public defense. Stone (1998, p.93) describes the impact of an experiment begun in the early 1990s in New York City—the local public defenders of the Neighborhood Defender Service of Harlem (N.D.S.):

> On May 30, 1996, an extraordinary event in the short history of community justice occurred in New York City. A large crowd of residents from Harlem—men, women, and children—appeared at City Hall to demonstrate their support for a local service that was threatened with elimination by the mayor's proposed budget. . . . No one had ever seen ordinary citizens turn out in such numbers for budget hearings.

Stone notes the reason so many citizens showed up to support the indigent defense program was because the experiment had worked: "The investigations had been more thorough, the representation more comprehensive, the sentences more humane and less costly, and the satisfaction among clients and their families far greater." He (p.99) also states: "The N.D.S. has shown that a community-based defense organization benefits not only clients, the community, and the criminal justice system, but also lawyers, for whom working to solve problems is its own reward."

Judges

Although most people think of trial judges when they hear the word *judge,* many different kinds of judges exist. In fact if a person comes to trial, he or she will already have encountered certain levels of the court system and judges acting within that system. The various types of judges and the functions they serve depend on the court to which they are appointed.

Judges have many important functions throughout the entire judicial process and can exercise great discretion by deciding in preliminary hearings if evidence is sufficient to justify prosecution; determining whether to grant bail, and if so, how much; deciding whether to grant delays; presiding over the trial; giving the jury instructions; and imposing the sentence if a defendant is found guilty.

Judicial discretion, however, can also lead to a significant amount of sentencing disparity. Carlson et al. (1999) note: "Studies seem to indicate that the race of the victim plays a large part in the determination of the offender's sentence, with crimes against Whites receiving stiffer penalties than crimes against others. . . . Sentencing structures such as presumptive and mandatory sentencing were designed to eliminate a degree of this disparity, yet, even these methods are not without fault."

Having looked at the nature of the adversary system and the key players, now consider the critical steps normally involved in the criminal justice process.

Critical Stages in the Criminal Justice System

The criminal justice process consists of the steps that occur between and including the filing of a complaint through the acquittal or sentencing of an offender. At various points along the way, a case may be dismissed, as illustrated in Figure 12.6.

The criminal justice system consists of several critical stages: the complaint or charge, the warrant, arrest, booking, preliminary hearing, grand jury hearing, the arraignment, the trial and sentencing.

Usually the criminal justice process begins when a police officer or a citizen approaches the prosecutor to obtain a complaint. A **complaint,** also called the **charge,** is a legal document drawn up by a prosecutor that specifies the alleged crime and the supporting facts providing probable cause.

The police officer or citizen then presents the complaint to a judge and, in the judge's presence, swears to the accuracy of the content of the complaint and signs a statement to that effect. If the judge concurs with the charge, he or she grants an arrest warrant ordering the police to arrest the suspect.

The arrest may occur at several points throughout the criminal justice process. For example, it may have occurred without a complaint or warrant if the crime was committed in the presence of the arresting officer. The prosecutor also may choose to present the case to a grand jury for indictment before arresting a suspect.

After a suspect is taken into custody, he or she is **booked** at the police station, that is they are formally entered into the police records system. The suspect is photographed and fingerprinted. The prints are placed on file with the FBI in Washington, DC, and the suspect has a police arrest record.

Marty Lederhandler/AP/Wide World Photos

Being arrested can change a person's life. Here Andrew Goldstein of Howard Beach, Queens, center, is escorted by police officers out of New York's 13th Precinct after being arrested for allegedly shoving a 32-year-old woman to her death under a Manhattan subway train. Goldstein, who was charged with second-degree murder, was carrying medical papers indicating he was under psychiatric care at an outpatient clinic. He was later found guilty.

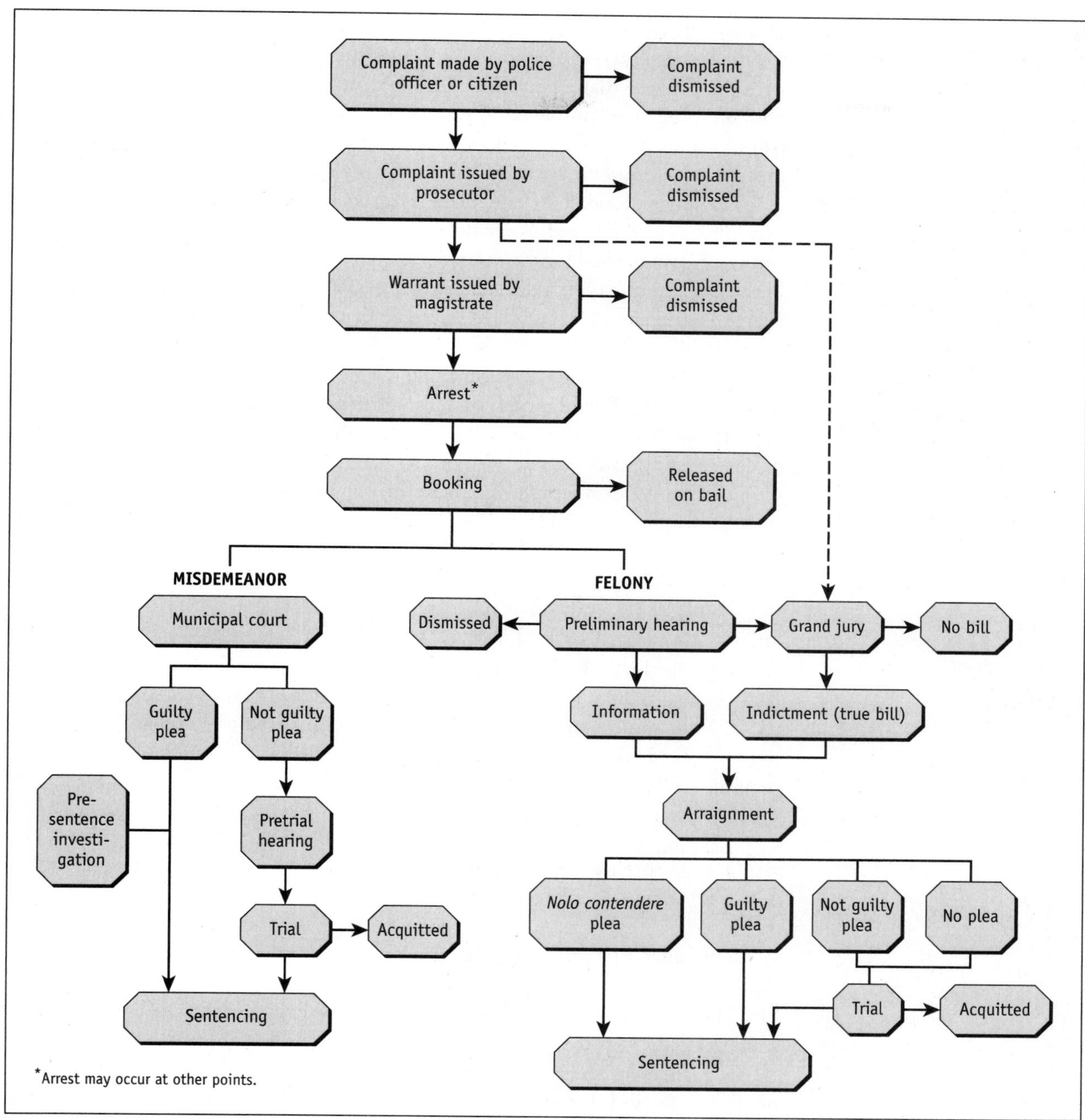

Figure 12.6
The Criminal Justice System from Complaint to Disposition

Bail and Writ of Habeas Corpus

Usually one right of the accused is the right to be released from custody. Not only is this essential to the accused's immediate freedom, but it is in keeping with the premise that a person is innocent until proven guilty. After the formal booking process is completed, the suspect is usually entitled to be *released* on bail or on his or her own *personal recognizance* **(R.P.R.d)** if the crime is a misdemeanor or released on a writ of habeas corpus or bond if the crime is a felony.

The judges decide how much bail is reasonable as a deposit to bring the defendant into court if released. Some defendants use a bail bondsman, a person or company that pays the bail for the defendant for an additional fee, typically a percentage of the amount of bail. If a defendant's bail is $100,000, the bail bondsman might charge 10 percent, or $10,000. Many argue that bail bonding discriminates against poor defendants and allows wealthy defendants to buy their way out of jail.

Periodically a person in jail may be released on a **writ of habeas corpus**—a legal court order literally meaning "bring forth the body you have"—which commands that a person being held be brought forth immediately. This means of determining whether the jailing of the suspect is legal is used primarily when the justice process moves slowly and a prisoner is detained for an unreasonable time before the court appearance. Most states have adopted guidelines as to how long a person may be jailed before being charged, released or making a court appearance. These guidelines range from 36 to 72 hours, taking into consideration Sundays and holidays.

The Preliminary Hearing

In the **preliminary hearing,** the judge determines whether probable cause exists for believing that an offense has been committed and that the accused committed it. Most statutes and rules of criminal procedure require a preliminary hearing to be held within a "reasonable time." Some jurisdictions require a preliminary hearing to be held immediately after arrest, some within 48 to 72 hours, others within 10 to 30 days.

> The preliminary hearing seeks to establish probable cause to prevent persons from being indiscriminately brought to trial.

The judge in a preliminary hearing is not bound by the rules of evidence that ordinarily control a trial. A far broader range of evidence is usually admissible. The prosecutor need only establish probable cause, not prove beyond a reasonable doubt that the crime was committed.

In reality the preliminary hearing is often a minitrial where the defense obtains as much information as possible to strengthen its case. Both prosecution and defense often use this stage of the criminal justice process for tactical purposes. In some instances overwhelming evidence may lead to a guilty plea or to a request for plea bargaining.

The **discovery process** requires that all pertinent facts on both sides be made available before the trial. Used properly the discovery process reduces questions of probable cause and other questions normally brought out in a preliminary hearing and encourages more final dispositions before trial, thereby saving court time. Available to both the prosecution and defense attorneys, it eliminates surprise as a legitimate trial tactic.

The preliminary hearing does not determine guilt or innocence. It merely determines whether further action should be taken. At this point the judge usually does not rule on complicated issues of evidence. The main intent is to add to the checks and balances of the criminal justice system by preventing the prosecutor from indiscriminately bringing someone to trial. The outcome of a preliminary hearing may be to (1) dismiss the charges, (2) present an information and bind the defendant over to a higher court or (3) send the case to a grand jury.

The Grand Jury

The U.S. Constitution requires an indictment by a federal grand jury before trial for most crimes against federal law. Grand juries often hear cases involving misconduct of public officials, violations of election laws, bankruptcy fraud, criminal conduct and the like.

The consideration of a felony charge by a grand jury is not a trial. Only the prosecution's evidence is usually presented and considered. Contrary to the popular portrayal of grand juries on television and in movies, suspected offenders are usually not heard nor are their lawyers present to offer evidence on their behalf.

A grand jury is usually composed of 23 voting citizens of the county, selected from voting lists. These juries may be called to duty any time the court is in session. A grand jury meets in secret sessions and hears from witnesses to and victims of a crime. Like a preliminary hearing, it determines only whether enough evidence exists to accuse a person of a crime.

In some states, by statute, a grand jury can hear evidence from suspects. However, the person being considered for indictment must sign a waiver of immunity and agree to answer all questions even though the testimony might be incriminating and may be used against them in a criminal trial. Their lawyers are not allowed to be present.

After the grand jury receives all testimony and evidence, it deliberates. If the majority of the grand jurors (or a specified number) agree that the person is guilty of a crime, they instruct the prosecutor to prepare an indictment specifying all the facts of the case. Grand juries may also issue what is called a **no bill** meaning the jurors believe there is no criminal violation.

The Coroner's Jury

Coroners investigate violent deaths where suspicion of foul play exists. By law coroners may conduct autopsies as to the cause of death, and they may conduct inquests. The coroner's jury usually consists of six members. In some states the coroner's jury system has been abandoned and its functions performed by a professional medical examiner.

The Arraignment

When defendants are charged with a felony, they must personally appear at an **arraignment.** As in the preliminary hearing, they are entitled to counsel. The procedures of the arraignment vary by state, but generally defendants appear before the court, are read the complaint, information or indictment, and if they have not received a copy, they are given one. They then enter a plea.

Defendants have several alternatives when they appear for the formal arraignment. **Standing mute,** that is, refusing to answer, is entered by the judge as a not guilty plea. ***Nolo contendere*** means "no contest." By entering a plea of *nolo contendere,* defendants, in effect, throw themselves on the court's mercy. A *guilty plea* means the accused admits the charge or a lesser charge agreed to in a plea bargaining session. *Not guilty* means the accused denies the charge. Some states require defendants to automatically plead not guilty to such capital crimes as first-degree murder.

If defendants plead guilty or *nolo contendere,* a sentencing time is set. Usually a presentence investigation is ordered to determine if probation is warranted. If defendants make no plea or plead not guilty, they have the choice of a trial by a judge or by a jury. If defendants wish a jury trial, the case is assigned to the court docket and a date set.

Before looking at the trial itself, consider some alternatives to a trial.

Alternatives to a Trial

Critics of our criminal justice system note that it is overburdened and that alternatives to a trial should be available. They suggest that often such alternatives would also be more equitable.

Alternatives to a trial include diversion and plea bargaining.

Diversion

Before cases go to court, defense attorneys may explore the possibility of diverting the case from the criminal justice system by using a community agency. For example in cases of mental incompetence, an attorney may seek to divert the case to a mental institution. **Diversion** is a discretionary decision that can occur at many points as the case progresses through the criminal justice system. For example a police officer who assumes custody of an intoxicated person and releases that person to the custody of family or a detoxification center diverts. Likewise a prosecutor who delays prosecution while a defendant participates in psychiatric treatment diverts. In both cases a discretionary decision is made that there is a more appropriate way to deal with the defendant than to prosecute.

As might be expected, diversion has its opponents. Some feel this is "letting criminals off easy." However major benefits can result, including saving court time; avoiding the stigma of conviction, particularly for first-time offenders; providing treatment for offenders whose criminal activity is the result of an addiction or disorder; allowing offenders to pay society back through community service or other work program; and easing overcrowding in correctional facilities by leaving room for the truly violent and dangerous offenders.

Plea Bargaining

The client and defense lawyer may also try to plea bargain their case. **Plea bargaining** is legal negotiation between the prosecutor and the defense lawyer or the client to reach an agreement that avoids a court trial, conserving time and expense. Carlson et al. (p.99) note: "Plea bargaining is highly used, involving more than 90 percent of all criminal convictions. Only 10 percent go to trial."

Basically plea bargaining involves compromises and promises. From the prosecutor it might mean that if a series of charges had been filed, the defendant would be charged with only one; the other charges would be dismissed. It also might mean the prosecutor would reduce a charge if only one charge had been filed. A charge of burglary might be reduced to breaking and entering, which carries a lesser penalty.

A hazard of plea bargaining is that it makes police officers feel left out. Often officers will ask about a case only to find it has been disposed of in plea bargaining. As criminals are placed back into society, the police officers' problems in dealing with crime grow. If police officers are to deal with these problems, they should be consulted.

The Trial

The trial is the climax in the criminal justice procedure. All previously made decisions now merge in one finality. How well the police have investigated the case, compiled evidence and reported it, and dealt with the victim and witnesses are weighed in the courtroom. The trial also tests how well the prosecutor prepared the case.

The key figures in the trial are the judge, members of the jury, the defendant and defense attorney(s), the prosecuting attorney(s), police officer(s) and witnesses. The judge has charge of the trial and decides all matters with respect to the law. He or she also assures that all rules of trial procedure are followed. The jury—people selected by law and sworn to examine the facts and determine the truth—decides all matters of fact. The trial begins with the jury selection.

A note: Before a jury can be assembled, the geographic location of the trial, called the **venue,** must be determined. A trial's venue is usually the same area in which the offense occurred. However, if a case has received such extensive publicity that picking an impartial jury from the local population is impossible, the trial may be moved to another part of the state, a process called a **change of venue.**

Jury Selection

Safeguards built into the jury selection process not only protect the defendant's rights but also assure the public that justice is done. Trial jurors are selected at random from voting or motor vehicle records or telephone directories by district or superior court judges or the commissioners of the county board. The defense attorney and then the prosecuting attorney question each person as to his or her qualifications to be a juror in this case. The judge may also question the prospective jurors. The random selection of potential jurors and the careful questioning of each, called ***voir dire,*** helps ensure selection of 6 or 12 fair and impartial jurors.

In *Williams v. Florida* (1970), the Court stated that jury size should be judged by whether the group is "large enough to promote group deliberation, to be free from outside attempts at intimidation, and to provide a fair possibility for obtaining a representative cross-section of the community." In this same case, the Court held that Florida's use of a six-person jury did not violate the defendant's rights to trial by jury.

Some critics of the present jury system claim that our legal system has gotten too complex for the average person to render a fair decision. Many advocate replacing the present system with a three-judge tribunal.

Testimony

After the jury is selected and instructed by the judge, opening statements are presented. The prosecutor informs the jury of the state's case and how he or she intends to prove the charges against the defendant. The defense lawyer makes an opening statement in support of the accused or may waive this opening statement.

The prosecutor then presents evidence and the witness testimony, attempting to prove a crime has been committed and that the defendant did it. Through **cross-examination** the defense attorney tries to discredit prosecution witnesses, the evidence and the testimony of the police officers.

The Police Officer in Court

Almost all officers have a day in court. Because of overloaded court dockets, cases usually come up well after the officers' investigations; therefore officers must refer to their reports and their original notes to refresh their memories. A court appearance is an important part of any police officer's duty. All elements of the investigation are brought together at this point: the report, the statements of the witnesses, the evidence collected and possibly even a confession.

The prosecution needs to establish the *corpus delicti* of the crime, which means it has to establish the elements of the crime by testimony of witnesses, physical evidence, documents, recordings or other admissible evidence. This information usually comes from police officers, their recollections, notes and reports. The prosecutor works with police officers in presenting the arguments for the prosecution.

According to Gil-Blanco (2001, p.74), police officers testify in approximately 90 percent of criminal cases brought to trial, and officers may be subpoenaed hundreds of times during their careers. In Gil-Blanco's survey of 78 San Jose police officers and sergeants, 52 percent said they had been subpoenaed in the range of 100 to 300 times; four reported being subpoenaed over 1,000 times (p.76). Thirty-eight percent reported having given "general" testimony 1 to 20 times, and 33 percent reported having given "general" testimony 100 to 300 times. In contrast, 70 percent reported having provided "expert" testimony 1 to 20 times; 4 percent reported having provided "expert" testimony 100 to 300 times.

Gil-Blanco (p.78) stresses: "The ability to present expert testimony persuasively is an essential skill every officer or investigator must have." In effect: "Whenever an officer gets on the stand, he or she is the subject of inquisition. Not only is that officer expected to know all the aspects of their case, they are also expected to know the law and to be above reproach. The officer is on 'stage' and expected to give vital and important information to their 'audience.' The testimony the officer gives is vital to a case and will not be available from other professional sources" (p.77). It is important for officers testifying in court to establish that they are experts by documenting their specialized training, experience and expertise (Kalk, 2001, p.39).

On the opposing side is the defense attorney, who uses several techniques to sway the jury away from the prosecution's argument. In a criminal case, the defense rarely expects to gain helpful information from police officers. The main intent is usually to discredit officers or their testimony.

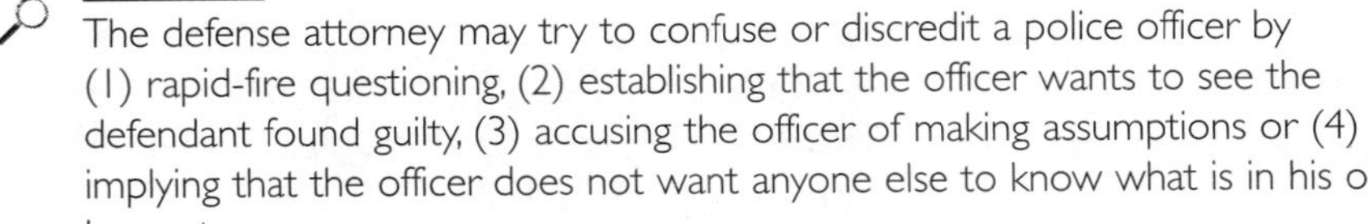

The defense attorney may try to confuse or discredit a police officer by (1) rapid-fire questioning, (2) establishing that the officer wants to see the defendant found guilty, (3) accusing the officer of making assumptions or (4) implying that the officer does not want anyone else to know what is in his or her notes.

Attorney General John Ashcroft announced on December 11, 2001, the first indictment of a key figure in the Sept. 11 attacks—six conspiracy charges against Zacarias Moussaoui, who has been held as a material witness. Moussaoui, a French citizen of Moroccan descent, faced the death penalty on four of the charges. He will be tried in a federal court and not a military tribunal as established by President George W. Bush. Moussaoui is shown in this undated police photograph.

© Reuters NewMedia Inc./CORBIS

An example of a defense team able to discredit a police officer occurred in the O. J. Simpson trial when defense attorneys were able to call into serious question the testimony given by former Los Angeles Police Department Detective Mark Fuhrman, in fact causing him to assert his Fifth Amendment right against self-incrimination.

Defense attorneys also attack a police officer's credibility by focusing on the officer's inferences.

Closing Statements and Jury Deliberation

After all testimony has been given, the jury hears the closing statements—a contest in persuasion first by the prosecution, stating that the jury should render a guilty verdict, then by the defense attorney, concluding that the client is surely innocent or at least not proven guilty beyond a reasonable doubt.

After the closing statements, the judge reads the instructions to the jury. This includes an explanation of the crime, what elements constitute the crime, alternate charges and the concepts of presumption of innocence and reasonable doubt. The jurors then retire behind closed doors to deliberate their findings. They can return one of three findings: guilty, not guilty or no verdict. No verdict simply means that no agreement can be reached; this is also sometimes referred to as a **hung jury.**

Sometimes a jury returns a not guilty verdict even when they believe the defendant did, indeed, commit the offense. This may occur when the jury feels the sentence expected to be handed down as a result of a guilty verdict is too harsh for the act, as with some mandatory sentences. This is one reason some jurisdictions no longer mandate rape as a capital offense.

After the jury has come to a decision, the judge is notified and the jury returns to the courtroom. With everyone present the jury foreman announces the verdict. Each juror is then polled as to how he or she voted and is asked if the verdict that the foreman has read is the verdict of the juror. If the finding is guilty, the defendant may either be sentenced immediately or may be given a sentencing date. If found not guilty, he or she is set free. If a hung jury results, the defendant may be retried at the prosecutor's discretion.

Sentencing

Sentences for people convicted of crimes vary considerably from lenient to extremely severe penalties, from probation to many years in prison or even death. In many jurisdictions the court has the authority to set, within limits established by state statute, both maximum and minimum sentences. Carlson et al. (p.100) note: "Twenty to thirty years ago, sentences were either prison or probation. Now judges have a host of intermediate choices available," as shown in Figure 12.7.

Three-Strikes Laws, Mandatory Minimums and Truth-in-Sentencing

In the effort to crack down on crime and get tough on criminals, sentences for repeat offenders and those convicted of certain crimes have become tougher. One popular sentencing reform has been "three-strikes" laws, first enacted in California, which require judges to impose life sentences on offenders who com-

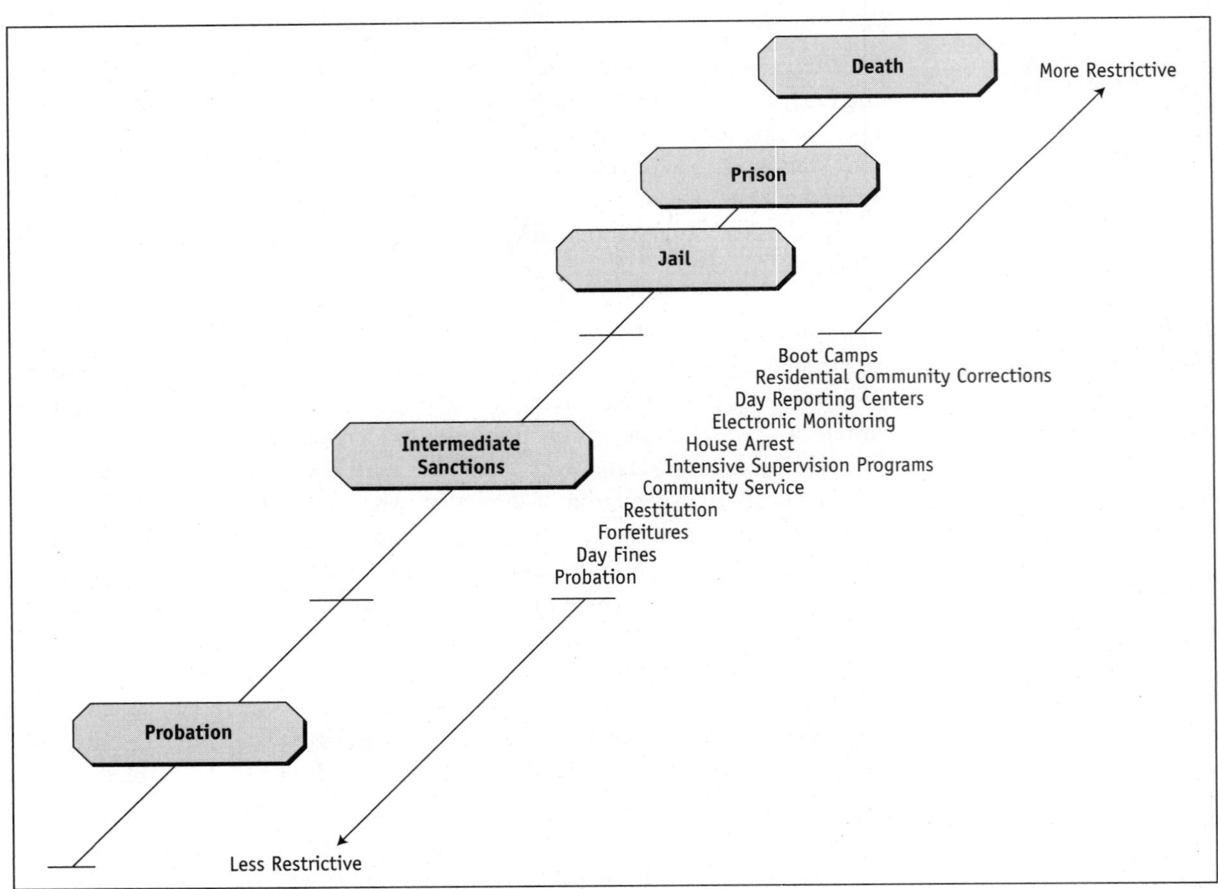

Figure 12.7 The Sentencing Continuum

Source: Norman A. Carlson; Kären M. Hess; and Christine M. H. Orthmann. *Corrections in the 21st Century: A Practical Approach.* Belmont, CA: West/Wadsworth Publishing Company, 1999, p.101. Reprinted by permission.

mit their third felony. Yet another get-tough-on-crime reform has come in the shape of mandatory minimum sentences for certain offenses, most notably drug and weapons offenses. Truth-in-sentencing laws aim to restrict or stop early release practices and keep offenders incarcerated for the duration of their sentences. Turner (2000, p.10) reports: "Thirty-seven states have adopted at least one of these get-tough-on-crime laws, many since 1994."

Such legislation, however, is being criticized for its inability to achieve the desired results and its significant contribution to the growing problem of prison overcrowding. According to Patch (1998, p.1): "The Three Strikes Law makes the average citizen feel as if something is being done, and indeed something is. It just isn't effective or theoretically sound." For example, he notes how, in California, the three-strikes law led in one year to 192 people "striking out" for marijuana possession while only 40 struck out for murder, 25 for rape and 24 for kidnapping: "At a cost of $21,885.00 per year per inmate, it cost the taxpayers of California $4.2 million per year to protect society from these dangerous marijuana smokers compared to $1.9 million per year for murderers, rapists, and kidnappers *combined.*" In addition, as Carlson et al. (p.112) note: "Most of these offenders are relatively young, with many years of life ahead of them. The cost to keep these offenders imprisoned into their 60s, 70s and beyond, and the increased medical care which frequently accompanies the aging process pose significant financial burdens to those states opting to impose such sanctions."

Mandatory minimums have also been blamed for filling up the nation's prisons with nonviolent offenders more in need of treatment than incarceration. Such sentencing schemes, however, are falling out of favor with many judges. For example, a Connecticut judge in sentencing a 20-year-old to 10 years in prison for selling crack cocaine told the defendant: "The sentence is one of the unfairest I have ever had to impose. I don't excuse your conduct. You deserve to go to jail. But 10 years is absolutely outrageous and I resent the fact that Congress has forced me to do this" (Dobbins, 1999, p.A19). Justice Department statistics show the number of prisoners nationwide has more than tripled, from 500,000 to 1.8 million, since 1980. Of that number, 1.1 million were locked up for nonviolent crimes, most of them drug-driven. Additional data from the Bureau of Justice Statistics indicates the U.S. prison rate, which has for 50 years held steady at 110 per 100,000 U.S. residents, skyrocketed between 1980 and 1990 to 450 per 100,000 U.S. residents. The BJS attributes nearly 80 percent of the increase to narcotics arrests (Dobbins, p.A19).

When combined with mandatory minimums, truth-in-sentencing laws nearly guarantee our country's correctional facilities will remain at or above capacity. Critics contend that by requiring a drug offender sentenced to 10 years to serve the entire 10-year sentence behind bars with no chance of parole, there is little incentive for inmates to reform, partake in treatment programs or even display "good behavior" as no hope exists that such efforts may lead to early release. Furthermore, such sentencing practices keep offenders isolated from society longer than may be necessary and, thus, might impede their reintegration into the community following their release.

Case Review and Appeal

To assure that justice is served, the court system provides for a **judicial review** of cases and for a person convicted to appeal the conviction in most instances. As Neubauer (p.435) suggests: "An appeal asks a higher court to review the actions of a lower court in order to correct mistakes or injustices. One of the few aspects of the American judicial process about which there is a consensus is that every loser in a trial court should have the right to appeal to a higher court."

Once sentence has been passed, the corrections component of the justice system—the final stage in the administration of U.S. criminal justice—takes over.

The Corrections System

Corrections is that portion of the criminal justice system that carries out the court's orders. It deals with both juvenile and adult offenders and consists of probation and parole systems, as well as jails, prisons and community-based programs to rehabilitate offenders. Data from the Justice Department's Bureau of Justice Statistics shows "the nation's combined federal, state and local adult correctional population reached a new high of almost 6.5 million men and women in 2000, having grown by 126,400 men and women during the year. . . . The total represents 3.1 percent of the country's total adult population, or 1 in every 32 adults (*National Correctional Population* . . ., 2001, p.1).

Purposes of Corrections

Throughout history, society has dealt with lawbreakers in many ways and has emphasized different goals and methods to accomplish those goals. The pendulum has swung from seeking pure revenge to viewing criminals as being ill and in need of treatment. It has swung from very public punishment, such as floggings and hangings, to very private punishment, such as solitary confinement. As the pendulum swings, the primary purposes to be served by corrections also shift. No matter where emphasis is placed, however, corrections generally serves four basic, often overlapping, purposes.

The primary purposes of corrections are retribution, deterrence, incapacitation and rehabilitation.

This simple statement belies the complexity of the issues. What purpose or purposes corrections should serve has been and continues to be the subject of heated debate.

Retribution is punishment for the sake of punishment. Retribution is also referred to as revenge, "just deserts" or "an eye for an eye." It assumes that offenders are responsible for their actions, that they chose to break the law and deserve to be punished. Recently retribution has come to include restitution.

Deterrence sees corrections as a way to prevent future criminal actions, a more functional, proactive view. Deterrence aimed at offenders is called **specific deterrence.** It tries to make the consequences of committing crime so severe that when offenders return to society, they will not commit crime. Deterrence that serves as an example to society of the consequences of crime is called **general deterrence.**

Incapacitation refers to making it impossible for offenders to commit further offenses. Incapacitation can take many forms. One of the earliest forms was banishment. Currently, the most common method of incapacitation is incarceration. While imprisoned a criminal is no longer a threat to society. The most extreme form of incapacitation is capital punishment.

Rehabilitation sees the purpose of corrections to be clear from its name—to *correct* deviant behavior. Rehabilitation is clearly proactive and focuses on the needs of offenders, as well as the needs of the community to which the offenders may return. The problem of **recidivism,** or offenders returning to crime, raises questions about whether corrections can effectively rehabilitate offenders. Closely related to this purpose is the goal of reintegrating offenders into society as productive, law-abiding citizens.

Purposes of Juvenile Corrections

While these four correctional purposes also exist within the juvenile justice system, the primary focus of juvenile corrections has traditionally been and continues to be rehabilitation. In Figure 12.8 the various correctional avenues for juvenile offenders are shown. This provides a sense of the emphasis placed on correcting deviant behavior in youths.

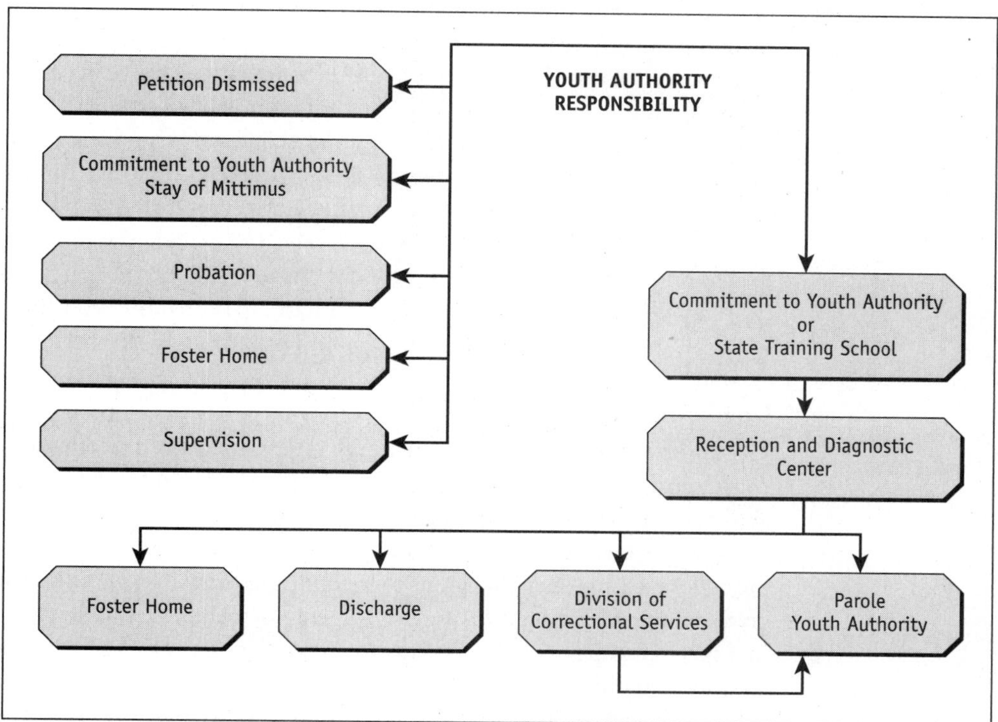

Source: Reprinted by permission of the International Association of Chiefs of Police.

Figure 12.8
Youth Authority Responsibility

Correctional Alternatives

As noted, the courts have several alternatives for sentencing persons convicted of crimes.

Correctional alternatives include probation, intermediate sanctions, incarceration and, in some states, the death penalty. These same options exist for juvenile offenders, although probation is by far the most frequent disposition in juvenile delinquency cases.

Probation

A person found guilty of a crime may be placed on probation, the least restrictive and most common alternative to a jail or prison sentence. The American Correctional Association (ACA) defines **probation** as "a court-ordered disposition alternative through which an adjudicated offender is placed under the control, supervision, and care of a probation field staff member in lieu of imprisonment, so long as the probationer meets certain standards of conduct." A major benefit of probation is that it allows offenders to remain in the community, able to maintain important family ties and fulfill vital work, family and community obligations.

Who Gets Probation?

The court considers the presentence investigation (PSI) report and state statutes in determining if an offender should be put on probation, but some statutes involving mandatory sentences preclude the option. Probation is most often used with first-time offenders, property offenders, low-risk offenders and nonviolent offenders, such as those convicted of white-collar crimes. Probation operates on a "second-chance" philosophy. Consequently if a person is convicted a second time for a crime, that person is very unlikely to receive probation.

Probation is also the most widely used correctional alternative for juveniles, and over half of all adjudicated youths receive this sentence. The main goal of probation is rehabilitation with secondary goals of (1) protecting the community, (2) making juvenile offenders accountable and (3) providing youthful offenders with skills needed to live productively and responsibly in the community.

Conditions of Probation

Conditions of probation vary depending on the nature of the offense and the court's goals. The general purpose of probation is to help offenders maintain law-abiding behavior. Some courts are more treatment oriented in assigning conditions, whereas other courts are more punitive. One universal condition for all probationers is to obey the law. Other conditions may include adherence to a program of supervision, maintaining steady employment or refraining from engaging in a specific employment or occupation, completing prescribed educational or vocational training, meeting family responsibilities, staying away from certain types of people or places, performing community service and making restitution.

Partnerships between Law Enforcement and Probation Services

A constant theme throughout this text has been the importance of partnerships between entities within the criminal justice field, as well as partnerships between such agencies and the communities and individuals they serve. This vital relationship also extends to law enforcement and probation services. According to McKay and Paris (1998, pp.27–28): "One resource seldom tapped by police agencies remains the local probation department. Perhaps as a result of interdepartmental rivalry or a perceived conflict of missions, many police departments have little, if any, contact or communication with the probation department serving the same jurisdiction. However, many law enforcement investigators who have explored this route have found that probation officers can become valuable resources and willing allies."

One way police and probation professionals build rapport and understanding is to participate in ride-along programs. McKay and Paris (p.29) note: "The conversations taking place in an 8-hour shift often serve to educate the officers in one field about the other, frequently culminating in enhanced appreciation and respect." Furthermore (p.29): "When citizens see probation and police officers working together, they realize that probation officers have an active interest in offenders complying with the conditions of their supervision."

Evans (2000, p.162) stresses: "There is a need for protocols between police and probation and parole for the emerging partnerships that focus on the high-risk offender."

The Growing Use of Probation

The first state to implement a formal probation program was Massachusetts in 1878. By 1927 juvenile probation programs were operating in every state, but it was not until 1957 that every state was providing similar services for adult offenders.

Probation is the fastest-growing sentencing alternative in the United States. On December 31, 2000, 3,839,532 adults were on probation in the United States, a 1.6 percent increase from 1999 (*National Correctional Population . . .*, p.3). In addition, probationers comprised 59 percent of all adults under correctional supervision.

The increased use of this disposition has led to an overload on the probation system and has fueled the increasing demand for an effective network of diversionary community-based programs known as intermediate sanctions. Often standard probation is combined with forms of intermediate punishment to increase the level of punishment and restriction imposed on the offender.

Intermediate Sanctions

Intermediate sanctions, also called community corrections, exist along a continuum of increasing control and are tougher than traditional probation but less restrictive and costly than imprisonment (recall Figure 12.7). Community corrections includes any activities in the community aimed at helping offenders become law-abiding citizens and requires a complicated interplay among judicial and correctional personnel from related public and private agencies, citizen volunteers and civic groups. Probation, as just discussed, is the oldest community-based correctional program and provides a foundation on which to build a wide range of community-based services. The use of control and surveillance is basic to a sound community corrections system. Regarding the variety of intermediate sanctions available, Carlson et al. (p.151) state:

> Day fines, forfeitures and restitution exist at the "low" end of control and restriction on the intermediate sanctions continuum and, when combined with probation, have been shown to provide an effective level of punishment for many offenders. Community service, intensive supervision, house arrest and electronic monitoring are sanctions further up the correctional continuum. Day reporting centers and residential community corrections programs exist at the most restrictive end of the correctional continuum, one step away from incarceration.

Day fines are based on an offender's daily income and differ from straight fines in that the judge considers not only the nature of the crime but also the offender's ability to pay. Day fines, while not particularly severe, do appear to provide effective punishment and deterrence while allowing the offender to remain in the community, able to tend to family needs.

Forfeiture, like day fines, imposes a financial penalty on offenders. However while fines are currency-based penalties, forfeiture involves seizing an offender's illegally used or acquired property or assets. Forfeiture is usually an add-on punishment used in conjunction with another sentence. Carlson et al. (p.155) state: "Civil forfeiture has been particularly useful in drug trafficking cases due to the abundance of assets needed to run a successful trafficking organization, including vehicles, aircraft, stash houses and cash."

Restitution has become an increasingly common criminal sanction, often imposed as a condition of probation, whereby an offender reimburses a victim, most often with money though occasionally with services. The three goals of restitution are to (1) punish and rehabilitate offenders, (2) deter future crimes and (3) provide compensation to victims. Perhaps restitution programs will encourage victims to report crimes as they see a financial incentive to do so. Offenders benefit by avoiding cell time and being allowed to remain in their communities. Closely related to restitution is the idea of community service, where an offender makes reparations not to a specific victim but to the community.

Community service, like restitution, is usually imposed not as a sole penalty but as a condition of probation. Community service often requires the offender to perform unpaid labor to pay a debt to society, with assignments ranging from cleaning litter along roadsides, to janitorial work in churches or schools, to building parks and playgrounds, repairing public housing and serving as a volunteer in a hospital or rehab center.

Intensive supervision programs (ISPs), also called intensive supervised probation, involve more supervision and greater restrictions than standard probation. They emphasize offender control and surveillance rather than treatment and rehabilitation. Although no single specific model exists for ISPs, common elements found in the various programs across the country include frequent personal contacts between the probation officer and the offender; strict enforcement of conditions, such as curfews and random drug and alcohol testing; fulfillment of restitution and community service obligations; mandatory employment; participation in treatment programs or educational classes; routine checks of local and state arrest records; and house arrest and electronic monitoring. Interestingly, several studies have found that the increased supervision and surveillance involved in ISPs leads to increased levels of probation violations (Giblin, 2002, p.116). This suggests the more one looks for something, the more likely it is one will find it.

House arrest, also known as home confinement or home detention, requires offenders to remain in their homes during specified times and to adhere to a strict curfew. Probation officers may monitor those under house arrest by random calls and home visits, or they may rely on technology to help keep track of offenders through **electronic monitoring (EM).** Such monitoring systems typically use radio frequency "tethers" consisting of a tamper-proof, water-resistant transmitter worn on the offender's ankle and a receiver placed in the offender's home. The transmitter communicates with the receiver, which has a preset range in which the offender must stay during the times they are to be at home, and sends an alarm to the supervising officer when the offender steps "out of bounds." More advanced monitoring systems use the Department of Defense's Global Positioning System (GPS) to provide satellite surveillance of offenders. Proximity limits are set for each offender, and a data center tracks offender movements around the clock, sounding an automatic alarm if a violation occurs.

Day reporting centers (DRCs) are nonresidential facilities where offenders must appear daily. First used in the United States during the 1970s for juvenile offenders and deinstitutionalized mentally ill persons, day reporting centers today serve as an alternative to sending both juvenile and adult offenders to jail or prison. While the emphasis at day reporting centers is on helping offenders find jobs, a variety of counseling and treatment programs are often also available.

For those offenders for whom live-in sanctions are more appropriate, **residential community corrections** are available—an alternative just a step away from incarceration. These residences provide a semisecure correctional environment within the community while addressing the dual objectives of community protection and offender reintegration. Such centers may take many forms, including halfway houses, prerelease centers, transition centers, work furlough and community work centers, community treatment centers and restitution centers. Offenders may live either part-time or full-time at these facilities, depending on the conditions set forth by the court.

Intermediate Sanctions for Juveniles

Community corrections programs for juvenile offenders include shelters; ranches, forestry camps and farms; group homes; and halfway houses. Juveniles requiring greater supervision and more security may be placed in correctional facilities such as detention centers, training schools and boot camps.

Boot Camps

For some offenders community corrections are not the answer. One alternative is **boot camp,** also known as **shock incarceration.** If a judge rules shock incarceration the appropriate sentence, the offender has a choice: consent to the

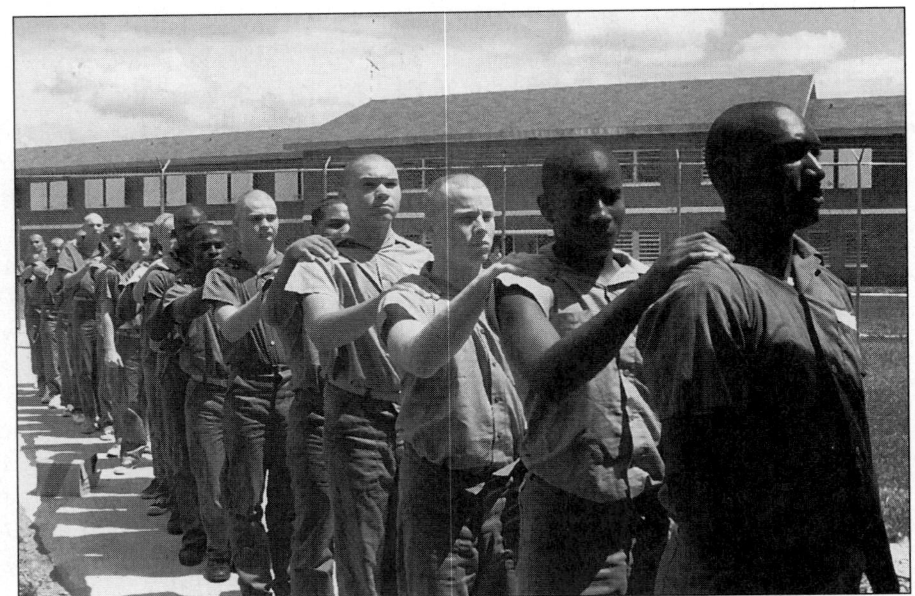

UPI/Bettmann Newsphotos

Sumter County Correctional Institution "Boot Camp" in Bushnell, Florida. Here juvenile offenders experience militaristic training and discipline.

placement and serve a relatively shorter sentence (typically 90 to 180 days), or refuse and be placed in prison to serve a longer sentence.

The dual goals of boot camps are to rehabilitate offenders and reduce prison overcrowding. Structured after the military boot camp, strict discipline and physical labor are elements of many shock incarceration programs. Education and behavior modification are also common elements of shock incarceration programs.

According to MacKenzie et al. (2001, p.1): "Despite their growing popularity, correctional boot camps are controversial. The controversy primarily is over whether the camps are an appropriate way to manage and treat juvenile delinquents and what impact the camps have on the adjustment and behavior of juveniles while they are confined and after they are released."

MacKenzie et al. (p.1) compared 27 boot camps to 22 more traditional facilities and found: "Juveniles in boot camps more frequently reported positive responses to their institutional environment. Boot camp juveniles said they were better prepared for release, were given more therapeutic programming, had more structure and control, and were more active than comparison facility youths." In assessing these results, it should be kept in mind that most boot camps are selective about who they admit, limiting admission to first-time, nonviolent offenders who have no psychological problems and are not suicide risks.

Although intermediate sanctions are growing in popularity, our nation's incarcerated population continues to climb, with more than 1.9 million adults, or nearly 30 percent of all adults under correctional supervision, confined in either jail or prison at year-end 2000 (*National Correctional Population . . .*, p.3).

Incarceration

Many types of correctional facilities exist for the **incarceration** (confining) of offenders. According to Beck and Harrison (2001, p.1): "Overall, the United States incarcerated 2,071,686 persons at year-end 2000," a total representing persons held in federal and state prisons, territorial prisons, local jails, facilities used by the U.S. Immigration and Naturalization Service, military facilities, tribal jails on Indian reservations and juvenile facilities. The primary goal of these correctional institutions is to protect society. Secondary goals may be to deter, rehabilitate and reintegrate offenders into society. While corrections tries to rehabilitate offenders, conditions cannot be such that the prison is a pleasant place to be. Inmates should dread a return. Unfortunately, however, too often our correctional institutions do not rehabilitate but actually contribute to and reward criminal behavior.

The type of correctional institution in which an offender is incarcerated, or imprisoned, usually depends on the type of crime committed and the offender's past record. Incarceration alternatives include local and county jails and state and federal prisons.

Jails

Jails are an important part of the U.S. criminal justice system and go by a variety of names, including houses of detention and houses of corrections, but their definitions are generally the same. A **jail** is a place of confinement, typically administered by local law enforcement, although occasionally by a regional or state law enforcement agency. At midyear 1999, 3,365 jails were operating throughout the United States (Stephan, 2001, p.5).

Jails serve the dual function of (1) detaining individuals waiting to appear before the court, either for trial (preconviction) or for sentencing (postconviction), and (2) holding those sentenced to a year or less of incarceration. Although jails vary considerably in their management and operational philosophies, the basic responsibilities of jail personnel remain constant, including the intake and classification of inmates, orientation of new residents, transportation of inmates between the jail and court and the release of inmates.

Jails differ from lockups in that lockups, commonly located in city halls or police stations, are temporary holding facilities, authorized to hold individuals for a maximum of 48 hours. Jails differ from prisons in that prisons are state or federally administered and hold only those convicted of a crime and sentenced, not those awaiting trial or sentencing.

Jail differs from prison in that its inmates are there for shorter terms, usually for less serious crimes.

According to the BJS, 621,149 inmates were held in the nation's local jails at midyear 2000, up from 605,943 at midyear 1999 ("Key Facts at a Glance . . .," 2001). From 1990 to 2000, the number of jail inmates per 100,000 U.S. residents rose from 163 to 226. However, from midyear 1999 to midyear 2000, the 12-month increase of 2.5 percent in the jail population was significantly smaller than the average annual increase of 4.4 percent since 1990.

The turnover rate of the jail population is relatively high, with offenders being booked and released, coming and going, much more often than inmates in prison. O'Toole (2001) notes: "It takes two years for the nation's prison population to turn over once, while the jail population turns over 20 to 25 times each [year]. . . . The reality of jail population dynamics is that the vast majority of inmates are released within a few days, and those who are not released early tend to remain in custody throughout the adjudication process."

The numbers of juveniles and female adults in the jail population have been increasing faster than the number of male adults, yet the vast majority of jail inmates, nearly 90 percent, remain male adults. The rate of jail incarceration for blacks is five times higher than the rate for whites ("Key Facts"). A significant proportion of those in jail have not yet been convicted of a crime. According to Stephan (p.5), at midyear 1999, more than half (54 percent) of all adult jail inmates were unconvicted and awaiting trial, up from 50 percent in 1993. In addition, approximately 74 percent of the federal inmates were unconvicted at midyear 1999—awaiting arraignment, trial or the completion of their trial (p.12).

Issues of concern vary slightly between state and federal jail facilities, including

- Overcrowding—the 11 federal jails had an aggregate occupancy rate of 39 percent over capacity while the national jail occupancy rate at midyear 1999 was 93 percent of capacity (Stephan, pp.9, 12).
- Assaults—nearly 9,300 inmate physical or sexual assaults on jail employees occurred between midyear 1998 and midyear 1999, 4 of which resulted in staff deaths (p.13).
- Inmate suicide—from midyear 1998 to midyear 1999, 324 jail inmates committed suicide and 4 more federal inmates died by suicide (pp.12, 13).
- Inmate rights—centers on the challenge posed to jail administration by the basic concept of "innocent until proven guilty," considering that most individuals in our nation's jails have not yet been tried or convicted of any crime.

The other major type of correctional institution in the United States, where the inmates *have* been convicted of a crime, is the prison.

Prisons

Prisons are often what come to people's minds when they think of *corrections.* A **prison** is administered by a warden or superintendent and holds convicted offenders sentenced to more than one year of incarceration. Just as the United States has both a state and federal court system, it also has a state and federal prison system. Since 1930 the Federal Bureau of Prisons (BOP), an agency within the Department of Justice, has been the authority charged with running our nation's federal facilities, which house those convicted of federal offenses.

The word *prison* usually conveys a mental picture of rows of cagelike cells several levels high, crowded mess halls and a "yard" where prisoners engage in

Laimute E. Druskis/Stock Boston

Because of overcrowding, newer institutions are being built with four tiers to accommodate more inmates. To many people this looks like warehousing prisoners.

physical activities, organized and not so organized, all patrolled by tight-lipped, heavily armed guards. While perhaps once accurate, this dramatic image no longer typifies modern prisons.

> Prisons may be punitive or treatment oriented. Punitive-oriented prisons are more formal and rigid, with an emphasis on obedience. Obedience is sought through negative incentives. Treatment-oriented prisons are more informal and flexible, with positive incentives for good behavior.

According to Austin and Irwin (2001, p.1): "The United States has been engaged in an unprecedented imprisonment binge. Between 1980 and 1998, the prison population ballooned from 329,821 to 1,302,019—a rise of 295 percent." By year-end 2000, the number of inmates in state and federal prison was 1,312,354, or 478 out of every 100,000 U.S. residents, which is markedly higher than the 1990 incarceration rate of 292 sentenced prisoners per every 100,000 residents (Beck and Harrison, pp.2, 4). However, the state prison population fell by 0.5 percent in the second half of 2000, the first such decline since 1972 (p.3).

Race and gender differences are noted among the prisoner population. Beck and Harrison (p.11) report: "At year-end 2000 black inmates represented an estimated 46% of all inmates with sentences of more than 1 year, while white inmates accounted for 36% and Hispanic inmates, 16%." In addition, they found nearly 1 out of every 10 black males age 25 to 29 were in prison in 2000 (p.11).

Women comprise a relatively small percentage of prisoners—6.6 percent (91,612) at year-end 2000 (Beck and Harrison, p.5). However, the number of women in prison has more than doubled since 1990. Austin et al. (2001, p.15) observe: "Between 1980 and 1999, the total number of incarcerated males increased 303 percent whereas that number increased 576 percent for females." The two most significant sources of growth for the female inmate population from 1990 to 2000 were a 28 percent increase in the number of violent women offenders and a 35 percent increase in female drug offenders (Beck and Harrison, p.12).

As with jails, our nation's prisons face several critical issues, including:

- Overcrowding—at year-end 2000, 22 states and the federal prison system were operating at 100 percent or more of their highest capacity (Beck and Harrison, p.9).
- Prison gangs—virtually every correctional system in the nation has had some experience with prison gangs. A survey of correctional facilities showed that, as of January 2000, the percentage of inmates identified as gang members ranged from less than 1 percent in the District of Columbia and Vermont, to 26 percent in Illinois, 30 percent in California and Arkansas and 47 percent in New Mexico ("Gangs Inside," 2000, pp.9–10).
- Criminalizing environment—socialization that occurs in prison may draw offenders away from a community's values and norms and strengthen their criminal tendencies. This phenomenon, which Clemmer (1971) identified as *prisonization,* leads prisoners to identify with and learn to coexist with other criminals and lose touch with any conventional values they may have had on the outside.
- Privatization—the provision of correctional services by organizations outside the governmental framework, either nonprofit or for profit—remains highly controversial. While proponents contend privatization will streamline and reduce the costs of corrections to the community, critics argue private prisons, motivated by the "bottom line," will cut corners, from cheaper, inferior construction materials to hiring inexperienced personnel, making decisions that enhance profits at the expense of security, quality of service and the rights and well-being of inmates. However, as Austin and Coventry (2001, p.38) report: "No data [exists] to support the contention that privately operated facilities offer cost savings over publicly managed facilities. Similarly, no definitive research evidence would lead to the conclusion that inmate services and the quality of confinement are significantly improved [or diminished] in privately operated facilities."

Regardless of whether an offender is housed in a public or private correctional facility, the reality for most inmates is that one day they will be released.

Parole

Parole is the conditional release from prison before the expiration of the sentence and the period of supervision in the community following this release. It is the most frequent type of release from a correctional institution. At year-end 2000, 652,199 adults were under state parole supervision (Hughes et al., 2001, p.1).

Parole differs from probation in that a person who is paroled has spent some time serving a prison sentence. It is similar to probation in that both require supervision of the offender and set up certain conditions the offender must meet.

Administratively parole, like law enforcement, is part of the executive branch of government; probation is under the courts and part of the judicial branch of government.

Factors influencing whether a person serving a sentence is eligible for or, indeed, is granted a parole include the type of offense committed, the offender's prior record, state statutes, the inmate's behavior while incarcerated, participation in programs, whether the inmate has a plan for life on the outside and if the inmate poses any public risk. In some jurisdictions parole is prohibited by statute for certain crimes. In other jurisdictions, however, people sentenced to prison are immediately eligible for parole. The type of parole release or reentry program granted depends on the inmate's individual needs and the variety of programs offered in a particular area. Common release programs include furloughs, work release, educational release, shock incarceration and halfway houses.

Conditions of parole typically include regular meetings between the parolee and the parole officer, a requirement to acquire and hold a job, a promise to act lawfully, a restriction on leaving the county or state without permission, a prohibition on purchasing or using a firearm and submission to random or routine drug testing. Violation of the conditions of parole typically send the offender back to prison.

Parole has had many advocates and critics over the years. Proponents assert parole plays an important role in relieving the pressures of our overcrowded prisons, while opponents claim parole lets offenders off by shortening their stay behind bars and exposes the public to criminals who haven't yet paid their debt or who still pose a threat to society. Clearly the parole process is not perfect, and many states have chosen to abolish it. However many states still rely on parole to return inmates to society. Once an inmate is released, it is the parole officer's task to supervise the parolee. For those offenders who are paroled, it is often a condition of their parole that they participate in some program to integrate them back into society.

Community-Based Reintegration Programs

Community-based institutional programs aimed at reintegration of the offender into society include halfway houses and restitution centers.

Halfway Houses

As the name implies, **halfway houses** are community-based institutions for people who are halfway into prison, that is on probation, or halfway out of prison, that is on or nearing parole. Halfway houses serving those nearing parole or actually discharged from prison are sometimes called "prerelease centers." Halfway houses typically provide offenders with a place to live, sleep and eat. Counselors help offenders return to society, sometimes helping them find suitable jobs or providing transportation to jobs.

Restitution Centers

A new variation of the halfway house is the restitution center. A **restitution center** differs from a halfway house in that in the restitution center offenders work to partially repay their victims. Like the halfway house, restitution centers offer an alternative to prison, either for those who are halfway into or halfway out of prison.

Other Reintegration Methods

Several other approaches to reintegrating offenders into society have been used, with varying degrees of success. Three common reintegration methods are furloughs, work release and study release. In all cases the possibility of escape from the directives of the criminal justice system must be considered.

Furloughs are short, temporary leaves from a prison or jail, supervised or unsupervised, although generally the latter. They are often used as positive motivators for good behavior. They may be granted for family emergencies, for a weekend with a spouse or for job interviewing. Work and study release are also positive motivators for good behavior that also help reintegrate offenders into society. Often such programs are conducted through halfway houses or through local jails.

The conditions of furloughs, work release and study release programs are usually very explicit and rigid. For example a strict curfew may be established; going into a bar may be prohibited; and associating with known criminals may be forbidden. People on work programs usually have their pay closely controlled. They may be required to pay a portion of their room and board, and, if married, to send part of their earnings to their dependents.

Recidivism

The problem of released criminals returning to crime is of great concern. According to Hughes et al. (p.10): "Of the 410,613 discharges from State parole in 1999, 42% successfully completed their term of supervision, 43% were returned to prison or jail, and 10% absconded." They (p.11) further report: "In every year during the 1990s, first releases to State parole were more likely to have been successful than re-releases. . . . In every year between 1990 and 1999, State prisoners released by a parole board had higher success rates than those released through mandatory parole."

Among the approximately 250,000 parole violators in state prisons in 1997, 70 percent (roughly 175,000) indicated their parole had been revoked because of an arrest or conviction for a new offense (Hughes et al., p.14). This pattern of "crime to prison to parole to crime and back to prison" ad infinitum describes what has become known as the "revolving door of criminal justice," a loop involving all three components of the justice system.

Nowhere is the issue of recidivism of greater concern than when considering how to handle offenders who have committed heinous and violent crimes. Because the general population and the courts agree such offenders should not be returned to society, the question then becomes a matter of life versus death: should we keep these offenders locked up forever (life) or execute them (death)?

The Death Penalty versus Life without Parole

During 2000, 14 states executed 85 prisoners and, at year-end, 3,593 remained on death row (Snell, 2001, p.1). Among those remaining, 54 were women, the average age of prisoner at time of arrest was 28, the youngest inmate was 18 and the oldest was 85 (p.1).

Many brutal methods have been used throughout history to execute condemned criminals, including being buried alive, thrown to wild animals, boiled in oil, stoned, pressed to death, stretched on a rack, disemboweled and beheaded. Capital punishment in the United States "evolved" as society searched

The gas chamber was invented in 1927 and continues to be used in several states. This is the gas chamber at San Quentin.

for more humane ways of killing its condemned—from hangings in the early years, to the first electrocution in 1890, the invention of the gas chamber in 1923, the use of a firing squad and finally the adoption of lethal injections in 1977. Today, lethal injection is the predominant method of execution in the United States, used in 34 states.

Despite attempts to make the methods of capital punishment more humane and, thereby more "palatable" to society, Manning and Rhoden-Trader (2000, p.22) note: "The United States is the only nation in the Western democratic world that has not abolished capital punishment. Virtually every other nation has done away with it or severely modified it. Moreover, only the United States, as a nation, uses the electric chair." In fact, the three most common methods of execution in the United States—electrocution, asphyxiation and lethal injection—are not used anywhere else in the world.

As correctional philosophies and practices fluctuate, and the pendulum swings from punishment to rehabilitation and back, so too do attitudes concerning capital punishment. Gallup polls conducted between 1936 and 2001 show support for the death penalty reached its lowest point in 1966 (42 percent favored it) and peaked in 1994, with 80 percent favoring capital punishment for someone convicted of murder ("Death Penalty," 2002). The Gallup poll, taken

October 11–14, 2001, showed 68 percent of adults polled were in favor of the death penalty.

Supporters of capital punishment see it as both a deterrent and as a form of retribution. They also assert that imprisoning for life those convicted of capital crimes will only further burden an already overcrowded prison system.

Those who argue against the death penalty contend it is morally reprehensible and self-defeating, sending the message "it's okay to punish an act of killing with an act of killing" or "it's okay to extinguish those who have done wrong." Some opponents assert that such state-sanctioned killings cheapen the value of human life and dull society to issues concerning intentional death. Others criticize the disparity shown by the court when deciding who should receive capital punishment. Indeed several studies have shown that the financial status of the offender and the location of the offense are factors in determining who receives a death sentence. Another disparity concerning the death penalty centers on the gender of the offender—women are conspicuously absent on death row.

Race of the offender, however, has been found not to be a factor in capital punishment cases. Citing a study of nearly 1,000 potential death penalty cases in U.S. Attorneys' offices across the country, Attorney General John Ashcroft concluded: "There is no evidence of racial bias in the administration of the federal death penalty. Our analysis has confirmed that black and Hispanic defendants were less likely at each stage of the department's review process to be subjected to the death penalty than white defendants" ("Expanded Study . . .," 2001, p.4).

It has been said that for a punishment to be effective, it must be both swift and certain. Critics of the death penalty argue this sanction fails on both counts. Snell (p.12) reports in 1983 the average elapsed time from sentence to execution was 51 months (4.25 years), but that by 2000 the average death row inmate had spent 137 months (11.4 years) awaiting execution. This delay between sentencing and actual execution has grown so long that the public often has forgotten the horror of the crime for which the death penalty was imposed, severely hindering any deterrent effect the capital punishment might have.

The certainty of execution is also in question, with some viewing the death penalty as an "empty threat." Death sentences are being handed down more frequently than they are being carried out. According to Snell (p.13) 6,930 prisoners were sentenced to death between 1973 and 2000, of which 683 were executed; 2,044 were removed from death row through an appeal or higher court overturning the state's death penalty statute, the conviction or the sentence; 157 had their sentence commuted; 223 died before execution; and 30 left death row for other unknown reasons; leaving a net accumulation over 28 years of 3,593 prisoners on death row.

Many opponents to capital punishment suggest life without parole (LWOP) as a suitable alternative, bolstering their argument by citing the potential good the inmate might do if allowed to live, including providing restitution to the victim's family and participating in the rehabilitation of other inmates (on and off death row). In fact, many death row inmates consider LWOP a worse alternative than execution, saying they would rather be put to death than rot behind bars for the rest of their lives, which may last decades.

Recall the average age of arrest for prisoners on death row—28 years old. Given the relatively young age at which many murderers commit their crimes and the likelihood these prisoners will spend many years behind bars if given LWOP, concern over the cost to warehouse these criminals has become another issue of the debate. Capital punishment proponents estimate that at $10,000 to $20,000 a year, a 20-year-old who lives 60 years in prison would cost society more than $1 million. However dollar estimates for executions that include the full cost of appeals are also often in the millions.

The execution of youths and the mentally handicapped is a hotly contested issue.

Juveniles and the Death Penalty

As noted by Carlson et al. (p.350): "When people think of the death penalty, they often do not consider its application to juvenile offenders." However according to Snell (p.9), among the 3,312 inmates under sentence of death at year-end 2000 for whom arrest information was available, 78 (2.4 percent) had been 17 years of age or younger at the time of their arrest. Since the first execution of a condemned juvenile in 1642, 361 persons have been executed for juvenile crimes (Streib, 2000), 14 executions having occurred between 1990 and 2000. Streib further elaborates that of the 6,881 death sentences imposed between 1973 and 2000 for crimes committed as juveniles, 13 offenders were age 15 at the time of their arrest, 47 were 16 years old, and 136 were 17 years old.

Many believe a lack of maturity and the inability to fully comprehend the nature of capital punishment are mitigating circumstances that should disqualify juveniles from receiving the death penalty. Cothern (2000, p.10) observes an increasing number of juvenile offenders are being sentenced to life in prison without the possibility of parole: "The overwhelming majority of American jurisdictions . . . allow life without parole for offenders younger than age 16. Some even make it mandatory for defendants convicted of certain offenses in criminal court. In Washington State, offenders as young as age 8 can be sentenced to life. In Vermont, 10-year-olds can face the sentence."

While LWOP is an increasingly popular sentencing option for juveniles who have committed capital offenses, and despite the apparent disdain shown by the rest of the civilized world toward sentencing juvenile capital offenders to death, 38 states persist in authorizing capital punishment for such offenders. In fact, according to Amnesty International USA, "the United States is currently the only nation in the world (since 1977) known to have executed inmates who committed crimes when they were younger than 18" (Manning and Rhoden-Trader, p.22). Nonetheless, the Supreme Court has continued to uphold the constitutionality of such executions.

Mental Competence and the Death Penalty

The Supreme Court has ruled that capital offenders are not necessarily or automatically exempt from receiving a death sentence simply because they are mentally retarded, although more than a dozen states and the federal government expressly prohibit such executions. Amnesty International USA ("Death Penalty

Facts," 2001) reports since 1976 and as of September 8, 2001, the United States has executed 35 mentally retarded offenders.

While *retardation* does not exclude the possibility of capital punishment as a sentence, a diagnosis of mental *illness* often does eliminate the death penalty as a sentencing option for capital offenders. The National Mental Health Association (2001) notes that over the past 30 years, the number of people with mental illness and other mental disabilities on death row has steadily increased, and it estimates 5 to 10 percent of death row inmates have a serious mental illness.

A person can be under a death sentence and become insane, at which time the death sentence is commuted until the prisoner regains sanity and is able to be executed. In 1986, the Supreme Court ruled that people with mental illness can be executed if they understand the punishment that awaits them and why they are being put to death, a ruling that prompted some states to provide psychiatric treatment and/or forced medication to mentally ill death row offenders to restore their competency. This practice, however, has generated much controversy. Furthermore, court rulings on this matter have been quite inconsistent (Slobogin, 2001).

Many courts have upheld the forcible medication of criminal defendants to restore their competency to stand trial, as long as the state does not *over*-medicate the defendant in its attempts to restore competency. Other courts have held that medicating an objecting person, with the ultimate goal of executing that offender once competent, constitutes cruel and unusual punishment. Noting the clear ethical stipulation in medicine that doctors should "do no harm" and, in fact, are expressly prohibited by governing professional organizations from participating or assisting in executions, some contend the physician who forcibly administers antipsychotic medication to restore a prisoner's competency so that the state may execute him is serving a role ethically indistinguishable from the physician who administers a lethal injection of barbiturates.

Of course, an issue always of concern is whether a defendant assessed as incompetent to stand trial is malingering (feigning the signs and symptoms of mental disorder). Another issue of grave concern regarding capital punishment is the execution of innocent people.

Innocence, Wrongful Conviction and the Death Penalty

Debate has also erupted over the possibility of innocent people being executed. According to Amnesty International USA, 350 people have been wrongfully convicted of capital or potentially capital crimes in the United States since 1990, 23 of whom were executed. From 1973 to 2001, 98 people were released from death row after evidence of their wrongful conviction surfaced. In January 2001, the case against Peter Limone was dropped by the state of Massachusetts after the main witness admitted fabricating much of his testimony. Limone had spent 33 years on death row.

Factors that may lead to wrongful convictions include inadequate defense, police and prosecutorial misconduct, perjured testimony, mistaken eyewitness testimony, racial prejudice, tainted jailhouse testimony, suppression of mitigating evidence, misinterpretation of evidence and community pressure (Amnesty International USA).

According to Manning and Rhoden-Trader (p.25): "The acceptance of advanced DNA technology in court is considered a powerful safeguard against wrongful executions that yield genetics susceptible to testing. . . . Utilizing such DNA technology, the FBI recently tested 100 inmates. Thirty-three of them, who had been identified by witnesses and serology as being criminals, were exonerated by DNA testing."

Many argue that the potential for even one mistake should be reason enough to abolish capital punishment. Others, however, assert that to abolish the death penalty out of fear of error is to second-guess the integrity of the system or to undermine the very credibility of our criminal justice system. The controversy regarding capital punishment and life without parole is likely to continue.

There is little doubt, however, that capital punishment is the ultimate form of retribution. Many argue that such retributive justice does not fit with the community justice discussed at the beginning of the chapter. Restorative justice might seem to be a better approach.

The Restorative Justice Model

Historically justice in this country has focused on offenders and the state punishing them. Victims and the community have traditionally been ignored. Quinn (1998, p.10) says of this retributive model of justice: "It does a good job of incarcerating violent, repeat offenders, but it does not—and many people argue that it *cannot*—adequately address victim and community harm. Nor does it give offenders an adequate opportunity to earn back their place in society."

In keeping with the trend of expanding community involvement in criminal justice, restorative justice is becoming an increasingly popular alternative to retributive justice. **Restorative justice** seeks to use a balanced approach involving offenders, victims, local communities and government to alleviate crime and violence and obtain peaceful communities.

More and more, crime is being viewed and redefined as a violation against another person, not simply a harm against the state. Bazemore and Umbreit (2001, p.1) report: "Reconciling the needs of victims and offenders with the needs of the community is the underlying goal of restorative justice. Unlike retributive justice, which is primarily concerned with punishing crime, restorative justice focuses on repairing the injury that crime inflicts."

The restorative justice approach is also having a positive impact on juvenile offenders, who, through victim-offender mediation, are required to make monetary restitution, provide community service and enter into direct service agreements with their victims. Crowley (1998, p.10) notes:

> It's not easy for juveniles to face their victims, or to humble themselves to doing work often required in the restitution agreements. Be that as it may, this restorative justice process works. Kids are learning that if caught, they can't just show up at juvenile court, pay a fine and call it a day. Instead they will be confronted by their victims and held accountable for their unlawful behavior. . . .
>
> For juveniles who have committed a crime, victim-offender mediation may be the only experience that leads them to see a victim's viewpoint—and its old-fashioned justice may touch the nerve that sparks changed attitudes and behavior.

According to Levrant et al. (1999, p.22): "Restorative justice is increasingly embraced—by criminologists and by policy makers—as an alternative correctional paradigm to the prevailing view that penal harm is the solution to crime. By offering something to everyone—victims, offenders, and the community—restorative justice is . . . seemingly deserving of the excitement that it is generating." Table 12.4 lists the various facets of restorative justice and how it involves crime victims, offenders, citizens, families and community groups.

Helfgott et al. (2000, p.5) conducted a pilot study on the restorative justice program at the Washington State Reformatory and found that the program was effective in achieving its program goals: (1) the program provided a safe environment for inmates to begin making amends for their crimes and for victims to heal; (2) it facilitated constructive communication between polarized groups;

Table 12.4
The Restorative Justice Response to Crime

Crime Victims

- Receive support, assistance, compensation, information, and services.
- Receive restitution and other reparation from the offender.
- Are involved and encouraged to provide input at all points in the system and direct input into how the offender will repair the harm done.
- Have the opportunity to face the offender and tell their story to the offender and others if they so desire.
- Feel satisfied with the justice process.
- Provide guidance and consultation to professionals on planning and advisory groups.

Offenders

- Pay restitution to their victims.
- Provide meaningful service to repay the debt to their communities.
- Face the personal harm caused by their crimes by participating in victim-offender mediation if the victim is willing or through other victim awareness process.
- Complete work experience and active and productive tasks that increase skills and improve the community.
- Improve decision-making skills and have opportunities to help others.
- Are monitored by community adults as well as juvenile justice providers and are supervised to the greatest extent possible in the community (if young offenders).

Citizens, Families and Community Groups

- Are involved to the greatest extent possible in offender accountability and rehabilitation and community safety initiatives.
- Work with offenders on local community service projects.
- Provide support to victims. Provide support to offenders as mentors, employers, and advocates.
- Provide work for offenders to pay restitution to victims and for service opportunities that provide skills and also allow offenders to make meaningful contributions to the quality of community life.
- Play an advisory role to courts and corrections and an active role in disposition through one or more neighborhood sanctioning processes.
- Assist families in helping young offenders repair the harm and in increasing competencies (if community groups).

Source: G. Bazemore. "What's New About the Balanced Approach?" *Juvenile and Family Court Journal*, Vol. 48, No. 1, 1997, pp.1–23. Reprinted by permission of the author.

and (3) it encouraged participants to develop creative ways of thinking about justice and strategies for dealing with crime.

Smith (2001, p.1) links restorative justice and public safety as important components of community corrections: "Public safety and restorative justice are big ideas now making claims on the future of community corrections." He (p.2) explains that traditionally public safety has been equated with more arrests, more prisoners, longer sentences and lower recidivism, but that these are "poor proxies" for public safety. Instead: "As an objective for community corrections, public safety is best conceived as the condition of a place, at times when people in that place are justified in feeling free of threat to their persons and property." In effect: "This view of public safety directly challenges offender-focused probation and parole case management. It emphasizes instead the need for unofficial, naturally occurring guardians of people and places." Guardians may include spouses, family members, friends, neighbors, employers and business people. When such guardians are in place, public safety exists. In their absence, public safety is in jeopardy.

Smith (p.3) notes the conceptual overlap between public safety and restorative justice: "Both public safety and restorative justice incorporate each other's essential features. The triangular "web of interdependency" (victims, offenders, community) on which restorative processes rely has much in common with the networks of naturally occurring guardians on which public safety depends." Following an in-depth examination of restorative justice, Quinn (pp.14–15) concludes:

> The evidence has convinced me that the restorative justice model has great potential to coexist with the existing incapacitative and retributive models and to contribute to greater well-being for victims and communities. . . .
>
> I've come to believe that restorative justice is a logical next step in a number of national trends. First, it is an integral part of the movement to involve communities in solving their crime problems and encourage justice components to participate in community solutions. . . .
>
> It is also an integral part of "reinventing" government, because it encourages flexibility and interdisciplinary efforts among the parties that are closest to the source of problems. . . .
>
> Thomas Jefferson acknowledged that our institutions must change as society evolves and matures. It is apparent that we are in a time of change, and our system of justice must change as well. Fortunately, the impending transition to involve the community and the victim has the potential to be a positive one.

Community Corrections and the Role of Police

Traditionally correctional institutions were isolated from other human service agencies and were required merely to hold prisoners and to provide some form of nominal supervision for those on probation and parole. More recently, however, corrections is expected to take a more positive approach, seeking rehabilitation whenever possible. These revised expectations make it necessary to link corrections to the community in every phase of operation.

A community approach to corrections has three significant advantages: humanitarian, restorative and managerial. The humanitarian aspect is obvious because no one should be subjected to custodial control unnecessarily. Second, restorative measures should help offenders achieve positions in the community in which they do not violate the law. Third, the managerial goal of cost effectiveness can often be achieved because any shift from custodial control saves money.

Community correctional programs cannot succeed without the understanding and cooperation of the police because those within these programs *will* come in contact with the police, and the nature of that contact will directly affect the offender's adjustment. The police can make affirmative contributions to community-based corrections programs. They know the resources available and the pitfalls to be avoided. In essence the police are an integral part of any successful corrections program, from using good judgment in making arrests to helping those on parole or probation to reenter the community.

Summary

Police officers aid the criminal justice process by (1) making arrests, (2) obtaining information and evidence, (3) writing reports, (4) identifying suspects and witnesses and (5) providing testimony in court. They routinely interact with both the courts and corrections.

Our judicial system operates at both the state and federal levels. The hierarchy at the state level often goes up from courts of special or limited jurisdiction called justice of the peace (J.P.) courts, to trial courts or original and general jurisdiction courts, to intermediate appellate courts, to the state supreme court. The federal court system is three tiered: district courts, appellate courts and the U.S. Supreme Court.

A specialized type of court is the juvenile court, historically informal, private and nonadversarial, stressing rehabilitation rather than punishment of youths. As juvenile justice has evolved, so too have juvenile rights, as defined by several landmark Supreme Court decisions. *Kent v. United States* established that if a juvenile court transfers a case to adult criminal court, juveniles are entitled to a hearing, their counsel must be given access to probation records used by the court in reaching its decision, and the court must state its reasons for waiving jurisdiction over the case. The *In re Gault* decision required that the due process clause of the Fourteenth Amendment be applied to proceedings in state juvenile courts, including the right of notice, the right to counsel, the right against self-incrimination and the right to confront witnesses. The *In re Winship* decision established that a juvenile defendant must be found guilty beyond a reasonable doubt, and *McKeiver v. Pennsylvania* established that a jury trial is not a constitutional right of juveniles.

Our criminal justice system is based on the adversary system, which requires that the accuser prove beyond a reasonable doubt to a judge or jury that the accused is guilty of a specified crime. The criminal justice system consists of several critical stages: the complaint or charge, the warrant, arrest, booking, preliminary hearing, grand jury hearing, the arraignment, the trial and sentencing. The preliminary hearing seeks to establish probable cause to prevent people from being indiscriminately brought to trial.

Not all cases go to court. Alternatives to a trial include diversion and plea bargaining. Police officers' testimony at the trial is of great importance. They should be aware of tactics often used by defense attorneys to confuse or discredit a police officer who is testifying: (1) rapid-fire questioning, (2) establishing that the officer wants to see the defendant found guilty, (3) accusing the officer of making assumptions or (4) implying that the officer does not want anyone else to know what is in his or her notes.

Once a case has passed through the court system and a disposition is reached, the case then moves into the corrections phase of the justice system. Corrections is that portion of the criminal justice system that carries out the court's orders. The primary purposes of corrections are retribution, deterrence, incapacitation and rehabilitation. Correctional alternatives available to the courts include probation, intermediate sanctions, incarceration and, in some states, the death penalty. These same options exist for juvenile offenders, although probation is by far the most frequent disposition in juvenile delinquency cases.

Many offenders, especially repeat offenders, are sentenced to correctional institutions, jails or prisons. Jail differs from prison in that its inmates are there for shorter terms, usually for less serious crimes. Prisons may be punitive oriented or treatment oriented. Punitive-oriented prisons are more formal and rigid, with an emphasis on obedience. Obedience is sought through negative incentives. In contrast, treatment-oriented prisons are more informal and flexible, with positive incentives for good behavior.

Most people sentenced to jail or prison become eligible for parole. Parole differs from probation in that a person who is paroled has spent some time serving a prison sentence. It is similar to probation in that both require supervision of the offender and set up certain conditions that must be met by the offender. Parole and probation often involve community-based institutional programs aimed at reintegrating offenders into society, including halfway houses, restitution centers, furloughs, and work release and study release programs.

Discussion Questions

1. Is the jury system really fair?
2. Should the police be consulted when plea bargaining is used?
3. Is our system truly an adversary system when the prosecutor also has to protect the accused's rights?
4. Do you feel diversion is an acceptable alternative in some instances? If so, when? If not, why?
5. Do juvenile courts too often stress rehabilitation and keeping youngsters in the home?
6. What correctional facilities are available for juvenile delinquents in your area? Your state?
7. What are your views on capital punishment? A sentence of life without parole? Which do you feel would be the harsher sentence?
8. Why do you think the United States has the highest rate and number of people behind bars?
9. Explain the relationships among community policing, community justice and restorative justice.
10. Does your community use any forms of community policing, community prosecution, community courts or community corrections? If so, what?

InfoTrac *College Edition Assignments*

Use InfoTrac College Edition to answer the Discussion Questions as appropriate.

- Use InfoTrac College Edition to research *restorative justice.* Find and outline at least two articles on the subject. OR
- Use InfoTrac College Edition to research *capital punishment.* Outline one article in favor and one article opposed to this form of "corrections." With either option, be prepared to share your findings with the class.

Internet Assignments

- Research *community justice* on the Web at www.communityjustice.org Outline at least two references. Be prepared to share your outline with the class.
- Look at the research on *drug courts* at http://www.ojp.usdoj.gov/dcpo/decade98.htm Summarize your finding, and be prepared to share with the class.

Book-Specific Web Site

The book-specific Web site at http://info.wadsworth.com/0534552803 hosts a variety of resources for students and instructors. Included are extended activities from each chapter in which students write a policy, use critical thinking skills to make choices in response to a given scenario, use InfoTrac College Edition with direct links to articles for participation in topical discussion forums, and analyze court cases using Web links for research. Many activities can be printed or emailed to instructors. Plus, cited cases with Web links, interactive key term FlashCards, PowerPoint presentations, chapter objectives, and an extensive collection of chapter-based Web links provide additional information and activities to include in the curriculum.

References

Amnesty International USA. "Death Penalty Facts." 2001. www.amnesty-usa.org/abolish/reports.html

Austin, James and Coventry, Garry. *Emerging Issues on Privatized Prisons.* Washington, DC: Bureau of Justice Assistance and the National Council on Crime and Delinquency, February 2001. (NCJ 181249)

Austin, James and Irwin, John. *It's About Time: America's Imprisonment Binge,* 3rd edition. Belmont, CA: Wadsworth Thomson Learning, 2001.

Austin, James; Bruce, Marino A.; Carroll, Leo; McCall, Patricia L.; and Richards, Stephen C. "The Use of Incarceration in the United States." *The Criminologist,* May/June 2001, pp.14–16.

Bazemore, Gordon and Umbreit, Mark. *A Comparison of Four Restorative Conferencing Models.* Washington, DC: OJJDP Juvenile Justice Bulletin, February 2001.

Beck, Allen J. and Harrison, Paige M. *Prisoners in 2000.* Washington, DC: Bureau of Justice Statistics Bulletin, August 2001. (NCJ 188207)

Boland, Barbara. "The Manhattan Experiment: Community Prosecution." In *Crime and Place: Plenary Papers of the 1997 Conference on Criminal Justice Research and Evaluation.* Washington, DC: National Institute of Justice, July 1998, pp.51–67. (NCJ 168618)

Boland, Barbara. *Community Prosecution in Washington, D.C.* Washington, DC: National Institute of Justice Research Report, April 2001.

Carlson, Norman A.; Hess, Kären M.; and Orthmann, Christine M. H. *Corrections in the 21st Century: A Practical Approach.* Belmont, CA: West/Wadsworth Publishing Company, 1999.

Clemmer, Donald. "The Process of Prisonization." In *The Criminal in Confinement,* edited by Leon Radzinowicz and Marvin Wolfgang. New York: Basic Books, 1971, pp.92–93.

Community Justice in Rural America: Four Examples and Four Futures. Washington, DC: Bureau of Justice Assistance Monograph. February 2001. (NCJ 182437)

Cooper, Caroline S. *Juvenile Drug Court Programs.* Washington, DC: Juvenile Accountability Incentive Block Grants Program Bulletin, May 2001.

Cothern, Lynn. *Juveniles and the Death Penalty.* Washington, DC: Office of Juvenile Justice and Delinquency Prevention, November 2000. (NCJ 184748)

Crowley, Jim. "Victim-Offender Mediation: Paradigm Shift or Old-Fashioned Accountability?" *Community Links,* Spring 1998, p.10.

"Death Penalty." Gallup Organization, 2002. www.gallup.com/poll/topics/death_pen.asp

"Death Penalty Facts." 2001.

Dobbins, Muriel. "Judge Decries Mandatory Minimum Sentences." (Pittsburgh) *Post-Gazette,* June 6, 1999, p.A19. http://users.ssm.ca/jhs/Library/war_on_drugs.htm

"Drug Courts." Washington, DC: *NCJRS Catalog,* May/June 2001, pp.18–21.

Evans, Donald G. "Common Probation Concerns." *Corrections Today,* December 2000, pp.162–163.

"Expanded Study Shows No Bias in Death Penalty, Ashcroft Says." *Criminal Justice Newsletter,* June 18, 2001, pp.4–5.

Feinblatt, John; Berman, Greg; and Sviridoff, Michele. "Neighborhood Justice at the Midtown Community Court." In *Crime and Place: Plenary Papers of the 1997 Conference on Criminal Justice Research and Evaluation.* Washington, DC: National Institution of Justice, July 1998, pp.81–92 (NCJ 168618)

"Gangs Inside." *Corrections Compendium,* April 2000, pp.9–18.

Giblin, Matthew J. "Using Police Officers to Enhance the Supervision of Juvenile Probationers: An Evaluation of the Anchorage CAN Program." *Crime and Delinquency,* January 2002, pp.116–137.

Gil-Blanco, Jorge. "Courtroom Coliseum." *Police,* October 2001, pp.74–78.

Goodwin, Tracy with Steinhart, David J. and Fulton, Betsy A. *Peer Justice and Youth Empowerment: An Implementation Guide for Teen Court Programs.* U.S. Department of Transportation, National Highway Traffic Safety Administration; American Probation and Parole Association; and the U.S. Department of Justice, Office of Juvenile Justice and Delinquency Prevention, no date.

Harrison, Paige; Maupin, James R.; and Mays, F. Larry. "Teen Courts, A Popular But Unproven Model." *Crime and Delinquency,* Vol. 47, No. 2, 2001.

Helfgott, Jacqueline B.; Lovell, Madeline L.; Lawrence, Charles F.; and Parsonage, William H. "Results from the Pilot Study of the Citizens, Victims, and Offenders Restoring Justice Program at the Washington State Reformatory." *Journal of Contemporary Criminal Justice,* January 2000, pp.5–31.

Hughes, Timothy A.; Wilson, Doris James; and Beck, Allen J. *Trends in State Parole, 1990–2000.* Washington, DC: Bureau of Justice Statistics Special Report, October 2001. (NCJ 184735)

Kalk, Dan. "Checkpoints, Pursuits and Court Dates." *Police,* March 2001, pp.39–41.

"Key Facts at a Glance: Correctional Populations 1980–2000." Washington, DC: Bureau of Justice Statistics, August 2001. www.ojp.usdoj.gov/bjs/glance/tables/corr2tab.htm

Levrant, Sharon; Cullen, Francis T.; Fulton, Betsy; and Wozniak, John F. "Reconsidering Restorative Justice: The Corruption of Benevolence Revisited?" *Crime and Delinquency,* January 1999, pp.3–27.

MacKenzie, Doris Layton; Gover, Angela R.; Armstrong, Gaylene Styve; and Mitchell, Ojmarrh. *A National Study Comparing the Environments of Boot Camps with Traditional Facilities for*

Juvenile Offenders. Washington, DC: National Institute of Justice Research in Brief, August 2001.

Manning, Will and Rhoden-Trader, Jacqueline. "Rethinking the Death Penalty." *Corrections Today,* October 2000, pp.22–25.

McKay, Brian and Paris, Barry. "Forging a Police-Probation Alliance." *FBI Law Enforcement Bulletin,* November 1998, pp.27–32.

National Correctional Population Reaches New High, Grows by 126,400 during 2000 to Total 6.5 Million Adults. Washington, DC: Department of Justice Press Release, August 28, 2001. www.ojp.usdoj.gov/bjs/pub/pdf/ppus00.pdf

National Mental Health Association. *Death Penalty and People with Mental Illness.* Policy Position: P-44. 2001. www.mha-mi.org/policy44.html

Neubauer, David W. *America's Courts and the Criminal Justice System,* 6th ed. Belmont, CA: West/Wadsworth Publishing Company, 1999.

O'Toole, Michael. "Jails and Prisons: The Numbers Say They Are More Different than Generally Assumed." *American Jails,* 2001. www.corrections.com/aja/mags/magazine.html

Patch, Peter C. "The Three Strikes Law and Control of Crime in California." *ACJS Today,* November/December 1998, pp.1, 3.

Quinn, Thomas. "Restorative Justice: An Interview with Visiting Fellow Thomas Quinn." *National Institute of Justice Journal,* March 1998, pp.10–16.

Senjo, Scott and Leip, Leslie A. "Examining the Judge's Role in Drug Courts." *Western Criminology Review,* Vol. 3, No. 1, 2001.

Slobogin, Christopher. "Mental Illness and the Death Penalty." *California Criminal Law Review,* Vol. 1, No. 3, 2001. www.boalt.org/CCLR/v1/v1slobogintext.htm

Smith, Michael E. *What Future for "Public Safety" and "Restorative Justice" in Community Corrections? Sentencing and Corrections Issues for the 21st Century.* Research in Brief. Papers from the Executive Sessions on Sentencing and Corrections, No. 11, June 2001.

Snell, Tracy L. *Capital Punishment 2000.* Washington, DC: Bureau of Justice Statistics Bulletin, December 2001. (NCJ 190598)

Stephan, James J. *Census of Jails, 1999.* Washington, DC: Bureau of Justice Statistics, August 2001. (NCJ 186633)

Stone, Christopher. "The Lessons of Neighborhood-Focused Public Defense." In *Crime and Place: Plenary Papers of the 1997 Conference on Criminal Justice Research and Evaluation.* Washington, DC: National Institution of Justice, July 1998, pp.93–100. (NCJ 168618)

Streib, Victor L. *The Juvenile Death Penalty Today: Death Sentences and Executions for Juvenile Crimes, January 1, 1973–June 30, 2000.* Ada, OH: Ohio Northern University Claude W. Pettit College of Law, 2000.

Swope, Ross E. "Community Prosecution." *Police Quarterly,* March 2000, pp.105–115.

Swope, Ross E. "Community Prosecution: The Real Deal." *Law Enforcement News,* January 15/31, 2001, pp.11, 14.

"Ten Years of Drug Courts; 'National Drug Court Week' Introduced." *NCJA Justice Bulletin,* April 1999, pp.6–7.

Territo, Leonard; Halsted, James B.; and Bromley, Max L. *Crime and Justice in America: A Human Perspective,* 5th ed. Boston: Butterworth-Heinemann, 1998.

Turner, Susan. "Impact of Truth-in-Sentencing and Three Strikes Legislation on Crime." In *Crime and Justice Atlas 2000.* Washington, DC: U.S. Department of Justice, June 2000, pp.10–11.

Cases Cited

Argersinger v. Hamlin, 407 U.S. 25 (1972)
Berger v. United States, 295 U.S. 78 (1935)
Betts v. Brady, 316 U.S. 455 (1942)
Breed v. Jones, 421 U.S. 519, 533, 95 (1975)
Commonwealth v. Fisher, 213 Pa. 48 (1905)
Escobedo v. Illinois, 378 U.S. 478 (1964)
Faretta v. California, 422 U.S. 806 (1975)
Gault, In re, 387 U.S. 187 (1967)
Gideon v. Wainwright, 372 U.S. 355 (1963)
Johnson v. Zerbst, 304 U.S. 458 (1938)
Kent v. United States, 383 U.S. 541 (1966)
McKeiver v. Pennsylvania, 403 U.S. 528 (1971)
Powell v. Alabama, 287 U.S. 45 (1932)
Shioutakon v. District of Columbia, 236 F.2d 666 (1956)
Williams v. Florida, 399 U.S. 78 (1970)
Winship, In re, 397 U.S. 358 (1970)

Glossary

The number following the definition refers to the chapter(s) in which the term is defined.

accreditation—being approved by an official review board as meeting specific standards. (11)

actus reus—a guilty, measurable act, including planning and conspiring. (2)

adjudicate—to judge juveniles as adults. (12)

administrative services—those services such as recruiting, training, planning and research, records, communications, crime laboratories and facilities, including the police headquarters and jail. (4)

administrative warrant—official permission to investigate the cause of a fire after the fire has been extinguished. (8)

adversary system—a system that puts the accuser versus the accused. The accuser must prove that the one accused is guilty. The criminal justice system used in the United States. (12)

affidavit—a statement reduced to writing, sworn to before a judge or notary having authority to administer an oath. (8)

affirmative action—results-oriented actions taken to ensure equal employment opportunity which may include goals to correct underutilization and backpay, retroactive seniority, makeup goals and timetables. (11)

aggravated assault—an unlawful attack upon a person for the purpose of inflicting severe bodily injury or death. (3)

aggravated rape—having sexual intercourse through use of force, threats or immediate use of force, or taking advantage of an unconscious or helpless person or a person incapable of consent because of mental illness or a defect reasonably known to the attacker. (3)

aggressive patrol—designed to handle problems and situations requiring coordinated efforts. Also called *specialized patrol* or *directed patrol.* (6)

American creed—the belief in individual freedom. (2)

American Dream—belief that anyone who works hard and is willing to sacrifice for a while can be successful. (5)

amphetamines—stimulants taken orally as tablets or capsules or intravenously to reduce appetite and/or to relieve mental depression. (9)

appeal—to ask a higher court to review the actions of a lower court to correct mistakes or injustices. (12)

appellate jurisdiction—a higher court with the power to hear and decide an appeal to the decision of an original court without holding a trial. (12)

arraignment—a court procedure whereby the accused is read the charges against him or her and is then asked how he or she pleads. (12)

arrest—to deprive a person of liberty by legal authority. Usually applied to the seizure of a person to answer before a judge for a suspected or alleged crime. (8)

arson—intentionally damaging or destroying, or attempting to damage or destroy, by means of fire or explosion the property of another without the consent of the owner or one's own property, with or without the intent to defraud. (3)

assault—an unlawful attack by one person upon another for the purpose of inflicting bodily harm. (3)

assembly-line justice—the operation of any segment of the criminal justice system in which excessive workload results in decisions being made with such speed and impersonality that defendants are treated as objects to be processed rather than as individuals. (12)

asset forfeiture—allows seizure of assets and property used in connection with a crime. (2)

authority—the right to direct and command. (2)

bail—payment by an accused of an amount of money, specified by the court based on the nature of the offense, to ensure the presence of the accused at trial. (12)

ballistics—a science dealing with the motion and impact of projectiles such as bullets and bombs. (7)

barbiturates—depressants usually taken orally as small tablets or capsules to induce sleep and/or to relieve tension. (9)

battery—physical assault. (3)

bias crime—unlawful action designed to frighten or harm an individual because of his or her race, religion, ethnicity or sexual orientation. Also called *hate crime.* (3)

Bill of Rights—the first 10 amendments to the Constitution. (2)

biometrics—measuring physical characteristics such as fingerprints or voice by computer. Often used as a means of access control. (7)

bioterrorism—involves such biological weapons of mass destruction (WMD) as anthrax, botulism and smallpox to cause fear in a population. (9)

Bloods—well-known African-American gang. Rivals of the Crips. (9)

body language—messages conveyed by how a person moves. Also called *kinesics.* (7)

bona fide occupational qualification (BFOQ)—skill or knowledge that is reasonably necessary to perform a job and, consequently, may be a requirement for employment. (11)

booked—formally entered into the criminal justice system. Includes the facts about a person's arrest, charges, identification and background information. (12)

boot camp—patterned after the traditional military boot camps for new recruits; a system of incarceration for youths that stresses strict and even cruel discipline, hard work and authoritarian decision-making and control by a drill sergeant. Also called *shock incarceration.* (12)

Bow Street Runners—the first detective unit; established in London by Henry Fielding in 1750. (1)

broken-window theory—maintains that if a neighborhood is allowed to run down, it will give the impression that no one cares and crime will flourish. (9)

burglary—an unlawful entry into a building to commit a theft or felony. (3)

burnout—a psychological state that occurs when someone is made exhausted and listless and rendered unserviceable or ineffectual through overwork, stress or intemperance. (11)

career criminal—an offender arrested five or more times as a juvenile. Also called a *chronic criminal.* (3)

carjacking—stealing a car from the driver by force. (3)

case law—a collection of summaries of how statutes have been applied by judges in various situations; the precedents that have been established by the courts. (2)

chain of evidence—documenting who has had possession of evidence from the time it was discovered and taken into custody until the present time. (7)

change of venue—shifting a trial to another part of the state because the court is convinced that a case has received such extensive publicity that picking an impartial jury is impossible. (12)

charge—the formal complaint against a suspect. Formal accusation of a crime. (12)

chronic criminal—an offender arrested five or more times as a juvenile. Also called a *career criminal.* (3)

circumstantial probable cause—incidents that, taken together, suggest that a crime has been or is about to be committed. (8)

civil injunction—a lawsuit that, if granted by the court, requires or limits certain actions by the defendants and serves, in essence, as a protective order from the city. (9)

civil law—all restrictions placed upon individuals that are noncriminal in nature; seeks restitution rather than punishment. (2)

civil liberties—an individual's immunity from governmental oppression. (2)

civil rights—claims that the citizen has to the affirmative assistance of government. (2)

civilian review—a process by which citizens' complaints about police behavior are reviewed by individuals who are not sworn police officers. (11)

civilian review board—consists of citizens who meet to review complaints filed against the police department or against individual officers. (11)

classical theory—sees people as free agents with free will, saying that people commit crimes because they want to. Theory developed by eighteenth-century Italian criminologist Cesare Beccaria. (3)

cocaine—a central nervous system stimulant narcotic derived from the Erythroxylon coca bush of South America. (9)

code of silence—a pact among officers that they will not make known any misconduct of fellow officers. (2)

cold crimes—crimes discovered after the perpetrator has left the scene. (6)

common law—in England, the customary law set by the judges as disputes arose; the law in force before and independent of legislation. (2)

community era—(1980–present) the third era of policing. Characterized by authority coming from community support, law and professionalism; broad provision of services, including crime control; decentralized organization with more authority given to patrol officers; an intimate relationship with the community; and use of foot patrol and a problem-solving approach. (1)

community justice—creates new relationships both within the justice system and with stakeholders in the community; has at its core partnerships and problem solving. (12)

community policing—a philosophy that emphasizes a problem-solving partnership between the police and the citizens in working toward a healthy, crime-free environment. Also called *neighborhood policing.* (4)

community service—usually imposed not as a sole penalty but rather as a condition of probation, often requiring the offender to perform unpaid labor to pay a debt to society. (12)

complainant—a person who makes a charge against another person. (7)

complaint—a legal document drawn up by a prosecutor that specifies the alleged crime and the supporting facts providing probable cause. (12)

cone of resolution—examining spacial patterns of crime rates at increasingly smaller scales of analysis to reveal variances. (5)

consent—to agree; to give permission; voluntary oral or written permission to search a person's premises or property. (8)

constable—an elected official of a hundred responsible to lead the citizens in pursuit of any lawbreakers. The first English police officer and, as such, in charge of the weapons and horses of the entire community. (1)

constitution—a system of fundamental laws and principles that prescribes the nature, functions and limits of a government or other body. The basic instrument of government and the supreme law of the United States; the written instrument defining the power, limitations and functions of the U.S. government and that of each state. (2)

constitutional law—statutes based on the federal or state constitutions. (2)

contamination—something foreign is introduced into or evidence is removed from a crime scene. (7)

contraband—any article forbidden by law to be imported or exported; any article of which possession is prohibited by law and constitutes a crime. (8)

corporate gangs—gangs that have strong leaders and focus on illegal money-making ventures, often drug trafficking. (9)

corpus delicti—the body of the crime, the elements making up a specific crime. (2)

corrections—that portion of the criminal justice system that carries out the court's orders. It consists of our probation and parole systems as well as our jails, prisons and community-based programs to rehabilitate offenders. (12)

corroborate—to support, tending to confirm. (7)

corruption—the misuse of authority by an officer for personal gain. Includes accepting gratuities and bribes as well as committing theft or burglary. (10)

court of last resort—the highest court to which a case may be appealed. (12)

CPTED—Crime Prevention Through Environmental Design. Focuses on "defensible space," using access control, lighting and surveillance as key strategies in preventing crime. (5)

crack—a form of cocaine available at greatly reduced cost. (9)

credentialing—process whereby individual police officers are approved by a board as meeting certain standards. (11)

crime—an action harmful to another person and/or to society and made punishable by law. (2)

criminal intent—a resolve, design or mutual determination to commit a crime, with full knowledge of the consequences and exercise of free will. (2)

criminal law—the body of law that defines crimes and fixes punishments for them. (2)

Crips—gang with the reputation of being the toughest African-American gang in Los Angeles. Rivals of the Bloods. (9)

cross-examination—questioning of an opposing witness in a trial or hearing. (12)

cultural gangs—neighborhood-centered gangs that exist independently of criminal activity. (9)

curtilage—that portion of property associated with the common use of land—for example, buildings, sheds and fenced-in areas. (8)

custodial interrogation—questioning a person who is not free to leave. (2)

custody—state of being kept or guarded, or being detained. (8)

cyanoacrylate—super glue; used in fingerprinting. (7)

cybercops—investigators of computer crimes. (3)

cybercrime—computer crime. (3)

cyberterrorism—terrorism that initiates or threatens to initiate the exploitation of or attack on computerized information systems. (9)

dangerous drugs—addicting, mind-altering drugs such as depressants, stimulants and hallucinogens. (9)

dark figure of criminality—the actual, unknown number of crimes being committed. (3)

day fines—fines based on an offender's daily income, differing from straight fines in that the judge considers not only the nature of the crime but also the offender's ability to pay when determining the fine amount. (12)

day reporting centers—nonresidential alternative to sending both juvenile and adult offenders to jail or prison, where offenders must appear daily and the emphasis is on finding jobs. (13)

deadly force—any force intended to cause death or serious physical injury. (10)

de facto segregation—actual separation, often geographically into ghettos. (5)

deinstitutionalization—releasing into society those who have been under the care of the state. Frequently refers to the massive release of mentally ill individuals into society in the 1960s and 1970s, many of whom became homeless. (5)

delinquency—actions or conduct by a juvenile in violation of criminal law or constituting a status offense. An error or failure by a child or adolescent to conform to society's expectations of social order, either where the child resides or visits. (3)

delinquent—a child judged to have violated a federal, state or local law; a minor who has done an illegal act or who has been proven in court to misbehave seriously. A child may be found delinquent for a variety of behaviors not criminal for adults (status offenses). (3)

deliriants—volatile chemicals that can be sniffed or inhaled to produce a "high" similar to that produced by alcohol. (9)

demographers—individuals who study the characteristics of human populations. (5)

determinism—maintains that human behavior is the product of a multitude of environmental and cultural influences. (3)

deterrence—sees corrections as a way to prevent future criminal actions. Tries to show offenders that the price of committing crimes is too great. (12)

differential response strategies—suiting the response to the call. (6)

digitizing—in photography, recording an image electronically rather than on a piece of light-sensitive film. (7)

directed patrol—uses crime statistics to plan shift and beat staffing, providing more coverage during times of peak criminal activity and in high-crime areas. Designed to handle problems and situations requiring coordinated efforts. Also called *specialized patrol* or *aggressive patrol.* (6)

direct victims—those who are initially harmed by injury, death or loss of property as a result of crimes committed. Also called *primary victims.* (3)

discovery crimes—illegal acts brought to the attention of the victim and law enforcement after the act has been committed—a burglary, for example. (7)

discovery process—a system that requires that all pertinent facts be available to the prosecutor and the defense attorney before the trial. (12)

discretion—the freedom of an agency or individual officer to make choices as to whether to act; freedom to act or judge on one's own. (4)

discrimination—showing a preference or prejudice in treating individuals or groups. (10)

diversion—bypassing the criminal justice system by assigning an offender to a social agency or other institution rather than trying him or her in court. (12)

DNA profiling—uses the material from which chromosomes are made to positively identify individuals. No two individuals except identical twins have the same DNA structure. (7)

double jeopardy—being tried for the same crime more than once. (2)

drug gangs—smaller than other gangs; more cohesive; focused on the drug business; strong, centralized leadership with market-defined roles. (9)

drug-defined offenses—illegal acts involving drugs, that is, the crime occurs as a part of the drug business or culture, for example marijuana cultivation or cocaine distribution. Also called *systemic* offenses. (9)

drug-related offenses—illegal acts in which the effect of a drug is a contributor, such as when a drug user commits crime because of drug-induced changes in physiological functions, cognitive ability, and mood, or in which the need for the drug is a factor, as when a drug user commits crime to obtain money to buy drugs. (9)

dual motive stop—when the officer has an ulterior motive for the stop. Also called a *pretext stop.* (8)

dual system—created by the Juvenile Court Act, in which poor and abused children are equated with criminal children and, consequently, treated in essentially the same way. (12)

due process of law—not explicitly defined, but embodies the fundamental ideas of American justice expressed in the Fifth and Fourteenth Amendments. (2)

ecclesiastical law—law of the church. (2)

eco-terrorism—terrorism to inflict economic damage on those who profit from the destruction of the natural environment. (9)

electronic monitoring (EM)—supervision of offenders via devices worn around their ankles, wrists or necks that send signals back to a control office. (12)

elements of the crime—the distinctive acts making up a specific crime. The elements make up the *corpus delicti* of the crime. (2)

embezzle—a person steals or uses for him- or herself money or property entrusted to him or her. (3)

emergency situations—circumstances where a police officer must act without a magistrate's approval (without a warrant). (8)

empathy—understanding. Being able to see things as someone else sees them. Not to be confused with sympathy. (7)

entrapment—occurs when an officer induces someone to commit a crime for the purpose of prosecuting that person. (8)

equal protection—requires that a state cannot make unreasonable, arbitrary distinctions between different persons as to their rights and privileges. (2)

equity—a concept that requires that the "spirit of the law" take precedence over the "letter of the law." (2)

ethics—involves moral behavior, doing what is considered right and just. The rules or standards governing the conduct of a profession. (10)

evidence—all the means by which any alleged matter or act is either established or disproved. (7)

excessive force—force beyond that which is reasonably necessary to accomplish a legitimate law enforcement purpose. (10)

Exclusionary Rule—a U. S. Supreme Court ruling that any evidence seized in violation of the Fourth Amendment will not be admissible in a federal or state trial. (2)

Exculpatory evidence—evidence favorable to the accused. (10)

exigent circumstances—the same as *emergency situations.* (8)

expertise—specialized knowledge and/or experience. (8)

extenuating circumstances—requiring immediate action; an emergency situation. (9)

eyewitness—an individual who has observed a crime, who expects no favors from the police and who does not exchange information for protection or act out of motives for revenge. (9)

federalism—a principle reserving for the states the powers not granted to the federal government or withheld from the states. (2)

felony—a major crime—for example, murder, rape, arson; the penalty is usually death or imprisonment for more than one year in a state prison or penitentiary. (2)

fence—a professional receiver and seller of stolen property. (3)

field detention—holding suspects with less than probable cause. (8)

field identification—at-the-scene identification, made within a reasonable time after a crime has been committed. (7)

field inquiry—briefly detaining or stopping persons to determine who they are and/or what they are up to. (8)

field services—the operations or line divisions of a law enforcement agency, such as patrol, traffic control, investigation and community services. (4)

fighting words—utterances likely to cause violence. (2)

first-degree murder—willful, deliberate and premeditated (planned) taking of another person's life. (3)

flake—a more refined form of cocaine than rock, extracted from cocaine paste. It comes in flat crystals and is approximately 95 percent pure. (9)

follow-up investigation—investigation after the preliminary investigation. (7)

force—action taken to compel an individual to comply with an officer's request. (10)

forced entry—an announced or unannounced entry into a dwelling or a building by force for the purpose of executing a search or arrest warrant to avoid the needless destruction of property, to prevent violent and deadly force against the officer and to prevent the escape of a suspect. (9)

forensic science—the study of evidence. (7)

forfeiture—usually an add-on punishment involving seizure of an offender's illegally used or acquired property or assets. (12)

Frankpledge system—Norman modification of the tithing system requiring loyalty to the king's law and mutual local responsibility in maintaining the peace. (1)

frisk—a patting down or minimal search of a person to determine the presence of a dangerous weapon. (8)

furloughs—short, temporary leaves from a prison or jail, supervised or unsupervised, although generally the latter. (12)

gang—a group of people who form an allegiance for a common purpose and engage in unlawful or criminal activity. (9)

general deterrence—deterrence to serve as an example to others of the consequences of crime. (12)

ghetto—area of a city inhabited by people of an ethnic or racial group who live in poverty and apparent social disorganization often resulting from involuntary segregation. (5)

ghetto syndrome—a vicious cycle of poverty and welfare dependency in which an individual's inability to go to college or prepare for well-paying jobs leads to lack of motivation, which leads to unemployment, poverty and welfare dependency, perpetuating the cycle. (5)

graffiti—writing or drawing on buildings and walls. A common form of communication used by gang members. Marks their territories. Sometimes called the newspaper of the street. (9)

grand jury—a group of citizens, usually 23, convened to hear testimony in secret and to issue formal criminal accusations (indictments) based upon probable cause if justified. (2)

grand larceny—theft of property valued above a certain amount, in contrast to petty larceny, a less serious offense. (3)

halfway houses—community-based institutions for individuals who are halfway into prison, that is, on probation, or halfway out of prison, that is, on or nearing parole. (12)

hallucinogens—drugs whose physical characteristics allow them to be disguised as tablets, capsules, liquids or powders; hallucinogens produce distortion, intensify sensory perception and lessen the ability to discriminate between fact and fantasy. (9)

hate crime—unlawful act designed to frighten or harm an individual because of his or her race, religion, ethnicity or sexual orientation. Also called *bias crime.* (3)

hearsay—see *hearsay evidence.* (2)

hearsay evidence—secondhand evidence. Facts not in the personal knowledge of a witness, but a repetition of what others said. (2)

hedonistic/social gangs—only moderate drug use and offending, involved mainly in using drugs and having a good time; little involvement in crime, especially violent crime. (9)

heroin—a commonly abused narcotic synthesized from morphine. Physically addictive and expensive. (9)

heuristic—a rule of thumb; a strategy that is powerful and general but not absolutely guaranteed to work. (5)

homicide—the willful killing of a human by another human; also *murder.* (3)

homophobia—a fear of gays and lesbians. (10)

hot spots—specific locations with high crime rates. (5)

house arrest—an intermediate sanction used with both juveniles and adults in which the offender is required to remain within the confines of the home during specified times and to adhere to a strict curfew. Also called *home confinement* or *home detention.* (12)

Hue and Cry—a shout by a citizen who witnessed a crime, enlisting the aid of others in the area to chase and catch the offender. May be the origin of the general alarm and the citizen's arrest. (1)

hundreds—groups of 10 tithings. (1)

hung jury—a jury that cannot reach a decision. The result is a "no verdict" decision which can result in a retrial. (12)

image—how one is viewed; the concept of someone or something held by the public. Police image results from the media portrayal of police and from everyday contacts between individual police officers and citizens. (4)

immediate control—within a person's immediate reach. Also called *wingspan.* (8)

implied consent—laws stating that any person driving a motor vehicle is deemed to have consented to a chemical test of the alcohol content of his or her blood if arrested while intoxicated. Refusal to take such a test can be introduced in court as evidence. (6)

in custody—not free to leave. (8)

incapacitation—making it impossible for offenders to commit further offenses. (12)

incarceration—being confined in jail or prison. (12)

incident-driven policing—where calls for service drive the department. A reactive approach with emphasis on rapidity of response. (6)

incorporation doctrine—holds that only those provisions of the Bill of Rights that are fundamental to the American legal process are made applicable to the states through the due process clause. Also called *selective incorporation.* (2)

Index Crimes—categories of crime used in the Uniform Crime Report: Part I or Part II depending on the seriousness of the crime. (3)

indicted—formally charged with a specific crime by a grand jury, based on probable cause. (2)

indigent—destitute, poverty-stricken, with no visible means of support. (2)

indirect victims—family members and friends of victims who also feel pain and suffering along with the victim. Also called *secondary victims.* (3)

inevitable discovery doctrine—holds that illegally obtained evidence may be admitted at trial if the prosecution can prove that the evidence would have been discovered sooner or later (inevitability). (8)

infamous crime—an especially heinous crime. (2)

informant—person who furnishes information concerning accusations against another person or persons. (7)

informational probable cause—statements made to officers that can be relied upon and are generally sufficient in themselves to justify an arrest. (8)

inspection warrant—see *administrative warrant.* (8)

instrumental gangs—gangs formed for the express purpose of criminal activity. They pose a greater threat than cultural gangs because they provide for a higher degree of organization. (8)

instruments of a crime—the means by which a crime is committed or the suspects and/or victims transported—for example, gun, knife, burglary tools, car, truck. (8)

integrated patrol—an operational philosophy that combines community-based policing with aggressive enforcement and provides a balanced, comprehensive approach to addressing crime problems throughout an entire jurisdiction rather than merely in targeted areas within a community. (5)

integrity—a series of concepts and beliefs that provide structure to an agency's operation and officers' professional and personal ethics, including, but are not limited to, honesty, honor, morality, allegiance, principled behavior and dedication to mission. (10)

intensive supervision programs (ISPs)—called the "heart of the intermediate sanction program," a correctional alternative that involves more supervision and greater restrictions than standard probation and places an overriding emphasis on offender control and surveillance rather than treatment. Also called *intensive supervised probation.* (12)

intent—see *criminal intent.* (2)

interdiction—cutting off or destroying a line of communication—in the case of drug control, halting the flow of drugs into the United States. (9)

intermediate sanctions—sanctions that are tougher than traditional probation but less stringent—and less expensive—than imprisonment. (12)

interrogate—questioning a suspect. (7)

interview—questioning a witness or person with information relating to an incident. (7)

involvement crimes—illegal acts discovered while being committed. (7)

jail—a place of confinement, typically administered by local law enforcement, although occasionally by a regional or state law enforcement agency, serving the dual function of (1) detaining individuals waiting to appear before the court, either for trial (preconviction) or for sentencing (postconviction), and (2) holding those sentenced to a year or less of incarceration. (12)

judicial review—a court's power to declare a statute unconstitutional, to interpret state laws and to review cases that are appealed. (12)

judicial waiver—the juvenile court waives its jurisdiction and transfers the case to criminal court. Also known as *binding over, transferring* or *certifying* juvenile cases to criminal courts. (12)

jurisdiction—the geographic area within which a court (or public official) has the right and power to operate. Also refers to individuals and subjects over which a court has the right and power to make binding decisions. (12)

justifiable homicide—includes killing in self-defense or in the defense of another person if the victim's actions and capability present imminent danger of serious injury or death. (3)

kinesics—messages conveyed by how a person moves. Also called *body language.* (7)

landmark decision—a ruling of the Supreme Court that becomes a precedent that must be honored by all lower courts. (12)

larceny/theft—the unlawful taking and removing of the property of another with the intent of permanently depriving the legal holder of the property. (3)

latent fingerprints—prints made by sweat or grease that oozes out of the pores from little wells under the ridges at the ends of the fingers. (7)

law—a body of rules for human conduct that are enforced by imposing penalties for their violation. (1)

lawful arrest—lawfully taking a person into custody (with or without a warrant) for the purpose of holding that person to answer for a public offense; all legal standards must be satisfied, particularly probable cause. (8)

Leges Henrici—a document that made law enforcement a public matter and separated offenses into felonies and misdemeanors. (1)

less-lethal force—force that has less potential for causing death or serious injury than traditional tactics. (10)

lex talionis—an eye for an eye. (1)

liability—a legal obligation incurred for an injury suffered/complained which results from failure to conduct a specific task/activity within a given standard. (10)

litigaphobia—fear of a lawsuit. (2,10)

magistrate—a judge. (8)

Magna Carta—a decisive document in the development of constitutional government in England that checked royal power and placed the king under the law (1215). (1)

mala in se—"bad in itself," a crime so offensive, such as murder or rape, that it is obviously criminal. (2)

mala prohibita—"bad because it is forbidden," a crime that violates a specific regulatory statute and would not usually be considered a crime if no law prohibited it, for example, certain traffic violations. (2)

malice—hatred or ill will, disregard for the lives of others. (3)

manslaughter—accidentally causing the death of another person. No malice or intent is involved. (3)

marijuana—the most socially acceptable of the illegal drugs, derived from the cannabis plant, a hardy weed adaptable to most climates. Variously classified as a narcotic, a depressant and a hallucinogen. Usually smoked. (9)

medical model—in corrections, assumes criminals are victims of society and need to be "cured." (5,13)

mens rea—guilty intent. Literally, a guilty mind. (2)

methamphetamine—a powerful stimulant emerging as a major problem for law enforcement because of its tendency to invoke violence in the user. (9)

misdemeanor—a minor offense—for example, breaking a municipal ordinance, speeding; the penalty is usually a fine or a short imprisonment, usually less than one year, in a local jail or workhouse. (2)

mobility—movable; not firm, stationary or fixed—for example, an automobile that is capable of being moved quickly with relative ease. (8)

modus operandi (M.O.)—a method of criminal attack specific to an individual offender. (7)

monikers—street names of gang members. (9)

moonlighting—working at a second, part-time job while fulfilling the obligations of a full-time position. (11)

moral law—laws made by society and enforced solely by social pressure. (2)

motive—reason for doing something. (2)

motor vehicle theft—the unlawful taking or stealing of a motor vehicle without the authority or permission of the owner. Includes automobiles, trucks, buses, motorcycles, motorized boats and aircraft. (3)

mules—individuals who smuggle cocaine for professional drug dealers. Often tourists or students. (9)

multiple hurdle procedure—the numerous tests that applicants for police positions must pass. (11)

murder—see *homicide.* (3)

narcoterrorism—hiring terrorists to protect the drug cartels as well as the sale and distribution of drugs by these cartels. (9)

narcotics—drugs that produce sleep and lethargy or relieve pain; usually opiates. (9)

negligence—failure to exercise a reasonable amount of care in a situation that causes harm to someone or something. (2)

negligent homicide—an accidental death that results from the reckless operation of a motor vehicle, boat, plane or firearm. (3)

nightcap warrants—a nighttime search or arrest warrant. (8)

nighttime search warrants—search or arrest warrants issued by a magistrate that authorize a police officer to execute the warrant during the night. (8)

no bill—issued by a grand jury if it decides that no crime has been committed. (12)

no-knock search warrant—authorization by a magistrate upon the issuance of a search warrant to enter a premise by force without notification to avoid the chance that evidence may be destroyed if the officers' presence was announced. (8)

nolo contendere—"I will not contest it." A defendant's plea of "no contest" in a criminal case. It means he or she does not directly admit guilt, but submits to sentencing or other punishment. (12)

nonverbal communication—includes everything but the actual words in a communication: tone, pitch, rate, inflection. (7)

nystagmus—an uncontrolled bouncing or jerking of the eyeball of an intoxicated person when he or she looks to the extreme right or left, and up or down. (9)

observational probable cause—what an officer sees, hears or smells; that is, evidence presented directly to the officer's senses. (8)

open fields doctrine—holds that land beyond what is normally associated with use of that land, that is, undeveloped land, can be searched without a warrant. (8)

ordinances—local laws or regulations. (2)

ordinary care—such degree of care, skills and diligence as a person of ordinary prudence would employ under similar circumstances. (8)

ordinary law—statutes passed at the federal or state level that are not based on the Constitution. (2)

organized crime—conspiratorial crime involving a hierarchy of persons who coordinate, plan and execute illegal acts using enforcement and corruptive tactics. (3)

organized gangs—heavy involvement in all kinds of crime, heavy use and sale of drugs; may resemble corporations, with separate divisions handling sales, marketing, discipline and so on; discipline is strict, and promotion is based on merit. Also called *corporate gangs.* (9)

original jurisdiction—a court's power to take a case, try it and decide it. In contrast to an appellate court which hears appeals to the decisions of the original court. (12)

paradigm shift—a change in the thinking and attitudes toward a concept or model. (5)

parens patriae—the right of the government to take care of minors and others who cannot legally take care of themselves. (1)

parish—the area in which people lived who worshipped in a particular parish church. (1)

parish constable system—an early system of law enforcement used primarily in rural areas of the United States. (1)

parole—a release from prison before a sentence is finished. Continued release depends on good behavior and reporting to a parole officer. The most frequent type of release from a correctional institution. (12)

party gangs—commonly called "party crews"; relatively high use and sale of drugs, but only one major form of delinquency—vandalism; compete over who throws the biggest party, with alcohol, marijuana, nitrous oxide, sex and music critical party elements. (9)

pat down—an exploratory search of an individual's clothing. The "search" phase of a stop and frisk. (8)

PCP—phencyclidine, also known as Angel Dust, a hallucinogen. (9)

perception—how something is seen or viewed. (7)

petition—a written request for some action, a form of communication with the government, guaranteed by the First Amendment. (2) In the juvenile justice system, a document alleging a juvenile is a delinquent, status offender or dependent and asking the court to assume jurisdiction of the child. (12)

petty larceny—theft of property valued below a certain amount, in contrast to grand larceny, the more serious offense. (3)

pilfer—a person steals or uses money or property entrusted to him or her. (3)

plain feel/touch doctrine—related to the plain view doctrine. An officer who feels/touches something suspicious during the course of lawful activity can investigate further. (8)

plain view—evidence that is not concealed and is seen by an officer engaged in a lawful activity; what is observed in plain view is not construed within the meaning of the Fourth Amendment as a search. (8)

plea bargaining—a compromise between the defense and prosecuting attorneys that prearranges the plea and the sentence, conserving time, effort and court expenses. (12)

police authority—the right to direct and command. (4)

police power—the power of the federal, state or municipal governments to pass laws regulating private interests, to protect the health and safety of the people, to prevent fraud and oppression and to promote public convenience, prosperity and welfare. (2)

political era—(1840–1930) the first era of policing. Characterized by authority coming from politicians and the law, a broad social service function, decentralized organization, an intimate relationship with the community and extensive use of foot patrol. (1)

positivist theory—sees criminals as "victims of society" and of their own biological, sociological, cultural and physical environments. Theory developed at the turn of the century by Italian criminologist Cesare Lombroso. (3)

posttraumatic stress disorder (PTSD)—a psychological illness that happens after a highly stressful event or series of events, commonly associated with shooting incidents. (11)

power—the force by which others can be made to obey. (2)

precedent—what has come before. (2)

predatory gangs—heavily involved in serious crimes (robberies, muggings) and the abuse of addictive drugs such as crack cocaine; may engage in selling drugs, but not in an organized fashion. (9)

preliminary hearing—that stage in the judicial system which seeks to establish probable cause for believing that an offense has been committed and that the accused committed it to prevent persons from being indiscriminately brought to trial. (12)

preliminary investigation—actions performed immediately upon receiving a call to respond to the scene of a crime. Usually conducted by patrol officers. (7)

premeditated—planned ahead of time, as in premeditated murder. (3)

preponderance of the evidence—the greater weight of the evidence. One side is more credible than the other. Used in civil trials. (12)

presumption of innocence—the accused is assumed innocent until proof to the contrary is clearly established. (12)

pretext stop—when an officer stops a vehicle for ulterior motives. Also called a *dual motive stop.* (8)

primary victims—individuals directly affected by an incident, such as the person who is robbed, burglarized or raped. (3)

prison—a correctional facility of confinement, administered by a warden or superintendent, holding convicted offenders sentenced to more than one year of incarceration. (12)

privatization—civilians performing duties normally performed by sworn personnel who may be volunteers, paid civilians or private security personnel. (11)

***pro bono* work**—work done for free. Lawyers volunteer their time to be public defenders. (12)

proactive—seeking to find the causes of crime and to rectify those problems, thereby deterring or even preventing crime. Acting before the fact rather than reacting to something that has already occurred. (1)

probable cause—reasonable grounds for presuming guilt; facts that lead a person of ordinary care and prudence to believe and conscientiously entertain an honest and strong suspicion that a person is guilty of a crime. (8)

probation—the conditional suspension of a sentence of a person convicted of a crime but not yet imprisoned for that crime. The defendant is placed under the supervision of a probation officer for a set period of time and must meet specific conditions. (12)

procedural criminal law—laws specifying how law enforcement officers are to carry out their responsibilities. (2)

procedural due process—deals with notices, hearings and gathering evidence in criminal matters. (2)

professional model—the style of policing used during the reform era, based on the thinking of August Vollmer and O.W. Wilson. (1)

protective sweep—a quick and limited search of premises, incident to an arrest and conducted to protect police officers and/or others. (8)

public health model—used to explain the partnership between the police and the community in which community citizens take an active role in achieving public safety, not expecting the police to take sole responsibility for it. Emphasis is on prevention rather than cure, on being proactive rather than reactive and on treating causes rather than symptoms. (5)

public offenses—any crime. Includes felonies and misdemeanors. (8)

public safety exception—allows police officers to question suspects without first giving the Miranda warning if the information sought sufficiently affects the officers' or the public's safety. (8)

pure speech—words without any accompanying action. (2)

pursuit—an active attempt by a law enforcement officer on duty in a patrol car to apprehend one or more occupants of a moving motor vehicle, providing the driver of such vehicle is aware of the attempt and is resisting apprehension by maintaining or increasing his speed or by ignoring the law enforcement officer's attempt to stop him. (10)

racial profiling—any police-initiated action that relies on the race, ethnicity or national origin rather than the behavior of an individual that leads the police to believe a particular individual is engaged in criminal activity. (6)

random patrol—having no set pattern; by chance; haphazard. (6)

rape—carnal knowledge of a woman or man through the use of force or the threat of force. (3)

rattle watch—a group of citizens patrolling at night armed with rattles to call for help. Used in New Amsterdam in the 1650s. (1)

reactive—responding to crimes after they have been committed. (1)

reasonable—sensible; just; well-balanced; good, sound judgment; that which would be attributed to a prudent person. (8)

reasonable doubt—that state of a case in which, after comparing and considering all the evidence, the jurors cannot say they feel an abiding conviction of the truth of the charge. Moral uncertainty of the truth of the charges. (12)

reasonable force—force not greater than that needed to achieve the desired end. (10)

reasonable search—a search conducted in a manner consistent with the Fourth Amendment. (8)

reasonable seizure—the seizure of evidence or persons according to constitutional standards set forth in the Fourth Amendment. (8)

recidivism—repeated or habitual offending. (13)

recidivist—one who habitually or repeatedly breaks the law. (3)

reeve—the top official of a hundred. (1)

reform era—(1930–1980) the second era of policing. Characterized by authority coming from the law and professionalism; crime control as the primary function of law enforcement; a centralized, efficient organization; professional remoteness from the community; and an emphasis on preventive motorized patrol and rapid response to crime. (1)

regulators—respectable settlers of average or affluent means who joined others as vigilantes to attack and break up outlaw gangs and restore order in the 1760s. (1)

rehabilitation—correcting deviant behavior. (12)

residential community corrections—semisecure correctional facilities within the community where offenders may live either part time or full time and which address the dual objectives of community protection and offender reintegration. Such centers may take many forms, including halfway houses, prerelease centers, transition centers, work furlough and community work centers, community treatment centers and restitution centers. (12)

restitution—compensating or making up for loss, damage or injury. Requiring an offender to repay the victim or the community in money or services. (12)

restitution center—a new variation of the halfway house where offenders work to partially repay their victims. (12)

restorative justice—seeks to use a balanced approach involving offenders, victims, local communities and government to alleviate crime and violence and obtain peaceful communities. (12)

retribution—punishment for the sake of punishment; revenge. (12)

reverse discrimination—giving preferential treatment in hiring and promoting to women and minorities to the detriment of white males. (11)

riflings—spiral grooves cut into a gun barrel in its manufacture. (7)

riot act—an order permitting the magistrate to call the military to quell a riot. (1)

risk factors—elements related to how and where people live that affect the likelihood of their victimization. (3)

ritual—a system of rites; a ceremonial act. (3)

ritualistic crime—an unlawful act committed during a ceremony related to a belief system. It is the crime, not the belief system, that must be investigated. (3)

road rage—an angry, frequently violent response to an aggressive-driving incident. Not the same as aggressive driving. (6)

robbery—stealing anything of value from the care, custody or control of a person in his or her presence, by force or by the threat of force. (3)

rock—cocaine extracted from cocaine paste. The extracted cocaine looks somewhat like rock sugar candy. Its purity varies from 70 to 80 percent. (9)

roll call—the briefing of officers before their tour of duty to update them on criminal activity and calls for service. (4)

R.P.R.d—release on personal recognizance. (12)

SARA model—four strategies used in problem-oriented policing: scan, analyze, respond, assess. (5)

scavenger gangs—gangs that have few goals and primarily provide an outlet for impulsive behavior and meet the need to belong. (9)

scienter—a degree of knowledge that makes an individual legally responsible for the consequences of his or her acts. (2)

scofflaws—people who habitually violate the law. (6)

search—examination of a person or property for the purpose of discovering evidence to prove guilt in relation to a crime. (8)

search warrant—a judicial order directing a peace officer to search for specific property, seize it and return it to the court; it may be a written order or an order given over the telephone. (8)

secondary victims—family members and friends of victims who also feel pain and suffering along with the victim. Also called *indirect victims.* (3)

second-degree murder—the unpremeditated but intentional killing of another person. (3)

seizure—a forcible detention or taking of a person or property in an arrest. (8)

selective enforcement—targets specific accidents and/or high-accident areas. (6)

selective incorporation—holds that only those provision of the Bill of Rights that are fundamental to the American legal process are made applicable to the states through the due process clause. Also called the *incorporation doctrine.* (2)

self-incrimination—an individual is required to provide answers to questions that might convict him or her of a crime. (2)

serious delinquent gangs—heavy involvement in both serious and minor crimes, but much lower involvement in drug use and drug sales than party gangs. (9)

sexual harassment—has two conditions: (1) it must occur in the workplace or an extension of the workplace (department sanctioned), and (2) it must be of a sexual nature that does not include romance or that is not of a mutually friendly nature. The harassment must be unwelcome, unsolicited and deliberate. (11)

sheriff—the principal law enforcement officer of a county. (1)

shire-reeve—the top official of a shire (county). The forerunner of our county sheriff. (1)

shires—counties in England. (1)

shock incarceration—patterned after the traditional military boot camps for new recruits, a system of incarceration for youths that stresses strict and even cruel discipline, hard work and authoritarian decision-making and control by a drill sergeant. Also called *boot camp.* (12)

simple assault—an unlawful attack by one person on another, but without the intention of causing serious, permanent injury. (3)

simple rape—misleading a victim into having sexual intercourse. (3)

sinsemilla—marijuana grown indoors in the United States. (9)

situational testing—job-related simulation exercises to assess a candidate's qualifications for a law enforcement position. (11)

social gangs—only moderate drug use and offending, involved mainly in using drugs and having a good time; little involvement in crime, especially violent crime. Also called *hedonistic gangs.* (9)

social law—law made by society and enforced solely by social pressure. (2)

solvability factors—factors affecting the probability of successfully concluding a case. (7)

specific deterrence—deterrence aimed at offenders. Attempts to make the consequences of committing crime so severe that when offenders return to society, they will not commit crime. (12)

speech plus—words accompanied by some sort of action, such as burning a flag. (2)

spoils system—a political system whereby "friends" of politicians were rewarded with key positions in the police department. (1)

standing mute—refusing to answer as to guilt or innocence at an arraignment. Is entered as a "not guilty" plea. (12)

status offenses—crimes restricted to persons under the legal age—for example, smoking, drinking, breaking curfew, absenting from home, truancy, incorrigibility. (3)

statutory law—law passed by a legislature. (2)

statutory rape—rape without force, but still against the law, as in having intercourse with an underage female. (3)

stereotype—oversimplified conception, opinion or belief, often associated with specific racial or ethnic groups; seeing all members of a group as the same with no individuality. (5)

stop—briefly detaining someone who is acting suspiciously. A stop is *not* an arrest. (8)

stop and frisk—a protective search for weapons that could be used to assault police officers and others—for example, knives, guns and clubs. (8)

stress—physical, chemical or emotional factors that cause bodily or mental tension; mentally or emotionally disruptive or disquieting influence; distress. (11)

strict liability—intent is not required; the defendant is liable regardless of his or her state of mind when the act was committed. (2)

styles—particular ways of doing something. (4)

subculture—any group demonstrating specific patterns of behavior that distinguish it from others within a society. Policing has been referred to as "The Blue Brotherhood." (4)

subpoena—a written legal document ordering the person named in the document to appear in court to give testimony. (2)

substantive criminal law—statutes specifying crimes and their punishments. (2)

substantive due process—protects individuals against unreasonable, arbitrary or capricious laws and limits arbitrary government actions. (2)

suppressible crimes—crimes that commonly occur in locations and under circumstances that provide police officers a reasonable opportunity to deter or apprehend offenders. Included in the category are robbery, burglary, car theft, assault and sex crimes. (7)

symbolic speech—tangible forms of expressions such as wearing buttons or clothing with political slogans or displaying a sign or flag. Protected by the First Amendment. (2)

target hardening—making it more difficult for crime to occur. For example, using access control, lighting and surveillance. (5)

territorial gangs—gangs that establish their turf and defend it. (9)

terrorism—the use of force or violence against persons or property in violation of the criminal laws of the United States for purposes of intimidation, coercion or ransom. (9)

theft—stealing of any kind. (3)

threshold inquiry—same as a *stop,* that is, briefly detaining an individual who is acting suspiciously. (8)

tithing—in Anglo-Saxon England, a unit of civil administration consisting of 10 families; established the principle of collective responsibility for maintaining law and order. (1)

tithing system—established the principle of collective responsibility for maintaining local law and order by organizing families into groups of 10 families known as a *tithing.* (1)

tort—a civil wrong for which the court seeks a remedy in the form of damages to be paid. (2)

totality of circumstances—taking into account all factors involved in a given situation. (7)

traditional gangs—gangs that can trace their heritage back several generations and have a strong system of tradition. (9)

turf—the geographic territory claimed by a gang. (9)

typologies—systematic classifications, as in styles of policing. (4)

undercover—long-term, ongoing investigations into criminal activity where officers do not wear uniforms or drive marked cars and may use assumed names and fictitious identities. (7)

union—any group authorized to represent the members of the law enforcement agency in negotiating such matters as wages, fringe benefits and other conditions of employment. (11)

union shop—an agency where people must belong to or join the union to be hired. (11)

venue—the local area where a case may be tried. It is usually required that the trial for an offense be held in the same area in which the offense occurred. (12)

victim impact statement (VIS)—a written or spoken statement detailing the medical, financial and emotional injuries resulting from a crime. The information is usually provided to a probation officer who writes a summary to be included in the defendant's presenting packet. (3)

victim statement of opinion (VSO)—a spoken or written statement to the judge in which victims tell the court their opinions on what sentence the defendant should receive. More subjective than the victim impact statement. (3)

vigilante—a person who takes the law into his or her own hands, usually in the absence of effective policing. (1)

voir dire—the random selection of potential jurors and the careful questioning of each. (12)

waiver—the intentional giving up of a right. (8)

wannabes—youths who dress and act like gang members and hang out on the fringes of the gang, hoping some day to be invited in. (9)

warrant—a written order issued by an officer of the court, usually a judge, directing a person in authority to arrest the person named, charge that person with the named offense and bring him or her before the issuing person or court of jurisdiction. (2)

Watch and Ward—a system of law enforcement that was used to protect citizens 24 hours a day; the day shift was called the "ward" and the night shift the "watch." (1)

white-collar crime—occupational or business-related crime. Also called *economic crime.* (3)

wingspan—the area within a person's reach. Also known as *immediate control.* (8)

witness—a complainant, an accuser, a victim, an observer of an incident. (7)

writ of certiorari—a request for a transcript of the proceedings of a case for review. Made when the Supreme Court decides to hear a case. (12)

writ of habeas corpus—see *habeas corpus.* (12)

xenophobia—fear or hatred of strangers or foreigners. (3)

zones of privacy—areas safe from governmental intrusion. (2)

Author Index

D

E

F

G

H

Y

Z

Subject Index

D

E

J

K

L

Photo Credits

P. 1, James L. Shaffer; p. 10, AP / Wide World Photos; p. 15, Brown Brothers; p. 31, © CORBIS; p. 37, © Aaron Haupt / Photo Researchers, Inc.; p. 54, Jeff Cadge / Image Bank; p. 63, Spencer Grant; p. 78, AP / Wide World Photos; p. 84, © Bob Self / Silver Image; p. 98, AP / Wide World Photos; p. 103, Michael Newman / PhotoEdit; p. 105, AP / Wide World Photos; p. 115, © Richard Bermack / Impact Visuals; p. 127, Photofest; p. 133, James L. Shaffer; p. 149, AP Photo / Anna Mia Davidson; p. 150, Mark Richards / PhotoEdit; p. 169, Michael Newman / PhotoEdit; p. 179, Associated Press / AP; p. 180, Shelley Boyd / PhotoEdit; p. 201, AP Photo / Carla M. Cataldi; p. 219, AP / Wide World Photos; p. 222, © Joel Gordon 2001; p. 229, © Mark Reinstein / Index Stock Imagery; p. 235, AP Photo / Jeff Klein; p. 267, © AP Photo / Jerry Torrens; p. 280, Mark Richards / PhotoEdit; p. 300, AP / Wide World Photos; p. 308, © Joel Gordon; p. 331, © Online USA, Inc.; p. 332, Richard Sheinwald / AP / Wide World Photos; p. 345, Photo by Stephen Ferry / Getty Images; p. 371, David R. Frazier; p. 391, Michael Newman / PhotoEdit; p. 413, Wayne Chasan / The Image Bank; p. 423, Wes Stafford / AP / Wide World Photos; p. 432, Marty Lederhandler / AP / Wide World Photos; p. 439, © Reuters NewMedia Inc./CORBIS; p. 448, UPI / Bettmann Newsphotos; p. 451, Laimute E. Druskis / Stock Boston, p. 455, UPI / Bettmann Newsphotos.